BIG ISLAND

O F   H A W A I I

HANDBOOK

INCLUDING **HAWAII VOLCANOES NATIONAL PARK,**
THE KONA COAST, AND WAIPIO VALLEY

D0448903

BIG ISLAND
OF HAWAII
HANDBOOK

INCLUDING HAWAII VOLCANOES NATIONAL PARK, THE KONA COAST, AND WAIPIO VALLEY

J.D. BISIGNANI

COMPILED AND REVISED BY
ROBERT NILSEN

MOON
TRAVEL
HANDBOOKS

BIG ISLAND HANDBOOK
THIRD EDITION

Published by
  Moon Publications, Inc.
  P.O. Box 3040
  Chico, California 95927-3040, USA

Printed by
  Colorcraft Ltd.

ISBN: 1-56691-100-1
ISSN: 1096-956X

Editor: Pauli Galin
Editorial Assistance: Carey Wilson
Copy Editor: Asha Johnson
Production & Design: Rob Warner
Cartography: Chris Folks and Mike Morgenfeld
Index: Deana Shields

Cover art: by Roy Tabora, courtesy of Kahn Galleries

All photos by J.D. Bisignani unless otherwise noted.

Distributed in the United States and Canada by Publishers Group West

Printed in China

Please send all comments,
corrections, additions,
amendments, and critiques to:

BIG ISLAND HANDBOOK
MOON TRAVEL HANDBOOKS
P.O. BOX 3040
CHICO, CA 95927-3040, USA
e-mail: travel@moon.com
www.moon.com

Printing History
  1st edition—September 1990
  3rd edition—May 1998

to Madame Pele and all women of heart

ACKNOWLEDGMENTS

Writing the acknowledgments for a book is supercharged with energy. It's a time when you look forward, hopefully, to a bright future for your work, and a time when you reflect on all that has gone into producing it. Mostly it's a time to say thank you. Thank you for the grace necessary to carry out the task, and thank you to all the wonderful people whose efforts have helped so much along the way. To the following people, I offer my most sincere thank you.

Firstly, to the Moon staff, professionals every one. As time has passed, and one book has followed another, they've become amazingly adept at their work, to the point where their mastery is a marvel to watch.

I would also like to thank the following people for their special help and consideration: Dr. Greg Leo, an adventurer and environmentalist who has done remarkable field research and provided me with invaluable information about the unique flora and fauna of Hawaii; Roger Rose of the Bishop Museum; Lee Wild, Hawaiian Mission Houses Museum; Marilyn Nicholson, State Foundation on Culture and the Arts; the Hawaii Visitors Bureau; Donna Jung, Donna Jung and Associates, who has shown confidence in me since day one; Haunani Vieira, Dollar Rent A Car; Keoni Wagner, Hawaiian Airlines; Jim and John Costello; Dr. Terry and Nancy Carolan; Aubrey Hawk, Bozelle Advertising; Constance Wright, Molokai Visitors Assoc.; Barbara Schonley, of Molokai; Elisa Josephsohn, Public Relations; Faith Ogawa, for helping me keep the faith; Joyce Matsumoto, Halekulani Hotel; Bernie Caalim-Polanzi, Hilton Hotels; Nancy Daniels, Outrigger Hotels; Donn Takahashi, Regional Manager Prince Hotels; Alvin Wong, Hawaii Prince Hotel Waikiki; Martin Kahn, Kahn Galleries; Allison Kneubuhl, Kahala Mandarin Oriental; Matt Bailey, Manele Bay Hotel; Kurt Matsumoto, Lodge at Koele; Stephanie Reid, Princeville Hotel; Margy Parker, Poipu Beach Resort Assoc.; Yvonne Landavazo, Ritz-Carlton Kapalua; Catherine Sharpe, Stryker Weiner; Adi Kohler, Percy Higashi, and Jon Fukuda, Mauna Kea Beach Hotel and Hapuna Prince Hotel; Donna Kimura, Orchid at Mauna Lani; Denise Anderson, Hawaiian Regent; Dennis Costa, Maui Hill; Kim Marshall, Grand Wailea Resort; Sheila Donnelly, of Sheila Donnelly and Associates; Sandi Kato-Klutke, Aston Kauai Beach Villa; Barbara Sheehan, Sheraton Moana Surfrider; Aston Hotels; Norm Manzione, Suntrips; Renee Cochran and Will Titus, Colony Resorts; Linda Darling-Mann, a helpful Kauai friend; Sonia Franzel, Public Relations; Alexander Doyle, Aston Wailea Resort. To all of you, my deepest *aloha*.

CONTENTS

INTRODUCTION . . . . **1~69**
Overview
The Land 5
Climate 10
Flora and Fauna 13
The Mystery of Migration; Plants, Flowers, and Trees; Birds; Other Hawaiian Animals;
Marine Life; The Hakalau Forest National Wildlife Refuge
History 21
The Road from Tahiti; The World Discovers Hawaii; The Unification of Old Hawaii;
Missionaries and Whalers; King Sugar; A Kingdom Passes; Modern Times
Government 40
Economy 41
Tourism; The Military; Agriculture; The "Big Five"; Land Ownership
People 47
The Hawaiians; The Chinese; The Japanese; Caucasians; Filipinos and Others
Language 55
Pidgin; Hawaiian
Religion 59
Hawaiian Beliefs; The Strifes of Maui; *Heiau* and Idols; Missionaries One and All
Arts and Music 63
Arts of Old Hawaii; Hula and Lei; That Good Old Island Music

SPECIAL TOPICS

Average Maximum/Minimum Temperature and Rainfall *11*
What Is a Hurricane? *12*
Ethnicity *47*
Capsule Pidgin *56*
The Arts in Hawaii *69*

OUT AND ABOUT . . . . **70~146**
Sports and Recreation 70
Camping and Hiking; Deep-Sea and Freshwater Fishing; Ocean Tours; Snorkeling, Scuba,
and Water Sports; Skiing; Golf; Tennis; Horseback Riding; Bicycling; Hunting
Shopping 93
Shopping Centers; Food Stores and Supermarkets; Bookstores; Specialty Shops;
Arts to Buy
Festivals, Holidays, and Events 99
January; February; March; April; May; June; July; August; September; October;
November; December
Accommodations 102
Hotels; Condominiums; Bed and Breakfasts; Hostels; Home Exchanges
Food and Drink 107
Hawaiian Cuisine; Tropical Fruits and Vegetables; Fish and Seafood;
Unique Island Drinks; Munchies and Island Treats; Money-Savers
Getting There 115
By Air; Domestic Carriers; Foreign Carriers; Interisland Carriers; Travel By Ship; Tour
Companies

Getting Around 127
    Car Rentals; Alternative Transportation; Sightseeing Tours; Special Needs
Health and Conduct 135
    Water Safety; Hawaiian Folk Medicine and Cures; Hospitals and Pharmacies;
    Alternative Health Care; Illegal Drugs; Theft and Hassles
What to Take 141
Information and Services 143
    Hawaii Visitors Bureau Offices; Local Resources; Other Information; Money
    and Finances

SPECIAL TOPICS

Golf Courses *87-88*
Tennis Courts *89*
Museums *97*
Kukui (Candlenut Tree) *137*

HILO . . . . **147~175**
Sights and Beaches . . . . . : 148
    Sights; Beaches
Practicalities 159   SPECIAL TOPICS
    Accommodations; Food; Entertainment;   *History of the Anthurium* *153*
    Shopping; Services and Information

THE SADDLE ROAD . . . . **176~180**
Mauna Kea 176
    Mauna Kea Observatory Complex; Mauna Kea State Recreation Area

HAMAKUA COAST . . . . **181~198**
Honomu to Laupahoehoe 181
    Honomu and Vicinity; Laupahoehoe
Honokaa to Kukuihaele 186
    Honokaa and Vicinity; Kukuihaele
Waipio Valley 191
    Activities; History; Staying in the Valley; Waimanu Valley, Camping and Hiking

PUNA . . . . **199~210**
Route 130 and the Southeast Coast 201
    Keeau; Pahoa and Vicinity; Kaimu and Kalapana; Beaches, Parks, and Campgrounds
The Hawaii Belt Road From Hilo 210

HAWAII VOLCANOES NATIONAL PARK . . . . **211~230**
Introduction 211
Kilauea Caldera 216
    Visitors Center Area; Crater Rim Drive; Small Detours
Chain of Craters Road 222
Practicalities 224   SPECIAL TOPICS
    Camping and Hiking; Accommodations,   *Volcano Activity* *213*
    Food, and Shopping

KAU .... 231~240
Sights and Beaches.. 232
  Pahala; Punaluu and Ninole; Naalehu and Vicinity; South Point

KONA .... 241~289
Kailua-Kona and Vicinity 243
  Sights; Beaches and Parks; Accommodations; Food; Entertainment and Activities;
  Shopping; Services and Information
Central and South Kona 273
  Holualoa; Sights from Honalo to Captain Cook and Vicinity; Accommodations; Food;
  Shopping; Hookena and Milolii

SOUTH KOHALA .... 290~310
The Coast 292
  Sights and Nearby Communities; Beaches, Parks, and Campgrounds
Practicalities 296
  Resorts; Other Accommodations; Food; Shopping and Activities

WAIMEA (KAMUELA) .... 311~323
Sights.. 313
  Historic Homes and Art Collection at Puuopelu; Sights in Town
Practicalities 316
  Accommodations; Food; Shopping; Services and Information

NORTH KOHALA... 324~335
Sights, Beaches, and Towns.. 326
  Kawaihae Coast; Hawi; Kapaau; Pololu Valley and Beyond

BOOKLIST... 336~342

CAPSULE HAWAIIAN GLOSSARY .... 343~347

ACCOMMODATIONS INDEX 348

RESTAURANT INDEX... 349~351

INDEX .... 352~360

MAPS

INTRODUCTION
Hawaii (The Big Island) 3
Mountains of Hawaii 5
Polynesian Triangle 24
Senatorial Districts/House Districts 41
Land Ownership 46

OUT AND ABOUT
Big Island Campgrounds 71
Big Island Snorkeling 82
Big Island Golf Courses 86
Pacific Crossroads 116
Interisland Air Routes 123

HILO
Hilo 149
Vicinity of Hilo 156

THE SADDLE ROAD
The Saddle Road 177

HAMAKUA
Hamakua Coast 182

PUNA
Puna 200

HAWAII VOLCANOES NATIONAL PARK
Volcanoes National Park 212

KAU
Kau 233

KONA
North Kona 242
Kailua-Kona 244
Central and South Kona 274

SOUTH KOHALA
South Kohala 291

WAIMEA (KAMUELA)
Waimea 312

NORTH KOHALA
North Kohala 325

MAP SYMBOLS

═══════	Main Road	○	Town or Village	▲	Mountain
═══════	Other Road	▪	Sight	Λ	Campground
- - - - - - - -	Unpaved Road	•	Accommodation	🏯	Heiau
· · · · · · · · · · ·	Trail	✈	Primary Airport		Water
○	Highway Shield	✈	Secondary Airport		Lava
🐟	Snorkeling	⚲	Golf Course	🍂	Waterfall

ABBREVIATIONS

d = double p/d = per day
4WD = Four wheel drive p/h = per hour
HVB = Hawaii Visitors Bureau p/w = per week
HVNP = Hawaii Volcanoes National Park s = single
pp = per person YH = youth hostel

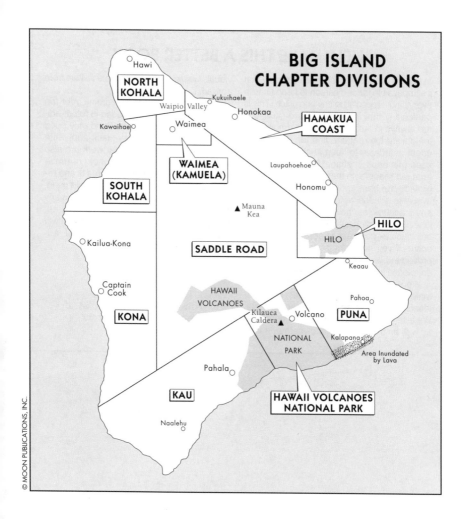

BIG ISLAND CHAPTER DIVISIONS

NORTH KOHALA

Hawi

Kukuihaele

Waipio Valley

Honokaa

HAMAKUA COAST

Kawaihae

Waimea

WAIMEA (KAMUELA)

Laupahoehoe

Honomu

SOUTH KOHALA

▲ Mauna Kea

HILO

Kailua-Kona

SADDLE ROAD

HILO

Keaau

Captain Cook

HAWAII VOLCANOES

Pahoa

KONA

Kilauea Caldera

Volcano

PUNA

NATIONAL PARK

Kalapana

Area Inundated by Lava

Pahala

HAWAII VOLCANOES NATIONAL PARK

KAU

Naalehu

HELP MAKE THIS A BETTER BOOK

In today's world, things change so rapidly that it's impossible for one person to keep up with everything happening in any one place. This is particularly true in Hawaii, where situations are always in flux. Travel books are like automobiles: they require fine tuning and frequent overhauls to keep in shape. Help us keep this book in shape! We require input from our readers so that we can continue to provide the best, most current information available. Please write to let us know about any inaccuracies, new information, or misleading suggestions. Although we try to make our maps as accurate as possible, errors do occur. If you have any suggestions for improvement or places that should be included, please let us know about them.

We especially appreciate letters from female travelers, visiting expatriates, local residents, and hikers and outdoor enthusiasts. We also like hearing from experts in the field as well as from local hotel owners and individuals wishing to accommodate visitors from abroad.

If you take a photograph during your trip that you feel might be included in future editions, please send it to us. Send only good slide duplicates or glossy black-and-white prints. Drawings and other artwork are also appreciated. If we use your photo or drawing, you'll be mentioned in the credits and receive a free copy of the book. Keep in mind, however, that the publisher cannot return any materials unless you include a self-addressed, stamped envelope. Moon Publications will own the rights on all material submitted. Address your letter to:

Big Island Handbook
Moon Publications
P.O. Box 3040
Chico, CA 95927-3040 USA
e-mail: travel@moon.com

BOB RACE

INTRODUCTION

The island of Hawaii is grand in so many ways. Its two nicknames, "The Orchid Island" and "The Volcano Island," are both excellent choices: the island produces more of the delicate blooms than anywhere else on earth; and Pele, the fire goddess who makes her mythological home here, regularly sends rivers of lava from the world's largest and most active volcanoes. However, to the people who live here, Hawaii has only one real nickname, "The Big Island." Big isn't necessarily better, but when you combine it with beautiful, uncrowded, traditional, and inexpensive, it's hard to beat.

The Big Island was the first to be inhabited by the Polynesian settlers, yet it's geologically the youngest of the Hawaiian Islands at barely a million years old. Like all the islands in the Hawaiian chain, it's a mini-continent whose geographical demarcations are much more apparent because of its size. There are parched deserts, steaming fissures, jet-black sand beaches, raw semi-cooled lava flows, snow-covered mountains, upland pastures, entire forests encased in hardened stone, and lush valleys where countless waterfalls break through the rock faces

of thousand-foot-high chasms. There are small working villages that time has passed by, the state's most tropical city, and an arid coast stretching over 90 miles where the sun is guaranteed to shine. You'll find some of the islands' least expensive accommodations as well as some of the world's most exclusive resorts.

Historically, the Big Island is loaded with religious upheavals, the births and deaths of great people, vintage missionary homes and churches, reconstructed *heiau,* and even a royal palace. Here is the country's largest privately owned ranch, where cowboy life is the norm; America's only coffee plantations; and enclaves of the counterculture, where people with alternative lifestyles are still trying to keep the faith of the '60s.

Sportspeople love it here, too. The Big Island is a Mecca for triathletes and offers snow skiing in season, plenty of camping and hiking, and the best marlin waters in all the oceans of the world.

There are direct flights to the Big Island, where the fascination of perhaps not "old" Hawaii, but definitely "simple" Hawaii, still lingers.

OVERVIEW

Hilo on the east coast and Kailua-Kona on the west are the two ports of entry to the Big Island. At opposite ends of the island as well as of the cultural spectrum, the two have a friendly rivalry. It doesn't matter at which one you arrive, because a trip to the Big Island without visiting both is unthinkable. Better yet, split your stay and use each as a base while you tour. The Big Island is the only Hawaiian island big enough that you can't drive around it comfortably in one day, nor should you try. Each of the districts is interesting enough to spend at least one day exploring.

Hilo and Vicinity
Hilo is the oldest port of entry, the most tropical town in Hawaii, and the only major city built on the island's windward coast. The city is one tremendous greenhouse where exotic flowers and tropical plants are a normal part of the landscape, and entire blocks canopied by adjoining banyans are taken for granted. The town, which hosts the yearly Merrie Monarch Festival, boasts an early morning fish market, Japanese gardens, the Lyman House Museum, and a profusion of natural phenomena, including Rainbow Falls and Boiling Pots. Plenty of rooms in Hilo are generally easily available, and its variety of restaurants will titillate anyone's taste buds. Both go easy on the pocketbook while maintaining high standards.

Saddle Road begins just outside of Hilo. It slices across the island through a most astonishing high valley or "saddle" separating the mountains of Mauna Loa and Mauna Kea. Passable, but the bane of car-rental companies, it slides down the western slope of Mauna Kea to meet the Belt Road, from where it's an easy drive to either Waimea or Kona. From the Saddle Road, a spur road heads up to the top of Mauna Kea at 13,796 feet, where a series of astronomical observatories peer into the heavens through the clearest air on earth.

Hamakua Coast
Hamakua refers to the entire northeast coast, where streams, wind, and pounding surf have chiseled the lava into towering cliffs and pre-

J.D. BISIGNANI

copter over lava

cipitous valleys known locally by the unromantic name of "gulches." Until recently, all the flatlands here were awash in a green sea of sugarcane; no commercial and few private fields remain. A spur road from the forgotten town of Honomu leads to Akaka Falls, whose waters tumble over a 442-foot cliff—the highest sheer drop of water in Hawaii. North along the coastal road is Honokaa, a one-street town of stores, restaurants, and crafts shops. The main road bears left here to the cowboy town of Waimea, but a smaller road inches farther north. It dead-ends at the top of Waipio Valley, cradled by cliffs on three sides with its mouth wide open to the sea. The valley is reachable only by foot, 4WD vehicle, or horseback. On its verdant floor a handful of families live simply by raising taro, a few head of cattle, and horses. Waipio was a burial ground of Hawaiian *ali'i*, where *kahuna* traditionally came to commune with spirits. The enchantment of this "power spot" remains.

Puna

Puna lies south of Hilo and makes up the majority of the southeast coast. Here are the greatest lava fields that have spewed from Kilauea, the heart of Volcanoes National Park. An ancient flow embraced a forest in its fiery grasp, entombing trees that stand like sentinels today in Lava Tree State Monument. Cape Kumukahi, a pointed lava flow that reached the ocean in 1868, is officially the easternmost point in Hawaii. Just below it is a string of beaches featuring ebony-black sand. Past the small village of Kala-

pana, the road skirts the coast before it dead-ends where it has been covered over by lava. Chain of Craters Road is now passable only *from* Hawaii Volcanoes National Park. This road spills off the mountain through a forbidding, yet vibrant, wasteland of old lava flows until it comes to the sea, where this living volcano fumes and throbs. Atop the volcano, miles of hiking trails crisscross the park and lead to the very summit of Mauna Loa. You can view the natural phenomena of steaming fissures, boiling mud, Devastation Trail, and Thurston Lava Tube, large

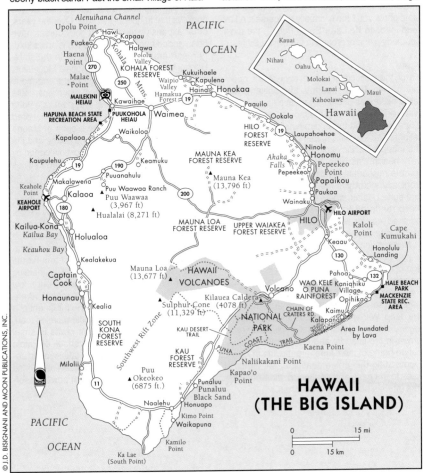

© J.D. BISIGNANI AND MOON PUBLICATIONS, INC.

HAWAII
(THE BIG ISLAND)

enough to accommodate a subway train. Here, too, you can lodge or dine at Volcano House, a venerable inn carved into the rim of the crater.

Kau

Kau, the southern tip of the island, is primarily a desert. On well-marked trails leading from the main road you'll discover ancient petroglyphs and an eerie set of footprints, the remnants of an ill-fated band of warriors who were smothered under the moist ash of a volcanic eruption and whose demise marked the ascendancy of Kamehameha the Great. Here are some lovely beaches and state parks you'll have virtually to yourself. A tiny road leads to Ka Lae ("South Point"), the most southerly piece of ground in the United States.

Kona

Kona, the west coast, is in every way the opposite of Hilo. It's dry, sunny, and brilliant, with large expanses of old barren lava flows. When watered, the rich soil blossoms, as in South Kona, renowned for its diminutive coffee plantations. The town of Captain Cook, named after the intrepid Pacific explorer, lies just above the very beach where he was slain because of a terrible miscommunication two centuries ago. Ironically, nearby is the restored Pu'uhonua o Honaunau Heiau, where mercy and forgiveness were rendered to any *kapu*-breaker or vanquished warrior who made it into the confines of this safe refuge.

Kailua-Kona is the center of Kona. The airport is just north of town and here is a concentration of condos and hotels. The town itself boasts an array of art and designer shops; world-class triathletes come here to train, and charter boats depart in search of billfish and other denizens of the deep. Within Kailua is Mokuaikua Church, a legacy of the very first packet of missionaries to arrive in the islands; and Hulihee Palace, vacation home of the Kamehameha line of kings. Dominating this entire coastline, Mt. Hualalai rises to the east, and northward, the Kona District offers a string of fine beaches.

Kohala

Up the coast in South Kohala is Hapuna Beach, best on the island. In 1965, Laurance Rockefeller opened the Mauna Kea Resort here. For the last three decades, this resort, along with its sculptured, coast-hugging golf course, has been considered one of the finest in the world. Just south is the Kona Village Resort, whose guests can arrive at a private airstrip to spend the night in a "simple" grass shack on the beach. Its serenity is broken only by the soothing music of the surf and by the not-so-melodious singing of "Kona nightingales," a pampered herd of wild donkeys that frequents this area. Over the years, other expansive resorts and golf courses have been added here, making this the island's luxury resort area, on a par with any in the state. Upcountry, at the base of the Kohala Mountains, is **Waimea** (Kamuela), center of the enormous Parker Ranch. Here in the cool mountains, cattle graze in chest-high grass, and *paniolo* astride their sturdy mounts ride herd in time-honored tradition. Hunters range the slopes of Mauna Kea in search of wild goats and boars, and the Fourth of July is boisterously acknowledged by the wild whoops of cowboys at the world-class Parker Ranch Rodeo.

North Kohala is primarily the hilly peninsular thumb on the northern extremity of the island. Along the coast are beach parks, empty except for an occasional local family picnic. A series of *heiau* dot the coast, and on the northernmost tip a broad plain overlooking a sweeping panorama marks the birthplace of Kamehameha the Great. The main town up here is Hawi, holding on after the sugar companies pulled out a few years ago. Down the road is Kapaau, where Kamehameha's statue resides in fulfillment of a *kahuna* prophecy. Along this little-traveled road, a handful of artists offer their crafts in small shops. At road's end is the overlook of Pololu Valley, where a steep descent takes you to secluded beaches and camping in an area once frequented by some of the most powerful sorcerers in the land.

THE LAND

The modern geological theory concerning the formation of the Hawaiian Islands is no less fanciful than the Polynesian legends sung about it. Science maintains that 30 million years ago, while the great continents were being geologically tortured into their rudimentary shapes, the Hawaiian Islands were a mere ooze of bubbling magma 20,000 feet below the surface of the primordial sea. For millions of years this molten rock flowed up through fissures in the sea floor. Slowly, layer upon layer of lava was deposited until an island rose above the surface of the sea. The island's great weight then sealed the fissures, whose own colossal forces progressively crept in a southeastern direction, then burst out again and again to build the chain. At the same time, the entire Pacific plate was afloat on a giant sea of molten magma, and it slowly glided to the northwest carrying the newly formed islands with it.

In the beginning the spewing crack formed Kure and Midway islands in the extreme northwestern sector of the Hawaiian chain. Today, more than 130 islands, islets, and shoals make up the Hawaiian Islands, stretching 1,600 miles across an expanse of the North Pacific. Geologists maintain that the "hot spot" now primarily under the Big Island remains relatively stationary, and that the 1,600-mile spread of the Hawaiian archipelago is due to a northwest drifting effect of about 3-5 inches per year. In conjunction with this drifting and presumably due to the immense weight of the mountains and their relative location over the molten mass under them, the Kona Coast is sinking about one inch a decade. Still, with the center of activity under the Big Island, Mauna Loa and Kilauea volcanoes regularly add more land to the only state in the U.S. that is literally still growing. About 20 miles southeast of the Big Island is Loihi Seamount, waiting 3,000 feet below the waves. Frequent eruptions bring it closer and closer to the surface; one day it will emerge as the newest Hawaiian island and later, perhaps, merge with the Big Island itself.

Science and *The Kumulipo* oral history differ sharply on the age of the Big Island. Scientists say that Hawaii is the youngest of the islands, being a little over one million years old; the chanters claim that it was the first "island-child" of Wakea and Papa. It is, irrefutably, closest to the "hot spot" on the Pacific floor, evidenced by Kilauea's frequent eruptions and by Loihi Seamount. The geology, geography, and location of the Hawaiian Islands, and their ongoing drifting and building in the middle of the Pacific, make them among the most fascinating pieces of real estate on earth. The Big Island is the *most* fascinating of them all—it is truly unique.

Size

The Big Island dwarfs all the others in the Hawaiian chain at 4,038 square miles and growing. It accounts for about 63% of the state's total land mass; the other islands could fit within it two times over. With 266 miles of coastline, the island stretches about 95 miles from north to south and 80 miles from east to west. Cape Kumukahi is the easternmost point in the state,

MOUNTAINS OF HAWAII

Mauna Loa (13,679 ft.) Mauna Kea (13,796 ft.)

Puu Okeokeo (6875 ft.) Hualalai (8271 ft.) Kohala (5480 ft.)

Waimea (2670 ft.) Kilauea (4078ft.)

Kona HILO

and Ka Lae ("South Point") is the southernmost point in the country.

The Mountains

The tremendous volcanic peak of **Mauna Kea** ("White Mountain"), located in north-central Hawaii, has been extinct for over 3,500 years. Its seasonal snowcap earns Mauna Kea its name and reputation as a good skiing area in winter. Over 18,000 feet of mountain below the surface rises straight up from the ocean floor—making Mauna Kea actually 31,796 feet tall, a substantial 2,768 feet taller than Mt. Everest; some consider it the tallest mountain in the world. At 13,796 feet above sea level, it is without doubt the tallest peak in the Pacific. Near its top, at 13,020 feet, is **Lake Waiau,** the highest lake in the state and third highest in the country. Mauna Kea was obviously a sacred mountain to the Hawaiians, and its white dome was a welcome beacon to seafarers. On its slope is the largest adze quarry in Polynesia, from which high-quality basalt was taken to be fashioned into prized tools. The atmosphere atop the mountain, which sits mid-Pacific far from pollutants, is the most rarefied and cleanest on earth. The clarity makes Mauna Kea a natural for astronomical observatories. The complex of telescopes on its summit is internationally staffed and provides data to scientists around the world.

The **Kohala Mountains** to the northwest are the oldest and rise only to 5,480 feet at Kaunu o Kaleiho'ohei peak. This section looks more like the other Hawaiian islands, with deep gorges and valleys along the coast and a forested interior. As you head east toward Waimea from Kawaihae on Route 19, for every mile that you travel you pick up about 10 inches of rainfall per year. This becomes obvious as you begin to pass little streams and rivulets running from the mountains.

Mount Hualalai, at 8,271 feet , is the backdrop to Kailua-Kona. It's home to many of the Big Island's endangered birds and supports many of the region's newest housing developments. Just a few years ago, Mt. Hualalai was thought to be extinct, since the last time it erupted was in 1801. It is now known that within the last 1,000 years, the mountain has erupted about every two or three centuries. In 1929 it suffered an earthquake swarm, which means that there was a large movement of lava inside the mountain which caused tremors. USGS scientists now consider Mt. Hualalai only dormant and very likely to erupt at some point in the future. When it does, a tremendous amount of lava is expected to pour rapidly down its steep sides. From the side of this mountain grows the cone Pu'u Wa'awa'a. At 3,967 feet, it's only slightly shorter than the very active Kilauea on the far side of Mauna Loa. Obsidian is found here and it's one of the few place in Hawaii where this substance has been quarried in large quantities.

Even though **Mauna Loa** ("Long Mountain") measures a respectable 13,679 feet, its height isn't its claim to fame. This active volcano, 60 miles long by 30 wide, is comprised of 10,000 cubic miles of iron-hard lava, making it the densest and most massive mountain on earth. In 1950, a tremendous lava flow belched from Mauna Loa's summit, reaching an astonishing rate of 6,750,000 cubic yards per hour. Seven lava rivers flowed for 23 days, emitting over 600 million cubic yards of lava that covered 35 square miles. There were no injuries, but the villages of Kaapuna and Honokua were partially destroyed along with the Magoo Ranch. Its last eruption, in 1984, was small by comparison yet created fountaining inside the summit crater and a "curtain of fire" along its eastern rift.

The lowest of the island's major peaks, **Kilauea** rises only to 4,078 feet. Its pragmatic name means "The Spewing," and it's the world's most active volcano. In the last hundred years, it has erupted on the average once every 11 months. The Hawaiians believed that the goddess Pele inhabited every volcano in the Hawaiian chain, and that her home is now Halemaumau Crater in Kilauea Caldera. Kilauea is the most scientifically watched volcano in the world, with a permanent observatory built right into the crater rim. When it erupts, the flows are so predictable that observers run toward the mountain, not away from it! The flows, however, can burst from fissures far from the center of the crater in areas that don't seem "active." This occurs mainly in the Puna District. In 1959, Kilauea Iki Crater came to life after 91 years, and although the flow wasn't as massive as others, it did send blazing fountains of lava 1,900 feet into the air. Kilauea has been very active within the last few years, with eruptions occurring at least once a month and expected to continue. Most activity has been from a vent below Pu'u O'o crater. You might be lucky enough to see this phenomenon while visiting.

Island Builders

The Hawaiians worshipped Madame Pele, the fire goddess. Her name translates equally as "volcano," "fire pit," or "eruption of lava." When she was angry, she complained by spitting fire which cooled and formed land. Volcanologists say that the islands are huge mounds of cooled basaltic lava surrounded by billions of polyp skeletons which have formed coral reefs. The Hawaiian Islands are shield volcanoes that erupt gently and form an elongated dome much like a turtle shell. The Big Island is a perfect example of this. Once the lava is above the surface of the sea, its tremendous weight seals the fissure below. Eventually the giant tube that carried lava to the surface sinks in on itself and forms a caldera, as evidenced atop Kilauea. More eruptions occur periodically, and they cover the already existing island like frosting on a titanic cake. Wind and water take over next and relentlessly sculpt the raw lava into deep crevices and cuts that become valleys. The once-smooth Kohala Mountains, once a single, smooth block typical of a shield volcano, are now a jagged, multispired mountain range due to this process.

Lava

Lava flows in two distinct types, for which the Hawaiian names have become universal geological terms: a'a and pahoehoe. They're easily distinguished in appearance, but chemically they're the same. A'a is extremely rough and spiny and will quickly tear up your shoes if you do much hiking over it. Also, if you have the misfortune to fall down, you'll immediately know why they call it a'a. Pahoehoe, a billowy, ropy lava that looks like burned pancake batter, can mold itself into fantastic shapes. Examples of both lavas are frequently encountered on various hikes throughout the Big Island. Other lava oddities that you may spot are peridots (green, gemlike stones called "Pele's Diamonds"); clear, feldspar-like, white cotton candy called "Pele's hair"; and gray lichens known as "Hawaiian snow" covering

pahoehoe lava

J.D. BISIGNANI

the older flows. For a full account of recent lava flows and eruptions, see the Hawaii Volcanoes National Park section below.

Tsunamis

"Tsunami" is the Japanese word for "tidal wave." It ranks up there with the worst of them in sparking horror in human beings. But if you were to count up all the people in Hawaii who have been swept away by tidal waves in the last 50 years, the toll wouldn't come close to those killed on bicycles in only a few Mainland cities in just five years. A Hawaiian tsunami is actually a seismic sea wave that has been generated by an earthquake that could easily have originated thousands of miles away in South America or Alaska. Some waves have been clocked at speeds up to 500 mph. The safest place during a tsunami, besides high ground well away from beach areas, is out on the open ocean where even an enormous wave is perceived only as a large swell—a tidal wave is only dangerous when it is opposed by land. Hilo has been struck with the two worst tidal waves in modern history. A giant wave smashed the islands on April 1, 1946, and swept away 159 people and over

1,300 homes; Hilo sustained most of these losses. Again, on May 23, 1960, Hilo took the brunt of a wave that rumbled through the business district, killing 61 people. There is an elaborate warning system throughout the island; warning procedures and inundation maps are listed in the front of the telephone directory.

Earthquakes

These rumblings are also a concern in Hawaii and offer a double threat because they can generate tsunamis. If you ever feel a tremor and are close to a beach, get as far away as fast as possible. The Big Island, because of its active volcanoes, experiences hundreds of technical earthquakes, although 99% can only be felt by very delicate equipment. In the last two decades, the Big Island has experienced about one earthquake a year in the range of 5.0-6.0 on the Richter scale, which is about 60% of all quakes of that magnitude in the state. The last major quake on the Big Island occurred in late November 1975, reaching 7.2 on the Richter scale and causing many millions of dollars' worth of damage in the island's southern regions. The only loss of life occurred when a beach collapsed and two people from a large camping party were drowned.

Beaches and Ponds

The Big Island takes the rap for having poor beaches—this isn't true! They are certainly few and far between, but they are spectacular. Hawaii is big and young, so distances are greater than on other islands, and the wave action hasn't had enough time to grind new lava and coral into sand. The Kona and Kohala coast beaches, along with a few nooks and crannies around Hilo, are gorgeous. Puna's beaches are incredible black sand, and the southern part of the island has a string of hidden beaches enjoyed only by those intrepid enough to get to them. Full listings are found in the various travel chapters under "Beaches."

Just north of Keahole Airport in Kona is Makalawena. Follow a rough coastal trail to a beautiful white-sand beach. Inland is its associated wetland pond, probably the most important one on the Big Island. This fragile and archaeologically important area is managed by the Bishop Estate. Currently, entry is not allowed except with a U.S. Fish and Wildlife Service official or a state biologist. However, the Sierra Club and Audubon Society are permitted to enter, and you can arrange to accompany them on a field trip. If you wish to visit this beautiful area, consider contacting these organizations long before your trip to the Big Island. Two other coastal ponds are located in Kaloko-Honokohau National Historical Park between the Kona airport and Kailua-Kona.

Protecting the Coral Reef

Currently controversy is raging over an attempt to place anchoring pins in the hard lava rock just off the Kailua-Kona Coast. Boats could latch onto them, and by doing so would not drag their anchors across the fragile coral reef, as is now the case. The Dive Council in Kona isn't known for agreeing on many issues because they represent so many different factions, but on this issue they agree unanimously that the pins should be put in place. So, they collectively decided to make a move in favor of the pins, which have been used successfully all over the world. The process is environmentally sound, and in fact the technology specifically needed for drilling in lava rock was worked out at the University of Hawaii. After three years elapsed, during which the Department of Land and Natural Resources debated whether it was their responsibility or that of the Hawaii Department of Transportation to implement the program, the Dive Council went ahead and put in the pins, without the moorings. Upstaged, the Department of Land and Natural Resources was furious and at meetings tried to find a scapegoat at which they could throw their bureaucratic book. They would be better served spending their energies protecting the reef.

Geothermal Controversy

Pele's blood-red lava is cool compared to the uncompromising debate now sizzling between natives' rights groups allied with environmentalists, and geothermal advocates who view the Big Island's molten core as an infinite source of power. Former governor John D. Waihee, with strong support from the state's legislators, sanctioned the construction of a geothermal well within the 27,000 acres that make up the **Wao Kele O Puna Rainforest**—the *only* tropical lowland rainforest in the United States! Another 20 power plants will bore into the east rift of Kilauea Volcano, and all will require huge steam collection systems, power plants, power lines, and towers that will march across the most expansive and pristine panoramas that the island has to offer. Adding to the magnitude of this engineering feat (the largest developmental plan of any type ever attempted in Hawaii) will be a deep ocean cable stretching from the Big Island to Maui, and on to Oahu. Transversing an unstable ocean canyon over 6,500 feet deep, the cable, with an estimated cost of $3 billion, will lie at more than seven times the depth of any cable laid thus far anywhere in the world. The major developers, Hawaii's Campbell Estates, and True Geothermal of Casper, Wyoming, envision generating about 500 megawatts of electricity, about four times the amount needed by the Big Island at the present rate of consumption. The power will be used to further develop Kona, on the Big Island; the substantial excess will be exported to Oahu and Maui. Residents of Puna, where the development will occur, can see no benefit in despoiling their homes and environment in order to fuel the ravenous demands generated by tourism on the islands.

One of the constituents of the anti-geothermal coalition, the Pele Defense Fund, views the development as a desecration of the land according to traditional religion, believing that each well is a puncture wound in Pele's side. To these local people, many of whom are native Hawaiians who trace their lineage directly to Pele and who feel protected by her, the drilling amounts to no less than sacrilege. Having recently lost a local court battle claiming that the area has religious significance, they plan to carry on the fight all the way to the Supreme Court. The Pele Defense Fund points out that the wells are being drilled over extremely unstable land that is susceptible to a rampaging lava flow at any time. A destroyed well could pump incalculable volumes of hydrogen sulfide gas into the atmosphere. They also contend that most of the jobs at the sites are low-paying maintenance jobs that will hardly benefit the local economy, and that the higher-paying managerial positions will be given to new arrivals brought in from the Mainland.

To environmentally aware botanists and entomologists, the despoiling of any of the precious and dwindling rainforest is a nightmare. Even one footfall in a 2,000-year-old bog-floored rainforest can take months and even years to disappear. Native species of plants could be made extinct through the introduction of foreign species inadvertently carried by workers and machinery, while the ruts left by construction could become stagnant pools breeding mosquito larvae that affect native birds. The destruction caused by heavy trucks, earth-moving machinery, site deforestation, and the constant maintenance of the site, in these fragile environs, is incalculable. All scientists agree that once a rainforest is destroyed, or disturbed, it is virtually gone forever. The Earthjustice Legal Defense Fund (formerly, Sierra Club Legal Defense Fund), in coalition with the Pele Defense Fund, Rainforest Action Network, and other island environmental groups, attempted to force the Environmental Protection Agency, Army Corps of Engineers, U.S. Geological Survey, Department of Energy, and National Park Service—the federal agencies involved in the project—to prepare an environmental impact statement which, unbelievably, had not been done previously. The coalition sought a moratorium placed on construction until a study was done. As a finale to their perseverance, in 1996, True Geothermal ceased participation in the project and the following year the state discontinued all efforts to promote future geothermal development in the Wao Kele O Puna rainforest.

Proponents of the geothermal power plants point to the fact that Hawaii is *the* most oil-dependent state in America. They say that the building of the pollution-free plants will save millions of barrels of oil over the years, reduce air pollutants, and help reduce the threat to Hawaii's coastline due to oil spills. Ormat Energy Systems of Sparks, Nevada, who purchased Puna Geothermal Venture, the previous plant operator, claims that its geothermal technology provides for a "closed system" that will pump any residual geothermal brine and steam back into the earth, while absolutely eliminating any foul smell of hydrogen sulfide gas. Opponents say that the vast majority of Hawaii's imported petroleum is used for automobiles and aircraft, and that the development of alternative sources of power like solar and wind energy, along with increased conservation, could easily make up for the purported savings.

The real issue in the development of geothermal electrical power generation on the Big Island is the priorities of modern American society: power and profits now for large developers and corporations, or the preservation of the earth's wild places for future generations. Neither seems able to wait.

Environmental Resource Groups

Anyone interested in Hawaii's environmental issues can contact the following for more information:

Earthjustice Legal Defense Fund (formerly Sierra Club Legal Defense Fund), 223 S. King St., 4th Fl., Honolulu, HI 96813, tel. 599-2436 (E-mail: eajushi@igc.apc.org).

Greenpeace, 1807 Waianuenue Ave., Hilo, HI 96720, tel. 969-9910.

The Nature Conservancy, 1116 Smith St., Suite 201, Honolulu, HI 96817, tel. 537-4508 (E-mail: TNCH1@aol.com; Web site: www.tnc .org/hawaii).

Pele Defense Fund, P.O. Box 404, Volcano, HI 96785, tel. 935-1663.

Rainforest Action Network, 301 Broadway, Suite A, San Francisco, CA 94133, tel. (415) 398-4404.

Sierra Club Hawaii Chapter, 233 Merchant St., 2nd Fl., Honolulu, HI 96813, tel. 538-6616.

A savvy monthly newsletter that focuses on environmental and political issues facing Hawaii today is *Environment Hawai'i,* 200 Kanoelehua Ave., Suite 103-325, Hilo, HI 96720, tel. 934-0115, fax 934-8321, individual subscription rate $35 per year. The well-researched and concisely written newsletter attempts to be fair to all parties concerned, explaining both sides to most controversies. Short on preaching and long on common sense, *Environment Hawaii* is an excellent resource for anyone interested in sociopolitical and environmental issues. E-mail: pattum@aloha.net.

For organizations offering environment-conscious tours in Hawaii, see "Sightseeing Tours" under "Getting Around" in the Out and About chapter below.

CLIMATE

The average temperature around the island varies between 72 and 78° F. Summers raise the temperature to the mid-80s and winters cool off to the low 70s. Both Kona and Hilo seem to maintain a year-round average of about 74 degrees, and the South Kohala coast is a few degrees warmer. As usual, it's cooler in the higher elevations, and Waimea sees most days in the mid-60s to low 70s, while Volcano maintains a relatively steady 60 degrees. Atop Mauna Kea, the temperature rarely climbs above 50° or dips below 30, while the summit of Mauna Loa is about 10 degrees warmer. The lowest recorded temperature on the Big Island (and for the state) was 1°F inside the Mauna Kea summit crater in January 1970, while the highest ever recorded was in April 1931 at Pahala in Kau—a scorching (for Hawaii) 100°F.

Rainfall

Weatherwise, the Big Island's climate varies not so much in temperature but precipitation. Hawaii has some of the wettest and driest coastal areas in the islands. The line separating wet from dry can be dramatic. Waimea, for example, has an actual dry and wet side of town, as if a boundary

line split the town in two! Houses on the dry side are at a premium. Kona and Hilo are opposites. The Kona Coast is almost guaranteed to be sunny and bright, receiving as little as 15 inches of rainfall per year but with an average of 28 inches. Both Kona and the Kau Desert to the south are in the rain shadow of Mauna Loa, and most rain clouds coming from east to west are pierced by its summit before they ever reach Kona. Hilo is wet, with predictable afternoon and evening showers—they make the entire town blossom. Though this reputation keeps many tourists away, the rain's predictability makes it easy to avoid a drenching while exploring the town. Hilo gets an average of 128 inches of rainfall per year, with a record of 153.93 inches set in 1971. It also holds the dubious honor of being the town with the most rainfall recorded by the National Weather Service in a 24-hour period—a drenching 22.3 inches in February 1979.

"So Good" Weather

The ancient Hawaiians had words to describe climatic specifics such as rain, wind, fog, and even snow, but they didn't have a general word for "weather." The reason is that the weather is just about the same throughout the year and depends more on where you are on any given island than on what season it is. The Hawaiians did distinguish between *kau* (summer, May-Oct.) and *hoo'ilo* (winter, Nov.-April), but this distinction included social, religious, and even navigational factors, far beyond a mere distinction of weather variations.

The average daytime temperature throughout Hawaii is about 80° F (26° C), with the average winter (January) day registering 78°, and the average summer (August) day raising the thermometer only seven degrees to 85. Nighttime temperatures drop less than 10 degrees. Altitude, however, does drop temperatures about three degrees for every 1,000 feet; if you intend to visit the mountain peaks of Mauna Loa and Mauna Kea (both over 10,000 feet), expect the temperature to be at least 30 degrees cooler than at sea level. Recently, snows lasted atop Mauna Kea well into June, with nighttime temperatures well below freezing.

The Trade Winds

Temperatures in the 50th state are both constant and moderate because of the trade winds. These breezes are so prevailing that the northeast sides of the islands are always referred to as **windward,** regardless of where the wind happens to blow on any given day. You can count on the trades to be blowing on an average of 300 days per year, hardly missing a day during summer, and occurring half the time in winter. They blow throughout the day but are strong during the heat of the afternoon, then weaken at night. Just when you need a cooling breeze, there they are, and when the temperature drops at night, it's as if someone turned down a giant fan.

The trade winds are also a factor in keeping down the humidity. They will suddenly disappear, however, usually in winter, and might not resume for a few weeks. The Tropic of Cancer runs through the center of Hawaii, yet the latitude's famed oppressively hot and muggy weather is joyfully absent in the islands. Honolulu, on the same latitude as sweaty Hong Kong and Havana, has only a 50-60% daily humidity factor.

Kona Winds

Kona means "leeward" in Hawaiian, and when the trades stop blowing, these southerly winds often take over. To anyone from Hawaii, *"kona* wind" is a euphemism for bad weather, for it brings in hot, sticky air. Luckily, *kona* winds are most common Oct.-April, when they appear roughly half the time. The temperatures drop slightly during the winter so these hot winds are tolerable, and even useful for moderating the thermometer. In the summer they are awful, but luckily again they hardly ever blow during this season.

A *kona* storm is another matter. These subtropical low-pressure storms develop west of the Hawaiian Islands, and as they move east draw

AVERAGE MAXIMUM/MINIMUM TEMPERATURE AND RAINFALL

TOWN		JAN.	MARCH	MAY	JUNE	SEPT.	NOV.
Hilo	high	79	79	80	82	82	80
	low	62	62	61	70	70	65
	rain	11	15	7	10	10	15
Kona	high	80	81	81	82	82	81
	low	62	64	65	68	68	63
	rain	4	3	2	0	2	1

temperature in °F, rainfall in inches

winds up from the south. Usual only in winter, they can cause considerable damage to crops and real estate. There is no real pattern to *kona* storms—some years they come every few weeks while in other years they don't appear at all.

Severe Weather

With all this talk of ideal weather it might seem as if there isn't any bad. Read on. When a storm does hit an island, conditions can be bleak and miserable. The worst storms occur in the fall and winter and often have the warped sense of humor to drop their heaviest rainfalls on areas that are normally quite dry. It's not infrequent for a storm to dump more than three inches of rain an hour; this can go as high as 10, making Hawaiian rainfalls some of the heaviest on earth.

Hawaii has also been hit with some walloping hurricanes in the last few decades. There haven't been many but they've been destructive. The vast majority of hurricanes originate far to the southeast off the Pacific coasts of Mexico and Latin America; some, particularly later in the season, start in the midst of the Pacific Ocean near the equator south of Hawaii. Hurricane season is generally considered June to November. Most pass harmlessly south of Hawaii but some, swept along by *kona* winds, strike the islands. The most recent and destructive was Hurricane Iniki, which battered the islands in 1992, killing eight people and causing an estimated 2 billion dollars in damage. It had its greatest effect on Niihau, the Poipu Beach area of Kauai, and the leeward coast of Oahu.

WHAT IS A HURRICANE?

Tropical Depression: low-pressure system or cyclone with winds below 39 mph.
Tropical Storm: cyclone with winds 39-73 mph.
Hurricane: cyclone with winds over 74 mph. These winds are often accompanied by torrential rains, destructive waves, and storm surges.

The National Weather Service issues a Hurricane Watch if hurricane conditions are expected in the area within 36 hours. A Hurricane Warning is issued when a hurricane is expected to strike within 24 hours. The state of Hawaii has an elaborate warning system against natural disasters. You will notice loudspeakers high atop poles along many beaches and coastal areas; these warn of tsunamis, hurricanes, and earthquakes. As the figures below attest, property damage has been great but the loss of life has, thankfully, been minimal.

Major Hurricanes Since 1950

NAME	DATE	ISLANDS AFFECTED	DAMAGES
Hiki	Aug. 1950	Kauai	1 death
Nina	Dec. 1957	Kauai	—
Dot	Aug. 1959	Kauai	$5.5 million
Fico	July 1978	Hawaii	—
Iwa	Nov. 1982	Kauai, Oahu	1 death; $234 million
Estelle	July 1986	Maui, Hawaii	$2 million
Iniki	Sept. 1992	Kauai, Oahu	8 deaths; $1,900 million

No alien land in all the world has any deep, strong charm for me, but that one; no other land could so longingly and beseechingly haunt my sleeping and waking, through half a lifetime, as that one has done. Other things leave me, but it abides.

—*Mark Twain, c. 1889*

FLORA AND FAUNA

THE MYSTERY OF MIGRATION

Anyone who loves a mystery will be intrigued by the speculation about how plants and animals first came to Hawaii. Most people's idea of an island paradise includes swaying palms, dense mysterious jungles ablaze with wildflowers, and luscious fruits just waiting to be plucked. In fact, for millions of years the Hawaiian chain consisted of raw and barren islands where no plants grew and no birds sang. Why? Because they are geological orphans that spontaneously popped up in the middle of the Pacific Ocean. The islands, more than 2,000 miles from any continental landfall, were therefore isolated from the normal ecological spread of plants and animals. Even the most tenacious travelers of the flora and fauna kingdoms would be sorely tried in crossing the mighty Pacific. Those that made it by pure chance found a totally foreign ecosystem. They had to adapt or perish. The survivors evolved quickly, and many plants and birds became so specialized that they were not only limited to specific islands in the chain but to habitats that frequently encompassed a single isolated valley. It was as if after traveling so far, and finding a niche, they never budged again. Luckily, the soil of Hawaii was virgin and rich, the competition from other plants or animals was nonexistent, and the climate was sufficiently varied and nearly perfect for most growing things.

The evolution of plants and animals on the isolated islands was astonishingly rapid. A tremendous change in environment, coupled with a limited gene pool, accelerated natural selection. For example, many plants lost their protective thorns and spines because there were no grazing animals or birds to destroy them. Before settlement, Hawaii had no fruits, vegetables, coconut palms, edible land animals, conifers, mangroves, or banyans. Tropical flowers, wild and vibrant as we know them today, were relatively few. In a land where thousands of orchids now brighten every corner, there were only four native varieties, the least in any of the 50 states. Today, the indigenous plants and animals have the highest rate of extinction anywhere on earth. By the beginning of this century, native plants growing below 1,500 feet in elevation were almost completely extinct or totally replaced by introduced species. The land and its living things have been greatly transformed by humans and their agriculture. This inexorable process began when Hawaii was the domain of its original Polynesian settlers, then greatly accelerated when the land was inundated by Western peoples.

The indigenous plants and birds of the Big Island have suffered the same fate as those of the other Hawaiian Islands; they're among the most endangered species on earth and disappearing at an alarming rate. There are some sanctuaries on the Big Island where native species still live, but they must be vigorously protected. Do your bit to save them; enjoy but do not disturb.

PLANTS, FLOWERS, AND TREES

Hawaii's indigenous and endemic plants, flowers, and trees are both fascinating and beautiful, but unfortunately, like everything else that was native, they are quickly disappearing. The majority of flora considered exotic by visitors was introduced either by the original Polynesians or by later white settlers. The Polynesians who colonized Hawaii brought foodstuffs, including coconuts, bananas, taro, breadfruit, sweet potatoes, yams, and sugarcane. They also carried along gourds to use as containers, *awa* to make a basic intoxicant, and the ti plant to use for offerings or to string into hula skirts. Non-Hawaiian settlers over the years have brought mangos, papayas, passion fruit, pineapples, and the other tropical fruits and vegetables associated with the islands. Also, most of the flowers, including protea, plumeria, anthuriums, orchids, heliconia, ginger, and most hibiscus, have come from every continent on earth. Tropical America, Asia, Java, India, and China have contributed their most beautiful and delicate blooms. Hawaii is blessed with national and state parks, gardens, undisturbed rainforests, private reserves, and commercial nurseries that offer an exhaustive botanical survey of the island. The following is a sampling of the common native and introduced flora that add dazzling color and exotic tastes to the landscape.

Native Trees

Koa and **ohia** are two indigenous trees still seen on the Big Island. Both have been greatly reduced by the foraging of introduced cattle and goats, and through logging and forest fires. The koa, a form of acacia, is Hawaii's finest native tree. It can grow to over 70 feet high and has a strong, straight trunk which can measure more than 10 feet in circumference. Koa is a very quickly growing legume that fixes nitrogen in the soil. It is believed that the tree originated in Africa, where it was very damp. It then migrated to Australia, where it was very dry, which caused the elimination of leaves so that all that was left were bare stems which could survive in the desert climate. When koa came to the Pacific islands, instead of reverting to the true leaf, it just broadened its leaf stem into sickle-shaped, leaflike foliage that produces an inconspicuous, pale-yellow flower. When the tree is young or damaged it will revert to the original feathery, fernlike leaf that evolved in Africa millions of years ago. The koa does best in well-drained soil in deep forest areas, but scruffy specimens will grow on poorer soil. The Hawaiians used koa as the main log for their dugout canoes, and elaborate ceremonies were per-

ohia

LOUISE FOOTE

formed when a log was cut and dragged to a canoe shed. Koa wood was also preferred for paddles, spears, even surfboards. Today it is still, unfortunately, considered an excellent furniture wood, and although fine specimens can be found in the reserve of Hawaii Volcanoes National Park, loggers elsewhere are harvesting the last of the big trees.

The ohia is a survivor, and therefore the most abundant of all the native Hawaiian trees. Coming in a variety of shapes and sizes, it grows as miniature trees in wet bogs or as 100-foot giants on cool, dark slopes at higher elevations. This tree is often the first life in new lava flows. The ohia produces a tuftlike flower—usually red, but occasionally orange, yellow, or white, the latter being very rare and elusive—that resembles a natural pompon. The flower was considered sacred to Pele; it was said that she would cause a rainstorm if you picked ohia blossoms without the proper prayers. The flowers were fashioned into lei that resembled feather boas. The strong, hard wood was used to make canoes, poi bowls, and especially temple images. Ohia logs were also used as railroad ties

LOUISE FOOTE

koa

and shipped to the Mainland from Pahoa. It's believed that the "golden spike" linking rail lines between the U.S. East and West coasts was driven into a Puna ohia log when the two railroads came together in Ogden, Utah.

Ferns

If you travel to Volcanoes National Park you will find yourself deep in an amazing, high-altitude tropical rainforest. This unique forest exists because of the 120 inches of annual rainfall, which turns the raw lava into a lush forest. Besides stands of ohia and koa, you'll be treated to a primordial display of ferns. All new fronds on ferns are called "fiddleheads" because of the way they unfurl and resemble the scrolls of violin heads. Fiddleheads were eaten by Hawaiians during times of famine. The most common ferns are *hapuu*, a rather large tree fern, and *amauamau*, a smaller type with a more simple frond. A soft, furry growth around the base of the stalks is

Fiddlehead ferns are prevalent along trails where the lava has weathered.

called *pulu*. At one time *pulu* was collected for stuffing mattresses, and a factory was located atop Volcanoes. But *pulu* breaks down and forms a very fine dust after a few years, so it never really became generally accepted for mattresses.

At high altitudes, young ferns and other plants will often produce new growth that turns bright red as protection against the sun's ultraviolet rays. You'll see it on new foliage before it hardens. Hawaiians called this new growth *liko*. Today, people still make lei from *liko* because it has so many subtle and beautiful colors. Ohia *liko* is a favorite for lei because it is so striking.

Other Flora

The Hawaiians called the **prickly pear cactus** *panini,* which translates as "very unfriendly," undoubtedly because of the sharp spines covering the flat, thick leaves. The cactus is typical of those found in Mexico and the southwestern United States. It was introduced to Hawaii before 1810 and established itself coincidentally with the cattle brought in at the time; *panini* is very common in North Kohala, especially on the Parker Ranch lands. It is assumed that Don Marin, a Spanish advisor to Kamehameha I, was responsible for importing the plant. Perhaps the early *paniolo* (cowboy) felt lonely without it. The *panini* can grow to heights of 15 feet and is now considered a pest but nonetheless looks as if it belongs. It develops small and delicious pear-shaped fruits. Hikers who decide to pick the fruit should be careful of small, yellowish bristles that can burrow under the skin and irritate. An attempt is being made to control the cactus in *paniolo* country. *El cosano rojo,* the red worm found in the bottom of Mexican tequila, has been introduced to destroy the plant. It burrows into the cactus and eats the hardwood center, causing the plant to wither and die.

More species of **lobelia** grow in Hawaii than anywhere else in the world. A common garden flower elsewhere, in Hawaii it grows to tree height. You'll see some unique species covered with hair or with spikes. The lobelia flower is tiny and resembles a miniature orchid with curved and pointed ends, like the beak of the native *i'iwi*. This bird feeds on the flower's nectar; it's obvious that both evolved in Hawaii together and exhibit the strange phenomenon of nature mimicking nature.

The Big Island has more species of **gesneriad,** the African violet family, than anywhere else on earth. Many don't have the showy flowers that you normally associate with African violets, but have evolved into strange species with huge, fuzzy leaves.

The *puahanui,* meaning "many flowers," is Hawaii's native hydrangea; it is common in the upland forests of the Big Island.

prickly pear

DIANA LASICH HARPER

Tropical Rainforests

When it comes to pure and diverse natural beauty, the U.S. is one of the finest pieces of real estate on earth. As if purple mountains' majesty and fruited plains weren't enough, it even received a tiny, living emerald of tropical rainforest. A tropical rainforest is where the earth takes a breath and exhales pure sweet oxygen through its vibrant green canopy. Located in the territories of Puerto Rico and the Virgin Islands and in the state of Hawaii, these forests comprise only one-half of one percent of the world's total, and they must be preserved. The U.S. Congress passed two bills in 1986 designed to protect the unique biological diversity of its tropical areas, but their destruction has continued unabated. The lowland rainforests of Hawaii, populated mostly by native ohia, are being razed. Landowners slash, burn, and bulldoze them to create more land for cattle and agriculture and, most distressingly, for wood chips to generate electricity! Introduced wild boar gouge the forest floor, exposing sensitive roots and leaving tiny, fetid ponds where mosquito larvae thrive. Feral goats roam the forests like hoofed locusts and strip all vegetation within reach. Maui's Nature Conservancy Preserve in Waikamoi has managed to fence in a speck of this forest, keeping it safe from these animals for the time being. Almost half the birds classified in the U.S. as endangered live in Hawaii, and almost all of these make their homes in the rainforests. For example, Maui's rainforests have yielded the *poouli,* a new species of bird discovered only in 1974. Another forest survey in 1981 rediscovered the Bishop's *o'o,* a bird thought to be extinct at the turn of the century. We can only lament the passing of the rainforests that have already fallen to ignorance, but if this ill-fated destruction continues on a global level, we will be lamenting our own passing. We must nurture the rainforests that remain, and with simple enlightenment, let them be.

BIRDS

One of the great tragedies of natural history is the continuing demise of Hawaiian birdlife. Perhaps only 15 original species of birds remain of the more than 70 native families that thrived before the coming of humans. Since the arrival of Captain Cook in 1778, 23 species have become extinct, with 31 more in danger. And what's not known is how many species were wiped out before the coming of white explorers. Experts believe that the Hawaiians annihilated about 40 species, including seven other species of geese besides the *nene,* a rare one-legged owl, ibis, lovebirds, sea eagles, and hunting creepers—all gone before Captain Cook arrived. Hawaii's endangered birds account for 40% of the birds officially listed as endangered or threatened by the U.S. Fish and Wildlife Service. In the last 200 years, more than four times as many birds have become extinct in Hawaii as in all of North America. These figures unfortunately suggest that a full 40% of Hawaii's endemic birds no longer exist.

The nene, the state bird, lives only on Haleakala on Maui and on the slopes of Mauna Loa, Mauna Kea, and Mt. Hualalai.

BOB RACE

Almost all of Oahu's native birds are gone and few indigenous Hawaiian birds can be found on any island below the 3,000-foot level.

Native birds have been reduced in number because of multiple factors. The original Polynesians helped wipe out many species. They altered large areas for farming, and used fire to destroy patches of pristine forests. Also, bird feathers were highly prized for the making of lei, for featherwork in capes and helmets, and for the large *kahili* fans that indicated rank among the *ali'i*. Introduced exotic birds and the new diseases they carried are another major reason for reduction of native bird numbers, along with predation by the mongoose and rat—especially upon ground-nesting birds. Bird malaria and bird pox are also devastating to the native species. Mosquitoes, unknown in Hawaii until a ship named the *Wellington* introduced them at Lahaina in 1826 through larvae carried in its water barrels, infect most native birds, causing a rapid reduction in birdlife. Feral pigs rooting deep in the rainforests knock over ferns and small trees, creating fetid pools in which mosquito larvae thrive. However, the most damaging factor by far is the assault upon native forests by agriculture and land developers. The vast majority of Hawaiian birds evolved into specialists. They lived in only one small area and ate a very limited number of plants or insects, which once removed or altered soon killed the birds.

You'll spot birds all over the Big Island, from the coastal areas to the high mountain slopes. Some are found on other islands as well, but the ones listed below are found only or mainly on the Big Island. Every bird listed is either threatened or endangered.

Hawaii's Own

The *nene,* or Hawaiian goose, deserves special mention because it is Hawaii's state bird and is making a comeback from the edge of extinction. The *nene* is found only on the slopes of Mauna Loa, Hualalai, and Mauna Kea on the Big Island, and in Haleakala Crater on Maui. It was extinct on Maui until a few birds were returned there in 1957, but some experts maintain that the *nene* lived naturally only on the Big Island. *Nene* are raised at the Wildfowl Trust in Slimbridge, England, which placed the first birds at Haleakala; and at the Hawaiian Fish and Game Station at Pohakuloa, along the Saddle Road on Hawaii. By the 1940s, fewer than 50 birds lived in the wild. Now approximately 125 birds live on Haleakala and 500 on the Big Island. Although the birds can be raised successfully in captivity, their life in the wild is still in question.

The *nene* is believed to be a descendant of the Canadian goose, which it resembles. Geese are migratory birds that form strong kinship ties, mating for life. It's speculated that a migrating goose became disabled, and along with its loyal mate, remained in Hawaii. The *nene* is smaller than its Canadian cousin, has lost a great deal of webbing in its feet, and is perfectly at home away from water, foraging and nesting on rugged and bleak lava flows.

Good places to view *nene* are in Volcanoes National Park at Kipuka Nene Campground, Summit Caldera, Devastation Trail, and Volcanoes Golf Course, at dawn and dusk. The birds gather at the golf course because they love to feed on grasses. The places to view them on the Kona side are Puulani, a housing development north of Kailua-Kona; or Kaloka Mauka, another housing development on the slopes of Mt. Hualalai. At the top of the road up Mt. Hualalai is a trail, also a good place to see the *nene.* Unfortunately, as the housing developments proliferate and the residents invariably acquire dogs and cats, the *nene* will disappear. The *nene* is a perfect symbol of Hawaii: let it be, and it will live.

The **Hawaiian crow,** or *alala,* is reduced to less than 12 birds living on the slopes of Hualalai and Mauna Loa above the 3,000-foot level. It looks like the common raven but has a more melodious voice and sometimes dull brown feathers. The *alala* breeds in early spring, and the greenish-blue, black-flecked eggs hatch from April to June. It is extremely nervous while nesting and any disturbance will cause it to abandon its young.

The **Hawaiian hawk** *('io)* primarily lives on the slopes of Mauna Loa and Mauna Kea below 9,000 feet. It travels from there to other parts of the island and can often be seen kiting in the skies over Hawaii Volcanoes National Park, upland from Kailua-Kona, and in remote spots like Waimanu Valley. This noble bird, the royalty of the skies, symbolized the *ali'i*. The *'io* population was once dwindling, and many scientists feared that the bird was headed for extinction. The hawk exists only on the Big Island for reasons that are not entirely clear. The good news is that the *'io* is making a dramatic comeback, also for reasons that are still unclear. Speculation has it that it may be gaining resistance to some diseases, including malaria, or that it may have learned how to prey on the introduced rats, or even that it may be adapting to life in macadamia nut groves and other alternate habitats.

The *akiapola'au,* a honeycreeper, is a five-inch yellow bird hardly bigger than its name. It lives mainly on the eastern slopes in ohia and koa forests above 3,500 feet. It has a long, curved upper beak for probing and a smaller lower beak that it uses woodpecker-fashion. The *akiapola'au* opens its mouth wide, strikes the wood with its lower beak, and then uses the upper beak to scrape out any larvae or insects. Listen for the distinctive rapping sound to spot this melodious singer. The *akiapola'au* can be seen at the Hakalau National Wildlife Refuge and along the Pu'u O'o Volcano Trail from Volcanoes National Park. It's estimated that only about 1,000 of these birds, the rarest of the island's rare winged creatures, are left.

In addition, two other endangered birds of the Big Island are the *koloa maoli,* a duck that resembles the mallard, and the slate gray or white *alae ke'oke'o* coot.

Marine Birds

Two coastal birds that breed on the high slopes of Hawaii's volcanoes and feed on the coast are the **Hawaiian dark-rumped petrel** *('ua'u)* and the **Newell's shearwater** *('a'o).* The *'ua'u* lives on the barren high slopes and craters, where it nests in burrows or under stones. Breeding season lasts from mid-March to mid-October. Only one chick is born and nurtured on regurgitated squid and fish. The *'ua'u* suffers heavily from predation. The *'a'o* prefers the forested slopes of the interior. It breeds from April-Nov., and spends its days at sea and nights inland. Feral cats and dogs reduce its numbers considerably. In addition, the *ae'o* Hawaiian black-necked stilt has become endangered.

'io

BOB RACE

Forest Birds

The following birds are found in the upland forests of the Big Island. The **elepaio** is found on other islands but is also spotted in Volcanoes National Park. This long-tailed (often held upright), five-inch brown bird (appearance can vary considerably) can be coaxed to come within touching distance of the observer. Sometimes it will sit on lower branches above your head and scold you. This bird was the special *amakua* (personal spirit) of canoe builders in ancient lore. Fairly common in the rainforest, it is basically a flycatcher.

The *amakihi* and *iiwi* are endemic birds not endangered at the moment. The *amakihi* is one of the most common native birds; yellowish green, it frequents the high branches of the ohia, koa, and sandalwood looking for insects, nectar, or fruit. It is less specialized than most other Hawaiian birds, the main reason for its continued existence. The *iiwi* is a bright red honeycreeper with a salmon-colored, hooked bill. It's found on Hawaii in the forests above 2,000 feet. It too feeds on a variety of insects and flowers. The *iiwi* is known for a harsh voice that sounds like a squeaking hinge, but it's also capable of a melodious song. The *iiwi* can be spotted at the top of Kaloka Mauka (a housing development north of Kailua-Kona), at Powerline Road, which goes south off the Saddle Road, and at Pu'u O'o Trail in Volcanoes National Park.

The *apapane* is abundant on Hawaii, especially atop Volcanoes, and being the most common native bird, is the easiest to see. It's a chubby, red-bodied bird about five inches long with a black bill, legs, wingtips, and tail feathers. It's quick and flitty and has a wide variety of calls and songs, from beautiful warbles to mechanical buzzes. Its feathers were sought by Hawaiians to produce distinctive capes and helmets for the *ali'i*.

The **Hawaiian thrush** *(oma'o)* is a fairly common bird found above 3,000 feet in the windward forests of Hawaii. This eight-inch gray bird is a good singer, often seen perching with distinctive drooping wings and a shivering body. The *oma'o* is probably descended from Townsend's solitaire. The best place to look for it is at the Thurston Lava Tube in Hawaii Volcanoes National Park, where you can see it doing its baby-bird shivering-and-shaking act. A great mimic, it can sound like a cat or even like an old-fashioned radio with stations changing as you turn the dial. Another good place to see the *oma'o* is along Powerline Road, off the Saddle Road.

The *akepa* is a four- to five-inch bird. The male is a brilliant orange to red, the female a drab green and yellow. It is found mainly on Hualalai and in windward forests. In ornithologic and environmental circles, the *akepa, akiapolaau,* and **Hawaii creeper** are lovingly referred to as the Big Three, as they are the rarest of the rare birds of the island and a true joy to spot.

The six-inch, bright yellow *palila* is found only on Hawaii in the forests of Mauna Kea above 6,000 feet. It depends exclusively upon *mamane* trees for survival, eating its pods, buds, and flowers. *Mamane* seedlings are destroyed by feral sheep. The Department of Land and Natural Resources for some inexplicable reason attempted to introduce sheep on the land that is the main refuge for the *palila,* which greatly endangered the bird's survival. The Sierra Club and Audubon Society immediately sued to prevent this environmental fiasco and were successful in winning their case in the local courts. The Department of Land and Natural resources insisted on fighting the decision all the way to the Supreme Court. They lost, and reluctantly got rid of the sheep. But instead of letting a bad decision fade away, they compounded their folly by introducing a different type of sheep. They were sued again, lost again, and again fought it all the way to the Supreme Court, wasting taxpayers money every laborious inch of the way. As goes the *mamane,* so goes the *palila.* As goes the *palila,* so goes humanity's attempt to live in harmony with nature.

The *po'ouli* is a dark-brown, five-inch bird with a black mask and dark-brown feet. Its tail is short, and it sports a conical bill. It was saved from extinction through efforts of the Sierra Club and Audubon Society, who successfully had it listed as the newest addition to the Federal List of Endangered Species. The bird has one remaining stronghold deep in the forests of Maui.

OTHER HAWAIIAN ANIMALS

Hawaii had only two indigenous mammals, the monk seal or *'ilio holu I ka uaua* (found throughout the Islands) and the hoary bat (found mainly on the Big Island); both are threatened or endangered. The remainder of the Big Island's mammals are transplants. But like anything else, including people, that has been in the islands long enough, they have taken on characteristics that make them "local."

The following animals are found primarily on the Big Island. The **Hawaiian hoary bat** *(ope 'ape'a)* is a cousin of the Mainland bat, a strong flier that made it to Hawaii eons ago and developed its own species. Its tail has a whitish coloration, hence its name. Small populations of the bat are found on Maui and Kauai, but the greatest numbers of them are on the Big Island, where they have been spotted even on the upper slopes of Mauna Loa and Mauna Kea. The hoary bat has a 13-inch wingspan. Unlike other bats, it is a solitary creature, roosting in trees. It gives birth to twins in early summer and can often be spotted over Hilo and Kealakekua Bays just around sundown.

The **feral dog** *(ilio)* is found on all the islands but especially on the slopes of Mauna Kea, where packs chase feral sheep. Poisoned and shot by local ranchers, their numbers are diminishing. Black dogs, thought to be more tender, are still eaten in some Hawaiian and Filipino communities.

The **feral sheep** is an escaped descendant of animals brought to the islands by Captain Vancouver in the 1790s, and of merinos brought to the island later and raised for their exceptional woolly fleece. It exists only on the Big Island, on the upper slopes of Mauna Loa, Mauna Kea, and Hualalai; by the 1930s, its numbers topped 40,000 head. The fleece is a buff brown, and its two-foot-wide curved horns are often sought as hunting trophies. Feral sheep are responsible for the overgrazing of young *mamane* trees, necessary to the endangered bird, *palila.* In 1979, a law was passed to exterminate or remove the sheep from Mauna Kea so that the native *palila* could survive.

The **Mouflon sheep** was introduced to Lanai and Hawaii to cut down on overgrazing and serve as trophy animals. This Mediterranean sheep can interbreed with feral sheep to produce a hybrid. It lives on the upper slopes of Mauna Loa and Mauna Kea. Unfortunately, its introduction has not been a success. No evidence concludes that the smaller family groups of mouflon cause less damage than the herding feral sheep, and hunters reportedly don't like the meat as much as feral mutton.

The **feral donkey,** better known as the "Kona nightingale," came to Hawaii as a beast of burden. Domesticated donkeys are found on all islands, but a few wild herds still roam the Big Island along the Kona Coast, especially near the exclusive Kona Village Resort at Kaupulehu.

Feral cattle were introduced by Captain Vancouver, who gave a few domesticated head to Kamehameha; immediately a *kapu* (taboo) against killing them went into effect for 10 years. The lush grasses of Hawaii were perfect and the cattle flourished; by the early 1800s they were out of control and were hunted and exterminated. Finally, Mexican cowboys were brought to Hawaii to teach the locals how to be range hands. From this legacy sprang the Hawaiian *paniolo.*

Drosophila, the Hawaiian Fly

Most people hardly pay attention to flies, unless one lands on their plate lunch. But geneticists from throughout the world, and especially from the University of Hawaii, make a special pilgrimage to the Volcano area of the Big Island and to Maui just to study the native Hawaiian drosophila. This critter is related to the fruit fly and housefly, but there are hundreds of native species that are singularly unique. The Hawaiian ecosystem is very simple and straightforward, so geneticists can trace the evolutionary changes from species to subspecies through mating behavior. The scientists compare the species between the two islands, and chart the differences. Major discoveries in evolutionary genetics have been made through these studies.

MARINE LIFE

The **humpback whale,** known in Hawaii as *kohola,* migrates to Hawaiian waters yearly, arriving in late December and departing by mid-March. The best places to view it are along the South Kona Coast, especially at Kealakekua Bay and

Ka Lae ("South Point"), with many sightings off the Puna coast around Isaac Hale Beach Park.

Hawaii Volcanoes National Park stretches from the top of Mauna Kea all the way down to the sea. It is here, around Apua Point, that three of the last-known nesting sites of the very endangered **hawksbill turtle** *(honu 'ea)* are found. This creature has been ravished in the Pacific, where it is ruthlessly hunted for its shell, which is made into women's jewelry, especially combs. It is illegal to bring items made from turtle shell into the U.S., but the hunt goes on.

Billfish

Although these magnificent game fish occur in various South Sea and Hawaiian waters, catching them is easiest in the clear, smooth waters off the Kona Coast. The billfish—swordfish, sailfish, marlin, and *a'u*—share two distinctive common features: a long, spearlike or swordlike snout, and a prominent dorsal fin. The three main species of billfish caught are the blue, striped, and black marlin. Of these three, the **blue marlin** is the leading game fish in Kona waters. The blue has tipped the scales at well over 1,000 pounds, but the average fish weighs in at 300-400 pounds. When alive, this fish is a striking cobalt blue, but death brings a color change to slate blue. It feeds on skipjack tuna; throughout the summer, fishing boats look for schools of tuna as a tip-off to blues in the area. The **black marlin** is the largest and most coveted catch for blue-water anglers. This solitary fish is infrequently found in the banks off Kona. Granddaddies can weigh 1,800 pounds, but the average is a mere 200. The **striped marlin** is the most common commercial billfish, a highly prized food served in finer restaurants and often sliced into *sashimi.* Its coloration is a remarkable royal blue. Its spectacular leaps when caught gives it a great reputation as a fighter. The striped marlin is smaller than the other marlins, so a 100-pounder is a very good catch.

THE HAKALAU FOREST NATIONAL WILDLIFE REFUGE

The Hakalau Forest National Wildlife Refuge, acquired with the help of the Nature Conservancy but administered solely by the U.S. Fish and Wildlife Service, is a large tract of land off the Saddle

Road that goes all the way up to the Parker Ranch lands. It's upland forest and scrub that drifts down into solid rainforest that is the home of such birds as the *akiapola'au, akepa, 'io,* Hawaiian creeper, *oma'o, apapane, amakihi, elepaio, nene,* and *pueo.* The U.S. Fish and Wildlife Service is working hard to reconvert this refuge into natural habitat, and efforts include fencing, snaring, and hunting to rid the area of feral pigs and cattle, and replanting with koa, ohia, *opeka, pilo,* and other native species while removing introduced and exotic foliage. It's a tremendous task that's mainly being shouldered by Dick Wass and Jack Jeffrey, rangers with the U.S. Fish and Wildlife Service. The refuge is not adequately staffed to accept visits by the general public at all times, but the Maulau Tract, the northernmost section of the refuge, is open for hiking and birding on the last

weekend of every month. This area is a two-hour drive from Hilo, half of which is over a rugged dirt road traversable only by a 4WD vehicle. Additionally, the refuge is open the first three weekends of the month for public hunting of feral pigs. Numerous volunteer opportunities are available for various ongoing projects, either in the field or at the greenhouse, for a weekend or week-long stint. If you *truly* have a dedication to help and aren't afraid to get your hands dirty, contact Dick or Jack for a very rewarding experience. To enter the refuge for any reason, contact the office at least three weeks in advance to make arrangements; call 933-6915, fax 933-6917, or write to the Refuge Manager, Hakalau Forest NWR, 32 Kinoole St., Suite 101, Hilo, HI 96720. The refuge is a very beautiful diamond in the rough, encompassing an incredible rainforest .

HISTORY

THE ROAD FROM TAHITI

Until the 1820s, when New England missionaries began a phonetic rendering of the Hawaiian language, the past was kept vividly alive only by the sonorous voices of special *kahuna* who chanted the sacred *mele.* The chants were beautiful, flowing word pictures that captured the essence of every aspect of life. These *mele* praised the land *(mele aina),* royalty *(mele ali'i),* and life's tender aspects *(mele aloha).* Chants were dedicated to friendship, hardship, and favorite children. Entire villages sometimes joined together to compose a *mele*—every word was chosen carefully, and the wise old *kapuna* would decide if the words were lucky or unlucky. Some *mele* were bawdy or funny on the surface but contained secret meanings, often bitingly sarcastic, that ridiculed an inept or cruel leader. The most important chants took listeners back into the dim past before people lived in Hawaii. From these genealogies *(ko'ihonua),* the *ali'i* derived the right to rule, since these chants went back to the gods Wakea and Papa from whom the *ali'i* were directly descended.

The Kumulipo

The great genealogies, finally compiled in the late 1800s by order of King Kalakaua, were collectively known as *The Kumulipo, A Hawaiian*

Creation Chant, basically a Polynesian account of Genesis. Other chants related to the beginning of this world, but *The Kumulipo* sums it all up and is generally considered the best. The chant relates that after the beginning of time, there is a period of darkness. The darkness, however, mysteriously brims with spontaneous life; during this period plants and animals are born, as well as Kumulipo, the man, and Po'ele, the woman. In the eighth chant darkness gives way to light and the gods descend to earth. Wakea is "the sky father" and Papa is "the earth mother," whose union gives birth to the islands of Hawaii. First born is Hawaii, followed by Maui, then Kahoolawe. Apparently, Papa becomes bushed after three consecutive births and decides to vacation in Tahiti. While Papa is away recovering from postpartum depression and working on her tan, Wakea gets lonely and takes Kaula as his second wife; she bears him the island-child of Lanai. Not fully cheered up, but getting the hang of it, Wakea takes a third wife, Hina, who promptly bears the island of Molokai. Meanwhile, Papa gets wind of these shenanigans, returns from Polynesia, and retaliates by taking up with Lua, a young and virile god. She soon gives birth to the island of Oahu. Papa and Wakea finally decide that they really are meant for each other and reconcile to conceive Kauai, Niihau, Kaula, and Nihoa. These two progenitors are the source from which the *ali'i* ultimately traced their lineage, and from which they derived their god-ordained power to rule.

Basically, there are two major genealogical families: the **Nana'ulu**, who became the royal *ali'i* of Oahu and Kauai; and the **Ulu**, who provided the royalty of Maui and Hawaii. The best sources of information on Hawaiian myth and legend are Martha Beckwith's *Hawaiian Mythology* and the monumental three-volume opus *An Account of the Polynesian Race* compiled by Abraham Fornander 1878-85. Fornander, after settling in Hawaii, married an *ali'i* from Molokai and had an illustrious career as a newspaperman, Maui circuit judge, and finally Supreme Court justice. For years Fornander sent scribes to every corner of the kingdom to listen to the elder *kupuna*. They returned with firsthand accounts, which they dutifully recorded.

The Big Island plays a significant role in Hawaii's history. A long list of "firsts" have occurred here. Historians generally believe (backed up by the oral tradition) that the Big Island was the first in the Hawaiian chain to be settled by the Polynesians. The dates now used are A.D. 600-700. Hawaii is geographically the closest island to Polynesia; Mauna Loa and especially Mauna Kea, with its white summit, present easily spotted landmarks. Psychologically, the Polynesian wayfarers would have been very attracted to Hawaii as a lost homeland. Compared to Tahiti and most other South Sea islands (except Fiji), it's huge. It *looked* like the promised land. Some may wonder why the Polynesians chose to live atop an obviously active volcano and not bypass it for a more congenial island. The volcanism of the Big Island is comparatively gentle; the lava flows follow predictable routes and rarely turn killer. The animistic Hawaiians would have been drawn to live where the godly forces of nature were so apparent. The mana (power) would be exceptionally strong, and therefore the *ali'i* would be great. Human sacrifice was introduced to Hawaii at Waha'ula Heiau in the Puna District in the 13th century, and from there *luakini* (human-sacrifice temples) spread throughout the islands.

The Great Navigators

No one knows exactly when the first Polynesians arrived in Hawaii, but the great deliberate migrations from the southern islands seem to have

LOUISE FOOTE

The Polynesians, attuned to every nuance in their environment, noticed that a migratory land bird called the golden plover arrived from the north every year. They reasoned that since the plover was not a seabird, there must be land to the north.

taken place A.D. 500-800; anthropologists keep pushing the date backward as new evidence becomes available. Even before that, however, it's reasonable to assume that the first people to set foot on Hawaii were probably fishermen, or perhaps defeated warriors whose canoes were blown hopelessly northward into unfamiliar waters. They arrived by a combination of extraordinary good luck and an uncanny ability to sail and navigate without instruments, using the sun by day and the moon and rising stars by night. They could feel the water and determine direction by swells, tides, and currents. The movements of fish and cloud formations were also utilized to give direction. Since their arrival was probably an accident, they were unprepared to settle on the fertile but barren lands, having no stock animals, plant cuttings, or women. Forced to return southward, undoubtedly many lost their lives at sea, but a few wild-eyed stragglers must have made it home to tell tales of a paradise to the north where land was plentiful and the sea bounteous. This is affirmed by ancient navigational chants from Tahiti, Moorea, and Bora Bora, which passing from father to son revealed how to follow the stars to the "heavenly homeland in the north." Possibly a few migrations followed, but it's known that for centuries there was no real reason for a mass exodus, so the chants alone remained and eventually became shadowy legend.

From Where They Came

It's generally agreed that the first planned migrations were from the violent cannibal islands that Spanish explorers called the Marquesas, 11 islands in extreme eastern Polynesia. The islands themselves are harsh and inhospitable, breeding a toughness into these people which enabled them to withstand the hardships of long, unsure ocean voyages and years of resettlement. Marquesans were a fiercely independent people whose chiefs could rise from the ranks because of bravery or intelligence. They must have also been a savage-looking lot. Both men and women tattooed themselves in complex blue patterns from head to foot. The warriors carried massive, intricately designed ironwood war clubs and wore carved whale teeth in slits in their earlobes, which became stretched to the shoulders. They shaved the sides of their heads with sharks' teeth, tied their hair in two topknots that looked like horns, and rubbed their heavily muscled and tattooed bodies with scented coconut oils. Their cults worshipped mummified ancestors; the bodies of warriors of defeated neighboring tribes were consumed. They were masters at building great double-hulled canoes launched from huge canoe sheds. Two hulls were fastened together to form

SHIP'S ARTIST JACQUES ARAGO (HAWAII STATE ARCHIVES)

Guerrier sandwichien

a catamaran, and a hut in the center provided shelter in bad weather. The average voyaging canoe was 60-80 feet long and could comfortably hold an extended family of about 30 people. These small family bands carried all the staples they would need in the new lands.

The New Lands

For five centuries the Marquesans settled and lived peacefully on the new land, as if Hawaii's *aloha* spirit overcame most of their fierceness. The tribes coexisted in relative harmony, especially since there was no competition for land. Cannibalism died out. There was much coming and going between Hawaii and Polynesia as new people came to settle for hundreds of years. Then, it appears that in the 12th century a deliberate exodus of warlike Tahitians arrived and subjugated the settled islanders. They came to conquer. This incursion had a terrific significance on the Hawaiian religious and social system. Oral tradition relates that a Tahitian priest, Paao, found the mana of the Hawaiian chiefs to be low, signifying that their gods were weak. Paao built a *heiau* at Waha'ula on the Big Island, then introduced the warlike god Ku and the rigid *kapu* system through which the new rulers became dominant. Voyages between Tahiti and Hawaii continued for about 100 years, and Tahitian customs, legends, and language became the Hawaiian way of life. Then suddenly, for no recorded or apparent reason, the voyages discontinued and Hawaii returned to total isolation.

The islands remained forgotten for almost 500 years until the indomitable English seaman, Capt. James Cook, sighted Oahu on January 18, 1778 and stepped ashore at Waimea on Kauai two days later. At that time Hawaii's isolation was so complete that even the Polynesians had forgotten about it. On an earlier voyage, Tupaia, a high priest from Raiatea, had accompanied Captain Cook as he sailed throughout Polynesia. Tupaia demonstrated his vast knowledge of existing archipelagos throughout the South Pacific by naming over 130 islands and drawing a map that included the Tonga group, the Cook Islands, the Marquesas, even tiny Pitcairn, a rock in far eastern Polynesia where the mutinous crew of the *Bounty* found solace. In mentioning the Marquesas, Tupaia said, *"He ma'a te ka'ata,"* which means "Food is man" or simply "Cannibals!" But

POLYNESIAN TRIANGLE

HAWAII

How shall we account for this nation spreading itself so far over this vast ocean? We find them from New Zealand to the south, to these islands to the north and from Easter Island to the Hebrides; . . . how much farther is not known.

—*Capt. James Cook*

Palmyra

Baker   Christmas

Phoenix   EQUATOR

Tokelau

Marquesas

Society   Tuamoto

Samoa   Niue   Tahiti

Tonga   Cook   Mangareva

Austral   Pitcairn

Rapa   Easter

Kermadec

NEW ZEALAND

Chathan

0 ___ 1000 mi

0 ___ 1000 km

© J.D. BISIGNANI AND MOON PUBLICATIONS, INC.

remarkably absent from Tupaia's vast knowledge was the existence of Easter Island, New Zealand, and Hawaii.

The next waves of people to Hawaii would be white, and the Hawaiian world would be changed quickly and forever.

THE WORLD DISCOVERS HAWAII

The late 18th century was an extraordinary time in Hawaiian history. Monumental changes seemed to happen all at once. First, Capt. James Cook, a Yorkshire farm boy fulfilling his destiny as the all-time greatest Pacific explorer, found Hawaii for the rest of the world. For better or worse, it could no longer be an isolated Polynesian homeland. For the first time in Hawaiian history, a charismatic leader named Kamehameha emerged, and after a long civil war he united all the islands into one centralized kingdom. The death of Captain Cook in Hawaii marked the beginning of a long series of tragic misunderstandings between whites and natives. When Kamehameha died, the old religious system of *kapu* came to an end, leaving the Hawaiians in a spiritual vortex. Many takers arrived to fill the void: missionaries after souls, whalers after their prey and a good time, traders and planters after profits and a home. The islands were opened and devoured like ripe fruit. Powerful nations, including Russia, Great Britain,

France, and the United States, yearned to bring this strategic Pacific jewel under their own influence. The 19th century brought the demise of the Hawaiian people as a dominant political force in their own land and with it the end of Hawaii as a sovereign monarchy. An almost bloodless yet bitter military coup followed by a brief Hawaiian Republic ended in annexation by the United States. As the U.S. became completely entrenched politically and militarily, a new social and economic order was founded on the plantation system. Amazingly rapid population growth occurred with the importation of plantation workers from Asia and Europe, which yielded a unique cosmopolitan blend of races like nowhere else on earth. By the dawning of the 20th century, the face of old Hawaii had been altered forever; the "sacred homeland in the north" was hurled into the modern age. The attack on Pearl Harbor saw a tremendous loss of life and brought Hawaii closer to the U.S. by a baptism of blood. Finally, on August 21, 1959, after 59 years as a "territory," Hawaii officially became the U.S.'s 50th state.

Captain Cook Sights Hawaii

In 1776 Capt. James Cook set sail for the Pacific from Plymouth, England, on his third and final expedition into this still vastly unexplored region of the world. On a fruitless quest for the fabled

Capt. James Cook

Northwest Passage across the North American continent, he sailed down the coast of Africa, rounded the Cape of Good Hope, crossed the Indian Ocean, and traveled past New Zealand, Tasmania, and the Friendly Islands (where an unsuccessful plot was hatched by the *friendly* natives to murder him). On January 18, 1778, Captain Cook's 100-foot flagship HMS *Resolution* and its 90-foot companion HMS *Discovery* sighted Oahu. Two days later, they sighted Kauai and went ashore at the village of Waimea on January 20, 1778. Though anxious to get on with his mission, Cook decided to make a quick sortie to investigate this new land and reprovision his ships. He did, however, take time to remark in his diary about the close resemblance of these newfound people to others he had encountered as far south as New Zealand, and he marveled at their widespread habitation across the Pacific.

The first trade was some brass medals for a mackerel. Cook also stated that he had never before met natives so astonished by a ship, and that they had an amazing fascination for iron, which they called *toe,* Hawaiian for "adze." There is even some conjecture that a Spanish ship under one Captain Gaetano had landed in Hawaii as early as the 16th century, trading a few scraps of iron that the Hawaiians valued even more than the Europeans valued gold. It was also noted that the Hawaiian women gave themselves freely to the sailors with the apparent good wishes of the island men. This was actually a ploy by the *kahuna* to test if the white newcomers were gods or men—gods didn't need women. These sailors proved immediately mortal. Cook, who was also a physician, tried valiantly to keep the 66 men (out of 112) who had measurable cases of V.D. away from the women. The task proved impossible as women literally swarmed the ships; when Cook returned less than a year later, it was logged that signs of V.D. were already apparent on some natives' faces.

Cook was impressed with the Hawaiians' swimming ability and with their well-bred manners. They had happy dispositions and sticky fingers, stealing any object made of metal, especially nails. The first item stolen was a butcher's cleaver. An unidentified native grabbed it, plunged overboard, swam to shore, and waved his booty in triumph. The Hawaiians didn't seem to care for beads and were not at all impressed with a mirror. Cook provisioned his ships by trading chisels for hogs, while common sailors gleefully traded nails for sex. Landing parties were sent inland to fill casks with fresh water. On one such excursion a Mr. Williamson, who was eventually drummed out of the Royal Navy for cowardice, unnecessarily shot and killed a native. After a brief stop on Niihau, the ships sailed away, but both groups were indelibly impressed with the memory of each other.

Cook Returns

Almost a year later, when winter weather forced Cook to return from the coast of Alaska, his discovery began to take on far-reaching significance. Cook had named Hawaii the Sandwich Islands, in honor of one of his patrons, John Montague, the Earl of Sandwich. On this return voyage, he spotted Maui on November 26, 1778. After eight weeks of seeking a suitable harbor, the ships bypassed it, but not before the coastline was duly drawn by Lt. William Bligh, one of Cook's finest and most trusted officers. (Bligh would find his own drama almost 10 years later as commander of the infamous HMS *Bounty*.) The *Discovery* and *Resolution* finally found safe anchorage at Kealakekua Bay on the Kona coast of the Big Island. It is very lucky for history that on board was Mr. Anderson, ship's chronicler, who left a handwritten record of the strange and tragic events that followed. Even more important were the drawings of John Webber, ship's artist, who rendered invaluable impressions in superb drawings and etchings. Other noteworthy men aboard were George Vancouver, who would lead the first British return to Hawaii after Cook's death and introduce many fruits, vegetables, cattle, sheep, and goats; and James Burney, who would become a long-standing leading authority on the Pacific.

The Great God Lono Returns

By all accounts Cook was a humane and just captain, greatly admired by his men. Unlike many other supremacists of that time, he was known to have a respectful attitude toward any people he discovered, treating them as equals and recognizing the significance of their cultures. Not known as a violent man, he would use his superior weapons against natives only in an absolute case of self-defense. His hardened

crew had been at sea facing untold hardship for almost three years; returning to Hawaii was truly like reentering paradise.

A strange series of coincidences sailed with Cook into Kealakekua Bay on January 16, 1779. It was *makahiki* time, a period of rejoicing and festivity dedicated to the fertility god of the earth, Lono. Normal *kapu* days were suspended and willing partners freely enjoyed each other sexually, as well as dancing, feasting, and the islands' version of Olympic games. It was long held in Hawaiian legend that the great god Lono would return to earth. Lono's image was a small wooden figure perched on a tall, mastlike crossbeam; hanging from the crossbeam were long, white sheets of tapa. Who else could Cook be but Lono, and what else could his ships with their masts and white sails be but his sacred floating *heiau?* This explained the Hawaiians' previous fascination with his ships, but to add to the remarkable coincidence, Kealakekua Harbor happened to be considered Lono's private sacred harbor. Natives from throughout the land prostrated themselves and paid homage to the returning god. Cook was taken ashore and brought to Lono's sacred temple, where he was afforded the highest respect. The ships badly needed fresh supplies so the Hawaiians readily gave all they had, stretching their own provisions to the limit. To the sailors' delight, this included full measures of the *aloha* spirit.

The Fatal Misunderstanding

After an uproarious welcome and generous hospitality for over a month, it became obvious that the newcomers were beginning to overstay their welcome. During the interim a seaman named William Watman died, convincing the Hawaiians that the *haole* were indeed mortals, not gods. Watman was buried at Hikiau Heiau, where a plaque commemorates the event to this day. Incidents of petty theft began to increase dramatically. The lesser chiefs indicated it was time to leave by "rubbing the Englishmen's bellies." Inadvertently many *kapu* were broken by the English, and once-friendly relations became strained. Finally, the ships sailed away on February 4, 1779.

After plying terrible seas for only a week, *Resolution*'s foremast was damaged. Cook sailed back into Kealakekua Bay, dragging the mast ashore on February 13. The natives, now totally hostile, hurled rocks at the sailors. Orders were given to load muskets with ball; firearms had previously only been loaded with shot and a light charge. Confrontations increased when some Hawaiians stole a small boat and Cook's men set after them, capturing the fleeing canoe, which held an *ali'i* named Palea. The English treated him roughly; to the Hawaiians' horror, they even smacked him on the head with a paddle. The Hawaiians then furiously attacked the marines, who abandoned the small boat.

Cook Goes Down

Next the Hawaiians stole a small cutter from the *Discovery* that had been moored to a buoy and partially sunk to protect it from the sun. For the first time Captain Cook became furious. He ordered Captain Clerk of the *Discovery* to sail to the southeast end of the bay and stop any canoe trying to leave Kealakekua. Cook then made a fatal error in judgment. He decided to take nine armed marines ashore in an attempt to convince the venerable King Kalaniopuu to accompany him back aboard ship, where he would hold him for ransom in exchange for the cutter. The old king agreed, but his wife prevailed upon him not to trust the *haole*. Kalaniopuu sat down on the beach to think while the tension steadily grew.

Meanwhile, a group of marines fired upon a canoe trying to leave the bay. A lesser chief, Nookemai, was killed. The crowd around Cook and his men reached an estimated 20,000. Warriors outraged by the killing of the chief armed themselves with clubs and protective straw-mat armor. One bold warrior advanced on Cook and struck him with his *pahoa* (dagger). In retaliation, Cook drew a tiny pistol lightly loaded with shot and fired at the warrior. His bullets spent themselves on the straw armor and fell harmlessly to the ground. The Hawaiians went wild. Lt. Molesworth Phillips, in charge of the nine marines, began a withering fire; Cook himself slew two natives.

Overpowered by sheer numbers, the marines headed for boats standing offshore, while Lieutenant Phillips lay wounded. It is believed that Captain Cook, the greatest seaman ever to enter the Pacific, stood helplessly in knee-deep water instead of making for the boats because he could not swim! Hopelessly surrounded, he was knocked on the head. Countless warriors then passed a knife around and hacked and mutilated his lifeless body. A sad Lieutenant King lamented in his diary, "Thus fell our great and excellent commander."

The Final Chapter

Captain Clerk, now in charge, settled his men and prevailed upon the Hawaiians to return Cook's body. On the morning of February 16 a grisly piece of charred meat was brought aboard: the Hawaiians, according to their custom, had afforded Cook the highest honor by baking his body in an underground oven to remove the flesh from the bones. On February 17 a group of Hawaiians in a canoe taunted the marines by brandishing Cook's hat. The English, strained to the limit and thinking that Cook was being desecrated, finally broke. Foaming with blood-lust, they leveled their cannons and muskets on shore and shot anything that moved. It is believed that Kamehameha the Great was wounded in this flurry, along with four *ali'i;* 25 *makaainana* (commoners) were killed. Finally, on February 21, 1779, the bones of Capt. James Cook's hands, skull, arms, and legs were returned and tearfully buried at sea. A common seaman, one Mr. Zimmerman, summed up the feelings of all who sailed under Cook when he wrote, ". . . he was our leading star." The English sailed next morning after dropping off their Hawaiian girlfriends who were still aboard.

Captain Clerk, in bad health, carried on with the fruitless search for the Northwest Passage. He died and was buried at the Siberian village of Petropavlovisk. England was at war with upstart colonists in America, so the return of the expedition warranted little fanfare. The *Resolution* was converted into an army transport to fight the pesky Americans; the once proud *Discovery* was reduced to a convict ship ferrying inmates to Botany Bay, Australia. Mrs. Cook, the great captain's steadfast and chaste wife, lived to the age of 93, surviving all her children. She was given a stipend of 200 pounds per year and finished her days surrounded by Cook's mementos, observing the anniversary of his death to the very end by fasting and reading from the Bible.

THE UNIFICATION OF OLD HAWAII

Hawaii was already in a state of political turmoil and civil war when Cook arrived. In the 1780s the islands were roughly divided into three kingdoms: venerable Kalaniopuu ruled Hawaii and the Hana district of Maui; wily and ruthless warrior-king Kahekili ruled Maui, Kahoolawe, Lanai, and later Oahu; and Kaeo, Kahekili's brother, ruled Kauai. War ravaged the land until a remarkable chief, Kamehameha, rose and subjugated all the islands under one rule. Kamehameha initiated a dynasty that would last for about 100 years, until the independent monarchy of Hawaii forever ceased to be. To add a zing to this brewing political stew, Westerners and their technology were beginning to come in ever-increasing numbers. In 1786, Captain LaPerouse and his French exploration party landed in what's now LaPerouse Bay near Lahaina, foreshadowing European attention to the islands. In 1786 two American captains, Portlock and Dixon, made landfall in Hawaii. Also, it was known that a fortune could be made on the fur trade between the Pacific Northwest and Canton, China; stopping in Hawaii could make it feasible. After this was reported, the fate of Hawaii was sealed.

Hawaii under Kamehameha was ready to enter its "golden age." The social order was medieval, with the ali'i as knights owing their military allegiance to the king, and the serflike *makaainana* paying tribute and working the lands. The priesthood of *kahuna* filled the posts of advisors, sorcerers, navigators, doctors, and historians. This was Polynesian Hawaii at its apex. But like the uniquely Hawaiian silversword, the old culture blossomed, and as soon as it did, began to wither. Ever since, all that was purely Hawaiian has been supplanted by the relentless foreign influences that began bearing down upon it.

Young Kamehameha

The greatest native son of Hawaii, Kamehameha, was born under mysterious circumstances in the Kohala District, probably in 1753. He was royal born to Keoua Kupuapaikalaninui, the chief of Kohala, and Kekuiapoiwa, a chieftess from Kona. Accounts vary, but one claims that before his birth, a *kahuna* prophesied that this child would grow to be a "killer of chiefs." Be-

King Kamehameha

cause of this, the local chiefs conspired to murder the infant. When Kekuiapoiwa's time came, she secretly went to the royal birthing stones near Mookini Heiau and delivered Kamehameha. She entrusted her baby to a manservant and instructed him to hide the child. He headed for the rugged and remote coast around Kapaau. Here Kamehameha was raised in the mountains, mostly by men. Always alone, he earned the nickname "the lonely one."

Kamehameha was a man noticed by everyone; there was no doubt he was a force to be reckoned with. He had met Captain Cook when the *Discovery* unsuccessfully tried to land at Hana on Maui. While aboard, he made a lasting impression, distinguishing himself from the multitude of natives swarming the ships by his royal bearing. Lt. James King, in a diary entry, remarked that Kamehameha was a fierce-looking man, almost ugly, but that he was obviously intelligent, observant, and very good-natured. Kamehameha received his early military training from his uncle Kalaniopuu, the great king of Hawaii and Hana who fought fierce battles against Alapai, the usurper who stole his hereditary lands. After regaining Hawaii, Kalaniopuu returned to his Hana district and turned his attention to conquering all of Maui. During this period young Kamehameha distinguished himself as a ferocious warrior and earned the nickname of "the hard-shelled crab," even though old

Kahekili, Maui's king, almost annihilated Kalaniopuu's army at the sand hills of Wailuku.

When the old king neared death, he passed on the kingdom to his son Kiwalao. He also, however, empowered Kamehameha as the keeper of the family war god Kukailimoku: Ku of the Bloody Red Mouth, Ku the Destroyer. Oddly enough, Kamehameha had been born not 500 yards from Ku's great *heiau* at Kohala, and had heard the chanting and observed the ceremonies dedicated to this fierce god from his first breath. Soon after Kalaniopuu died, Kamehameha found himself in a bitter war that he did not seek against his two cousins, Kiwalao and his brother Keoua, with the island of Hawaii at stake. The skirmishing lasted nine years until Kamehameha's armies met the two brothers at Mokuohai in an indecisive battle in which Kiwalao was killed. The result was a shaky truce with Keoua, a much-embittered enemy. During this fighting, Kahekili of Maui conquered Oahu, where he built a house of the skulls and bones of his adversaries as a reminder of his omnipotence. He also extended his will to Kauai by marrying his half-brother to a high-ranking chieftess of that island. A new factor would resolve this stalemate of power—the coming of the *haole*.

The Olowalu Massacre

In 1790 the American merchant ship *Ella Nora,* commanded by Yankee Capt. Simon Metcalfe, was looking for a harbor after its long voyage from the Pacific Northwest. Following a day behind was the *Fair American,* a tiny ship sailed by Metcalfe's son Thomas and a crew of five. Simon Metcalfe, perhaps by necessity, was a stern and humorless man who would broach no interference. While his ship was anchored at Olowalu, a beach area about five miles east of Lahaina, some natives slipped close in their canoes and stole a small boat, killing a seaman in the process. Metcalfe decided to trick the Hawaiians by first negotiating a truce and then unleashing full fury upon them. Signaling he was willing to trade, he invited canoes of innocent natives to visit his ship. In the meantime, he ordered that all cannons and muskets be readied with scatter shot. When the canoes were within hailing distance, he ordered his crew to fire at will. Over 100 people were slain; the

Hawaiians remembered this killing as "the day of spilled brains." Metcalfe then sailed away to Kealakekua Bay and in an unrelated incident succeeded in insulting Kameiamoku, a ruling chief, who vowed to annihilate the next *haole* ship that he saw.

Fate sent him the *Fair American* and young Thomas Metcalfe. The little ship was entirely overrun by superior forces. In the ensuing battle, the mate, Isaac Davis, so distinguished himself by open acts of bravery that his life alone was spared. Kameiamoku later turned over both Davis and the ship to Kamehameha. Meanwhile, while harbored at Kealakekua, the senior Metcalfe sent John Young to reconnoiter. Kamehameha, having learned of the capture of the *Fair American,* detained Young so he could not report, and Metcalfe, losing patience, marooned his own man and sailed off to Canton. (Metcalfe never learned of the fate of his son Thomas, and was later killed with another son while trading with the Native Americans along the Pacific coast of the Mainland.) Kamehameha quickly realized the significance of his two captives and the *Fair American* with its brace of small cannons. He appropriated the ship and made Davis and Young trusted advisors, eventually raising them to the rank of chief. They would all play a significant role in the unification of Hawaii.

Kamehameha the Great

Later in 1790, supported by the savvy of Davis and Young and the cannons from the *Fair American* which he mounted on carts, Kamehameha invaded Maui, using Hana as his power base. The island's defenders under Kalaniekupule, son of Kahekili who was lingering on Oahu, were totally demoralized, then driven back into the deathtrap of Iao Valley. There, Kamehameha's forces annihilated them. No mercy was expected and none given, although mostly commoners were slain with no significant *ali'i* falling to the victors. So many were killed in this sheer-walled, inescapable valley that the battle was called *"ka pani wai"* which means "the damming of the waters"—literally with dead bodies.

While Kamehameha was fighting on Maui, his old nemesis Keoua was busy running amok back on Hawaii, again pillaging Kamehameha's lands. The great warrior returned home flushed with victory, but in two battles he could not subdue Keoua. Finally, Kamehameha had a prophetic dream in which he was told that Ku would lead him to victory over all the lands of Hawaii if he would build a *heiau* to the war god at Kawaihae. Even before the temple was finished, old Kahekili attempted to invade Waipio, Kamehameha's stronghold. But Kamehameha summoned Davis and Young, and with the *Fair American* and an enormous fleet of war canoes defeated Kahekili at Waimanu. Kahekili had no choice but to accept the indomitable Kamehameha as the king of Maui, although he himself remained the administrative head until his death in 1794.

Now only Keoua remained in the way and he would be defeated not by war, but by the great mana of Ku. While Keoua's armies were crossing the desert on the southern slopes of Kilauea, the fire goddess Pele trumpeted her disapproval and sent a huge cloud of poisonous gas and mud-ash into the air. It descended upon and instantly killed the middle legions of Keoua's armies and their families. The footprints of this ill-fated army remain to this day outlined in the mud-ash as clearly as if they were deliberately encased in wet cement. Keoua's intuition told him that the victorious mana of the gods had swung to Kamehameha and that his own fate was sealed. Kamehameha sent word that he wanted Keoua to meet with him at Ku's newly dedicated temple in Kawaihae. Both knew that Keoua must die. Riding proudly in his canoe, the old nemesis came gloriously outfitted in the red-and-gold feathered cape and helmet signifying his exalted rank. When he stepped ashore he was felled by Kamehameha's warriors. His body was ceremoniously laid upon the altar along with 11 others who were slaughtered and dedicated to Ku, of the Maggot-dripping Mouth.

Increasing Contact

By the time Kamehameha had won the Big Island, Hawaii was becoming a regular stopover for numerous ships seeking the lucrative sandalwood trade with China. In February 1791, Capt. George Vancouver, still seeking the Northwest Passage, returned to Kealakekua where he was greeted by a throng of 30,000. The captain at once recognized Kamehameha, who was wearing a Chinese dressing gown that he had received in tribute from another chief who in turn had received it directly from the hands of Cook himself. The diary of a crew member, Thomas Manby, relates that Kamehameha, missing his front teeth, was more fierce-looking than ever as he approached the ship in an elegant double-hulled canoe sporting 46 rowers. The king invited all to a great feast prepared for them on the beach. Kamehameha's appetite matched his tremendous size. It was noted that he ate two sizable fish, a king-sized bowl of poi, a small pig, and an entire baked dog. Kamehameha personally entertained the English by putting on a mock battle in which he deftly avoided spears by rolling, tumbling, and catching them in midair, all the while hurling his own spear a great distance. The English reciprocated by firing cannon bursts into the air, creating an impromptu fireworks display. Kamehameha requested from Vancouver a full table setting with which he was provided, but his request for firearms was prudently denied. Captain Vancouver became a trusted advisor of Kamehameha and told him about the white man's form of worship. He even interceded for Kamehameha with his headstrong queen, Kaahumanu, and coaxed her from her hiding place under a rock when she sought refuge at Pu'uhonua O Honaunau. The captain gave gifts of beef cattle, fowl, and breeding stock of sheep and goats. The ship's naturalist, Archibald Menzies, was the first *haole* to climb Mauna Kea; he also introduced a large assortment of fruits and vegetables. The Hawaiians were cheerful and outgoing, and showed remorse when they indicated that the remainder of Cook's bones had been buried at a temple close to Kealakekua. John Young, by this time firmly entrenched into Hawaiian society, made no request to sail away with Vancouver. During the next two decades of Kamehameha's rule, the French, Russians, English, and Americans discovered the great whaling waters off Hawaii. Their increasing visits shook and finally tumbled the ancient religion and social order of *kapu*.

Finishing Touches

After Keoua was laid to rest, it was only a matter of time until Kamehameha consolidated his power over all of Hawaii. In 1794 the old warrior Kahekili of Maui died and gave Oahu to his son, Kalanikupule, while Kauai and Niihau went to his brother Kaeo. In wars between the two, Kalanikupule was victorious, though he did not possess the grit of his father nor the great mana of Kamehameha. He had previously murdered a Captain Brown, who had anchored in Honolulu, and seized his ship, the *Jackal*. With the aid of this ship, Kalanikupule now determined to attack Kamehameha. However, while en route, the sailors regained control of their ship and cruised to the Big Island to inform and join with Kamehameha. An army of 16,000 was raised and sailed for Maui, where they met only token resistance, destroyed Lahaina, pillaged the countryside, and subjugated Molokai in one bloody battle.

The war canoes sailed next for Oahu and the final showdown. The great army landed at Waikiki, and though defenders fought bravely, giving up Oahu by the inch, they were steadily driven into the surrounding mountains. The beleaguered army made its last stand at Nuuanu Pali, a great precipice in the mountains behind present-day Honolulu. Kamehameha's warriors mercilessly drove the enemy into the great abyss. Kalanikupule, who hid in the mountains, was captured after a few months and sacrificed to Ku, the Snatcher of Lands, thereby ending the struggle for power.

Kamehameha put down a revolt on Hawaii in 1796. The king of Kauai, Kaumuali, accepting the inevitable, recognized Kamehameha as supreme ruler without suffering the ravages of a needless war. Kamehameha, for the first time in Hawaiian history, was the undisputed ruler of all the islands of "the heavenly homeland in the north."

Kamehameha's Rule

Kamehameha was as gentle in victory as he was ferocious in battle. Under his rule, which lasted until his death on May 8, 1819, Hawaii enjoyed a peace unlike any the warring islands had ever known. The king moved his royal court to Lahaina, where in 1803 he built the "Brick Palace," the first permanent building of Hawaii. The benevolent tyrant also enacted the "Law of the Splintered Paddle." This law, which protected the weak from the exploitation of the strong, had its origins in an incident of many years before. A brave defender of a small overwhelmed village had broken a paddle over Kamehameha's head and taught the chief—literally in one stroke—about the nobility of the commoner.

However, just as Old Hawaii reached its "golden age," its demise was at hand. The relentless waves of *haole* both innocently and determinedly battered the old ways into the ground. With the foreign ships came prosperity and fanciful new goods after which the *ali'i* lusted. The *makaainana* were worked mercilessly to provide sandalwood for the China trade. This was the first "boom" economy to hit the islands, but it set the standard of exploitation that would follow. Kamehameha built an observation tower in Lahaina to watch for ships, many of which were his own returning laden with riches from the world at large. In the last years of his life Kamehameha returned to his beloved Kona Coast, where he enjoyed the excellent fishing renowned to this day. He had taken Hawaii from the darkness of warfare into the light of peace. He died true to the religious and moral *kapu* of his youth, the only ones he had ever known, and with him died a unique way of life. Two loyal retainers buried his bones after the baked flesh had been ceremoniously stripped away. A secret burial cave was chosen so that no one could desecrate the remains of the great chief, thereby absorbing his mana. The tomb's whereabouts remains unknown, and disturbing the dead remains one of the strictest *kapu* to this day. The Lonely One's kingdom would pass to his son, Liholiho, but true power would be in the hands of his beloved but feisty wife Kaahumanu. As Kamehameha's spirit drifted from this earth, two forces sailing around Cape Horn would forever change Hawaii: the missionaries and the whalers.

MISSIONARIES AND WHALERS

The year 1819 was of the utmost significance in Hawaiian history. It marked the death of Kamehameha, the overthrow of the ancient *kapu* system, the arrival of the first "whaler" in Lahaina, and the departure of Calvinist missionaries from New England determined to convert the heathen islands. Great changes began to rattle the old order to its foundations. With the *kapu* system and all of the ancient gods abandoned (except for the fire goddess Pele of Kilauea), a great void permeated the souls of the Hawaiians. In the coming decades Hawaii, also coveted by Russia, France, and England, was finally consumed by America. The islands had the first American school, printing press, and newspaper *(The Polynesian)* west of the Mississippi. Lahaina, in its heyday, became the world's greatest whaling port, accommodating over 500 ships during its peak years.

The Royal Family

Maui's Hana District provided Hawaii with one of its greatest queens, Kaahumanu, born in 1768 in a cave within walking distance of Hana Harbor. At the age of 17 she became the third of Kamehameha's 21 wives and eventually the love of his life. At first she proved to be totally independent and unmanageable, and was known to openly defy her king by taking numerous lovers. Kamehameha placed a *kapu* on her body and even had her attended by horribly deformed hunchbacks in an effort to curb her carnal appetites, but she continued to flaunt her authority. Young Kaahumanu had no love for her great, lumbering, unattractive husband, but in time (even Captain Vancouver was pressed into service as a marriage counselor) she learned to love him dearly. She in turn became his favorite wife, although she remained childless throughout her life. Kamehameha's first wife was the supremely royal Keopuolani, who so outranked even him that the king himself had to approach her naked and crawling on his belly. Keopuolani produced the royal children Liholiho and Kauikeaouli, who became King Kamehameha II and III, respec-

tively. Just before Kamehameha I died in 1819 he appointed Liholiho his successor, but he also had the wisdom to make Kaahumanu the *kuhina nui* or queen regent. Initially, Liholiho was weak and became a drunkard. Later he became a good ruler, but he was always supported by his royal mother Keopuolani and by the ever-formidable Kaahumanu.

Kapu Is Pau

Kaahumanu was greatly loved and respected by the people. On public occasions, she donned Kamehameha's royal cloak and spear: so attired and infused with the king's mana, she demonstrated that she was the real leader of Hawaii. For six months after Kamehameha's death, Kaahumanu counseled Liholiho on what he must do. The wise *kuhina nui* knew that the old ways were *pau* ("finished") and that Hawaii could not hope to function in a rapidly changing world under the *kapu* system. In November 1819, Kaahumanu and Keopuolani prevailed upon Liholiho to break two of the oldest and most sacred *kapu* by eating with women and by allowing women to eat previously forbidden foods such as bananas and certain fish. Heavily fortified with strong drink and attended by other high-ranking chiefs and a handful of foreigners, Kaahumanu and Liholiho ate together in public. This feast became known as *Ai Noa* ("free eating"). As the first morsels passed Kaahumanu's lips, the ancient gods of Hawaii tumbled. Throughout the land, revered *heiau* were

the great Queen Kaahumanu, by ship's artist Louis Choris from the Otto Von Kotzebue expedition, circa 1816

HAWAII STATE ARCHIVES

burned and abandoned and the idols knocked to the ground. Now the people had nothing but their weakened inner selves to rely on. Nothing and no one could answer their prayers; their spiritual lives were empty and in shambles.

Missionaries

Into this spiritual vortex sailed the brig *Thaddeus* on April 4, 1820. It had set sail from Boston on October 23, 1819, lured to the Big Island by Henry Opukahaia, a local boy born at Napoopoo in 1792. Coming ashore at Kailua-Kona, the Reverends Bingham and Thurston were granted a one-year trial missionary period by King Liholiho. They established themselves on the Big Island and Oahu and from there began the transformation of Hawaii. The missionaries were people of God, but also practical-minded Yankees. They brought education, enterprise, and most importantly, unlike the transient seafarers, a commitment to stay and build. By 1824 the new faith had such a foothold that Chieftess Keopuolani climbed to the firepit atop Kilauea and defied Pele. This was even more striking than the previous breaking of the food *kapu* because the strength of Pele could actually be seen. Keopuolani ate forbidden *ohelo* berries and cried out, "Jehovah is my God." Over the next decades the governing of Hawaii slipped away from the Big Island and moved to the new port cities of Lahaina on Maui and later, Honolulu, Oahu. In 1847, the Parker Ranch began with a two-acre grant given to John Parker. He coupled this with 640 acres given to his *ali'i* wife Kipikane by the land division known as the Great *Mahele*.

Rapid Conversions

The year 1824 also marked the death of Keopuolani, who was given a Christian burial. She had set the standard by accepting Christianity, and a number of the *ali'i* had followed the queen's lead. Liholiho had sailed off to England, where he and his wife contracted measles and died. Their bodies were returned by the British in 1825, on the HMS *Blonde* captained by Lord Byron, cousin of *the* Lord Byron. During these years, Kaahumanu allied herself with Rev. Richards, pastor of the first mission in the Islands, and together they wrote Hawaii's first code of laws based upon the Ten Commandments. Foremost was the condemnation of murder, theft, brawling, and the desecration of the Sabbath by work or play. The early missionaries had the best of intentions, but like all zealots they were blinded by the single-mindedness that was also their greatest ally. They weren't surgically selective in their destruction of native beliefs. *Anything* native was felt to be inferior, and they set about wiping out all traces of the old ways. In their rampage they reduced the Hawaiian culture to ashes, plucking self-will and determination from the hearts of a once-proud people. More so than the whalers, they terminated the Hawaiian way of life.

The Early Seamen

A good portion of the common seamen of the early 19th century came from the dregs of the Western world. Many a whoremongering drunkard had awoken from a stupor and found himself on the pitching deck of a ship, discovering to his dismay that he had been "pressed into naval service." For the most part these sailors were a filthy, uneducated, lawless rabble. Their present situation was dim, their future hopeless, and they would live to be 30 if they were lucky and didn't die from scurvy or a thousand other miserable fates. They snatched brief pleasure in every port and jumped ship at every opportunity, especially in an easy berth like Lahaina. They displayed the worst elements of Western culture—which the Hawaiians naively mimicked. In exchange for *aloha* they gave drunkenness, sloth, and insidious death by disease. By the 1850s the population of native Hawaiians tumbled from the estimated 300,000 reported by Captain Cook in 1778 to barely 60,000. Common conditions such as colds, flu, venereal disease, and sometimes smallpox and cholera decimated the Hawaiians, who had no natural immunities to these foreign ailments. By the time the missionaries arrived, *hapa haole* children were common in Lahaina streets.

The earliest merchant ships to the Islands were owned or skippered by lawless opportunists who had come seeking sandalwood after first filling their holds with furs from the Pacific Northwest. Aided by *ali'i* hungry for manufactured goods and Western finery, they raped Hawaiian forests of this fragrant wood so coveted in China. Next, droves of sailors came in search of whales. The whalers, decent men at home, left their morals back in the Atlantic and lived by the slogan "no conscience east of the Cape." The delights of Hawaii were just too tempting for most.

Two Worlds Tragically Collide

The 1820s were a time of confusion and soul-searching for the Hawaiians. When Kamehameha II died the kingdom passed to Kauikeaouli (Kamehameha III), who made his lifelong residence in Lahaina. The young king was only nine years old when the title passed to him, but his power was secure because Kaahumanu was still a vibrant *kuhina nui*. The young prince, more so than any other, was raised in the cultural confusion of the times. His childhood was spent during the very cusp of the change from old ways to new, and he was often pulled in two directions by vastly differing beliefs. Since he was royal born, he was bound by age-old Hawaiian tradition to mate and produce an heir with the highest-ranking *ali'i* in the kingdom. This mate happened to be his younger sister, the Princess Nahienaena. To

Kamehameha III

the old Hawaiian advisors, this arrangement was perfectly acceptable and encouraged. To the increasingly influential missionaries, incest was an unimaginable abomination in the eyes of God. The problem was compounded by the fact that Kamehameha III and Nahienaena were drawn to each other and were deeply in love. The young king could not stand the mental pressure imposed by conflicting worlds. He became a teenage alcoholic too royal to be restrained by anyone in the kingdom, and his bouts of drunkenness and womanizing were both legendary and scandalous.

Meanwhile, Nahienaena was even more pressured because she was a favorite of the missionaries, baptized into the church at age 12. She too vacillated between the old and the new. At times a pious Christian, at others she drank all night and took numerous lovers. As the prince and princess grew into their late teens, they became even more attached to each other and hardly made an attempt to keep their relationship from the missionaries. Whenever possible, they lived together in a grass house built for the princess by her father.

In 1832, the great Kaahumanu died, leaving the king on his own. In 1833, at the age of 18, Kamehameha III announced that the "regency" was over and that all the lands in Hawaii were his personally, and that he alone was the ultimate law. Almost immediately, however, he decreed that his half-sister Kinau would be "premier," signifying that he would leave the actual running of the kingdom in her hands. Kamehameha III fell into total drunken confusion, until one night he attempted suicide. After this episode he seemed to straighten up a bit and mostly kept a low profile. In 1836, Princess Nahienaena was convinced by the missionaries to take a husband. She married Leleiohoku, a chief from the Big Island, but continued to sleep with her brother. It is uncertain who fathered the child, but Nahienaena gave birth to a baby boy in September 1836. The young prince survived for only a few hours, and Nahienaena never recovered from her convalescence. She died in December 1836 and was laid to rest in the mausoleum next to her mother, Keopuolani, on the royal island in Mokuhina Pond (still in existence in modern-day Lahaina). After the death of his sister, Kamehameha III became a sober and righteous ruler. Often seen paying his respects at the royal mausoleum, he ruled longer than any other king until his death in 1854.

The Missionaries Prevail

In 1823, the first mission was established in Lahaina under the pastorage of Rev. Richards and his wife. Within a few years, many of the notable *ali'i* had been, at least in appearance, converted to Christianity. By 1828 the cornerstones for Wainee Church, the first stone church on the island, were laid just behind the palace of Kamehameha III. The struggle between missionaries and whalers centered around public drunkenness and the servicing of sailors by native women. The normally God-fearing whalers had signed on for perilous duty that lasted up to three years, and when they anchored in Lahaina they demanded their pleasure. The missionaries were instrumental in placing a curfew on sailors and prohibiting native women from boarding ships, which had become customary. These measures certainly did not stop the liasons between sailor and *wahine,* but they did impose a modicum of social sanction and tolled the end of the wide-open days. The sailors were outraged; in 1825 the crew from the *Daniel* attacked the home of the meddler, Rev. Richards. A year later a similar incident occurred. In 1827, confined and lonely sailors from the whaler *John Palmer* fired their cannons at Rev. Richards' newly built home.

Slowly the tensions eased, and by 1836 many sailors were regulars at the Seamen's Chapel adjacent to the Baldwin home. Unfortunately, even the missionaries couldn't stop the pesky mosquito from entering the islands through the port of Lahaina. The mosquitoes arrived from Mexico in 1826 aboard the merchant ship *Wellington.* They were inadvertently carried as larvae in the water barrels and democratically pestered everyone in the islands from that day forward, regardless of race, religion, or creed.

Foreign Influence

By the 1840s Honolulu was becoming the center of commerce in the islands; when Kamehameha III moved the royal court there from Lahaina, the ascendant fate of the new capital was guaranteed. In 1843, Lord Paulet, commander of the warship *Carysfort,* forced Kamehameha III to sign a treaty ceding Hawaii to the British. London, however, repudiated this act, and Hawaii's independence was restored within a few months when Queen Victoria sent Admiral Thomas as her personal agent of good intentions. The king memorialized the turn of events by a speech in which he uttered the phrase, *Ua mau ke ea o ka aina i ka pono* ("The life of the land is preserved in righteousness"), now Hawaii's motto. The French used similar bullying tactics to force an unfavorable treaty on the Hawaiians in 1839; as part of these heavy-handed negotiations they exacted a payment of $20,000 and the right of Catholics to enjoy religious freedom in the islands. In 1842 the U.S. recognized and guaranteed Hawaii's independence without a formal treaty, and by 1860 over 80% of the islands' trade was with America.

The Great *Mahele*

In 1840 Kamehameha III ended his autocratic rule and instituted a constitutional monarchy. This brought about the Hawaiian Bill of Rights, but the most far-reaching change was the transition to private ownership of land. Formerly, all land belonged to the ruling chief, who gave wedge-shaped parcels called *ahupua'a* to lesser chiefs to be worked for him. The commoners did all the real labor, their produce heavily taxed by the *ali'i.* The fortunes of war, the death of a chief, or the mere whim of a superior could force a commoner off the land. The Hawaiians, however, could not think in terms of "owning" land. No one could *possess* land; one could only *use* land, and its *ownership* was a strange foreign concept. (As a result, naive Hawaiians gave up their lands for a song to unscrupulous traders, which remains an integral, unrectified problem to this day.) In 1847 Kamehameha III and his advisors separated the lands of Hawaii into three groupings: crown land (belonging to the king), government land (belonging to the chiefs), and the people's land (the largest parcels). In 1848, 245 *ali'i* entered their land claims in the *Mahele Book,* assuring them ownership. In 1850 the commoners were given title in fee simple to the lands they cultivated and lived on as tenants, not including house lots in towns. Commoners without land could buy small *kuleana* (farms) from the government at 50 cents per acre. In 1850, foreigners were also allowed to purchase land in fee simple, and the ownership of Hawaii from that day forward slipped steadily from the hands of its indigenous people.

KING SUGAR

The sugar industry began at Hana, Maui, in 1849. A whaler named George Wilfong hauled four blubber pots ashore and set them up on a rocky hill in the middle of 60 acres he had planted in sugar. A team of oxen turned "crushing rollers" and the cane juice flowed down an open trough into the pots, under which an attending native kept a roaring fire burning. Wilfong's methods of refining were crude but the resulting high-quality sugar turned a neat profit in Lahaina. The main problem was labor. The Hawaiians, who made excellent whalers, were basically indentured workers. They became extremely disillusioned with their contracts, which could last up to 10 years. Most of their wages were eaten up by manufactured commodities sold at the company store, and it didn't take long for them to realize that they were little more than slaves. At every opportunity they either left the area or just refused to work.

Imported Labor
The **Masters and Servants Act of 1850,** which allowed importation of laborers under the contract system, ostensibly guaranteed an endless supply of cheap labor for the plantations. Chinese laborers were imported but were too enterprising to remain in the fields for a meager $3 per month. They left as soon as opportunity permitted, and went into business as small merchants and retailers. In the meantime, Wilfong had sold out, releasing most of the Hawaiians previously held under contract, and his plantation fell into disuse. In 1860 two Danish brothers, August and Oscar Unna, bought land at Hana to raise sugar. They solved the labor problem by importing Japanese laborers who were extremely hard-working and easily managed. The workday lasted 10 hours, six days a week, for a salary of $20 per month with housing and med-

ical care thrown in. Plantation life was very structured, with stringent rules governing even bedtimes and lights out. A worker was fined for being late or for smoking on the job. Even the Japanese couldn't function under these circumstances, and improvements in benefits and housing were slowly gained.

Sugar Grows
The demand for "Sandwich Island Sugar" grew as California was populated during the gold rush, and increased dramatically when the American Civil War demanded a constant supply. The only sugar plantations on the Mainland were small plots confined to the Confederate states, whose products would hardly be bought by the Union and whose fields, later in the war, were destroyed. By the 1870s it was clear to the planters, still mainly New Englanders, that the U.S. was their market; they tried often to gain closer ties and favorable tariffs. The Americans also planted rumors that the British were interested in annexing Hawaii; this put pressure on the U.S. Congress to pass the long-desired **Reciprocity Act,** which would exempt sugar from import duty. It finally passed in 1875, in exchange for U.S. long-range rights to the strategic naval port of Pearl Harbor, among other concessions. These agreements gave increased political power to a small group of American planters whose outlooks were similar to those of the post-Civil War South, where a few powerful whites were the virtual masters of a multitude of dark-skinned laborers. Sugar was now big business and the Hana District alone exported almost 3,000 tons per year. All of Hawaii would have to reckon with the "sugar barons."

Changing Society
The sugar plantation system changed life in Hawaii physically, spiritually, politically, and economically. Now boatloads of workers came not only from Japan, but from Portugal, Germany, and even Russia. The white-skinned workers were most often the field foremen *(luna)*. With the immigrants came new religions, new animals and plants, unique cuisines, and a plantation language known as *pidgin,* or better yet, *da'kine.* Many Asians and, to a lesser extent, the other groups, including the white plantation owners, intermarried with Hawaiians. A new

class of people properly termed "cosmopolitan" but more familiarly and aptly known as "locals" was emerging. These were the people of multiple race backgrounds who couldn't exactly say *what* they were but it was clear to all just *who* they were. The plantation owners became the new "chiefs" of Hawaii who could carve up the land and dispense favors. The Hawaiian monarchy was soon eliminated.

A KINGDOM PASSES

The fate of Lahaina's Wainee Church through the years has been a symbol of the political and economic climate of the times. Its construction heralded the beginning of missionary dominance in 1828. It was destroyed by a tornado or "ghost wind" in 1858, just when whaling began to falter and the previously dominant missionaries began losing their control to the merchants and planters. In 1894, Wainee Church was burned to the ground by royalists supporting the besieged Queen Liliuokalani. Rebuilding was begun in 1897—while Hawaii was a republic ruled by the sugar planters—with a grant from H.P. Baldwin. It wasn't until 1947 that Wainee was finally completed and remodeled.

The Beginning of the End
Like the Hawaiian people themselves, the Kamehameha dynasty in the mid-1800s was dying from within. King Kamehameha IV (Alexander Liholiho) ruled 1854-63; his only child died in 1862. He was succeeded by his older brother Kamehameha V (Lot Kamehameha), who ruled until 1872. With his passing, the Kamehameha line ended. William Lunalilo, elected king in 1873 by popular vote, was of royal, but not Kamehameha, lineage. He died after only a year in office, and being a bachelor left no heirs. He was succeeded by David Kalakaua, known far and wide as "The Merrie Monarch," who made a world tour and was well received wherever he went. He built Iolani Palace in Honolulu and was personally in favor of closer ties with the U.S., helping push through the Reciprocity Act. Kalakaua died in 1891 and was replaced by his sister Lydia Liliuokalani, last of the Hawaiian monarchs.

HAWAII STATE ARCHIVES

Queen Liliuokalani

The Revolution
When Liliuokalani took office in 1891, the native population was at a low of 40,000 and she felt that the U.S. had too much influence over her homeland. She was known to personally favor the English over the Americans. She attempted to replace the liberal constitution of 1887 (adopted by her pro-American brother) with an autocratic mandate in which she would have had much more political and economic control of the islands. When the McKinley Tariff of 1890 brought a decline in sugar profits, she made no attempt to improve the situation. Thus, the planters saw her as a political obstacle to their economic growth; most of Hawaii's American planters and merchants were in favor of a rebellion. She would have to go! A central spokesperson and firebrand was Lorrin Thurston, a Honolulu publisher who, with a central core of about 30 men, challenged the Hawaiian monarchy. Although Liliuokalani rallied some support and had a small military potential in her personal guard, the coup was ridiculously easy—

it took only one casualty. Captain John Good shot a Hawaiian policeman in the arm and that did it. Naturally, the conspirators could not have succeeded without some solid assurances from a secret contingent in the U.S. Congress as well as outgoing President Benjamin Harrison, who favored Hawaii's annexation. Marines from the *Boston* went ashore to "protect American lives," and on January 17, 1893, the Hawaiian monarchy came to an end.

The provisional government was headed by Sanford B. Dole, who became president of the Hawaiian Republic. Liliuokalani surrendered not to the conspirators but to U.S. Ambassador John Stevens. She believed that the U.S. government, which had assured her of Hawaiian independence, would be outraged by the overthrow and would come to her aid. Incoming President Grover Cleveland *was* outraged and Hawaii wasn't immediately annexed as expected. When queried about what she would do with the conspirators if she were reinstated, Liliuokalani said that they would be hung as traitors. The racist press of the times, which portrayed the Hawaiians as half-civilized, bloodthirsty heathens, publicized this widely. Since the conspirators were the leading citizens of the land, the queen's words proved untimely. In January 1895 a small, ill-fated counterrevolution headed by Liliuokalani failed, and she was placed under house arrest in Iolani Palace. Officials of the republic insisted that she use her married name (Mrs. John Dominis) to sign the documents forcing her to abdicate her throne. She was also forced to swear allegiance to the new republic. Liliuokalani went on to write *Hawaii's Story* and the lyric ballad "Aloha O'e." She never forgave the conspirators and remained "queen" to the Hawaiians until her death in 1917.

Annexation

The overwhelming majority of Hawaiians opposed annexation and desired to restore the monarchy. But they were prevented from voting by the new republic because they couldn't meet the imposed property and income qualifications—a transparent ruse by the planters to control the majority. Most *haole* were racist and believed that the "common people" could not be entrusted with the vote because they were child-ish and incapable of ruling themselves. The fact that the Hawaiians had existed quite well for 1,000 years before the white man even reached Hawaii was never considered. The Philippine theater of the Spanish-American War also prompted annexation. One of the strongest proponents was Alfred Mahon, a brilliant naval strategist who, with support from Theodore Roosevelt, argued that the U.S. military must have Hawaii in order to be a viable force in the Pacific. In addition, Japan, victorious in its recent war with China, protested the American intention to annex, and in so doing prompted even moderates to support annexation for fear that the Japanese themselves coveted the prize. On July 7, 1898, President McKinley signed the annexation agreement, and this "tropical fruit" was finally put into America's basket.

MODERN TIMES

Hawaii entered the 20th century totally transformed from what it had been. The old Hawaiian language, religion, culture, and leadership were all gone; Western dress, values, education, and recreation were the norm. Native Hawaiians were now unseen citizens who lived in dwindling numbers in remote areas. The plantations, new centers of social order, had a strong Asian flavor; more than 75% of their work force was Asian. There was a small white middle class, an all-powerful white elite, and a single political party ruled by that elite. Education, however, was always highly prized, and by the turn of the century all racial groups were encouraged to attend school. By 1900, almost 90% of Hawaiians were literate (far above the national norm) and schooling was mandatory for all children ages 6-15. Intermarriage was accepted, and there was a mixing of the races like nowhere else on earth. The military became increasingly important to Hawaii. It brought in money and jobs, dominating the island economy. The Japanese attack on Pearl Harbor, which began U.S. involvement in WW II, bound Hawaii to America forever. Once the islands had been baptized by blood, the average Mainlander felt that Hawaii was American soil. A movement among Hawaiians to become part of the Union began to grow. They wanted a real voice in Washington, not merely a voteless delegate as provided under their territory status. Hawaii became the 50th state in 1959 and the jumbo-jet revolution of the 1960s made it easily accessible to growing numbers of tourists from all over the world.

Military History

A few military strategists realized the importance of Hawaii early in the 19th century, but most didn't recognize the advantages until the Spanish-American War. It was clearly an unsinkable ship in the middle of the Pacific from which the U.S. could launch military operations. Troops were stationed at Camp McKinley, at the foot of Diamond Head, the main military compound until it became obsolete in 1907. Pearl Harbor was first surveyed in 1872 by General Schofield. Later, a military base named in his honor, Schofield Barracks, was a main military post in central Oahu. It first housed the U.S. 5th Cavalry in 1909 and was heavily bombed by the Japanese at the outset of WW II. Pearl Harbor, first dredged in 1908, was officially opened on December 11, 1911. The first warship to enter was the cruiser *California*. Ever since, the military has been a mainstay of island economy. Unfortunately, there has been long-standing bad blood between locals and military personnel. Each group has tended to look down upon the other.

The Honolulu Star Bulletin *banner headline announces the beginning of U.S. involvement in WW II on Sunday, December 7, 1941.*

Pearl Harbor Attack

On the morning of December 7, 1941, the Japanese carrier *Akagi*, flying the battle flag of the famed Admiral Togo of the Russo-Japanese War, received and broadcast over its PA system island music from Honolulu station KGMB. Deep in the bowels of the ship a radio man listened for a much different message, coming thousands of miles from the Japanese mainland. When the ironically poetic message "east wind rain" was received, the attack was launched. At the end of the day, 2,325 U.S. servicemen and 57 civilians were dead; 188 planes were destroyed; 18 major warships were sunk or heavily damaged; and the U.S. was in the war. Japanese casualties were ludicrously light. The ignited conflict would rage for four years until Japan, through Nagasaki and Hiroshima, was vaporized into total submission. At the end of hostilities, Hawaii would never again be considered separate from America.

Statehood

A number of economic and political reasons explain why the ruling elite of Hawaii desired statehood, but put simply, the vast majority of people who lived there, especially after WW II, considered themselves Americans. The first serious mention of making "The Sandwich Islands" a state was in the 1850s under President Franklin Pierce, but it wasn't taken seriously until the monarchy was overthrown in the 1890s. For the next 50 years statehood proposals were made repeatedly to Congress, but there was stiff opposition, especially from the southern states. With Hawaii a territory, an import quota system beneficial to Mainland producers could be enacted on produce, especially sugar. Also, there was prejudice against creating a state in a place where the majority of the populace was not white. This situation was illuminated by the infamous Massie Rape Case of 1931 (see "People," below), which went down as one of the greatest miscarriages of justice in American history.

During WW II, Hawaii was placed under martial law, but no serious attempt to intern the Japanese population was made, as in California. There were simply too many Japanese, who went on to gain the respect of the American people by their outstanding fighting record during the war. Hawaii's own 100th Battalion became the famous 442nd Regimental Combat Team, which gained notoriety by saving the Lost Texas Battalion during the Battle of the Bulge and went on to be *the* most decorated battalion in all of WW II. When these GIs returned home, *no one* was going to tell them that they were *not* loyal Americans. Many of these AJAs (Americans of Japanese Ancestry) took advantage of the GI Bill and received higher education. They were from the common people, not the elite, and they rallied grassroots support for statehood. When the vote finally occurred, approximately 132,900 voted in favor of statehood with only 7,800 votes against. Congress passed the Hawaii State Bill on March 12, 1959, and on August 21, 1959, President Eisenhower announced that Hawaii was officially the 50th state.

GOVERNMENT

The only difference between the government of the state of Hawaii and those of other states is that it's "streamlined" and in theory more efficient. There are only two levels of government: the state and the county. With no town or city governments to deal with, considerable bureaucracy is eliminated. Hawaii, in anticipation of becoming a state, drafted a constitution in 1950 and was ready to go when statehood came. Politics and government are taken seriously in the Aloha State, which consistently turns in the best national voting record per capita. For example, in the first state elections 173,000 of 180,000 registered voters voted—a whopping 94% of the electorate. In the election to ratify statehood, hardly a ballot went uncast, with 95% of the voters opting for statehood. The bill carried every island of Hawaii except Niihau, where, coincidentally, most of the people (total population 250 or so) are of relatively pure Hawaiian blood. The U.S. Congress passed the Hawaii State Bill on March 12, 1959, and on August 21, 1959, President Eisenhower proclaimed Hawaii the 50th state. Honolulu became the state capital. The present governor is Benjamin

J. Cayetano, the second Hawaiian governor of the state, and the first with any Filipino heritage. Mr. Cayetano has held this office since 1994.

County of Hawaii
The county of Hawaii is almost entirely Democratic and currently has only one Republican elected state legislative member. The current mayor is Stephen K. Yamashiro, Democrat. The mayor is assisted by an elected county council consisting of nine members, one from each council district around the island.

Of the 25 State Senatorial Districts, Hawaii County is represented by three, all Democrats. The First District takes in the whole northern section of the island: the Hamakua Coast, Mauna Kea, North and South Kohala, and part of North Kona. The Second District is mainly Hilo and its outlying area. The Third comprises Puna, Kau, South Kona, and most of North Kona. Hawaii County has six of 51 seats in the State House of Representatives. At this time, all representatives are Democrats, except for a Republican representing North and South Kona, the Fifth District.

ECONOMY

Hawaii's mid-Pacific location makes it perfect for two primary sources of income: tourism and the military. Tourists come in anticipation of endless golden days on soothing beaches, while the military is provided with the strategic position of an unsinkable battleship. Each economic sector nets Hawaii about $4 billion annually, money which should keep flowing smoothly and even increase in the foreseeable future. These revenues remain mostly aloof from the normal ups and downs of the Mainland U.S. economy. Together they make up 60% of the islands' income, and both attract either gung-ho enthusiasts or rabidly negative detractors. The remaining 40% comes in descending proportions from manufacturing, construction, and agriculture (mainly sugar and pineapples). As long as the sun shines and the balance of global power requires a military presence, the economic stability of Hawaii is guaranteed.

TOURISM

"The earthly paradise! Don't you want to go to it? Why, of course!" This was the opening line of *The Hawaiian Guide Book* by Henry Whitney which appeared in 1875. In print for 25 years, it sold for 60 cents during a time when a roundtrip sea voyage between San Francisco and Honolulu cost $125. The technique is a bit dated, but the human desires remain the same: some of us seek paradise, all seek escape, some are drawn to play out a drama in a beautiful setting. Tourists have been coming to Hawaii ever since steamship service began in the 1860s. Until WW II, luxury liners carried the financial elite on exclusive voyages to the islands. By the 1920s 10,000 visitors a year were spending almost $5 million—cementing the bond between Hawaii and tourism.

A $25,000 prize offered by James Dole of pineapple fame sparked a trans-Pacific air race in 1927. The success of the aerial daredevils who answered the challenge proved that commercial air travel to Hawaii was feasible. Two years later, **Hawaiian Air** was offering regularly scheduled flights between all of the major islands. By 1950, airplanes had captured over 50% of the transportation market, and ocean voyages were relegated to "specialty travel" catering to the elite. By 1960 the large airbuses made their debut; 300,000 tourists arrived on eight designated airlines. The Boeing 747 began operating in 1969. These enormous planes could carry hundreds of passengers at reasonable rates, so travel to Hawaii became possible for the average-income person. In 1970, two million ar-

SENATORIAL DISTRICTS   HOUSE DISTRICTS

© J.D. BISIGNANI AND MOON PUBLICATIONS, INC.

rived, and by 1990 close to six million passengers arrived on 22 international air carriers.

The first hotel in Hawaii was the **Volcano House,** which overlooked Kilauea Crater and was built in 1866. Over 3,000 island residents are directly employed by the hotel industry, and many more indirectly serve the tourists. Of the slightly more than 9,500 hotel and condo rooms, the greatest concentration is in Kona. The Kona hotels have the lowest occupancy rate in the state, rarely rising above 60%. The occupancy rates for Kohala and Hilo are only slightly higher. Hawaii receives about 1.2 million tourists annually, about 19,500 on any given day. Of the major islands, it ranks third in number of annual visitors, following Oahu and Maui.

Tourists: Who, When, and Where

Tourism-based income outstripped pineapples and sugar by the mid-'60s and the boom was on. Most visitors (54%) are Americans, and by far the largest numbers come from the West Coast. Sun-seeking refugees from Alaska, however, make up the greatest proportional number, according to state population figures. The remaining arrivals are, in descending proportions, from Japan, Canada, Korea, Australia, Germany, England, and Taiwan. Europe, as a whole, sends proportionally fewer visitors than North America or Asia, while the fewest come from South America. The Japanese market is constantly growing, reaching about 2 million Japanese visitors per year in 1995. This is particularly beneficial to the tourist market because the average Western tourist spends about $135 per day, while a Japanese counterpart spends $340 per day. The average Japanese tourist, however, stays only about six days as opposed to 10 days for westbound travelers. Up until very recently the Japanese traveled only in groups and primarily stayed on Oahu. Now the trend is to travel independently or to come with a group and then peel off, with a hefty percentage heading for the "Neighbor Islands" (all islands other than Oahu).

The typical visitor is slightly affluent, and female visitors outnumber males three to two. The average age (35) is a touch higher than in most vacation areas because it reflects an inflated proportion of retirees heading for Hawaii, especially Honolulu, to fulfill lifelong "dream" vacations. A typical stay lasts about 10 days, down from a month in the 1950s; a full 56% are repeat

visitors. On any given day there are about 80,000 travelers on Oahu, 35,000 on Maui, 19,000 on Hawaii, and about 8,000 on Kauai. Molokai and Lanai get so few visitors, 1,400 and 1,000, respectively, that the figures are hardly counted. In 1964 only 10% of the islands' hotel rooms were on the Neighbor Islands, but by 1966 the figure jumped to 25%, with more than 70% of the tourists opting to visit the Neighbor Islands. Today four out of 10 hotel rooms are on the Neighbor Islands and that figure should reach 50% shortly.

Joaquin Miller, the 19th-century poet of the Sierra, said, "I tell you my boy, the man who has not seen the Sandwich Islands, in this one great ocean's warm heart, has not seen the world." The times have certainly changed, but the sentiments of most visitors to Hawaii remain the same.

Tourism-Related Problems

Tourism is both boon and blight to Hawaii. It is the root cause of two problems: one environmental, the other socioeconomic. The environmental impact is obvious and best described by the lament in songstress Joni Mitchell's "Big Yellow Taxi": "They paved paradise and put up a parking lot." Put simply, tourism can draw too many people to an area and overburden it. In the process, it stresses the land and destroys the natural beauty that attracted people in the first place. Tourists come to Hawaii for what has been called its "ambient resource": a balanced collage of indulgent climate, invigorating waters, intoxicating scenery, and exotic people all wrapped up neatly in one area which can both soothe and excite. It is in the best interest of Hawaii to preserve this "resource."

Like the land, humans are stressed by tourism. Local people, who once took the "Hawaiian lifestyle" for granted, become displaced and estranged in their own land. Some areas, predominantly along gorgeous beaches that were average- to low-income communities, are now overdeveloped, with prices going through the roof. The locals are not only forced to move out, but often must come back as service personnel in the tourist industry and cater to the very people who displaced them. At one time the psychological blow was softened because, after all, the newcomers were merely benign tourists who would stay a short time, spend a wad of money, and leave.

Today, condos are being built and a different sort of visitor is arriving. Many condo owners are well-educated businesspeople and professionals in above-average income brackets. The average condo owner is a Mainlander who purchases one as a second or retirement home. These people are not islanders and have a tough time relating to the locals, who naturally feel resentment. Moreover, since they don't *leave* like normal tourists, they use community facilities, find those special nooks and crannies for shopping or sunbathing that were once the exclusive domain of locals, and have a say as voters in community governments. The islanders become more and more disenfranchised. Many believe that the new order instigated by tourism is similar to what has always existed in Hawaii: a few from the privileged class being catered to by many from the working class. In a way it's an extension of the plantation system, but instead of carrying pineapples, most islanders find themselves carrying luggage, cocktails, or broiled fish. One argument, however, remains undeniable: whether it's people or pineapples, one has to make a living. The days of a little grass shack on a sunny beach aren't gone; it's just that you need a wallet full of credit cards to afford one.

THE MILITARY

Hawaii is the most militarized state in the U.S.: all five services are represented. Camp H.M. Smith, overlooking Pearl Harbor, is the headquarters of CINCPAC (Commander in Chief Pacific), which is responsible for 70% of the earth's surface, from California to the east coast of Africa and to both poles. The U.S. military presence dates back to 1887, when Pearl Harbor was given to the Navy as part of the Sugar Reciprocity Treaty. The sugar planters were given favorable duty-free treatment for their sugar, while the U.S. Navy was allowed exclusive rights to one of the best harbors in the Pacific. In 1894, when the monarchy was being overthrown by the sugar planters, the USS *Boston* sent a contingency of U.S. Marines ashore to "keep order," which really amounted to a show of force backing the revolution. The Spanish-American War saw U.S. troops billeted at Camp McKinley at the foot of Diamond Head, and Schofield Barracks opened to receive the 5th Cavalry in 1909. Pearl Harbor's flames ignited WW II, and there has been no looking back since then.

On average, about 60 military personnel are stationed on the Big Island at any one time, with about the same number of dependents. Most of these people are attached to the enormous Pohakuloa Military Reserve in the center of the island; a lesser number are at a few minor installations around Hilo and at Kilauea.

The Military Has No Aloha
Not everyone is thrilled by the strong military presence in Hawaii. Two factions, native Hawaiians and antinuclear groups, are downright angry. Radical contingencies of native Hawaiian-rights groups consider Hawaii an independent country,

Missiles stand ready to defend America's unsinkable "Battleship Hawaii."

J.D. BISIGNANI

besieged and "occupied" by the U.S. government. They date their loss of independence to Liliuokalani's overthrow in 1894. The vast majority of ethnic Hawaiians, though they consider themselves Americans, are concerned about loss of their rightful homelands with no financial reparation, and about continuing destruction and disregard for their traditional religious and historical sites. A long list of grievances is cited by native Hawaiian action groups, but the best and clearest example was the controversy over the sacred island, Kahoolawe, which, until 1994, was used as a bombing target by the U.S. Navy.

A major controversy raised by the military presence focuses on Hawaii as a nuclear target. The ultimate goal of the antinuclear protesters is to see the Pacific, and the entire world, free from nuclear arms. They see Hawaii as a big target used by the international power merchants on the Mainland as both pawn and watchdog— if war breaks out, they say, the Hawaiian Islands will be reduced to cinders. The military naturally counters that a strong Hawaii is a deterrent to nuclear war and that Hawaii is not only a powerful offensive weapon, but one of the best-defended regions of the world. Unfortunately, when you are on an island there is no place to go: like a boxer in a ring, you can run, but you can't hide. Also, the military has been recently cited for disposing of stockpiles of chemical weapons by incineration on Johnston Island, a military installation southwest of the Big Island. Because there was no environmental impact study, scientists fear that wind and currents could carry the pollutants to the main Hawaiian islands, destroying delicate coral reefs along the way.

AGRICULTURE

The Big Island's economy is the state's most agriculturally based. Over 6,000 farmhands, horticultural workers, and *paniolo* work the land to produce about one-third of the state's vegetables and melons and over 75% of the fruit, especially papaya. The Big Island also produces 60 million pounds of macadamia nuts, the state's entire crop except for what's produced by small farms here and there on the other islands. Hawaii has the only commercial coffee plantations in the country. Each year due to the increased interest

in gourmet Kona coffee, the coffee industry's share in the economy of the island is increasing. About 300 or more horticultural farms produce the largest number of orchids and anthuriums in the state, leaving the Big Island awash in color and fragrance. In the hills, entrepreneurs raise *pakalolo* (marijuana), which has become the state's most productive cash crop. Over $400 million worth is confiscated every year by law enforcement agencies (two-thirds of the total taken in the state), so you can imagine how much remains to hit the street.

LOUISE FOOTE

young sugarcane

Sugar

Hawaii used to be the state's largest sugar grower, with over 90,000 acres in cane. These commercial fields produced four million tons of refined sugar, 40% of the state's output. The majority of sugar land was along the Hamakua Coast, long known for its abundant water supply. At one time, the cane was even transported to the mills by water flumes. Another large pocket of cane fields was found on the southern part of the island, mostly in Puna. With the closing of the last mill in 1996, sugar is no longer grown commercially on the island. Still, small entrepreneurial farms grow it on greatly reduced acreage. The big cane trucks have ceased to roll and the smokestacks stand in silent testimony to a bygone era.

Coffee

The Kona District is a splendid area for raising coffee; it gives the beans a beautiful tan. Lying in Mauna Loa's rain shadow, the district gets dewy mornings followed by sunshine and an afternoon cloud shadow. The coffee has long been accepted as gourmet quality, and is sold in the better restaurants throughout Hawaii and in fine coffee shops around the world. It's a dark, full-bodied coffee with a rich aroma. Approximately 650 small farms produce nearly $7 million a year in coffee revenue. Few, however, make it a full-time business. The production of Kona coffee makes up only about one-tenth of one percent of the coffee grown around the world. The rare bean is often blended with other varieties. When sold unblended it is quite expensive.

Cattle

Hawaii's cattle ranches produce over 5 million pounds of beef per year, 50% of the state's total. More than 400 independent ranches are located on the island, but they are dwarfed both in size and production by the massive Parker Ranch (now held as a public trust), which alone is three-quarters the size of Oahu.

THE "BIG FIVE"

Until statehood, Hawaii was ruled economically by a consortium of corporations known as the "Big Five": **C. Brewer and Co.,** sugar, ranching, and chemicals, founded in 1826; **Theo. H. Davies & Co.,** sugar, investments, insurance, and transportation, founded in 1845; **Amfac Inc.** (originally H. Hackfield Inc.—a German firm that changed its name and ownership during the anti-German sentiment of WW I to American Factors), sugar, insurance, and land development, founded in 1849; **Castle and Cooke Inc.,** (Dole) pineapple, food packing, and land development, founded in 1851; and **Alexander and Baldwin Inc.,** shipping, sugar, and pineapple, founded in 1895. This economic oligarchy ruled Hawaii with a velvet glove and a steel grip.

With members on all important corporate boards, they controlled all major commerce, including banking, shipping, insurance, hotel development, agriculture, utilities, and wholesale and retail merchandising. Anyone trying to buck the system was ground to dust, finding it suddenly impossible to do business in the islands. The Big Five were made up of the islands' oldest and most well-established *haole* families; all included bloodlines from Hawaii's own nobility. They looked among themselves for suitable husbands and wives, so that breaking in from the outside even through marriage was hardly possible. The only time they were successfully challenged prior to statehood was when Sears, Roebuck and Co. opened a store on Oahu. Closing ranks, the Big Five decreed that their steamships would not carry Sears's freight. When Sears threatened to buy its own steamship line, the Big Five relented.

Actually, statehood, and more to the point, tourism, broke their oligarchy. After 1960 too much money was at stake for Mainland-based corporations to ignore. Eventually the grip of the Big Five was loosened, but they are still enormously powerful and richer than ever. These days, however, they don't control everything; now their power is land. With only five other major landholders, they control 65% of the privately held land in Hawaii.

LAND OWNERSHIP

Landwise, Hawaii is a small pie, and its slices are not at all well divided. Of the state's 6,423 square miles of land, the six main inhabited islands make up 98% of it. This figure does not include Niihau, which is privately owned by the Robinson family and inhabited by some of the last re-

LAND OWNERSHIP

Hawaii
1,477,886 Acres

- STATE
- FEDERAL
- HAWAIIAN HOMES
- SMALL PRIVATE
- LARGE PRIVATE

© J.D. BISIGNANI AND MOON PUBLICATIONS, INC.

maining pure-blooded Hawaiians; nor does it include uninhabited Kahoolawe. Of the 4,110,966 acres that make up the inhabited islands, 34% is owned by the state and 16% by the federal government; the remaining 50% is in private hands. While only 40 owners, with 5,000 or more acres each, own 75% of all private lands, the top seven control 46% of it. To be more specific, Castle and Cooke Inc. owns 99% of Lanai, while 40-60% of Maui, Oahu, Molokai, Kauai, and Hawaii is owned by less than a dozen private parties. The largest private landowner, with over 336,000 acres or 8% of the total land area of the state, is the Kamehameha Schools/Bishop Estate, which recently lost a Supreme Court battle that ended with a ruling allowing the state of Hawaii to acquire privately owned land for "the public good." Second in line is the Big Island's Parker Ranch with 140,000 acres, now administered as a public trust after the death of its last owner, Richard Smart.

More than in any other state, Hawaii's landowners tend to lease land instead of sell it, and many private homes are on rented ground. Many feel that with land prices going up all the time, only the very rich land developers will be able to purchase, and the "people" of Hawaii will become even more land-poor.

PEOPLE

Nowhere else on earth can you find such a kaleidoscopic mixture of people. Every major race is accounted for, and over 50 ethnic groups are represented throughout the islands, making Hawaii the most racially integrated state in the U.S. Its population of 1.2 million includes 100,000 permanently stationed military personnel and their dependents. It is the only state where whites are not the majority. About 56% of the people living in Hawaii were born there, 26% were born on the Mainland U.S., and 18% are foreign-born.

The population of Hawaii has been growing steadily in recent times, but it fluctuated wildly in times past. In 1876 it ebbed to its lowest, with only 55,000 permanent residents in the islands. This was the era of large sugar plantations; their constant demand for labor was the primary cause of the importation of various peoples from around the world, which is what led to Hawaii's racially integrated society. WW II saw Hawaii's population swell from 400,000 just prior to the war to 900,000 during the war. Naturally, 500,000 were military personnel who left at war's end, but many returned to settle after getting a taste of island living.

Of the 1,200,000 people in the islands today (1995 est.), 870,000 live on Oahu, with slightly less than half of these living in the Honolulu Metropolitan Area. The rest of the population is distributed as follows: 137,000 on Hawaii, with 47,000 living in Hilo; 115,000 on Maui, with the largest concentration, 53,000, in Wailuku/Kahului; 56,000 on Kauai, including 230 pure-blooded Hawaiians on Niihau; 6,700 on Molokai; and just under 3,000 on Lanai. The population density, statewide, is 186 people per square mile, approximately that of California's. The population is not at all evenly distributed, with Oahu claiming about 1,430 people per square mile, and Hawaii barely 34 residents per square mile. Statewide, city dwellers outnumber those living in the country by nine to one. For the Big Island, 61% are urban while 39% live rurally.

Population Figures

With 137,000, the Big Island has the second-largest island population in Hawaii, just under 9% of the state's total. However, it has the small-

est population density of the main islands, with about 34 people per square mile. The Hilo area has the largest population with 47,000 residents, followed by North and South Kona with about 33,000, Puna at 28,000, South Kohala at 12,000, and the Hamakua Coast, North Kohala, and Kau each between 5,000-6,000. Within the last five years, the areas of Puna and South Kohala have experienced the greatest increases in population. The ethnic breakdown of the Big Island's 137,000 people is as follows: 40% Caucasian, 20% Japanese, 19% Hawaiian, 13% Filipino, 2% Chinese, 6% other.

THE HAWAIIANS

The study of the native Hawaiians is ultimately a study in tragedy because it ends in their demise as a viable people. When Captain Cook first sighted Hawaii in 1778, there were an estimated 300,000 natives living in relative harmony with their ecological surroundings; within 100 years a scant 50,000 demoralized and dejected Hawaiians existed almost as wards of the state. Today, although more than 210,000 people claim varying degrees of Hawaiian blood, experts say that fewer than 1,000 are pure Hawaiian, and this is stretching it.

It's easy to see why people of Hawaiian lineage can be bitter over what they have lost, being strangers in their own land now, much like Native Americans. The overwhelming majority of "Hawaiians" are of mixed heritage, and the wisest take the best from all worlds. From the Hawaiian side comes simplicity, love of the land, and acceptance of people. It is the Hawaiian legacy of *aloha* that remains immortal and adds that special elusive quality that *is* Hawaii.

Polynesian Roots

The Polynesians' original stock is muddled and remains an anthropological mystery, but it's believed that they were nomadic wanderers who migrated from both the Indian subcontinent and Southeast Asia through Indonesia, where they learned to sail and navigate on protected waterways. As they migrated they honed their sailing skills until they could take on the Pacific, and as they moved, they absorbed people from other cultures and races until they had coalesced into what we now know as Polynesians.

Abraham Fornander, still considered a major authority on the subject, wrote in his 1885 *Account of the Polynesian Race* that he believed the Polynesians started as a white (Aryan) race that was heavily influenced by contact with the Cushite Chaldeo-Arabian civilization. He estimated their arrival in Hawaii at A.D. 600, based on Hawaiian genealogical chants. Modern science seems to bear this date out, although it remains skeptical about his other surmises. According to others, the intrepid Polynesians who actually settled Hawaii are believed to have come from the Marquesas Islands, 1,000 miles southeast of Hawaii. The Marquesans were cannibals known for their tenacity and strength, attributes that would serve them well.

The Caste System

Hawaiian society was divided into rankings by a strict caste system determined by birth, and from which there was no chance of escaping. The highest rank was the *ali'i,* the chiefs and royalty. The impeccable genealogies of the *ali'i* were traced back to the gods themselves, and the chants *(mo'o ali'i)* were memorized and sung by professionals (called *ku'auhau)* who were themselves *ali'i.* Ranking passed from both father and mother, and custom dictated that the

JOHN WEBBER (HAWAII STATE ARCHIVES)

first mating of an *ali'i* be with a person of equal status.

A *kahuna* was a highly skilled person whose advice was sought before any major project was undertaken, such as building a house, hollowing a canoe log, or even offering a prayer. The *mo'o kahuna* were the priests of Ku and Lono, and they were in charge of praying and following rituals. They were very powerful *ali'i* and kept strict secrets and laws concerning their various functions.

Besides this priesthood of *kahuna,* there were other *kahuna* who were not *ali'i* but commoners. The two most important were the healers *(kahuna lapa'au)* and the black magicians *(kahuna ana'ana),* who could pray a person to death. The *kahuna lapa'au* had a marvelous pharmacopoeia of herbs and spices that could cure over 230 diseases common to the Hawaiians. The *kahuna ana'ana* could be hired to cast a love spell over a person or cause his or her untimely death. They seldom had to send out a reminder of payment!

The common people were called the *makaainana,* "the people of land"—the farmers, artisans, and fishermen. The land that they lived on was owned by the *ali'i,* but they were not bound to it. If the local *ali'i* was cruel or unfair, the *makaainana* had the right to leave and reside on another's lands. The *makaainana* mostly loved their local *ali'i* much like a child loves a parent, and the feeling was reciprocal. *Makaainana* who lived close to the *ali'i* and could be counted on as warriors in times of trouble were called *kanaka no lua kaua,* "a man for the heat of battle." They were treated with greater favor than those who lived in the backcountry, *kanaka no hii kua,* whose lesser standing opened them up to discrimination and cruelty. All *makaainana* formed extended families called *ohana* who usually lived on the same section of land, called *ahupua'a.* Those farmers who lived inland would barter their produce with the fishermen who lived on the shore, and thus all shared equally in the bounty of land and sea.

A special group called *kauwa* was a landless, untouchable caste confined to living on reservations. Their origins were obviously Polynesian, but they appeared to be descendants of castaways who had survived and become perhaps the aboriginals of Hawaii before the main migrations. It was *kapu* for anyone to go onto *kauwa* lands, and doing so meant instant death. If a human sacrifice was needed, the *kahuna* would simply summon a *kauwa,* who had no recourse but to mutely comply. To this day, to call someone *kauwa,* which now supposedly only means servant, is considered a fight-provoking insult.

Kapu And Day-to-Day Life

Occasionally there were horrible wars, but mostly the people lived quiet and ordered lives based on a strict caste society and the *kapu* system. Famine was known but only on a regional level, and the population was kept in check by birth control, crude abortions, and the distasteful practice of infanticide, especially of baby girls. The Hawaiians were absolutely loving and nurturing parents under most circumstances, and would even take in a *hanai* (adopted child or oldster), a lovely practice that lingers to this day.

A strict division of labor existed among men and women. Men were the only ones permitted to have anything to do with taro: this foodstuff was so sacred that there were a greater number of *kapu* concerning taro than concerning man himself. Men pounded poi and served it to the women. Men also were the fishermen and the builders of houses, canoes, irrigation ditches,

and walls. Women tended to other gardens and shoreline fishing, and were responsible for making tapa cloth. The entire family lived in the common house called the *hale noa.*

Certain things were *kapu* between the sexes. Primarily, women could not enter the *mua* (man's house), nor could they eat with men. Certain foods, such as pork, coconut, red fish, and bananas, were forbidden to women, and it was *kapu* for a man to have intercourse before going fishing, engaging in battle, or attending a religious ceremony. Young boys lived with the women until they underwent a circumcision rite called *pule ipu.* After this was performed, they were required to keep the *kapu* of men. A true Hawaiian settlement required a minimum of five huts: the men's eating hut; women's menstruation hut; women's eating hut; communal sleeping hut; and prayer hut. Without these five separate structures, Hawaiian "society" could not happen, since the *ia kapu* (forbidden eating between men and women) could not be observed.

Ali'i could also declare a *kapu,* and often did so. Certain lands or fishing areas were temporarily made *kapu* so that they could revitalize. Even today, it is *kapu* for anyone to remove all the *opihi* (a type of limpet) from a rock. The great King Kamehameha I even placed a *kapu* on the body of his notoriously unfaithful child bride, Kaahumanu. It didn't work! The greatest *kapu (kapu moe)* was afforded to the highest ranking *ali'i:* anyone coming into their presence had to prostrate themselves. Lesser ranking *ali'i* were afforded the *kapu noho:* lessers had to sit or kneel in their presence. Commoners could not let their shadows fall upon an *ali'i* or enter an *ali'i's* house except through a special door. Breaking a *kapu* meant immediate death.

Fatal Flaws

Less than 100 years after Captain Cook's arrival, King Kalakaua found himself with only 48,000 Hawaiian subjects. Wherever the king went, he would beseech his people, *"Hooulu lahui,"* "Increase the race," but it was already too late. It was as if nature herself had turned her back on these once-proud people. Many of their marriages were barren; in 1874, when only 1,400 children were born, a full 75% died in infancy. The Hawaiians could do nothing but watch as their race faded from existence.

The Causes of Decline

The ecological system of Hawaii has always been exceptionally fragile and this included its people. When the first whites arrived they found a great people who were large, strong, and virile. But when it came to fighting off the most minor diseases, the Hawaiians proved as delicate as hothouse flowers. To exacerbate the situation, the Hawaiians were totally uninhibited toward sexual intercourse between willing partners, and they engaged in it openly and with abandon. Unfortunately, the sailors who arrived were full of syphilis and gonorrhea. The Hawaiian women brought these diseases home and, given the nature of Hawaiian society at the time, they spread like wildfire. By the time the missionaries came in 1820 and helped halt the unbridled fornication, they estimated the native population at only 140,000, less than half of what it had been only 40 years since initial contact! In the next 50 years measles, mumps, influenza, and tuberculosis further ravaged the people. Furthermore, Hawaiian men were excellent sailors, and it's estimated that during the whaling years at least 25% of all able-bodied Hawaiian men sailed away, never to return.

But the coup de grace that really ended the Hawaiian race, as such, was that racial newcomers to the islands were attracted to the Hawaiians and the Hawaiians were in turn attracted to them. With so many interracial marriages, the Hawaiians literally bred themselves out of existence. By 1910, there were still twice as many full-blooded Hawaiians as mixed-bloods, but by 1940 mixed-blooded Hawaiians were the fastest-growing group, and full-blooded the fastest declining.

Hawaiians Today

Many of the Hawaiians who moved to the cities became more and more disenfranchised. Their folk society stressed openness and a giving nature, but downplayed the individual and the ownership of private property. These cultural traits made them easy targets for the users and schemers until they finally became either apathetic or angry. Most surveys reveal that although Hawaiians number only 13% of the population, they account for almost 50% of the financially destitute families and about half of all arrests and illegitimate births. Niihau, a privately owned island, is home to about 230 pure-blooded Hawaiians, representing the largest concentration of them, per capita, in the islands. The Robinson family, which owns the island, restricts visitors to invited guests only.

The second-largest concentration is on Molokai, where 2,700 Hawaiians, living mostly on 40-acre *kuleana* of Hawaiian Homes Lands, make up 40% of that island's population. The majority of mixed-blooded Hawaiians, 80,000 or so, live on Oahu, where they are particularly strong in the hotel and entertainment fields. People of Hawaiian extraction are still a delight to meet, and anyone so lucky as to be befriended by one long regards this friendship as the highlight of his or her travels. The Hawaiians have always given their *aloha* freely to all the peoples of the world, and it is we who must acknowledge this precious gift.

THE CHINESE

Next to Yankees from New England, the Chinese are the oldest migrant group in Hawaii, and their influence has far outshone their meager numbers. They brought to Hawaii, along with their individuality, Confucianism, Taoism, and Buddhism, although many have long since become Christians. The Chinese population, at 68,000, makes up only six percent of the state's total, and the vast majority reside on Oahu. As an ethnic group they account for the least amount of crime, the highest per capita income, and a disproportionate number of professionals.

The First Chinese

No one knows his name, but an unknown Chinese immigrant is credited with being the first person in Hawaii to refine sugar. This Asian wanderer tried his hand at crude refining on Lanai in 1802. Fifty years later the sugar plantations desperately needed workers, and the first Chinese brought to Hawaii under the newly passed Masters and Servants Act were 195 coolies from Amoy, who arrived in 1852. These conscripts were contracted for three to five years and given $3 per month plus room and board. This was for 12 hours a day, six days a week, and even in 1852 these wages were the pits.

The Chinese almost always left the plantations the minute their contracts expired. They went into business for themselves and promptly monopolized the restaurant and small-shop trades.

The Chinese Niche

Although many people in Hawaii considered all Chinese ethnically the same, they were actually quite different. The majority came from Guangdong Province in southern China. They were two distinct ethnic groups: the Punti made up 75% of the immigrants, and the Hakka made up the remainder. In China, they remained separate from each other, never mixing; in Hawaii, they mixed out of necessity. For one thing, hardly any Chinese women came over at first, and the ones who followed were at a premium and gladly accepted as wives, regardless of ethnic background. The Chinese were also one of the first groups who willingly intermarried with the Hawaiians, from whom they gained a reputation for being exceptionally caring spouses.

The Chinese accepted the social order and kept a low profile. For example, during the turbulent labor movements of the 1930s and '40s in Hawaii, the Chinese community produced not one labor leader, radical intellectual, or left-wing politician. When Hawaii became a state, one of the two senators elected was Hiram Fong, a racially mixed Chinese. Since statehood, the Chinese community has carried on business as usual as they continue to rise both economically and socially.

THE JAPANESE

Most scholars believe that (inevitably) a few Japanese castaways floated to Hawaii long before Captain Cook arrived, and might have introduced the iron with which the islanders seemed to be familiar before the white explorers arrived. The first official arrivals from Japan were ambassadors sent by the Japanese shogun to negotiate in Washington; they stopped en route at Honolulu in March 1860. But it was as plantation workers that the Japanese were brought en masse to the islands. A small group arrived in 1868, and mass migration started in 1885.

In 1886, because of famine, the Japanese government allowed farmers mainly from southern Honshu, Kyushu, and Okinawa to emigrate. Among these were members of Japan's little-talked-about untouchable caste, called *eta* or *burakumin* in Japan and *chorinbo* in Hawaii. They gratefully seized this opportunity to better their lot, an impossibility in Japan. The first Japanese migrants were almost all men. Between 1897 and 1908 migration was steady, with about 70% of the immigrants being men. Afterwards, migration slowed because of a "gentlemen's agreement," a euphemism for racism against the "yellow peril." By 1900 there were over 60,000 Japanese in the islands, constituting the largest ethnic group.

AJAs, Americans of Japanese Ancestry

Parents of most Japanese children born before WW II were *issei* (first generation), who considered themselves apart from other Americans and clung to the notion of "we Japanese." Their children, the *nisei* or second generation, were a different matter altogether. In one generation they had become Americans, and they put into practice the high Japanese virtues of obligation, duty, and loyalty to the homeland; that homeland was now unquestionably America. After Pearl Harbor was bombed, the FBI kept close tabs on the Japanese community, and the menace of the "enemy within" prompted the decision to place Hawaii under martial law for the duration of the war. It has since been noted that not a single charge of espionage or sabotage was ever reported against the Japanese community in Hawaii during the war.

AJAs as GIs

Although Japanese had formed a battalion during WW I, they were insulted by being considered unacceptable as American soldiers in WW II. Some Japanese-Americans volunteered to serve in labor battalions, and because of their flawless work and loyalty, it was decided to put out a call for a few hundred volunteers to form a combat unit. Over 10,000 signed up! AJAs formed two distinguished units in WW II: the 100th Infantry Battalion, and later the 442nd Regimental Combat Team. They landed in Italy at Salerno and even fought from Guadalcanal to Okinawa. They distinguished themselves by becoming *the* most decorated unit in American military history.

The Japanese-American GIs returned as "our boys."

The AJAs Return

Many returning AJAs took advantage of the G.I. Bill and received college educations. The "Big Five" corporations for the first time accepted former AJA officers as executives, and the old order was changed. Many Japanese became involved with Hawaiian politics and the first elected to Congress was Daniel Inouye, who had lost an arm fighting in WW II. Hawaii's past governor, George Ariyoshi, elected in 1974, was the country's first Japanese-American to reach such a high office. Most Japanese, even as they climb the economic ladder, tend to remain Democrats.

Today, one out of every two political offices in Hawaii is held by a Japanese-American. In one of those weird quirks of fate, it is now the Hawaiian Japanese who are accused by other ethnic groups of engaging in unfair political practices—nepotism and reverse discrimination. Many of these accusations against AJAs are undoubtedly motivated by jealousy, but the AJAs' record in social fairness issues is not without blemish; true to their custom of family loyalty, they do stick together.

There are now 250,000 people in Hawaii of Japanese ancestry, nearly one-quarter of the state's population. They are the least likely of any ethnic group in Hawaii to marry outside of their group—especially the men—and they enjoy a higher-than-average standard of living.

CAUCASIANS

White people have a distinction separating them from all other ethnic groups in Hawaii: they are lumped together as one. You can be anything from a Protestant Norwegian dockworker to a Greek Orthodox shipping tycoon, but if your skin is white, in Hawaii you're a *haole*. What's more, you could have arrived at Waikiki from Missoula, Montana, in the last 24 hours, or your *kama'aina* family can go back five generations, but again, if you're white, you're a *haole*.

The word *"haole"* has a floating connotation that depends upon the spirit in which it's used. It can mean everything from a derisive "honky" or "cracker" to nothing more than "white person." The exact Hawaiian meaning is clouded, but some say it meant "a man of no background," because white men couldn't chant a genealogical *kanaenae* telling the Hawaiians who they were. The word eventually evolved to mean "foreign white man" and today, simply "white person."

White History

Next to Hawaiians themselves, white people have the oldest stake in Hawaii. They've been there as settlers in earnest since the missionaries of the 1820s, and were established long before any other migrant group. From last century until statehood, old *haole* families owned and controlled everything, and although they were generally benevolent, philanthropic, and paternalistic, they were also racist. They were established *kama'aina* families, many of whom made up the boards of the Big Five corporations or owned huge plantations and formed an inner social circle that was closed to the outside. Many managed to find mates from among close family acquaintances.

Their paternalism, which they accepted with grave responsibility, at first only extended to the Hawaiians, who saw them as replacing their own *ali'i*. Asians were considered primarily instruments of production. These supremacist attitudes tended to drag on in Hawaii until quite recent times. They are today responsible for the sometimes sour relations between white and nonwhite people in the islands. Today, all individual white people are resented to a certain degree because of these past acts, even though they personally were in no way involved.

White Plantation Workers

In the 1880s the white landowners looked around and felt surrounded and outnumbered by Asians, so they tried to import white people for plantation work. None of their schemes seemed to work out. Europeans were accustomed to a much higher wage scale and better living conditions than were provided on the plantations. Although only workers and not considered the equals of the ruling elite, they still were expected to act like a special class. They were treated preferentially, which meant higher wages for the same jobs performed by Asians. Some of the imported workers included: 600 Scandinavians in 1881; 1,400 Germans 1881-85; 400 Poles 1897-98; and 2,400 Russians 1909-12. Many proved troublesome, like the Poles and Russians who staged strikes after only months on the job. Many quickly moved to the Mainland. A contingency of Scots, who first came as mule skinners, did become successful plantation managers and supervisors. The Germans and Scandinavians were well received and climbed the social ladder rapidly, becoming professionals and skilled workers.

The Depression years, not as economically bad in Hawaii as in the continental U.S., brought many Mainland whites seeking opportunity, mostly from the South and the West. These new people were even more racist toward brown-skinned people and Asians than the *ka-ma'aina haole,* and they made matters worse. They also competed more intensely for jobs. The racial tension generated during this period came to a head in 1932 with the infamous "Massie Rape Case."

The Massie Rape Case

Thomas Massie, a naval officer, and his young wife, Thalia, attended a party at the Officers Club. After drinking and dancing all evening, they got into a row and Thalia rushed out in a huff. A few hours later, Thalia was at home, confused and hysterical, claiming to have been raped by some local men. On the most circumstantial evidence, Joseph Kahahawai and four friends of mixed ethnic background were accused. In a highly controversial trial rife with racial tensions, the verdict ended in a hung jury.

While a new trial was being set, Kahahawai and his friends were out on bail. Seeking revenge, Thomas Massie and Grace Fortescue, Thalia's mother, kidnapped Joseph Kahahawai with a plan of extracting a confession from him. They were aided by two enlisted men assigned to guard Thalia. While questioning Joseph, they killed him and attempted to dump his body in the sea but were apprehended. Another controversial trial—this time for Mrs. Fortescue, Massie, and the accomplices—followed. Clarence Darrow, the famous lawyer, sailed to Hawaii to defend them. For killing Kahahawai, these people served *one hour* of imprisonment in the judge's private chambers. The other four, acquitted with Joseph Kahahawai, maintain innocence of the rape to this day. Later, the Massies divorced, and Thalia went on to become a depressed alcoholic who took her own life.

The Portuguese

The last time anyone looked, Portugal was still attached to the European continent, but for some anomalous reason the Portuguese weren't considered *haole* in Hawaii for the longest time. About 12,000 arrived between 1878 and 1887 and another 6,000 came between 1906 and 1913. Accompanied during this period by 8,000 Spanish, they were considered one and the same. Most of the Portuguese were illiterate peasants from Madeira and the Azores, and the Spanish hailed from Andalusia. They were very well received, and because they were white but not *haole,* they made a perfect "buffer" ethnic group. Committed to staying in Hawaii, they rose to be skilled workers—the *"luna* class" on the plantations. However, they deemphasized education and became very racist toward Asians, regarding them as a threat to their job security.

By 1920, the 27,000 Portuguese made up 11% of the population. After that they tended to blend with the other ethnic groups and weren't counted separately. Portuguese men tended to marry within their ethnic group, but a good portion of Portuguese women married other white men and became closer to the *haole* group, while another large portion chose Hawaiian mates and grew further away. Although they didn't originate pidgin English (see "Language"), the unique melodious quality of their native tongue did give pidgin that certain lilt it has today. Also, the ukulele ("jumping flea") was closely patterned after the *cavaquinho,* a Portuguese stringed folk instrument.

The Caucasian Population
Today Caucasians make up the largest racial group in the islands, at 33% (about 370,000) of the population. There are heavy white concentrations throughout Oahu, especially in Waikiki, in Kailua-Kaneohe, and around Pearl City. In terms of pure numbers, the white population is the fastest growing in the islands because most people resettling in Hawaii are white Americans predominantly from the West Coast.

FILIPINOS AND OTHERS

The Filipinos who came to Hawaii brought high hopes of amassing personal fortunes and returning home as rich heroes; for most it was a dream that never came true. Filipinos had been American nationals ever since the Spanish-American War of 1898, and as such weren't subject to immigration laws that curtailed the importation of other Asian workers at the turn of this century. The first to arrive were 15 families in 1906, but a large number came in 1924 as strikebreakers. The majority were illiterate peasants called *Ilocanos* from the northern Philippines, with about 10% Visayans from the central cities. The Visayans were not as hard-working or

thrifty, but were much more sophisticated. From the first, Filipinos were looked down upon by all the other immigrant groups, and were considered particularly uncouth by the Japanese. The value they placed on education was the least of any group, and even by 1930 only about half could speak rudimentary English, the majority remaining illiterate. They were billeted in the worst housing, performed the most menial jobs, and were the last hired and first fired.

One big difference between Filipinos and other groups was that the men brought no Filipino women to marry, so they clung to the idea of returning home. In 1930 there were 30,000 men and only 360 women. This hopeless situation led to a great deal of prostitution and homosexuality; many of these terribly lonely bachelors would feast and drink on weekends and engage in their gruesome but exciting pastime of cockfighting on Sundays. When some did manage to find wives, their mates were inevitably part Hawaiian. Today, there are still plenty of old Filipino bachelors who never managed to get home, and the Sunday cockfights remain a way of life.

The Filipinos constitute 15% of Hawaii's population (170,000), with almost 75% living on Oahu. Many visitors to Hawaii mistake Filipinos for Hawaiians because of their dark skin, and this is a minor irritant to both groups. Some streetwise Filipinos even claim to be Hawaiians, because being Hawaiian is "in" and goes over well with the tourists, especially the young women tourists. For the most part, these people are hard-working, dependable laborers who do tough work for little recognition. They remain low on the social totem pole and have not yet organized politically to stand up for their rights.

Other Groups
About 10% of Hawaii's population is made up of a conglomerate of other ethnic groups. Of these, one of the largest and fastest growing is Korean, with 25,000 people. About 8,000 Koreans came to Hawaii from 1903 until 1905, when their government halted emigration. During the same period about 6,000 Puerto Ricans arrived, but they have become so assimilated that only 4,000 people in Hawaii today consider themselves Puerto Rican. There were also two attempts made last century to import other Polynesians to strengthen the dying Hawaiian race, but they were fail-

ures. In 1869 only 126 central Polynesian natives could be lured to Hawaii, and from 1878 to 1885 2,500 Gilbert Islanders arrived. Both groups became immediately disenchanted with Hawaii. They pined away for their own islands and departed for home as soon as possible.

Today, however, 15,000 Samoans have settled in Hawaii, and with more on the way they are the fastest-growing minority in the state. For unexplainable reasons, Samoans and native Hawaiians get along extremely poorly and have the worst racial tensions and animosity of any groups. The Samoans ostensibly should represent the archetypal Polynesians that the Hawaiians are seeking, but it doesn't work that way. Samoans are criticized by Hawaiians for their hot tempers, lingering feuds, and petty jealousies. They're clannish and are often the butt of "dumb" jokes. This racism seems especially ridiculous, but that's the way it is.

Just to add a bit more exotic spice to the stew, there are about 27,000 blacks, 5,000 Native Americans, and 6,000 Vietnamese refugees living on the islands.

LANGUAGE

Hawaii is part of America and people speak English there, but that's not the whole story. If you turn on the TV to catch the evening news, you'll hear "Walter Cronkite" English, unless of course you happen to tune in to a Japanese-language broadcast designed for tourists from that country. You can easily pick up a Chinese-language newspaper or groove to the music on a Filipino radio station, but let's not confuse the issue. All your needs and requests at airports, car-rental agencies, restaurants, hotels, or wherever you happen to travel will be completely understood, as well as answered, in English. However, when you happen to overhear islanders speaking, what they're saying will sound somewhat familiar but you won't be able to pick up all the words, and the beat and melody of the language will be noticeably different.

Hawaii—like New England, the Deep South, and the Midwest—has its own unmistakable linguistic regionalism. All the ethnic peoples who make up Hawaii have enriched the English spoken there with words, expressions, and subtle shades of meaning that are commonly used and understood throughout the islands. The greatest influence on English has come from the Hawaiian language itself, and words such as "aloha," "hula," and "muumuu" are familiarly used and understood by most Americans.

Other migrant peoples, especially the Chinese, Japanese, and Portuguese, influenced the local dialect to such an extent that the simplified plantation lingo they spoke has become known as "pidgin." A fun and enriching part of the "island experience" is picking up a few words of Hawaiian and pidgin. English is the official language of the state, business, education, and perhaps even the mind; but pidgin is the language of the people, the emotions, and life, while Hawaiian remains the language of the heart and the soul.

Note: Many Hawaiian words are commonly used in English, appear in English dictionaries, and therefore would ordinarily be subject to the rules of English grammar. The Hawaiian language, however, does not pluralize nouns by adding an "s"; the singular and plural are differentiated in context. For purposes of this book, and to highlight the Hawaiian culture, the Hawaiian style of pluralization will be followed for common Hawaiian words. The following are some examples of plural Hawaiian nouns treated this way in this book: *haole* (not haoles), hula, *kahuna,* lei, luau, and *nene.*

PIDGIN

The dictionary definition of pidgin is: a simplified language with a rudimentary grammar used as a means of communication between people speaking different languages. Hawaiian pidgin is a little more complicated than that. It had its roots during the plantation days of last century when white owners and *luna* (foremen) had to communicate with recently arrived Chinese, Japanese, and Portuguese laborers. It was designed as a simple language of the here and now, and was primarily concerned with the necessary functions of working, eating, and sleep-

CAPSULE PIDGIN

The following are a few commonly used words and expressions that should give you an idea of pidgin. It really can't be written properly, merely approximated, but for now, *"Brah, study da' kine an' bimbye you be hele on, brah! Okay? Lesgo."*

an' den—and then?; big deal; so what's next; how boring

bimbye—after a while; bye and bye. "Bimbye, you learn pidgin."

blalah—brother, but refers to a large, heavyset, good-natured Hawaiian man

brah—all the bro's in Hawaii are brahs; brother; pal. Used to call someone's attention. One of the most common words used even among people who are not acquainted. After a fill-up at a gas station, a person would say "Tanks, brah."

cockaroach—steal; rip off. If you really want to find out what *cockaroach* means, just leave your camera on your beach blanket when you take a little dip.

da' kine—a catch-all word of many meanings that epitomizes the essence of pidgin. *Da' kine* is easily used as a euphemism and is substituted whenever the speaker is at a loss for a word or just wants to generalize. It can mean: you know?; whatchamacallit; of that type.

geev um—give it to them; give them hell; go for it. Can be used as an encouragement. If a surfer is riding a great wave, the people on the beach might yell, "Geev um, brah!"

hana ho—again. Especially after a concert, the audience shouts "Hana ho!" (One more!).

hele on—right on!; hip; with it; groovy

howzit?—as in "howzit brah?"; what's happening?; how is it going? The most common greeting, used in place of the more formal "How do you do?"

huhu—angry! "You put the make on the wrong da' kine wahine brah, and you in da' kine trouble, if you get one big Hawaiian blalah plenty hu hu."

kapu—a Hawaiian word meaning "forbidden." If *kapu* is written on a gate or posted on a tree, it means "No trespassing." *Kapu*-breakers are still very unpopular in the islands.

lesgo—let's go!; do it!

li'dis an' li'dat—like this or that; a catch-all grouping used especially if you want to avoid details; like, ya' know?

lolo buggah—stupid or crazy guy (person). Words to a tropical island song go, "I want to find the lolo who stole my pakalolo."

mo' bettah—real good!; great idea. An island sentiment used to be "Mo' bettah you *come* Hawaii." Now it has subtly changed to "Mo' bettah you *visit* Hawaii."

ono—number one!; delicious; great; groovy. "Hawaii is ono, brah!"

pakalolo—literally "crazy smoke"; marijuana; grass; reefer. "Hey, brah! Maui-wowie da' kine ono pakalolo."

pakiki head—stubborn; bull-headed

pau—a Hawaiian word meaning finished; done; over and done with. *Pau hana* means end of work or quitting time. Once used by plantation workers, now used by everyone.

stink face—basically frowning at someone; using facial expression to show displeasure. Hard looks. What you'll get if you give local people a hard time.

swell head—burned up; angry

talk story—spinning yarns; shooting the breeze; throwing the bull; a rap session. If you're lucky enough to be around to hear *kapuna* (elders) "talk story," you can hear some fantastic tales in the tradition of old Hawaii.

tita—sister, but only used to describe a fun-loving, down-to-earth country girl

waddascoops—what's the scoop?; what's up?; what's happening?

ing. It has an economical noun-verb-object structure (although not necessarily in that order).

Hawaiian words make up most of pidgin's non-English vocabulary. It includes a good smattering of Chinese, Japanese, and Samoan; the distinctive rising inflection is provided by the melodious Mediterranean lilt of the Portuguese. Pidgin is not a stagnant language. It's kept alive by hip new words introduced by people who are "so radical," or especially by slang words introduced by teenagers. It's a colorful English, like "jive" or "ghettoese" spoken by American blacks, and is as regionally unique as the speech of Cajuns from Louisiana's bayous. *Makaainana* of all socioethnic backgrounds can at least understand pidgin. Most islanders are proud of it, while some consider it a low-class jargon. The Hawaiian House of Representatives has given pidgin an official sanction, and most people feel that it adds a real local style and should be preserved.

Pidgin Lives

Pidgin is first learned at school, where all students, regardless of background, are exposed to it. The pidgin spoken by young people today is "fo' real" different from that of their parents. It's no longer only plantation talk but has moved to the streets and picked up some sophistication. At one time there was an academic movement to exterminate it, but that idea died away with the same thinking that insisted on making left-handed people write with their right hand. It is strange, however, that pidgin has become the unofficial language of Hawaii's grass-roots movement, when it actually began as a white owners' language which was used to supplant Hawaiian and all other languages brought to the islands.

Although hip young *haole* use pidgin all the time, it has gained the connotation of being the language of the nonwhite locals, and is part of the "us against them" way of thinking. All local people, *haole* or not, do consider pidgin their own island language and don't really like it when it's used by *malihini* (newcomers). If you're in the islands long enough, you don't have to bother learning pidgin; it'll learn you. There's a book sold all over the islands called *Pidgin to da Max*, written by (you guessed it) a *haole* from Nebraska named Doug Simonson. You might not be able to understand what's being said by locals speaking pidgin (that's usually the idea), but you should be able to *feel* what's being meant.

HAWAIIAN

The Hawaiian language sways like a palm tree in a gentle wind. Its words are as melodious as a love song. Linguists say that you can learn a lot about people through their language; when you hear Hawaiian you think of gentleness and love, and it's hard to imagine the ferocious side so evident in Hawaii's past. With its many Polynesian root words easily traced to Indonesian and Malay, Hawaiian is obviously from this same stock. The Hawaiian spoken today is very different from old Hawaiian. Its greatest metamorphosis occurred when the missionaries began to write it down in the 1820s. There is a movement to reestablish the Hawaiian language, and courses in it are offered at the University of Hawaii. Many scholars have put forth translations of Hawaiian, but there are endless, volatile disagreements in the academic sector about the real meanings of Hawaiian words. Hawaiian is no longer spoken as a language except on Niihau, and the closest tourists will come to it is in place-names, street names, and words that have become part of common usage, such as *aloha* and *mahalo*. A few old Hawaiians still speak it at home and there are sermons in Hawaiian at some local churches. Kawaiahao Church in downtown Honolulu is the most famous of these. (See the Glossary for a list of commonly used Hawaiian words.)

Wiki Wiki Hawaiian

Thanks to the missionaries, the Hawaiian language is rendered phonetically using only 12 letters. They are the five vowels, a-e-i-o-u, sounded as they are in Italian; and seven consonants, h-k-l-m-n-p-w, sounded exactly as they are in English. Sometimes "w" is pronounced as "v," but this only occurs in the middle of a word and always follows a vowel. A consonant is always followed by a vowel, forming two-letter syllables, but vowels are often found in pairs or even triplets. A slight oddity about Hawaiian is the glottal stop. This is an abrupt break in sound in the middle of a word such as "oh-oh" in English, and is denoted with an apostrophe ('). A good example is *ali'i;* or even better, the Oahu town of Ha'iku, which actually means "abrupt break."

Pronunciation Key

For those unfamiliar with the sounds of Italian or other Romance languages, the vowels are sounded as follows:

A—in stressed syllables, pronounced as in "**ah**" (that feels good!). For example, Haleakala is pronounced "**hah** lay **Ah** kah lah." Unstressed syllables, pronounced as in "**a**gain" or "**a**bove." For example, Kamehameha "**ka** May ha May ha.**

E—short "e" as in "pen" or "dent" *(hale.)* Long "e" sounded as "ay" as in "sw**ay**" or "d**ay**." For example, the Hawaiian goose *(nene)* is a "n**ay** n**ay**," not a "knee knee."

I—pronounced "ee" as in "s**ee**" or "w**e**" *(pali).*

O—pronounced as in "n**o**" or "**oh**" (k**o**a, or **o**no).

U—pronounced "oo" as in "d**o**" or "st**ew**" (*kapu,* or P**u**na).

Diphthongs

There are also eight vowel pairs known as "diphthongs" (ae-ai-ao-au-ei-eu-oi-ou). These are the sounds made by gliding from one vowel to another within a syllable. The stress is placed on the first vowel. In English, examples would be s**oil** and **eu**phoria. Common examples in Hawaiian are "lei" (lay) and "*heiau*" (hay-ow).

Stress

The best way to learn which syllables are stressed in Hawaiian is by listening closely. It becomes obvious after a while. Also, some vowel sounds are held longer than others; these can occur at the beginning of a word, such as the first "a" in "*aina,*" or in the middle of a word, like the

cover page of the first Hawaiian primer, showing the phonetic rendering of the ancient Hawaiian language before five of the consonants were dropped

first "a" in "*lanai.*" Again, it's a matter of tuning your ear and paying attention. No one is going to give you a hard time if you mispronounce a word. It's good, however, to pay close attention to the pronunciation of street and place-names because many Hawaiian words sound alike and a misplaced vowel here or there could be the difference between getting where you want to go and getting lost.

In what other land save this one is the commonest form of greeting not 'Good Day,' . . . but 'Love?' . . . Aloha . . . It is the positive affirmation of one's own heart giving.

—Jack London, 1916

RELIGION

The Lord saw fit to keep His island paradise secret from humans for a few million years, but once we finally arrived we were awfully thankful. Hawaii sometimes seems like a floating tabernacle; everywhere you look there's a church, temple, shrine, or *heiau*. The islands are either a very holy place, or there's a powerful lot of sinning going on that would require so many houses of prayer. Actually, it's just America's "right to worship" concept fully employed in microcosm. All the peoples who came to Hawaii brought their own forms of devotion. The Polynesian Hawaiians praised the primordial creators, Wakea and Papa, from whom their pantheon of animistically inspired gods sprang. Obviously, for a modern world these old gods would never do. Unfortunately for the old gods, there were too many of them, and belief in them was looked upon as superstition, the folly of semicivilized pagans. So the famous missionaries of the 1820s brought Congregational Christianity and the "true path" to heaven.

Inconveniently, the Catholics, Mormons, Reformed Mormons, Adventists, Episcopalians, Unitarians, Christian Scientists, Lutherans, Baptists, Jehovah's Witnesses, Salvation Army, and every other major and minor denomination of Christianity that followed in their wake brought their own brands of enlightenment and never quite agreed with each other. Chinese and Japanese immigrants established the major sects of Buddhism, Confucianism, Taoism, and Shintoism. Allah is praised, the Torah is chanted in Jewish synagogues, and nirvana is available at a variety of Hindu temples. If the spirit moves you, a Hare Krishna devotee will be glad to point you in the right direction and give you a free flower for only a dollar or two. If the world is still too much with you, you might find peace at a Church of Scientology, or meditate at a Kundalini yoga institute, or perhaps find relief at a local assembly of Baha'i. Anyway, rejoice, because in Hawaii you may find not only paradise, but salvation.

HAWAIIAN BELIEFS

The Polynesian Hawaiians worshipped nature. They saw its forces manifested in a multiplicity of forms to which they ascribed godlike powers, and based daily life on this animistic philosophy. Hand-picked and specially trained storytellers chanted the exploits of the gods. These ancient tales, kept alive in a special oral tradition called *moolelo*, were recited only by day. Entranced listeners encircled the chanter; in respect for the gods and in fear of their wrath, they were forbidden to move once the tale was begun. This was serious business during which a person's life could be at stake. It was not like the telling of *kaao*, which were simple fictions, tall tales, and yarns of ancient heroes related for amusement and to pass the long nights. Any object, animate or inanimate, could be a god. All could be infused with mana, especially a dead body or respected ancestor.

Ohana had personal family gods called *amakua* on whom they called in times of danger or strife. There were children of gods called *kupua* who were thought to live among humans and were distinguished either for their beauty and strength or for their ugliness and terror. It was told that processions of dead *ali'i*, called "Marchers of the Night," wandered through the land of the living and unless you were properly protected it could mean death if they looked upon you. There were simple ghosts known as *akua lapu* who merely frightened people. Forests, waterfalls, trees, springs, and a thousand forms of nature were the manifestations of *akua li'i*, "little spirits" who could be invoked at any time for help or protection. It made no difference who or what you were in old Hawaii; the gods were ever-present and they took a direct and active role in your life.

Behind all of these beliefs was an innate sense of natural balance and order. It could be interpreted as positive-negative, yin-yang, plus-minus, life-death, light-dark, whatever, but the main idea was that everything had its opposite. The time of darkness when only the gods lived was *po*. When the great gods descended to the earth and created light, this was *ao* and humanity was born. All of these *moolelo* are part of the *Kumulipo*, the great chant that records the Hawaiian version of creation. From the time the gods descended and touched the earth at Ku

Moku on Lanai, the genealogies were kept. Unlike the Bible, these included the noble families of female as well as male *ali'i*.

THE STRIFES OF MAUI

Of all the heroes and mythological figures of Polynesia, Maui is the best known. His "strifes" are like the great Greek epics, and they make excellent tales of daring that elders loved to relate to youngsters around the evening fire. Maui was abandoned by his mother, Hina of Fire, when he was an infant. She wrapped him in her hair and cast him upon the sea where she expected him to die, but he lived and returned home to become her favorite. She knew then that he was a born hero and had strength far beyond that of ordinary mortals. His first exploit was to lift the sky. In those days the sky hung so low that humans had to crawl around on all fours. A seductive young woman approached Maui and asked him to use his great strength to lift the sky. In fine heroic fashion, the big boy agreed, if the beautiful woman would euphemistically "give him a drink from her gourd." He then obliged her by lifting the sky, and he might even have made the earth move for her once or twice.

More Land

The territory of humankind was small at that time. Maui decided that more land was needed, so he conspired to "fish up islands." He descended into the land of the dead and petitioned an ancestress to fashion him a hook from her jawbone. She obliged and created the mythical hook, *Manai ikalani*. Maui then secured a sacred *alae* bird that he intended to use for bait and bid his brothers to paddle him far out to sea. When he arrived at the deepest spot, he lowered *Manai ikalani* baited with the sacred bird, and his sister, Hina of the Sea, placed it into the mouth of "Old One Tooth," who held the land fast to the bottom of the waters. Maui then exhorted his brothers to row, but warned them not to look back. They strained at the oars with all their might and slowly a great land mass arose. One brother, overcome by curiosity, looked back, and when he did so, the land shattered into all of the islands of Polynesia.

Further Exploits

Maui still desired to serve mankind. People were without fire, the secret of which was held by the sacred *alae* birds, who learned it from Maui's far distant mother. Hina of Fire gave Maui her burning fingernails, but he oafishly kept dropping them into streams until all had fizzled out and he had totally irritated his generous progenitor. She pursued him, trying to burn him to a cinder; Maui chanted for rain to put out her scorching fires. When she saw that they were being quenched, she hid her fire in the barks of special trees and informed the mud hens where they could be found, but first made them promise never to tell humans. Maui knew of this and captured a mud hen, threatening to wring its scrawny, traitorous neck unless it gave up the secret. The bird tried trickery and told Maui first to rub together the stems of sugarcane, then banana and even taro. None worked, and Maui's determined rubbing is why these plants have hollow roots today.

Finally, with Maui's hands tightening around the mud hen's gizzard, the bird confessed that fire could be found in the *hau* tree and also the sandalwood, which Maui named *ili aha* ("fire bark") in its honor. He then rubbed all the feathers off the mud hen's head for being so deceitful, which is why their crowns are featherless today.

The Sun is Snared

Maui's greatest deed, however, was in snaring the sun and exacting a promise that it would go slower across the heavens. The people complained that there were not enough daylight hours to fish or farm. Maui's mother could not dry her tapa cloth because the sun rose and set so quickly. She asked her son to help. Maui went to his blind grandmother, who lived on the slopes of Haleakala and was responsible for cooking the sun's bananas, which he ate every day in passing. She told him to personally weave 16 strong ropes with nooses from his sister's hair. Some say these came from her head, but other versions insist that it was no doubt Hina's pubic hair that had the power to hold the sun god. Maui positioned himself with the rope, and as each of the 16 rays of the sun came across Haleakala, he snared them until the sun was defenseless and had to bargain for his life. Maui agreed to free him if he promised to go more slowly. From that time forward the sun agreed to move slowly and Haleakala ("The House of the Sun") became his home.

HEIAU AND IDOLS

A *heiau* is a Hawaiian temple. The basic *heiau* was a masterfully built and fitted rectangular stone wall that varied in size from about as big as a basketball court to as big as a football field. Once the restraining outer walls were built, the interior was backfilled with smaller stones and the top dressing was expertly laid and then rolled, perhaps with a log, to form a pavement-like surface. All that remains of Hawaii's many *heiau* are the stone platforms. The buildings upon them, made from perishable wood, leaves, and grass, have long since disappeared.

Some *heiau* were dreaded temples where human sacrifices were made. Tradition says that this barbaric custom began at Waha'ula Heiau on the Big Island in the 12th century and was introduced by a ferocious Tahitian priest named Paao. Other *heiau*, such as Pu'uhonua o Honaunau, also on the Big Island, were temples of refuge where the weak, widowed, orphaned, and vanquished could find safety and sanctuary.

Idols

The Hawaiian people worshipped gods who took the form of idols fashioned from wood, feathers, or stone. The eyes were made from shells and until these were inlaid, the idol was dormant. The hair used was often human hair, and the arms and legs were usually flexed. The mouth was either gaping or formed a wide figure-eight lying on its side, and more likely than not was lined with glistening dog teeth. Small figures made of woven basketry were expertly covered with feathers. Red and yellow feathers were favorites taken from specific birds by men whose only work was to roam the forests in search of them.

Ghosts

The Hawaiians had countless superstitions and ghost legends, but two of the more interesting involve astral travel of the soul and the "Marchers of the Night." The soul, *uhane*, was considered by Hawaiians to be totally free and indepen-dent of its body, *kino*. The soul could separate, leaving the body asleep or very drowsy. This disincorporated soul *(hihi'o)* could visit people and was considered quite different from a *lapu* or ordinary spirit of a dead person. A *kahuna* could immediately recognize if a person's *uhane* had left the body, and a special wreath was placed upon the head to protect the person and to facilitate reentry.

If confronted by an apparition, you could test to see if it was indeed dead or still alive by placing leaves of an *ape* plant upon the ground. If the leaves tore when they were walked upon, the spirit was merely human, but if they remained intact it was a ghost. Or you could sneak up and startle the vision, and if it disappeared it was a ghost. Also, if no reflection of the face appeared when it drank water from an offered calabash, it was a ghost. Unfortunately, there were no instructions to follow once you had determined that you indeed had a ghost on your hands. Maybe it was better not to know! Some people would sprinkle salt and water around their houses, but this kept away evil spirits, not ghosts.

There are also many stories of *kahuna* restoring a soul to a dead body. First they had to catch it and keep it in a gourd. They then placed beautiful tapa and fragrant flowers and herbs about the body to make it more enticing. Slowly, they would coax the soul out of the gourd until it reentered the body through the big toe.

Death Marchers

One inexplicable phenomenon that many people attest to is *ka huakai o ka po,* "Marchers of the Night." This march of the dead is fatal if you gaze upon it unless one of the marchers happens to be a friendly ancestor who will protect you. The peak time for "the march" is 7:30 p.m.-2 a.m. The marchers can be dead *ali'i* and warriors, the gods themselves, or the lesser *amakua.* When the *amakua* march there is usually chanting and music. *Ali'i* marches are more somber. The entire procession, lit by torches, often stops at the house of a relative and might even carry him or her away. When the gods themselves march, there is often thunder, lightning, and heavy seas. The sky is lit with torches, and they walk six abreast, three gods and three goddesses. If you get in the way of a march, remove your clothing and prostrate yourself. If the marching gods or *amakua* happen to be ones to which you prayed, you might be spared. If it's a march of the *ali'i,* you might make it if you lie face upward and feign death. If you *do* see a death march, the last thing that you'll worry about is lying naked on the ground looking ridiculous.

MISSIONARIES ONE AND ALL

In Hawaii, when you say "missionaries," it's taken for granted you're referring to the small and determined band of Congregationalists who arrived aboard the brig *Thaddeus* in 1820, and the follow-up groups called "companies" or "packets" that reinforced them. They were sent from Boston by the American Board of Commissioners for Foreign Missions (ABCFM), which learned of the supposed sad and godless plight of the Hawaiian people through returning sailors and especially through the few Hawaiians who had come to America to study.

The person most instrumental in bringing the missionaries to Hawaii was a young man named Opukahaia. He was an orphan befriended by a ship's captain and taken to New England, where he studied theology. Obsessed with the desire to return home and save his people from certain damnation, Opukahaia wrote accounts of life in Hawaii that were published and widely read. These accounts were directly responsible for the formation of the Pioneer Company to the Sandwich Islands Missions in 1819. Unfortunately, Opukahaia died in New England from typhus the year before they left.

"Civilizing" Hawaii
The first missionaries had the straightforward task of bringing the Hawaiians out of paganism and into Christianity and civilization. They met with terrible hostility—not from the natives, but from the sea captains and traders who were very happy with the open debauchery and wanton whoremongering that was status quo in the Hawaii of 1820. Many direct confrontations between these two factions even included the cannonading of missionaries' homes by American sea captains who were denied the customary visits of island women, thanks to meddlesome "do-gooders." The most memorable of these incidents involved "Mad Jack" Percival, the captain of the USS *Dolphin,* who bombed a church in Lahaina to show his rancor. In actuality, the truth of the situation was much closer to the sentiments of James Jarves, who wrote, "The missionary was a far more useful and agreeable man than his Catholicism would indicate; and the trader was not so bad a man as the missionary would make him out to be." The missionaries' primary aim might have been conversion, but the most fortuitous by-product was education, which raised the consciousness of every Hawaiian, regardless of religious affiliation. In 40 short years Hawaii was considered a civilized nation well on its way into the modern world, and the American Board of Missions officially ended its support in 1863.

Non-Christians
By the turn of the century, both Shintoism and Buddhism, brought by the Japanese and Chinese, were firmly established in Hawaii. The first official Buddhist temple was Hongpa Hongwanji, established on Oahu in 1889. All the denominations of Buddhism account for 17% of the island's religious total, and there are about 50,000 Shintoists. The Hindu religion has perhaps 2,000 adherents, and about the same number of Jewish people live throughout Hawaii with only one synagogue, Temple Emanuel, on Oahu. The largest number of people in Hawaii (300,000) remains unaffiliated, and about 10,000 people are in new religious movements and lesser-known faiths such as Baha'i and Unitarianism.

ARTS AND MUSIC

Referring to Hawaii as "paradise" is about as hackneyed as you can get, but when you combine it into "artists' paradise" it's the absolute truth. Something about the place evokes art (or at least personal expression) from most people. The islands are like a magnet: they not only draw artists to them, but they draw art *from* the artists.

The inspiration comes from the astounding natural surroundings. The land is so beautiful yet so raw; the ocean's power and rhythm are primal and ever-present; the riotous colors of flowers and fruit leap from the deep-green jungle background. Crystal water beads and pale mists turn the mountains into mystic temples, while rainbows ride the crests of waves. The stunning variety of faces begging to be rendered suggests that all the world sent delegations to the islands. And in most cases it did! Inspiration is everywhere, as is art, good or bad.

Sometimes the artwork is overpowering in itself and in its sheer volume. Though geared to the tourist's market of cheap souvenirs, there is hardly a shop in Hawaii that doesn't sell some item that falls into the general category of "art." You can find everything from carved monkey-face coconut shells to true masterpieces. The Polynesian Hawaiians were master craftspeople, and their legacy still lives in a wide variety of woodcarvings, basketry, and weavings. The hula is art in swaying motion, and the true form is rigorously studied and taken very seriously. There is hardly a resort area that doesn't offer the "bump and grind" tourist's hula, but even these revues are accompanied by proficient local musicians. Nightclubs offer "slack key" balladeers; island music performed on ukuleles and on Hawaii's own steel guitars spills from many lounges.

Vibrant fabrics that catch the spirit of the islands are rendered into muumuu and aloha shirts at countless local factories. They're almost a mandatory purchase! Pottery, heavily influenced by the Japanese, is a well-developed craft at numerous kilns. Local artisans fashion delicate jewelry from coral and olivine, while some ply the whaler's legacy of etching on ivory, called scrimshaw. There are fine traditions of quilting, flower art in lei, and street artists working in everything from airbrush to glass.

ARTS OF OLD HAWAII

Since everything in old Hawaii had to be fashioned by hand, almost every object was either a genuine work of art or the product of a highly refined craft. With the "civilizing" of the natives, most of the "old ways" disappeared, including the old arts and crafts. Most authentic Hawaiian art exists only in museums, but with the resurgence of Hawaiian roots, many old arts are being revitalized, and a few artists are becoming proficient in them.

Magnificent Canoes

The most respected artisans in old Hawaii were the canoe makers. With little more than a stone adze and a pump drill, they built canoes that could carry 200 people and last for generations—sleek, well proportioned, and infinitely seaworthy. The main hull was usually a gigantic koa log, and the gunwale planks were minutely drilled and sewn to the sides with sennit rope. Apprenticeships lasted for years, and a young man knew that he had graduated when one day he was nonchalantly asked to sit down and eat with the master builders. Small family-sized canoes with outriggers were used for fishing and perhaps carried a spear rack; large oceangoing double-hulled canoes were used for migration and warfare.

On these, the giant logs had been adzed to about two inches thick. A mainsail woven from pandanus was mounted on a central platform, and the boat was steered by two long paddles. The hull was dyed with plant juices and charcoal, and the entire vil-

BOB RACE

lage helped launch the canoe in a ceremony called "drinking the sea."

Carving and Weaving

Wood was a primary material used by Hawaiian craftsmen. They almost exclusively used koa because of its density, strength, and natural luster. It was turned into canoes, woodware, calabashes, and furniture used by the *ali'i*. Temple idols were another major product of woodcarving. Various stone artifacts were also turned out, including poi pounders, mirrors, fish sinkers, and small idols.

Hawaiians became the best basket makers and mat weavers in all of Polynesia. *Ulana* (mats) were made from *lau hala* (pandanus) leaves. Once split, the spine was removed and the leaves stored in large rolls. When needed they were soaked, pounded, and then fashioned into various floor coverings and sleeping mats. Intricate geometrical pattterns were woven in, and the edges were rolled and well fashioned. Coconut palms were not used to make mats in old Hawaii, but a wide variety of basketry was made from the aerial root *'ie'ie*. The shapes varied according to use. Some baskets were tall and narrow, some were cones, others were flat like trays, while many were woven around gourds and calabashes.

A strong tradition of weaving and carving has survived in Hawaii, and the time-tested material of *lau hala* is still the best, although much is now made from coconut fronds. You can purchase anything from beach mats to a woven hat, and all share the desirable qualities of strength, lightness, and ventilation.

Featherwork

This highly refined art was practiced on the islands of Tahiti, New Zealand, and Hawaii, but the fashioning of feather helmets and idols was unique to Hawaii. Favorite colors were red and yellow, which came only in a very limited supply from a small number of birds such as the *'o'o*, *'i'iwi*, *mamo*, and *apapane*. Professional bird hunters in old Hawaii paid their taxes to *ali'i* in prized feathers. The feathers were fastened to a woven net of *olona* cord and made into helmets, idols, and beautiful flowing capes and cloaks. These resplendent garments were made and worn only by men, especially during battle when a fine cloak became a great trophy of war.

Featherwork was also employed in the making of *kahili* and lei which were highly prized by the noble *ali'i* women.

Tapa Cloth

Tapa, cloth made from tree bark, was common throughout Polynesia and was a woman's art. A few trees such as the *wauke* and *mamaki* produced the best cloth, but a variety of other types of bark could be utilized. First the raw bark was pounded into a feltlike pulp and beaten together to form strips (the beaters had distinctive patterns that also helped make the cloth supple). The strips were decorated by stamping (using a form of block printing) and then were dyed with natural colors from plants and sea animals in shades of gray, purple, pink, and red. They were even painted with natural brushes made from pandanus fruit, with an overall gray color made from charcoal. The tapa cloth was sewn together to make bed coverings, and fragrant flowers and herbs were either sewn or pounded in to produce a permanent fragrance. Tapa cloth is still available today, but the Hawaiian methods have been lost, and most comes from other areas of Polynesia.

HULA AND LEI

The hula is more than an ethnic dance; it is the soul of Hawaii expressed in motion. It began as a form of worship during religious ceremonies and was only danced by highly trained men. It gradually evolved into a form of entertainment, but in no regard was it sexual. The hula was the opera, theater, and lecture hall of the islands all rolled into one. It was history portrayed in the performing arts. In the beginning an androgynous deity named Laka descended to earth and taught men how to dance the hula. In time the male aspect of Laka departed for the heavens, but the female aspect remained. The female Laka set up her own special hula *heiau* at Haena Point on the Na Pali coast of Kauai, where it still exists. As time went on women were allowed to learn the hula. Scholars surmise that men became too busy wresting a living from the land to maintain the art form.

Men did retain a type of hula for themselves called *lua*. This was a form of martial art em-

classic hula troupe

ployed in hand-to-hand combat that evolved into a ritualized warfare dance called *hula kui*. During the 19th century, the hula almost vanished because the missionaries considered it vile and heathen. King Kalakaua is generally regarded as saving it during the 1800s, when he formed his own troupe and encouraged the dancers to learn the old hula. Many of the original dances were forgotten, but some were retained and are performed to this day. Although professional dancers were highly trained, everyone took part in the hula. *Ali'i*, commoners, young, and old all danced.

Today, hula *halau* (schools) are active on every island, teaching hula, and keeping the old ways and culture alive. Performers still spend years perfecting their techniques. They show off their accomplishments during the fierce competition of the Merrie Monarch Festival in Hilo every April. The winning *halau* is praised and recognized throughout the islands.

Hawaiian hula was never performed in grass skirts; tapa or ti-leaf skirts were worn. Grass skirts came to Hawaii from the Gilbert Islands, and if you see grass and cellophane skirts in a "hula revue," it's not traditional. Almost every major resort offering entertainment or a luau also offers a revue. Most times, young island beauties accompanied by local musicians put on a floor show for the tourists. It'll be fun, but it won't be traditional. A hula dancer has to learn how to control every part of her/his body, including facial expressions, which help set the mood. The hands are extremely important and provide instant background scenery. For example, if the hands are thrust outward in an aggressive manner, this can mean a battle; if they sway gently overhead, they refer to the gods or to creation; they can easily become rain, clouds, sun, sea, or moon. Watch the hands to get the gist of the story, but remember the words of one wiseguy, "You watch the parts you like, and I'll watch the parts I like!" The motion of swaying hips can denote a long walk, a canoe ride, or sexual intercourse. Foot motion can portray a battle, a walk, or any kind of conveyance. The overall effect is multi-directional synchronized movement. The correct chanting of the *mele* is an integral part of the performance. These story chants, accompanied by musical instruments, make the hula very much like opera; it is especially similar in the way the tale unfolds.

Lei Making

Any flower or blossom can be strung into a lei, but the most common are carnations or the lovely smelling plumeria. Lei, like babies, are all beautiful, but special lei are highly prized by those who know what to look for. Of the different stringing styles, the most common is *kui*—stringing the flower through the middle or side. Most "airport-quality" lei are of this type. The *humuhumu* style,

HAWAIIAN *LEI*

plumeria

ilima

crown

lau hala

fern

DIANA LASICH HARPER

reserved for making flat lei, is made by sewing flowers and ferns to a ti, banana, or sometimes *hala* leaf. A *humuhumu* lei makes an excellent hatband. *Wili* is the winding together of greenery, ferns, and flowers into short, bouquet-type lengths. The most traditional form is *hili,* which requires no stringing at all but involves braiding fragrant ferns and leaves such as *maile.* If flowers are interwoven, the *hili* becomes the *haku* style, the most difficult and most beautiful type of lei.

The Lei of the Land

Every major island is symbolized by its own lei made from a distinctive flower, shell, or fern. Each island has its own official color as well, though it doesn't necessarily correspond to the color of the island's lei. The island of Hawaii's lei is made from the red (or rare creamy white or orange) lehua lehua blossom. The lehua tree grows from sea level to 9,000 feet and produces an abundance of tufted flowers. The official color of Hawaii Island, like the lava from its active volcanoes, is red.

THAT GOOD OLD ISLAND MUSIC

The missionaries usually take a beating when it's recounted how much Hawaiian culture they destroyed while "civilizing" the natives. However, they seem to have done one thing right. They introduced the Hawaiians to the diatonic musical scale and immediately opened a door to latent and superbly harmonious talent. Before the missionaries, the Hawaiians knew little about melody. Though sonorous, their *mele* were repetitive chants in which the emphasis was placed on historical accuracy and not on "making music." The Hawaiians, in short, didn't *sing.* But within a few years of the missionaries' arrival, they were belting out good old Christian hymns, and one of their favorite pastimes became group and individual singing.

Early in the 1800s, Spanish *vaqueros* from California were imported to teach the Hawaiians how to be cowboys. With them came guitars and moody ballads. The Hawaiian *paniolos* (cowboys) quickly learned how to punch cows and croon away the long lonely nights on the range. Immigrants who came along a little later in the 19th century, especially from Portugal, helped create a Hawaiian-style music. Their biggest influence was a small, four-stringed instrument called a *braga* or *cavaquinho.* One owned by Augusto Dias was the prototype of a homegrown Hawaiian instrument that became known as the ukulele. "Jumping flea," the translation of ukulele, is an appropriate name devised by the Hawaiians when they saw how nimble the fingers were as they "jumped" over the strings.

The Merry Monarch, King Kalakaua, and Queen Liliuokalani were both patrons of the arts who furthered the Hawaiian musical identity at the turn of the century. Kalakaua revived the hula and was also a gifted lyricist and balladeer. He wrote the words to "Hawaii Pono," which became the national anthem of Hawaii and later the state anthem. Liliuokalani wrote the hauntingly beautiful "Aloha Oe," which is often pointed to as the "spirit of Hawaii" in music. Detractors say that its melody is extremely close to the old Christian hymn, "Rock Beside the Sea," but the lyrics are so beautiful and perfectly fitted that this doesn't matter.

Just prior to Kalakaua's reign, a Prussian bandmaster, Capt. Henri Berger, was invited to head the fledgling Royal Hawaiian Band, which he turned into a very respectable orchestra lauded by many visitors to the islands. Berger was open-minded and learned to love Hawaiian music. He collaborated with Kalakaua and other island musicians to incorporate their music into a Western format. He headed the band for 43 years until 1915, and was instrumental in making music a serious pursuit of talented Hawaiians.

Popular Hawaiian Music

Hawaiian music has a unique twang, a special feeling that says the same thing to everyone who hears it: "Relax, sit back in the moonlight, watch the swaying palms as the surf sings a lullaby." This special sound is epitomized by the bouncy ukulele, the falsettos of Hawaiian crooners, and the smooth ring of the "steel" or "Hawaiian" guitar. The steel guitar is a variation originated by Joseph Kekuku in the 1890s. Stories abound of how Joseph Kekuku devised this instrument; the most popular versions say that Joe dropped his comb or pocketknife on his guitar strings and liked what he heard. Driven by the faint rhythm of an inner sound, he went to the machine shop at the Kamehameha Schools and turned out a steel bar for sliding over the strings. To complete the sound he changed the cat-gut strings to steel and raised them so they wouldn't hit the frets. Voilà!—Hawaiian music as the world knows it today.

The first melodious strains of **slack-key guitar** *(ki ho'alu)* can be traced back to the time of Kamehameha III and the *vaqueros* from California. The Spanish had their way of tuning the guitar and played difficult and aggressive music that did not sit well with Hawaiians, who were much more gentle and casual in their manners.

Hawaiians soon became adept at making their own music. At first, one person played the melody, but it lacked fullness. There was no body to the sound. So, as one *paniolo* fooled with the melody, another soon learned to play bass, which added depth. But, a player was often alone, and by experimenting he learned that he could get the right hand going with the melody, and at the same time could play the bass note with the thumb to improve the sound. Singers also learned that they could "open tune" the guitar to match their rich voices.

Hawaiians believed knowledge was sacred, and what is sacred should be treated with utmost respect—which meant keeping it secret, except from sincere apprentices. Guitar playing became a personal art form whose secrets were closely guarded, handed down only to family members, and only to those who showed ability and determination. When old-time slack-key guitar players were done strumming, they loosened all the strings so no one could figure out how they had them tuned. If they were playing, and some folks came by who were interested and weren't part of the family, the Hawaiians stopped what they were doing, put their guitars down, and put their feet across the strings to wait for the folks to go away. As time went on, more and more Hawaiians began to play slack key, and a common repertoire emerged.

An accomplished musician could easily figure out the simple songs, once they had figured out how the family had tuned the guitar. One of the most popular tunings was the "open G." Old Hawaiian folks called it the "taro patch tune." Different songs came out, and if you were in their family and were interested in the guitar, they took the time to sit down and teach you. The way they taught was straightforward—and a test of your sincerity at the same time. The old master would start to play. He just wanted you to listen and get a feel for the music—nothing more than that. You brought your guitar and *listened*. When you felt it, you played it, and the knowledge was transferred. Today, only a handful of slack-key guitar players know how to play the classic tunes classically. The best-known and perhaps greatest slack-key player was Gabby Pahinui, with The Sons of Hawaii. He passed away recently but left many recordings behind. A slack-key master still singing and playing is Raymond Kane. Raymond now teaches a handful of students his wonderful and haunting music. None of his students are from his own family, and most are *haole* musicians trying to preserve the classical method of playing.

Hawaiian music received its biggest boost from a remarkable radio program known as "Hawaii Calls." This program sent out its music from the Banyan Court of the Moana Hotel from 1935 until 1975. At its peak in the mid-1950s, it was syndicated on over 700 radio stations throughout the world. Ironically, Japanese pilots heading for Pearl Harbor tuned in island music as a signal beam. Some internationally famous classic tunes came out of the '40s and '50s. Jack Pitman composed "Beyond the Reef" in 1948; over 300 artists have recorded it and it has sold well over 12 million records. Other million-sellers include: "Sweet Leilani," "Lovely Hula Hands," "The Crosseyed Mayor of Kaunakakai," and "The Hawaiian Wedding Song."

By the 1960s, Hawaiian music began to die. Just too corny and light for those turbulent years, it belonged to the older generation and the good times that followed WW II. One man was instrumental in keeping Hawaiian music alive during this period. Don Ho, with his "Tiny Bubbles," became the token Hawaiian musician of the '60s and early '70s. He's persevered long enough to become a legend in his own time, and his Polynesian Extravaganza at the Hilton Hawaiian Village packed visitors in until the early 1990s. He's now at the Waikiki Beachcomber. Al Harrington, "The South Pacific Man," until his recent retirement had another Honolulu "big revue" that drew large crowds. Of this type of entertainment, perhaps the most Hawaiian is Danny Kaleikini, still performing at the Kahala Hilton, who entertains his audience with dances, Hawaiian anecdotes, and tunes on the traditional Hawaiian nose flute.

The Beat Goes On

Beginning in the mid-'70s islanders began to assert their cultural identity. One of the unifying factors was the coming of age of "Hawaiian" music. It graduated from the "little grass shack" novelty tune and began to include sophisticated jazz, rock, and contemporary rhythms. Accomplished musicians whose roots were in traditional island music began to highlight their tunes with this distinctive sound. The best embellish their arrangements with ukuleles, steel guitars, and traditional percussion and melodic instruments. Some excellent modern recording artists have become island institutions. The local people say that you know if the Hawaiian harmonies are good if they give you "chicken skin."

Each year special music awards, **Na Hoku Hanohano**, or Hoku for short, are given to distinguished island musicians. The following are recent Hoku winners considered by their contemporaries to be among the best in Hawaii. Though most do not perform on the Big Island, if they're playing on one of the other islands while you're in Hawaii, don't miss them. **Barney Isaacs and George Kuo** won Instrumental Album of the year for *Hawaiian Touch*. **Na Leo Pilimihana (Flying With Angels)** won Song of the Year, Album of the Year, Contemporary Album of the Year, and Group of the Year. **Robi Kahakalau**'s *Sistah Robi* earned Female Vocalist and Island Contemporary Album of the Year. "Friends in Me" won Single of the Year for **Brothers and Sister. Keali'i Reichel**'s *Lei Hali'a* was voted Popular Hawaiian Album of the Year (and the artist also won Male Vocalist of the Year and Favorite Entertainer of the Year). *Broken Hearts* earned **Darren Benitez** a Most Promising Artist of the Year award; **Sonny Kamahele** received a Lifetime Achievement Award; and **Ledward Ka'apana** is a Slack Key Award winner.

Past Hoku winners who have become renowned performers include: **Brothers Cazimero**, who are blessed with beautiful harmonic voices; **Krush**, who are highly regarded for their contemporary sounds; **The Peter Moon Band**, fantastic performers with a strong traditional sound; **Karen Keawehawai'i**, who has a sparkling voice and can be very funny when the mood strikes her; and **Henry Kapono**, formerly of Cecilio and Kapono, who keeps a low profile but is an incredible performer and excellent songwriter (his shows are noncommercial and very special). **Cecilio** is now teamed up with **Maggie Herron**; they are hot together and have a strong following in Honolulu. **The Beamer Brothers** are excellent performers and can be seen at various nightspots. **Loyal Garner**, who was awarded Female Vocalist of the Year for *I Shall Sing*, is a truly wonderful artist. **Del Beazley** is a talented, energized performer. **Makaha Sons Of Niihau** are the best traditional Hawaiian band and shouldn't be missed. **Hawaiian Style Band** is known for

THE ARTS IN HAWAII

This section includes the names and addresses of guilds, centers, and organizations that dispense information on Hawaiian arts and crafts.

Arts Council of Hawaii, Box 50225, Honolulu, HI 96850, tel. 524-7120, Karl Ichida, Exec. Director. A citizens' advocacy group for the arts providing technical assistance and information to individuals and groups. Publishes the *Cultural Climate,* a newsletter covering what's happening in the arts of Hawaii. Includes a calendar of events, feature articles, and editorials. Membership fee, $15, includes newsletter (50 cents per issue to nonmembers).

Bishop Museum, 1525 Bernice St., Honolulu, HI 96819, tel. 847-3511. The world's best museum covering Polynesia and Hawaii. Exhibits, galleries, archives, demonstrations of Hawaiian crafts, and a planetarium. On the premises, Shop Pacifica has a complete selection of books and publications on all aspects of Hawaiian art and culture. Shouldn't be missed.

Contemporary Arts Center, 605 Kapiolani Blvd., Honolulu, HI 96813, tel. 525-8047. Promotes public awareness of contemporary art by providing gallery space, publicity, and exposure for local artists. Also houses a permanent collection and monthly exhibitions.

East Hawaii Cultural Council, Box 1312, Hilo, HI 96721, tel. 961-5711. Publishes *The Center Newspaper,* a monthly newsletter of what's happening artistically and culturally primarily on the Big Island. Includes a good monthly calendar of events with listings from exhibit openings to movies.

East-West Center Culture Learning Institute, Burns Hall 4076, 1777 East-West Rd., Honolulu, HI 96848, tel. 944-7691. At the University of Hawaii campus. Dedicated to the sharing, exhibiting, and appreciation of arts, culture, and crafts from through-

out Asia and the Western world. Bimonthly *Centerviews* includes an events calendar and topical editorials on the Pacific. Free.

East-West Journal, 1633 Kapiolani Blvd., Honolulu, HI 96814. Yearly guide to exhibition galleries featuring the work of locally renowned artists.

Hawaii Craftsmen, Box 22145, Honolulu, HI 96823, tel. 523-1974. Increases awareness of Hawaiian crafts through programs, exhibitions, workshops, lectures, and demonstrations.

Honolulu Academy of Arts, 900 S. Beretania St., Honolulu, HI 96814, tel. 532-8700. Collects, preserves, and exhibits works of art. Offers public art education programs related to their collections. Also offers tours, classes, lectures, films, and a variety of publications.

Honolulu Symphony Society, 1000 Bishop St., Honolulu, HI 96813, tel. 537-6171. Provides professional-level music, primarily symphonic concerts.

Pacific Handcrafters Guild, P.O. Box 15491, Honolulu, HI 96818, tel. 538-7227. Focuses on developing and preserving handicrafts in Hawaii and the Pacific. They sponsor four major crafts fairs annually.

State Foundation on Culture and the Arts, 335 Merchant St., Room 202, Honolulu, HI 96813, tel. 586-0330. Begun by the state legislature in 1965 to preserve Hawaii's diverse cultural and artistic heritage. Publishes *Hawaii Cultural Resource Directory,* which lists most of the arts organizations, galleries, councils, co-ops, and guilds throughout Hawaii. Very complete.

University of Hawaii at Manoa Art Gallery, 2535 The Mall, Honolulu, HI 96822, tel. 948-6888. Showcases contemporary artwork. Theme changes periodically.

Vanishing Treasures, a terrific album filled with contemporary music. **Bryan Kessler & Me No Hoa Aloha** perform songs like "Heiau," a haunting melody. **Susan Gillespie** and **Susi Hussong** are first-rate instrumentalists, and **Kealohi,** who recorded *Kealohi,* is very promising.

Other top-notch performers with strong followings are Ledward Kaapana; Mango; Oliver Kelly; Ka'eo; Freitas Brothers; Brickwood Galuteria, who won a double Hoku for Best Male Vocalist and Most Promising Artist; and Third Road Delite.

BOB RACE

OUT AND ABOUT

SPORTS AND RECREATION

You'll have no problem having fun on the Big Island. Everybody goes outside to play. You can camp and hike, drive golf balls over lagoons, smack tennis balls at private and public courts, ski, snorkel, windsurf, gallop a horse, bag a wild turkey, spy a rare bird, or latch on to a marlin that'll tail-walk across a windowpane sea. Choose your sport and have a ball.

CAMPING AND HIKING

The Big Island has the best camping in the state, with more facilities and less competition for campsites than on the other islands. Nearly three dozen parks fringe the coastline and sit deep in the interior; almost half offer camping. The others boast a combination of rugged hikes, easy strolls, self-guided nature walks, swimming, historical sites, and natural phenomena. The ones with campgrounds are state-, county-, and national-ly operated, ranging from remote walk-in sites to

housekeeping cabins. All require camping per-mits—inexpensive for the county and state parks, free for the national park. Camping permits can be obtained by walk-in application to the appro-priate office or by writing. Although there is usu-ally no problem obtaining sites, when writing, request reservations well in advance, allowing a minimum of one month for letters to go back and forth.

General Information
Most campgrounds have pavilions, fireplaces, toilets (sometimes pit), and running water, but usually no individual electrical hookups. Pavilions often have electric lights, but sometimes campers appropriate the bulbs, so it's wise to carry your own. Drinking water is available, but at times brackish water is used for flushing toilets and for showers, so read all signs regarding water. Backcountry shelters have catchment water, but never hike without an adequate supply of your own. Cooking fires are allowed in established

firepits, but no wood is provided. Charcoal is a good idea. When camping in the mountains, be prepared for cold and rainy weather. Women, especially, should never hike or camp alone, and everyone should exercise precaution against theft, though it's not as prevalent as on the other islands.

County Parks

The county-maintained parks are open to the public for day use, and permits are only required for overnight camping (tents or RVs). For information write: Department of Parks and Recreation, County of Hawaii, 25 Aupuni St., Hilo, HI 96720, tel. 961-8311. You can obtain a permit by mail or pick it up in person, Mon.-Fri. 8 a.m.-4:30 p.m. If you'll be arriving after hours or on a weekend, have the permits mailed to you. Branch offices (most with reduced hours) are located at Hale Halawai in Kailua-Kona, tel. 329-5277; in Waimea Community Center in Waimea, tel. 885-5454; in Yano Hall in Captain Cook, tel. 323-

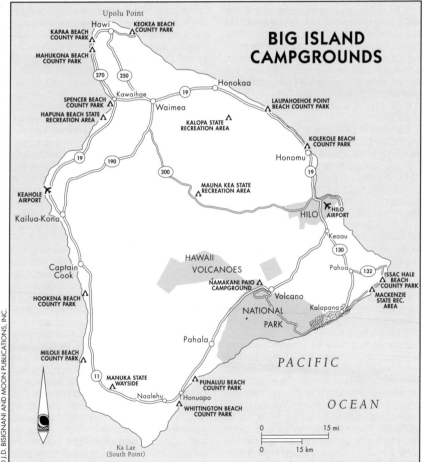

BIG ISLAND CAMPGROUNDS

3060; in Naalehu, tel. 929-9166; and in Pahala, tel. 928-6206. Fees are adult $1 p/d; children 13-17, 50 cents p/d; youngsters free. Pavilions for exclusive use are $5 p/d with kitchen, $2 without. Camping is limited to one week at any one site June-Aug. and to two weeks at any one site for the rest of the year.

State Parks and Cabins

Day use of state parks is free, with no permit required, but you will need one for tent camping and for cabins. Five consecutive nights is the limit for either camping or cabins at any one site. If you want a permit, at least one week's notice is required regardless of availability. You can pick up your permit at the state parks office 8 a.m.-4 p.m. (applications accepted only 8 a.m.-noon), but again it saves time if you do it all by mail. Write: Department of Land and Natural Resources, Division of State Parks, P.O. Box 936 (75 Aupuni St. #204), Hilo, HI 96721, tel. 974-6200.

Camping is permitted only at Kalopa and MacKenzie State Recreation Areas (SRA). Cabins are located at Mauna Kea SRA's Pohakuloa Camp, tel. 935-7237; and Kalopa SRA, tel. 775-7114. A-frames are located only at Hapuna Beach SRA, tel. 882-7995. A-frames are a flat $20 per night. The housekeeping cabins at Mauna Kea SRA are $45 for up to four persons, and group cabins at Mauna Kea and Kalopa SRAs are $55 for up to eight people. When writing for permits, specify exactly which facility you require, for how long, and for how many people.

Hawaii Volcanoes National Park

The day use of campgrounds in Hawaii Volcanoes National Park is free but for overnight camping, permits are required and available through the park Visitors Center. The drive-in campgrounds throughout the park can be reserved but usually operate on a first-come, first-served basis. Your stay is limited to seven days per campground per year. A-frame cabins are provided at Namakani Paio Campground, and arrangements are made through Volcano House, Hawaii Volcanoes National Park, HI 96718, tel. 967-7321. There are free walk-in trail cabins and shelters throughout the park; you can't reserve them and you should expect to share them with other hikers. Coleman stoves and lanterns

are sometimes provided (check), but you provide the fuel. Basic bedding and cooking utensils are also there for your convenience. Shelters, in the park along the coast, are three-sided, open affairs that offer only a partial covering against the elements. For information on camping and hiking in the park, write Hawaii Volcanoes National Park, P.O. Box 52, Hawaii National Park, HI 96718.

Equipment

Like everything else you take to Hawaii, your camping and hiking equipment should be lightweight and durable. Camping equipment size and weight should not cause a problem with baggage requirements on airlines: if it does, it's a tip-off that you're hauling too much. One odd luggage strategy you might consider is to bring along a small **styrofoam cooler** packed with equipment. Substitute food items for the equipment when you get to Hawaii; if you intend to car-camp successfully and keep food prices down, you'll definitely need a cooler. You can also buy one on arrival for only a few dollars.

You'll need a lightweight **tent,** preferably with a rainfly and a sewn-in floor. This will save you from getting wet and miserable, and will keep out mosquitoes, cockroaches, ants, and the few stinging insects in Hawaii. Atop Mauna Loa, where you can expect cold and wind, a tent is a must; in fact you won't be allowed to camp without one. **Sleeping bags** are a good idea, although you can get along at sea level with only a blanket. Down-filled or high-quality synthetic bags are necessary for Mauna Kea, Mauna Loa, or any high-altitude camping—you'll freeze without one. **Camp-stoves** are needed because there's very little wood in some volcanic areas, it's often wet in the deep forest, and open fires are often prohibited. If you'll be car-camping, take along a multi-burner stove; for trekking, a backpacker's stove will be necessary. The grills found at some campgrounds are popular with many families who go often to the beach parks for an open-air dinner. You can buy a very inexpensive charcoal grill at many variety stores throughout Hawaii. It's a great idea to take along a **lantern.** This will give car-campers added safety. Definitely take a **flashlight,** replacement batteries, and a few small **candles.** A complete **first-aid kit** can mean the difference between life and death and is worth the extra bulk. Hikers, especially those leaving the coastal areas, should take **rain gear,** plastic ground cloth, utility knife, compass, safety whistle, mess kit, water purification tablets, canteen, nylon twine, and waterproof matches. (For additional suggestions, see "What To Take" later in this chapter.)

You can find plenty of stores that sell, and a few stores that rent, **camping equipment.** Try **Hilo Surplus Store,** tel. 935-6398, at 148 Mamo Ave. in downtown Hilo; **Pacific Rent All,** 1080 Kilauea Ave., Hilo, tel. 935-2974; **Kona Rent All,** tel. 329-1644; and **C&S Cycle and Surf,** tel. 885-5005, in Waimea.

Hiking the Big Island

Hiking on the Big Island is stupendous. There's something for everyone, from civilized walks to the breathtaking Akaka Falls to huff-puff treks to the summit of Mauna Loa. The largest number of trails, and the most outstanding according to many, are laced across Volcanoes National Park. After all, this is the world's most active volcano. You can hike across the crater floor, spurred on by the knowledge that it can shake to life at any moment. Or dip down off the mountain and amble the lonely trails in the Kau desert or remnants of the King's Coastal Trail in Puna.

The most important thing to do, before heading out in Volcanoes, is to stop at park headquarters and inquire about trail conditions. Make absolutely sure to register, giving the rangers your hiking itinerary. In the event of an eruption, they will be able to locate you and send a helicopter if necessary. Follow this advice; your life may depend upon it! Everyone can enjoy vistas on Devastation Trail or Sulfur Bank or at the Thurston Lava Tube without any danger whatsoever. In the north you'll find Waipio, Waimanu, and Pololu Valleys. All offer secluded hiking and camping where you can play Robinson Crusoe on your own beach and gather a variety of island fruits from once-cultivated trees gone wild.

Safety

There are two things in Hawaii that you must keep your eye on in order to remain safe: humans and nature. The general rule is, the farther you get away from towns, the safer you'll be from human-induced hassles. If possible, don't hike or camp alone, especially if you're a woman. Don't leave your valuables in your tent, and always carry your money, papers, and camera with you. Don't tempt the locals by being overly friendly or unfriendly, and make yourself scarce if they're drinking. While hiking, remember that many trails are well maintained, but trailhead markers are often missing. The trails themselves can be muddy, which can make them treacherously slippery and often knee-deep. Always bring food because you cannot, in most cases, forage from the land. Water in most streams is biologically polluted and will give you bad stomach problems if you drink it without purifying it first by boiling, filtering, or adding purification tablets. For your part, please don't use the streams as a toilet.

Precautions

Always tell a ranger or official of your hiking intentions. Supply an itinerary and your expected route, then stick to it. Twilight is short in the islands, and night sets in rapidly. In June sunrise and sunset are around 6 a.m. and 7 p.m.; in December these occur at 7 a.m. and 6 p.m. If you become lost at night, stay put, light a fire if possible, and stay as dry as you can. Hawaii is made of volcanic rock which is brittle and crumbly. Never attempt to climb steep *pali* (cliffs). Be aware of current lava flows, and heed all posted advice. If lost, walk on ridges and avoid the gulches, which have more obstacles and make it harder for rescuers to spot you. Be careful of elevation sickness, especially on Mauna Loa and Mauna Kea. The best cure is to descend as soon as possible.

Heat can cause you to lose water and salt. If you become woozy or weak, rest, take salt, and drink water as you need it. Remember, it takes much more water to restore a dehydrated person than to keep hydrated; take small, frequent sips. Be mindful of flash floods. Small creeks can turn into raging torrents with upland rains. Never camp in a dry creekbed. Fog is only encountered at elevations of 1,500-5,000 feet, but be careful of disorientation. Generally, stay within your limits, be careful, and enjoy yourself.

Birdwatching and Hiking Tours

Hawaii has its fair share of birds. One type or other of the state's many species can be seen and heard wherever you are on the island, whether you're sunbathing along the shore, putting on a golf green, or hiking high on the mountainside. The most common will soon be obvious, but to see some of Hawaii's rare winged creatures you have to be adventurous, quiet, and willing to walk. Be sure to bring your binoculars. Anyone can appreciate birds where you are, but hard-core birders might want to go to spots where the chance of getting a fleeting glimpse of that "rare one" will be greater.

If you're not familiar with good birdwatching spots on Hawaii, contact Rob or Cindy Pacheco at **Hawaii Forest & Trail,** tel. 322-8881 or (800) 464-1993, fax 322-8883, P.O. Box 2975, Kailua-Kona, HI 96745. This well-established naturalist company uses 4WD vehicles to get you to where the less common birds are. Its two exclusive birdwatching tours take you to the rainforests of the Pu'u O'o Ranch and the Hakalau National Wildlife Refuge, both on the eastern slope of Mauna Kea. Other tours include the Rainforest Discovery Adventure to the Pu'u O'o Ranch, the Palani Ranch Mountain Adventure on the slopes of Hualalai Volcano, the Valley Waterfall Adventure to the spectacular Pololu Valley of North Kohala, and a tour to Hawaii Volcanoes National Park. Other birdwatching and custom tours can be arranged. All tours are kept to a minimum of 10 people, are guided by knowledgeable naturalists, are fully catered, provide the necessary equipment, and include pickup and drop off at Kona accommodations or the Kona airport. The birdwatching, rainforest, and volcano tours run $130 pp, the valley waterfall tour $110 ($79 half-day), and the geologic and natural history Palani Ranch tour $110. Children ages 5-12 are discounted 15%; kids below age 5 are free. E-mail: hitrail@aloha.net.

The Big Island **Audubon Society** group also runs periodic birdwatching excursions. For information, contact them at P.O. Box 1371, Kailua-Kona, HI 96745; or call 329-9141.

A well-established and reputable hiking company that will help you stretch your legs in the great outdoors yet have minimal impact on the land is **Hawaiian Walkway,** P.O. Box 2193, Kamuela, Hawaii 96743, tel./fax 885-7759 or (800) 457-7759. Not for the lighthearted, hikes last 6-10 hours. Custom hikes and hiking/camping tours can also be arranged. Six basic hikes take you to

Hawaii Volcanoes National Park, to the north Kohala mountains and valleys, along the north Kona coast, or up on the slope of Mt. Hualalai. Scheduled day-hikes run $110 for adults and $80 for children under age 13; custom hikes are $125 and 95, respectively. A small day pack, rain gear, lunch, and drinks are provided.

The **Kona Hiking Club,** tel. 328-8192, offers organized hikes on the island. Write them for information: P.O. Box 569, Captain Cook, HI 96704.

For a more educational, "guided geologic adventure" on one of the earth's most changeable pieces of real estate, try **Hawaii Volcano GeoVentures,** P.O. Box 794, Volcano, HI 96785, tel. 985-8972. Or e-mail them at jbabb@aloha .net. Also check out their web site: planet-hawaii.com/hea/volcano.

Helpful Departments and Organizations
The **Department of Land and Natural Resources,** Division of Forestry and Wildlife, 1151 Punchbowl St., Honolulu, HI 96813, tel. 587-0166, is helpful in providing trail maps, accessibility information, hunting and fishing regulations, and general forest rules. Their "Recreation Map" (one for each island) is free. On the Big Island, contact the DLNR, Division of Forestry and Wildlife, P.O. Box 4849, Hilo, HI 96720. The DLNR, **State Parks Division,** tel. 587-0300, puts out a brochure on camping, permits, general rules, and recreational opportunities. The following organizations can provide general information on wildlife, conservation, and organized hiking trips: **Hawaiian Audubon Society,** P.O. Box 22832, Honolulu, HI 96822; and **The Sierra Club,** tel. 885-3575, P.O. Box 3220, Kailua-Kona, HI 96745. Write or call for current information.

Hiking and Camping Books
The best guidebooks to camping and hiking on the Big Island are **Hawaii: A Camping Guide** by George Cagala; and **Hawaii Trails** by Kathy Morey. If you plan on doing any independent camping and hiking while here, check out these two for good introductory information and specifics on sites and trails.

Topographical and Nautical Charts, Etc.
For detailed topographical maps, write **U.S. Geological Survey, Information Services** P.O. Box 25286, Denver, CO 80225; or call (800)

USA-MAPS or (703) 648-4888. Website: www .usgs.gov. For nautical charts, write **National Ocean Service,** Riverdale, MD 20737-1199, tel. (301) 436-6990 or (800) 638-8972. In Hawaii, a wide range of topographical maps, nautical charts, and local maps can be purchased at **Pacific Map Center,** 560 N. Nimitz Hwy., Suite 206A, Honolulu, HI, tel. 545-3600.

On the Big Island, **Basically Books,** downtown Hilo at 46 Waianuenue St., tel. 961-0144, has an unbeatable selection of maps. You can get anywhere you want to go with their nautical charts, road maps, and topographical maps, which include sectionals for serious hikers and trekkers. Their collection covers most of the Pacific. Also try **Big Island Marine, Inc.,** 73-4840 Kanalani St., #A-1, Kailua-Kona, HI 96740, tel. 329-3719.

DEEP-SEA AND FRESHWATER FISHING

Hawaii has some of the most exciting and productive "blue waters" in all the world. You'll find a sportfishing fleet made up of skippers and crews who are experienced professional anglers. You can also fish from jetties, piers, rocks, or the shore. If rod and reel don't strike your fancy, try the old-fashioned throw net, or take along a spear when you go snorkeling or scuba diving. There's nighttime torch fishing that requires special skills and equipment, and freshwater fishing in public areas. Streams and irrigation ditches yield introduced trout, bass, and catfish. While you're at it, you might want to try crabbing for Kona and Samoan crabs, or working low-tide areas after sundown hunting octopus, a tantalizing island delicacy.

Deep-Sea Fishing
Most game-fishing boats work the waters on the calmer Kona side of the island. Some skippers, carrying anglers who are accustomed to the sea, will also work the much rougher windward coasts and island channels where the fish bite just as well. Trolling is the preferred method of deep-sea fishing; this is done usually in waters of 1,000-2,000 fathoms (a fathom is six feet). The skipper will either "area fish," which means running in a crisscross pattern over a known productive area, or "ledge fish," which involves

weigh-in at Honokohau Harbor

J.D. BISIGNANI

trolling over submerged ledges where the game fish are known to feed. The most advanced marine technology, available on many boats, sends sonar bleeps searching for fish. On deck, the crew and anglers scan the horizon in the age-old Hawaiian tradition—searching for clusters of seabirds feeding on baitfish pursued to the surface by the huge and aggressive game fish. "Still fishing," or "bottom fishing" with hand-lines, yields some tremendous fish.

The Game Fish
The most thrilling game fish in Hawaiian waters is marlin, generically known as "billfish" or *a'u* to the locals. The king of them is the blue marlin, with record catches of well over 1,000 pounds The mightiest caught in the waters off this island was a huge 1,656 pounds. There are also striped marlin and sailfish, which often go over 200 pounds. The best times for marlin are during spring, summer, and fall. The fishing tapers off in January and picks up again by late February. "Blues" can be caught year-round but, oddly enough, when they stop biting it seems as

though the striped marlin pick up. Second to the marlin are tuna. *Ahi* (yellowfin tuna) are caught in Hawaiian waters at depths of 100-1,000 fathoms. They can weigh 300 pounds, but 25-100 pounds is common. There are also *aku* (skipjack tuna) and the delicious *ono,* which average 20-40 pounds.

Mahimahi is another strong, fighting, deepwater game fish abundant in Hawaii. These delicious fish can weigh up to 70 pounds. Shore fishing and bait casting yield *papio,* a jack tuna. *Akule,* a scad (locally called *halalu*), is a smallish schooling fish that comes close to shore and is great to catch on light tackle. *Ulua* are shore fish and can be found in tidepools. They're excellent eating, average two to three pounds, and are taken at night or with spears.

O'io are bonefish that come close to shore to spawn. They're caught by bait casting and bottom fishing with cut bait. They're bony, but they're a favorite for fish cakes and *poki. Awa* is a schooling fish that loves brackish water. It can grow up to three feet long, and is a good fighter. A favorite for throw-netters, it's even raised commercially in fishponds. Besides these there are plenty of goatfish, mullet, mackerel, snapper, sharks, and even salmon.

Fishing Boats and Charters

The fishing around the Big Island's Kona Coast ranges from excellent to outstanding! It's legendary for marlin fishing, but there are other fish in the sea. A large fleet of charter boats with skilled captains and tested crews is ready, willing, and competent to take you out. The vast majority are berthed at Honokohau Small Boat Harbor just north of Kailua-Kona. The best times of year for marlin are July-Sept. and Jan.-March (when the generally larger females arrive). August is the optimum month. Rough seas can keep boats in for a few days during December and early January, but by February all are generally out.

You can hire a boat for a private or share charter, staying out for a full day or half day. Boat size varies, but four anglers per mid-size boat is about average. No matter the size, most boats will take no more than six anglers. Approximate rates are: private, full day $400-600, half day $250-350; share, full day $125, half day $85. Full days are eight hours, half days

four, with three-quarter days and overnighters available too. No licenses are required and all gear is provided. Bring your own lunch, beverages, and camera.

To charter a boat contact the individual captains directly, check at your hotel activities desk, or book through one of the following agencies. **Charter Services Hawaii,** operated by Ed Barry, tel. 334-1881, or (800) 567-5662, offers more than 50 boats in all sizes and price ranges from which to choose. Ed also offers complete packages including room, car, and boat along with a cash prize of $1 million if you book through his agency and top the world record. If you're after a company that's knowledgeable about getting you onto a boat that will bring you to waters where you'll have the opportunity to catch one of the twirling and gigantic "big blues," this is the place to come. (E-mail: fishing@aloha.com; Web site: www.aloha.com/~hdc/charter.) Located on the dock at Honokohau Harbor, the **The Charter Desk,** tel. 329-5735 or (800) 566-2487, is another reputable booking agency that tries to match you and your desire with the right boat and captain for best results. Other general booking agencies include: **Kona Activities Center** in Kailua-Kona, tel. 329-3171; and **Kona Charter Skippers Assoc.,** P.O. Box 806, Kailua-Kona, HI 96740, tel. 329-3600.

Most of the island's 80 charter boats are berthed at Honokohau Harbor off Route 19, about midway between downtown Kailua and Kona Airport. Fish are **weighed in** daily 11 a.m.-1 p.m., and again 3-6 p.m. Big fish are sometimes still weighed in at Kailua Pier, in front of the King Kamehameha's Kona Beach Hotel for the benefit of the tourists. But Honokohau Harbor has eclipsed Kailua Pier, which is now tamed and primarily for swimmers, triathletes, and body-boarders. Congestion makes it difficult for charter boats to get in and out so the majority of the trade has moved up to Honokohau.

An excellent publication listing boats and general deep-sea fishing information is *Fins and Fairways, Hawaii,* P.O. Box 9014, Kailua-Kona, HI 96745, tel. 325-6171 or (800) 367-8014 from the Mainland, or fax 325-6378 (E-mail: fishkona @fishkona.com; Web site: www.fishkona.com.) This tabloid, published by Capt. Tom Armstrong and available free at newsstands and in hotel/condo lobbies, is filled with descriptions of boats, phone numbers, captains' names, maps, and photos of recent catches. Write for subscription rates. For general fishing information and a listing of tournaments throughout the islands, pick up a copy of the *Hawaii Fishing News* at a newsstand or supermarket.

You can also contact **The Hawaiian International Billfish Assoc.,** 74-381 Kealakehe Pkwy., Kailua-Kona, HI 96740, tel. 329-6155, for details on upcoming tournaments and on "what's biting and when."

Coastal Fish

You don't have to hire a boat to catch fish! The coastline is productive too. *Ulua* are caught all along the coast south of Hilo, and at South Point and Kealakekua Point. *Papio* and *halalu* are caught in bays all around the island, while *manini* and *ama'ama* hit from Kawaihae to Puako. Hilo Bay is easily accessible to anyone, and the fishing is very exciting, especially at the mouth of the Wailuku River. Catch limits for 21 species of marine fish and eight crustaceans and shellfish are regulated, so check state guidelines.

Freshwater Fish

Hawaii has only one native freshwater game fish, the *o'opu*. This goby is an oddball with fused ventral fins. It grows to 12 inches long and is found on all islands, especially Kauai. Introduced species include largemouth and smallmouth bass, bluegill, catfish, *tucunare,* oscar, carp, and tilapia. The *tucunare* is a tough, fighting, good-tasting game fish introduced from South America, similar to the oscar from the same region. Both have been compared to bass but are of a different family.

The tilapia is from Africa and has become common in Hawaii's irrigation ditches. It is a "mouth breeder" and the young will take refuge in their parents' protective jaws even a few weeks after hatching. The snakehead is an eel-like fish that inhabits the reservoirs and is a great fighter. The channel catfish can grow to over 20 pounds; it bites best after sundown. Or go for carp—with its broad tail and tremendous strength, it's the poor man's game fish. All of these species are best caught with light spinning tackle or with a bamboo pole and trusty old worm. The catch limit of eight species of freshwater fish is regulated.

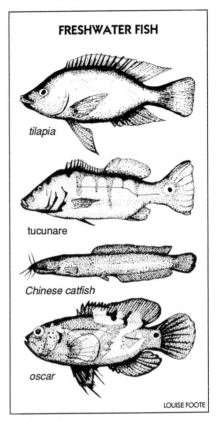

FRESHWATER FISH

tilapia

tucunare

Chinese catfish

oscar

LOUISE FOOTE

Fishing Rules

All game fish may be taken year-round, except trout, *ama'ama, moi,* and certain crustaceans (check specific regulations). Licensed fishing is limited to the **Waiakea Public Fishing Area,** a state-operated facility in downtown Hilo. This 26-acre pond offers a variety of saltwater and brackish-water species. Licenses are needed for freshwater fishing only. A **Freshwater Game Fishing License** is good July 1-June 30. Licenses cost $7.50 for nonresidents, $3.50 for tourists (good for 30 days), $3.75 for residents over age 15 and military personnel and their dependents over age 15, $1.50 for children ages 9-15; they are free to senior citizens and children under age nine when accompanied by an adult with a license. You can pick up a license at sporting goods stores or at the Division of Aquatic Resources, 75 Aupuni St., Hilo, HI 96720, tel. 974-6201. Be sure to ask for their "Hawaii Fishing Regulations" and "Freshwater Fishing in Hawaii" booklets. Fishing is usually allowed in most State Forest Reserve Areas. Owner's permission must be obtained to fish on private property.

OCEAN TOURS

Whether it's skimming across the ocean surface on a trim sloop, diving by submarine to view coral fields, or watching whales breach and play, there are many and various ocean tours to excite visitors to the Big Island. Some of the more popular options follow.

Captain Zodiac, 74-425 Kealakehe Pkwy., Suite 16, Kailua-Kona, 96740, tel. 329-3199 or (800) 422-7824, will take you on a fantastic ocean odyssey beginning at Honokohau Small Boat Harbor just north of Kailua-Kona, from where you'll skirt the coast south all the way to Kealakekua Bay. A Zodiac is a very tough, motorized rubber raft. It looks like a big, horseshoe-shaped inner-tube that bends itself and undulates with the waves like a floating waterbed. These seaworthy craft, powered by twin Mercury 280s, have five separate air chambers for unsinkable safety. They'll take you for a thrilling ride down the Kona coast, pausing along the way to whisk you into sea caves, grottoes, and caverns. The Kona coast is also marked with ancient ruins and the remains of villages, which the captains point out, and about which they relate historical anecdotes as you pass by. You stop at Kealakekua Bay, where you can swim and snorkel in this underwater conservation park. Roundtrips departing at 8 a.m., and again at 1 p.m., take about four hours and cost $62 adults, $52 children under 11. Captain Zodiac also provides a light tropical lunch of fresh exotic fruit, taro chips, fruit juice, iced tea, and sodas. All you need are a bathing suit, sun hat, towel, suntan lotion, camera, and sense of adventure.

Atlantis Submarine, tel. 329-6626 or (800) 548-6262, allows everyone to live out the fantasy of Captain Nemo on a silent cruise under the waves off Kailua-Kona. After checking in at their office in the King Kamehameha's Kona Beach Hotel Mall, you board a launch at Kailua Pier that takes you on a 10-minute cruise to the waiting submarine tethered offshore. You're given all of your safety tips on the way there. The underwater portion lasts about one half hour. As you descend to 120 feet, notice that everything white, including teeth, turns pink because the ultraviolet rays are filtered out. The only colors that you can see clearly beneath the waves are blues and greens because water is 800 times denser than air and filters out the reds and oranges. Everyone gets an excellent seat with a viewing port; there's not a bad seat in this 48-passenger submarine, so you don't have to rush to get on. Don't worry about being claustrophobic either—the sub is amazingly airy and bright, with white space-age plastic on the inside walls, and aircraft-quality air blowers above the seats.

The Atlantis Sub is getting some competition from the **Nautilus II,** tel. 326-2003, a semi-submersible very similar to the famous "ironsides" first used in the Civil War. This high-tech model offers a narrated one-hour tour in its spacious, air-conditioned lower deck. Departures are daily from Kailua Pier: adults $29.95, children under 12 $19.95.

The **Maile,** berthed at Kawaihae Harbor, P.O. Box 44335, Kamuela, HI 96743, tel. 326-5174 or (800) 726-SAIL, is a 50-foot Gulfstar sloop available for luxury sailing charters and shorter-term whalewatching, snorkeling, and fishing expeditions. Skippered by Ralph Blancato, a U.S. Coast Guard-certified Master, the sloop offers competitive prices on half- or full-day charters, sunset sails, and long-term rental. Offering more than just a sailing trip, Blantaco teaches his guests about marinelife, reef ecology, and island environment. Aside from her commercial use, the *Maile* also functions as the research boat for both the Ocean Mammal Institute and the Oceanic Society.

For more conventional sailing and boating adventures, try one of the following. **Captain Beans',** tel. 329-2955, is a Kona institution that will take you aboard its glass-bottom boat daily at 5:15 p.m. from Kailua Pier at $45 adults; only open to those age 21 and older. During the very tame cruise you'll spot fish, listen to island music, and enjoy a sunset dinner. **Captain Cook VII,** tel. 329-6411, is also a glass-bottom boat. Its tour includes snorkeling and lunch for $25 adults.

Whalewatch Cruises

In season (Nov.-April), these fascinating adventures are provided by **Royal Hawaiian Cruises,** tel. 329-6411. Morning and afternoon cruises usually last about three hours and cost $35 adults, $17 for children 5-12. Accompanied by naturalists from the University of Hawaii, the educational cruise advertises that you will "see a whale, or get a coupon for another whale watch free."

Three-hour whalewatching tours on the 40-foot boat *Land Ann* are offered by **Dan Mc-Sweeney's Whalewatching Adventures,** P.O. Box 139, Holualoa, HI 96725, tel. 322-0028 or (888) WHALES6. While many are interested in looking only for the humpback whale, Dan, a marine biologist and whale researcher, takes visitors year-round so they can also learn about different kinds of whales and other ocean mammals that inhabit this coast. (E-mail: dmcswwa@interpac.net.)

For a day of snorkeling, sailing, and whalewatching in season, contact **Kamanu Charters,** tel. 329-2021. From Waikoloa, try **Ocean Sports,** tel. 885-5555; they offer snorkeling and whalewatching cruises with five departures per day.

SNORKELING, SCUBA, AND WATER SPORTS

If you think that Hawaii is beautiful above the sea, wait until you explore below. The warm tropical waters and coral growth make it a fascinating haven for reef fish and aquatic plantlife. You'll soon discover that Hawaiian waters are remarkably clear, with excellent visibility. Fish in every fathomable color parade by. Lavender clusters of coral, red and gold coral trees, and over 1,500 different types of shells carpet the ocean floor. In some spots the fish are so accustomed to humans that they'll eat bread from your hand. In other spots, lurking moray eels add the special zest of danger. Sharks and barracuda pose less danger than scraping your knee on the coral or being driven against the rocks by a heavy swell. There are enormous but harmless sea bass and a profusion of sea turtles. All this awaits you below Hawaii's waters

Hawaii has particularly generous underwater vistas open to anyone donning a mask and fins. Snorkel and dive sites, varying in difficulty

and challenge, are accessible from the island. Sites can be totally hospitable, good for families and first-time snorkelers who want an exciting but safe frolic; or they can be accessible only to the experienced diver. Specific sites are listed under "Beaches" in the travel sections.

Scuba

Those in the know consider the deep diving along the steep drop-offs of Hawaii's geologically young coastline some of the best in the state. The ocean surrounding the Big Island has not had a chance to turn the relatively new lava to sand, which makes the visibility absolutely perfect, even to depths of 150 feet or more. There's also 60-70 miles of coral belt around the Big Island, which adds up to a magnificent diving experience. Only advanced divers should attempt deep-water dives, but beginners and snorkelers will have many visual thrills inside the protected bays and coves.

If you're a scuba diver you'll have to show your C Card before local shops will rent you gear, fill your tanks, or take you on a charter dive. Plenty of outstanding scuba instructors will give you lessons toward certification, and they're especially reasonable because of the stiff competition. Prices vary, but you can take a three- to five-day semiprivate certification course including all equipment for about $350 (instruction book, dive tables, logbook extra charge). Divers unaccustomed to Hawaiian waters should not dive alone regardless of their experience. Most opt for dive tours to special dive grounds guaranteed to please. These vary also, but an *accompanied* single-tank dive where no boat is involved goes for about $50; for a two-tank boat dive, expect to spend $80. There are special charter dives, night dives, and photography dives. Most companies pick you up at your hotel, take you to the site, and return you home. Basic equipment costs $20-30 for the day, and most times you'll only need the top of a wetsuit.

Snorkeling

Scuba diving takes expensive special equipment, skills, and athletic ability. Snorkeling, in comparison, is much simpler and enjoyable to anyone who can swim. In about 15 minutes you can be taught the fundamentals of snorkeling—you really don't need formal instructions. Other

REEF FISH

blue-spotted cowfish

Hawaiian lionfish

saddleback wrasse

manta ray

Potter's angelfish

mottled moray

bluestripe butterflyfish

manini

trumpetfish

lagoon humu

moorish idol

threadfin butterflyfish

red-lipped parrotfish

Achilles tang

uhu

BIG ISLAND SNORKELING

Upolu Point
KAPAA BEACH PARK
Hawi
MAHUKONA BEACH PARK
270 250
SPENCER BEACH PARK
Kawaihae
PUAKO/ BOAT RAMP
Waimea
Honokaa
19
19 190
200
Honomu
19
LELEIWI BEACH PARK
KEAHOLE AIRPORT
HILO
RICHARDSON'S OCEAN CENTER
Kailua-Kona
Keaau
130
Kapoho Point
KAHALUU BEACH PARK
Captain Cook
HAWAII VOLCANOES
Pahoa
132
ISAAC HALE BEACH PARK
PUUHONUA O HONAUNAU NATIONAL HISTORICAL PARK
Volcano
Kalapana
HOOKENA BEACH PARK
NATIONAL PARK
Pahala
PACIFIC
11
OCEAN
Honuapo
Ka Lae (South Point)

0   15 mi
0   15 km

© J.D. BISIGNANI AND MOON PUBLICATIONS, INC.

snorkelers or dive-shop attendants can tell you enough to get you started. Because you can breathe without lifting your head, you get great propulsion from the fins and hardly ever need to use your arms. You can go for much greater distances and spend longer periods in the water than if you were swimming. Experienced snorkelers make an art of this sport and you, too, can see and do amazing things with a mask, snorkel, and flippers. Don't, however, get a false sense of invincibility and exceed your limitations.

Larger hotels often have snorkel equipment for guests, but if it isn't free, it always costs more than if you rent it from a dive shop.

Snuba

Part scuba, part snorkeling, snuba is a fairly recent underwater concept (from 1988) that is perfect for an introductory underwater adventure. Tethered to a flotation raft bearing a scuba tank, you are unencumbered by the normal scuba equipment and your descent is limited to under 20 feet. For those who feel timid about scuba diving or who just want a new, fun-filled adventure, snuba might be the answer.

Snorkel, Scuba, Snuba Companies and Equipment Rental

There are over two dozen companies on the Big Island, mostly in Kona, that offer scuba instruction and escorted dives, and rent scuba and snuba equipment.

One of the best outfits to dive with on the Big Island is **Dive Makai** in Kona, tel. 329-2025, operated by Tom Shockley and Lisa Choquette. These very experienced divers have run this service for years and have many dedicated customers. Both Tom and Lisa are conservationists who help preserve the fragile reef. They've worked very hard with the Diver's Council to protect dive sites from fish collectors and to protect the reef from destruction by anchors. Their motto, "We care," is not a trite saying, as they continue to preserve the reef for you and your children.

Another excellent diving outfit is **Jack's Diving Locker,** 75-5819 Ali'i Dr., tel. 329-7585, (800) 345-4807—a responsible outfit that does a good job of watching out for their customers and taking care of the reef. Owners Teri and Jeff Leicher, along with their crew, run diving and snorkeling excursions along the Kona Coast from Kealakekua Bay to Keahole Point, which takes in over 50 dive sites (most of which have permanent moorings to protect the reef from damage by anchoring). Jack's also specializes in snorkel sales and rentals, scuba rentals, certification classes, and dive classes. You can do a five-hour snorkel/sail on the *Blue Dolphin* departing at 8:30 a.m., or on their larger *Na Pali Kai II.*

Hawaiian Divers in the King Kamehameha's Kona Beach Hotel, Kailua-Kona, tel. 329-5662, offers a daily boat charter that gives you a two-tank certified dive with your own gear for $85, $95 with their gear. An introductory dive is $95, and snorkeling is $45. This includes continental breakfast, lunch, and soft drinks.

Big Island Divers at 75-5467 Kaiwi St., tel. 329-6068 or (800) 488-6068, departing from Honokohau Harbor on their custom-built 35-foot dive boat, offers a very inexpensive scuba certification course that's given on four consecutive Saturdays or Wednesdays, so you must intend to stay on the Big Island for that length of time. The normal four-day course costs about $450. Dives range from a two-tank two-location dive for $69.95 to a three-tank three-location dive for $110. They also rent complete snorkel gear (only $6 for 24 hours) and offer introductory and night dives.

Kohala Divers along Route 270 in the Kawaihae Shopping Center, tel. 882-7774, open daily 8 a.m.-5 p.m., offers scuba certification for $300, snorkel rentals for $10 (24 hours), and scuba rentals for $22. They lead two-tank dives for $75, and will take snorkelers along if they have room on the boat ($15). It's a bit far to go from Kailua-Kona but it's a big savings, and they're the only dive company along the Kohala coast. (E-mail: theboss@kohaladivers.com; Web site: www.kohaladivers.com.)

Kona Coast Divers, 74-5614 Palani Rd., Kona, tel. 329-8802, (800) 562-3483, is owned and operated by longtime Kona Coast diver Jim Robertson. This outfit is efficient and to the point. Rates are: two-tank boat dive $70; night dive $55; introductory dive $95; boat riders and snorkelers $30. Full underwater gear is sold and rented. (E-mail: divekona@ilhawaii.net; Web site: konacoastdivers.com.)

Snorkel Bob's, tel. 329-0770, in the parking lot next to the Royal Kona Resort right in front of Huggo's Restaurant, offers snorkel gear for $15 per week for basic equipment. Upgrading to a comfortable surgical silicone mask with Italian fins is $27. Boogie boards are $9-15 p/d, $22-35 p/w depending on quality.

For those still dancing to the primordial tune of residual DNA from our one-celled, ocean-dwelling ancestors, *Kona Aggressor II* is a "live-aboard" dive boat, tel. 329-8182 or (800) 344-5662, departing Kona every Saturday for six days of diving along the Kona coast toward South Point. Passengers dive up to five times per day and night, as the *Aggressor* completely fulfills its motto to "Eat, Sleep, and Dive."

A Sea Paradise Scuba, tel. 322-2500, offers introductory dives at $80-90, and an array of morning and night dives priced at $57-85. Owners and divers John and Roy have had well over a decade of experience off the Kona coastline. They're reputable, fun, and well tested. A good choice.

Sandwich Isle Divers, tel. 329-9188, is owned and operated by Steve and Larry, longtime Kona coast divers who know all the spots. They have a custom, six-passenger dive boat, great for small personalized trips for avid divers.

The **Nautilus Dive Center,** 382 Kamehameha Ave., Hilo, tel. 935-6939, open Mon.-Sat. 9 a.m.-4 p.m., Sunday by appointment, owned and operated by certified instructor William DeRooy, is one of the longest established dive companies on the Hilo side. This full-service dive center offers PADI certification (group session) at a very reasonable $125, new and used dive gear, shore and boat dives at $55 including transportation from Hilo, snorkeling excursions starting at $40, and snorkel gear rental at $5 for 24 hours. Mr. DeRooy is also willing to offer information over the phone for anyone coming to the Hilo side to dive or snorkel. He updates you on ocean conditions, suggests spots compatible with your ability, and even offers a free dive and snorkel map whether you're a customer or not. Bill is a font of information about the Big Island's water sports and is willing to share in the true *aloha* spirit. Definitely stop in!

An alternative to boat dives is shore diving. *Shore Diving in Kona* is a great book listing sites, equipment, regulations, and suggestions for successful and safe dives. If your budget is limited and you're an experienced shore diver, it's a way to have a great outing at a reasonable price.

Snuba Tours of Kona at the King Kamehameha's Kona Beach Hotel, tel. 326-7446; or **Snuba Big Island, Inc.,** tel. 326-7446, can both set you up for this new adventure. Prices vary depending on services provided, such as an additional cruise and lunch, but a basic snuba experience costs about $60.

Snorkel, Scuba, and Snuba Boats

Snorkeling, scuba, and snuba excursions are also provided by the following. The **Fair Wind,** tel. 322-2788 or (800) 677-9461 off island, a well-established company with a 60-foot catamaran, has a great reputation and is sure to please. Its boat leaves daily from magnificent Keauhou Bay and stops at Kealakekua Bay in front of the Captain Cook monument. **The Body Glove,** tel. 326-7122, (800) 551-8911, a full-fledged snorkel, scuba, and snuba company offering a bar, lunch, and plenty of other snorkelers, departs from the Kailua pier. **Kamanu Charters,** tel. 329-2021, Kona's original snorkel sail, in business over 30 years, provides a full day of fun with beer and snacks included in the price. They pilot Kona's only sailing catamaran, maximum of 24 passengers. Or try **Capt. Cook VI,** tel.

329-6411, which sails a 79-foot glass-bottom boat twice a day.

Scuba and snorkel cruises can also be booked through the various activity centers along the Kona and Kohala coasts and at your hotel travel desk.

Surfing and Sailboarding

The surfing off the Big Island is rather uninspiring compared to that off the other islands. The reefs are treacherous and the surf is lazy. Some surfers bob around off the Hilo Bay, and sometimes in Kealakekua and Wailua Bays on the Kona side. Puna also attracts a few off Isaac Hale and Kaimu beaches, and up north off Waipio Valley Beach. Generally, the north and west shores boast better swells during the winter, the east and south shores in summer. Surfboards are for rent only on the Kona side. Try Honolua Surf Co., tel. 329-1001, for starters. While surfing is not the best, the winds are great for sailboarding.

Parasailing, Etc.

UFO Parasailing, tel. 325-5836, (800) 359-4836, offers boat platform take-off and landing. Costs are: an early bird special for $37; a "400 feet for seven minutes" standard ride for $42; an "800 feet for 10 minutes" ride for $52; and boat ride-alongs for $17. You, too, can dangle from a parachute and put your life in the hands of these fun-filled Kona guys who will streak you through the air. For an alternative, try **Kona Water Sports,** tel. 329-1593.

Kayaking

Kona Kai-Yaks, owned and operated by David Johnson—who claims to be paddling so long that he actually entered this life by kayak directly from the womb—is located at Honokohau Harbor, tel. 326-2922, open Mon.-Fri. 9 a.m.-5 p.m., Saturday 9 a.m.-1 p.m. David opened this shop in 1987, and from here rents kayaks and offers tours. Rental kayaks are of different types: the Frenzy (name is a bit of a confidence buster), the Pro Prism, and the Malibu; each rents for $5-13 per hour and $9.95-39.95 per day, depending upon the kayak chosen (weekend and weekly discounts available). David offers guided day tours for around $80 per person. Overnight camping trips are also offered for the intrepid outdoor enthusiast, and are custom designed to fit group or individual needs. Overnight trips are

$100/person per night plus $100 per day for the guide (food included). A "liquid luxury" overnight trip that pampers you with gourmet meals, night dives with manta rays, and even hot showers is another option. You paddle by day trailed by a mother ship, *The Sun Seeker,* a 53-foot yacht upon which you spend the night at $250 per person per night, plus $100 per day for the guide. Try to tough it out!

A twist on the kayak business is offered by **Kohala Mountain Kayak Cruise,** P.O. Box 660, Kapa'au, HI 96755, tel. 899-6922. On an outing with this company, you'll float several scenic miles of the Kohala irrigation canal flumes, over small ravines, and through several tunnels in the remote, private lands of the north Kohala coast. Completed in the early part of this century and considered a feat of engineering, this 22-mile-long irrigation system (better known as the Kohala Ditch) supplied the Kohala Sugar mills with a steady supply of water until the plantation ceased business in 1975. Guided by experts using large, flat-bottom, double-hulled kayaks, you'll not only experience the beauty of the surrounding rainforest and rugged scenery but will also absorb a lesson in the history and culture of this area. No experience required. Bring an extra set of dry clothes. Floats are offered Mon.-Fri. at 9:00 a.m. and 1:00 p.m. Children 5-18 $55, adults $75, and seniors age 60 and older $60. Meet across from the King Kamehameha statue in Kapaau.

SKIING

Bored with sun and surf? Strap the "boards" to your feet and hit the slopes of Mauna Kea. There are no lifts so you'll need a 4WD to get to the top, and someone willing to pick you up again at the bottom. You can rent 4WDs from the car-rental agencies already mentioned, but if that seems like too much hassle, contact **Ski Guides Hawaii,** P.O. Box 1954, Kamuela, HI 96743, tel. 885-4188 or 889-6747. Here you can rent skis, and they'll provide the "lifts" to the top. Skis, boots, and poles rent for $20 a day; the popular full-day ski tour with equipment, ride and driver, ski guide, and lunch goes for $120. Other ski packages are available and priced on request. You can expect snow Dec.-May, but you can't always count on it.

GOLF

The Big Island has some of the most beautiful golf links in Hawaii. The Kohala-area courses taken together are considered by some to be the crown jewel of the state's golf options. Robert Trent Jones Sr. and Jr. have both built exceptional courses here. Dad built the Mauna Kea Beach Hotel course, while the kid built his at the Waikoloa Beach Resort. The Mauna Kea course bedevils many as the ultimate challenge. If the Kohala courses are too rich for your blood, you can hit nine holes in Hilo for about $25. How about golfing at Volcano Golf Course, where if you miss a short putt, you can blame it on an earthquake?

For rates, tee times, and reservations, call each clubhouse direct. Golfing can be expensive on Hawaii, so if you're interested in saving more than a few bucks and don't mind playing later in the day, ask for twilight rates and hours. For the golf fanatic, individual and group golf packages at courses on two or more of the islands for one to two weeks can be arranged through **Fore Golf Hawaii,** 73-1150 Oluolu St., Kailua-Kona, HI 96740, tel. 325-6755 or (800) 729-1490.

TENNIS

Many tennis courts dot the Big Island, and plenty of them are free. County courts are under the control of the Department of Parks and Recreation, which maintains a combination of lighted and unlit courts around the island. Some private and hotel courts are open to the public for a fee, while others restrict play to guests only.

HORSEBACK RIDING

Waipio Na'alapa Trail Rides, operated by Sherri Hannum, tel. 775-0419, offers the most unique rides on Hawaii. Sherri and her family have lived in Waipio Valley for over 20 years and know its history, geology, and legends intimately. She offers pick-up service from Kukuihaele for the 9:30 a.m. and 1 p.m. rides ($75). Sherri treats guests like family. If you have time, don't miss this wonderful adventure!

H.R.T. Waipio Tour Desk, tel. 775-7291, located in the Hawaiian Holiday Macadamia Nut

BIG ISLAND GOLF COURSES

Factory in Honokaa, offers horseback riding through fabulous Waipio Valley. The rides start at 9:30 a.m. and 1:30 p.m., last two and one-half hours, and cost $65, including transportation from Honokaa to Waipio. Make reservations 24 hours in advance.

Enjoyable rides are also offered by the **Mauna Kea Resort Stables** (for nonguests also), tel. 882-4288. They have an arrangement with the Parker Ranch, which will supply a *paniolo* to guide you over the quarter-million acres of open range

on the slopes of Mauna Kea, morning or afternoon. The stable is open Mon.-Sat. 9 a.m.-3 p.m. Rates are $40 pp for a one-hour ride and $70 for the two-hour ride; special trail rides available on request. Eight years old is the minimum age for riders; 210 pounds is the maximum weight. The stables are at Parker Ranch headquarters in Waimea.

Paniolo Riding Adventures, tel. 889-5354, offers horseback riding on a working ranch in the Kohala Mountains. With your comfort in mind, they offer chaps, rain slickers, cowboy hats,

BIG ISLAND GOLF COURSES

LOCATION	COURSE	PAR	YARDS	FEES	CART	CLUB RENTAL
Hilo	Naniloa Country Club 120 Banyan Dr. Hilo, HI 96720 tel. 935-3000	35	2740 (9 holes)	$30 (9 holes) $40 (18 holes)	$14	$19
Hilo	Hilo Municipal Golf Course 340 Haihai St. Hilo, HI 96720 tel. 959-7711	71	6006	$25	$14.50	$10
Hamakua Coast	Hamakua Country Club Box 344 Honokaa, HI 96727 tel. 775-7244	33	2520 (9 holes)	$10	(no carts)	(no club rental)
Kau	Volcano Golf and Country Club Box 46 Hawaii Volcanoes National Park, HI 96718 tel. 967-7331	72	6180	$60	incl.	$16
Kau	Seamountain Golf Course P.O. Box 190 Pahala, HI 96777 tel. 928-6222	72	6492	$40	incl.	$15
Kau	Discovery Harbor Golf and Country Club P.O. Box 621 Naalehu, HI 96772 tel. 929-7353	72	6326	$28	incl.	$12
Kailua-Kona	Kona Country Club 78-7000 Ali'i Dr. Kailua-Kona, HI 96740 tel. 322-2595	Ali'i Course 72 Ocean Course 72	5841 6155	$125 $125	incl. incl.	$25 $25
Kailua-Kona	Makalei Hawaii Country Club 72-3890 Hawaii Belt Rd. Kailua-Kona, HI 96740 tel. 325-6625	72	6161	$110	incl.	$25
Kailua-Kona	Hualalai Golf Club P.O. Box 1119 Kailua-Kona, HI 96745 tel. 325-8480	72	6032	$125 (Four Seasons Hotel guests only)	incl.	$40

(continues on next page)

BIG ISLAND GOLF COURSES

(continued)

LOCATION	COURSE	PAR	YARDS	FEES	CART	CLUB RENTAL
Kohala Coast	Waikoloa Beach Golf Club 1020 Keana Place Waikoloa, HI 96743 tel. 885-6060	Beach 70	5958	$120	incl.	$30
Kohala Coast	Waikoloa King's Golf Club 600 Waikoloa Beach Dr. Waikoloa, HI 96743 tel. 885-4647	72	6010	$120	incl.	$30
Kohala Coast	Mauna Lani Resort, Frances H. I'i Brown Golf Courses 68-1310 Mauna Lani Dr. Kohala Coast, HI 96743 tel. 885-6655	South Course 72 North Course 72	5940 6086	$170 $160	incl. incl.	$30 $30
Kohala Coast	Mauna Kea Beach Resort Golf Course 62-100 Mauna Kea Beach Dr. Kamuela, HI 96743 tel. 880-3480	72	6737	$150	incl.	$35
Kohala Coast	Hapuna Golf Course 62-100 Kauna'oa Dr. Kamuela, HI 96743 tel. 880-3000	72	6029	$130	incl.	$30
Waikoloa	Waikoloa Village Golf Club P.O. Box 383910 Waikoloa, HI 96738 tel. 883-9621	72	6230	$55	incl.	$25
Waimea	Waimea Country Club Box 2155, Kamuela, HI 96743 tel. 885-8777	72	6210	$60	incl.	$25

and fleece saddle covers to keep you happy where the sun don't shine. Prices vary according to ride chosen, from novice to cowpoke.

Kohala Na'alapa Trail Rides, tel. 889-0022, offers trail rides onto the historic Kahua and Kohala Ranch, high in the Kohala Mountains. Rides are offered daily at 9 a.m. and 1:30 p.m., with prices $55-75.

Using horses from their own working ranch in Waimea, **Dahana Ranch,** tel. 885-0057, gives riders free range trail rides on their own property.

King's Trail Rides O'Kona, tel. 323-2388, has offices along Route 11, at mile marker 111, high above the Kona Coast on the outskirts of Kealakekua. Their wranglers will lead you (4-6 people maximum) on a custom trail ride down to Captain Cook's Monument on the shores of Kealakekua Bay. This four-hour trip, departing at 9 a.m. (two hours of actual riding), includes snorkeling in the bay, along with a delicious picnic lunch. The price is $95. The office, which doubles as a retail shop, is open daily 7:30 a.m.-

5 p.m.; there you can purchase chocolate-covered coffee beans, bottled salad dressings made in the area, honey, and koa boxes, along with cowboy items like spurs, western belts, and a full assortment of tack. Dave "Bones" Inkster, owner and top hand, spent his life in the saddle and taught his twin daughters Melissa and Nicole to ride like the wind. The girls were chosen to represent Hawaii in 1996 at the National Finals held in Pueblo, Colorado on the Dally Team (heading, heeling, and roping). Ride 'em cowgirls! E-mail: bones@interpac.net; Web site: interpac.net/~hit/ktr.hmtl.

Rain Forest Trailrides, tel. 322-7126, takes you on horseback across the face of the Hualalai Mountains. Open daily 9 a.m.-5 p.m., it offers rides from one to two and a half hours (latter with lunch included) for $45-80.

BIG ISLAND TENNIS COURTS
PUBLIC COURTS

Under jurisdiction of the County Department of Parks and Recreation, 25 Aupuni St., Hilo, HI 96720. Tel. 961-8311.

LOCATION	NAME OF COURT	NO. OF COURTS	LIGHTED
Hilo	Ainaole Park	1	No
Hilo	Hakalau Park	2	No
Hilo	Hoolulu Park	8	Yes
Hilo	Lincoln Park	4	Yes
Hilo	Lokahi Park	2	Yes
Hilo	Malama Park	2	Yes
Hilo	Mohouli Park	2	No
Hilo	Panaewa Park	2	Yes
Hilo	Papaaloa Park	2	Yes
Honokaa	Honokaa Park	2	Yes
Puna	Kurtistown Park	1	No
Keaau	Keaau Park	2	No
Kau	Kau High School	2	Yes
Kau	Naalehu Park	2	Yes
Kona	Greenwell Park	1	Yes
Kona	Keauhou Park	1	No
Kona	Kailua Park (Old Kona Airport)	4	Yes
Kona	Kailua Playground	1	Yes
Waimea	Waimea Park	2	Yes
Kapaau	Kamehameha Park	2	Yes

HOTEL AND PRIVATE COURTS OPEN TO THE PUBLIC

LOCATION	NAME OF COURT	NO. OF COURTS	LIGHTED
Hilo	Hilo High School	1	No
Hilo	University of Hawaii-Hilo College	2	No
Pahala	Seamountain Tennis Center (fee)	4	No
Keauhou-Kona	Kona Surf Hotel Racket Club (fee)	7	Yes
Keauhou-Kona	Keauhou Beach Hotel (fee)	6	Yes
Kona	Country Club Villas	2	No
Kailua-Kona	Royal Kona Resort	6	Yes
Kailua-Kona	King Kamehameha Kona Beach Hotel (fee)	2	Yes
Waikoloa	Waikoloa village (fee)	2	Yes
Waimea	Hawaii Prep Academy	4	Yes
Waimea	Waimea Park	2	Yes

J.D. BISIGNANI

Explore the Big Island on horseback with a paniolo guide.

Also offering rides over the slopes of Hualalai between 1,500-3,000 feet is **Waiono Meadows Trail Rides,** tel. 329-0888. A one-hour ride costs $15, a two-hour ride $28. Breakfast, lunch, and sunset rides are also available.

Horse-Drawn Wagon Rides

Waipio Valley Wagon Tour, tel. 775-9518, owned and operated by Peter Tolin, is a mule-drawn tour of the magnificent Waipio Valley. The one and a half-hour tours leave five times daily at 9 a.m., 10:30 a.m., 12:30 p.m., 2 p.m., and 4 p.m. The cost is $35 adults; children under 12 pay half price, children two and under are free.

BICYCLING

Pedaling around the Big Island can be both fascinating and frustrating. The roads are well paved, but the shoulders are often torn up. With all the triathletes coming to Hawaii, and all the fabulous, little-trafficked roads, you'd think the island would be great for biking! It is, but you are better off bringing your own bike than renting. If you do rent, instead of a delicate road bike, you're better off getting a **cruiser** or **mountain bike** that can handle the sometimes poor road conditions as well as open up the possibilities of offroad biking. Even experienced mountain bikers should be careful on the often extremely muddy and rutted trails.

For those who desire off-street trails to paved roads, pick up a copy of the Big Island Mountain Bike Association's comprehensive offroad, public-access trail guide at either HVB office or at most bike shops on the island. This guide is also available on their Web site: www.interpac.net/~mtbike. Aside from an introduction to the organization and safety tips, each trail is briefly described and accompanied by a rudimentary map, directions to the start of the trail, and any additional information that's necessary to complete the ride. The type of ride, length in distance, ride time, elevation change, and level of expertise needed is also listed. Trails vary from flat shoreline jaunts to rugged mountain workouts, for beginners to the advanced rider. Check it out before you ride; this information comes from experienced island riders. For additional information contact BIMBA at P.O. Box 6819 Hilo, HI 96720-8934, or call 961-4452.

For general information on biking in Hawaii, contact **Hawaii Bicycling League,** P.O. Box 4403, Honolulu, HI 96812-4403. This nonprofit organization promotes biking as recreation, sport, and transportation, encourages safe biking practices, conducts biking education, and advocates for biking issues. It publishes a monthly newsletter, *Spoke-n-Words,* filled withnews of the organization's business, its bicycle safety program for kids, and rides that are open to the public, as well as current bicycle issues and sponsored bicycle competitions throughout the state. If you are a bicycle rider living in the islands or simply want a subscription to the newsletter, write for membership information.

For additional information, have a look at the *Bicycle Regulations and Illustrated Safety Tips* booklet, put out by the Department of Transportation Services, City and County of Honolulu. Although written for the island of Oahu, the information is applicable to all the islands, except for a few minor details on Oahu. On Oahu pick up a copy at any city hall or satellite city hall and most bike shops. From the neighbor islands or if coming from outside the state, write or call for a copy: Chris Sayers, Bicycle Coordinator, City and County of Honolulu, 711 Kapiolani Blvd., 1200, Honolulu, HI 96813, tel. 527-5044.

Bicycle Shops

For rentals, try the following. **Hawaiian Pedals Ltd,** tel. 329-2294, in the Kona Inn Shopping Plaza, rents mountain bikes at $15 for five hours, $20 for 24 hours, $15 p/d for 2-3 days, $12 p/d for 4-5 days, $10 p/d for 6-7 days, and $9 p/d for over one week. Performance bikes are slightly more expensive; tandems cost $35 all day. Bike racks and baby seats are also for rent. They deliver. Ask about their tours. **Island Cycle Rentals** is at Jack's Diving Locker at the Kona Inn Plaza, tel. 329-7585.

Dave's Bike and Triathlon Shop, owned and pedaled by triathlete Dave Bending, is located just a long stride or two from the beginning of the Ironman Triathlon across from the King Kamehameha's Kona Beach Hotel in the Kona Square Shopping Center, at 75-5669 Ali'i Dr., tel. 329-4522. Dave rents competition-quality road bikes at $25 p/d, and *Caloi* mountain bikes at $15 first day, $12 second day, $10 third day, or $60 p/w. Prices include helmet, water bottles, map, bicycle lock and, most importantly, road advice. Dave knows his stuff, so pay heed!

In Waimea, try either **C&C Cycle and Surf,** tel. 885-5005; or **Mauna Kea Mountain Bikes,** tel. 883-0130, for wheels that will get you up to the high country.

Teo's Safaris in Keaau, just south of Hilo, tel. 982-5221, rents bicycles and leads mountain tours. Rentals for 21-speed mountain bikes are $10 p/d, $15 for 24 hours, $20 for two days, or $50 for the week. Teo leads a two- to three-hour rainforest ride which includes bike and helmet for $20 (call 24 hours in advance). Teo also has panniers, bike racks, and camping equipment available for people renting his bikes (rates subject to length of rental). **Pacific United Rental** at 1080 Kilauea Ave., Hilo, tel. 935-2974, has rentals limited to the Hilo area at $10 p/d for single-speed bikes. Also in Hilo is **Mid Pacific Wheels,** at 1133C Manono St., tel. 935-6211.

Bicycle Tours

For those interested in bicycle touring, contact one of the following for their specialized bike trips.

The owners and tour leaders of **Island Bicycle Adventures,** 569 Kapahulu Ave., Honolulu, HI 96815, tel. 734-0700 or (800) 233-2226, are intimately familiar with bicycle touring and are members of the Hawaii Bicycling League. They offer tours to Maui, the Big Island, and Kauai. **Hawaiian Eyes Big Island Bicycle Tours,** P.O. Box 1500, Honokaa, HI 96727, tel. 775-7335, offers a variety of guided rides including along the Hamakua Coast, down the Saddle Road, and around the island. **Mauna Kea Mountain Bikes,** tel. 883-0180, offers cross-country, downhill, and offroad guided tours. Customized tours can be arranged. **Backroads,** 1516 Fifth St., Suite PR, Berkeley, CA 94710, tel. (510) 527-1555, (800) 462-2848, goes easy on the environment with their bicycle and hiking trips to the Big Island.

HUNTING

Most people don't think of Hawaii as a place for hunting, but actually it's quite good. Seven species of introduced game mammals and 15 species of game birds are regularly hunted. Not all species of game animals are open on all islands, but every island offers hunting. Huge unpopulated expanses of grassland, forest, and scrubby mountainside are very good for hunting. The Big Island's game includes wild pig, sheep, and goats, plus a variety of pheasant, quail, dove, francolin, and wild turkey. Public game lands are located throughout the island; a license is required to take birds and game.

Information

Hunting rules and regulations are always subject to change. Also, environmental considerations often change bag limits and seasons. Make sure to check with the State Division of Forestry and Wildlife for the most current information. Request "Rules Regulating Game Bird Hunting," "Rules Regulating Game Mammal Hunting," and "Hunting in Hawaii." Direct inquiries to: Department of Land and Natural Resources, Division of Forestry and Wildlife Office, P.O. Box 4849, Hilo, HI 96720, tel. 974-4221.

General Hunting Rules

Hunting licenses are mandatory in order to hunt on public, private, or military land anywhere in Hawaii. They're good for one year beginning July 1 and cost $15 residents and servicemen, $95 nonresidents; free to senior citizens. Licenses are available from sporting goods stores and from the various offices of the Division of Forestry and Wildlife. This government organization also sets and enforces the rules, so contact them with any questions. Generally, hunting hours are from a half-hour before sunrise to a half-hour after sunset. Checking stations are maintained, where hunters must check in before and after hunting.

Rifles must have a muzzle velocity greater than 1,200-foot-pounds. Shotguns larger than .20 gauge are allowed, and muzzleloaders must have a .45 caliber bore or larger. Bows must have a minimum draw of 40 pounds for straight bows, 35 pounds for a recurve bow, and 30 pounds for compounds. Arrows must be broadheads. The use of hunting dogs is permitted only for certain species of birds and game, and when dogs are permitted, only smaller caliber rifles and shotguns, and spears and knives, may be used—no big bore guns/shotguns. Hunters must wear orange safety cloth on front and back no smaller than a 12-inch square. Certain big-game species are hunted only by lottery selection; contact the Division of Forestry and Wildlife two months in advance. Guide service is not mandatory but is advised if you're unfamiliar with hunting in Hawaii. You can hunt on private land only with permission, and you must possess a valid hunting license. Guns and ammunition brought into Hawaii must be registered with the chief of police of the corresponding county within 48 hours of arrival.

gray francolin

Game Animals

All game animals on Hawaii have been introduced. Some have adapted admirably and are becoming well entrenched, while the existence of others is still precarious. **Feral pigs** are escaped domestic pigs that have gone wild and are found on all islands except Lanai. The stock is a mixture of original Polynesian pigs and subsequently introduced species. The pigs are hunted with dogs and usually killed with a spear or long knife—not recommended for the timid or tenderhearted. These beasts' four-inch tusks and fighting spirit make them tough and dangerous. **Feral goats** come in a variety of colors. Found on all islands except Lanai, they have been known to cause erosion and are viewed as a pest in some areas, especially on Haleakala. Openly hunted on all islands, their meat when done properly is considered delicious. **Mouflon sheep** are native to Corsica and Sardinia. They do well on Lanai and on the windswept slopes of Mauna Loa and Mauna Kea, where they're hunted at various times by public lottery. **Feral sheep** haunt the slopes of Mauna Kea and Mauna Loa at 7,000-12,000 feet. They travel in flocks and destroy vegetation. It takes determination and a good set of lungs to bag one, especially with a bow and arrow.

BOB RACE

Game Birds

A number of game birds are found on most of the islands. Bag limits and hunting seasons vary, so check with the Division of Forestry and Wildlife for details. **Ring-necked pheasant** is one of the best game birds; it is found on all the islands. The **kalij pheasant** from Nepal is found only on the Big Island, where the **green pheasant** is also prevalent. **Francolins,** gray and black, from India and the Sudan, are similar to partridges. They are hunted on all islands with dogs and are great roasted. There are also **chukar** from Tibet, found on the slopes of all islands; a number of **quail,** including the Japanese and California varieties; **doves;** and the **wild Rio Grande turkeys** which are found on all islands except Kauai and Oahu (although a few of the "featherless variety" have been known to walk the streets of Waikiki).

SHOPPING

The following is an overview of the main shopping areas and their locations around the island. Almost every town has at least a gas station and market, and they will be listed in the travel chapters. Look under "Shopping" for directions to and descriptions of specific malls, art shops, and boutiques in the area. Supermarkets, health food stores, and local markets are listed in the individual travel chapters, generally in the "Food" sections.

SHOPPING CENTERS

General shopping centers are found in Hilo, Kailua-Kona, Waimea, and Captain Cook. Like most shopping malls, these have a variety of stores whose offerings include apparel, dry goods, sporting goods, food, photography supplies, or outdoor rentals.

Hilo Malls

The main shopping center in Hilo is the **Prince Kuhio Plaza** at 111 E. Puainako. This shoppers' paradise is Hilo's newest and the island's largest shopping mall. An older but still full-service shopping center is **Kaiko'o Mall** at 777 Kilauea Avenue. The **Hilo Shopping Center** is about one-half mile south on Kilauea Ave. at the corner of Kekuanoa Street. This smaller mall has only a handful of local shops. **Puainako Town Center** is located at 2100 Kanoelehua Avenue. **Waiakea Kai Shopping Plaza**, at 88 Kanoelehua Ave., has a small clutch of stores.

Kona Malls

Two commodities that you're guaranteed in Kailua-Kona are plenty of sunshine and plenty of shopping. **Kona Inn Shopping Village** is located in central Kailua at 75-5744 Ali'i Dr. and has more than 40 shops selling everything from fabrics to fruits. **World Square** is smaller and just across the road. **Kona Banyan Court**, also in central Kailua, has a dozen shops with a medley of goods and services. **Kailua Bay Inn Shopping Plaza** is along Ali'i Drive, **Akona Kai Mall** is across from Kailua Pier, and the **Kona Coast Shopping Plaza** and the **North Kona**

Shopping Center are both along Palani Road. **Lanihau Center,** at 75-5595 Palani Rd., is one of Kailua-Kona's newest shopping additions. **King Kamehameha's Kona Beach Hotel Mall** is an exclusive shopping haven on the first floor of the hotel, while **Rawson Plaza,** at 74-5563 Kaiwi St., is in the industrial area and offers bargains. **Waterfront Row** is a new shopping and food complex at the south end of downtown Kailua-Kona that's done in period architecture with rough-cut lumber.

Keauhou Shopping Center is conveniently located at the corner of Ali'i Dr. and Kamehameha III Rd. at the far end of Kailua-Kona. Here you'll find everything from a post office to a supermarket. Continuing south on Route 11, you'll spot **Kainaliu Village Mall** along the main drag.

Kealakekua Ranch Center, in Captain Cook, is a two-story mall with fashions and general supplies.

Waimea (Kamuela) Malls

After the diversity of shopping malls in Kailua and Hilo, it's like a breath of fresh air to have fewer choices. In Waimea try the **Parker Ranch Shopping Center,** which has over 30 shops, including a pharmacy, grocery, and general merchandise. A small herd of shops in this center also features ranch and Western-wear with a Hawaiian twist. **Parker Square Shopping Mall,** along Route 19, has a collection of fine boutiques and shops. **Waimea Shopping Center,** also along Route 19, is one of Waimea's newest shopping malls.

The "Martinizing" of the Big Island

The Big Island has been "martinized:" Wal-Mart is here, along with Kmart, the largest store in the Hawaii chain (oh joy), and Costco Warehouse, causing a bit of spindling, mutilating, and . . . folding of the local small retail shops. But to some consumers, these shopping meccas have had a positive effect upon the island—sort of.

These retail behemoths have definitely lowered prices and made more goods available, but with an eye toward corporate gain they've put the squeeze on local "mom and pop" shops, the traditional retailers of The Big Island. We have all been programmed to accept the dubious concept that "progress is our most important product," and in consequence the demise of the neighborhood store has been repeated countless times in towns and cities around the nation. However, in the encapsulated island economy of Hawaii, this brand of progress has been particularly devastating, since there is only a limited number of shoppers to go around, especially "tourist shoppers" whose dollars are the lifeblood of the small shops. In a free economy, all have the right to trade, and you may even feel that the coming of the "big boys" was inevitable. However, some of their business practices seem to be particularly aimed at crushing their small competitors. For example, both large stores have added "Hawaiiana" sections offering traditional Hawaiian arts and crafts. Part of the enjoyment in purchasing a traditional Hawaiian craft item has always been in obtaining it either directly from the person who made it, or off the plain wood shelves of a local store closely connected to the source. Since the "marts" have entered the retail scene, plenty of locally owned stores and boutiques have gone under. Keep this in mind when making that "special purchase," which can just as easily be bought from a local merchant tending his or her counter, as from a blue-smocked, name-tagged Assistant Manager in Training striding the antiseptic aisles. Wal-Mart, Kmart, and Costco have stores in Kailua-Kona, and Wal-Mart also has one in Hilo.

FOOD STORES AND SUPERMARKETS

Groceries and supplies can be purchased in almost every town on the island. Many of the markets in the smaller towns also sell a limited supply of sundries and dry goods. The general rule is: the smaller the market, the higher the prices. The largest and least expensive stores with the biggest selections are found in Hilo and Kailua-Kona. The following is a sampling of what you'll find. More extensive listings are found under "Shopping" in the individual district chapters.

Hilo and Kona
Supermarkets in Hilo include **Food Fair,** 194 Kilauea Ave.; **Safeway,** 333 Kilauea Ave.; **Sack 'n Save Foods** at Puainako Shopping Center; **Sure Save Supermarket** in Kaiko'o Mall; and **KTA Super Stores** at Puainako Shopping Center and along Kilauea Ave. downtown.

In Kona, **K. Tanaguchi Market** at Kona Coast Shopping Center and **Food for Less** in Lanihau Center are two of the main supermarkets. **KTA Super Stores** are at both the Kona Coast Shopping Center and at the Keauhou Shopping Center, at the extreme south end of Ali'i Drive.

Around the Island
These smaller markets should meet your needs as you travel around the Big Island. Along the eastern Hamakua Coast you'll find **Ishigo's General Store** in Honomu Village en route to Akaka Falls. Further north along Route 24 in Honokaa are **T. Kaneshiro Store** and **K.K. Super-Mart.** In Kukuihaele, the last village before Waipio Valley, look for **The Last Chance Store.**

In Waimea, **Sure Save Supermarket** is at the Parker Ranch Shopping Center. Meat lovers can't go wrong at the **Kamuela Meat Market,** also at the center, selling Parker Ranch beef at home-town prices. On the Kohala Peninsula look for **Kohala Market** in Kawaihae, **M. Nakahara** for general supplies and liquor in Hawi, and Kapaau's **Union Market** for a good assortment of grains, nuts, fruit, and locally made pastries and breads.

South of Hilo you'll find in Pahoa Town **Pahoa Cash and Carry.** Along the Puna coast is the **Kalapana General Store.** In Volcano Village try **Kilauea General Store** along Route 11 just before entering Hawaii Volcanoes National Park.

Kamigaki Market and **Sure Save** are in Kealakekua. **Shimizu Market** is south on Route 11 in Honaunau. Farther south between mile markers 77 and 78 you'll find the very well-stocked **Ocean View General Store.** In the Kau District look for **Wong Yuen Store** in Waiohinu, and **Pick and Pay** in Naalehu, which bills itself as the southernmost market in the United States.

Health Food, Fruit Stores, and Farmers' Markets
Abundant Life Natural Foods is in downtown Hilo at 292 Kamehameha Avenue. Kona keeps you healthy with **Kona Healthways** in the Kona Coast Shopping Center. The **Aloha Village Store,** just next door to the Aloha Cafe in Kainaliu, sells gifts, sundries, and natural foods. In Kealakekua look for the well-stocked **Ohana O Ka Aina Food Co-op.** In Naalehu the **Naalehu Fruit Stand** is a favorite with local people for its fresh fruit, grains, minerals, vitamins, and health foods.

While heading south from Hilo to Volcanoes, stop along Route 11 at **Keaau Natural Foods** or in Pahoa at **Pahoa Natural Groceries,** which specializes in organic fruits and juices and is one of the finest health food stores on the Big Island.

On Wednesday and Saturday mornings, check out the **Hilo Farmers' Market** (best produce and deals are early in the morning) at Kamehameha Ave. and Mamo St., fronting the bay in the center of the downtown area. For a real treat visit the early morning (over by 8 a.m.) **Suisan Fish Market** at 85 Lihiwai St. in Hilo. In Pahoa, the **"Caretakers of Our Land" Farmers' Market** puts out their wares on Saturday 7:30 a.m.-12 p.m. at the Sacred Heart Church. At the Cooper Center in Volcano, you'll find produce, flowers, and baked goods at the **Volcano Farmers' Market** every Sunday 8:30-11 a.m. For locally grown produce on the west side of the island try the **Kona Farmers' Market** every Saturday and Sunday 8 a.m.-2:30 p.m. at Kaiwi Square in Kona; the **Kailua Village Farmers' Market** across from Hale Kalawai on Wednesday, Friday, Saturday, and Sunday; or the **Kona Country Farmers' Market** every Saturday and Sunday along Hwy. 11 between mile markers 112 and 113 near Kealakekua. The **Hawaiian Homestead Market** held in Waimea every Saturday 7 a.m.-noon is where local farmers come to sell their produce, much of which is organic. Look for a dozen or so stalls in the parking lot of the Hawaiian Homelands Building located along Route 19, about two miles east of town center heading toward Honokaa. Alternately, in Waimea, shop at the **Kamuela Farmers' Market** every Saturday 8 a.m.-12 p.m. at the Parker School.

BOOKSTORES

Two aspects of a quality vacation are knowing what you're doing and thoroughly relaxing while doing it. Nothing helps you do this better than a good book. The following stores offer full selections.

Hilo has some excellent bookstores. **Basically Books,** downtown at 46 Waianuenue St., has a good selection of Hawaiiana and out-of-print books, and an unbeatable selection of maps. You can get anywhere you want to go with their nautical charts, road maps, and topographical maps, which include sectionals for serious hikers and trekkers. Their collection covers most of the Pacific. They also feature a very good selection of travel books, and flags from countries throughout the world. The **Book Gallery,** at Prince Kuhio Plaza, is a full-selection bookstore featuring Hawaiiana, hardcovers, and paperbacks. **Waldenbooks,** also at Prince Kuhio Plaza, is the largest and best-stocked bookstore in the Hilo area.

Kailua-Kona bookstores include **Waldenbooks** in Lanihau Center on Palani Rd.; **Middle Earth Bookshop** at 75-5719 Ali'i Dr., in the Kona Plaza Shopping Arcade; and **Keauhou Village Bookshop** at Keauhou Shopping Village.

Waimea offers the **Waimea General Store,** located at the Parker Square Shopping Mall, and **Pueo Bookshop,** at the Waimea Center.

SPECIALTY SHOPS

You can stroll in and out of flower shops, T-shirt factories, and a panoply of boutiques offering ceramics, paintings, carvings, and all manner of island handicrafts. Art and crafts shops are always a part of the Big Island's shopping malls, and in even the smallest village you can count on at least one local artist displaying his or her creations. The following list of artists and shops is by no means exhaustive, but most are in out-of-the-way places and worth a visit. Art shops and boutiques in specific areas will be covered in the travel sections under "Shopping."

In Hilo, **Hawaiian Handicrafts** specializes in woodcarvings. **Sugawara Lauhala and Gift Shop** is a virtually unknown Hilo institution making genuine *lau hala* weavings. **Old Town Printer and Stationers** has been in business for 35 years selling stationery, office supplies, postcards, note cards, and a terrific selection of calendars. They also have a fax and copy center for travelers. **Sig Zane Design** is one of the most unique and distinctive shops on the island, selling island wearables in 100% cotton.

While heading up the Hamakua Coast, make sure to visit **The Hawaiian Artifacks Shop** along the main drag in Honokaa. **Waipio Valley Artworks** in Kukuihaele showcases exclusive artwork of distinguished island artists.

If you are after an exquisite piece of art, a unique memento, or an inexpensive but distinctive souvenir, make sure to visit the **Volcano Art Center** in Hawaii Volcanoes National Park.

J.D. BISIGNANI

ipu, a drum used to accompany hula

Collectors Fine Art in the Kona Inn Shopping Village is a perfect labyrinth of rooms and hallways showcasing fine art from around the world. **Kona Inn Jewelry,** for world treasures, is one of the oldest and best-known shops for a square deal in Kona. **Alapaki's,** at Keauhou Shopping Center, sells traditional island arts and crafts; **Showcase Gallery** here offers glasswork, beadwork, featherwork, enameling, and shell lei from the islands, with emphasis on the Big Island.

The mountain village of Holualoa has become an artists' haven. As you enter the village you'll spot **Kimura's Lauhala Shop,** which has been selling and producing its famous *lau hala* hats ever since local weavers began bartering their creations for groceries in 1915. In town you'll find a converted and brightly painted coffee mill that's the home of the **Kona Art Center,** a community art-cooperative since 1965. The premier shop in town, **Studio 7,** showcases the work of Hiroki Morinoue and his wife Setsuko, famous *raku* potter Chiu Leong, and numerous other island artists. A separate shop in the same

building is **Goldsmithing by Sam Rosen,** featuring unusual, one-of-a-kind works mostly in gold, silver, and precious stones.

The Little Grass Shack is an institution in Kealakekua. It looks like a tourist trap, but don't let that stop you from going in and finding some authentic souvenirs, most of which come from the surrounding area. **Tropical Temptations** in Kealakekua turns the best available grade of local fruits, nuts, and coffee beans into delicious candies. In the nearby village of Kainaliu, look for **The Blue Ginger Gallery,** displaying art of owners Jill and David Bever as well as artists' works from all over the island.

In the *paniolo* town of Waimea you can pick up down-home cowboy items or sophisticated artwork. One of the galleries in town, **Gallery of Great Things,** really is loaded with great things—everything from a carousel horse to koa hair sticks. Along the north shore in Kapaau across from the Kamehameha statue is **Ackerman Gallery,** where you'll find the work of artist Gary Ackerman along with displays of local pottery, carvings, and one-of-a-kind jewelry. Many other artists and galleries call Kohala home.

ARTS TO BUY

Wild Hawaiian shirts or bright muumuus, especially when worn on the Mainland, have the magical effect of making wearers "feel" like they're in Hawaii, while at the same time eliciting spontaneous smiles from passers-by. Maybe it's the colors, or perhaps it's just the "vibe" that signifies "party time" or "hang loose," but nothing says Hawaii like alohawear does. There are more than a dozen fabric houses in Hawaii turning out distinctive patterns, and many dozens of factories creating their own personalized designs. These factories often have attached retail outlets, but in any case you can find hundreds of shops selling alohawear. Aloha shirts were the brilliant idea of a Chinese merchant in Honolulu, who used to hand-tailor them and sell them to the tourists who arrived by ship in the glory days before WW II. They were an instant success. Muumuus or "Mother Hubbards" were the idea of missionaries, who were appalled by Hawaiian women running about *au naturelle* and insisted on covering their new Christian converts from head to foot. Now the roles are reversed, and it's

MUSEUMS OF THE BIG ISLAND

Hilo Tsunami Museum, tel. 935-0926, is housed in the art deco-style First Hawaiian Bank building near the bayfront in Hilo. It's dedicated to those who lost their lives in the destructive tidal waves that hit and virtually destroyed the city in 1946 and 1960.

Hulihee Palace, a Victorian-style building in downtown Kailua-Kona, is one of two royal palaces in the state. Used by the Hawaiian monarchs until 1916, it now contains countless items owned and used by the royal families. It's a treasure house and well worth a look. Open Mon.-Fri. 9 a.m.-4 p.m. Admission is $5. Call 329-1877 for information.

Kamuela Museum, tel. 885-4724, is an eclectic private collection of Hawaiiana, upcountry *paniolo* life, Asian artifacts, and photos of the Parker family. Located west of downtown Waimea, it's open daily 8 a.m.-5 p.m.; $5 admission.

Kona Historical Society Museum, tel. 323-3222, near Captain Cook, is open Mon.-Fri. 8 a.m.-4 p.m. and Saturday 10 a.m.-2 p.m.; $2 admission. Housed in a native stone and lime mortar general store from 1875, this museum has a small collection of glassware and photographs. An archive of Kona-area historical items is housed in the basement and is open by appointment only.

Lyman House Memorial Museum was first opened in 1932. The main building is a New England-style frame structure from 1839, the oldest wood frame house on the island. It contains furniture and household goods from Rev. and Mrs. Lyman and other missionary families on the island. In an annex are a collection of Hawaiian artifacts and items of daily use in the Island Heritage Gallery and a very fine collection of rocks and minerals in the Earth Heritage Gallery. Located at 276 Haile St. in Hilo, tel. 935-5021, this museum is open Mon.-Sat. 9 a.m.-5 p.m. and Sunday 1-4 p.m.; $5 admission.

Onizuka Space Center, tel. 329-3441, is at the Kona International Airport. Its hours are 8:30 a.m.-4:30 p.m. daily except Thanksgiving, Christmas, and New Year's Day; $2 admission. This center is a memorial to Hawaii's first astronaut and a space education facility for adults and children. It includes interactive and static exhibits, models, audiovisual displays, and lots of reading material.

Parker Ranch Historic Homes are located a few miles outside Waimea and are open daily 10 a.m.-5 p.m.; $7.50 admission. Puuopelu, the ranch home of the Parker family, is a structure to be appreciated in and of itself, but it also houses artwork of world-prominent artists collected by Richard Smart, the last of the Parker line. Reconstucted nearby is Mana House, the original Parker ranch home from 1847.

Mainlanders who come to Hawaii and immediately strip down to as little clothing as possible.

Alohawear

At one time alohawear was made exclusively from cotton or from manmade, natural fiber-based rayon, and these materials are still the best for any tropical clothing. Beware, however: polyester has slowly crept into the market! No material could possibly be worse for the island climate, so when buying your alohawear make sure to check the label for material content. Muumuus now come in various styles and can be worn for the entire spectrum of social occasions in Hawaii. Aloha shirts are basically cut the same as always, but the patterns have undergone changes, and apart from the original flowers and ferns, modern shirts might depict an island scene in the manner of a silk-screen painting. A basic good-quality muumuu or aloha shirt is guaranteed to be worth its price in good times and happy smiles. The connoisseur might want to purchase *The Hawaiian Shirt, Its Art and History* by R. Thomas Steele. It's illustrated with more than 150 shirts that are now considered works of art by collectors the world over.

Woodcarvings

One surviving Hawaiian art is woodcarving. Old Hawaiians used koa almost exclusively because of its density, strength, and natural luster, but koa is becoming increasingly scarce—though many items are still available—and costly. Milo and monkeypod are also excellent woods for carving and have largely replaced koa. You can buy tikis, bowls, and furniture at numerous shops. Countless inexpensive carved items are sold at variety stores, such as hula dancers or salad

woven palm frond baskets and hats

J.D. BISIGNANI

servers, but most of these are imported from Asia or the Philippines and can be bought at any variety store.

Weaving

The minute you arrive in Hawaii, you should shell out $2 for a woven beach mat. This is a necessity, not a frivolous purchase, but it definitely won't have been made in Hawaii. What is made in Hawaii is *lau hala*. This is traditional Hawaiian weaving from the leaves *(lau)* of the pandanus *(hala)* tree. These leaves vary greatly in length, with the largest over six feet, and they have a thorny spine that must be removed before they can be worked. The color ranges from light tan to dark brown. The leaves are cut into strips one-eighth to one inch wide and are then employed in weaving. A great variety of items can be made or at least covered in *lau hala*. It makes great purses, mats, baskets, and table mats.

Woven into a hat, it's absolutely superb but should not be confused with a palm-frond hat. A *lau hala* hat is amazingly supple and even when squashed will pop back into shape. A good one is expensive ($25) and with proper care will last for years. All *lau hala* should be given a light application of mineral oil on a monthly basis, especially if it's exposed to the sun. For flat items, iron over a damp cloth and keep purses and baskets stuffed with paper when not in use. Palm fronds also are widely used in weaving. They,

too, are a great natural raw material, but not as good as *lau hala*. Almost any woven item, such as a beach bag woven from palm, makes a good authentic yet inexpensive gift or souvenir; a wide selection is available in countless shops.

Gift Items

Jewelry is always an appreciated gift, especially if it's distinctive, and Hawaii has some of the most original. The sea provides the basic raw materials of pink, gold, and black corals that are as beautiful and fascinating as gemstones. Harvesting coral is very dangerous work. The Lahaina beds off Maui have one of the best black coral lodes in the islands, but unlike reef coral, these trees grow at depths bordering the outer limits of a scuba diver's capabilities. Only the best can dive 180 feet after the black coral, and about one diver per year dies in pursuit of it. Conservationists have placed great pressure on the harvesters of these deep corals, and the state of Hawaii has placed strict limits and guidelines on the firms and divers involved.

Pink coral has long been treasured by humans. The Greeks considered it a talisman for good health, and there's even evidence that it has been coveted since the Stone Age. Coral jewelry is on sale at many shops throughout Hawaii. The value comes from the color of the coral and the workmanship.

Puka shells (with small, naturally occurring holes) and *opihi* shells are also made into jewelry. Many times these items are very inexpensive, yet they are authentic and are great purchases for the price. Hanging macrame planters festooned with seashells are usually quite affordable and are sold at roadside stands along with shells.

Hawaii produces some unique food items that are appreciated by most people. Various-sized jars of macadamia nuts and butters are great gifts, as are tins of rich, gourmet-quality Kona coffee, the only coffee produced in the U.S. Guava, pineapple, passion fruit, and mango are often gift-boxed into assortments of jams, jellies, and spicy chutneys. And for that special person in your life, you can bring home island fragrances in bottles of perfumes and colognes in the exotic odors of gardenia, plumeria, and even ginger. All of the above items are reasonably priced, lightweight, and easy to carry.

FESTIVALS, HOLIDAYS, AND EVENTS

In addition to all the American national holidays, Hawaii celebrates its own festivals, pageants, ethnic fairs, and a multitude of specialized exhibits. They occur throughout the year, some particular to only one island or locality, others, such as the Aloha Festivals and Lei Day, celebrated on all the islands. Check local newspapers and the free island magazines for dates. Some of the smaller local happenings are semi-spontaneous, so there's no *exact* date when they're held. These are some of the most rewarding, because they provide the best times to have fun with the local people.

The following events and celebrations are either particular to the Big Island, or they're celebrated here in a special way. Everyone is welcome to join in the fun, and most times the events are either free or nominally priced. There's no better way to enjoy yourself while vacationing than by joining in a local party or happening.

JANUARY

Thump in the New Year with a traditional Japanese **Mochi Pounding Festival** at Volcano Art Center, Volcanoes National Park.

The athletes gear up with the Big Island **Triathlon Invitational** held in late December or early January. This is a three-day event that ranges all over the island and includes an overnight stay at Volcanoes National Park. During **The Volcano Wilderness Marathon and Rim Runs** the truly energetic run 26 miles through the desolate Kau Desert, while a 10-mile race around the Caldera Crater Rim features over 1,000 participants.

FEBRUARY

Early February
February offers everything from the links to skiing at the **Mauna Kea Ski Meet** atop the Big Island's 13,000-foot volcano—weather and snow conditions dictate the exact time, which can vary from early January to March. Skiers from around the world compete in cup and cross-country skiing.

Mid- to Late February
Enjoy the authentic Western flavor of the **Great Waikoloa Horse Races and Rodeo** at Waikoloa Stables, Waikoloa. Major rodeo events draw skilled *paniolo* from around the islands.

The **Annual Keauhou-Kona Triathlon** at Keauhou Bay is open to athletes unable to enter the Ironman and to anyone in good health. Each of its three events is half as long as in the Ironman, and it allows relay-team racing for each grueling segment.

MARCH

Mid-March rumbles in with the **Kona Stampede** at Honaunau Arena, Honaunau, Kona. *Paniolo* provide plenty of action during the full range of rodeo events.

Mid-month features feminine beauty, grace, and athletic ability at the **Miss Aloha Hawaii Pageant** at Hilo Civic Auditorium, Hilo.

The end of March is dedicated to Prince Kuhio, a member of the royal family and Hawaii's first delegate to the U.S. Congress. **Prince**

Kuhio Day is a state holiday honoring the prince, held on March 26, his birthday.

APRIL

Wesak, or **Buddha Day,** is on the closest Sunday to April 8 and celebrates the birthday of Gautama Buddha. Ornate offerings of tropical flowers are placed at temple altars throughout Hawaii.

The **Paniolo Ski Meet** features exciting skiing atop the Big Island's Mauna Kea, conditions permitting.

The **Merrie Monarch Festival** in Hilo sways with the best hula dancers that the islands' *hula halau* have to offer. Gentle but stiff competition features hula in both its ancient *(kahiko)* and modern *(auana)* forms. The festival runs for a week on a variable schedule from year to year. It's immensely popular with islanders, so hotels, cars, and flights are booked solid. For information call the Hawaii Naniloa Hotel at 935-9168, or the HVB at 961-5797.

The **Kona Sports Festival,** Kailua-Kona, is a solid week of sports entertainment and frivolity held toward the end of the month.

MAY

May 1 is May Day to the communist world, but in Hawaii red is only one of the colors when everyone dons a lei for Lei Day. Festivities abound throughout Hawaii.

The **Captain Cook Festival** at Kailua-Kona offers Hawaiian games, music, and fishing.

Look skyward on May 5, **Japanese Boys' Day,** and you'll see paper carp (koi) flying from rooftops. Carp symbolize the virtues of strength and courage. The number of koi kites corresponds to the number of sons in the family, with the largest, highest koi for the eldest, and then down the line.

Filipino Fiesta is a month-long celebration of the islands' Filipino population. Food, various festivities, and a beauty contest are part of the fiesta.

Costumed riders from the annals of Hawaiian history ride again at **Hawaii on Horseback.** Horsemanship and a Western flair mark these days held in and around Waimea and the Parker Ranch on the Big Island.

Annual Western Week at Honokaa is a fun-filled week with a Western theme. It includes a cookout, parade, rodeo, and dance.

JUNE

King Kamehameha Day, June 11, is a state holiday honoring Kamehameha the Great, a Big Island native son, with festivities on all islands. Check local papers for times and particulars. Kailua-Kona is hospitable with a *ho'olaule'a* (large, festive party), parades, art demonstrations, entertainment, and contests.

The **Kamehameha Ski Meet** atop Mauna Kea takes place in early June, when bikini-clad contestants add a little extra spice on those bouncy moguls.

Hilo flashes its brilliant colors with the **Annual Hilo Orchid Society Show** at the Hilo Civic Auditorium, and the **Annual Big Island Bonsai Show,** Wailoa Center, Hilo (both sometimes scheduled for early July).

Bon Odori, the Japanese festival of departed souls, features dances and candle-lighting ceremonies held at numerous Buddhist temples throughout the island. These festivities change yearly and can be held anytime from late June to early August.

JULY

The week of the **Fourth of July** offers the all-American sport of rodeo along with parades. Don't miss the **July 4 Parker Ranch Rodeo and Horseraces,** Paniolo Park, Waimea. The epitome of rodeo by Hawaii's top cowboys is set at the Parker Ranch, the largest privately owned ranch in all of America, including Texas, pardner!

Annual Naalehu Rodeo, in Naalehu, includes rodeo events, motorcycle and dune buggy races, luau, food booths, and Hawaiian entertainment.

The **Big Island Marathon** in Hilo consists of full and half marathons starting and ending at the Hilo Hawaiian Hotel.

Four-person teams of one pro and three amateurs compete in the 54-hole **Mauna Kea Beach Hotel's Annual Pro-Am Golf Tournament** held at the hotel links along the Kohala Coast.

The **International Festival of the Pacific** in mid-July features a "Pageant of Nations" in Hilo. Folk dances, complete with authentic costumes from throughout Asia and the Pacific, add a rare excitement to the festivities.

The beauty and grace of one of Hawaii's ethnic groups is apparent at the **Miss Hawaii Filipina Pageant,** Hawaii Naniloa Hotel, Hilo.

The annual **Crater Rim Run and Marathon** is held over rough lava, in and out of volcanic craters, and through ohia and fern forests within the Hawaii Volcanoes National Park.

AUGUST

The first August weekend is **Establishment Day.** Traditional hula and lei workshops are presented at the Puukohala Heiau in Kawaihae, where traditional artifacts are also on display.

The **Pro-Am Billfish Tournament,** held in the waters off Kona, precedes and is a qualifying meet for the more famous **Annual Hawaiian International Billfish Tournament,** held about one week later. A world-renowned tournament and the Big Daddy of them all, the HIBT has been held every year since 1959. Contact organizer Peter Fithian, tel. 922-9708, for information.

The macadamia nut harvest is celebrated with sporting events, horse racing and a "Harvest Ball" at the **Macadamia Nut Harvest Festival,** Honokaa.

August 17 is **Admission Day,** a state holiday recognizing the day that Hawaii became a state.

Kailua-Kona hosts the annual **Queen Liliuokalani Long Distance Canoe Race** every Labor Day weekend. Single-hull, double-hull, and one-person events are held over a two-day period. For those who really like the sport, head up the coast to Kawaihae for the **Moikeha Hawaiian Sailing Canoe Race.**

SEPTEMBER

In early September don't miss the **Parker Ranch Round-Up Rodeo** at Paniolo Park in Waimea.

The **Million Dollar Golden Marlin Fishing Tournament** catches plenty of fishermen at Kailua-Kona.

The **Hawaii County Fair** at Hilo is an old-time fair held on the grounds of Hilo Civic Auditorium.

Aloha Festivals celebrates Hawaii's own "intangible quality," aloha. This two-month series of several dozen individual festivals includes parades, luau, athletic competitions, historical pageants, balls, and various entertainment. The spirit of *aloha* is infectious and all are welcome. Check local papers and tourist literature for happenings near you.

OCTOBER

When they really "wanna have fun," super-athletes come to the **Ironman World Triathlon Championship** at Kailua-Kona. A 2.4-mile open-ocean swim, followed by a 112-mile bike ride and topped off with a full marathon, is their idea of a good day. Ironman Office, tel. 329-0063.

NOVEMBER

Taste the best and only coffee commercially grown in the U.S. at the **Annual Kona Coffee Cultural Festival** in Kailua-Kona. Parades, arts and crafts, plus ethnic foods and entertainment are part of the festivities.

The **Annual King Kalakaua Keiki Hula Festival** is for children from around the state who come to Kailua-Kona to perform their hula. Plenty of fun, but the competition is serious.

November 11, **Veterans Day,** is a national holiday celebrated by parades.

Christmas in the Country, atop Hawaii's volcano, is a delight. Merrymakers frolic in the crisp air or relax around a blazing fire, drinking hot toddys. Also, plenty of arts and crafts, food, and Santa for the *keiki.* Contact the Volcano Art Center, Hawaii Volcanoes National Park, tel. 967-8222.

DECEMBER

The **Hamakua Music Festival,** held around the first week of December in Honokaa, lasts for four days and attracts island musicians proficient in everything from Hawaiian to jazz.

Christmas Fantasyland of Trees at Honokaa is an early showing of gaily decorated trees. The right Christmas spirit auctions them off for charity.

The people of Hilo celebrate a New England Christmas in memory of the missionaries with **A**

Christmas Tradition. Held at the Lyman House Memorial Museum, Hilo, tel. 935-5021.

Bodhi Day is ushered in with ceremonies at Buddhist temples to commemorate Buddha's day of enlightenment.

At the **Mauna Kea Beach Hotel's Annual Invitational Golf Tournament,** men and women play at this fabulous golf course on the Kohala Coast.

On **New Year's Eve** hold onto your hat, because they do it up big in Hawaii. The merriment and alcohol flow all over the islands. Firecrackers are illegal, but they go off everywhere. Beware of hangovers and "amateur" drunken drivers.

ACCOMMODATIONS

Finding suitable accommodations on the Big Island is never a problem. The 9,500-plus rooms available at the island's 170 properties have the lowest annual occupancy rate of any in the islands at only 60%. Except for the height of the high seasons and during the Merrie Monarch Festival in Hilo, you can count on finding a room at a bargain. The highest concentration of rooms is strung along Ali'i Dr. in Kailua-Kona—over 5,000 in condos, apartment hotels, and standard hotels. Hilo has almost 2,000 rooms; many of its hotels have "gone condo," and you can get some great deals. The rest are scattered around the island in small villages from Naalehu in the south to Hawi in the north, where you can almost count on being the only off-island guest. You can comfortably stay in the cowboy town of Waimea, or perch above Kilauea Crater at one of the oldest hotel sites in the islands. There are bed and breakfasts, and the camping is superb, with a campsite almost guaranteed at any time.

The Range

The Big Island has a tremendous range of accommodations. A concentration of the world's greatest luxury resorts are within minutes of each other on the Kohala coast: The Mauna Kea, Hapuna, Mauna Lani, Royal Waikoloa, and Kona Village. The Mauna Kea, built by Laurence Rockefeller, has everything the name implies. The others are just as superb, with hideaway "grass shacks," exquisite art collections as an integral part of the grounds, world-ranked golf courses, and perfect crescent beaches.

Kona has fine hotels like the King Kamehameha's Kona Beach Hotel and Royal Kona Resort in downtown Kailua. Just south towards Keauhou is a string of reasonably priced yet luxurious hotels like the Keauhou Beach Hotel. Interspersed among the big hotels are smaller hotels and condominiums with homey atmospheres and great rates. Hilo offers the best accommodations bargains. Luxury hotels such as the Hilo Hawaiian and Naniloa are priced like mid-range hotels on the other islands. There are also semi-fleabags in town that pass the basic cleanliness test, along with gems like the Dolphin Bay Hotel that gives you so much for your money it's embarrassing. And for a real treat, head to Hawaii Volcanoes National Park and stay at one of the bed and breakfasts tucked away there, or at Volcano House where raw nature has thrilled kings, queens, and luminaries like humorist Mark Twain for over a century.

If you want to get away from everybody else, it's no problem, and you don't have to be rich to do it. Pass-through towns like Captain Cook and Waimea have accommodations at very reasonable prices. You can try a self-growth retreat in Puna at Kalani Honua Oceanside Eco-resort or at the Wood Valley Buddhist Temple above Pahala. Want ultimate seclusion? Head down to Tom Araki's Hotel in Waipio Valley.

HOTELS

Hotels come in all shapes and sizes, from 10-room, family-run affairs to high-rise giants. A recent trend has turned some into condominiums. The Neighbor Islands have learned an aesthetic lesson from Waikiki, however, and build low-rise resorts that don't obstruct the view and blend more readily with the surroundings. Every year more hotels are built and older ones renovated.

Types of Hotel Rooms

Most readily available and least expensive is a bedroom with bath, the latter sometimes shared in the more inexpensive hotels. Some hotels can also offer you a studio, a large sitting room that converts to a bedroom; a suite, a bedroom with

KONA HILTON BEACH AND TENNIS RESORT

Royal Kona Resort

sitting room; or an apartment with full kitchen plus at least one bedroom. Kitchenettes are often available and contain a refrigerator, sink, and stove usually in a small corner nook or fitted together as one space-saving unit. Kitchenettes cost a bit more but save you a bundle by allowing you to prepare some of your own meals. To get that vacation feeling while keeping costs down, eat breakfast in, pack a lunch for the day, and go out to dinner. If you rent a kitchenette, make sure all the appliances work as soon as you arrive. If they don't, notify the front desk immediately, and if the hotel will not rectify the situation, ask to be moved or ask for a reduced rate. Hawaii has cockroaches, so put all food away.

Amenities

All hotels have some of them, and some hotels have all of them. Air-conditioning is available in most, but under normal circumstances you won't need it. Balmy trade winds provide plenty of breezes, which flow through louvered windows and doors in many hotels. Casablanca room fans are better. TVs are often included in the rate, but not always. In-room phones are provided, but a service charge is usually tacked on, even for local calls. Swimming pools are very common, even though the hotel may sit right on the beach. There is always a restaurant of some sort, a coffee shop or two, a bar, a cocktail lounge, and sometimes a sundries shop. Some hotels also offer tennis courts or golf courses either as part of the premises or affiliated with the hotel; usually an "activities desk" can book you

into a variety of daily outings. Plenty of hotels offer laundromats on the premises, and hotel towels can be used at the beach. Bellhops get about $1 per bag, and maid service is free, though maids are customarily tipped $1-2 per day and a bit more if kitchenettes are involved. Parking is free. Hotels can often arrange special services like baby-sitters, all kinds of lessons, and special entertainment activities. A few even have bicycles and snorkeling equipment to lend. They'll receive and send mail for you, cash your traveler's checks, and take messages.

Hotel Rates: Add 10% Room Tax

Every year Hawaiian hotels welcome in the New Year by hiking their rates by about 10%. A room that was $90 this year will be $99 next year, and so on. Hawaii, because of its gigantic tourist flow and tough competition, offers hotel rooms at universally lower rates than those at most developed resort areas around the world; so, even with the 10% room tax (6% transient accommodations tax, plus 4% state excise tax), there are still many reasonable rates to be had. Package deals, especially to Waikiki, almost throw in a week's lodging for the price of an air ticket. The basic **daily rate** is geared toward double occupancy; singles are hit in the pocketbook. Single rates are cheaper than doubles, but never as low as half the double rate; the most you get off is 40%. **Weekly and monthly** rates will save you approximately 10% off the daily rate. Make sure to ask because this information won't be volunteered. Many hotels will charge for a double and then add an additional charge ($3-25) for extra persons. Some hotels—not always the budget ones—let you cram in as many as can sleep on the floor with no additional charge, so again, ask. Others have a policy of **minimum stay**, usually three days, but their rates can be cheaper, and **business/corporate rates** are usually offered to anyone who can at least produce a business card. Senior citizens are sometimes offered special discount rates of 10-20%. This information will usually not be offered so you must inquire.

Hawaii's **peak season** runs from just before Christmas until after Easter, and then again in early summer. Rooms are at a premium, and peak-season rates are an extra 10% above the normal daily rate. Oftentimes they'll also suspend weekly and monthly rates during peak season. The **off-peak** season is late summer and fall, when rooms are easy to come by and most hotels offer off-peak rates. Subtract about 10% from the normal rate.

In Hawaiian hotels you always pay more for a good view. Terms vary slightly, but usually "oceanfront" means that your room faces the ocean and your view is mostly unimpeded. "Ocean view" is slightly more vague. It could be a decent view, or it could require standing on the dresser and craning your neck to catch a tiny slice of the sea sandwiched between two skyscrapers. Rooms are also designated and priced upward as **standard, superior,** and **deluxe.** As you go up, this could mean larger rooms with more amenities or can merely signify a better view.

Plenty of hotels offer the **family plan,** which allows children under a certain age to stay in their parents' room free, if they use the existing bedding. If another bed or crib is required, there is an additional charge. Only a limited number of hotels offer the **American plan,** where breakfast and dinner are included with the night's lodging. In many hotels, you're provided with a refrigerator and a heating unit for coffee and tea at no extra charge.

Paying, Deposits, and Reservations

The vast majority of Hawaiian hotels accept foreign and domestic traveler's checks, personal checks preapproved by the management, foreign cash, and most major credit cards. Reservations are always the best policy, and they're easily made through travel agents or directly

by contacting the hotel. In all cases, bring documentation of your confirmed reservations with you in case of a mix-up.

Deposits are not always required to make reservations, but they do secure them. Some hotels require the first night's payment in advance. Reservations without a deposit can be legally released if the room is not claimed by 6 p.m. Remember too that letters "requesting reservations" are not the same as "confirmed reservations." In letters, include your dates of stay, type of room you want, and price. Once the hotel answers your letter, *confirm* your reservations with a phone call or follow-up letter and make sure that the hotel sends you a copy of the confirmation. All hotels and resorts have **cancellation requirements** for refunding deposits. The time limit on these can be as little as 24 hours before arrival, to a full 30 days. Some hotels require full **advance payment** for your length of stay, especially during peak season or during times of crowded special events such as the Merrie Monarch Festival in Hilo. Be aware of the time required for a cancellation notice *before* making your reservation deposit, especially when dealing with advance payment. If you have confirmed reservations, especially with a deposit, and there is no room for you, or one that doesn't meet prearranged requirements, you should be given the option of accepting alternate accommodations. You are owed the difference in room rates if there is any. If there is no room whatsoever, the hotel is required to find you one at a comparable hotel and to refund your deposit in full.

CONDOMINIUMS

The main qualitative difference between a condo and a hotel is in amenities. At a condo, you're more on your own. You're temporarily renting an apartment, so there won't be any bellhops and rarely a bar, restaurant, or lounge on the premises, though many times you'll find a sundries store. The main lobby, instead of having that grand-entrance feel of many hotels, is more like an apartment-house entrance, although there might be a front desk. Condos can be efficiencies (one big room), but mostly they are one- or multiple-bedroom affairs with a complete kitchen. Reasonable housekeeping items should be provided: linens, all furniture, and a fully equipped kitchen. Most have TVs and phones, but remember that the furnishings provided are up to the owner. You can find brand-new furnishings that are top of the line, right down to "garage sale" bargains. Inquire about the furnishings when you make your reservations. Maid service might be included on a limited basis (for example, once weekly), or you might have to pay extra for it.

Condos usually require a minimum stay, although some will rent on a daily basis, like hotels. Minimum stays when applicable are often three days, but seven is also commonplace, and during peak season, two weeks isn't unheard of. Swimming pools are common, and depending on the "theme" of the condo, you can find saunas, weight rooms, jacuzzis, and tennis courts. Rates are about 10-15% higher than at comparable hotels, with hardly any difference between doubles and singles. A nominal extra fee is charged for more than two people; condos can normally accommodate four to six guests. You can find clean, decent condos for as little as $200 per week, all the way up to exclusive apartments for well over $1500. The method of paying for and reserving a condo is just about the same as for a hotel. However, requirements for deposits, final payments, and cancellation charges are much stiffer than in hotels. Make absolutely sure you fully understand all of these requirements when you make your reservations.

Their real advantage is for families, friends who want to share, and especially long-term stays, for which you will always get a special rate. The kitchen facilities save a great deal on dining costs, and it's common to find units with their own mini-washers and dryers. Parking space is ample for guests, and like hotels, plenty of stay/drive deals are offered.

Hotel/Condominium Information
The best source of hotel/condo information is the **Hawaii Visitors Bureau.** While planning your trip, either visit one nearby or write to them in Hawaii. (Addresses are given in the "Information and Services" section later in this chapter.) Request a copy of their (free) current *Member Accommodation Guide.* This handy booklet lists all the hotel/condo members of the HVB, with addresses, phone numbers, facilities, and rates. General tips are also given.

Hotel/Condo Booking and Reservations
The following is a partial list of booking agents handling a number of properties on the Big Island. **Aston Hotels and Resorts,** 2250 Kuhio Ave., Honolulu, HI 96815, tel. 931-1400 or (800) 922-7886 Mainland, (800) 445-6633 Canada, or (800) 321-2558 in Hawaii.

Go Condo Hawaii, tel. (800) 452-3463 (Web site: www.gocondohawaii.com).

Hawaii Resort Management, 75-5776 Kuakini Hwy., Suite 105C, Kailua-Kona, HI 96740, tel. 329-9393, fax 326-4136.

Homes and Villas in Paradise, 116 Hekili St., Suite 201, Kailua, HI 96734, tel. (808) 262-4663 or (800) 282-2736 (Web site: planet-hawaii.com/homes-villas).

Keahou Property Management, 76-6225 Kuakini Hwy., Suite C105, Kailua-Kona, HI 96740, tel. 326-9075 or (800) 745-5662, fax 326-2055,

Marc Resorts Hawaii, 2155 Kalakaua Ave., Honolulu, HI 96815, tel. 926-5900 or (800) 535-0085.

SunQuest Vacations, 77-6435 Kuakini Hwy., Kailua-Kona, HI 96740, tel. 329-6488, (800) 367-5168 Mainland, or (800) 800-5662 Canada.

BED AND BREAKFASTS

Bed-and-breakfast (B&B) inns are hardly a new idea. The Bible talks of the hospitable hosts who opened the gates of their homes and invited the wayfarer in to spend the night. B&Bs have a long tradition in Europe and were commonplace in Revolutionary America. Nowadays, lodging in private homes called bed and breakfast homes is becoming increasingly fashionable throughout America, and Hawaii is no exception with about 100,000 B&B guests yearly. Not only can you visit the Big Island, you can "live" there for a time with a host family and share an intimate experience of daily life.

Points to Consider
The primary feature of bed-and-breakfast homes is that every one is privately owned and therefore uniquely different from every other. The range of B&Bs is as wide as the living standards in America. You'll find everything from a semi-mansion in the most fashionable residential area to a little grass shack offered by a down-home fisherman and his family. This means that it's particularly im-

portant for the guest to choose a host family with whom his or her lifestyle is compatible.

Unlike at a hotel or a condo, you'll be living *with* a host (usually a family), although your room will be private, with private baths and separate entrances being quite common. You can make arrangements directly or you might want to go through an agency (listed below) which acts as a go-between, matching host and guest. Write to them and they'll send you a booklet with a complete description of the B&B, its general location, the fees charged, and a good idea of the lifestyle of your host family. With the reservations application they'll include a questionnaire that will basically determine your profile: Are you single? Do you have children? Smoker? etc., as well as arrival and departure dates and all pertinent particulars.

Since B&Bs are run by individual families, the times that they will accept guests can vary according to what's happening in their lives. This makes it imperative to write well in advance: three months is good; earlier is too long and too many things can change. Four weeks is about the minimum time required to make all necessary arrangements. Expect a minimum stay (three days is common) and a maximum stay. B&Bs are not long-term housing, although it's hoped that guest and host will develop a friendship and that future stays can be as long as both desire.

B&B Agencies

A top-notch B&B agency with over 150 homes is **Bed and Breakfast Hawaii,** operated by Evelyn Warner and Al Davis. They've been running this service since 1978, and their reputation is excellent. B&B Hawaii has a membership fee of $10 yearly. For this they mail you their "Directory of Homes," a periodic "hot sheet" of new listings, and all pertinent guest applications; add $1 handling. Write Bed and Breakfast Hawaii, P.O. Box 449, Kapaa, HI 96746, tel. 822-7771 or (800) 733-1632. (E-Mail: bandb@aloha.net; Web site: planet-hawaii.com/bandb.)

Operating strictly for establishments on the Big Island is **Hawaii Island Bed and Breakfast Association.** For information about their member accommodations write HIBBA, P.O. Box 1890, Honokaa, HI 96727, or E-mail: hibba@aloha.net. Their Web site, www.stayhawaii.com, lists member accommodations with addresses, telephone and fax numbers, E-mail and Web site addresses, rates, and descriptions. It's a local organization. They know their business so give them a try.

One of the most experienced agencies, **Bed And Breakfast Honolulu Statewide,** at 3242 Kaohinanai Dr., Honolulu, HI 96817, tel. 595-7533, 595-2030, or (800) 288-4666, owned and operated by Marylee and Gene Bridges, began in 1982. Since then, they've become masters at finding visitors the perfect accommodations to match their desires, needs, and pocketbooks. Their repertoire of guest homes offers more than 350 rooms, with half on Oahu and the other half scattered around the state. When you phone, they'll match your needs to their computerized in-house guidelines. (E-mail: bnbshi@aloha.net; Web site: planet-hawaii.com/bnb-honolulu.)

Other well-known agencies include the following:

Go Native Hawaii will send you a directory and all needed information if you write to them at 65 Halaulani Pl., P.O. Box 11418, Hilo, HI 96721, tel. 935-4178 or (800) 662-8483.

All Island Bed and Breakfast, 463 Iliwahi Loop, Kailua, HI 96734, tel. 263-2342 or (800) 542-0344, can match your needs up with about 700 homes throughout the state. (E-mail: cac@aloha.net; Web site: planet-hawaii.com/all-island.)

Run by Susan Campbell, **Hawaii's Best Bed and Breakfast,** P.O. Box 563, Kamuela, HI 96743, tel. 885-4550 or (800) 262-9912, fax 885-0559, is a smaller business but has listings all over the state. (E-mail: bestbnb@aloha.net; Web site: www.bestbnb.com.)

Volcano Reservations, owned and operated by Brian and Lisha Crawford, P.O. Box 998, Volcano Village, HI 96785, tel. 967-7786, (800) 937-7786, is an agency specializing in the Volcano area, but with rentals available throughout the state.

Hawaiian Islands Vacation Rentals, 1277 Mokulua Dr., Kailua, HI 96734, tel. 261-7895 or (800) 258-7895, is owned and operated by Rick Maxey, who can arrange stays on all islands and help with interisland flights and car rental.

Babson's Vacation Rentals and Reservation Service, 3371 Keha Dr., Kihei, Maui, HI 96753, tel. 874-1166 or (800) 824-6409, is owned and operated by Ann and Bob Babson, a delightful couple who will try hard to match your stay with your budget.

Agencies specializing in beachfront villas, luxury condominiums, and exclusive estates are **Villas of Hawaii,** 4218 Waialae Ave., Suite 203, Honolulu, HI 96816, tel. 735-9000; and **Vacation Locations Hawaii,** P.O. Box 1689, Kihei, HI 96753, tel. 874-0077.

HOSTELS

The Big Island has three very reasonably priced hostels operating at this time. **Arnott's Lodge,** 98 Apapane Rd., Hilo, HI 96720, tel. 969-7097, (800) 368-8752 Mainland, (800) 953-7773 Hawaii, offers a dormitory bunk for $17, and semiprivate rooms with a shared bath, kitchen, and living room for $30 s, $40 d. Arnott's also offers inexpensive hiking and snorkeling excursions.

Patey's Place, 75-5731 Ala Hou St., Kailua-Kona, HI 96740, tel. 326-7018, will set you up in a bunk for $15, a private room for $35, or a room with bath and kitchen for $45.

The **Hotel Honokaa Club,** tel. 775-0678, P.O. Box 247, Honokaa, HI 96727, has three

private ($20) and two communal ($15) rooms in its basement level. All rooms share a bath and kitchen facilities, and upstairs is a dining room.

HOME EXCHANGES

One other method of staying in Hawaii, open to homeowners, is to offer the use of your home for use of a home in Hawaii. This is done by listing your home with an agency that facilitates the exchange and publishes a descriptive directory. To list your home and to find out what is available, contact one of the following agencies:

Vacation Exchange Club (Affiliate of Homelink, Int'l), P.O. Box 650, Key West, FL 33041, tel./fax (305) 294-1448 or (800) 638-3841.

Intervac U.S., P.O. Box 590504, San Francisco, CA 04159, tel. (415) 535-3497, fax (415) 435-7440.

Worldwide Home Exchange Club, 806 Brantford Ave., Silver Spring, MD 20904, tel. (301) 680-8950.

FOOD AND DRINK

Hawaii is a gastronome's Shangri-La, a sumptuous smorgasbord in every sense of the word. The varied ethnic groups that have come to Hawaii in the last 200 years have each brought their own special enthusiasm and culture—and lucky for all, they didn't forget their cook pots, hearty appetites, and exotic taste buds. The Polynesians who first arrived found a fertile but barren land. Immediately they set about growing taro, coconuts, and bananas, and raising chickens, pigs, fish, and even dogs, though consumption of the latter was reserved for the nobility. The harvests were bountiful and the islanders thanked the gods with the traditional feast called the luau. The underground oven, the *imu,* baked most of the food. Participants were encouraged to feast while relaxing on straw mats and enjoying the hula and various entertainments. The luau is as popular as ever and is a treat that's guaranteed to delight anyone with a sense of eating adventure.

The missionaries and sailors came next; their ships' holds carried barrels of ingredients for the puddings, pies, dumplings, gravies, and roasts—the sustaining "American foods" of New England

farms. The mid-1800s saw the arrival of boatloads of Chinese and Japanese peasants, who wasted no time making rice instead of bread the staple of the islands. The Chinese added their exotic spices, cooking complex Sichuan dishes as well as workers' basics like chop suey. The Japanese introduced *shoyu* (soy sauce), sashimi, *bento* boxed lunches, delicate tempura, and rich, filling noodle soups. The Portuguese brought their luscious Mediterranean dishes of tomatoes, peppers and plump, spicy sausages; nutritious bean soups; and mouth-watering sweet treats like *malasadas* (holeless donuts) and *pao dolce* (sweet bread). Koreans carried crocks of zesty kimchi and quickly fired up grills for *pulgogi,* a grilled, marinated beef. Filipinos served up their delicious *adobo* stews—fish, meat, or chicken in a rich sauce of vinegar and garlic.

Recently, Thai and Vietnamese restaurants have been offering their irresistible dishes next door to restaurants serving fiery burritos from Mexico and elegant Marsala cream sauces from France. The ocean breezes of Hawaii not only cool the skin but waft with them some of the

*Hawaiian family
eating poi*

A. PLUM, CIRCA 1846 (HAWAII STATE ARCHIVES)

most delectable aromas on earth, making the taste buds tingle and the spirit soar.

HAWAIIAN CUISINE

Hawaiian cuisine, the oldest in the islands, consists of wholesome, well-prepared, and delicious foods. All you have to do on arrival is notice the size of some of the local boys (and women) to know immediately that food to them is indeed a happy and serious business. An oft-heard island joke is that "local men don't eat until they're full; they eat until they're tired." Many Hawaiian dishes have become standard fare at a variety of restaurants, eaten at one time or another by anyone who spends time in the islands. Hawaiian food in general is called *kaukau;* cooked food is *kapahaki,* and something broiled is called *kaola.* Any of these prefixes on a menu will let you know that Hawaiian food is served. Usually inexpensive, it will definitely fill you and keep you going.

Traditional Favorites
In old Hawaii, although the sea meant life, many more people were involved in cultivating beautifully tended garden plots of taro, sugarcane, breadfruit, and various sweet potatoes *(uala)* than with fishing. They husbanded pigs and barkless dogs *(ilio),* and prized *moa* (chicken) for their feathers and meat, but found eating the eggs repulsive. Their only farming implement

was the *o'o,* a sharpened hardwood digging stick. The Hawaiians were the best farmers of Polynesia, and the first thing they planted was taro, a tuberous root that was created by the gods at the same time as humans. This main staple of the old Hawaiians was made into poi. Every luau will have poi, a glutinous purple paste made from pounded taro root. It comes in liquid consistencies referred to as one-, two-, or three-finger poi. The fewer fingers you need to eat it, the thicker it is. Poi is one of the most nutritious carbohydrates known, but people unaccustomed to it find it bland and tasteless. Some of the best, fermented for a day or so, has an acidic bite. Poi is made to be eaten *with* something, but locals who love it pop it in their mouths and smack their lips. Those unaccustomed to it will suffer constipation if they eat too much.

A favorite popular dessert is *haupia,* a custard made from coconut. *Limu* is a generic term for edible seaweed, which many people still gather from the shoreline and eat as a salad, or mix with ground *kukui* nuts and salt as a relish. A favorite Hawaiian snack is *opihi,* small shellfish (limpets) that cling to rocks. Those who gather them always leave some on the rocks for the future. Cut from the shell and eaten raw by all peoples of Hawaii, *opihi* sell for $150 per gallon in Honolulu—a testament to their popularity. A general term that has come to mean hors d'oeuvres in Hawaii is *pu pu.* Originally the name of a small shellfish, it is now used for any finger food. A traditional liquor made from ti root is *okolehao.*

It literally means "iron bottom," reminiscent of the iron blubber pots used to ferment it.

Pacific Rim Specialties
(a.k.a. "Hawaiian Regional") Cuisine

At one time the "tourist food" in Hawaii was woeful. Of course, there has always been a handful of fine restaurants, but for the most part the food lacked soul, with even the fine hotels opting to offer second-rate renditions of food more appropriate to large Mainland cities. Surrounded by some of the most fertile and pristine waters in the Pacific, you could hardly find a restaurant offering fresh fish, and it was an ill-conceived boast that even the fruits and vegetables lying limply on your table were "imported." Beginning with a handful of extremely creative and visionary chefs in the early 1980s, who took the chance of perhaps offending the perceived simple palates of visitors, a delightfully delicious new cuisine was born. Based upon the finest traditions of continental cuisine—including, to a high degree, its sauces, pastas, and presentations—the culinary magic of Pacific Rim boldly adds the pungent spices of Asia, the fantastic fresh vegetables, fruits, and fish of Hawaii, and, at times, the earthy cooking methods of the Southwest. The result is a cuisine of fantastic tastes, subtle yet robust, and satiating but health-conscious—the perfect marriage of fresh foods prepared in a fresh way. Now restaurants on every island proudly display menus labeled "Hawaiian Regional." As always, some are better than others, but the general result is that the "tourist food" has been vastly improved and everyone benefits. Many of these exemplary chefs left lucrative and prestigious positions at many of Hawaii's five-diamond hotels and opened signature restaurants of their own, making this fine food much more available and affordable.

Luau

Following is a list of the luau presently available on the Big Island. For full descriptions, including prices, menus, and times, see the listings in the appropriate district chapters.

Tihati's Drums of Polynesia Luau at the Royal Kona Resort, tel. 329-3111.

Royal Luau at the Royal Waikoloan Hotel, tel. 885-6789.

Island Breeze Luau at King Kamehameha's Kona Beach Hotel, tel. 326-4969.

Hale Ho'okipa—Friday Night Luau at Kona Village Resort, tel. 325-5555.

Old Hawaiian Aha'aina Luau at the Mauna Kea Beach Hotel, tel. 822-7222.

Kamehameha Court Luau at Hilton Waikoloa Village, tel. 885-1234.

TROPICAL FRUITS AND VEGETABLES

Some of the most memorable taste treats from the islands require no cooking at all: the luscious tropical and exotic fruits and vegetables sold in markets and roadside stands or just found hanging on trees, waiting to be picked. Make sure to experience as many as possible. The general rule in Hawaii is that you are allowed to pick fruit on public lands, but the amount should be limited to personal consumption. The following is a sampling of some of Hawaii's best produce.

Bananas

No tropical island is complete without them. There are over 70 species in Hawaii, with hundreds of variations. Some are for peeling and eating while others are cooked. A "hand" of bananas is great for munching, backpacking, or picnicking. Available everywhere—and cheap.

Avocados

Brought from South America, avocados were originally cultivated by the Aztecs. They have

common banana

DIANA LASICH HARPER

a buttery consistency and nutty flavor. Hundreds of varieties in all shapes and colors are available fresh year-round. They have the highest fat content of any fruit next to the olive.

Coconuts

What tropical paradise would be complete without coconuts? Indeed, these were some of the first plants brought by the Polynesians. When a child was born, a coconut tree was planted to provide fruit for the child throughout his or her lifetime. Truly tropical fruits, coconuts know no season. Drinking nuts are large and green, and when shaken you can hear the milk inside. You get about a quart of fluid from each. It takes

The coconut was very important to the Hawaiians and every part was utilized. A tree was planted when a child was born as a prayer for a good food supply throughout life. The trunks were used for building homes and heiau and carved into drums to accompany hula. The husks became bowls, utensils, and even jewelry. 'Aha, sennit rope braided from the husk fiber, was renowned as the most saltwater-resistant natural rope ever made.

DIANA LASICH HARPER

skill to open one, but a machete can handle anything. Cut the stem end flat so that it will stand, then bore a hole into the pointed end and put in a straw or hollow bamboo. Coconut water is slightly acidic and helps balance alkaline foods. Spoon meat is a custardlike gel on the inside of drinking nuts. Sprouted coconut meat is also an excellent food. Split open a sprouted nut, and inside is the yellow fruit, like a moist sponge cake. "Millionaire's salad" is made from the heart of a coconut palm. At one time an entire tree was cut down to get to the heart, which is just inside the trunk below the fronds and is like an artichoke heart except that it's about the size of a watermelon. In a downed tree, the heart stays good for about two weeks.

Breadfruit

This island staple provides a great deal of carbohydrates, but many people find the baked, boiled, or fried fruit bland. It grows all over the islands and is really thousands of little fruits growing together to form a ball.

Mangos

These are some of the most delicious fruits known to humans. They grow wild all over the islands; the ones on the leeward sides of the islands ripen April-June, while the ones on the windward sides can last until October. They're found in the wild on trees up to 60 feet tall. The problem is to stop eating them once you start!

Papayas

This truly tropical fruit has no real season but is mostly available in the summer. Papayas grow on branchless trees and are ready to pick as soon as any yellow appears. Of the many varieties, the "solo papaya," meant to be eaten by one person, is the best. Split them in half, scrape out the seeds and have at them with a spoon.

Passion Fruit

Known by their island name of lilikoi, passion fruit make excellent juice and pies. The small yellow fruit (similar to lemons but smooth-skinned) is mostly available in summer and fall. Many grow wild on vines, waiting to be picked. Slice off the stem end, scoop the seedy pulp out with your tongue, and you'll know why they're called "passion fruit."

Guavas

These small, round, yellow fruits are abundant in the wild, where they ripen from early summer to late fall. They're considered a pest—so pick all you want. A good source of vitamin C, they're great for juice, jellies, and desserts.

Macadamia Nuts

The king of nuts was brought from Australia in 1892. Now it's the state's fourth-largest agricultural product. Available roasted, candied, or buttered.

Litchis

Called nuts but really small fruit with thin red shells, litchis have sweet, juicy white flesh when fresh and appear nutlike when dried.

breadfruit

Potpourri

Along with the above, you'll find pineapples, oranges, limes, kumquats, thimbleberries, and blackberries in Hawaii, as well as carambolas, wild cherry tomatoes, and tamarinds.

FISH AND SEAFOOD

Anyone who loves fresh fish and seafood has come to the right place. Island restaurants specialize in seafood, and it's available everywhere. Pound for pound, seafood is one of the best dining bargains on the Big Island. You'll find it served in every kind of restaurant, and often the fresh catch-of-the-day is proudly displayed on ice in a glass case. The following is a sampling of the best.

Mahimahi

This excellent eating fish is one of the most common and least expensive in Hawaii. It's referred to as "dolphin" but is definitely a fish, not a mammal. Mahimahi can weigh 10-65 pounds; the flesh is light and moist. This fish is broadest at the head. When caught it's a dark olive color, but after a while the skin turns iridescent shades of blue, green, and yellow. It can be served as a main course or as a patty in a fish sandwich.

DIANA LASICH HARPER

A'u

This true island delicacy is a broadbill swordfish or marlin. It's expensive even in Hawaii because the damn thing's so hard to catch. The meat is moist and white and truly superb. If it's offered on the menu, order it. It'll cost a bit more, but you won't be disappointed.

Ono

Ono means "delicious" in Hawaiian, so that should tip you off to the taste of this wahoo, or king mackerel. *Ono* is regarded as one of the finest eating fishes in the ocean, and its flaky white meat lives up to its name.

Manini

These five-inch fish are some of the most abundant in Hawaii and live in about 10 feet of water. They school and won't bite a hook but are easily taken with spear or net. Not often on menus, they're favorites with local people, who know best.

Ulua

This member of the crevalle jack family ranges 15-100 pounds. Its flesh is white and has a steaklike texture. Delicious and often found on the menu.

Uku

This gray snapper is a favorite with local people. The meat is light and firm and grills well.

Ahi

A yellowfin tuna with distinctive pinkish meat, *ahi* is a great favorite cooked or served raw in sushi bars.

Moi

This is the Hawaiian word for "king." The fish has large eyes and a sharklike head. Considered one of the finest eating fishes in Hawaii, it's best during the autumn months.

Seafood Potpourri

Other island seafood found on menus include *opihi*, a small shellfish (limpet) that clings to rocks and is considered one of the best island delicacies, eaten raw; *aloalo*, similar to tiny lobsters; crawfish, plentiful in taro fields and irrigation ditch-

HAWAIIAN GAME FISH

mahimahi

ahi

ulua

uku

ono

a'u

LOUISE FOOTE/DIANA LASICH HARPER

es; *ahipalaka*, albacore tuna; various octopuses and squids (calamari); and shark of various types.

A'ama are the ubiquitous little black crabs that you'll spot on rocks and around pier areas. They're everywhere. For fun, local fishermen will try to catch them with poles, but the more efficient way is to throw a fish head into a plastic bucket and wait for the crabs to crawl in and trap themselves. The *a'ama* are about as big as two fingers and make delicious eating.

Limu is edible seaweed that has been gathered as a garnish since pre-contact times and is frequently found on traditional island menus. There's no other seaweed except *limu* in Hawaii. Because of this, the heavy, fishy-ocean smell that people associate with the sea but which is actually that of seaweed is absent in Hawaii.

UNIQUE ISLAND DRINKS

To complement the fine dining in the islands, bartenders have been busy creating their own tasty concoctions. The standard range of beers, wines, and well drinks is served in Hawaii, but for a real treat you should try mixed drinks inspired by the islands. Most look very innocent because they come in pineapples, coconut shells, or tall frosted glasses. They're often garnished with little umbrellas or sparklers, and most have enough fruit in them to give you your vitamins for the day. Rum is used as the basis of many of them; it's been an island favorite since it was introduced by the whalers of last century. Here are some of the most famous: Mai Tai, a mixture of light and dark rum, orange curaçao, orange and almond flavoring, and lemon juice; Chi chi, a simple concoction of vodka, pineapple juice, and coconut syrup—a real sleeper because it tastes like a milk shake; Blue Hawaii, vodka and blue curaçao; Planter's Punch, light rum, grenadine, bitters, and lemon juice—a great thirst quencher; and Singapore Sling, a sparkling mixture of gin and brandy with cherry and lemon juice.

Local Brews

Khalsa and Cameron Healy, a father-and-son team known to their friends and family as "Pops" and "Spoon," are the owners and hands-on brewmasters at **Kona Brewing Company**, 75-5629 Kuakini Hwy., Kailua-Kona, Big Island, Hawaii 96740, tel. 334-1133—tours offered Mon.-Fri. 3-5 p.m. Originally from Portland, Oregon, they moved to Hawaii on a whim. Spoon, who called himself a beach bum, was in reality, like other self-professed beach bums, a highly intelligent and energetic young man who was searching for a worthwhile life mission. In the midst of meditating on his future, he saw there were no locally brewed beers to quaff. With this fact in mind he approached Pops with an idea to "make a really better beer." Pops considered the proposition, concluding Spoon was a chip off the old block. (Pops had a similar idea a few years back when he felt much improvement could be made to the "too common" potato chip. Like his son, Pops decided to make "really great ones," and started producing the now famous Kettle Chips.) Later, Spoon and Pops started producing a home brew that barely covered their own needs. With plenty of hard work, mixed with experimentation and a dollop of luck, their efforts have yielded a small, spotless state-of-the-art brewery producing about 500 barrels per month of absolutely excellent beer. At this stage, they produce three basic beers available on all the islands: **Lilikoi Wheat Beer,** a fruity yet hardy beer made with *lilikoi* (passion fruit); **Pacific Golden Ale,** a classic malty ale, light and perfect for sipping at the beach; and **Firerock Pale Ale,** a darker, hoppy beer, perfect with a meal. Spoon and Pops are still hard at work perfecting new brews for your ultimate enjoyment. You can find beer from the Kona Brewing Co. at many bars and fine restaurants throughout Hawaii. Do yourself a flavor and order a frosty mug of this truly wonderful beer. Spoon and Pops are also working on opening a brew pub restaurant at their brewery in which they intend to serve healthful sandwiches, salads, and pizza to go with their brew (call for information).

In March, Kona hosts the **Kona International Brewers' Festival,** another great endeavor started by the dynamic dad and son duo in 1995. Call 329-2911 for information and location.

A locally brewed beer, **Primo,** manufactured under the auspices of the Joseph Schlitz Brewing Co. of Milwaukee, is a serviceable American brew in the German style, but it lacks that full, hearty flavor of the European imports. In the early '70s it enjoyed an estimated 65% of the local market share, the highest in the nation, but after a bad batch was inadvertently released, sales plummeted and the local share fell to five percent, where it has since remained. In the early 1990s two local breweries folded: the Pacific Brewing Company that produced **Maui Lager,** and the Honolulu Brewing Company that produced **Koolau Lager,** among others. Both breweries were critically acclaimed but geared their beers to the full-bodied European taste. Local beer drinkers enjoy a much lighter brew, so sales of the new beers never really took off.

Undaunted, Paula Thompson, a young and energetic ad executive turned *bier meister,* has been brewing small batches of beer in her Kula home on Maui for years. A visiting uncle, involved in an Oregon brewery, suggested after tasting and enjoying one of her beers that Maui was perfect for a microbrewery of its own. Paula agreed, but to keep start-up costs down, she is brewing her **Whale Ale** and **Aloha Lager** at the Blitz Weinhard Brewery in Portland, Oregon. Once the beer has been established, she hopes to move operations to Maui.

Coffee

Kona coffee is the only coffee grown in the United States. It comes from the Kona District of the Big Island and is a rich, aromatic, truly fine coffee. If it's offered on the menu, have a cup. Recently, small coffee farms have been started on Maui and Kauai, but so far these are small-scale operations having little commercial impact.

Drinking Laws

There are no state-run liquor stores; all kinds of spirits, wines, and beers are available in markets and shops, generally open during normal business hours, seven days a week. The drinking age is 18, and no towns are "dry." Legal hours for serving drinks depend on the type of establishment. Hours generally are: hotels, 6 a.m.-4 a.m.; discos, and nightclubs where there is dancing, 10 a.m.-4 a.m.; bars, lounges where there is no dancing, 6 a.m.-2 a.m. Most restaurants serve alcohol, and in many that don't, you can bring your own.

MUNCHIES AND ISLAND TREATS

Certain finger foods, fast foods, and island treats are unique to Hawaii. Some are meals in themselves, others are snacks. Here are some of the best and most popular.

Pu Pu

Pronounced as in "Winnie the Pooh Pooh," these are little finger foods and hors d'oeuvres. They can be anything from crackers to cracked crab. Often, they're given free at lounges and bars and can even include chicken drumettes, fish kabobs, and tempura. At a good display of them you can have a free meal.

Crackseed

A sweet of Chinese origin, crackseed is preserved and seasoned fruits and seeds. Favorites include coconut, watermelon, pumpkin seeds, mango, plum, and papaya. Distinctive in taste, they take some getting used to but make great trail snacks. Available in all island markets. Also look for dried fish (cuttlefish) on racks, usually near the crackseed. Nutritious and delicious, it makes a great snack.

Shave Ice

This real island institution makes the Mainland "snow cone" melt into insignificance. Special machines literally shave ice to a fluffy consistency. It's mounded into a paper cone, and your choice from dozens of exotic island syrups is generously poured over it. Given a straw and spoon, you just slurp away.

Malasadas and Pao Dolce

Two sweets from the Portuguese, *malasadas* are holeless donuts and *pao dolce* is sweet bread. Sold in island bakeries, they're great for breakfast or as treats.

Lomi Lomi Salmon

This salad of salmon, tomatoes, and onions with garnish and seasonings often accompanies "plate lunches" and is featured at buffets and luaus.

MONEY-SAVERS

Only one thing is better than a great meal: a great meal at a reasonable price. The following are island institutions and favorites that will help you eat well and keep prices down.

Kaukau Wagons

These are lunch wagons, but instead of slick, stainless-steel jobs, most are old delivery trucks converted into portable kitchens. Some say they're a remnant of WW II, when workers had to be fed on the job; others say that the meals they serve were inspired by the Japanese *bento,* a boxed lunch. You'll see the wagons parked along beaches, in city parking lots, or on busy streets. Usually a line of local people will be placing their orders, especially at lunchtime—a tip-off that the wagon serves delicious, nutritious island dishes at reasonable prices. They might have a few tables, but basically they serve food to go. Most of their filling meals are about $3.50, and they specialize in the "plate lunch."

Plate Lunch

One of the best island standards, these lunches give you a sampling of authentic island food that can include teriyaki chicken, mahimahi, *lau lau,* and *lomi* salmon, among others. They're on paper or Styrofoam plates, are packed to go, and usually cost less than $3.50. Standard with a plate lunch is "two-scoop rice" and a generous dollop of macaroni or other salad. Full meals, they're great for keeping down food costs and for instant picnics. Available everywhere, from *kaukau* wagons to restaurants.

Saimin

Special "saimin shops," as well as restaurants, serve this hearty, Japanese-inspired noodle soup. Saimin is a word unique to Hawaii. In Japan, these soups would be called *ramin* or *soba,* and it's as if the two were combined into saimin. A large bowl of noodles in broth, stirred with meat, chicken, fish, or vegetables, costs only a few dollars and is big enough for an evening meal. The best place to eat saimin is in a local hole-in-the-wall shop run by a family.

Tips

Even some of the island's best restaurants in the fanciest hotels offer "early-bird specials"—the regular-menu dinners offered to diners who come in before the usual dinner hour, which is approximately 6 p.m. You pay as little as half the normal price and can dine in luxury on some of the best foods. The specials are often advertised in the "free" tourist books, which might include coupons for two-for-one meals or limited dinners at much lower prices. Just clip them out.

GETTING THERE

With the number of visitors each year over six million—and double that number of travelers just passing through—the state of Hawaii is one of the easiest places in the world to get to . . . by plane. About half a dozen large U.S. airlines (and other small ones) fly to and from the islands; about the same number of foreign carriers, mostly from Asia and Oceania, touch down on a daily basis. In 1978, airlines were "deregulated." In 1984, the reign of the Civil Aeronautics Board (CAB), which controlled exactly which airlines flew where and how much they could charge, ended. Routes, prices, and schedules were thrown open to free competition. Airlines that had previously monopolized preferred destinations found competitors prying loose their strangleholds. Thus, Hawaii is now one of the most hotly contested air markets in the world. The competition between carriers is fierce, and this makes for "sweet deals" and a wide choice of fares for the money-wise traveler. It also makes for pricing chaos. It's impossible to quote airline prices that will hold true for more than a month, if that long. But it's comforting to know that flights to Hawaii are cheaper today than they have been in years, and mile for mile they are one of the best travel bargains in the industry. Familiarize yourself with the alternatives at your disposal so you can make an informed travel selection. Now more than ever, you should work with a sharp travel agent who's on your side.

Almost all travelers to the Big Island arrive by air. A few lucky ones come by private yacht, and the cruise ship SS *Independence* docks both at Hilo and Kailua-Kona. For the rest, the island's two major airports are at Hilo and Kona, with a few commercial flights going to Kamuela. While a few airlines offer flights directly to the Big Island, most still make stopovers in Honolulu, but these are efficient and at no extra cost.

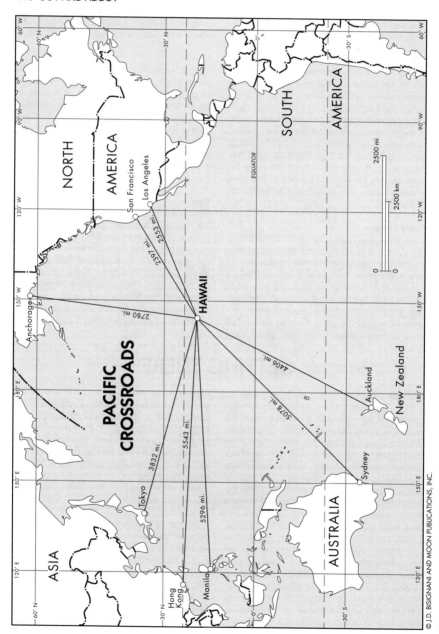

PACIFIC
CROSSROADS

NORTH
AMERICA

SOUTH
AMERICA

ASIA

AUSTRALIA

New Zealand

Anchorage

San Francisco
Los Angeles

HAWAII

Tokyo

Hong
Kong

Manila

Sydney

Auckland

EQUATOR

2280 mi.
2397 mi.
2553 mi.
3832 mi.
5543 mi.
5296 mi.
4406 mi.
5078 mi.

2500 mi

2500 km

© J.D. BISIGNANI AND MOON PUBLICATIONS, INC.

When to Go

The prime tourist season starts two weeks before Christmas and lasts until Easter. It picks up again with summer vacation in early June and ends once more in late August. Everything is usually booked solid and prices are inflated. Hotel, airline, and car reservations, which are a must, are often hard to coordinate at this time of year. You can save 10-50% and a lot of hassling if you go in the artificially created off-season—September to early December, and mid-April (after Easter) until early June. Recently, the numbers of tourist during the off-season has not been nearly as substantial as in years past, indicating the increasing popularity of the island at this time of year, but you'll still find the prices better and the beaches, trails, campgrounds, and even restaurants less crowded. The people will be happier to see you, too.

BY AIR

There are two categories of airlines that you can take to Hawaii: **domestic,** meaning American-owned, and **foreign**-owned. An American law, penned at the turn of the century to protect American shipping, says that "only" an American carrier can transport you to and from two American cities. In the airline industry, this law is still very much in effect. It means, for example, that if you want a roundtrip between San Francisco and Honolulu, you *must* fly on a domestic carrier, such as United or American. If, however, you are flying from San Francisco to Tokyo, you are at liberty to fly a "foreign" airline such as Japan Air Lines, and you may even have a stopover in Hawaii, but you must continue to Tokyo or some other foreign city and cannot fly JAL back to San Francisco. Canadians have no problem flying Canadian Pacific roundtrip from Toronto to Honolulu because this route does not connect two American cities, and so it is with all foreign travel to and from Hawaii. Travel agents know this, but if you're planning your own trip be aware of this fact; if you're traveling roundtrip it must be on a domestic carrier.

Kinds of Flights

The three kinds of flights are the "milk run," direct, and nonstop. Milk runs are the least convenient. On these, you board a carrier—say in your home town—fly it to a gateway city, change planes and

carriers, fly on to the West Coast, change again, and then fly to Hawaii. They're a hassle—your bags have a much better chance of getting lost, you waste time in airports, and to top it off, they're not any cheaper. Avoid them if you can.

On direct flights you fly from point A to point B without changing planes; it doesn't mean that you don't land in between. Direct flights do land usually once to board and deplane passengers, but you sit cozily on the plane along with your luggage and off you go again. Nonstop is just that, but it can cost a bit more. You board and when the doors open again you're in Hawaii. All flights from the West Coast gateway cities are nonstop "God willing"—because there is only the Pacific in between!

Nonstop Flights

Most island flights in the past landed at Hilo International Airport. With the Kona Coast gaining popularity, domestic flights from the Mainland have shifted to that side of the island, and the only direct international connection to the Big Island lands there as well. United Airlines operates the only nonstop flights to the Big Island from the Mainland—daily flights from San Francisco and Los Angeles to Kona. In past peak seasons, United has run a flight to Hilo International Airport, but it's an on-and-off affair depending on the number of travelers. Japan Airlines offers daily flights from Tokyo to Kona.

Stopover Flights

All major carriers have arrangements for getting you to the Big Island. American carriers such as Hawaiian Air, Western, Continental, and American, along with foreign carriers like Canadian Pacific, Qantas, and Japan Airlines, land at Honolulu. There they have an inter-line agreement with island carriers, including Hawaiian Air and Aloha Airlines, which then take you to the Big Island. This sometimes involves a plane change, but your baggage can be booked straight through. Hawaiian Air has expanded to Mainland flights from San Francisco and Los Angeles, with connecting flights in Honolulu to Kona or Hilo. They offer the added convenience of dealing with just one airline.

Travel Agents

At one time people went to a travel agent the same way they went to a barber or beautician, loyally sticking with one. Most agents are reputable professionals who know what they're doing. They should be members of the American Society of Travel Agents (ASTA) and licensed by the Air Traffic Conference (ATC). Most have the inside track on the best deals, and they'll save you countless hours calling 800 numbers and listening to elevator music while on hold. Unless you require them to make very special arrangements, their services are free—they are paid a commission by the airlines and hotels that they book for you.

If you've done business with a travel agent in the past, and were satisfied with the services and prices, by all means stick with him or her. If no such positive rapport exists, then shop around. Ask friends or relatives for recommendations; if you can't get any endorsements go to the Yellow Pages. Call two or three travel agents to compare prices. Make sure to give all of them the same information and to be as precise as possible. Tell them where and when you want to go, how long you want to stay, which class you want to travel, and any special requirements. Write down their information. It's amazing how confusing travel plans can be when you have to keep track of flight numbers, times, prices, and all the preparation info. When you compare, don't look only for the cheapest price. Check for convenience in flights, amenities of hotels, and any other fringe benefits that might be included. Then make your choice of agent, and if he or she is willing to give you individualized service, stick with that agent from then on.

Agents become accustomed to offering the same deals to many clients because they're familiar with the arrangements and because the deals have worked well in the past. Sometimes these are indeed the best, but if they don't suit you, don't be railroaded into accepting them. Any good agent will work with you. After all, it's your trip and your money.

Package Tours

For the independent traveler, practical package deals that include only flight, car, and lodging are okay. Agents put these together all the time and they just might be the best, but if they don't suit you, make arrangements separately. A package *tour* is totally different. On these you get your hand held by an escort, eat where they want you to eat, go where they want you to go, and watch Hawaii slide by your bus window. For some people, especially groups, this might be the

way to do it, but everyone else should avoid the package tour. You'll see Hawaii best on your own, and if you want a tour you can arrange one there, often more cheaply. Once arrangements have been made with your travel agent, make sure to take all receipts and letters of confirmation (hotel, car) with you to Hawaii. They probably won't be needed, but if they are, nothing will work better in getting results.

Mainland and International Fares

There are many categories of airline fares, but only three apply to the average traveler: first class, coach, and excursion (APEX). Traveling **first class** seats you in the front of the plane, gives you free drinks and movie headsets, a wider choice of meals, more leg room, and access to VIP lounges, if they exist. There are no restrictions, no penalties for advance-booking cancellations or rebooking of return flights, and no minimum-stay requirements.

Coach, the way that most people fly, is totally adequate. You sit in the plane's main compartment behind first class. Your seats are comfortable, but you don't have as much leg room or as wide a choice of meals. Movie headsets and drinks cost you a few dollars, but that's about it. Coach offers many of the same benefits as first class and costs about 30% less. You can buy tickets up until takeoff; you have no restrictions on minimum or maximum stays; you receive liberal stopover privileges, and you can cash in your return ticket or change your return date with no penalties.

Excursion or advance payment excursion (APEX) fares are the cheapest. You are accommodated on the plane exactly the same as if you were flying coach. There are, however, some restrictions. You must book and pay for your ticket in advance (usually 7-14 days). At the same time, you must book your return flight, and under most circumstances you can't change either without paying a penalty. Also, your stopovers are severely limited and you will have a minimum/maximum stay period. Only a limited number of seats on any one plane are set aside for APEX fares, so book as early as you can. Also, if you must change travel plans, you can go to the airport and get on as a standby passenger using a discounted ticket, even if the airline doesn't have an official standby policy. There's always the risk that you won't get on, but you do have a chance, as well as priority over an actual standby customer.

Standby is exactly what its name implies: you go to the airport and wait around to see if any flights going to Hawaii have an empty seat. You can save some money, but you cannot have a firm itinerary or limited time. Since Hawaii is such a popular destination, standbys can wait days before catching a plane.

Charters

Charter flights were at one time only for groups or organizations that had memberships in travel clubs. Now they're open to the general public. A charter flight is an entire plane or a block of seats purchased at a quantity discount by a charter company and then sold to customers. Because they are bought at wholesale prices, charter fares can be the cheapest available. As in package deals, only take a charter flight if it is a "fly only" or perhaps includes a car. You don't need one that includes a guide and a bus. Most importantly, make sure that the charter company is reputable. They should belong to the same organizations (ASTA and ATC) as most travel agents. If not, check into them at the local chamber of commerce.

More restrictions apply to charters than to any other flights. You must pay in advance. If you cancel after a designated time, you can be penalized severely or lose your money entirely. You cannot change departure or return dates and times. However, up to 10 days before departure the charter company is legally able to cancel, raise the price by 10%, or change time and dates. They must return your money if cancellation occurs or if changed arrangements are unacceptable to you. Mostly they are on the up-and-up and flights go smoothly, but there are horror stories. Be careful. Be wise. Investigate!

Tips

Flights from the West Coast take about five hours; you gain two hours over Pacific standard time when you land in Hawaii. From the East Coast it takes about 11 hours and you gain five hours over eastern standard time. Flights from Japan take about seven hours and there is a five-hour difference between the time zones. Travel time between Sydney, Australia or Auckland, New Zealand, and Hawaii is about nine hours. They are ahead of Hawaii time by 20 and 22 hours, respectively. Try to fly Mon.-Thurs., when flights are cheaper and easier to book. Pay for your ticket as soon as your plans

are firm. If prices go up there is no charge added, but merely booking doesn't guarantee the lowest price. Make sure that airlines, hotels, and car agencies get your phone number too—not only your travel agent's—in case any problems with availability arise (travel agents are often closed on weekends). It's not necessary, but it's a good idea to call and reconfirm flights 24-72 hours in advance.

First-row (bulkhead) seats are good for people who need more leg room, but bad for watching the movie. Airlines will give you special meals (vegetarian, kosher, low cal, low salt) often at no extra charge, but you must notify them in advance. If you're "bumped" from an overbooked flight, you're entitled to a comparable flight to your destination within one hour. If more than an hour elapses, you get denied-boarding compensation which goes up proportionately with the amount of time you're held up. Sometimes this is cash or a voucher for another flight to be used in the future. You don't have to accept what an airline offers on the spot, if you feel they aren't being fair.

Traveling with Children

Fares for children ages 2-12 are 50% of the adult fare; children under two not occupying a seat travel free. If you're traveling with an infant or active toddler, book your flight well in advance and request the bulkhead seat or first row in any section and a bassinet if available. Many carriers have fold-down cribs with restraints for baby's safety and comfort. Toddlers appreciate the extra space provided by the front-row seats. Be sure to reconfirm, and arrive early to ensure this special seating. On long flights you'll be glad that you took these extra pains.

Although most airlines have coloring books, puppets, etc., to keep your child busy, it's always a good idea to bring your own. These can make the difference between a pleasant flight and a harried ordeal. Also, remember to bring baby bottles, formula, diapers, and other necessities, as many airlines may not be equipped with exactly what you need. Make all inquiries ahead of time so you're not caught unprepared.

Baggage

You are allowed two free pieces of luggage—one large, the other smaller—and a carry-on bag. The two main pieces can weigh up to 70 pounds each; an extra charge is levied for extra weight.

The larger bag can have an overall added dimension (height plus width plus length) of 62 inches; the smaller, 55 inches. Your carry-on must fit under your seat or in the overhead storage compartment. Purses and camera bags are not counted as carry-ons and may be taken aboard. Surfboards and bicycles are about $15 extra. Although they make great mementos, remove all previous baggage tags from your luggage; they can confuse handlers. Attach a sturdy holder with your name and address on the handle, or use a stick-on label on the bag itself. Put your name and address inside the bag, and the address where you'll be staying in Hawaii if possible. Carry your cosmetics, identification, money, prescriptions, tickets, reservations, change of underwear, camera equipment, and perhaps a change of shirt or blouse in your carry-on.

Visas

Entering Hawaii is like entering anywhere else in the U.S. Foreign nationals must have a current passport and proper visa, an ongoing or return air ticket, and sufficient funds for the proposed stay in Hawaii. Canadians do not need a visa or passport but must have proper identification (such as a passport, driver's license, or birth certificate).

Agricultural Inspection

Remember that before you leave Hawaii for the Mainland, all of your bags are subject to an agricultural inspection, a usually painless procedure taking only a minute or two. To facilitate your departure, leave all bags unlocked until after inspection. There are no restrictions on beach sand, coconuts, dried flower arrangements, fresh flower lei, pineapples, certified pest-free plants, seashells, seed lei, and wood roses. However, avocado, litchi, and papaya must be treated before departure. Some other restricted items are berries, fresh gardenias, roses, jade plants, live insects, snails, cotton, plants in soil, soil itself, and sugarcane. For any questions pertaining to plants that you want to take to the Mainland, call the Agricultural Quarantine Inspection office, tel. 933-6930 in Hilo or 326-1252 in Kona.

Big Island Airports

The largest airport on the Big Island is **Hilo International Airport,** tel. 935-0809, which services Hilo and the eastern half of the island. It's a modern facility with full amenities and its runways can handle all jumbo jets. Flights from here connect to Kona, Lihue, Kahului, and Honolulu The two-story terminal has an information center, a restaurant, a number of vendors (including lei shops), and lockers. Most major car-rental agencies have booths outside the terminal; a taxi for the three-mile ride to town costs about $8. The airport features 20 acres of landscaped flowers and an assortment of fountains and waterfalls supplied by rainwater collected on the terminal's roof.

Kona International Airport, tel. 329-2484, is nine miles north of Kailua-Kona and handles the air traffic for Kona, a much prettier town to fly into than Hilo. This airport handles a growing amount of air traffic from other island cities and all the Mainland and international flights, eclipsing Hilo as the island's major air transportation hub. Interisland flights arrive from Hilo, Honolulu, Kahului, and Lihue; Mainland and international flights arrive from San Francisco, Los Angeles, and Tokyo. In the winter season charter flights also fly in from Vancouver. The terminal is a series of open-sided, Polynesian-style buildings which, because of the increasing volume of traffic into Kona, is being expanded. Here too are lockers, food, visitor information, various vendors, and most car-rental agencies. A private cab to your hotel will be $15 or more.

Waimea-Kohala Airport, tel. 885-4520, is just outside Waimea (Kamuela). There are few amenities and no public transportation to town. Only commuter flights are scheduled between here and Honolulu. **Upolu Airport** is a lonely strip on the extreme northern tip of the island, with no facilities whatsoever and no scheduled flights. Both airports are serviced on request by small charter airlines.

DOMESTIC CARRIERS

The following are the major domestic carriers to and from Hawaii. The planes used are primarily DC-10s and 747s, with a smaller 727 flown now and again. A list of the "gateway cities" from which they fly direct and nonstop flights is given, but "connecting cities" are not. All flights, by all carriers, land at Honolulu International Airport except the limited direct flights to Maui and Hawaii. Only the established companies are listed. Entrepreneurial small airlines such as the now-defunct Hawaii Express pop up now and

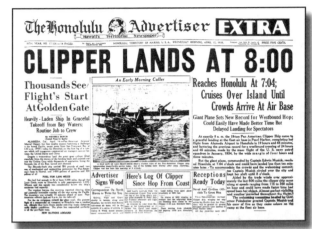

Pan American Airlines, now out of business in the Pacific, opened Hawaii to mass air travel with this historic flight on Wednesday, April 17, 1935. The flight from Alameda Airport to Pearl Harbor took 19 hours and 48 minutes.

again and specialize in dirt-cheap fares. There is a hectic frenzy to buy their tickets and business is great for a while, but then the established companies lower their fares and the gamblers fold.

Hawaiian Airlines

One of Hawaii's own domestic airlines has entered the Mainland market. They operate a daily flights from Los Angeles, San Francisco, Las Vegas, Seattle, and Portland to Honolulu, with twice-weekly flights from San Francisco and Seattle to Kahului, Maui. The "common fare" ticket price includes an ongoing flight to any of the Neighbor Islands, and if you're leaving Hawaii, a free flight from a Neighbor Island to the link-up in Honolulu. Senior-citizen discounts for people age 60 or older are offered on trans-Pacific and interisland flights. Scheduled flights to the South Pacific run between Honolulu and Pago Pago twice a week and once a week to Papeete, Tahiti. Hawaiian Air offers special discount deals with Dollar rental cars and select major-island hotels. Contact Hawaiian Air at (800) 367-5320 Mainland and Canada, (800) 882-8811 in Hawaii.

United Airlines

Since their first island flight in 1947, United has become top dog in flights to Hawaii. Their Mainland routes connect over 100 cities to Honolulu. The main gateway cities of San Francisco, Los Angeles, Chicago, and Vancouver have direct flights to Honolulu; flights from all other cities connect through these. They also offer direct flights to Maui from San Francisco and Los Angeles, and from San Francisco and Los Angeles to Kona on the Big Island. Continuing through Honolulu, United flights go to Tokyo, where connections can be made for other Asian cities. United offers a number of packages, including flight and hotel on Oahu, and flight, hotel, and car on the Neighbor Islands. They inter-line with Aloha Airlines and deal with Hertz rental cars. They're the "big guys" and they intend to stay that way—their packages are hard to beat. Call (800) 241-6522.

American Airlines

American offers direct flights to Honolulu from Los Angeles, San Francisco, Dallas, and Chicago. They also fly from Los Angeles to Maui, with a connection in Honolulu. Call (800) 433-7300.

Continental Airlines

Flights from all Mainland cities to Honolulu connect via Los Angeles, San Francisco, and Houston. Also available are direct flights from Guam to Honolulu. Call (800) 525-0280 or (800) 231-0856 for international information.

Northwest Airlines

Northwest flies into Honolulu from Los Angeles, San Francisco, and Seattle. There are onward flights to Tokyo, Osaka, Nagoya, Manila, Guam, Bangkok, Singapore, Hong Kong, Taipei, and Seoul. Call (800) 225-2525.

Delta Airlines

In 1985, Delta entered the Hawaiian market; when it bought out Western Airlines its share became even bigger. They have nonstop flights to Honolulu from Dallas/Fort Worth, Los Angeles, and Atlanta; and flights to Kahului, Maui, from Los Angeles. Call (800) 221-1212.

FOREIGN CARRIERS

The following carriers operate throughout Asia and Oceania but have no U.S. flying rights. This means that in order for you to vacation in Hawaii using one of these carriers, your flight must originate or terminate in a foreign city. You can have a stopover in Honolulu with a connecting flight to a Neighbor Island. For example, if you've purchased a flight on Japan Air Lines from San Francisco to Tokyo, you can stop in Hawaii, but you must then carry on to Tokyo. Failure to do so will result in a stiff fine, and the balance of your ticket will not be refunded.

Canadian Airlines International

Nonstop flights from Canada to Honolulu originate in Vancouver and Toronto. Call (800) 426-7000 in the U.S. or (800) 665-7530 in Canada.

Air Canada

Air Canada has weekly direct flights from Vancouver to both Honolulu and Maui. Call (800) 776-3000 for information and schedules.

Air New Zealand

Flights link New Zealand, Australia, and numerous South Pacific islands with Los Angeles via Honolulu. Also offered are special APEX fares from Los Angeles to Australia and New Zealand, with stops in Honolulu and up to five other island points. Call (800) 926-7255 or (800) 262-1234 in the U.S. and (800) 663-5494 in Canada for current information.

Japan Air Lines

The Japanese are the second-largest group, next to Americans, to visit Hawaii. JAL flights to Honolulu originate in Tokyo (Narita), Nagoya, Osaka (Kansai), Sendai, and Fukuoka. In addition, there are flights between Tokyo (Narita) and Kona on the Big Island. There are no JAL flights between the Mainland and Hawaii. Call (800) 525-3663.

Philippine Airlines

Philippine Airlines flies between San Francisco and Manila via Honolulu. Connections in Manila are available to most Asian cities. Call (800) 435-9725.

Qantas

Daily flights connect Sydney and Auckland, New Zealand, with Honolulu; flights from other cities go through these hubs. Call (800) 227-4500.

China Airlines

Routes to Honolulu with China Airlines are from Taipei direct or through Tokyo, but flights are not available year-round. Connections in Taipei to most Asian capitals. Call (800) 227-5118.

Korean Air

Korean Air offers some of the least expensive flights to Asia. All flights to/from Honolulu go directly to Seoul. Connections to many Asian cities. Call (800) 438-5000.

Asiana Airlines

Direct daily flights are offered from Honolulu to Seoul, with connections to other Asian cities. Call (800) 227-4262

INTERISLAND CARRIERS

Getting to and from the Big Island via the other islands is easy and convenient. The only effective way for most visitors to travel between the Hawaiian islands is by air. Luckily, Hawaii has excellent air transportation that boasts one of the industry's safest flight records. The following airlines have competitive prices, with interisland flights at about $75 each way. You can also save money (about $15) if you **take the first or last daily scheduled flight.** This offer usually applies only to flights to and from Honolulu, but do check because the policy often changes. Another alternative is to **purchase a booklet of six flight vouchers.** You save about $7 per ticket, and they are *transferable.* Just book a flight as normal and present the filled-in voucher to board the plane. Perfect for families or groups of friends, vouchers can be purchased at any ticket office or at Honolulu International Airport.

Note: Although every effort has been made for up-to-date accuracy, remember that sched-

INTERISLAND
AIR ROUTES

Major Airports With
Full Facilities

Secondary Airport

© J.D. BISIGNANI AND MOON PUBLICATIONS, INC.

ules are constantly changing. The following should be used only as a point of reference. Please call the airlines listed below for their latest schedules.

Hawaiian Airlines

Hawaiian Airlines can be contacted at tel. (800) 367-5320 nationwide, (800) 882-8811 statewide, or 326-5615 on the Big Island. From Honolulu to Kona, 11 flights (about 40 minutes) are spread throughout the day from approximately 5:20 a.m. to 7 p.m. From Kona to Honolulu, there are 14 daily flights, 6:25 a.m.-8:05 p.m., two of which stop in Kahului, Maui. A similar scheduling applies to Hilo, with a few flights stopping in either Kahului, Maui, or Kona on the way. Hawaiian Airlines offers fewer daily flights from Kauai and Maui to both Hilo and Kona (about one hour and 40 minutes). Website: www.hawaiianair.com.

Aloha Airlines

Aloha Airlines, tel. (800) 367-5250 Mainland, (800) 235-0936 Canada, 935-5771 Big Island, also services the Big Island with flights from the neighboring islands. Their 19 daily Honolulu-Kona runs start at 5:25 a.m., with the last at 7:20 p.m.; 16 Honolulu-to-Hilo flights depart throughout the day, 5:25 a.m.-7 p.m. There are the same number of flights in the reverse direction to both destinations, leaving between 6:30 a.m.-8:25 p.m. Aloha also flies from Kona and Hilo to Kahului with about a dozen or so flights to each spread throughout the day. Flights to/from Maui are much fewer, with two from Hilo and three from Kona. Aloha also has one flight daily from Hilo to Kona. Website: www.alohaair.com.

A subsidiary of Aloha Airlines, **Aloha Island Air,** tel. (800) 323-3345 nationwide, (800) 652-6541 statewide, has no flights to the Big Island. It services Honolulu; Lanai; Molokai; and Kahului, Kapalua, and Hana on Maui.

Mahalo Air

Mahalo Air, tel. 833-5555 on Oahu, (800) 277-8333 from the Neighbor Islands, and (800) 462-4256 from the U.S. and Canada, is the newest competitor to the market and serves only Kona on the Big Island. Eight flights a day connect Kona to Honolulu, departing Kona 7:25 a.m.-7:45 p.m. One of the late afternoon flights stops at Kahului, Maui, on the way. (Website: www.is-lander-magazine.com/mahaloschedule.html.)

Trans Air
Trans Air, tel. 885-5134 in Kamuela or (800) 634-2094, runs one commuter route between Honolulu and Kamuela (Waimea), aside from their charter services. Flights from Honolulu run daily at 4:30 p.m.; Thursday, Friday, and Saturday at 4:45 p.m.; and Sunday, Monday, and Tuesday at 6 a.m. For each flight, there is a layover of about a half hour in Kamuela before the return to Honolulu. (Website: www.travelocity.com.)

TRAVEL BY SHIP

American Hawaii Cruises
This American cruise ship company operates the 800-passenger SS *Independence*. This ship offers a seven-day itinerary that calls at five ports on the four main islands. For those who want just a taste of a cruise through the islands, three- and four-day trips are also offered. The seven-day fares start at $1,230 pp double occupancy, three- and four-day fares from $670 and 805, respectively. Fares go up from there according to the class and location of your cabin. Children under 18 are often given special rates and cruise free June-Sept. when they share a cabin with their parents. All cruises leave on Saturday from the Aloha Towers in Honolulu. After leaving Honolulu, the seven-day cruise first stops at Nawiliwili on Kauai, followed by Kahului on Maui, and Hilo and Kona on the Big Island, before returning to Honolulu. For the three-day cruise, you board in Honolulu and alight in Kahului. Those on the four-day trip board in Kahului and get off in Honolulu. Each ship is a luxury seagoing hotel and gourmet restaurant; swimming pools, health clubs, movies, and nightclubs are all part of the amenities. Onshore excursions are offered at each port of call. Airfare to Hawaii, interisland air flights, rental cars, and accommodation on any island after your cruise can be arranged for you by American Hawaii Cruises. For details contact: American Hawaii Cruises, Robin St. Wharf, 1380 Port of New Orleans Place, New Orleans, LA 70130-1890, tel. (800) 765-7000, fax (504) 585-0690. (Website: www.cruisehawaii.com.)

Alternatives
Other companies offering varied cruises include **P&O Lines,** which operates the *Sea Princess* through the South Pacific, making port at Honolulu on its way from the West Coast once a year.

Royal Cruise Line out of Los Angeles, or Auckland alternatively, sails the *Royal Odyssey,* which docks in Honolulu on its South Pacific and Orient cruise, $2,200-4,000.

The **Holland America Line** sails a year-long World Cruise, calling at Honolulu. Call (800) 426-0327.

Society Expeditions offers a 42-day cruise throughout the South Pacific departing from Honolulu. Fares range $3,000-9,000. Call (800) 426-7794.

American Hawaii Cruises'
SS Independence

AMERICAN HAWAII CRUISES

Information

Most travel agents can provide information on the above cruise lines. If you're especially interested in traveling by freighter, contact: **Freighter Travel Club of America,** P.O. Box 12693, Salem, OR 97309; or **Ford's Freighter Travel Guide,** P.O. Box 505, 22151 Clarendon St., Woodland Hills, CA 91367.

TOUR COMPANIES

Many tour companies advertise packages to Hawaii in large city newspapers every week. They offer very reasonable airfares, car rentals, and accommodations. Without trying, you can get roundtrip airfare from the West Coast and a week in Hawaii for $400-500 using one of these companies. The following companies offer great deals and have excellent reputations. This list is by no means exhaustive.

SunTrips

This California-based tour and charter company sells vacations all over the world. They're primarily a wholesale company but will work with the general public. SunTrips often works with Rich International Air, tel. (305) 871-5113. When you receive your SunTrip tickets, you are given discount vouchers for places to stay that are convenient to the airport of departure. Many of these hotels have complimentary airport pickup service and will allow you to park your car, free of charge, for up to 14 days, which saves a considerable amount on airport parking fees. SunTrips does not offer assigned seating until you get to the airport. They recommend that you get there two hours in advance, and they ain't kidding! This is the price you pay for getting such inexpensive air travel. SunTrips usually has a deal with a car-rental company. Remember that everyone on your incoming flight is offered the same deal, and all make a beeline for the rental car's shuttle van after landing and securing their baggage. If you have a traveling companion, work together to beat the rush by leaving your companion to fetch the baggage and heading directly for the van as soon as you arrive. Pick your car up, then return for your partner and the bags. Even if you're alone, you could zip over to the car-rental center and then return for your bags without having them sit very long on the carousel. Contact SunTrips,

2350 Paragon Dr., P.O. Box 18505, San Jose, CA 95158, tel. (800) 786-8747 in California, (808) 941-2697 in Honolulu.

Council Travel Services

These full-service, budget-travel specialists are a subsidiary of the nonprofit Council on International Educational Exchange, and the official U.S. representative to the International Student Travel Conference. They'll custom-design trips and programs for everyone from senior citizens to college students. Bona fide students have extra advantages, however, including eligibility for the International Student Identification Card (CISC), which often gets you discount fares and waived entrance fees. Groups and business travelers are also welcome. For full information, call (800) 226-8624, or write to Council Travel Services at one of these offices: 530 Bush St., San Francisco, CA 94108, tel. (415) 421-3473; or 205 E. 42nd St., New York, NY 10017, tel. (212) 661-1450. Other offices are in Austin, Berkeley, Boston, Davis, Long Beach, Los Angeles, Miami, Portland, San Diego, and Seattle.

Student Travel Network

STA Travel is a full-service travel agency specializing in student travel, regardless of age. Those under 26 do not have to be full-time students to get special fares. Older independent travelers can avail themselves of services, although they are ineligible for student fares. STA works hard to get you discounted or budget rates. STA's central office is at 7202 Melrose Ave., Los Angeles, CA 90046, tel. (213) 934-8722 or (800) 777-0112. STA maintains 39 offices throughout the USA, Australasia, and Europe, along with **Travel Cuts,** a sister organization operating in Canada. Many tickets issued by STA are flexible, allowing changes with no penalty, and are open-ended for travel up to one year. STA also maintains **Travel Help,** a service available at all offices designed to solve all types of problems that may arise while traveling. STA is a well-established travel agency with an excellent and well-deserved reputation.

Nature Expeditions International

These quality tours have nature as the theme. Trips are nine- or 15-day, four-island, natural-history expeditions, with emphasis on plants, birds, and geology. Their guides are experts in their fields and give personable and attentive service. Contact Nature Expeditions International at 6400 E. El Dorado, Suite 200, Tucson, AZ 85714, tel. (520) 721-6712 or (800) 869-0639.

Ocean Voyages

This unique company offers seven- and 10-day itineraries aboard a variety of yachts in the Hawaiian Islands. The yachts, equipped to carry 2-10 passengers, ensure individualized sail training. The vessels sail throughout the islands, exploring hidden bays and coves, and berth at different ports as they go. This opportunity is for anyone who wishes to see the islands in a timeless fashion, thrilling to sights experienced by the first Polynesian settlers and Western explorers. For rates and information contact Ocean Voyages, 1709 Bridgeway, Sausalito, CA 94965, tel. (415) 332-4681.

Pleasant Hawaiian Holidays

A California-based company specializing in Hawaii, Pleasant Hawaiian Holidays makes arrangements for flights, accommodations, and transportation only. At 2404 Townsgate Rd., Westlake Village, CA 91361, tel. (800) 242-9244.

Travelers with Disabilities

Accessible Vans of Hawaii (formerly Wheelers of Hawaii), 186 Mehani Circle, Kihei, HI 96753, tel. 879-5521, fax 879-0649, (800) 303-3750 Hawaii or (888) AVAVANS Mainland, is a private company, owned and operated by Dave McKown, who has traveled the world with his paraplegic brother. Dave knows first-hand the obstacles faced by disabled people, and his disabled associate does as well. Accessible Vans of Hawaii provides a full service travel agency, booking rooms, flights, and activities for the physically disabled. Wheelchair lift equipped vans are rented on Oahu, Maui, and the Big Island for $109 a day or $560 a week, plus tax. If a van is needed on Kauai, it must be shipped at the renter's expense. Dave and his associate are good sources of information for any disabled traveler.

EcoTours to Hawaii

Sierra Club Trips offers Hawaii trips for nature lovers who are interested in an outdoor experience. Various trips include hikes over Maui's Haleakala and, on Kauai, a kayak trip along the Na Pali Coast and a family camping spree in Kauai's Koke'e region. All trips are led by experienced guides and are open to Sierra Club members only ($35 per year to join). For information contact the Sierra Club Outing Department, 85 2nd St., 2nd Fl., San Francisco, CA 94105, tel. (415) 775-5500.

Earthwatch allows you to become part of an expeditional team dedicated to conservation and the study of the natural environment. An expedition might include studying dolphins in Kewalo Basin Marine Mammal Laboratory, diving Maui's threatened reefs. If you become an assistant field researcher, your lodgings may be a dorm room at the University of Hawaii, and your meals may come from a remote camp kitchen. Fees vary and are tax deductible. If you're interested in this learning experience, contact Earthwatch, 680 Mt. Auburn St., P.O. Box 403-P, Watertown, MA 02272, tel. (617) 926-8200.

Backroads, 1516 Fifth St., Suite PR, Berkeley, CA 94710, tel. (510) 527-1555 or (800) 462-2848, arranges easy-on-the-environment bicycle and hiking trips to the Big Island. Basic tours include a six-day hiking/camping tour ($698), a six-day hiking/inn tour ($1,295), and a five-day bicycle/camping tour ($649). Prices include hotel/inn accommodations or tent when applicable, most meals, and professional guide service. Airfare is not included, and bicycles and sleeping bags can be rented (BYO okay) for reasonable rates.

Crane Tours, 15101 Magnolia Blvd., Sherman Oaks, CA 91403, tel. (800) 653-2545, owned and operated by Bill Crane, has been taking people kayaking and backpacking to the Big Island, Maui, and Kauai since 1976. Basic prices for these eco-adventures start at $650, with the most expensive tour around $1,145 (airfare not included).

GETTING AROUND

The first thing to remember when traveling on the Big Island is that it *is* big, over four times larger than Rhode Island. A complete range of vehicles is available for getting around—everything from helicopters to mopeds. Hawaii, like Oahu, has good public transportation. Choose the conveyance that fits your style, and you should have no trouble touring the Big Island.

CAR RENTALS

The best way to tour the island is in a rented car, but keep these tips in mind. Most car companies charge you a fee if you rent the car in Hilo and drop it off in Kona, and vice versa. The agencies are prejudiced against the Saddle Road and the spur road leading to South Point, both of which offer some of the *most* spectacular scenery on the island. Their prejudice is unfounded because both roads are paved, generally well maintained, and no problem if you take your time. They'll claim the insurance will not cover you if you have a mishap on these roads. A good automobile policy at home will cover you in a rental

car, but definitely check this before you take off. It's even possible, but not recommended, to drive to the top of Mauna Kea if there is no snow. Plenty of signs to the summit say "4WD only"; heed them, not so much for going up, but for needed braking power coming down. Don't even hint of these intentions to the car-rental agencies, or they won't rent you a car.

No way whatsoever should you attempt to drive down to Waipio Valley in a car! The grade is unbelievably steep, and only a 4WD compound first gear can make it. Put simply, you have a good chance of being killed if you try it in a car.

Gas stations are farther apart than on the other islands, and sometimes they close very early. As a rule, fill up whenever the gauge reads half full.

Both Hilo International Airport and Kona International Airport have a gauntlet of car-rental booths and courtesy phones outside the terminals.

Requirements

A variety of requirements are imposed on the renter by car agencies, but the most important clauses are common. Some of the worst practices being challenged are: no rentals to people

HAWAII STATE ARCHIVES

under 25 and over 70, and no rentals to military personnel or Hawaiian residents! Before renting, check that you fulfill the requirements. Generally, you must be 21, although some agencies rent to 18-year-olds, while others still require you to be 25. You must possess a valid driver's license, with licenses from most countries accepted, but if you are not American, get an International Driver's License to be safe. You should have a major credit card in your name. This is the easiest way to rent a car. Some companies will take a deposit, but it will be very stiff. It could easily be $50 per day on top of your rental fees and sometimes much more. In addition, they may require a credit check on the spot, complete with phone calls to your employer and bank. If you damage the car, charges will be deducted from your deposit, and the car company itself determines the extent of the damages. Some companies *will not* rent you a car without a major credit card in your name, no matter how much of a deposit you are willing to leave.

When to Rent

On this one, you'll have to make up your own mind, because it's a "bet" that you can either win or lose big. But it's always good to know the odds before you plop down your money. You can reserve your car in advance when you book your air ticket, or play the field when you get there. If you book in advance, you'll obviously have a car waiting for you, but the deal that you made is the deal that you'll get—it may or may not be the best around. On the other hand, if you wait, you can often take advantage of excellent on-the-spot deals. However, you're betting that cars are available. You might be totally disappointed and not be able to rent a car at all, or you might make a honey of a deal.

If you're arriving during the peak seasons of Christmas, Easter and late summer vacation, absolutely *book your car in advance*. They are all accounted for during this period, and even if you can find a junker from a fly-by-night, they'll price-gouge you mercilessly. If you're going off-peak, you stand a good chance of getting the car you want at the price you want. It's generally best to book ahead, but the majority of car companies have toll-free 800 numbers (listed below). At least call them for an opinion of your chances of getting a car upon your intended arrival.

Rates

If you pick up a car-rental brochure at a travel agency, notice that the prices for Hawaii rentals are about the lowest in the U.S. The two rate options for renting are mileage and flat rate. A third type, mileage/minimum, is generally a bad idea unless you plan to do some heavy-duty driving. Mileage rate costs less per day, but you are charged for every mile driven. Mileage rates are best if you drive less than 30 miles per day—but even on an island that isn't much! The flat rate is best, providing a fixed daily rate and unlimited mileage. With either rate, you buy the gas; don't buy the cheapest because the poor performance from low octane eats up your savings.

Discounts of about 10-15% for weekend, weekly, and monthly rates are available. It's sometimes cheaper to rent a car for the week even if you're only going to use it for five days. Both weekly and monthly rates can be split between Neighbor Islands.

The average price of a subcompact standard shift, without a/c, is $30 per day, $120 per week (add about $8 per day—$50 per week—for an automatic), but rates vary widely. Luxury cars are about $10 per day more, with a comparable weekly rate. Most of the car companies, local and national, offer special rates and deals. These deals fluctuate too rapidly to give any hard-and-fast information. They are common, however, so make sure to inquire. Also, peak periods have "black outs" where normally good deals no longer apply.

Warning: If you keep your car beyond your contract, you'll be charged the highest daily rate unless you notify the rental agency beforehand. *Don't keep your car longer than the contract without notifying the company.* Companies are *quick* to send out their repossession specialists. You might find yourself in a situation with your car gone, a warrant issued for your arrest, and an extra charge on your bill. A simple courtesy call notifying them of your intentions saves a lot of headaches and hassle.

What Wheels to Rent

The super-cheap rates on the eye-catcher brochures refer to subcompact standard shifts. The price goes up with the size of the car and with an automatic transmission. As with options on a new car, the more luxury, the more you pay. If you can drive a standard shift, get one! They're cheaper to rent and operate and a standard shift gives you greater control. AM/FM radios are good to have for entertainment and for weather and surf conditions. If you have the choice, take a car with cloth seats instead of sticky vinyl.

Insurance

Before signing your car-rental agreement, you'll be offered "insurance" for around $10 p/d. Since insurance is already built into the contract (don't expect the rental agency to point this out), what you're really buying is a waiver on the deductible ($500-1,000), in case you crack up the car. If you have insurance at home, you will almost always have coverage on a rental car—including your normal deductible—although not all policies are the same, so check with your agent. Also, if you haven't bought their waiver, and you have a mishap, the rental agencies will put a claim against your major credit card on the spot for the amount of deductible, even if you can prove that your insurance will cover. They'll tell you to collect from your insurance company because they don't want to be left holding the bag on an across-the-waters claim. If you have a good policy with a small deductible, it's hardly worth paying the extra money for the waiver, but if your own policy is inadequate, buy the insurance. Also, most major credit cards offer complimentary car-rental insurance as an incentive for using their cards to rent the car. Simply call the toll-free number of your credit card company to see if this service is included.

Driving Tips

Protect your children as you would at home with car seats. Their rental prices vary considerably: Alamo offers them free of charge; National charges $3 per day; Hertz needs 48 hours notice; Dollar gives them free but they're not always available at all locations. Almost all the agencies can make arrangements if you give them enough notice. Check before you go and if all else fails, bring one from home.

There are few differences between driving in Hawaii and on the Mainland. Just remember that many people on the roads are tourists and can be confused about where they're going. Since many drivers are from somewhere else, there's hardly a "regular style" of driving in the islands. A farmer from Iowa accustomed to poking along on back roads can be sandwiched between a frenetic New Yorker who's trying to drive over his roof and a super-polite but horribly confused Japanese tourist who normally drives on the left.

In Hawaii, drivers don't honk their horns except to say hello, or in an emergency. It's considered rude, and honking to hurry someone might earn you a knuckle sandwich. Hawaiian drivers reflect the climate: they're relaxed and polite. Oftentimes, they'll brake to let you turn left when they're coming at you. They may assume you'll do the same, so be ready, after a perfunctory turn signal from another driver, for him or her to turn across your lane. The more rural the area, the more apt this is to happen.

It may seem like common sense, but remember to slow down when you enter the little towns strung along the circle-island route. It's easy to bomb along on the highway and flash through these towns, missing some of Hawaii's best scenery. Also, rural children expect *you* to be watchful, and will assume that you are going to stop for them when they dart out into the crosswalks.

BYO Car

If you want to bring your own car, write for information to: Director of Finance, Division of Licenses, 1455 S. Beretania St., Honolulu, HI 96814. However, unless you'll be in Hawaii for a bare minimum of six months and will spend all your time on one island, don't even think about it. It's an expensive proposition and takes time and plenty of arrangements. From California, the cost is at least $600 to Honolulu, and an additional $100 to any other island. To save on rental costs, it would be better to buy and sell a car there, or to lease for an extended period. For information about licensing and insurance on the Big Island, contact the Hawaii Police Department, 349 Kapiolani St., Hilo, HI 96720.

Auto Rental Companies

The following are major firms that are represented at both the Hilo and Kona airports. Kona numbers begin with "329" and "327," Hilo numbers with "961" or "935."

Dollar, tel. 961-6059, 329-2744, (800) 342-7398 statewide or (800) 800-4000 worldwide has an excellent reputation and very competitive prices. Dollar rents mostly Chrysler vehicles: sedans, jeeps, convertibles, and 4WDs. Great weekly rates, and all major credit cards accepted. (Website: www.dollarcar.com.)

Alamo, tel. 961-3343, 329-8896, or (800) 327-9633, has good weekly rates. Mostly GM cars. (Website: www.goalamo.com.)

National, tel. 935-0891, 329-1674, or (800) 227-7368 worldwide, features GM and Nissan cars and accepts all major credit cards. They sometimes rent without a credit card if you leave a $100/day deposit—less if you take full insurance coverage.

Avis, tel. 935-1290, 327-3000, or (800) 321-3712 nationwide, features late model GM cars as well as most imports and convertibles.

Budget, tel. 935-6878, 329-8511, or (800) 527-0700 nationwide, offers competitive rates on a variety of late model Ford and Lincoln-Mercury cars and specialty vehicles.

Hertz, tel. 935-2896, 329-3566, (800) 654-3011 worldwide, is competitively priced with many fly/drive deals. They feature Ford vehicles. (Website: www.hertz.com.)

A few short years ago, local companies abounded, but today only two have survived. As always *caveat emptor*. The firms are: **Harper,** in Hilo at tel. 969-1478 and in Kona at 329-6688, where you can rent a car, truck, 7-15-passenger van, or 4WD; and **V/N Rental** at 75-5799 Ali'i Dr., tel. 329-7328, that rents used but not too abused longer term cars.

Motorcycles and Mopeds

D.J.'s Rentals, tel. 329-1700, open daily 7:30 a.m.-6 p.m., at 75-5663 Palani Rd., across from the King Kamehameha's Hotel in an outdoor booth, rents mopeds, jogs (faster version of a moped but for only one person), scooters, and motorcycles. Costs are: mopeds $8 hourly,

$24.95 daily, and $29.95 for 24 hours; jogs $12 hourly, $34.95 daily, and $39.95 for 24 hours; two-person scooters (capable of attaining highway speeds), $15 hourly, $44.95 daily, $49.95 for 24 hours. Motorcycles: a Big Twin Harley Davidson costs $125 daily or $80 half day, and all other motorcycles cost $99 daily or $65 half day. A half day is 7:30 a.m.-noon, and then again noon-6 p.m. A good deal is to rent noon-6 p.m. and then pay an extra $10 to keep the cycle overnight. Weekly and three-day special rates are also available.

ALTERNATIVE TRANSPORTATION

Buses

The county of Hawaii maintains the Mass Transportation System (MTS), known throughout the island as the **Hele-On Bus.** For information, schedules, and fares contact the Mass Transit Agency at 25 Aupuni St., Hilo 96720, tel. 961-8744 or 935-8241. The main bus terminal is in downtown Hilo at Mooheau Park, just at the corner of Kamehameha Ave. and Mamo Street. Recently, it's been completely rebuilt and modernized. Like bus terminals everywhere, it has a local franchise of derelicts and down-and-outers, but they leave you alone. What the Hele-On Bus lacks in class, it more than makes up for in *color* and affordability. The Hele-On operates Mon.-Fri. approximately 6 a.m.-6 p.m., depending on the run, except for the routes to Kona and Kohala, which operate Saturday and/or Sunday. There are a number of intra-Hilo routes with additional intercity routes to points around the periphery of the island. If you're in a hurry then definitely forget about taking it, but if you want to meet the people of Hawaii, there's no better way. The base fare is 75 cents, which increases whenever you go into another zone. Have change for exact fare when you board. You can also be charged an extra $1 for a large backpack or suitcase. Don't worry about that—the Hele-On is one of the best bargains in the country. There are five basic intercity routes connecting to Hilo. One goes from Kealia, south of Captain Cook, all the way to Hilo on the east coast via Kailua, Waimea, Honokaa, and Honomu. This journey (operating Mon.-Sat.) covers 110 miles in just over four hours and costs about $6, the most expensive fare in the system. From Kohala a daily bus from the Hilton Waikoloa Village Resort makes its way through Waimea to Hilo. You can take the southern route from Ocean View Estates through Kau, passing through Naalehu and Volcano, and continuing on to Hilo. This trip takes just over two hours and costs $5.25. A fourth runs from Pahoa through Keaau to Hilo, while the fifth goes down the coast from Honokaa to Hilo. In the Kohala district, a bus runs every weekday morning from Kapaau to Hilton Waikoloa Village and returns in the late afternoon.

The county also maintains the **Banyan Shuttle** in Hilo. This bus does five runs Mon.-Fri. 9 a.m.-2:55 p.m. The Shuttle costs 75 cents but you can buy a $2 pass for one-day unlimited use. The Shuttle runs from the Hukilau Hotel at the end of Banyan Dr. to the Mooheau Bus Terminal in downtown Hilo. En route it stops at the better hotels, Puainako Town Center, Hilo and Kaikoo Malls, Lyman Museum, and Rainbow Falls, where you're allowed 10 minutes for a look.

Kailua-Kona has the **Ali'i Shuttle,** tel. 775-7121, that cruises Ali'i Drive. This red, white, and blue bus runs every 30-45 minutes or so, 8:30 a.m.-10 p.m. Rides are $2 each way, $5 for a day pass, $20 for a weekly pass, or $40 for a monthly pass.

Van Shuttle

Arnott's Lodge and Hiking Adventures runs an around-island van expedition called the "Big Island Experience" oriented toward the budget traveler, camper, and backpacker. Their van makes a counterclockwise run around the north side of the island from Hilo to Kona on Tuesday, Friday, and Sunday, and continues south around the island from Kona to Hilo on Monday, Wednesday, and Saturday, stopping at a variety of historical and scenic sites, towns, eateries, and accommodations on the way. Each one-day, half-island segment of this trip costs $20 if you stay on the van and enjoy the ride to its destination. A one-way pass for each half-segment, good for one month, costs $36. With it you can get off and on at any or all of the stops, but they ask that you give them 24-hour notice for pick-up. Call 969-7097 or fax 961-9638 for information and reservations.

Taxis

Both the Hilo and Kona airports always have taxis waiting for fares. From Hilo's airport to downtown costs about $12, and from Kona to most hotels along Ali'i Dr. in Kailua is $22. Obviously, a taxi is no way to get around if you're trying to save money. Most taxi companies, both in Kona and Hilo, run sightseeing services for fixed prices. In **Kona** try: Kona Taxi, tel. 329-7779; Paradise Taxi, tel. 329-1234; Marina Taxi, tel. 329-2481. In **Hilo** try: Hilo Harry's Taxi, tel. 935-7091; A-1 Bob's Taxi, tel. 959-4800; ABC Taxi, tel. 9692076; Hawaii Taxi, tel. 959-6359.

Note: Inquire from the County Transit Agency, tel. 935-8241, about money-saving coupons for "shared-ride taxi service." They allow door-to-door taxi service within nine miles of the urbanized areas of Hilo and Kona. Service hours and other restrictions apply.

Hitchhiking

The old thumb works on the Big Island about as well as anywhere else. Some people hitchhike rather than take the Hele-On Bus not so much to save money but to save time! It's a good idea to check the bus schedule (and routes), and set out about 30 minutes before the scheduled departure. If you don't have good luck, just wait for the bus to come along and hail it. It'll stop.

SIGHTSEEING TOURS

Tours are offered that will let you literally cover the Big Island from top to bottom. You can drive it, fly it, sail around it, hike it, or bike it.

Note: For ocean, bicycling, and hiking tours, see the "Sports and Recreation" section above.

Bus and Van Tours

Narrated and fairly tame island bus tours are operated by**Robert's Tours,** tel. 329-1688 or 966-5483; and by **Polynesian Adventure Tours,** tel. 329-8008. Tours run $40-60 pp and either circle the island or have Kilauea Volcano as their main feature.

Four-wheel-drive van tours include: **Waipio Valley Shuttle,** tel. 775-7121, offering a two-hour tour down to Waipio Valley ($25) and a Mauna Kea summit tour ($75), minimum four people; and **Hawaiian Resorts Transportation Com-**

free Kailua-Kona Shuttle

J.D. BISIGNANI

pany, tel. 775-7291, which also offers a trip into Waipio Valley ($26). In addition, Arnott's Lodge in Hilo, tel. 969-7097, offers a Mauna Kea tour on Tuesday and Friday 10 a.m.-7 p.m. for $75. At other times, the van can be chartered for $300 for four people, $75 for each extra person.

Paradise Safaris, tel. 322-2366 or (800) 545-5662, owned and operated by Pat Wright, has been taking visitors on high-adventure trips around the Big Island for the last 10 years. Pat, originally from New Mexico, is a professional guide who's plied his trade from the Rockies to New Zealand and has taken people on trips ranging from mountaineering to whitewater rafting. Your comfort and safety, as you roam the Big Island, are ensured as you ride in sturdy GMC High Sierra vans with 4WD and a/c. The premier trip offered by Paradise Safaris is an eight-hour journey to the top of Mauna Kea. Pat not only fills your trip with stories, anecdotes, and fascinating facts during the ride, he tops off the safari by setting up an eight-inch telescope so you can get a personal view of the heavens through the rarefied atmosphere atop the great mountain. Pat will pick you up at your hotel in Kailua-Kona at about 4 p.m. If you're staying on the Hilo side, he will meet you at a predetermined spot along the Saddle Road. The price is $125, with hot savory drinks and good warm parkas included. Paradise Safaris will also tailor special trips for photography, hiking, astronomy, and shore fishing. E-mail: parsaf@maunakea.com; Web site: www.maunakea.com.

Arnott's Lodge and Hiking Adventures, 98 Apapane Road, Hilo, HI 96720, tel. 967-7097, will take you on hiking and swimming trips in a relaxed atmosphere.

Tour Tapes and Brochures
For a unique concept, rent Tour Tapes, narrated by Russ Apple, Ph.D., a retired national-park ranger and 1987 winner of the *Historic Hawaii Foundation Award.* Russ dispenses his knowledge about the Big Island as you drive along prescribed routes, mostly in and around Hawaii Volcanoes National Park. Tapes and decks are available in Hilo from the Hilo Hawaiian Hotel, Hawaii Naniloa Resort, and Lyman House Museum. They are also available at the Volcano Art Center.

The Big Island chapter of the HVB puts out the free "Hawaii's Big Island Driving Tour" brochure. Maps, photos, and text detail one and multiple-day self-drive itineraries of major historical and cultural points of interest, scenic spots, and other highlights around the island. Cursory coverage, but it introduces all areas of the island. Pick one up at either the Hilo or Kona HVB office.

Helicopter and Air Tours
Air tours are a great way to see the Big Island, but they are expensive especially when the volcano is putting on a mighty display. Expect to spend a minimum of $135-275 for a front-row seat to watch the amazing light show from the

air. Kilauea volcano erupting is like winning the lottery for these small companies, and many will charge whatever the market will bear.

Tip: To get the best view of the volcanic activity, schedule your flight for the morning, and no later than 2 p.m. Later, clouds and fog can set in to obstruct your view.

Volcano Helitours, tel. 967-7578, owned and operated by David Okita, is intimately familiar with the volcano area. Their heliport sits atop Kilauea and is located just off a fairway of the Volcano Golf and Country Club. Rates are extremely competitive, and because your flight originates atop the volcano, you waste no air time going to or from the eruption sites. The helicopter is a four-passenger (all seats have windows) Hughes 500D.

Helicopter flights from Hilo International Airport are very competitively priced, with savings over the companies operating out of Kailua-Kona. Try **Io Aviation,** tel. 935-3031, or **Kainoa Aviation,** tel. 961-5591. **Safari Helicopters,** tel. 969-1259 or (800) 326-3356 from other islands, also flies from Hilo. Its prices run $130-249. (E-

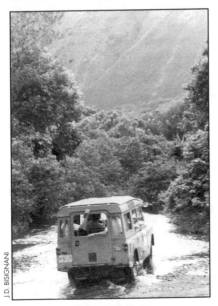

Waipio Valley Shuttle

mail: safari@safariair.com; Web site: www.safariair.com.)

Mauna Kea Helicopters, tel. 885-6400, flies from the small Kamuela Airport in Waimea.

Helicopter tours also leave from the Kona side. One of the oldest and most knowledgeable helicopter companies on the Big Island is **Kenai Helicopters,** tel. 329-7424 in Kona, 969-3131 in Hilo, or (800) 622-3144 from the Mainland. They offer a "Creations of Pele and Hidden Treasures of Kohala" tour for $299, leaving from the Hapuna helipad. From Hilo are the "Fire and Rain Tour," which includes a rainforest and Puna Coast flyover for $160, "Formations of Pele" for $160, and "Hidden Treasures of Kohala" for $140. A ride with Kenai is a once-in-a-lifetime thrill. With its spotless safety record, **Blue Hawaiian Helicopters,** tel. 961-5600 or (880) 786-2583, operates from the Waikoloa Heliport on the Kona side and from the Hilo airport. (E-mail: blue@maui.net.) **Hawaii Helicopters,** tel. 329-4700, flies from the Kona airport. (E-mail: pchild@pixi.com; Web site: www.hawaiiheli.com.)

For fixed-wing air tours try one of the following: **Big Island Air** offers small-plane flights from Kona Airport, two-person minimum, tel. 329-4868 or (800) 303-8868. They fly a volcano tour in an eight-passenger Cessna 402 for $199 pp or $119 for the early bird special. Every seat is a window seat. The plane can be chartered for $550 an hour from Kona or $660 an hour from Hilo. From either Kona or Hilo, **Classic Aviation,** tel. 329-8687, (800) 695-8100, offers a number of flying adventures at $125-250 pp in their open-cockpit biplane. (E-mail: biplane@ilhawaii.net; Web site: www.planet-hawaii.com/biplane.)

Ecotourism in Hawaii

Ecotourism is economically, culturally, socially, and environmentally sensitive and sustainable tourism that helps promote local communities and organizations and works in harmony with nature. Although small potatoes yet in the Hawaiian (and worldwide) tourism economy, ecotourism and its goals are growing in importance and will become a major factor in the economic vitality of tourism in the state. For more information on ecotourism in Hawaii, contact the Hawaii Ecotourism Association, P.O. Box 61435, Honolulu, HI 96839, tel. 956-2866. (E-Mail: hea@aloha.net; Web site: www.planet-hawaii.com/hea.) In addition, the following organizations also can provide related information and contacts: Ecotourism Society International, P.O. Box 755, North Bennington, VT 05257, tel. (802) 447-2121, fax (802) 447-2122 (E-mail: ecotsocy@iga.apc.org; Web site: www.ecotourism.org); and the Center For Responsible Travel, P.O. Box 827, San Anselmo, CA 94979, tel. (415) 258-6594.

The following is a partial list of organizations and companies, both public and private, that offer environmentally sound tours and outings on the Big Island.

Hawaii Audubon Society, 212 Merchant St., Suite 320, Honolulu, HI 96813, tel. 528-1432 (hiking and birding).

Hawaii Volcanoes National Park/Interpretation, P.O. Box 52, Hawaii Volcanoes National Park, HI 96718, tel. 967-7311 (hikes and talks).

Sierra Club, P.O. Box 3220, Kailua-Kona, HI 96745, tel. 885-3575 (hikes and service trips).

Hawaiian Walkways, P.O. Box 2193, Kamuela, HI 96743, tel./fax 885-7759 or (800) 457-7759 (hiking).

Hawaii Forest and Trail, P.O. Box 2975, Kailua-Kona, HI 96745, tel. 322-8881, fax 322-8883, or (800) 464-1993 (hiking and birding).

Hawaii Volcano GeoVentures, P.O. Box 794, Volcano, HI 96785, tel./fax 985-8972 (hiking).

Waipio Valley Shuttle and Tours, P.O. Box 5128, Kukuihaele, HI 96727, tel. 775-7121 (van tour).

Dan MacSweeney's Whalewatching Adventures. P.O. Box 139, Holualoa, HI 96725, tel. 332-0028 (sailing and whalewatching).

Maile **Charters,** P.O. Box 44335, Kamuela, HI 96743, tel. 326-5174 or (800) 726-SAIL (sailing and whalewatching).

Paradise Safaris, P.O. Box 9027, Kailua-Kona, HI 96745, tel. 322-2366 or (800) 545-5662 (van tours).

SPECIAL NEEDS

Help for the Handicapped

A handicapped or physically disabled person can have a wonderful time in Hawaii; all that's needed is a little pre-planning. The following is general advice that should help your planning.

Commission on Persons with Disabilities

This commission was designed with the express purpose of aiding handicapped people. They are a source of invaluable information and distribute self-help booklets free of charge. Any handicapped person heading to Hawaii should write first or visit their offices on arrival. For the *Aloha Guide To Accessibility* ($3) write or visit the head office at: Commission on the Handicapped, 500 Ala Moana Blvd., Honolulu, HI 96813, tel. 586-8121; on Maui, 54 High St., Wailuku, Maui, HI 96793, tel. 243-5441; on Kauai, 3060 Eiwa St. #207, Lihue, Kauai, HI 96766, tel. 241-3308; on Hawaii, P.O. Box 1641, Hilo, HI 96820, tel. 933-7747.

General Information

The key for a smooth trip is to make as many arrangements ahead of time as possible. Tell the transportation companies and hotels you'll be dealing with the nature of your handicap in advance so that they can make arrangements to accommodate you. Bring your medical records and notify medical establishments of your arrival if you'll be needing their services. Travel with a friend or make arrangements for an aide on arrival (see below). Bring your own wheelchair if possible and let airlines know if it is battery-powered; boarding interisland carriers requires steps. No problem: they'll board you early on special lifts, but they must know that you're coming. Most hotels and restaurants accommodate disabled persons, but always call ahead just to make sure.

Hawaii Services

At Hilo Airport there are no facilities for deplaning non-ambulatory people from propeller planes, only from jets and on the jetways. Interisland flights should be arranged only on jets. Ramps and a special elevator provide access in the bi-level terminal. Parking is convenient in designated areas. At Kona airport, boarding and deplaning is possible for the handicapped. Ramps make the terminal accessible. To get around, **Handi-Vans** are available in Hilo, tel. 961-6722. **Kamealoha Unlimited** has specially equipped vans, tel. 966-7244. **Parking permits** are available from the Department of Finance, tel. 961-8231. Medical help, nurses, and companions can be arranged through **Big Island**

Center for Independent Living, tel. 935-3777. Doctors are referred by **Hilo Hospital,** tel. 961-4211, and **Kona Hospital,** tel. 322-9311. Medical equipment is available from **Kamealoha Unlimited,** tel. 966-7244; **Medi-Home,** tel. 969-1123; **Pacific Rent-All,** tel. 935-2974.

HEALTH AND CONDUCT

In a recent survey published by *Science Digest,* Hawaii was cited as the healthiest state in the U.S. in which to live. Indeed, Hawaiian citizens live longer than anywhere else in America: men to 76 years and women to 82. Lifestyle, heredity, and diet help with these figures, but Hawaii is still an oasis in the middle of the ocean, and germs just have a tougher time getting there. There are no cases of malaria, cholera, or yellow fever. Because of a strict quarantine law, rabies is also nonexistent. On the other hand, tooth decay, perhaps because of a wide use of sugar and the enzymes present in certain tropical fruits, is 30% above the national average. With the perfect weather, a multitude of fresh-air activities, soothing negative ionization from the sea, and a generally relaxed and carefree lifestyle, everyone feels better there. Hawaii is just what the doctor ordered: a beautiful, natural health spa. That's one of its main drawing cards. The food and water are perfectly safe, and the air quality is the best in the country.

Handling the Sun

Don't become a victim of your own exuberance. People can't wait to strip down and lie on the sand like beached whales, but the tropical sun will burn you to a cinder if you're silly. The burning rays come through easier in Hawaii because of the sun's angle, and you don't feel them as much because there's always a cool breeze. The worst part of the day is 11 a.m.-3 p.m. You'll just have to force yourself to go slowly. Don't worry; you'll be able to flaunt your best souvenir, your golden Hawaiian tan, to your green-with-envy friends when you get home. It's better than showing them a boiled lobster body with peeling skin! If your skin is snowflake white, 15 minutes per side on the first day is plenty. Increase by 15-minute intervals every day, which will allow you a full hour per side by the fourth day. Have faith; this is enough to give you a deep golden, uniform tan.

Haole Rot

A peculiar condition caused by the sun is referred to locally as *haole* rot. It's called this because it supposedly affects only white people, but you'll notice some dark-skinned people with the same condition. Basically, the skin becomes mottled with white spots that refuse to tan. You get a blotchy effect, mostly on the shoulders and back. Dermatologists have a fancy name for it, and they'll give you a fancy prescription with a not-so-fancy price tag to cure it. It's common knowledge throughout the islands that Selsun Blue shampoo has some ingredient that stops the white mottling effect. Just wash your hair with it and then make sure to rub the lather over the affected areas, and it should clear up.

Bugs

Everyone, in varying degrees, has an aversion to vermin and creepy crawlers. Hawaii isn't infested with a wide variety, but it does have its share. Mosquitoes were unknown in the islands until their larvae stowed away in the water barrels of the *Wellington* in 1826 and were introduced at Lahaina. They bred in the tropical climate and rapidly spread to all the islands. They are a particular nuisance in the rainforests. Be prepared, and bring a natural repellent like citronella oil, available in most health stores on the islands, or a commercial product available in all groceries or drugstores. Campers will be happy to have mosquito coils to burn at night as well. Cockroaches are very democratic insects. They hassle all strata of society equally. They breed well in Hawaii and most hotels are at war with them, trying desperately to keep them from being spotted by guests. One comforting thought is that in Hawaii they aren't a sign of filth or dirty housekeeping. They love the climate like everyone else, and it's a real problem keeping them under control.

Beware the Slipper Dog

Every neighborhood has one, and they always strike in the middle of the night, never during the day. Because of the custom of no shoes inside, a pile of slippers invariably graces the entrance to most homes, somewhat like a free form sculpture or cosmic artificial plant. In the morning, a slipper or multiple slippers, never two from the same pair, is missing. Instantly resignation and recognition set in. Slipper Dog! So, if you see a local person, or even a tourist, walking down the street a bit lopsided wearing one pink, size 9 slipper, and one black, size 12 slipper, you will be observing at close hand a victim of Slipper Dog.

WATER SAFETY

Hawaii has one very sad claim to fame: more people drown here than anywhere else in the world. Moreover, there are dozens of yearly swimming victims with broken necks and backs or with injuries from scuba and snorkeling accidents. These statistics shouldn't keep you out of the sea, because it is indeed beautiful, benevolent in most cases, and a major reason to go to Hawaii. But if you're foolish, the sea will bounce you like a basketball and suck you away for good. The best remedy is to avoid situations you can't handle. Don't let anyone dare you into a situation that makes you uncomfortable. "Macho men" who know nothing about the power of the sea will be tumbled into Cabbage Patch dolls in short order. Ask lifeguards or beach attendants about conditions, and follow their advice. If local people refuse to go in, there's a good reason. Even experts get in trouble in Hawaiian waters. Some beaches, such as Waikiki, are as gentle as a lamb and you would have to tie an anchor around your neck to drown there. Others, especially on the north coasts during the winter months, are frothing giants.

While beachcombing, or especially when walking out on rocks, never turn your back to the sea. Be aware of undertows (the waves drawing back into the sea). They can knock you off your feet. Before entering the water, study it for rocks, breakers, reefs, and riptides. Riptides are powerful currents, like rivers in the sea, that can drag you out. Mostly they peter out not too far from shore, and you can often see their choppy waters on the surface. If caught in a "rip," don't fight to swim directly against it; you'll lose and only exhaust yourself. Swim diagonally across it, while going along with it, and try to stay parallel to the shore. Don't waste all your lung power yelling, and rest by floating.

When bodysurfing, never ride straight in; come to shore at a 45-degree angle. Remember, waves come in sets. Little ones can be followed by giants, so watch the action awhile instead of plunging right in. Standard procedure is to duck under a breaking wave. You can survive even thunderous oceans using this technique. Don't try to swim through a heavy froth and never turn your back and let it smash you. Don't swim alone if possible, and obey all warning signs. Hawaiians want to entertain you and they don't put up signs just to waste money. The last rule is, "If in doubt, stay out."

Yikes!

Sharks live in all the oceans of the world. Most mind their own business and stay away from shore. Hawaiian sharks are well fed—on fish—and don't usually bother with unsavory humans. If you encounter a shark, don't panic! Never thrash around because this will trigger their attack instinct. If they come close, scream loudly.

Portuguese man-o-wars put out long, floating tentacles that sting if they touch you. Don't wash the sting off with fresh water, as this will only aggravate it. Hot salt water will take away the sting, as will alcohol (the drinking or the rubbing kind), after-shave lotion, and meat tenderizer (MSG), which can be found in any supermarket or Chinese restaurant.

Coral can give you a nasty cut, and it's known for causing infections because it's a living organism. Wash the cut immediately and apply an antiseptic. Keep it clean and covered, and watch for infection.

Poisonous sea urchins, such as the lacquer-black *wana,* can be beautiful creatures. They are found in shallow tidepools and will hurt you if you step on them. Their spines will break off, enter your foot, and burn like blazes. There are cures. Vinegar and wine poured on the wound will stop the burning. If not available, the Hawaiian solution is urine. It might seem ignominious to have someone pee on your foot, but it'll put the fire out. The spines will disintegrate in a few days, and there are generally no long-term effects.

Hawaiian reefs also have their share of moray eels. These creatures are ferocious in appearance but will never initiate an attack. You'll have to poke around in their holes while snorkeling or scuba diving to get them to attack. Sometimes this is inadvertent on the diver's part, so be careful where you stick your hand while underwater.

HAWAIIAN FOLK MEDICINE AND CURES

Hawaiian folk medicine is well developed, and its cures for common ailments have been used effectively for centuries. Hawaiian *kahuna* were highly regarded for their medicinal skills, and Hawaiians were by far some of the healthiest people in the world until the coming of the Europeans. Many folk remedies and cures are used to this day and, what's more, they work. Many of the common plants and fruits that you'll encounter provide some of the best remedies. When roots and seeds and special exotic plants are used, the preparation of the medicine is as painstaking as in a modern pharmacy. These prescriptions are exact and take an expert to prepare. They should never be prepared or administered by an amateur.

Common Curative Plants

Arrowroot, for diarrhea, is a powerful narcotic used in rituals and medicines. The pepper plant *(Piper methisticum)* is chewed and the juice is spat into a container for fermenting. Used as a medicine for urinary tract infections, rheumatism, and asthma, it also induces sleep and cures headaches. A poultice for wounds is made from the skins of ripe bananas. Peelings have a powerful antibiotic quality and contain vitamins A, B, and C, phosphorous, calcium, and iron. The nectar from the plant was fed to babies as a vitamin juice. Breadfruit sap is used for healing cuts and as a moisturizing lotion. Coconut is used to make moisturizing oil, and the juice was chewed, spat into the hand, and used as a shampoo. Guava is a source of vitamins A, B, and C. Hibiscus has been used as a laxative. *Kukui* nut oil makes a gargle for sore throats and a laxative, plus the flowers are used to cure

LOUISE FOOTE

KUKUI (CANDLENUT TREE)

Reaching heights of 80 feet, the *kukui* (candlenut) was a veritable department store to the Hawaiians, who made use of almost every part of this utilitarian giant. Used as cure-alls, its nuts, bark, or flowers were ground into potions and salves and taken as a general tonic, applied to ulcers and cuts as an effective antibiotic, or administered internally as a cure for constipation or asthma attacks. The bark was mixed with water and the resulting juice was used as a dye in tattooing, tapa-cloth making, and canoe painting, and as a preservative for fishnets. The oily nuts were burned as a light source in stone holders, and ground and eaten as a condiment called *inamona*. Polished nuts took on a beautiful sheen and were strung as lei. Lastly, the wood itself was hollowed into canoes and sed as fishnet floats.

diarrhea. *Noni,* an unappetizing hand-grenade-shaped fruit that you wouldn't want to eat unless you had to, reduces tumors, diabetes, and high blood pressure, and the juice is good for diarrhea. Sugarcane sweetens many concoctions, and the juice of toasted cane was a tonic for sick babies. Sweet potato is used as a tonic during pregnancy, and juiced as a gargle for phlegm. Tamarind is a natural laxative and contains the most acid and sugar of any fruit on earth. Taro has been used for lung infections and thrush, and as suppositories. Yams are good for coughs, vomiting, constipation, and appendicitis.

HOSPITALS AND PHARMACIES

Hospitals

Medical help is available from Hilo Medical Center, tel. 974-4700; Kona Community Hospital in Kealakekua, tel. 322-9311; Honokaa Hospital, tel. 775-7211; North Hawaii Community Hospital in Kamuela, tel. 889-6211; and Kau Hospital in Pahala, tel. 928-8331.

Drugstores

Of the numerous drug stores throughout the island, the following should meet your needs: Longs Drugs, Hilo, tel. 935-3357, or Kona, tel. 329-1380; Village Pharmacy, Waimea, tel. 885-4418.

ALTERNATIVE HEALTH CARE

The Big Island is blessed with some of the finest natural healers and practitioners in the state. For a holistic healing experience of body, mind, and soul, the following are highly recommended.

At the **School of Hawaiian Lomi Lomi,** P.O. Box 221, Captain Cook, HI 96704, tel. 323-2416 or 328-2472, Margaret Machado, assisted by her husband Daniel, provides the finest *lomi lomi* and traditional Hawaiian herbal cures in the islands. Both are renowned *kapuna* who dispense a heavy dose of love and concern with every remedy prescribed.

Acupuncture and Herbs is the domain of Angela Longo. This remarkable woman is not only a superbly trained, licensed practitioner of traditional Chinese medicine and acupuncture, but she covers all bases by holding a Ph.D. in biochemistry from U.C. Berkeley. For a totally holistic health experience, contact Angela at her Waimea office, tel. 885-7886.

Angela's top student, **Karen MacIsaac,** has opened a Chinese herb and acupuncture clinic by appointment only, tel. 329-4393, at 75-5995 Kuakini Hwy., Suite 126, Kailua-Kona, HI 96740.

The **Hawaiian Islands School of Body Therapy,** tel. 322-0048, owned and operated by Peter Wind and Lynn Filkins-Wind, offers state-certified massage courses and mini-courses for the beginning or experienced therapist. A full range of massage, anatomy, and physiology are part of the coursework preparing the student for a Hawaii

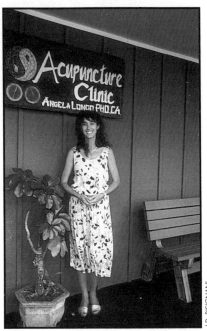

Ms. Angela Longo

State License. Programs include a basic massage program taking 150 hours, an advanced massage program of 450 hours, and a third-level course designed for the professional that takes a minimum of one year's intensive study to complete. Under Peter and Lynn's tutelage you'll learn *lomi lomi,* reflexology, hydrotherapy, aroma therapy, trigger point therapy, and treatment therapy. Lynn specializes in treatment therapy, which she teaches by the European, hands-on approach, while Peter is a hydrotherapist and colonics therapist. They are assisted by Gigi Goochey, the anatomy and physiology instructor. Lynn and Peter are dedicated professionals who have clued-in, body and soul, to the art of healing.

To revitalize those aching muscles and put a spring in your step, visit massage practitioners with magic in their hands: **Kiauhou Massage and Spa** at the Keauhou Beach Hotel, Room 227, tel. 322-0048, is open Tuesday, Thursday, and Saturday 10 a.m.-5 p.m., and Monday, Wednesday, and Friday 5-8 p.m.

To get that just-right chiropractic adjustment, visit the **Chiropractic Clinic** of Dr. Kenneth C. Williams, tel. 885-7719.

A wonderful healing center is **Halemana** in Pahoa, tel. 965-7783, where they'll soothe you with acupuncture and massage.

Academy of Therapeutic Massage, c/o Nancy Kahalewai P.M.T., 197 Kinoole St., Hilo, HI 96720, tel. 935-1405, focuses on pre-licensing programs with an emphasis on sports massage, injury prevention and care, inner changes of body psychology, and *lomi lomi.* Semesters include a summer intensive and regular winter and fall classes. Nancy, a longtime member of the Hawaii Board of Massage Advisory Committee and nationally certified, has been practicing her healing arts in the islands for over 15 years. She not only has the "golden touch" but is a terrific resource for all types of alternative medicines available on the Big Island. All massages, given by students and graduates, are completely supervised! This is a great opportunity to receive a quality massage at a reasonable price while visiting Hilo.

ILLEGAL DRUGS

The use and availability of illegal, controlled, and recreational drugs are about the same in Hawaii as throughout the rest of America. Cocaine constitutes the fastest-growing recreational drug and is available on the streets of the main cities, especially Honolulu. Although most dealers are small-time, the drug is brought in by organized crime. The underworld here is mostly populated by men of Asian descent, and recently the Japanese *yakuza* is said to be displaying a heightened involvement in Hawaiian organized crime. Cocaine trafficking fans out from Honolulu.

Another drug menace infesting Hawaii is "ice." Ice is smokable methamphetamine that wires a user for up to 24 hours. The high lasts longer and the drug is cheaper than cocaine or its derivative, "crack." Users become quickly dependent, despondent, and violent because ice robs them of their sleep as well as their dignity. Its use is particularly prevalent among late-night workers. Many of the violent deaths in Honolulu have been linked to the growing use of ice.

However, the main drug available and commonly used in Hawaii is marijuana, which is locally called *pakalolo.* There are also three varieties of psychoactive mushrooms that contain the hallucinogen psilocybin. They grow wild but are considered illegal controlled substances.

Pakalolo Growing

About 30 years ago, mostly *haole* hippies from the Mainland began growing pot in the more remote sections of the islands, such as Puna on Hawaii and around Hana on Maui. They discovered what legitimate planters had known for 200 years: plant a broomstick in Hawaii, treat it right, and it'll grow. *Pakalolo,* after all, is a weed, and it grows in Hawaii like wildfire. The locals quickly got into the act when they realized that they, too, could grow a "money tree." As a matter of fact, they began resenting the *haole* usurpers, and a quiet and sometimes dangerous feud has been going on ever since. Much is made of the viciousness of the backcountry "growers" of Hawaii. There are tales of booby traps and armed patrols guarding their plants in the hills, but mostly it's a cat-and-mouse game between the authorities and the growers. If you, as a tourist, are tramping about in the forest and happen upon someone's "patch," don't touch anything. Just back off and you'll be okay. Pot has the largest monetary turnover of any crop in the islands, and as such, is now considered a major source of agricultural revenue. There are all kinds of local names and varieties of pot in Hawaii, the most potent being "Kona Gold," "Puna Butter," and "Maui Wowie." These names are all becoming passé. It's possible that a dealer will approach you. Their normal technique is to stroll by and in a barely audible whisper say, "Buds?"

Hawaiian *pakalolo* is sold slightly differently than on the Mainland. The dealers package it in heat-sealed "Seal-a-Meal" plastic bags. The glory days are over, and many deals, especially on the streets, are rip-offs. All passengers leaving Hawaii are subject to a thorough "agricultural inspection," and you can bet they're not only looking for illegal papayas. In 1984 there was an uproar involving a particular post office on the Big Island. It turned out that a staggering 80% of the outgoing packages contained *pakalolo.* The authorities are getting wise.

THEFT AND HASSLES

From the minute you sit behind the wheel of your rental car, you'll be warned not to leave valuables unattended and to lock up your car tighter than a drum. Signs warning about theft at most major tourist attractions help fuel your paranoia. Many hotel rooms offer coin-operated safes so you can lock your valuables away and relax while getting sunburned. Stories abound about purse snatchings and surly locals just itching to give you a hard time. Well, they're all true to a degree, but Hawaii's reputation is much worse than the reality. In Hawaii you'll have to observe two golden laws: if you look for trouble, you'll find it; and a fool and his camera are soon parted.

Theft
The majority of theft in Hawaii is of the "sneak thief" variety. If you leave your hotel door unlocked, a camera sitting on the seat of your rental car, or valuables on your beach towel, you'll be inviting a very obliging thief to pad away with your stuff. You have to learn to take precautions, but they won't be anything like those employed in rougher areas like South America or Southeast Asia; just normal American precautions.

If you must walk alone at night, stay on the main streets in well-lit areas. Always lock your hotel door and windows and place valuable jewelry in the hotel safe. When you leave your hotel for the beach, there is absolutely no reason to carry all your traveler's checks and credit cards or a big wad of money. Just take what you'll need for drinks and lunch. If you're uptight about leaving money in your beach bag, stick it in your bathing suit or bikini. American money is just

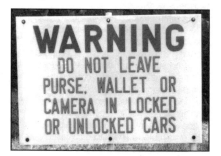

as negotiable if it is damp. Don't leave your camera or portable stereo on the beach unattended. Ask a person nearby to watch them for you while you go for a dip. Most people won't mind at all, and you can repay the favor.

While sightseeing in your shiny new rental car, which immediately brands you as a tourist, again, don't take more than what you'll need for the day. Why people leave a camera sitting on the seat of their car is a mystery! Many people lock valuables in the trunk, but remember that most good car thieves can "jimmy" it open as quickly as you can open it with your key. If you must, for some reason, leave camera or valuables in your car, lock them in the trunk, stash them under a seat back that's been reclined, or consider putting them under the hood. Thieves usually don't look there, and on most modern cars you can only pop the hood with a lever inside the car. It's not fail-safe, but it's worth a try.

Campers face special problems because their entire scene is open to thievery. Most campgrounds don't have any real security, but who, after all, wants to fence an old tent or a used sleeping bag? Many tents have zippers that can be secured with a small padlock. If you want to go trekking and are afraid to leave your gear in the campground, take a large green garbage bag with you. Transport your gear down the trail and then walk off through some thick brush. Put your gear in the garbage bag and bury it under leaves and other light camouflage. That's about as safe as you can be. You can also use a variation on this technique instead of leaving your valuables in your rental car.

Hassles
Another self-perpetuating myth about Hawaii is that "the natives are restless." An undeniable animosity exists between locals (especially those with some Hawaiian blood) and *haole*. Fortunately, this prejudice is directed mostly at the group and not at the individual. The locals are resentful of those *haole* who came, took their land, and relegated them to second-class citizenship. They realize that this is not the average tourist and they can tell what you are at a glance. Tourists usually are treated with understanding and are given a type of immunity. Besides, Hawaiians are still among the most friendly, giving, and understanding people on earth.

Haole who live in Hawaii might tell you stories of their children having trouble at school. They could even mention an unhappy situation at some schools called "beat-up-a-*haole*" day, and you might hear that if you're a *haole* it's not a matter of "if" you'll be beaten up, but "when." Truthfully, most of this depends upon your attitude and your sensitivity. The locals feel infringed upon, so don't fuel these feelings. If you're at a beach park and there is a group of local people in one area, don't crowd them. If you go into a local bar and you're the only one of your ethnic group in sight, you shouldn't have to be told to leave. Much of the hassle involves drinking. Booze brings out the worst prejudice on all sides. If you're invited to a beach party, and the local guys start getting drunk, make this your exit call. Don't wait until it's too late.

Most trouble seems to be directed toward white men. White women are mostly immune from being beaten up, but they have to beware of the violence of sexual abuse and rape. Although plenty of local women marry white men, it's not a good idea to try to pick up a local girl. If you're known in the area and have been properly introduced, that's another story. Also, women out for the night in bars or discos can be approached if they're not in the company of local guys. If you are with your bikini-clad girlfriend, and a bunch of local guys are, say, drinking beer at a beach park, don't go over and try to be friendly and ask, "What's up?" You, and especially your girlfriend, just might find out. Maintain your own dignity and self-respect by treating others with dignity and respect. Most times you'll reap what you sow.

WHAT TO TAKE

It's a snap to pack for a visit to the Big Island. Everything is on your side. The weather is moderate and uniform on the whole, and the style of dress is delightfully casual. The rule of thumb is to pack lightly: few items, and clothing light in both color and weight. What you'll need will depend largely on your itinerary and your desires. Are you drawn to the nightlife, the outdoors, or both? If you forget something at home, it won't be a disaster. You can buy everything you'll need in Hawaii. As a matter of fact, Hawaiian clothing, such as muumuus and aloha shirts, is one of the best purchases you can make, both in comfort and style. It's quite feasible to bring only one or two changes of clothing with the express purpose of outfitting yourself while there. Prices on bathing suits, bikinis, and summer wear in general are quite reasonable.

Matters of Taste

A grand conspiracy in Hawaii adhered to by everyone—tourist, traveler, and resident—is to "hang loose" and dress casual. Best of all, alohawear is just about all you'll need for comfort and virtually every occasion. The classic muumuu is large and billowy, and aloha shirts are made to be worn outside the pants. The best of both are made of cool cotton. Rayon is a natural fiber that isn't too bad, but polyester is hot, sticky, and not

authentic. Not all muumuus are of the "tent persuasion." Some are very fashionable and form-fitted with peek-a-boo slits up the side, down the front, or around the back. *Holomuu* are muumuus fitted at the waist with a flowing skirt to the ankles. They are not only elegant, but perfect for "stepping out."

In the Cold and Rain

Two occasions for which you'll have to consider dressing warmly are visits to mountaintops and boat rides where wind and ocean sprays are a factor. You can conquer both with a jogging suit (sweat suit) and a featherweight, water-resistant windbreaker. If you intend to visit Mauna Kea or Mauna Loa, it'll be downright chilly. Your jogging suit with a hooded windbreaker/raincoat will do the trick for all occasions. If you're going to camp or trek, you should add another layer, a woolen sweater being one of the best. Wool is the only natural fiber that retains most of its warmth-giving properties even if it gets wet. Several varieties of "fleece" synthetics currently on the market also have this ability. If your hands get cold, put a pair of socks over them. Tropical rain showers can happen at any time so you might consider a fold-up umbrella, but the sun quickly breaks through and the warming winds blow.

Shoes

Dressing your feet is hardly a problem. You'll most often wear zoris (rubber thongs) for going to and from the beach, leather sandals for strolling and dining, and jogging shoes for trekking and sightseeing. A few discos require leather shoes, but it's hardly worth bringing them just for that. If you plan on heavy-duty trekking, you'll definitely want your hiking boots. Lava, especially a'a, is murderous on shoes. Most backcountry trails are rugged and muddy, and you'll need those good old lug soles for traction. If you plan moderate hikes, you might want to consider bringing rubberized ankle supports to complement your jogging shoes. Most drugstores sell them, and the best are a rubberized sock with toe and heel cut out.

SUE STRANGIO EVERETT

Specialty Items

Following is a list of specialty items that you might consider bringing along. They're not necessities but most will definitely come in handy. A pair of binoculars really enhances sightseeing—great for viewing birds and sweeping panoramas, and almost a necessity if you're going whalewatching. A folding, Teflon-bottomed travel iron makes up for cotton's one major shortcoming, wrinkles; you can't always count on hotels to have irons. Nylon twine and miniature clothespins are handy for drying garments, especially bathing suits. Commercial and hotel laundromats abound, but many times you'll get by with hand-washing a few items in the sink. A transistor radio/tape recorder provides news, weather, and entertainment, and can be used to record impressions, island music, and a running commentary for your slide show. Hair dryer: although the wind can be relied upon to dry wet hair, it leaves a bit to be desired in the styling department. An inflatable raft for riding waves, along with flippers, mask, and snorkel, can easily be bought in Hawaii but don't weigh much or take up much space in your luggage. If you'll be camping, trekking, or boating with only seawater available for bathing, take along "Sea Saver Soap," available from good sporting goods stores. This special soap will lather in

seawater and rinse away the sticky salt residue with it.

For the Camper

If you don't want to take it with you, all necessary camping gear can be purchased or rented while in Hawaii. Besides the above, you should consider taking the following: framed backpack or the convertible packs that turn into suitcases, daypack, matches in a waterproof container, all-purpose knife, mess kit, eating utensils, flashlight (remove batteries), candle, nylon cord, and sewing kit (dental floss works as thread). Take a first-aid kit containing Band-Aids, all-purpose antiseptic cream, alcohol swabs, tourniquet string, cotton balls, elastic bandage, razor blade, Telfa pads, and a small mirror for viewing private nooks and crannies. A light sleeping bag is good, although your fleecy jogging suit with a ground pad and light blanket or even your rain poncho will be sufficient. Definitely bring a down bag for Haleakala or mountainous areas. In a film container pack a few nails, safety pins, fishhooks, line, and bendable wire. Nothing else does what these do and they're all handy for a million and one uses.

Basic Necessities

As previously mentioned, you really have to consider only two "modes" of dressing in Hawaii: beachwear and casual clothing. The following is designed for the mid-range traveler carrying one suitcase or a backpack. Remember that there are laundromats and that you'll be spending a considerable amount of time in your bathing suit. Consider the following: one or two pairs of light cotton slacks for going out and about, and one pair of jeans for trekking, or better yet, corduroys which can serve both purposes; two or three casual sundresses—muumuus are great; three or four pairs of shorts for beachwear and for sightseeing; four to five short-sleeved shirts or blouses and one long-sleeved; three or four colored and printed T-shirts that can be worn anytime from trekking to strolling; a beach coverup—the short terry cloth type is the best; a brimmed hat for rain and sun—the crushable floppy type is great for purse or daypack; two or three pairs of socks are sufficient, nylons you won't need; two bathing suits (nylon ones dry quickest); plastic bags to hold wet bathing suits and laundry; five to six pairs of underwear; towels (optional, because hotels provide them, even for the beach); a first-

aid kit, pocket-size is sufficient; suntan lotion and insect repellent; a daypack or large beach purse. And don't forget your windbreaker, perhaps a shawl for the evening, and an all-purpose jogging suit.

Pets and Quarantine

Hawaii has a very rigid pet quarantine policy designed to keep rabies and other Mainland disease from reaching the state. All domestic pets are subject to a **120-day quarantine** (a 30-say quarantine is allowed by meeting certain pre-arrival and post-arrival requirements—inquire). Unless you are contemplating a move to Hawaii, it is not feasible to take pets. For complete information, contact the Department of Agriculture, Animal Quarantine Division, 99-951 Halawa Valley Street, Aiea, HI 96701, tel. 483-7151.

INFORMATION AND SERVICES

HAWAII VISITORS BUREAU OFFICES

The **HVB** is a top-notch organization providing help and information to all of Hawaii's visitors. Anyone contemplating a trip to Hawaii should visit or write the HVB and inquire about any specific information that might be required. Their advice and excellent brochures on virtually every facet of living, visiting, or simply enjoying Hawaii are free. The material offered is too voluminous to list, but for basics, request individual island brochures (including maps), and ask for their copies of *Member Accommodation Guide* and *Member Restaurant Guide*. Allow two to three weeks for requests to be answered.

HVB Offices Statewide

The best information on the Big Island is dispensed by the **HVB Hilo Branch,** 250 Keawe St., Hilo, HI 96720, tel. 961-5797; or **HVB Kona Branch,** 75-5719 W. Ali'i Dr., Kailua-Kona, HI 96740, tel. 329-7787.

Statewide offices include: **HVB Administrative Office,** Waikiki Business Plaza, 2270 Kalakaua Ave., Suite 801, Honolulu, HI 96815, tel. 923-1811; **Maui HVB,** 1727 Wili Pa Loop, Wailuku, HI 96793, tel. 244-3530; **Kauai HVB,**

3016 Umi St., Suite 207, Lihue, HI 96766, tel. 245-3971.

North American Offices

HVB New York, Empire State Bldg., 350 5th Ave., Suite 1827, New York, NY 10018, tel. (212) 947-0717.

HVB Washington DC, 3975 University Dr., #335, Fairfax, VA 22030, tel. (703) 691-1800.

HVB San Diego, 11835 Carmel Mountain Rd., #1304-353, San Diego, CA 92128, tel. (619) 485-7278.

HVB Canada, c/o Comprehensive Travel, 1260 Hornby St., #104, Vancouver, B.C., Canada V6Z1W2, tel. (604) 669-6691.

European Office

HVB United Kingdom, P.O. Box 208, Sunbury on Thames, Middlesex, England, TW165RJ, tel. 44-181-941-4009.

Asia/Pacific Offices

HVB Japan, Kokusai Bldg., #2F, 1-1, Marunouchi 3-chome, Chiyoda-ku, Tokyo 100, tel. 011-81-3-3201-0430.

HVB Korea, c/o Travel Press, Inc., Samwon Bldg., 10th Floor, 112-5, Sokong-dong, Chung-gu, Seoul 100-070, tel. 82-2-773-6719.

The "HVB Warrior" is posted alongside the roadway, marking sites of cultural and historical importance.

HVB New Zealand, c/o Walshes World, 87 Queen St., 2nd Fl., Dingwall Bldg., Auckland, tel. 64-9-379-3708.

HVB Taiwan, c/o Federal Transportation Co., 8th Fl., 61 Nanking E. Road, Section 3, Taipei, tel. 886-2-507-8133.

Other Tourism-Related Information Sources
The **State Visitor Information** centers at the airports, tel. 934-5840 (Hilo) or 329-3423 (Kona), are good sources of information available on arrival.

LOCAL RESOURCES

For **police, fire, and ambulance** anywhere on the island, dial **911.**

Civil Defense: In case of natural disaster such as hurricanes or tsunamis on the Big Island, call 935-0031.

Coast Guard Search and Rescue: tel. (800) 552-6458.

Sexual Assault Crisis Line: tel. 935-0677.

Aloha Pages, tel. 935-1666, is a free 24-hour "talking telephone" information service on a variety of topics including weather, news, sports, community service, and entertainment. For specific information, dial the above number, followed by a four-digit code number as directed, or check your local Hawaiian phone book for a complete listing of available topics.

Weather, Marine, and Volcano Reports
For recorded information on **local island weather,** call 961-5582; for the **marine report,** call 935-9883; and for **volcano activity,** call 967-7977.

Consumer Protection
If you encounter problems with accommodations, bad service, or downright rip-offs, try the following: the chamber of commerce in Hilo, tel. 935-7178, or in Kailua-Kona, tel. 329-1758; the Hawaii Hotel Association, tel. 923-0407; the Office of Consumer Protection, tel. 974-6230; or the Better Business Bureau, tel. 941-5222.

Post Office
Branch post offices are found in most major towns. Window service is offered Mon.-Fri. 8:30 a.m.-4 p.m.; some offices are open Saturday 10 a.m.-noon. The following are the main offices: Hilo, tel. 933-7090; Kailua, tel. 329-1927; Captain Cook, tel. 323-3663; Waimea/Kamuela, tel. 885-4026; Volcano, tel. 967-7611; Hawi, tel. 889-5301.

Laundromats
There are perhaps a dozen laundromats on the Big Island. **Tyke's Laundromat** is located both in Hilo, at 1454 Kilauea Ave., and in Kona, at 74-5483 Kaiwi Street. Also in Hilo is **Hilo Quality Washerette** at 210 Hoku St., and in Kona you'll find **Hele Mai Laundromat** near the King Kamehameha's Beach Hotel.

Reading Material
Make sure to pick up copies of the following free literature. Besides maps and general information, they often include money-saving coupons. Available at most hotels/condos and at all tourist areas, the weekly publications include: *Guide: Big Island, Beach and Activity Guide: Big Island,*

and *This Week: Big Island.* Island newspapers include: *Hawaii-Tribune Herald,* a Hilo publication; *West Hawaii Today,* published in Kona; and the *Ka'u Landing,* a monthly out of Ocean View.

Libraries are located in towns and schools all over the island. The main branch is at 300 Waianuenue Ave., Hilo, tel. 933-4650. They provide all information regarding libraries. In Kailua-Kona, the library is at 75-140 Hualalai Rd., tel. 327-3077. For bookstores, please refer to the "Shopping" section in the Introduction.

OTHER INFORMATION

Telephone: All-Hawaii Area Code 808
Local calls from public telephones (anywhere on the same island is a local call) cost 25 cents. Calling between islands is a toll call, and the price depends on when and from where you call and for how long you speak. Emergency calls are always free. As they do everywhere else in the U.S., long-distance rates go down at 5 p.m. and again at 11 p.m. until 8 a.m. the next morning. From Friday at 5 p.m. until Monday morning at 8 a.m. rates are cheapest. For directory assistance: local, 1-411; interisland, 1-555-1212; Mainland, 1-area code-555-1212; toll free, (800) 555-1212.

> The area code for all Hawaii is 808.

Time Zones
There is no daylight saving time in Hawaii. When daylight saving time is not observed on the Mainland, Hawaii is two hours behind the West Coast, four hours behind the Midwest, five hours behind the East Coast, and 11 hours behind Germany. Hawaii, being just east of the international date line, is almost a full day behind most Asian and Oceanic cities. Hours behind these countries and cities are: Japan, 19 hours; Singapore, 18 hours; Sydney, 20 hours; New Zealand, 22 hours; Fiji, 22 hours.

Electricity
The same electrical current is in use in Hawaii as on the U.S. Mainland and is uniform throughout the islands. The system functions on 110 volts, 60 cycles of alternating current (AC). Appliances from Japan will work but there is some danger of burnout, while those requiring the normal European voltage of 220 will not work.

Distance, Weights, and Measures
Hawaii, like all of the U.S., employs the "English method" of measuring weights and distances. Basically, dry weights are in ounces and pounds; liquid measures are in ounces, quarts, and gallons; and distances are measured in inches, feet, yards, and miles. The metric system, based on units of 10, is known but is not in general use. The conversion charts at the back of this book should be helpful.

Island Radio
More than a dozen radio stations broadcast on the Big Island. Among those that are popular are: **K-BIG** 106.1 FM in Kona and 97.9 FM in Hilo, playing contemporary music; **KIPA** 620 AM Rainbow Radio out of Hilo with contemporary sounds and requests; **KKOA** 107.7 FM with hot country in Hilo; **KKON** 790 AM with contemporary songs from Kealakekua; **KPUA** 670 AM with news and sports broadcasting from Hilo; **The WAVE** at 97.1 FM broadcasting contemporary sound from Hilo; and Y101.5 FM for island rock.

Island Facts
Hawaii has three fitting nicknames: the Big Island, the Volcano Island, and the Orchid Island. It's the youngest, most southerly, and largest (4,038 square miles) island in the Hawaiian chain. Its color is red, the state flower is the red hibiscus, and the island lei is fashioned from the ohia-lehua blossom.

MONEY AND FINANCES

Currency
U.S. currency is among the drabbest in the world. It's all the same size and color; those unfamiliar with it should spend some time getting acquainted so that they don't make costly mistakes. U.S. coinage in use is: one cent, five cents, ten cents, twenty-five cents, fifty cents, and $1 (uncommon); paper currency is $1, $2 (uncommon), $5, $10, $20, $50, $100. Bills larger than $100 are not in common usage.

Banks

Full-service banks tend to open slightly earlier than Mainland banks, at 8:30 a.m. Mon.-Friday. Closing is at 3 p.m., except for late hours on Friday when most banks remain open until 6 p.m. Of most value to travelers, banks sell and cash traveler's checks, give cash advances on credit cards, exchange and sell foreign currency, and have 24-hour ATM machines. Major banks on the Big Island are American Savings Bank, Bank of Hawaii, and First Hawaiian Bank. All have branches in Hilo, Kona, and Waimea. First Hawaiian also has offices in Honokaa, Kealakekua, Pahoa, and Waikoloa.

Traveler's Checks

Traveler's checks are accepted throughout Hawaii at hotels, restaurants, and car-rental agencies, and in most stores and shops. However, to be readily acceptable they should be in American currency. Some larger hotels that often have Japanese and Canadians guests will accept their currency. Banks accept foreign-currency traveler's checks, but it'll mean an extra trip and inconvenience. It's best to get most of your traveler's checks in $20-50 denominations; anything larger will be hard to cash in shops and boutiques, though not in hotels.

Credit Cards

More and more business is transacted in Hawaii using credit cards. Almost every form of accommodation, shop, restaurant, and amusement accepts them. For renting a car they're almost a must. With "credit card insurance" readily available, they're as safe as traveler's checks and sometimes even more convenient. However, don't rely on them completely because some establishments won't accept them, or perhaps won't accept the kind that you carry.

BOB RACE

HILO

Hilo is a blind date. Everyone tells you what a beautiful personality she has, but . . . But? . . . it rains: 133 inches a year. Mostly the rains come in winter and are limited to predictable afternoon showers, but they do scare some tourists away, keeping Hilo reasonably priced and low key. In spite of, and because of, the rain, Hilo is gorgeous. It's one of the oldest permanently settled towns in Hawaii, and the largest on the windward coast of the island. Hilo's weather makes it a natural greenhouse. Twenty acres of exotic orchids and flowers line the runways at the airport! Botanical gardens and flower farms surround Hilo like a giant lei, and shoulder-to-shoulder banyans canopy entire city blocks. To counterpoint this tropical explosion, Mauna Kea's winter snows backdrop the town. The crescent of Hilo Bay blazes gold at sunrise, while a sculpted lagoon, Asian pagodas, rock gardens, and a tiny island connected by footbridge line its shores. Downtown's waterfront has the perfect false-front buildings that always need a paint job. They lean on each other like "old salts" who've had one too many. Don't make the mistake of underestimating Hilo, or of counting it out because of its rainy reputation.

For most, the blind date with this exotic beauty turns into a fun-filled love affair.

Hilo is a unique town in a unique state in America. You can walk down streets with names like Puueo and Keawe, and they could be streets in Anywhere, U.S.A., with neatly painted houses surrounded by white picket fences. Families live here. There are roots, and traditions, but the town is changing. Fishermen still come for the nightly ritual of soul-fishing and story-swapping from the bridge spanning the Wailuku River, while just down the street newly arrived chefs prepare Cajun blackened fish at a yuppie restaurant as midnight philosophers sip gourmet coffee and munch sweets next door. Hilo is a classic tropical town. Some preserved buildings, proud again after new face-lifts, are a few stories tall and date from the turn of the century when Hilo was a major port of entry to Hawaii. Sidewalks in older sections are covered with awnings because of the rains and add a turn-of-the-century gentility. Because Hilo is a town, most Americans can relate to it: it's big enough to have one-way streets and malls, but not so big that it's a metropolis like Honolulu, or so small that it's a village like Hana. You can walk the central area comfortably in an afternoon, but the town does sprawl, and it's *happening*. Teenagers in "boom box" cars cruise the main strip, which is lined with fine restaurants, high-tech discos, and mom-and-pop shops. There's even a down-and-out section where guys hunker down in alleyways, smoking cigarettes and peering into the night. In the still night, there's the deep-throated sound of a ship's foghorn, a specter of times past when Hilo was a vibrant port. Hilo is the opposite of Kailua-Kona both spiritually and physically. There, everything runs super fast; it's a clone of Honolulu. In Hilo the old beat, the old music, that feeling of a tropical place where rhythms are slow and sensual, still exist. Hilo nights are alive with sounds of the tropics and the heady smell of fruits and flowering trees wafting on the breeze. Hilo remains what it always was—a town, a place where people live.

Hilo is the eastern hub of the island. Choose a direction, and an hour's driving puts you in a time-lost valley deep in *paniolo* country, or on the blackness of a recent lava flow, or above the steaming fumaroles of Hawaii Volcanoes National Park. In and around town are museums, riverbank fishing, cultural centers, plenty of gardens, waterfalls, a potholed riverbed, and lava caves. Hilo's beaches are small, rocky, and hard to find—perfect for keeping crowds away. Hilo is bite-sized, but you'll need a rental car or the Banyan Shuttle to visit most of the sights around town.

The main thoroughfares through town are Kilauea St., which merges into Keawe St. and runs one-way toward the Wailuku River; and Kinoole St., which runs one-way away from the river. Basically they feed into each other and make a big loop through the downtown area. Kamehameha Ave. fronts the town area and runs along the bay.

SIGHTS AND BEACHES

SIGHTS

Lyman Mission House and Museum

The preserved New England-style homestead of David and Sarah Lyman, Congregationalist missionaries who built it in 1839, is the oldest frame building still standing on the Big Island. Lyman House, at 276 Haili St., Hilo, HI 96720, tel. 935-5021, open Mon.-Sat. 9 a.m.-5 p.m., Sunday 1-4 p.m., admission $5 adults, $2.50 children 6-18, opened as a museum in 1932! In 1856, a second story was added, which provided more room and a perfect view of the harbor. In 1926, Haili St. was extended past the home, and at that time the Wilcox and Lyman families had the house turned parallel to the street so that it would front the entrance.

The furniture is authentic "Sandwich Isles" circa 1850, the best pieces fashioned from koa. Much of it has come from other missionary homes, although many pieces belonged to the original occupants.

The floors, mantels, and doors are deep, luxurious koa. The main door is a "Christian door," built by the Hilo Boys Boarding School. The top panels form a cross and the bottom depicts an open Bible. Many of the artifacts on the deep windowsills are tacked down because of earthquakes. One room was used as a schoolroom/dayroom where Mrs. Lyman taught arithmetic, map-making, and proper manners. The dining room holds an original family table that was set with the "Blue Willow" china seen in a nearby hutch. Some of the most interesting exhibits are of small personal items like a music box that still plays, and a collection of New England autumn leaves that Mrs. Lyman had sent over to show her children what that season was like. Upstairs are bedrooms that were occupied by the parents and the eight children (six were boys). Their portraits hang in a row. Mrs. Lyman kept a diary and faithfully recorded eruptions, earthquakes, and tsunamis. Scientists still refer to it for some of the earliest recorded data on these natural disturbances. The master bedroom has a large bed with pineapples carved into the bedposts, crafted by a ship's carpenter who lived with the family for about eight months. The bedroom mirror is an original, in which many Hawaiians received their first surprised look at themselves. A nursery holds a cradle used by all eight children. It's obvious that the Lymans did not live luxuriously, but they were comfortable in their new island home.

© J.D. BISIGNANI AND MOON PUBLICATIONS, INC.

To Hamakua coast and Waimea

HILO

Keokea Point

Hilo Breakwater

Hilo Bay

Alcalea Point

ONEKAHAKAHA BEACH PARK

KEAUKAHA BEACH PARK

137

KAANIANAOE AVE.

SILVA ST.

REEDS BAY BEACH PARK

Reeds Bay

HAWAII NANILOA HOTEL

HILO HAWAIIAN HOTEL

BANYAN DR.

Coconut Island

LILIUOKALANI GARDENS

FISH AUCTION

BOAT SLIPS

WAIAKEA MALL

SWIMMING POOL

BASEBALL STADIUM

CIVIC AUDITORIUM

INFORMATION CENTER

STATE BUILDING

Waiakea Fish Pond

KAMEHAMEHA AVE.

BAYFRONT HWY.

BUS

COUNTY BUILDING

KAIKO'O MALL

VISITORS BUREAU

POST OFFICE

MAUI'S CANOE

SUGAR MILL

YWCA

CHURCH

LIBRARY

LYMAN HOUSE MUSEUM

POLICE STATION

KINOOLE ST.

ULULANI ST.

KAPIOLANI ST.

PONAHAWAI ST.

HAILI ST.

KUKUAU ST.

KINOOLE ST.

WAIANUENUE AVE.

Wailuku River

SCHOOL

Rainbow Falls

HILO HOSPITAL

20

KAUMANA DR.

KOMOHANU ST.

KOMOHANO ST.

MOHOULI ST.

HILO SHOPPING CENTER

YMCA

HILO COLLEGE

KANOELEHUA AVE.

HUALALAI

LEILANI ST.

KILAUEA ST.

HAWAII COMMUNITY COLLEGE

PRINCE KUHIO PLAZA

PUAINAKO TOWN CENTER MALL

11

123

PUAINAKO ST.

KANOELEHUA AVE.

KEAWE ST.

HILO INTERNATIONAL AIRPORT (GENERAL LYMAN FIELD)

POST OFFICE

TERMINAL

CAR RENTALS

2 mi

2 km

0

19

To Saddle Road, Kona, and Kamuela

To Puna and Volcano

Hilo Bay

J.D. BISIGNANI

Next door to the Lyman House, in a modern two-story building, is the museum. The first floor is designated the **Island Heritage Gallery.** The entry is a replica of a Hawaiian grass house, complete with thatched roof and floor mats. Nearby are Hawaiian tools: hammers of clinkstone, chisels of basalt, and state-of-the-art "stone age" polishing stones with varying textures used to rub bowls and canoes to a smooth finish. Hawaiian fiberwork, the best in Polynesia, is the next display. As well as coconut and pandanus, the Hawaiians used the pliable air root of the *ie'ie*. The material, dyed brown or black, was woven into intricate designs. You'll also see fishhooks, stone lamps, mortars and pestles, *lomi lomi* sticks, even a display on *kahuna*, with a fine text on the *kapu* system. Pre-contact displays give way to kimonos from Japan, a Chinese herbal medicine display, and a nook dedicated to Filipino heritage. Saying good-bye is a bust of Mark Twain, carved into a piece of the very monkeypod tree that he planted in Waiohinu in 1866.

Upstairs is the **Earth Heritage Gallery.** The mineral and rock collection here is rated one of the top 10 in the entire country, and by far the best in Polynesia. Marvel at thunder eggs, agates, jaspers, India blue mezolite, aquamarine lazurite from Afghanistan, and hunks of weirdly shaped lava. These displays are the lifelong collection of the great-grandson of the original Rev. Lyman. Anything coming from the earth can be exhibited here: shells named and categorized from around the world, petrified wood, glass pa-

perweights, crystals, and Chinese artifacts. Other exhibits explain the geology and volcanology of Kilauea and Mauna Kea, and an entire section is dedicated to the vanishing flora and fauna of Hawaii. The museum is an educational delight.

Natural Sites and Walking Tour

Start your tour of Hilo by picking up a pamphlet/map entitled *Discover Downtown Hilo, A Walking Tour of Historic Sites,* free at most restaurants, hotels, and shops. This self-guiding pamphlet takes you down the main streets and back lanes where you discover the unique architecture of Hilo's glory days. The majority of the vintage buildings have been restored and the architecture varies from the continental style of the Hawaiian Telephone Building to the Zen Buddhist Taishoji Shoto Mission.

A remarkable building is the old police station just across from Kalakaua Park. Behind it, in a classic plantation building, is the home of the **East Hawaii Cultural Center,** a nonprofit organization which supports local arts and hosts varying festivals, performances, and workshops throughout the year.

Hilo suffered a devastating tsunami is 1946 and again in 1960. Both times, most of the city was destroyed, but the 1930s First Hawaiian Bank building survived, owing to its structural integrity. Appropriately, the **Tsunami Museum** is now housed in this fine art deco structure and dedicated to those who lost their lives in the devastating tidal waves that raked the island.

After you leave the Lyman Museum, it's a short walk over to Hilo's library, 300 Waianuenue Avenue. Sitting at the entrance are two large stones. The larger is called the **Naha Stone,** known for its ability to detect any offspring of the ruling Naha clan. The test was simple: place a baby on the stone, and if the infant remained silent, he or she was Naha; if the baby cried, he or she wasn't. It is believed that this 7,000-pound monolith was brought from Kauai by canoe and placed near Pinao Temple in the immediate vicinity of what is now Wailuku Dr. and Keawe Street. Kamehameha the Great supposedly fulfilled a prophecy of "moving a mountain" by budging this stone. The smaller stone is thought to be an entrance pillar of the Pinao Temple. Just behind the library is the Wailuku River. Pick any of its bridges for a panoramic view down to the sea. Often, local fishermen try their luck from the Wailuku's grassy banks. The massive boulder sitting in the river's mouth is known as Maui's Canoe.

Rainbow Falls

A few miles out of town, heading west on Waianuenue Ave., are two natural spectacles definitely worth a look. Just past Hilo High School a sign directs you to Wailuku River State Park. Here is **Rainbow Falls,** a most spectacular yet easily visited natural wonder. You'll look down on a circular pool in the river below that's almost 100 feet in diameter; cascading into it is a lovely waterfall. The 80-foot falls deserve their name because as they hit the water below, their mists throw flocks of rainbows into the air. Underneath the falls is a huge cavern, held by legend to be the abode of Hina, mother of the god Maui. Most people are content to look from the vantage point near the parking lot, but if you walk to the left a stone stairway leads to a private viewing area directly over the falls. Here the river, strewn with volcanic boulders, pours over the edge. Follow the path for a minute or so along the bank to a gigantic banyan tree and a different vantage point.

Follow Waianuenue Ave. for two more miles past Hilo Hospital to the heights above town. A sign to turn right onto Pe'epe'e Falls Street points to the **Boiling Pots.** Usually no one is here. At the parking lot is an emergency phone and toilets. Follow the path past No Swimming signs to an overlook. Indented into the riverbed below is a series of irregularly shaped holes that look as though a peg-legged giant left his peg prints in the hot lava. Seven or eight resemble naturally bubbling jacuzzis. Best after a heavy rain. Turn your head upriver to see **Pe'epe'e Falls,** a gorgeous, five-spouted waterfall. You'll have this area to yourself, and it's great for a quiet picnic lunch.

Around Banyan Drive

If your Hilo hotel isn't situated along Banyan Dr., go there. This bucolic road skirts the edge of the Waiakea Peninsula that sticks out into Hilo Bay. Lining the drive is an almost uninterrupted series of banyans forming a giant hedgerow, while the fairways and greens of the Banyan Golf Course take up the center of the tiny peninsula. Park your car at one end and take a 15-minute stroll through this parklike atmosphere; the banyans have been named for well-known American luminaries. Boutiques and a variety of restaurants sit in the coolness under the trees.

J.D. BISIGNANI

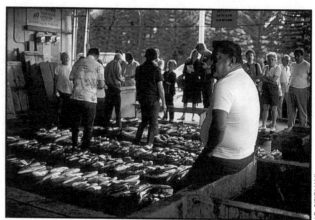

Suisan Fish Auction is perfect for bargains and local color.

J.D. BISIGNANI

Liliuokalani Gardens are formal Japanese-style gardens located along the west end of Banyan Drive. Meditatively quiet, they offer a beautiful view of the bay. **Coconut Island** just offshore is connected by a footbridge leading from the gardens. Along the footpaths are pagodas designed for relaxing, *torii* gates, stone lanterns, and half-moon bridges spanning a series of ponds and streams. Few people visit, and if it weren't for the striking fingers of black lava and the coconut trees, you could easily be in Japan. The peninsula, now blanketed by the gardens and the adjacent hotels, was once a populated residential area, an offshoot of central Hilo.

Suisan Fish Market is at the corner of Banyan Dr. and Lihiwai St., which crosses Kamehameha Avenue. This fish auction draws island fishermen of every nationality. The auctioneer's staccato is pure pidgin. Restaurateurs, housewives, and a smattering of tourists gather by 7:30 a.m. to eyeball the catch of the day. Boats tie up and fishermen talk quietly about the prices. Next door, a small snack shop sells sandwiches and piping-hot coffee. Grab a cup and walk over to the gardens through a nearby entrance—you'll have them to yourself.

Cross Lihiwai St. heading south. **Waiakea Pond,** a brackish lagoon where people often fish, is on your right. To the left are **Hoolulu County Park, Civic Center Auditorium,** and a city nursery brimming with orchids. The **Culture Center Nihon** is here too, at 123 Lihiwai St.; it displays artwork and cultural exhibits from Japan. The center is also a restaurant and sushi bar, with a special room set aside for the "tea ceremony."

On the opposite side of Waiakea Fish Pond (drive down Kamehameha Ave. and make a left onto Pauahi St. since no bridges cross), you'll find **Wailoa Center,** dispensing all manner of brochures and pamphlets on Hilo and Big Island activities. The walls of this 10-sided building are used to display works of local artists and cultural/historic exhibits, changed on a monthly basis.

Hilo's Gardens

Hilo's greatest asset is its flowers. Its biggest cash crops are orchids and anthuriums. Flowers grow everywhere, but to see them in a more formalized way, visit one of the following nurseries in and around town. Most have excellent prices for floral arrangements sent back to the Mainland. They'll do a Hawaiian bouquet with heliconia, anthuriums, and orchids for around $25 including shipping. The flowers arrive neatly packaged but unassembled, with a picture of the arrangement so that you can put them together yourself. These hearty cut flowers will look fresh and vibrant for as long as two weeks, so a few days in the mail won't hurt them.

Hilo Tropical Gardens and Gallery (formerly Kong's Floraleigh), 1477 Kalanianaole Ave., Hilo, HI 96720, tel. 935-4957, is open daily 9 a.m.-5 p.m. The admission price of $3 (children under 12 free) includes a free cup of Kona coffee. Here you can go on a self-guided tour through the gardens; all plants have been labeled. Everything's here: plumeria, lipstick trees, anthuriums, orchids, birds of paradise, even pineapples, coconuts, and papayas. You can purchase all manner of dried and fresh-cut flowers, seeds, packaged plants, seedlings, and corsages. The Gallery Gift Shop features art and local crafts of the Big Island, including prints, books, wood items, and pottery. The "no-pressure" salespeople are courteous and friendly. Shipping purchases is no problem.

Along Kilauea Ave., between Lanikaula and Kawili Streets, the Department of Natural Resources, Division of Forestry maintains the **Hilo Arboretum,** open Mon.-Fri. 7:45 a.m.-4:30 p.m., closed Saturday, Sunday, and holidays; free. This tree nursery contains most of the trees present in Hawaii, including indigenous and imported specimens. The office will provide you with a mimeographed sheet entitled "Hilo Nursery Arboretum." It's basically a self-guided tour, but the clerks will warn you that it's not very good. It attempts to name the trees by matching them with points on the map as you pass by, instead of referring to signs on each specimen. However, the

Anthurium, obake variety

DIANA LASICH HARPER

HISTORY OF THE ANTHURIUM

Originally a native of Central America, the anthurium was introduced into Hawaii in 1889 by Samuel M. Damon, an English missionary. Damon discovered that Hawaii's climate and volcanic soil made an ideal environment for this exotic flower. Over the years since then, anthurium production has turned into a million-dollar export industry with all the major growers located on the Big Island.

trees are magnificent and you will have this quiet area virtually to yourself. Originally the site was an animal quarantine station operated by the Territory of Hawaii; the 19.4 acres of the arboretum were established in 1920 by Brother Mathias Newell. Brother Newell was a nurseryman employed by the Catholic boys' school in Hilo. At that time the Division of Forestry was already actively introducing plant species from all over the world. For the 40 years between 1921 and 1961 the department was engaged in the development and maintenance of arboretums consisting primarily of plant species from Australia and Africa. Arboretum sites ranged from sea level to Mauna Kea. Plant materials were exchanged and thousands of breadfruit cuttings were exported. Over 1,000 different tree species and 500 different fruit trees were field tested. Here at the Hilo Arboretum over 1,000 trees were planted. A few trees such as the paper bark and some pines are more than 50 years old. Presently a small number of timber species are grown for reforestation purposes. Essentially the Hilo site is utilized for the propagation of rare and endangered plant species, for research, and for experimental pursuits.

Nani Mau Gardens are some of the largest in and around Hilo, and touring these spectacular displays is well worth an afternoon. Located at 421 Makalika St. (off Route 11), Hilo, HI 96720, tel. 959-3541, the gardens are open daily 8 a.m.-5 p.m. Admission is $5, $2 pp for an optional tram tour, or $6 for a self-drive golf cart. The gardens consist of 20 sculpted acres; 33 more are being developed. More than a botanical garden, Nani Mau is a "floral theme park" designed as a tourist attraction. Walks throughout the garden are very tame but very beautiful; umbrellas are provided during rainy weather, which adds its own dripping, crystalline charm to the experience. Plants are labeled in English, Latin, and Japanese. The gardens are a huge but ordered display of flowers, flowering trees, and shrubbery. The wildly colored plumage of tropical birds here and there competes with the colors of the exotic blooms. The gardens are broken off into separate areas: fruit orchards, heliconia garden, ginger garden, anthurium garden, orchid garden, orchid pavilion, gardenia garden, and bromeliad garden. The new 33 acres include an annual garden, white-sand beach, small vol-

Nani Mau Gardens

J.D. BISIGNANI

cano, picture garden for photos, and orchids and more orchids. It also features floral sculptures, a small reflective pond, and an assortment of flowers and shrubs laid out in geometric patterns, hearts, mountains, and even "aloha" and "Hilo Hawaii" spelled out. The tourist shop and snack area is exactly like a Japanese *omiyagi* (souvenir) shop. No wonder, since it's owned by Japanese, and the tour buses coming here are all filled with Japanese. If you enjoy a clean, outdoor experience surrounded by magnificent flowers, this is the place.

Tanaka's is an excellent nursery from which to buy and to send flowers. They call themselves Jewel Box Orchids and also The Orchidarium, Hawaii Inc., at 524 Manono St., Hilo, HI. It's off the main track. Follow Route 11 toward Volcano, make a right on Kekuanaoa St., and go down four blocks to Manono. Make a right and they're a few hundred yards down on the left. For beautiful orchids at unbeatable prices, search them out.

While in the neighborhood, visit **Paradise Plants** at 575 Hinano St., tel. 935-4043, a complete garden center specializing in indoor-outdoor plants and tropical fruit trees. They send orchids and other live flowers to the Mainland. Also featured is a large gift area with gifts from around the world. While browsing, check out their free orchid garden, which ranks as Hilo's oldest.

Kualoa Farms is at the corner of Mamaki (off Route 11) and Kealakai Streets, tel. 959-4565, open daily 8 a.m.-4 p.m. A guided tour takes you over some of the 62 acres planted in anthuriums,

ti plants, torch gingers, and macadamia and papaya orchards.

Mauna Loa Macadamia Nut Factory is located along Mauna Loa Rd., eight miles out of Hilo on Route 11 heading towards Volcanoes National Park. Head down the drive until you come to the Visitors Center. Inside will be a free video explaining the development and processing of macadamia nuts in Hawaii. Take a self-guided tour through the orchards, where all trees and plants are identified. Then return to the snack shop for mac-nut goodies like ice cream and cookies. The gift shop has a wide assortment of mac-nut items at considerably lower prices than anywhere else on the island. Open daily 8:30 a.m.-5 p.m.; tel. 966-8612.

Panaewa Rainforest Zoo

Not many travelers can visit a zoo in such a unique setting ,where the animals virtually live in paradise. The road to the zoo is a trip in itself, getting you back into the country. Follow Route 11 toward Volcanoes National Park for a few miles until you see the sign pointing down Mamaki St. to the zoo. On a typical weekday, you'll have the place to yourself. The zoo, operated by the county Department of Parks and Recreation, is open daily 9 a.m.-4 p.m., closed Christmas and New Year's Day. Admission is free. For information, call 959-7224.

Here you have the feeling that the animals are not "fenced in" so much as you are "fenced out." The collection of about 50 species includes ordinary and exotic animals from around the world.

You'll see a giant anteater from Costa Rica, pygmy hippos from Africa, and a wide assortment of birds like pheasants and peacocks. The zoo is also a botanical garden with many of the trees, shrubs, and ferns labeled. The zoo hosts many endangered animals indigenous to Hawaii like the Laysan duck, Hawaiian coot, *pueo*, Hawaiian gallinule, and even a feral pig in his own stone mini-condo. There are some great iguanas and mongooses, lemurs, and an aviary section with exotic birds like yellow-fronted parrots and blue and gold macaws. The central area is a tigers' playground; a tall fence marks this rather large area where tigers still rule their domain. It's got its own pond and tall grasses that make the tigers feel at home but also make them hard to spot.

A touching spot is the **Astronaut Grove,** in memory of the astronauts who were killed on the regrettable explosion of the space shuttle *Columbia.* All are remembered, especially Ellison Onizuka, a native son of the Big Island. The zoo makes a perfect side trip for families or for anyone wishing to get off the beaten track.

Kaumana Caves

In 1881 Mauna Loa's tremendous eruption discharged a huge flow of lava. The river of lava crusted over, forming a tube through which molten lava continued to flow. Once the eruption ceased, the lava inside siphoned out, leaving the tube now called Kaumana Caves. The caves are only five miles out of Hilo along Route 200, clearly marked next to the road. Oddly enough,

Kaumana Caves

they are posted as a fallout shelter. Follow a staircase down into a gray hole draped with green ferns and brightened by wildflowers. You can walk about 50 yards into the cave before you'll need a flashlight. It's a thrill to turn around and look at the entrance, where blazing sunlight shoots through the ferns and wildflowers. The floor of the cave is cemented over for easy walking. Another cave visible across the way is undeveloped and more rugged to explore.

Two miles past Kaumana Caves is **Hilo Municipal Golf Course,** a 6,006-yard, par-71 course where you can golf for $25.

Scenic Drive

Route 19 heading north from Hilo toward Honokaa is a must, with magnificent inland and coastal views one after another. (See the "Hamakua Coast" chapter for full coverage of the northern section leading to Waipio.) Only five minutes from Hilo, you'll come to Papaikou town. Look for a small convenience store on the right. Just here is a road posted as a scenic drive which dips down toward the coast. Take it. Almost immediately a sign says Narrow Winding Road, 20 MPH, letting you know what kind of area you're coming into. Start down this lane past some very modest homes and into the jungle that covers the road like a living green tunnel. Prepare for tiny bridges crossing tiny valleys. Stop, and you can almost hear the jungle growing. For those who have heard of the road to Hana, Maui, the Scenic Drive is a mini-version of what it has to offer.

In a few minutes you'll come to **Hawaii Tropical Botanical Gardens,** tel. 964-5233, open daily 9 a.m.-5 p.m., with the last shuttle van departing for the garden from the registration area at 4 p.m.Admission is $15, children 6-16 $5, and kids five and under are free. Remember that the $12 entrance fee not only allows you to walk through the best-tamed tropical rainforest on the Big Island, but helps preserve the area in perpetuity. The gardens were established in 1978 when Dan and Pauline Lutkenhouse purchased the property in order to educate the public to the beauty of tropical plants in their natural setting. The gardens have been open for viewing since 1984. Mr. Lutkenhouse, a retired San Francisco businessman, purchased the 25-acre valley and personally performed the work that transformed it into one of the most exotic spots in all of Hawaii. The locality was amazingly beautiful but inac-

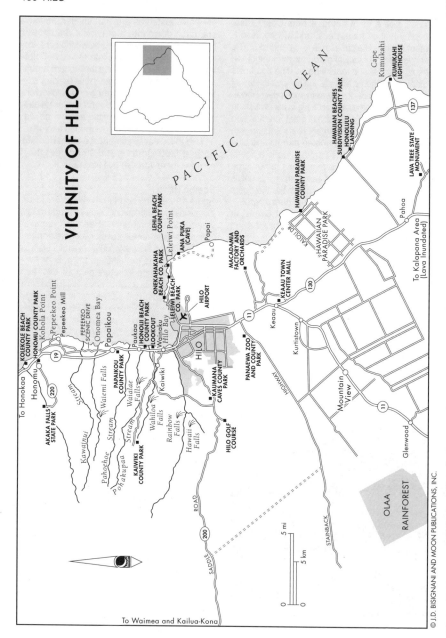

VICINITY OF HILO

PACIFIC OCEAN

Cape Kumukahi

KUMUKAHI LIGHTHOUSE

137

LAVA TREE STATE MONUMENT

HAWAIIAN BEACHES SUBDIVISION COUNTY PARK

HONOLULU LANDING

HAWAIIAN PARADISE COUNTY PARK

Pohoa

HAWAIIAN PARADISE PARK

KAPOHO

LEHIA BEACH COUNTY PARK

Papai

ANA PUKA (CAVE)

Leleiwi Point

ONEKAHAKAHA BEACH CO. PARK

MACADAMIA FACTORY AND ORCHARDS

KEAAU TOWN CENTER MALL

130

LELEIWI BEACH CO. PARK

HILO AIRPORT

Keaau

To Kalapana Area (Lava Inundated)

KOLEKOLE BEACH COUNTY PARK

Pepeekeo Point

Kohola Point

HONOMU COUNTY PARK

PEPEEKEO SCENIC DRIVE

Pepeekeo Mill

Onomea Bay

Papaikou

19

Honomu

Paukaa

IHONOLII BEACH COUNTY PARK

Wainaku

Hilo Bay

HILO

To Honokaa

220

PAPAIKOU COUNTY PARK

Waiemi Falls

Kaiwiki

11

PANAEWA ZOO AND COUNTY PARK

Kurtistown

AKAKA FALLS STATE PARK

Kawainui Stream

Pahoehoe Stream

Waialae Falls

Waiaiae Stream

KAIWIKI COUNTY PARK

Pohakupaa Stream

Wahiloa Falls

Rainbow Falls

KAUMANA CAVES COUNTY PARK

HILO GOLF COURSE

Hawaii Falls

Mountain View

11

Glenwood

OLAA RAINFOREST

SADDLE ROAD

STAINBACK

To Waimea and Kailua-Kona

5 mi

5 km

0

0

© J.D. BISIGNANI AND MOON PUBLICATIONS, INC.

cessible because it was so rugged. Through a personal investment of nearly $1 million and six painstaking years of toil aided only by two helpers, he hand-cleared the land, built trails and bridges, developed an irrigation system, acquired more than 2,000 different species of trees and plants, and established one mile of scenic trails and a large water lily lake stocked with *koi* and tropical fish. A shuttle van takes you on a five-minute ride down to Onomea Bay where the gardens are located. Onomea was a favorite spot with the Hawaiians, who came to fish and camp for the night. The valley was a fishing village called Kahlili in the early 1800s. Later on it became a rough-water seaport used for shipping sugarcane and other tropical products. Recently, a remake of *Lord of the Flies* was filmed here, and it's easy to see why the area made the perfect movie set.

The van drops you off at a staging area in the garden where you'll find self-guiding maps, drinking water, restrooms, umbrellas for your convenience, and jungle perfume—better known as mosquito repellent! Plants from the four corners of the globe, including Iran, Central China, Japan, tropical Africa, India, Borneo, Brazil, East Indies, South Pacific Islands, tropical America, and the Philippines, are named with a full botanical description. Native plants from Hawaii are included. Listen for the songs of birds: the white-tailed tropic bird, black-crowned heron, Pacific golden plover, Hawaiian hawk, Japanese white eye, common mynah, and northern cardinal. Choose one of the aptly named trails like Ocean Trail or Waterfall Trail and lose yourself in the beauty of the surroundings. You are in the middle of a tamed jungle, walking along manicured paths. Stroll the Ocean Trail down to the sea, where the rugged coastline is dramatically pummeled by frothy waves. You can hear the waves entering submerged lava caves, where they blow in and out like a giant bellows. Away from the sea you'll encounter screened gazebos filled with exotic birds like cockatoos from Indonesia and blue-fronted Amazon parrots. Walk the inland trails past waterfalls, streams, a bamboo grove, and innumerable flowers. For at least a brief time you get to feel the power and beauty of a living Garden of Eden.

Hawaiian Artifacts, just a minute down Scenic Drive past the gardens, is a shop owned and operated by Paul Gephart, tel. 964-1729, open Mon.-Sat. 9 a.m.-5 p.m. Paul creates wood sculptures mainly from koa and ohia that he turns into whales, dolphins, birds, and poi bowls. Here's also a small but tasteful collection of jewelry and seashells, all at very decent prices.

Continue for another two to three miles, and you'll come to a wooden bridge with a white railing overlooking a cascading mountain stream with a big swimming hole. Great for a freshwater dip, but always be careful: these streams can be torrential during a heavy rain. The side road rejoins Route 19 at Papeeko, a workers' village where you can get gas or supplies.

BEACHES

If you define a beach as a long expanse of white sand covered by a thousand sunbathers and their beach umbrellas, then Hilo doesn't have any. If a beach, to you, can be a smaller, more intimate affair where a good but not gigantic number of tourists and families can spend the day on pockets of sand between fingers of black lava, then Hilo has plenty. Hilo's best beaches all lie to the east of the city along Kalanianaole Ave., an area also known as the Keaukaha Strip, which runs six miles from downtown Hilo to its dead end at Leleiwi Point. Not all beaches are clearly marked, but they are easily spotted by cars parked along the road or in makeshift parking lots.

Hilo Bayfront Park is a thousand yards of black sand that narrows considerably as it runs west from the Wailoa River toward downtown. At one time it went all the way to the Wailuku River and was renowned throughout the islands for its beauty, but commercialism of the harbor has ruined it. By the 1960s, so much sewage and industrial waste had been pumped into the bay that it was considered a public menace, and then the great tsunami came. Reclamation projects created the Wailoa River State Recreation Area at the east end, and shorefront land became a buffer zone against future inundation. Few swimmers come to the beach because the water is cloudy and chilly, but the sharks don't seem to mind! The bay is terrific for fishing and picnicking, and the sails of small craft and windsurfers can always be seen. It's a perfect spot for

Richardson Beach

J.D. BISIGNANI

canoe races, and many local teams come here to train. Notice the judging towers and canoe sheds. Toward the west end, near the mouth of the Wailuku River, surfers catch long rides during the winter months, entertaining spectators.

The **Wailoa River State Recreation Area** is a 134-acre preserve set along the spring-fed Wailoa River in downtown Hilo. City residents use the area for picnics, pleasure walks, informal get togethers, and launching boats. Stop at the Wailoa Center off Pauahi St. for information and cultural displays. Additional parking for this landscaped, parklike area is at the end of Pi'ilani Street.

Coconut Island Park is reached by footbridge from a spit of land just outside Liliuokalani Gardens. It was at one time a *pu'uhonua* ("place of refuge") opposite a human sacrificial *heiau* on the peninsula side. Coconut Island has restrooms, a pavilion, and picnic tables shaded by tall coconut trees and ironwoods. A favorite picnic spot for decades, it has a diving tower and a sheltered natural pool area for children. The only decent place to swim in Hilo Bay, it also offers the best panorama of the city, bay, and Mauna Kea beyond.

Reeds Bay Beach Park is on the east side of the Waiakea Peninsula at the end of Banyan Drive. It too is technically part of Hilo Bay and offers good swimming, though the water is notoriously cold because of a constantly flowing freshwater spring. Most people just picnic here, and fishermen frequent the area.

Keaukaha Beach, located on Puhi Bay, is the first in a series of beaches as you head east on Kalanianaole Avenue. Look for Baker Ave. and pull off to the left into a parking area near an old pavilion. This is a favorite spot with local people, who swim at "Cold Water Pond," a spring-fed inlet at the head of the bay. A sewage treatment plant fronts the western side of Puhi Bay. Much nicer areas await you just up Kalanianaole Avenue.

Onekahakaha Beach Park has it all: safe swimming, white-sand beach, lifeguards, and all amenities. Turn left onto Machida Ln. and park in the lot of Hilo's favorite "family" beach, although very recently a number of local homeless people have been living in this area. Swim in the large, sandy-bottomed pool protected by the breakwater. Outside the breakwater the currents can be fierce and drownings have been recorded. Walk east along the shore to find an undeveloped area of the park with many small tidal pools. Beware of sea urchins.

James Kealoha Park, also known locally as "4 Mile," is next; people swim, snorkel, and fish here, and during winter months it's a favorite surfing spot. A large grassy area is shaded by trees and a picnic pavilion. Just offshore is an island known as Scout Island because local Boy Scouts often camp here. This entire area was known for its fishponds, and inland, just across Kalanianaole Ave., is the 60-acre Loko'aka Pond. This site of ancient Hawaiian aquaculture is now a commercial operation that provides the best mullet on the island.

Leleiwi Beach Park lies along a lovely residential area carved into the rugged coastline. Part of the park is dedicated to the Richardson Ocean Center, and the entire area is locally called **Richardson's Beach.** Look for Uwau St., just past the Mauna Loa Shores Condo, and park along the road here. Look for a fancy house surrounded by tall coconut trees and follow the pathway through the grove. Use a shower that's coming out of the retaining wall surrounding the house. Keep walking until you come to a seawall. A tiny cove with a black-sand beach is the first in a series. This is a terrific area for snorkeling, with plenty of marinelife, including *humu,* green sea turtles. Walk east to a natural lava breakwater. Behind it are pools filled and flushed by the surging tide. The water breaks over the top of the lava and rushes into the pools, making natural jacuzzis. This is one of the most picturesque swimming areas on the island. At Leleiwi Beach Park proper (three pavilions), the shore is open to the ocean and there are strong currents; it's best to head directly to Richardson's.

Lehia Park is the end of the road. When the pavement stops, follow the dirt track until you come to a large, grassy field shaded by a variety of trees. This unofficial camping area has no amenities whatsoever. A series of pools like those at Richardson's are small, sandy-bottomed, and safe. Outside of the natural lava breakwater, currents are treacherous. Winter often sends tides surging inland here, making Lehia unusable. This area is about as far away as you can get and still be within a few minutes of downtown Hilo.

PRACTICALITIES

ACCOMMODATIONS

Accommodations in Hilo are hardly ever booked out, and they're reasonably priced. Sounds great, but many hotels have "gone condo" to survive while others have simply shut their doors, so there aren't as many as there once were. During the Merrie Monarch Festival (late April), the entire town is booked solid! The hotels are clustered along Banyan Dr., with a few gems tucked away on the city streets.

Banyan Drive Hotels

The following hotels lie along Banyan Drive. They range from moderate to deluxe; all are serviced by the Banyan Shuttle (See "Alternate Transportation).

Prices at the classy **Hilo Hawaiian Hotel,** 71 Banyan Dr., Hilo, HI 96720, tel. 935-9361 or (800) 272-5275, are $104-325; all rooms have a/c, phone, and TV, plus there's a pool. The Hilo Hawaiian occupies the most beautiful grounds of any hotel in Hilo. From the vantage of the hotel's colonnaded veranda, you overlook formal gardens, Coconut Island, and Hilo Bay. Designed as a huge arc, the hotel's architecture blends well with its surroundings and expresses the theme set by Hilo Bay, that of a long, sweeping crescent. The hotel buffet, especially the Friday and Saturday seafood version, is absolutely out of this world (see "Food," below). As a deluxe hotel, the Hilo Hawaiian is the best that Hilo has to offer.

Hawaii Naniloa Resort, 93 Banyan Dr., Hilo, HI 96720, tel. 969-3333 or (800) 442-5845, is a massive, 317-room hotel offering deluxe accommodations. Rates start at $100 standard, $120 superior, $140-160 deluxe with private balcony. Private suites are available from $190. A third person costs $15 additional; children under 17 sharing with parents are free. They offer a/c, TV, hotel parking, restaurant, and a pool setting—just above the lava—that is the nicest in Hilo. The original hotel dates back over 60 years and has built up a fine reputation for value and service. The Hawaii Naniloa has recently undergone extensive renovations and is now as beautiful as ever.

Uncle Billy's Hilo Bay Hotel is sandwiched between much larger hotels at 87 Banyan Dr., Hilo, HI 96720, tel. 935-0861, (800) 367-5102 Mainland, (800) 442-5841 in Hawaii. Rooms here begin at $69 d, $79 including breakfast for two, and $95 for a room-and-car package. The Hilo Bay's blue metal roof and white louvered shutters make it look a bit like "Long John Silver's Meets Polynesia." The lobby's rattan furniture and thatched longhouse theme are pure '50s-kitsch Hawaii. Definitely have a look. There are parking and a pool, all rooms are clean and air-conditioned, and each room has a TV and phone. The hotel offers excellent value for the money. Uncle Billy's Polynesian Marketplace, where you can buy everything from beer to sundries, is part of the complex. (Website: aloha.net/~uncleb.)

You can't miss the orange-and-black **Hilo Seaside Hotel,** 126 Banyan Dr., tel. 935-0821 or (800) 367-7000. This is the budget hotel on Banyan Drive. It's island-owned by the Kimi family, and like the others in this small chain, it's clean and well kept and has Polynesian-inspired decor. Room prices are $50 standard, $60 superior, $70 deluxe, and $80 kitchenette. Add approximately $20 for a room/car package. Ask about off-season rates, and they will sometimes offer a better rate depending on the amount of business at the time. The grounds are laid out around a central courtyard and the pool is secluded away from the street. At this family-style hotel with a motel atmosphere, the friendly staff goes out of its way to make you feel welcome.

The **Country Club Condo Hotel,** 121 Banyan Dr., tel. 935-7171, is a very basic hotel/condo with reasonable rates. Rates based on double occupancy are: standard with kitchenette $50, standard oceanfront $60, one-bedroom suite $100; extra person $10, daily rental deposit $20, weekly rental deposit $100. Monthly rates range from fully furnished standard studio for $400 ($440 with

weekly maid service), up to a deluxe one-bedroom suite at $700 ($760 with weekly maid service). Since this is a condo hotel, the rooms vary from unit to unit, but most have either double beds or a queen-size bed.

Downtown Accommodations
The following hotels are found along Hilo's downtown streets. Some are in quiet residential areas, while others are along busy thoroughfares. They are moderately to inexpensively priced.

Dolphin Bay Hotel is a sparkling little gem— simply the best hotel bargain in Hilo, one of those places where you get more than you pay for. It sits on a side street in the Puueo section of town at the north end of Hilo Bay: 333 Iliahi St., Hilo, HI 96720, tel. 935-1466. John Alexander, the owner/manager, is at the front desk every day. He's a font of information about the Big Island and will happily dispense advice on how to make your day-trips fulfilling. The hotel was built by his father, who spent years in Japan, and you'll be happy to discover this influence when you sink deep into the *ofuro*-type tubs in every room. All 24 units have full modern kitchens. Rates are single studio apartment $59, superior $69, one bedroom $79, two-bedroom fully furnished unit $89, additional guest $10. Deluxe units upstairs have open-beam ceilings and lanais, and with three spacious rooms feel like apartments. No swimming pool or a/c, but there are color TVs

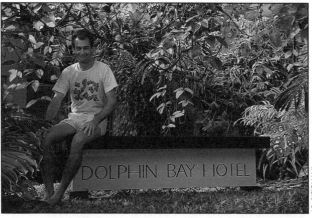

*John Alexander of the
Dolphin Bay Hotel*

J.D. BISIGNANI

and fans with excellent cross ventilation. The grounds and housekeeping are immaculate. Hotel guests can partake of free bananas, papayas, and other exotic fruits found in hanging baskets in the lobby, as well as free coffee. Weekly rates range from $325 for a studio to $550 for a two-bedroom deluxe. Make reservations, because everyone who has found the Dolphin Bay comes back again and again.

The Wild Ginger Inn, at 100 Puueo St., Hilo, HI 96720, tel. 935-5556, (800) 882-1887, is a refurbished plantation-style hotel, painted shocking pink and green, that bills itself as a bed-and-breakfast inn. An open-aired lobby leads to an encircling veranda overlooking the central courtyard area, with a view of the bay in the distance. Each of the 25 wainscoted rooms, very basic but very clean, has a refrigerator, private shower-bath, cross ventilation, and one double and one twin bed. A double hammock and vintage chairs in the lobby area are for your relaxation. Rates for standard rooms are $39, deluxe rooms with cable TV $50. Discounts are available for three nights or longer. The homestyle Hawaiian buffet is terrific: guava-passion juice, milk, local coffee, macadamia nuts, granola, yogurt, muffins, hard-boiled eggs, island fruits in season, turkey-ham, cheese, and toast. The inn is completely nonsmoking, with a special area provided for smokers in the garden. The Wild Ginger Inn, with a friendly staff and good service, is an excellent choice for budget accommodations and gives more than full value for the money.

B&Bs and Hostels

A house can have presence, and, if it's brushed by magic like the Tin Man in *The Wizard of Oz,* it can even attain a heart. The home we're referring to was a purchase motivated by love and occupied by a large, dynamic family who shared it with friends whose lives created drama and changed the course of history and human thought. **The Shipman House,** known locally as "The Castle," perched on five verdant acres high above Hilo, has such a heart.

After a quarter century on the Mainland, Barbara Ann Andersen, great-granddaughter of William H. "Willie" Shipman, the original owner, returned with her children and her husband Gary to restore to its former grandeur the residence where she spent her childhood Easters and Christmases.

The house was figuratively stripped to its petticoats, and Spencer Leineweber, of the prestigious historic architectural firm of *Spencer Mason Architects,* was given the job of outfitting her in grand style.

Shipman House B&B Inn, tel. 934-3002, (800) 627-8447, at 131 Ka'iulani St., Hilo, HI 96720, is the grandest B&B in all Hawaii, and to appreciate it fully, you must know its history, which goes back as far as the first tall ships that arrived from New England bearing the missionaries and their new faith to the old kingdom. The first members of the family to reside in Hawaii were The Rev. William C. Shipman and his wife Jane, who arrived in the 1850s. The Rev. Shipman died young, leaving Jane alone and in need of a means to support herself and their three children; she accomplished this by opening a Hawaiian girls' boarding school in Hilo. While working as a schoolmistress she met and married Mr. Reed, a famous engineer responsible for most of Hilo's bridges and for whom, by strange coincidence, "Reed's Island," the section of Hilo where the mansion sits, was named. Reed was 14 years senior to Jane, not an extraordinary age difference even by today's standards, but the family was concerned. As it turned out, he proved to be a loving husband and a good father to his three adopted children.

One of the boys, William H. "Willie" Shipman, became enamored with Mary Melekahuia Johnson, one of the young Hawaiian ladies at his mother's school, asking soon for her hand in marriage. Mary was descended from the ruling *ali'i,* and her grandfather was a high chief and advisor to King Kamehameha. Willie originally determined to study medicine, but one day his stepfather, Mr. Reed, made him an offer he couldn't refuse, saying, "Son, if you will give up medicine and take up the study of business, I'll give you a ranch to run." Willie knew a good opportunity when he saw it, and over the years he became one of the largest landholders on the Big Island, founding *W.H. Shipman, Ltd.,* which is today chaired by his grandson, Roy Blackshear—Barbara Ann's father.

Around the turn of the century, Mary often implored Willie to take her for a drive, which would invariably pass by a lovely home being built on Ka'iulani Street. Holding his hand and looking into his eyes she would ask, "Willie, won't you buy me that house?" and he would reply, " I can't. The Wilsons own it." Finally, one day as they passed the house, Mary asked once again, but this time Willie smiled, brandished his cigar, and said, "Yes, my dear. It's been ours for 30 days."

The Shipmans, who already had seven children, moved into the house in April 1903; they eventually had three more children in their new residence.

Mary was a dear friend of Hawaii's last queen, Liliuokalani, who would stay at the Shipman house whenever she was in Hilo. While there the queen would preside over simple but elegant "poi luncheons," always seated at the place of honor at the huge round koa dining room table, where she could look out the bay windows at Hilo below. While the queen sat eating, she had to be kept cool, so two of the Shipman's youngest girls, Barbara Ann's grandmother being one of them, got the job of fanning her. There was a rule that you must not touch the queen, so as the interminable afternoons droned on the girls made a game of inching closer and closer, seeing who could be the one to fan closest without actually touching the royal personage.

After lunch, Liliuokalani would slip away to the "Library" to clandestinely savor a fine cigar, sheltered from the prying eyes of the press.

Of the 10 original Shipman children, none of the five boys had children. Three died in childhood; one, Uncle Oliver, died of cancer as a young man; and Uncle Herbert, known for his efforts to save Hawaii's official bird, the *nene,* and for introducing orchids to what would become "The Orchid Isle," remained a bachelor. Of the five girls, three married, including Florence Lukini Shipman, Barbara Ann's grandmother.

To arrive at the Castle, ascend Waianuenue Ave. until you come to the fourth bridge from the sea; the creaking of its wood is whispers from times past. Cross it, turn left, and you'll see the Castle. Climb the steps to the wraparound lanai, a necessity even for well-to-do families, who, like all Hawaii residents, spend a great deal of time outdoors. The broad landing provides a wonderful view of Hilo and the sea in the distance, with wild flowers and tangled greenery cascading into a tropical bowl at your feet. Two stained glass windows, encircled by a laurel wreath, the classic sign of a congenial home, greet you on entering. The Double Parlor, the first floor of the rounded three-story Tower that caps the home, is magnificent. Everywhere is glass—old-fashioned, handmade curved glass—its mottled and rippled texture giving a surrealistic twist to the panorama.

Pad along on the burnished fir flooring past koa-wainscoted walls to enter the Dining Room, where an enormous round dining table and *punee* are still very functional. The back area of the home is called The Conservatory, really the center of the home for day-to-day life where the family took their meals. Just off it is a Solarium and the Butler's Pantry, next to an "Otis in-home elevator," installed in the 1930s and probably Hilo's first. Here, too, is the back bedroom, formerly reserved for guests like Jack London and his wife Charmagne. The peaceful Library, waiting to engulf an afternoon reader within its impressive 12-foot ceilings, is warmed by a brick fireplace with a koa mantel, and is fringed by built-in floor-to-ceiling koa bookcases.

Take the ancient elevator or ascend the central staircase to the second floor, where once upon a time a ballroom adorned in white wallpaper with twinkling stars swayed with dancing and music; nowadays it's been converted into two bedrooms. Notice a window opening to a catwalk that leads to a small room built over the water tank. This served as great-grandfather Willie's "Office," his haven from the clamor of 10 children! Enter the circular second-floor section of the Tower, which contains the Master Bedroom; the four-poster, koa bed is simply enormous, with the headboard about 8 eightfeet tall, and the mattress itself well above waist level. The bed's size and height served a practical purpose, placing the occupants at window level so that they could luxuriate and look out, while at the same time allowing the breeze to flow under the bed and help keep its occupants cool.

A spiral staircase ascends to the attic where a "canvas room" was the children's dormitory. A large, free-standing credenza holds hats and antique clothing still bearing labels like "extra quality A. J. White, hatter to the royal family, 74 German Street, Saint James, and 10 Regent Street." Also in the attic is the entrance to the Tower, a wine barrel of a room with wraparound windows.

The main house offers one guest room with antique koa twin beds, mosquito netting, private bath, and doors that open to a 10' wide *lanai.* Other guests will lodge in the Cottage, a separate building on the grounds, originally built for the express purpose of accommodating visitors. The Cottage contains two spacious bedrooms, each with queen-size bed, window seats, and private bath. Both rooms have private entrances, ceiling fans, and a small refrigerator, with TVs available upon request. The rate is $130/d; $25 per extra person.

In the early afternoons, lemonade, iced tea, soft drinks, and hors d'oeuvres are served on the main house's lanai. The Library is open to guests, along with use of the 1903 Steinway piano whose keys were once tinkled by Liliuokalani. A complete historical tour is offered daily. Breakfast, served 7:30-9 a.m. (earlier upon request, and special diets accommodated), is an expanded continental with homemade cereals, hot cereals on request, assorted local fruits (there are 20 varieties of fruit trees on the property), fruit juices, Kona coffee, yogurt, fruit bread, muffins, popovers, and cinnamon rolls. Check in is 3-6 p.m., and checkout is at 10 a.m. Shipman House is once again one of *the* finest homes in all Hawaii in which to spend a quiet and elegant visit. E-mail: bighouse@bigisland.com.

If you would appreciate something a little more . . . well, homey, try **Holmes' Sweet Home B&B,** at 107 Koula St., Hilo, HI 96720, tel. 961-9089, the residence of John and Charlotte Holmes. Located on a quiet cul-de-sac with a view of Hilo Bay, the home provides two rooms priced $60-70 (no credit cards) that feature their own private entrances, baths, and guest refrigerator and microwave. A continental breakfast is included. E-mail: homswhom@gte.com; Web site: www .hawaii-bnb.com/holmes.html.

Arnott's Lodge, 98 Apapane Rd., Hilo, HI 96720, tel. 969-7097, fax. 961-9638, is a very reasonably priced hostel, extremely well run, safe, clean, and friendly. Follow Kamehameha Ave. south until it turns into Kalanianaole Ave.; in about five minutes you'll see a white sign pointing to Arnott's. Those without private transportation can be picked up by a free shuttle service operating 8 a.m.-9 p.m., with outbound departures set at 8 a.m., 12:30 p.m., and 5:30 p.m. A ride downtown or to the airport costs only $1, and share-ride taxi service can be arranged for $5. Arnott's staff can also help with inexpensive interisland air tickets, along with an in-house eight-hour hiking and snorkeling excursions for

$36 (gear included) that take you Volcano National Park, the Puna coast, South Point, or the Hilo waterfalls, depending upon the day; non-guests pay $50. The premier excursion, however, is the Mauna Kea Expedition, $75 including snacks, offered on Tuesday and Friday. Other services are bicycle rental at $10 p/d, snorkel gear at $5 p/d, coin laundry, telephones, and safe storage of valuables and backpacks at no cost. If you're traveling around the island but don't have your own transportation, ask about Arnott's "Big Island Experience," which is a van trip that circles the island stopping at various sights, parks, eateries, and accommodations on the way. Dormitory bunks—male, female, and coed—at $17 are spotlessly clean and cooled by cross ventilation and ceiling fans. Single rooms with bath, kitchen, and living room shared with one other room are $30; a double room with the same setup is $40. A self-contained suite with two bedrooms, one with a double bed and the other with twins, includes a bathroom, kitchen, and living room for $105 for up to five people; each additional person ($10). Chick-in until 10 p.m. only. Tenting on the lawn with your own tent is now an option for $7 per person.Leisure time can be spent in a central courtyard or in a separate gazebo (for those who want to burn the midnight oil or watch one of ahuge selection of videos). A backyard covered lanai has pink, blue, and green picnic tables so enormous that you feel like you're back in kindergarten, along with barbecue grills for your convenience, and a meditation platform built in a tree. To help keep prices down, Arnott's hosts an all-you-can-eat barbecue/mixer on Wednesday and Saturday from 7 p.m., where you can have teriyaki or veggie burgers, salsa and chips, fresh fruit salads, ice cream, and tossed salads for only $6. Arnott's is an excellent hostel offering a quality, hassle-free stay at very reasonable prices.

Just four miles north of town is **Our Place Papaikou's B&B,** P.O. Box 469, Papaikou, HI 96781, tel. 964-5250 or (800) 245-5250. Set amongst thick vegetation, the four rooms of this cedar home open onto a large lanai that overlooks Kupua Stream. The Early American and Oriental Rooms run $55 a night, and the Master Bedroom and Treehouse Room are $80, two-night minimum. E-mail: rplace@aloha.met; Web site: www.best.com/~ourplace.

FOOD

Inexpensive Dining

Lodged in a gray and white building with matching awning over four picnic tables, **Broke the Mouth** at 55 Mamo St.,tel. 934-7670, open Tuesday, Thursday and Friday 9 a.m.-2 p.m. and Wednesday and Saturday 7 a.m.-2 p.m., is owned and operated by organic farmers Tip and Penny Davis, who grow and then cook the food served at this all-natural vegetarian restaurant. Their philosophy is "Farm-fresh, organically grown, local food is the best." Since 1992 the couple have owned and worked 16 acres of the island's finest soil, growing a variety of herbs, greens, and veggies. Gregarious, they had dinner guests who said, "You guys should open up a restaurant." Voilà! Hearty plates include The Mamo, which is fresh greens, *ono* pesto pasta, and a "big aloha" vegetarian hot dog for $4.50; and The Bomboola— fresh greens, *ono* pesto pasta, and Hawaiian salad with summer roll for $5.50. All plates include *manapua* and a side of *kulolo,* a dessert that's a mixture of steamed and grated taro and coconut cream. The Hawaiian salad is a healthy bowl of taro root, sweet potato, and green onion with mac-gado-gado sauce, and the greens include basil, mizuna, kale, collards, red chard, sorrel. and edible flowers. *Manapua,* made with whole wheat, are stuffed with *kulolo,* sweet potato basil pesto, or tofu and dill, and sell for 75 cents each, or $4 for a half dozen. Beverages are coffee for 50 cents; smoothie (fresh fruit and juice) $2.50; teas including ginger and lemongrass, mint, or anise $1; and fresh-squeezed, lemon-lime tangerinade. They also offer bottled sauces and dressings like"Mac-Gado," a sweet-and-sour dressing with macadamia nuts, ginger, and lemongrass; "Pesto" with fresh herbs, mac nuts, taro, and garlic; "Hinges of Hell" with fresh jalapeño, basil, sage, macadamia-nut oil, tahini, miso, and ginger; and "Guava Lava," which is catsup with guava, taro, and ginger. Broke The Mouth is *the* choice for anyone into hearty, nutritious, deliciously healthy food.

Named after the famous all-Japanese fighting battalion that predated even the famous "442," the **Cafe 100,** at 969 Kilauea Ave., open Mon.-Thurs. 6:45 a.m.-8:30 p.m., Fri.-Sat. until 9:30 p.m., is a Hilo institution. The Miyashiro family has been serving food at their indoor-outdoor restaurant here since the late '50s. Although the loco moco, a cholesterol atom bomb containing a hamburger and egg atop rice smothered in gravy, was invented at Hilo's Lincoln Grill, the Cafe 100, serving it since 1961, has actually patented this belly-buster and turned it into an art form. There are the regular loco moco, the teriyaki loco, the sukiyaki loco, the hot dog loco, the *oyako* loco, and for the health conscious, the mahi loco. With a few exceptions, they cost $2 or less. So, if your waistline, the surgeon general, and your arteries permit, this is *the* place to have one. Breakfast choices include everything from bacon and eggs to coffee and donuts, while lunches feature beef stew $3.75, mixed plate $3.95, fried chicken $3.25, and an assortment of sandwiches from teri-beef to good old BLT for $2 or so. Make your selection and sit at one of the picnic tables under the veranda to watch the people of Hilo go by.

All trips to Hilo must include a brief stop at **Low's International Food,** long occupying the corner of Kilauea and Ponahawai Streets, tel. 969-6652, open daily except Wednesday, 9 a.m.-8 p.m., where *everyone* comes for the unique bread. Some of the more fanciful loaves are made from taro, breadfruit, guava, mango, passion fruit, coconut, banana, pumpkin, and cinnamon. The so-you-want-to-taste-it-all rainbow bread is a combination of taro, guava, and sweetbread. Loaves cost $4.25-5.25, and arrangements can be made to ship them home by Federal Express. Lunches, most under $5, range from their famous pot-roast pork tail with black bean sauce to turkey plate to lamb curry stew. Choose a table under the pavilion and enjoy your picnic in downtown Hilo.

Open every day 7 a.m.-9 p.m., a place that's getting praise from local people is **Freddie's,** tel. 935-1108, at 454 Manono Street. What might be called upscale Formica, it serves down-home food, all for under $6. Lunch and all entrees are served with two scoops of rice, fries, or mashed potatoes. Among the items on the menu are saimin, teri steak sandwich, chili dogs, and burgers.

If you want to eat anything but uninspired "American standard" in Hilo after 9 p.m., go to **Nori's Saimin and Snacks,** 688 Kinoole St., tel. 935-9133, stuck away and hard to spot (but worth it) in a little alley across from the bowling alley. Here you can have a totally "island experience" in a humble but proud restaurant that specializes in authentic "local grinds." Inside, where the service is slow but friendly, are Formica tables and chairs, counter stools, and the "that's what you really look like" glow of fluorescent lighting. Boiling pots hold saimin of all sorts, ranging in price from $2.80 to $5, that is generously ladled into steaming bowls and topped with fresh vegetables. Plate lunches like yakitori chicken with a scoop of rice and a scoop of macaroni salad are under $5. Two people can eat until they waddle at Nori's for about $15. There's no atmosphere, but the food is authentic and good.

Mun Cheong Lau is a cheap Chinese joint in downtown Hilo at 172 Kilauea Ave., tel. 935-3040 (takeout too), open daily 11 a.m.-11 p.m., closed Tuesday. If you want to eat with "the people," this is the spot. Soups on the front of the menu are $3.50; those on the back are $2.50 and are about the same except that they don't contain noodles. The servings are generous. Entrees like crispy chicken in oyster sauce for under $5 are delicious at any price. Seafoods include abalone with veggies for $3.40, abalone with black mushrooms $4.50, and shrimp with corn $3.75. A variety of pork or beef dishes are all priced under $3.50, while pineapple spareribs are $2.70 and boneless chicken with mushrooms is $3.75. These are full plates served with steamed rice, 60 cents extra if you want fried rice. For under $4 you can fill up in this place. It's clean, service is friendly, and the dining experience, while certainly not fancy, is definitely authentic.

Owned and operated by Dotty and Rey Frasco, **Dotty's Coffee Shop and Restaurant,** tel. 959-6477, at the Puainako Town Center, is open for breakfast daily 7-11 a.m., for lunch Mon.-Sat. 10:30 a.m.-2 p.m., and for dinner Mon.-Thurs. 5-8 p.m., Friday 5-9 p.m. Dotty's is an institution where local people come for the large and hearty portions. Breakfast is known for the corned beef hash and eggs and for French toast made with thick slices of sweet bread from Punaluu covered with real maple or coconut syrup at $3.75. Lunch favorites are grilled chicken supreme with mushrooms and Swiss cheese $4.65, or Dotty's ultimate steak sandwich with slices of sirloin, sautéed mushrooms, onions, and Swiss cheese

on a grilled potato roll $5.65. Those in the know come from around the island to dine on Dotty's famous oven-roasted turkey, fresh catch of the day, barbecued pork ribs with their own smoke-flavored sauce, and an amazing combination plate for $9.85 that gives you a choice of two: top sirloin, teriyaki steak, ribs, scampi, sautéed shrimp, or the catch-of-the-day. Fresh vegetables, real mashed potatoes, and homemade soups (great chowder on Friday) come with all full meals. For a hearty Hawaiian meal, stop in on Friday when Ray does the cooking for this special offering, all for $7.29—a lot less than you would pay for a $60 luau feast. The decor is "American standard" with a Formica counter and leatherette booths. Check out the black-and-white photos hanging on the walls.

Ting Hao Mandarin Kitchen is a family affair run by Alice Chang and her sister, also in the Puainako Town Center, tel. 959-6288, open weekdays 11 a.m.-8:30 p.m., weekends 5-8:30 p.m. Seek them out for a mouth-watering, home-cooked meal. The two most expensive items on the menu are Seafood Treasure for $6, and half a tea-smoked duck for $7; all others are under $5. Service is slow due to individual-order cooking, and those in the know pick up a hand-out menu and call to place their orders 30 minutes before arriving. Also at Puainako Town Center is **Five Spice** with an assortment of *bento* for under $4 and quick snacks like chili and rice $1.90 and chili dogs $1.95.

Bear's Coffee Shop, at 106 Keawe, tel. 935-0708, is an upscale coffee shop renowned for its breakfast, served daily 7-11:30 a.m. It features Belgian waffles (made from malted flour) and an assortment of egg dishes for $2.95. Lunch is hearty sandwiches of turkey, pastrami, chicken fillet, tuna, or ham for under $5, along with a small but zesty selection of Mexican food as well as salads. Beverages include Italian sodas, homemade lemonade, and a large selection of coffee, cappuccino, and caffe latte from their full espresso bar. All perfect with desserts like carrot cake, Bear's brownies, cheesecake, and pies. A great place to relax, read the morning paper, and watch Hilo life go by.

Kay's Lunch Center, at 684 Kilauea Ave., tel. 969-1776, open Tues.-Sun. 5 a.m.-2 p.m. and 5-9 p.m., can't be beat for a good square meal of Asian, Hawaiian, or American standards. Sandwich favorites like hamburgers, fish burgers, grilled cheese, and tuna are all under $3. Large bowls of saimin and wonton soups are under $4. Their grilled plates, like Korean barbecued beef or *kalbi* (short ribs), are cooked over an open wood fire and are delicious. Combo plates of their grilled offerings are $5.95 for one choice, $6.95 for two choices, and $7.95 for three choices, and include rice, miso soup, four kinds of kimchi, and vegetables. Kay's isn't much to look at, with leatherette booths and Formica tables, but it's a winner.

The **Ichiban Deli,** at 415 Kilauea Ave., across from the Hilo Hongwanji Temple, open Tues.-Sat. 7 a.m.-2 p.m. and 5-8:30 p.m., takeout available, is a basic Japanese-Hawaiian-American restaurant with breakfast like eggs with bacon or link sausage or corned beef hash $3.35, and lunches like fried chicken or spareribs, each at $4.25. The Japanese meals are standards like *bento* or tempura for under $5. No decor at all, but the prices are very reasonable.

Satsuki's, along the 200 block of Keawe St., receives the highest recommendation because when local people want a good meal at an inexpensive price they head here. Open for lunch 10 a.m.-2 p.m., dinner 4:30-9 p.m., closed Tuesday. Specialties are oxtail soup, the lunch special for $4.25, and the Okinawa *soba* plate lunch for only $3.95. Dinner specials are beef teriyaki for $5.70, *tonkatsu* $5.65, and fish teriyaki $7.50. Plenty of traditional favorites like *donburi* and *nabemono*. All meals come with miso soup, Japanese pickles and condiments, rice, and tea. No decor, but spotlessly clean and friendly. Excellent food at excellent value.

Sachi's Gourmet, only a few seconds away at 250 Keawe St., open Monday 8 a.m.-2 p.m. only, Tues.-Sat. 8 a.m.-2 p.m. and dinner 5-9 p.m., Sunday dinner only 5-9 p.m., is the same type of restaurant as Satsuki's, with its own loyal local clientele. The food is excellent here, too, and the prices are unbeatable. You'll walk away stuffed on traditional Japanese food for about $8 for a full meal.

Hukilau Restaurant at the Hilo Seaside Hotel, 136 Banyan Way, is open daily 7 a.m.-1 p.m. and 4-9 p.m. For breakfast you can have steak and eggs $6.95, fish and eggs $2.95, two eggs and toast $1.85, ham omelette $2.75, or a full choice of hotcakes and waffles at reasonable

prices. The lunch menu offers a choice of Reuben sandwich, steak and rice, baked chicken, or hamburger deluxe; each choice comes with a buffet salad bar for a fixed price of $5.25. The dinner menu is reasonable with T-bone steak $10.95, steak and lobster $14.95, oven roast prime rib $9.95, or the captain's platter (fried fish, shrimp, scallops, and oysters) for $9.95. All dinners come with soup of the day and salad bar. The decor is orange Naugahyde booths and brown Formica tables. Some of the vegetables come out of a can, and the deep-fried offerings have enough grease to clog the Alaska pipeline, but the view of Hilo Bay is exceptional and helps digestion.

The **New China Restaurant,** at 510 Kilauea Ave., tel. 961-5677, open daily 10 a.m.-10 p.m., serves basic Chinese combo plates of chicken, duck, pork, beef, and seafood. The most expensive seafood on the menu is $7 for abalone and Chinese mushrooms. Special plates include steamed chicken with ginger, onion sauce, and steamed rice for $3.80; beef broccoli and crispy chicken for $2.80. Not much class—almost like a McDonald's of Chinese food—but it's bright, shiny, and sparkly.

When a Hilo resident wants a plate lunch, and that's saying something, they go to **Hilo Lunch Shop,** tel. 935-8273, at the corner of Kalanikoa and Piilani, open daily except Sunday 6:15 a.m.-1:30 p.m. At this very basic restaurant, you pick and choose each separately priced item for your plate: tempura 90 cents; mahimahi 50 cents; vegetables 45 cents; for about $3 your plate will be huge.

Down Piilani, just at the Kentucky Fried Chicken, make a right onto Hinano St. and in a minute you'll see **Don's Grill,** tel. 935-9099, open daily except Monday 10:30 a.m.-9 p.m., and to 10 p.m. on Friday. This American/Hawaiian restaurant is known for good food at reasonable prices. Inside find wood-trimmed blue Formica tables in a very modern yet functionally tasteful setting. Breakfast starts with two eggs and toast $2.50, omelettes $4.95, and on weekends only, sweet bread French toast $2.75. Lunch can be taco salad $4.95, Philadelphia cheese steak $5.95, club sandwich $4.50, or your own burger creation starting at $4.25. Entrees are barbecued ribs, pork chops, or fillet of fish, all priced under $6. There's homemade pie, cheesecake, and pudding to top off your meal. Don's is a basic

American standard restaurant where you can get a good square meal for a good price.

Shooter's, at 121 Banyan Dr., tel. 969-7069, open 11 a.m.-2 a.m., is a bar and restaurant where you can dance seven nights a week, but you might not want to tell your mommy that you went there! DJ music ranges from reggae to rock to rap depending upon the crowd and the night. The cavernous interior is like a giant rumpus room with cement floors, neon beer signs, a graffiti wall, and TVs at every angle. The decor is industrial chic–the bar is galvanized metal, the liquor shelves are made from pipe, and the cement supporting pillars have been painted purple and gold to add a touch of tropical color. The mainly appetizer-and-burger menu offers a basket of grilled garlic bread for $2.50, Buffalo wings for $6.50, fried calamari for $5.75, Thai chicken salad for $6.75, and burgers with a variety of toppings around $6. There's a small selection of pasta, from linguine with fresh basil pesto for $6.75 to seafood marinara at $11.75. Limited main dishes are New York steak for $13.75, fresh *ahi* for $11.75, and char-broiled chicken for $11.50. Don't be put off by the atmosphere, which can seem a bit stark and hard at first glance. Shooter's is friendly, has security, and boasts that "there hasn't been one confrontation since the day we opened." That's nice!

Fast Foods and Snacks

Okay! For those who must, **McDonald's** is at 88 Kanoelehua Ave. and 177 Ululani Street. **Pizza Hut,** which actually has a decent salad bar, is at 326 Kilauea Avenue. Fast-food junkies will be totally happy at the **Puainako Town Center,** where glass and Formica cubes hold an endless supply of munchies from **McDonald's, Pizza Hut, Subway Sandwiches,** and **Taco Bell.**

The Hilo Hawaiian Hotel, a landmark on Banyan Dr., has expensive and romantic dining, but you can get terrific snacks and *pu pu* at the hotel's **Wai'ole Lounge** after 11 a.m., with savory items like sautéed chicken with macadamia peanut sauce for only $3, toasted garlic bread topped with mozzarella and parmesan cheeses and served with marinara sauce on the side for $2, and the chopped steak (real steak cut into bite-sized pieces) for $2.75. The setting is congenial, overlooking Hilo Bay with palm trees and flowers right outside the windows. For a light lunch at unbelievable prices, try the Wai'ole Lounge.

On Banyan Dr. just outside of the Hilo Hawaiian Hotel, get delicious scoops of ice cream in island flavors like macadamia nut at the **Ice Cream Factory.** Nearby is the **Banyan Snack Shop,** which dispenses whopping plate lunches like the loco moco—two scoops of rice and a hamburger covered in fried egg and gravy—for only $2.75. The breakfast specials here are very cheap too.

Two other places for a refreshing scoop of dessert are the **Hilo Homemade Ice Cream** at Hilo Tropical Gardens and **Tropical Dreams Ice Cream** at the refurbished Kress Building downtown.

Hilo Seeds and Snacks next to Lehua's Restaurant at 15 Waianuenue Ave. sells sandwiches and authentic crackseed. The **Kilauea Preserve Center,** at the corner of Kilauea and Ponahawai Streets, also sells authentic crackseed.

Lanky's Pastries and Deli, Hilo Shopping Center, tel. 935-6381, open 6:30 a.m.-9 p.m., deli side from 6 a.m., is a perfect place to head if you have a sweet tooth that *must* be satisfied. The deli/bakery is especially known for its "long johns,"—long, thin sugar donuts filled with custard—but they also have all kinds of baked goods from bread to apple turnovers. Their deli case holds sandwiches priced under $3, along with an assortment of *bento,* perfect for a picnic lunch.

Cathy's Lunch Shop, at 270 Kamehameha Ave., is a tiny little place with two tables, where only a few dollars will get you breakfast, a plate lunch, a hamburger, or even a taco.

Island Grinds serves plate lunches, burgers, a salad bar, and vegetarian entrees from its lunchwagon at the bayfront beach Mon.-Fri., 10 a.m.-2 p.m.

Moderately Priced

Restaurant Miwa, at Hilo Shopping Center, 1261 Kilauea Ave., tel. 961-4454, is open daily 10 a.m.-9 p.m., sometimes until 10 p.m. for meals and until 2 a.m. at the bar. Very beautifully appointed, Miwa is a surprise, especially since it's stuck back in the corner of the shopping center. Enter to find traditional *shoji* screens and wooden tables adorned with fine linens, along with a classic sushi bar. The waitresses wear kimonos, though most are local women and not necessarily Japanese. The menu is excellent, with appetizers like sake-flavored steamed clams for $4.95 and crab *sunomono* (seaweed, cucumber slices, and crab meat) for $4.25. A specialty is *nabemono,* a hearty and zesty soup/stew prepared at your table with a two-order minimum. Traditional favorites popular with Westerners include beef sukiyaki and *shabu shabu* (each $14), and there's also a variety of combination dinners that give you a wider sampling of the menu at good value. Restaurant Miwa is an excellent choice for a gourmet meal at a reasonable price in a congenial setting.

Very clean and down-home proud, the **Royal Siam Thai Restaurant,** at 68 Mamo St., tel. 961-6100, serves up tasty Thai treats Mon.-Sat. 11 a.m.-2:30 p.m. and 5-9 p.m. Appetizers include a crispy Thai noodle dish for $4.95 or fish patty for $5.95. Two of the several soups are coconut chicken soup for $4.95 and a seafood soup for $7.95. Entrees range from an inexpensive water chestnut fried rice dish for $4.95 through curries and meat dishes to a reasonable red snapper for $16.95.

Modern and chic with a checkerboard floor, gray-on-black tables and chairs, ceiling fans, and the calming effect of ferns and flowers, **Cafe Pesto,** at 308 Kamehameha Ave., tel. 969-6640, is open Sun.-Thurs. 11 a.m.-9 p.m., Fri.-Sat. 11 a.m.-10 p.m. One of Hilo's established restaurants, it offers affordable gourmet food in an unpretentious and comfortable setting. The pizza from their ohia wood-fired oven can be anything from *quatro formaggio* (four cheeses) $5.95 to Southwestern pizza with fresh cilantro, pesto, *cipolte,* barbecued chicken, and red onions $9.95 small and $15.95 large. Another pizza that lets you know that you are in Hawaii is Pizza Luau, which is topped with *kalua* pork, local sweet onions, and fresh Hawaiian pineapple for $8.95 and $14.95. (Plenty of calzone choices, too, at $12.95.) Combined with dinner salads of "wild greens" at $3.50, the pizza or a calzone makes a great meal for two. Delectable yet inexpensive items are *focaccia* with rosemary and Gorgonzola $3.50, *crostini* (fresh bread with a creamy, fresh herb garlic butter) $2.95, and soup of the day for only $3.25; or try the seared *poke,* sesame marinated with green onion, ginger, and tamarind honey vinaigrette on a bed of spinach with fresh baked bread at $8.95. Heartier appetites will be satisfied with chicken Lallo Rosa, a breast of chicken, greens, Maui onions, cherry tomatoes, and coriander dressing for $7.95; *ceviche* pasta salad at $7.95; smoked salmon with fettuccine $12.95; wild chicken and mushroom risotto for $14.95; Island Seafood risotto with fresh fish, prawns, lobster, and corn served in a sweet chili risotto for $16.95; and New York steak with wild mushrooms, grilled onions, and wasabi mashed potatoes for $19.95. Cafe Pesto also has a brass-railed espresso bar where you can order caffe latte or iced cappuccino to top off your meal in one of the best "budget gourmet" restaurants on the Big Island.

Fiasco's, a good restaurant and nightspot, is at the Waiakea Shopping Center, 200 Kanoelehua St., tel. 935-7666, open Sun.-Thurs. 11 a.m.-10 p.m., weekends to 11 p.m., with dancing 9 p.m. until closing on weekends (see the following "Entertainment" section). Featuring a country inn flavor, Fiasco's has a cobblestoned entrance that leads you to the cozy, post-and-beam dining room appointed with stout wooden tables and captain's chairs, with semi-private booths lining the walls. The mahogany bar, a classic with polished lion's-head brass rails, offers comfortable stools and black leather booths. The menu begins with appetizers like fried mozzarella $4.25, escargots $5.95, or a big plate of onion rings $2.75. Lighter appetites might enjoy the salad bar buffet $6.50 or a taco salad with beef or chicken $6.25 (with refried beans $5.25). Sandwiches range from the croissant club $6.75 to French dip $5.95 to a classic burger $5.25. Entrees include Mexican fare like tacos $6.25 and American standards like rib eye steak or prime rib $14.95. Families can save money with a special children's menu.

Uncle Billy's at the Hilo Bay Hotel along Banyan Dr., tel. 935-0861, is open for breakfast 7-8:30 a.m., dinner 5:30-8:30 p.m. Enjoy the free nightly hula show 6-7:30 p.m. The interior of the banquet hall-style restaurant is neo-Polynesian, and hanging from the open beam ceiling are thatched umbrella-type chandeliers and mobiles with cascading white shells. Chairs are comfortable bent bamboo and every table is brightened by an orchid. Breakfast can be the *wiki wiki,* which is a scrambled eggs, rice, and ham for a very reasonable $2.99; a chef's omelette for $5.50; Hawaiian French toast with sausage for $4.50; or the "Sunrise Special," a short stack of pancakes served with link sausages for $3.95. Dinner can be fresh catch, charbroiled or sautéed, that includes a salad, vegetable of the day, and rice pilaf, at market price; golden fried shrimp dinner $13.95; shellfish sauté $15.95; lemon macadamia nut chicken $10.95; or broiled hibachi chicken and New York steak for $14.95. Treat yourself by coming to Uncle Billy's Bar, open daily from 5:30 p.m., and order an exotic drink while you peer through the louvered windows into the central garden bursting with the magical colors of tropical plants and flowers.

Ken's House of Pancakes is one of a chain but you can have a good meal for a good price. Open 24 hours every day of the year, it's conveniently located on the way to the airport at 1730 Kamehameha Ave., tel. 935-8711.

Nihon Culture Center, 123 Lihiwai St., tel. 969-1133 (reservations required), presents authentic Japanese meals, an excellent sushi bar, and combination dinners along with cultural and artistic displays. Open daily for breakfast, lunch, and dinner until 9 p.m., sushi bar until 10 p.m.

Reuben's Mexican Restaurant, tel. 961-2552, at 336 Kamehameha Ave., open Mon.-Fri. 11 a.m.-9 p.m., Saturday 12-9 p.m., will enliven your palate with its zesty dishes. The interior has a Mexican flair accomplished with a good selection of wall-hung sombreros and gaily colored serapes. The menu is reasonable, with selections like *carne asada* $8, steak tacos $7, chicken or beef tostadas $7, and vegetarian bean chili verde burrito $8. All are served with beans and rice. The bar has a large selection of *cerveza,* including Pacifico, Negra Modelo, and Carte Blanca for $3, and most domestics for $2. But Reuben's is most famous for their margaritas—more than one will get you acting like a human *chimichanga.* ¡Olé!

Expensive Restaurants

Queen's Court Restaurant at the Hilo Hawaiian Hotel on Banyan Dr., tel. 935-9361, offers a nightly buffet that is *the* best in Hilo. Connoisseurs usually don't consider buffets to be gourmet quality, but the Queen's Court proves them wrong. Throughout the week, buffets include: Monday and Thursday, prime rib and crab buffet for $19.95; Friday and Saturday, the legendary seafood buffet for $22.50; Sunday, Hawaiian and seafood buffet for $22.50. All are extraordinary and would give the finest restaurants anywhere a run for their money. The dining room is grand, with large archways and windows overlooking Hilo Bay. On buffet nights, a massive table is laden with fresh island vegetables and 15 different salads. For example, on seafood night, you choose from oysters, shrimp, crab, sushi, and sashimi. Then the chefs take over. Resplendent in white uniforms and chef's hats, they stand ready to sauté or broil your choice of fish, which always includes best selections like swordfish or *ono.* Beverages include white, rosé, and rich red wines, plus fresh-squeezed guava and orange juice. The dessert table entices you with fresh fruits and imported cheeses, and dares you to save room for cream pies, fresh-baked cookies, and éclairs. Sunday champagne brunch is more of the same quality at $19.95. A breakfast buffet is served daily 6:30 a.m.-9:30 a.m., with the continental breakfast buffet priced at $5.95, hot entrees for $6.95, and both (don't explode) for $8.25. You can also order from the menu items like two eggs any style with toast for $3.75; a short stack of griddle cakes for $3.75; an "Omelette by the Bay" with mushrooms, shrimp and mozzarella cheese for $7.50; or a local scramble with Portuguese sausage or green onions for $6.75. Lunch is reasonable, with yakitori chicken sauté for $6.30, saimin Supreme for $3.75, a Banyan tossed salad for $2.50 (or $5 as an entree). Cold sandwiches range from a stuffed crab salad sandwich for $9 to a good old BLT for $5.25; for the hungry a New York steak is $14. For dinner, if you don't choose the buffet, start with a Queens Court fruit salad for $6.50, followed by filet mignon for $16.50, seafood brochette for $16, fresh catch, broiled, blackened or sautéed at market price, or vegetarian linguine for $6. Make reservations, especially on seafood night, because the Hilo Hawaiian attracts many Hilo residents who love great food. (For an inexpensive lunch see the hotel's "Waiole Lounge" under "Fast Foods and Snacks.")

Sicilian fishermen would feel right at home at **Pescatore Ristorante,** 235 Keawe St., tel. 969-9090, open daily for lunch 11 a.m.-2 p.m., dinner 5:30-9 p.m., and until 10 p.m. Friday and Saturday. The building housing Pescatore is part of the *Main Street U.S.A. Project* evident in downtown Hilo. The building has had multiple uses over the years, and as part of its colorful past, served as a house of ill repute. Completely redone, it has been transformed into a bright, cheery room with high-backed, red velvet armchairs and formally set tables with green linen tablecloths. Italian-style chandeliers, lace curtains, exposed beams, and koa trim add to the elegance. You can also request a "Portofino Room," a separate area for romance and privacy. Lunch fare begins with antipasto of marinated fish with olive oil, garlic, and vinegar, or of fresh clams, when available. Primo piati can be pollo marsalla $8.95, or fresh steamed garden vegetables, plain or with extra virgin olive oil, served with marinara sauce and Romano cheese for $8.95. If your taste turns to pasta, go for the primavera with fresh vegetables in tomato sauce for a very reasonable $7.95. Or try the putanesca, a famous dish cooked by the Italian ladies of the evening for their clientele; it's made from garlic, anchovies, sun-dried tomatoes, black olives, capers, and olive oil and costs $7.95. For dinner, start with their special minestrone $3.50, or with the ensalata of sliced tomatoes, mozzarella, and spinach with Italian vinaigrette dressing $4.95. For a dinner antipasto try the hearts of artichokes sautéed with fresh basil, garlic, and tomatoes and sprinkled with Parmesan cheese $5.95. Dinner entrees can be cioppino clasico alla pescatore, swimming with morsels of lobster, mussels, clams, shrimp, fish, and scallops served with garlic bread $24.95; *gamberetti Alfredo* (large shrimp sautéed in butter, garlic, fresh basil, and Parmesan cheese in a white-wine sauce); or *vongole* (steamed clams and choice of red or white clam sauce) $17.95. Also, a dinner special includes soup or salad, one dinner entree from the menu, coffee or tea, and dessert for $19.95. Pescatore's offers good food for reasonable prices.

Lehua's Bar and Restaurant, at 11 Waianuenue Ave., tel. 935-8055, open for lunch 11 a.m.-4 p.m., dinner 5-9 p.m., is another upscale restaurant in a restored building. The mood is set with track lighting, Casablanca fans, and an excellent sound system. The decor is gray-on-gray with cane chairs and art deco silverware; the walls hold works of local artists. Owners Mark and Larry, transplanted from Oahu where they

spent years in the nightclub business, have joined to create a restaurant inspired by island-style cuisine. Lunch offerings feature Lehua's homemade soup at $3.95 per bowl, Caesar salad for $5.95 (with chicken $7.50 or shrimp $9.95), Lehua's chicken clubhouse sandwich for $7.95, and a full salad bar for $7.95, children under 10 $3.95. Lunch also brings pasta like linguine, fettuccine, or penne pasta smothered with a fresh tomato basil and garlic cream sauce for $7.50, or with charbroiled chicken and cilantro-pesto sauce for $8.95. Lighter appetites will enjoy yakitori sticks for $1.95; Lehua's quesadilla with cilantro-pesto, cheese, and salsa fresca for $4.25 (with chicken $5.25); or juicy *paniolo* ribs for $5.95. Evening brings the dinner menu, with selections like Thai coconut shrimp with sweet chili basil sauce for $10.95; sautéed garlic shrimp with grilled sourdough bread for $10.95; catch-of-the-day $16.95; mixed grill of prawns, chicken, and teriyaki steak $16.95; and country pork spareribs $12.95. The dinner menu also includes a medley of stir-fried vegetables over white or brown rice with teriyaki or oyster sauce $9.95, with boneless marinated chicken $10.25; and a New York or rib eye steak charbroiled to order for $17.95. Friday and Saturday nights bring live entertainment, mostly rock and blues. Lehua's is upbeat, with delicious food, and fun thrown in for free.

Sandalwood Room is the main restaurant of the Hawaii Naniloa Hotel on Banyan Dr., tel. 935-0831. Here, in an elegant room overlooking the bay and lined with aromatic sandalwood, you can feast on dishes from around the world. Zesty curries, rich French sauces, chops done in wine, and Polynesian-inspired dishes are offered on this full and expensive menu.

KK Tei Restaurant, 1550 Kamehameha Ave., tel. 961-3791, is a favored restaurant of many local people. The centerpiece is a bonsai garden complete with pagodas and arched moon bridges. Cook your own beef, chicken, or fish at your tableside hibachi and dip it into an array of savory sauces—or the chefs will prepare your selection from their full menu of Japanese dishes. Entrees cost about $10 in this unique Asian setting. Those in the know accord this restaurant gourmet status. From 5 p.m. to 8 p.m., the place is packed for the $1 draft beers and free *pu pu.*

Harrington's, at 135 Kalanianaole St., tel. 961-4966, is open nightly for dinner 5:30-10 p.m., Sunday 5:30-9 p.m.; lounge open 5:30-closing. The setting couldn't be more brilliant, as the restaurant overlooks the bay. A sunset cocktail or dinner is even more romantic with the melodic strains of live jazz, contemporary, or Hawaiian music playing softly in the background. The continental cuisine features appetizers like shrimp cocktail $7.50, seafood chowder $3.50, mushroom tempura $5.25, escargots in casserole $7.50, and a variety of salads. Special vegetarian dishes like eggplant parmigiana are $12.50, while seafood selections of prawns scampi are $19.95, scallops chardonnay $18.25, and calamari meunière $15.25. Meat and fowl dishes are tempting: Slavic steak $15.50, prime rib au jus $18.95, and chicken Marsala $15.25.

ENTERTAINMENT

Hilo doesn't have a lot of nightlife, but it's not a morgue either. You can dance, disco, or listen to quiet piano music at a few lounges and hotels around town.

In a classic plantation building behind the old police station, on Kalakaua between Keawe and Kinoole Streets, is the **East Hawaii Culture Center,** a nonprofit organization that supports local art and culture by showcasing the works of different artists monthly on a revolving basis in the large entrance hall of the old police station and an annex building. They also host **Shakespeare in the Park,** a local repertory of performers who stage, direct, design, and enact Shakespearean plays under the large banyan in Kalakaua Park during the month of July. If you're in Hilo at this time, it shouldn't be missed. The Big Island Arts Guild and the Dance Council also meet here. The bulletin board is always filled with announcements of happenings in the local art scene.

Lehua's Bar and Restaurant, 11 Waianuenue Ave., offers a mixed bag of jazz, Hawaiian, or contemporary music on weekends. Occasionally there is a comedy night. Upbeat vibes with good food as well.

Hilo has its own little sleaze bar, **The Green Onion,** at 885 Kilauea Ave., where exotic dancers can *sometimes* be coaxed on stage if the clientele takes up a collection and offers them a minimum amount of money. Sound good to you? Things *can't* be that bad!

Fiasco's at the Waiakea Shopping Mall, 200 Kanoelehua Ave., tel. 935-7666, swings with a full venue of live music on weekends. Doors open at 9 p.m., with a cover and relaxed dress code.

If you're looking for a night out, you can't beat the **Wai'oli Lounge** at the Hilo Hawaiian Hotel, where there is live music every night ranging from contemporary Hawaiian to rock. **Uncle Billy's Restaurant** at the Hilo Bay Hotel has a free hula show nightly 6-7:30 p.m. **Harrington's,** one of Hilo's most romantic night spots, offers live jazz, contemporary, or Hawaiian music nightly. Perfect for dinner or just for relaxing.

Others
To catch a flick, try the **Waiakea Theaters,** tel. 935-9747, at Waiakea Mall on Kanoelehua Ave.; the **Prince Kuhio Theaters,** tel. 959-4595, at the Prince Kuhio Plaza; or the newer **Kress Cinemas** downtown, tel. 961-3456. You'll enjoy great listening on **KIPA Rainbow Radio** (AM 620). This station plays an excellent selection of contemporary music with few commercial interruptions. It sounds the way FM used to. K-BIG FM 106 is worth listening to, and the Wave at 97.1 FM sends out easy listening jazz and Hawaiian music.

SHOPPING

Shopping Malls
Hilo has the best general-purpose shopping on the island. Stock up on film and food before you do any touring or camping. **Prince Kuhio Plaza,** at 111 E. Puainako, open weekdays 9:30 a.m.-9 p.m., Saturday to 5:30 p.m., Sunday 10 a.m.-5 p.m., is Hilo's newest and the island's largest shopping mall. Restaurants, jewelry shops, shoe stores, supermarkets, and large department stores like Sears and Liberty House make it a one-stop shopper's paradise. Here too you'll find Longs Drugs for film, and Waldenbooks for an extensive selection of reading material. An older but still full-service shopping center is **Kaiko'o Mall** at 777 Kilauea Avenue. **Hilo Shopping Center** is about one-half mile south on Kilauea

one of Hilo's many vintage buildings

J.D. BISIGNANI

Ave. at the corner of Kekuanaoa Street. This smaller mall has only a handful of local shops, but it does have some excellent inexpensive restaurants and a fine pastry shop. **Puainako Town Center** is located at 2100 Kanoelehua Ave. (Route 11 south toward Volcanoes), with lots of shops, Sack 'n' Save Market, and plenty of fast foods. Nearby are Wal-Mart, Denny's Restaurant, and a Barnes and Noble bookstore. **Waiakea Shopping Plaza,** handy to the airport at 100 Kanoelehua Ave., has a small clutch of stores.

Hilo's real treasures are its commercial flower gardens. The proprietors of these gardens are experts at preparing and shipping vibrant and colorful floral arrangements. Prices are reasonable and no other gift says Hawaii like a magnificent bouquet of exotic flowers.

Food Markets

For groceries and supplies try: **KTA Super Store,** 321 Kiawe Ave. or in the Puainako Town Center; **Safeway,** 111 E. Puainako; **Sack 'n' Save** at Puainako Town Center; or **Sure Save Supermarket** in Kaiko'o Mall. For a real treat visit the early morning **Suisan Fish Auction** at 85 Lihiwai St., one of only a few open-air fish auctions in the state. Their retail fresh-fish market is next door.

The Macadamia Nut Factory Outlet in front of Uncle Billy's Hotel on Banyan Dr., open daily 8 a.m.-9 p.m., is stocked with liquor, beer, pantry and deli items, and curios and gifts.

Health Food and Fruit Stores

Abundant Life Natural Foods, owned and operated by Leslie Miki since 1977, is in downtown Hilo at 292 Kamehameha Ave., open daily 8:30 a.m.-6 p.m., Saturday until 5 p.m., and Sunday 11 a.m.-3 p.m., tel. 935-7411. The store's kitchen puts out daily specials of soup, salads, sandwiches, and *bento,* all for well under $5, while the shelves are stocked with an excellent selection of fresh fruits and veggies, bulk foods, cosmetics, vitamins, and herbs. The bookshelves cosmically vibrate with a selection of tomes on metaphysics and new-age literature.

On Wednesday and Saturday morning, check out the **farmers' market** along Kamehameha Ave. fronting the bay in the center of the downtown area. Great for bargains and local color.

Bookstores

Hilo has excellent bookstores. **Basically Books,** downtown at 46 Waianuenue St., tel. 961-0144, (800) 903-6277, has a good selection of Hawaiiana, out-of-print books, and an unbeatable selection of maps. You can get anywhere you want to go with their nautical charts, road maps, and topographical maps. The selection includes sectionals for serious hikers and trekkers. Their collection covers most of the Pacific. They also feature a very good selection of travel books, and flags from countries throughout the world. Owner and proprietress Christine Reed can help you with any of your needs.

The **Book Gallery** at Prince Kuhio Plaza, tel. 959-7744, is a full-selection bookstore featuring Hawaiiana, hardcovers, and paperbacks.

Waldenbooks, also at Prince Kuhio Plaza, tel. 959-6468, open daily 9 a.m.-9 p.m., is the largest and best-stocked bookstore in the Hilo area.

Gifts and Crafts

If you're looking for that special island memento or souvenirs to bring home to family and friends, Uncle Billy covers all the bases and along with everything else offers the **Polynesian Market Place,** adjacent to the Hilo Bay Hotel. Open daily 8 a.m.-8 p.m., the marketplace sells a lot of good junk, liquor, and resortwear. The **Hilo Hattie** store at Prince Kuhio Plaza has all you need in island clothing, tourist style. **Hawaiian Handcrafts** at 760 Kilauea Ave., tel. 935-5587, specializes in woodcarvings. Here, Dan DeLuz uses exotic woods to turn out bowls, boxes, and vases, and sells shells from around the Pacific.

Sugawara Lauhala and Gift Shop at 59 Kalakaua St. is a virtually unknown Hilo institution operated by the Sugawara sisters, who have been in business for most of their 70-plus years. They make genuine *lau hala* weavings right on the premises of their character-laden shop. Their best hats sell for $75 up, and they also have baskets from $15. If you are after the genuine article, made to last a lifetime, you'll find it here. One by one, the old-timers—the best weavers—are dying or losing their eyesight, so these unique woven products are becoming more and more scarce and will undoubtedly increase in value as time goes by.

Just down from Sugawara's at 38 Kalakala St., tel. 935-4555, is **Hanahou.** Open Mon.-Sat. 10 a.m.-5 p.m., this wonderful little shop sells mostly vintage island treasures like *lau hala* weavings, baskets, pillows, hats, and sandals. Most of the items are made here on the Big Island but some are imported from Niue, east of Tonga.

Old Town Printer and Stationers, at 201 Kinoole St., open weekdays 8 a.m.-5 p.m., has been in business for 35 years selling stationery, office supplies, postcards, notecards, and a terrific selection of calendars.

At 35 Waianuenue Ave. is the classy little shop called **Etsko's,** tel. 961-3778. It's Ginza and Paris in Hilo. This eclectic little shop sells all sorts of arts and craft items, gifts, furniture, jewelry, and a small selection of silk and natural fiber clothing. Perhaps a hand-painted silk tie for him or a Japanese *tansu* chest for her is just the piece you're looking for. After you've shopped yourself into oblivion, head for the espresso bar at the back of the shop to rejuvenate yourself on coffee, Italian soda, or a wide variety of baked goods. Open Mon.-Fri. 9 a.m-6 p.m. and until 4 p.m. on Saturday; closed Sunday.

Sig Zane Design, at 122 Kamehameha Ave., tel. 935-7077, open Mon.-Sat. 9 a.m.-5 p.m., is one of the most unique and distinctive shops on the island. Here, owner and designer Sig Zane creates distinctive island wearables in 100% cotton. All designs are not only Hawaiian/tropical but also chronicle useful and medicinal Hawaiian plants and flowers. Sig's wife, Nalani, who helps in the shop, is a *kumu hula* who learned the intricate dance steps from her mother, Edith Kanakaole, a legendary dancer who has been memorialized with a local tennis stadium that bears her name. You can get shirts for $59, dresses around $75, and *pareau* $30, as well as affordable house slippers, sweatshirts, T-shirts, *hapi* coats, and even futon covers. The shelves also hold *lau hala* hats, handbound koa notebooks, and basketry made from natural fibers. Outfit yourself from head to toe at Sig's shop and be totally in style and comfort.

Dragon Mama, a lovely boutique at 266 Kamehameha Ave., features natural-fiber futons, fine bedding, wool, cotton fabrics, custom covers, meditation pillows, and Japanese rice paper.

Dreams of Paradise, at 308 Kamehameha Ave. (the restored S. Hata Building, erected in 1912), tel. 935-5670 or (800) 935-5670, open Mon.-Sat. 10 a.m.-9 p.m., Sunday noon-7 p.m., shipping available, is a combination boutique and gallery owned and operated by Susan Starr, who is herself a talented artist capturing the heart of Hawaii's *aina* in oils, pastels, and textiles. Some artists showcased in Dreams of Paradise are: Andrew Plack, a nature artist specializing in the flora and fauna of Hawaii; Gerard Beauvalet, a multitalented artist producing fine koa furniture as well as distinctive acrylic paintings—mostly depicting Polynesian women in natural poses of meditation and serenity—that are also reproduced as distinctive T-shirt designs; Beverly Jackson, who catches the sun in her stained glass renditions of breadfruit, lotus blossoms, and various Hawaiian flowers; and Terry Taube, a sculptor producing lava sculptures and renditions of animal life, especially *honu,* the green sea turtle. Shelves also hold gourmet food items, incidental bags, distinctive cooking aprons, and plenty of inexpensive but tasteful souvenirs.

The **Rift Zone,** at 106 #1 Kamehameha Ave., tel. 969-9976, is open Tues.-Sat. 9 a.m-6 p.m. Owned and operated by the husband-and-wife team of Robert and Cathy Joiner (he the potter, she the glazier), this gallery features about 50 artists, predominantly from the Big Island. Works include paintings by Avi Kriaty, fantastic fiber-sculptured baskets by Mika McCann, gorgeous hand-painted silks by Kalalani, outrageous photographs of volcanoes and lava by Brad Lewis, a multitude of furniture made from island woods, and of course pottery by the owners. If you care to have a look at the Rift Zone pottery studio, they are located at 13-3522 Kaupilai St. in Pahoa, tel. 965-9509.

Watch as your T-shirt is screen-printed at **Hawaiian Arts,** 284 Kamehameha Ave., tel. 935-1860, a functioning T-shirt factory. Most shirts are $12.99, and hanging on the wall is *the* biggest T-shirt in all of Hawaii.

Caravan Town at 194 Kamehameha Ave. is open daily except Sunday 8 a.m.-4:30 p.m., Friday until 5:30 p.m., and Saturday until 4 p.m. It is one of the most interesting junk stores in Hilo. The shelves hold an internationally eclectic mix of merchandise that includes pendulum clocks, plaster Greek goddesses, luggage, and paper lanterns. Also, the shop specializes in over-the-counter Chinese herbs and medicines purportedly effective for everything from constipation to impotence.

Big Island Estate Jewelry, at 300 Kamehameha Ave., open Mon.-Fri. 9 a.m.-6 p.m., Saturday 9 a.m.-4 p.m., is much more than its name implies, functioning as a pawn shop and discovery shop. Inside are antiques, collectibles, knickknacks, vases, musical instruments, and a good selection of used camera gear.

The Kipuka Smoke Shop, at 308 Kamehameha Ave., Suite 102, tel. 961-5082, open Mon.-Thurs. 9 a.m.-6 p.m., Friday 9 a.m.-8 p.m., Saturday 9 a.m.-4 p.m., is a tiny, aromatic closet of a shop selling cigars, cigarettes, pipe tobacco, rolling papers, lighters, and even walking sticks.

The 100 block of Keawe Ave., between Shipman and Kalakaua Streets, is Hilo's **yuppie row.** Here are **The Most Irresistible Shop in Hilo,** with Ciao backpacks and bags; and **The Fire Place Store,** featuring coffeepots, Mexican *piñatas,* children's toys, greeting cards, *pareau,* T-shirts, and a good selection of cosmetics.

The other side of yuppie row is down-home Hilo. One downtown shop along Keawe St. is **Kodani's Florist,** for fresh-cut flowers and lei. Gift shops, antique stores, and use- book emporiums fill this area.

Hawaii Sales and Surplus, featuring raincoats, hats, military supplies, knives, backpacks, rubber rafts, and plenty of old and new military uniforms, can be found on Mamo Street. Also along this street at #64 is **Pacific Isle Pawn.** Open Mon.-Fri. 9:30 a.m.-5 p.m., Saturday 9:30 a.m.-2 p.m., this is one of those places where you might come across a treasure, especially old gold jewelry. **Northern Lights Antiques,** not far away on Ponahawai St., is another treasure chest overflowing with antiques, curios, lamps, beads, and Asian heirlooms.

The **Modern Camera Center,** at 165 Kiawe St., tel. 935-3279, is one of the few full-service camera shops in Hilo.

SERVICES AND INFORMATION

Emergencies

When in need call: **police,** tel. 935-3311; **Hilo Hospital** at 1190 Waianuenue St., tel. 974-4700.

Keiko Gibo has an office at 321 Kinoole St., where she practices the ancient healing arts of **acupuncture** and shiatsu and various therapeutic massages.

Also for massage, *lomi lomi,* and herbal and nutritional products, contact the **Academy of Therapeutic Massage,** tel. 935-1405, at 180 Kinoole St.; it offers classes too.

The Hilo Pharmacy, tel. 961-9267, in the 300 block of Kamehameha Ave., open Mon.-Fri. 8:30 a.m.-5:30 p.m., Saturday 8:30 a.m.-12:30 p.m., is a full-service pharmacy.

Information

Two good sources of maps and helpful brochures are **Hawaii Visitors Bureau,** at the corner of Keawe and Haili Streets, tel. 961-5797, open Mon.-Fri. 8 a.m.-noon and 1-4:30 p.m.; and the **Chamber of Commerce,** 202 Kamehameha Ave., tel. 935-7178. Also try the **Hilo Public Library,** 300 Waianuenue St., tel. 933-4650; or the **University of Hawaii at Hilo** information, tel. 974-7516.

Banks and Post Office

For your money needs try the following: **City Bank** at Kaiko'o Mall, tel. 935-6844; **Central Pacific,** 525 Kilauea Ave., tel. 935-5251; **Bank of Hawaii,** 120 Pauahi, tel. 935-0084; or **First Hawaiian Bank,** 1205 Kilauea Ave., tel. 969-2211.

The central **post office,** open weekdays 9 a.m.-4:30 p.m., Saturday 9 a.m.-12:30 p.m., is an efficiently run, modern post office, clearly marked on the access road to the airport. It is extremely convenient for mailings prior to departure.

DIANA LASICH HARPER

BOB RACE

THE SADDLE ROAD

Slicing west across the Hilo District with a north-ward list is Route 200, the Saddle Road. Every-one with a sense of adventure loves this bold cut across the Big Island along a high valley separating the two great mountains, Mauna Loa and Mauna Kea. Along it you pass explorable caves, a *nene* sanctuary, camping areas, and spur roads leading to the tops of Mauna Kea and Mauna Loa. Besides, it's a great adventure for anyone traveling between Hilo and Kona. Keep your eyes peeled for convoys of tanks and armored personnel carriers as they sometimes sally forth from Pohakuloa Military Camp.

Getting There
The car-rental companies cringe when you men-tion the Saddle Road. Some even intimidate you by saying that their insurance won't cover

you on this road. They're terrified you'll rattle their cars to death. For the most part these fears are groundless. For a few miles the Saddle Road is corrugated because of heavy use by the military but, by and large, it's a good road, no worse than many others around the island. How-ever, it *is* isolated, and there are no facilities along the way. If you bypass it, you'll miss some of the best scenery on the Big Island. From Hilo, follow Waianuenue Ave. west past Rainbow Falls. Saddle Road (Route 200) splits left within a mile or two and is clearly marked. If you follow it across the island, you'll intersect Route 190 on which you can turn north to Waimea or south to Kona. For information on professional guide service to the top of Mauna Kea, see below, or see "Bus and Van Tours" under "Sightseeing Tours" in the "Getting Around" chapter.

MAUNA KEA

The lava along both sides of the road is old as you approach Mauna Kea ("White Mountain"). The lowlands are covered with grass, ferns, small trees, and mossy rocks. Twenty-seven miles out of Hilo, a clearly marked road to your right leads to the summit of 13,796-foot Mauna

Kea. A sign warns you that this road is rough, unpaved, and narrow, with no water, food, fuel, restrooms, or shelters. Moreover, you can ex-pect winds, rain, fog, hail, snow, and altitude sickness. Intrigued? Proceed: It's not as bad as it sounds. A 4WD vehicle is highly advised, and if there's snow it's impossible without one. A normal rental car isn't powerful enough, mainly because you're gaining more than 8,000 feet of elevation in 15 miles, which plays havoc with carburetors. But the real problem is coming down. For a small car with not very good gearing you're going to be riding your brakes for 15 miles. If they fail, you'll stand a very good chance of becoming a resident spirit of the mountain!

Four miles up you pass **Hale Pohaku** ("House of Stone"), which looks like a ski resort; many of the scientists from the observatory atop the mountain live here. A sign says that you need a permit from the Department of Land and Natural Resources (in Hilo) and a 4WD vehicle to proceed. Actually, the road is graded, banked, and well maintained, with the upper four miles paved so that dust is kept to a minimum to protect the sensitive "eyes" of the telescopes. As you climb, you pass through the clouds to a barren world devoid of vegetation. The earth is a red, rolling series of volcanic cones. You get an incredible vista of Mauna Loa peeking through the clouds and what seems like the entire island lying at your feet. In the distance the lights of Maui flicker. **Lake Waiau,** which unbelievably translates as "Swim Water," is almost at the top at 13,020 feet, making it the third-highest lake in the U.S. For some reason, ladybugs love this area.

If the vistas aren't enough, bring a kite along and watch it soar in the winds of the earth's upper atmosphere. Off to your right is Pu'u Kahinahina,

a small hill whose name means "hill of the silver sword." It's one of the only places on the Big Island where you'll see this very rare plant. The mountaintop was at one time federal land, and funds were made available to eradicate feral goats, one of the worst destroyers of the silver sword and many other native Hawaiian plants.

Mauna Kea is the only spot in the tropical Pacific that was glaciated. The entire summit of the mountain was covered in 500 feet of ice. Toward the summit, you may notice piles of rock which are the terminal moraine of these ancient glaciers. The snows atop Mauna Kea are unpredictable. Some years it is merely a dusting, while in other years, as in 1982, there was enough snow to ski from late November to late July. The ski run comes all the way down from the summit, giving you about a four-mile trail. For skiing guides, see "Skiing" under "Sports and Recreation" in the Out and About chapter.

Here and there around the summit are small caves, remnants of ancient quarries where Hawaiians came to dig a special kind of fired rock that is the hardest in all Hawaii. They hauled roughed-out tools down to the lowlands, where they refined them into excellent implements that became coveted trade items.

A natural phenomenon is the strange thermal properties manifested by the cinder cones that dot the top of the mountain. Only 10 feet or so under their surface is permafrost which dates back 10,000 years to the Pleistocene Epoch. If

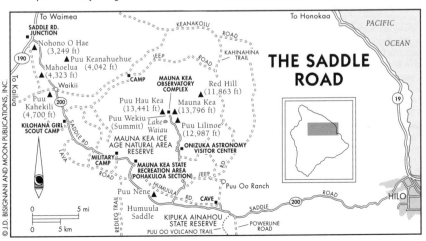

you drill into the cones for only 10-20 feet and put a pipe in, during daylight hours air will be sucked into the pipe. At night, warm air comes out of the pipe with sufficient force to keep a hat levitating.

Evening brings an incredibly clean and cool breeze that flows down the mountain. The Hawaiians called it the Keihau Wind, whose source, according to ancient legend, is the burning heart of the mountain. To the Hawaiians, this inspiring heavenly summit was the home of Poliahu, The Goddess of Snow and Ice, who vied with the fiery Pele across the way on Mauna Loa for the love of a man. He could throw himself into the never-ending embrace of a mythical ice queen, or of a red-hot mama. Tough choice, poor fellow!

MAUNA KEA OBSERVATORY COMPLEX

Atop the mountain is a mushroom grove of astronomical observatories, as incongruously striking as a futuristic earth colony on a remote planet of a distant galaxy. The crystal-clear air and lack of dust and light pollution make the Mauna Kea Observatory site *the* best in the world. At close to 14,000 feet, it is above 40% of the earth's atmosphere and 98% of its water vapor. Although temperatures generally hover around freezing, there's only 9-11 inches of precipitation annually, mostly in the form of snow. The astronomers have come to expect an average of 325 crystal-clear nights per year, perfect for observation. The state of Hawaii leases the tops of the cinder cones, upon which various institutions from all over the world construct telescopes. These institutions in turn give the University of Hawaii up to 15% of their viewing time. The university sells the excess viewing time for $5,000-10,000 a night, which supports the entire astronomy program and makes a little money on the side. Those who work up here must come down every four days because the thin air seems to make them forgetful and susceptible to making minor calculation errors.

Scientists from around the world book months in advance for a squint through one of these phenomenal telescopes. Teams from Great Britain, The Netherlands, Canada, France, and Japan as well as from the U.S. maintain permanent outposts here.

The first telescope that you see on your left is the U.K.'s **James Clerk Maxwell Telescope,** a radio telescope with a primary reflecting surface over 15 meters in diameter. It was dedicated by Britain's Prince Philip, who rode all the way to the summit in a Rolls Royce. The **Canada-France-Hawaii Telescope,** built in 1977 for $33 million, was the first to spot Halley's comet in 1983.

The newest eye to the heavens atop Mauna Kea is the **W.M. Keck Observatory,** completed in March 1993 at a cost of $94 million. The Keck Foundation, a philanthropic organization from Los Angeles, funded the telescope, one of the world's most high tech, powerful, and expensive. Operated by the California Association for Research in Astronomy (CARA), a joint project of the University of California and Cal Tech, the telescope has an aperture of 400 inches and employs entirely new and unique types of technology. The primary reflector is fashioned from a mosaic of 36 hexagonal mirrors, each only three inches thick and six feet in diameter. These "small" mirrors have been very carefully joined together to form one incredibly huge, actively controlled light reflector surface. Each of the mirror segments is separately positionable to an accuracy of a millionth of an inch, and is computer-controlled to bring the heavenly objects into perfect focus. This titanic eyeball has already spotted both the most distant known galaxy and the most distant known object in the universe, 12 and 13 billion light years from earth, respectively. The light received from these objects today was emitted not long after the "Big Bang" creating the universe theoretically occurred. In a very real sense, these scientists are looking back toward the beginning of time! The Keck Observatory includes a public gallery. Keck II, Son of Cyclops, is an copy of Keck I and was operational in 1996. Scientists now have an immensely more powerful tool for their earthbound exploration of the heavens.

In addition to these are the following: The **NASA Infrared Telescope Facility** does only infrared viewing with its three-meter mirror. Also only with infrared capabilities, the **United Kingdom Infrared Telescope (UKIRT),** in operation since 1979, searches the sky with its 3.8-meter lens. The **California Institute of**

Technology 10.4-meter Submillimeter Telescope has been looking into the sky since 1987. Completed in 1970, the **University of Hawaii 2.2-meter Telescope** is one of the smaller telescopes at the top. **Subaru (Japan National Large Telescope),** with a monolithic 8.3-meter mirror capable of both optical and infrared viewing, will come into operation in 1998. And the **Gemini Northern 8-meter Telescope,** also with both optical and infrared viewing, is run by a consortium from the U.S., U. K., Canada, Chile, Argentina, and Brazil, and should be completed around 1999. Also under construction is the **Submillimeter Array.** About two miles distant from the top is the **Hawaii Antenna of the Very Long Baseline Array,** a series of 25-meter-wide, centimeter wavelength, radio dishes.

The entire mountaintop complex, plus almost all of the land area above 12,000 feet, is managed by the University of Hawaii. Visitors are welcome to tour the complex and to have a look through the telescopes on weekends, starting at 1 p.m. Reservations are a must; arrangements can be made by calling the **Mauna Kea Support Services** in Hilo at 935-3371 or the Visitors Center at 961-2180. The **Onizuka Visitor Center** at the 9,200-foot level, named in honor of astronaut Ellison Onizuka who died in the *Challenger* tragedy, is a must-stop for stargazers. It allows visitors a chance to acclimatize to the thin, high-mountain air, another must—a stay of one hour here is recommended before you head up to the 13,796-foot summit. (Because of the high altitude and the remoteness of the mountaintop from emergency medical facilities, children under age 16 are prohibited from venturing to the summit. People with cardiopulmonary or respiratory problems or with physical infirmities or weakness, and those who are very obese, are also discouraged from attempting the trip.) The Visitors Center provides the last public restrooms before the summit and is a good place to stock up on water, also unavailable higher up. The Visitors Center is open Fri.-Sun. 9 a.m.-noon and 1-4:30 p.m. It also conducts free stargazing tours Thurs.-Sun 6:30-10 p.m. and an observatory tour every Saturday and Sunday at 1 p.m. (weather permitting). Call 961-2180 for more information, or 969-3218 for the weather report. For information on the Internet about the mountaintop observatory, the individual telescope installations, or the Visitors Center, log onto the Mauna Kea Observatory Web site (www.ifa.hawaii.edu/mko.html) or the University of Hawaii Institute for Astronomy Web site (www.ifa.hawaii.edu/) and follow the links from there.

If you plan on continuing up to the summit, you must provide your own transportation. Observatory personnel suggest calling **Harper Car and Truck Rentals** in Hilo, tel. 969-1478, or 329-6688 in Kona, which offers 4WD rentals. Alternately, make arrangements for a guided tour to the top with **Paradise Safaris** of Kona, tel. 322-2366 or (800) 545-5662, parsaf@il-hawaii.net; or with Arnott's Lodge in Hilo, tel. 969-7097. Take extra layers of warm clothing—it can snow up there any month of the year—and your camera. Photographers, using fast film, get some of the most dazzling shots *after* sunset. During the gloaming, the light show begins. Look down upon the clouds to see them filled with fire. This heavenly light is reflected off the mountain to the clouds and then back up like a celestial mirror in which you get a fleeting glimpse of the soul of the universe.

MAUNA KEA STATE RECREATION AREA

This area, known as Pohakuloa ("Long Stone"), is five miles west of the Mauna Kea Observatory Road (35 miles from Hilo). The altitude is 6,500 feet and the land begins to change into the rolling grasslands for which this *paniolo* country is famous. Here you'll find a cluster of seven cabins that can be rented (arrange in advance) from the Department of Land and Natural Resources, Division of State

The Hawaiians were the finest adze makers in Polynesia. One of the best stone quarries was atop Mauna Kea.

LOUISE FOOTE

Parks, 75 Aupuni St., Hilo, HI 96720, tel. 974-6200. The cabins are completely furnished with cooking facilities and hot showers. You'll need warm clothing, but the days and nights are unusually clear and dry with very little rain. The park is within the Pohakuloa Game Management Area, so expect hunting and shooting in season. A few minutes west is the Pohakuloa Military Camp, whose maneuvers can sometimes disturb the peace in this high mountain area. Follow the Saddle Road about 20 miles west to intersect Route 190, on which you can turn right (north) to Waimea—seven miles—or left (south) to Kailua—33 miles.

Birdwatchers or nature enthusiasts should turn into Koa Kipuka, a bite-sized hill just near mile marker 28. (A *kipuka* is a very special area, usually a hill or gully, in the middle of a lava flow that was never inundated by lava and therefore provides an old, original, and established ecosystem.) Look for Powerline Road and Pu'u O'o Volcano Trail. Follow either for a chance to see the very rare *akiapola'au* or *apapane,* and even wild turkeys.

J. ARCHER (HAWAII STATE ARCHIVES)

HAMAKUA COAST

Along the shore, cobalt waves foam into razor-sharp valleys where cold mountain streams meet the sea at lonely pebbled beaches. Inland, the Hamakua Coast, once awash in a rolling green sea of sugarcane, has been put to other uses. Along a 50-mile stretch of the Belt Road (Route 19) from Hilo to Waipio, the Big Island grew its cane for 100 years or more. Water was needed for sugar, a ton to produce a pound, and this coast has plenty. Huge flumes once carried the cut cane to the mills. Last century so many Scots worked the plantations hereabouts that Hamakua was called the "Scotch Coast." Now most residents are a mixture of Scottish, Japanese, Filipino, and Portuguese ancestry. Side roads dip off Route 19 into one-family valleys where modest, weather-beaten homes of plantation workers sit surrounded by garden plots on tiny, hand-hewn terraces. These valleys, as they march up the coast, are unromantically referred to as "gulches." From the Belt Road's many bridges, you can trace silvery-ribboned streams that mark the valley floors as they open to the sea. Each valley is jungle-lush with wildflowers and fruit trees transforming the steep sides to emerald-green velvet.

HONOMU TO LAUPAHOEHOE

The ride alone, as you head north on the Belt Road, is gorgeous enough to be considered a sight. But there's more! You can pull off the road into sleepy one-horse towns where dogs are safe snoozing in the middle of the road. You can visit a plantation store in Honomu on your way to Akaka Falls, or take a cautious dip at one of the seaside beach parks. If you want solitude, you can go inland to a forest reserve and miles of trails. The largest town on the coast is Honokaa, with supplies, handmade mementos, and a macadamia nut factory. You can veer west to Waimea from Honokaa, but don't. Take the spur road, Route 240, to Waipio Valley, known as the "Valley of Kings," one of the most beautiful in all of Hawaii.

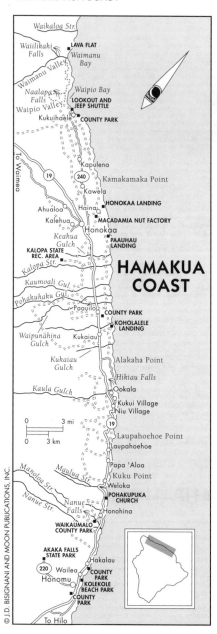

HONOMU AND VICINITY

During its heyday, Honomu ("Silent Bay") was a bustling center of the sugar industry boasting saloons, a hotel/bordello, and a church or two for repentance. Now Honomu mainly serves as a stop as you head somewhere else, but definitely take the time to linger and soak in the feel of classic village life that still permeates its streets. Honomu is 10 miles north of Hilo and a mile or so inland on Route 220, which leads to Akaka Falls. On entering, you'll find a string of false-front buildings that are doing a great but unofficial rendition of a "living history museum." The town has recently awoken from a long nap and is now bustling—if that's possible in a two-block town—with wonderful art galleries, small gourmet cafes, and a B&B inn. At the south end of town, just at the turn to Akaka Falls, notice the **Odaishasan,** a beautifully preserved Buddhist Temple. Honomu is definitely worth a stop. It takes only minutes to walk the main street, but those minutes can give you a glimpse of history that will take you back 100 years.

Practicalities: Food, Lodging, and Shopping
Before entering town proper you'll spot **Jan's,** a convenience store selling cold beer and groceries.

As you enter town look for **Akaka Falls Flea Market,** tel. 963-6171, open daily 9 a.m.-5 p.m., shipping available, where owner Dennis Sevilla claims "all new quality merchandise at reduced prices." Although the merchandise constantly changes, you might find Baltic amber necklaces for $85, Chinese hole-coins, Niihau shell lei, Czech crystals, batiks from Indonesia, wind chimes, plenty of furniture, and of course T-shirts. Can't forget those! Especially look for Hawaiian *pahu* (temple drums) made by master drum maker Tuifua (whose work is displayed at the prestigious Bishop Museum), hula instruments, a Polynesian *toere* (a split bamboo mouth drum), and a "can't live without" crocheted Budweiser Beer Can hat.

On the left as you drive along the main street is **Aloha Akaka Plate Lunch,** open daily except Wednesday 10 a.m.-5 p.m., where Nancy Tanemoto serves up *charsiu,* Chinese barbecued pork, for $5.50; *miso* with limpets for $4.50; and saimin for $3.50. Sandwiches include a ham and cheese sub for $4.50, hot tuna melt for

Ishigo's General Store

$4.25, and cheeseburger for $1.75. The interior of the old building holds a few tables with chairs salvaged from Honomu's defunct theater, and a counter with little red stools. The shelves are lined with pieces of remarkable driftwood, all natural sculptures made by Mother Nature. Aloha Akaka Plate Lunch is clean, friendly, and caught in a time warp harkening back to the days when a burger and a Nehi were the treat of the week!

The Woodshop Gallery, tel. 963-6363, open daily 10:30 a.m.-5:30 p.m., along Honomu's main street, offers a wonderful opportunity for browsing among fine tropical wood furniture and artworks, and for an afternoon pick-me-up, an espresso, or a homemade ice cream (fresh every Monday) at the bar. Shelves shine with the lustrous patina of bowls, calabashes, mirrors, and furniture fashioned from koa, mango, milo, and macadamia wood, as well as from Norfolk pine, which can be turned so thin it becomes translucent. Some of the fine artists and woodworkers displayed are: Jeanette and Peter McLaren, the shop owners, who create stained glass works and furniture, respectively; Jack Straker, a master woodworker; Gene Buscher, who turns natural-edge koa calabashes; Rift Zone pottery from Hilo; Moon Road Pottery, another local pottery, specializing in a floral glaze design; and Pachini, a well-known island potter who often renders a simple Asian design. Less expensive items include chopsticks, wooden spoons made of coconut and wood, combs,

barrettes, or lovely vanity mirrors that come in a velvet bag. If you've worked up an appetite, head for the espresso bar and order a coffee for $1.50, a smoothie for $2.65, sandwiches like tuna, turkey, or pastrami priced at $3.50, or an ice cream cone or even a banana split. Choose a table inside, or head for the lanai where you can watch the "action" in the two-block downtown of Honomu.

Clifford and Nara Chow share the philosophy that Hawaii's culture, history, and beauty are alive in the art of its people. Together they operate **The Hawaii Artists O'Hana,** tel. 963-5467, open daily except Wednesday 10 a.m.-5 p.m., a combination fine arts cooperative gallery, gift shop, and gourmet cafe that occupies the Ishigo Building, built in 1880 and the oldest building in Honomu. Gracing the shelves and walls of the two-story gallery are works by some of the island's best artists, including: Avi Kiriaty, who uses bold colors to capture the emotions of Hawaii in the expressive faces of its women; Edward Kayton, who sees the "soul fire" of Hawaii in its ancient warriors; Raymond Helgeson, whose canoe paddlers match rippling muscle with rippling sea; Andrew Plack, who gives wings to color, offering bouquets of "birds of paradise"; Kathleen Kan, who travels in spirit with Polynesian voyagers and the animals of the sea; and Brad Lewis, a photographer who sees lava, colored like the *ali'i* feathered cape, as the red and yellow mana of Hawaii. Indigenous water gourds are grown from seed by Olivia Ling, who then carves them into beautifully functional art pieces; and paddles are expertly carved by Mal Pauole from curly *koa* and mango wood. The downstairs gallery offers more works, such as an *'io*, a Hawaiian hawk sculpted from Norfolk pine, whose wings promise magic and adventure; a carved "story board" entitled *The Pride of the People;* lustrous bowls and calabashes smooth and sensual to the touch; and a carved sculpture of Kamehameha on a pedestal of koa.In a nook is a clothing boutique with truly distinctive T-shirts by artist Bob Hackney, who prints them with a famous design titled *Out Of Hand,*along with geckos, petroglyph designs, and paddlers. There are handmade vests by Carolyn Ainsworth, aromatherapy care products, essential oils handmade by a local Hawaiian woman, an extensive collection of Niihau shells, and dark, naturally burnished *kukui* nut lei. All guests are treated to a glass of lemongrass iced tea, but if you're hungry head for the Bamboo Lanai, a covered and screened veranda appointed with *lau hala* weaving, where you can order specialties like fresh *ahi* (tuna) salad for $6.95, homemade meatloaf for $6.50, lasagna (vegetarian or with Italian sausage) with garlic bread and salad for $7.50, and a garden burger deluxe for $6.95. The Hawaii Artists O'Hana is a jewel of a shop where the spirit, heart, and vision of old Hawaii are very much alive.

You'd feel comfortable in your bowler hat or calico dress ordering up a root beer float in the **Akaka Falls Inn, Gift Gallery and Cafe,** 28-1676 Main St., P.O. Box 190, Honomu, HI 96728, tel. 963-5468, a semi-converted 1920s ice cream parlor that still retains the original ambiance with bent iron stools, a foot rail, a marble countertop, and a mirrored breakfront. The cafe section offers a turkey sandwich on potato bread with lettuce, tomato, and sprouts for $4.50; quiche for $2.50; curried veggies in puff pastry for $2.95; or a simple old-fashioned peanut butter and jelly sandwich for $1.75. Sides include potato or macaroni salad, apple and macadamia nut slaw, and Greek pasta—only 75 cents each. Shelves hold gourmet items like mango syrup and ginger mango dressing, and a small freezer is packed with various flavors of ice cream, sold by the cone. Two back rooms, serving as the gift gallery, are stuffed with quality souvenir items like koa bracelets, mirrors, beaded necklaces, calendars, cutting boards, earrings, books, and

artwork. As you meander through, look for potions and lotions, candles, *pareau,* T-Shirts, and real Hawaiian quilts made by "a lady from Hilo." Ascend a wainscoted stairway to the two-room bed-and- breakfast inn furnished in "plantation style" with hardwood floors, sash windows, and Casablanca fans. One guest room, at $55, features twin beds and a rollaway cot, while the other, at $65, holds a queen bed and a day bed; both are bright with Hawaiian quilts and rattan furniture. A large tiled bathroom, with tub and shower, is shared by the two guest rooms, as is the comfortable parlor—perfect for relaxing. Peer through the windows into the backyards of Honomu, and in a few short few days you will be absorbed in the life of this simple village.

As you walk the main street of Honomu, make sure to stop into **Ishigo's General Store,** tel. 963-6128, open Mon.-Fri. 7 a.m.-6 p.m., Saturday and Sunday 7 a.m.-5 p.m., to see a real plantation store still in operation. Owned and operated by Hideo Ishigo, the original store began in 1910 when his forebears, Inokichi Ishigo and his wife Maki, emigrated from Fukuoka, Japan, to begin a new life in Hawaii. They began with a bakery, employing recipes that they learned from all the ethnic groups in Hawaii. They passed their knowledge down to their children, who still use the same recipes in the bakery section of the store. The general store section has food, ice cream, sandwiches, and pizza, but the real treats are in the bakery. Here in a self-serve case are munchies like blueberry, pineapple, and coconut turnovers, along with taro bread. But according to Mr. Ishigo, the old-timers around here go right for the cream buns and the *anpan* with *adzuki* beans. So if you want to get some *real* local flavor, pick one of these and sit out front sipping a cup of Kona coffee. Mr. Ishigo is very friendly and will "talk story" about Honomu, and he may even invite you to a relative's orchid farm in the nearby area. If he's around, it's an added treat, but you can give yourself a small history course of Honomu by checking out the antiques, mementos, and vintage photos that have been placed around the store. Most photos are of Japanese couples who immigrated to the area. Check out the bottles of *okolehau,* local moonshine, that could easily fuel the space shuttle, and an old HVB roadside warrior that's made of wood.

Another establishment worth a visit is **Glass of the Past,** with vintage bottles and collectibles.

Akaka Falls State Park

Follow Route 220 from Honomu past sugarcane fields for 3.5 miles to the parking lot of Akaka Falls. From here, walk counterclockwise along a paved "circle route" that takes you through everybody's idea of a pristine Hawaiian valley. For 40 minutes you're surrounded by heliconia, gingers, orchids, ferns, and bamboo groves as you cross bubbling streams on wooden footbridges. Many varieties of plants that would be in window pots anywhere else are giants here, almost trees. An overlook views Kahuna Falls as it spills into a lush green valley below. The trail becomes an enchanted tunnel through hanging orchids and bougainvillea. In a few moments you arrive at Akaka Falls. The mountain cooperates with the perfect setting, forming a semicircle from which the falls tumble 442 feet in one sheer drop, the tallest single-tier waterfall in the state. After heavy rains, expect a mad torrent of power; during dry periods marvel at liquid-silver threads forming mist and rainbows. The area, maintained by the Division of State Parks, is one of the most easily accessible forays into Hawaii's beautiful interior.

Kolekole Beach Park

Look for the first tall bridge (100 feet high) a few minutes past Honomu, where a sign points to a small road that snakes its way down the valley to the beach park below. Amenities include restrooms, grills, electricity, picnic tables, and a camping area (county permit). Kolekole is very popular with local people, who use its five pavilions for all manner of special occasions, usually on weekends. A black-sand beach fronts an extremely treacherous ocean. The entire valley was inundated with over 30 feet of water during the great 1946 tsunami. The stream running through Kolekole comes from Akaka Falls, four miles inland. It forms a pool complete with waterfall that is safe for swimming but quite cold.

LAUPAHOEHOE

This wave-lashed peninsula is a finger of smooth pahoehoe lava that juts into the bay. Located about halfway between Honomu and Honokaa, the valley at one time supported farmers and fishermen who specialized in catching turtles. Laupahoehoe was the best boat landing along the coast, and for years canoes and, later, schooners would stop here. A plaque commemorates the tragic loss of 20 schoolchildren and their teacher who were taken by the great tsunami of 1946. Afterwards, the village was moved to the high ground overlooking the point. **Laupahoehoe Beach Park** now occupies the low peninsula; it has picnic tables, showers, electricity, and a county camping area. The sea is too rough to swim but many fishermen come here, along with some daring surfers. Laupahoehoe makes a beautiful rest stop along the Belt Road.

Ten miles inland from Laupahoehoe Point along a very rugged jeep trail is **David Douglas Historical Monument.** This marks the spot where the naturalist, after whom the Douglas fir is named, lost his life under mysterious circumstances. Douglas, on a fact-gathering expedi-

DAVID STANLEY

Akaka Falls

The Local Cafe in Laupahoehoe

J.D. BISIGNANI

tion on the rugged slopes of Mauna Kea, never returned. His body was found at the bottom of a deep pit that was used at the time to catch feral cattle. Douglas had spent the previous night at a cabin occupied by an Australian who had been a convict. Many suspected that the Australian had murdered Douglas in a robbery attempt and thrown his body into the pit to hide the deed. No hard evidence of murder could be found, and the death was officially termed accidental.

Practicalities

Just before Laupahoehoe on the Hilo side, look for a sign to **Papaaloa.** Turn here, and head down the road to the **Papaaloa Neighborhood Store,** where local people go to buy the area's *best* smoked meats and fish, including marlin, beef, pork, and *laulau*— made right at the store; they'll also fix a plate lunch to go.

In Laupahoehoe along Route 19, look for **Sakado Store,** open 7:30 a.m.-5:30 p.m., an old-fashioned Hawaiian-style convenience store. They sell basic items like milk, bread, and soft drinks, enough for a picnic.

Keoki's Place, tel. 962-0011, open Tues.-Sat. 10 a.m.-7 p.m., Sunday 10 a.m.-5 p.m., in a white and turquoise painted vintage building in Laupahoehoe Village, is a combination plate lunch restaurant and pizza parlor. Pizzas range $8-12 plus $1 for extra toppings; $2 by the slice. Deli sandwiches like ham, turkey, chicken, tuna, avocado, veggie, or eggplant parmigiana are all under $5, while a salami, meatball, sausage, or pastrami sandwich is $5.50, a hamburger $4.75, and a salmon burger $5.50. Plate lunches priced under $5 are the standards, from mahimahi to teriyaki beef. Desserts are homemade cheesecake $2.50, pies $1.75, and ice cream one scoop $1.75, two scoops $2.50. Keoki's also offers milk shakes and malteds at $3.10 and $3.95 respectively. The atmosphere is as local as you can get!

HONOKAA TO KUKUIHAELE

HONOKAA AND VICINITY

With a population of nearly 2,000, Honokaa ("Crumbling Bay") is the major town on the Hamakua Coast. Here you can continue on Route 19 to Waimea, or take Route 240 through Honokaa and north to Waipio, which you should not miss. First, however, stroll the main street of Honokaa, Mamane Street, where a number of shops specialize in locally produced handicrafts. This is also the best place to stock up on supplies or gasoline. The surrounding area is the center of the macadamia nut industry. If you are proceeding north along Route 240, the coastal route heading to Waipio Valley, just past mile marker 6 on the left, keep an eye peeled for a lava-tube cave right along the roadway. This is just a tease of the amazing natural sights that follow.

Kalopa State Recreation Area

This spacious natural area is 12 miles north of Laupahoehoe (five miles southeast of Honokaa), three miles inland on a well-marked secondary road, and 2000 feet in elevation. Little used by tourists, it's a great place to get away from it all. Hiking is terrific throughout the park on a series of nature trails where much of the flora has been identified. All trails are well marked and vary widely in difficulty. The park provides an excellent opportunity to explore some of the lush gulches of the Hamakua Coast, as well as tent camping and furnished cabins (state permit required) that can house up to eight people.

Hawaiian Holiday Macadamia Nut Factory

This factory, open 9 a.m.-6 p.m., is on a side road that leads from the middle of town down a steep hill toward the sea. A self-guided tour explains how John MacAdams discovered the delicious qualities of these nuts, and how they were named after him. The macadamia nut industry was started in Honokaa when W.H. Purvis, a British agriculturalist who had been working in Australia, brought the first trees to Honokaa in 1881, one of which is still bearing! In 1924, W. Pierre Naquin, then manager of the Honokaa Sugar Co., started the first commercial nut farm in the area. You can buy a large variety of macadamia items, from butters to candies. A delicious and nutritious munchie is a five-ounce, vacuum-packed can of nuts that make a great souvenir or add a special touch to a picnic lunch. The Nut Factory also has a small deli selection and ice cream. Inside the same facility is the **H.R.T. Waipio Tour Desk,** tel. 775-7291, where you can arrange a van or horseback tour through fabulous Waipio.

Food and Lodging

Centrally located along Route 240, in downtown Honokaa, is the **Hotel Honokaa Club,** P.O. Box 247, Honokaa, HI 96727, tel. 775-0678 or (800) 808-0678. What it lacks in elegance it makes up for in cleanliness and friendliness. The hotel, mostly used by local people, is old and well used, but clean and comfortable. Follow a wainscoted

hallway to the upstairs rooms, priced at $55; all are upgraded with carpeting and fluffy quilts; each features a view and TV. The more Spartan but very clean downstairs rooms, with private baths, go for $40. **Hostel** rooms, located in the basement, all with shared bath and kitchen facilities, are separated into three private rooms at $20 and two communal rooms (one sleeping three people and the other six people) that rent for $15. The basement hostel rooms—although a bit dungeonesque—are clean, with windows to catch the breeze. The hotel's dining room is open daily except Monday, serving breakfast 7:30-10:30 a.m., lunch 11 a.m.-1:30 p.m., and dinner 5-8:30 p.m., with all meals prepared in a new and much upgraded kitchen. The breakfast menu offers a low-cholesterol breakfast like Eggbeaters and turkey bacon for $5.50; local standards like two eggs and choice of Spam, bacon, Portuguese sausage, ham or Vienna sausage with homemade hashbrowns, toast, and coffee for only $4.70; and the hotel's famous pancakes and homemade corned beef hash patties. The "Sunrise Special," which is one egg, breakfast meat, and toast or rice for only $2.75, is served Mon.-Fri. 6:30-7:30 a.m. only. Lunch brings entrées like hamburger steak for $6.50, boneless and skinless chicken for $6.50, and their famous pork chops with onions and gravy for $6.75. You can also choose sandwiches, everything from a burger to a tuna melt or a mushroom cheeseburger, for around $4.85. The restaurant features dinner specials daily, but they always serve local cuisine like an authentic Japanese dinner with a choice of shrimp tempura, chicken *katsu,* mahimahi, or stir-fried vegetables for $9.25; 10-oz teriyaki steak for $12.95; or chicken *katsu* for $8.75. The specialty is lobster that must be ordered by phone a day ahead and that sells at market price, usually around $25. The meals, although not gourmet, are wholesome, with plenty of well-prepared food.

Luana Ola B&B and Cottages, at P.O. Box 430, Honokaa, HI 96727, tel. 775-7727 or (800) 357-7727, fax 775-0949, owned by Tim and Jeannie Mann, are located on a side street in the residential area of Honokaa, overlooking lands once owned by Hamakua Sugar that slope directly to the sea. Each cottage (handicapped accessible) has a kitchen, laundry room, full bath, lanai, and private phone. The B&B rooms come with a full continental breakfast. Prices range from $75, with weekly discounts available. E-mail: luana@aloha.net; Web site: www.stay-hawaii.com/luana.html

Local people thought that Jolene was such a good cook, they talked her into opening **Jolene's Kau Kau Corner** in downtown Honokaa, tel. 775-9498, open daily except Sunday 10 a.m.-8 p.m., and Saturday 10 a.m.-3 p.m. Most tried-and-true recipes were handed down by her extended family, who also lend a hand in running the restaurant. They currently serve only lunch and dinner, with breakfast a possibility in the near future. The restaurant, located in a vintage storefront, is trim and neat, and the menu includes a variety of plate lunches like beef tips teriyaki $5.95, shrimp plate $5.95, and a steaming bowl of beef stew $4.95. Saimin in two sizes is $2.50 and $3.95, while most burgers and fries are under $5. The dinner menu brings broiled mahimahi $8.75, shrimp tempura $9.25, shrimp and chicken baskets around $5, a steak and seafood combination for $16.95, and vegetarian stir-fry $8.25. Jolene's is as down-home and local as you can get, and what she lacks in atmosphere, she more than makes up for in friendly service, hearty dishes, and reasonable prices. One of the best places to eat along the northern Hamakua Coast!

Follow the comforting aroma of fresh-baked bread to **Mamane Street Bakery & Café,** tel. 775-9478, open Mon.-Fri. 7 a.m.-5:30 p.m., Saturday 7 a.m.-4 p.m., closed Sunday, owned and operated by Eliahu "Ely" Pessah, and assisted by his fiancée Emma, who has a smile sweeter than the cupcakes on the shelves. Ely bakes goodies including coconut turnovers, Danish pastries, and *ensemada,* a special type of cinnamon roll, all priced $1-1.50, but what the local people come in for are the honey-nut bran muffins, crunchy with chunks of macadamia nuts. Ely's oven also turns out ham and cheese croissants, mozzarella or marinara focaccia, or three-cheese focaccia, all under $5.95. Eat in or take out while enjoying your purchase with a cup of steaming coffee or tea. Make sure to visit the "Gift Shop," constructed in free-form design with 52 different kinds of wood. Here, you'll discover painted fish, glass fish, wooden earrings, *lau hala* bracelets, carved elephants, a smattering of pottery, notecards, and Hawaiian dolls.

Also ask to see the plaster of Paris "castings" of old lava flows, a very unique expression of "art."

"On a Wing and a Prayer" is part of the logo welcoming you to **Simply Natural Ice Cream Parlor, and More,** tel. 775-0119, open Mon.-Sat. 9 a.m.-5 p.m., Sunday 11 a.m.-5 p.m., where the owner, Sharon, does the praying and Bernie the Cockatoo and official greeter is the wing man. Besides ice cream in tropical and standard flavors, which comes in cones, cups, or waffle cones, a board offers a full sandwich and burger menu with plenty of vegetarian items. Choose a garden salad sandwich for $4.25, garden burger $4.25, or delicious bowl of Thai coconut curry soup with chicken or vegetarian. Other sandwiches are grilled mahimahi for $5.50, teriyaki chicken for $4.50, and the handmade and "old-fashioned real" Awesome Burger at $2.75-4.50 depending upon what you want on it. Sharon is also adding a full Mexican menu with everything from tacos to tostadas, available with beef or chicken, or vegetarian. Beverages include soft drinks, fresh squeezed carrot juice, Kona coffee, espresso, and cappuccino.

Genuine cowpokes as well as city slickers from the Mainland pretending to be *paniolo* will have the urge to fling their Stetsons in the air and yell "yuppie yi yo kai yea!" when their trail leads to the **Texas Drive-In and Restaurant,** open daily 5 a.m.-9 p.m., a little later on weekends. The long-established Hamakua restaurant is known for its fresh *malasadas.* Get some! Upon entering Honokaa along Route 240 coming from Hilo, look for the chain-link fence of the Honokaa High and Elementary School. Make a left where it ends up Pakalana St. and follow it to the top of the hill where you'll see the Texas Drive-In on your left, a plain cinder-block building with a yellow and red exterior. Basically a walk-up window restaurant, it has a few tables out front; a cavernous dining room in the back will remind you of a school cafeteria. They specialize in inexpensive local food like *kalua* pork, teriyaki chicken and beef, hamburgers, and fresh fish. There is no item over $8; most dinners are priced around $5, and sandwiches are only $2-3. Local people and (an even better sign) the local police come here to chow down on good, easy-on-the-wallet food.

Herb's Place, in downtown Honokaa, is open for breakfast, lunch, and dinner Mon.-Fri. from

5:30 a.m., Saturday from 8:30 a.m., closed Sunday. You get basic meals and cocktails in this little roadside joint.

C.C. Jon's is a plate-lunch, local fast-food stand, just as you enter town. Most of their dishes are under $4.50.

Shopping

World-renowned art critic and author Amaury St. Giles just can't seem to get enough of volcanic islands. After residing in Japan for over 30 years, where he became an expert in Japanese pottery—publishing *Earth and Fire,* an acclaimed book on the subject—and where he was a columnist appearing in the *Mainichi Shimbun,* an English-language daily, he decided to move to the Big Island. Luckily for us, he's continued his lifelong love affair with art and now operates the **Amaury St. Giles Modern Art Gallery,** tel. 775-9278, open daily except Wednesday 10 a.m.-5 p.m., major credit cards accepted, shipping available, located in a vintage building in downtown Honokaa that has been remodeled to display perfectly the personally chosen art that graces its walls. Some of the fine artists represented are: Phil Gallagher, who uses watercolors to capture the simple yet evocative figures in ancient petroglyphs; Wailehua Gray, a native Hawaiian whose spiritual heart sees the legends of old Hawaii, allowing him to render them on canvas; octogenarian John Young, one of Hawaii's premiere artists, who has tuned into the soul of Hawaii; Tom Adolf, a local Honokaa artist who has perfected painting in a series of panels depicting circular panoramas of places and things Hawaiian; Raymond Helgeson, who realistically paints the joy and power of Hawaiian canoe paddlers, creating an amazing correlation between the ripples in the sea and the ripples in their muscled arms and sinewy backs; Lauan Okano, a calligrapher who uses words to create what looks from a distance like a painted fan, koi, or rose, but on close inspection is revealed as fine calligraphy rendered repeatedly to form the simple but powerful images. Amaury St. Giles has a superb eye for art, honed to fine sharpness over the years. If he has chosen a work to appear in his gallery, you know that it is one of great merit.

If you are at all interested in the history of Hawaii, make sure to stop by the **The Hawaiian "Artifacks" Shop** along the main drag in downtown Honokaa. Just look for a carved mermaid and a strobe light blinking you into the shop. This amazing curio and art shop is owned and operated by Lokikamakahiki "Loki" Rice, who ran it for many years with her husband James; unfortunately, he passed away in the spring of 1996. Loki, elderly and in failing health, keeps no set hours, opening when she feels like it, usually for a few hours in the afternoon, but never before 2 p.m. At first glance the shop may look inauthentic, but once you're inside, that impression quickly melts away. Loki, a full-blooded Hawaiian, was born and raised in Waipio Valley, and James traveled the Pacific for years. The stories from the old days are almost endless. Notice a tiki that serves as a main beam, and two giant shields against the back wall. They belonged to Loki's father, a giant of a man just under seven feet tall and over 450 pounds who had to have a special coffin made when he was buried on the island of Niihau. Local people bring in their carvings and handicrafts to sell, many of which are hula implements and instruments like drums and rattles. Some of the bric-a-brac is from the Philippines or other South Sea islands, but Loki will identify them for you. Mingled in with what seems to be junk are some real artifacts like poi pounders, adzes, and really good drums. Many have come from Loki's family, while others have been collected by the Rices over the years. But the real treasure is Loki, who will share her *aloha* as long as time and the call from above permits.

Hamakua Woodworks, tel. 775-9910, open Mon.-Sat. 9 a.m.-5 p.m., Sunday 11 a.m.-4 p.m. in downtown Honokaa, offers custom koa woodwork by island artists, including the furniture of Dennis and Marie Smith, koa fans and lazy Susans for $125 by Kayong Walton, and lovely koa boxes for $125 by the proprietors Walker and Susan Sanders assisted by their daughter, Elizabeth. Simple items include koa mirrors for $35, candleholders for $4.50, chopsticks at $9.50 , a koa napkin holder for $18, and barrettes for $18. A display case also holds glass earrings, sterling silver jewelry, and a smattering of beadwork.

Kanani Woods and Crafts, tel. 775-0109, open Mon.-Sat. 10 a.m.-5 p.m., owned by Kanani Weller and Dave Moniz, showcases *lau hala* weavings and woodwork made on the Big Island. Dave does all the woodwork, creating everything from bowls to keychains using island woods that include koa, milo, mango, and ohia. A specialty item is a *makini,* the owl-eyed helmet with a *hau* headdress used by warriors in the ancient days. The people in Hawaii often dangle them from their rear view mirrors, but Mainlanders will appreciate them more as artpieces.

Kama'aina Woodworks, tel. 775-7722, in Honokaa halfway down the hill leading to Hawaiian Holiday Macadamia Nut Factory, is usually open daily 9 a.m.-5 p.m. except Sunday but this depends on the weather, their inclination, and how the spirits are moving on any particular day. The shop is owned and operated by Bill Keb and Roy Mau, talented woodworkers who specialize in fabulous bowls turned from native woods like koa, milo, extremely rare *kou,* and a few introduced woods like mango and Norfolk Island pine. All of the wooden artpieces, priced at $20-1,000, are one-of-a-kind and utilitarian. Less expensive items are koa or milo bracelets $10-20, letter openers $5, and rice paddles $4. When you first enter the shop, don't be surprised if it looks like someone's home, with a TV on in the sitting room and glass cases filled with Hawaiian flora and fauna.

The Honokaa Trading Company, tel. 775-0808, open daily 10 a.m.-5 p.m., is a discovery shop owned and operated by Denise Walker. Items come and go, but you can expect to find classic artwork from the Matson Steamship Lines, hula dolls, Japanese netsuke, poi bowls, costume jewelry, pots and pans, bottles, and old crockery. Denise has also filled this rambling building with a good selection of old books, Hawaiian instruments, Japanese fans, and vintage signs. Denise focuses not only on things *from* Hawaii, but on things *brought to* Hawaii. Much of the furniture and many of the antique items were brought to Hawaii by *kama'aina* and GI families.

At the south end of town, **Seconds To Go,** open daily except Sunday 9:30 a.m.-5 p.m., is owned and operated by Elaine Carlsmith. The collectibles-and-antique shop specializes in Hawaiian artifacts; it brims with classic Hawaiian ties and shirts from the '50s, dancing hula-doll lamps, antique hardware and building materials, clawfoot bathtubs, old books, Japanese bowls, a good collection of plates and saucers,

and a ukulele. Elaine also sells used fishing gear in case you want to try your luck.

In town, **S. Hasegawa** has a few racks of local fashions and a few bolts of traditional Japanese cloth. Look for the very ethnic **Filipino Store** along the main drag to soak up a cultural experience and to find an array of exotic spices and food ingredients. You can pick up supplies and even a few health food items at **T. Kaneshiro Store** and **K.K. Super-Mart,** two well-stocked markets in town.

Practicalities

The once run-down and classic "Last Picture Show" **Honokaa Movie Theater,** along the main drag , is now renovated and showing slightly late, first-run movies for a mere $4.

You can take care of most of your banking needs at **Bank of Hawaii,** also located in the downtown area. Gas can be purchased at either a **Union 76** or a **Chevron,** both well marked along the main drag.

The **Hamakua Music Festival,** held around the first week of December and lasting four days, attracts island musicians proficient in everything from Hawaiian to jazz.Contact Hamakua Music Festival, P.O. Box 1757, Honokaa, HI 96727 for a newsletter regarding the festivities and the performing artists.

KUKUIHAELE

For all of you looking for the "light at the end of the tunnel," Kukuihaele ("Traveling Light") is it. On the main road, the **Last Chance** grocery and gas station, open daily 9 a.m.-6 p.m., stocks basic supplies plus a small assortment of handicrafts and gift items. The Last Chance has an excellent selection of domestic and imported beers, along with light snacks for a picnic lunch. The store attendants are friendly and don't mind answering a few questions about the Waipio area if they are not too busy.

Waipio Valley Artworks, tel. 775-0958, open daily 9 a.m.-5 p.m., is an excellent shop in which to pick up an art object. There are plenty of offerings in wood by some of the island's best woodworkers that include carvings and bowls, but the shop also showcases various Hawaii-based artists working in different mediums. Definitely check out inspired prints by Sue Sweardlow, who has tuned in to the soul of Hawaii; paintings by Carli Oliver and Kim Starr; and the inspired art of Cathy Long and her mother, Mary Koskie. You'll also find tikis, earrings, basketry made from natural fibers, and ceramics by Robert Joiner and Ann Rathbun. The shop features a snack window serving ice cream, sandwiches, and soft drinks. Out back, a small boutique offers designer T-shirts, alohawear, a smattering of souvenir items, and a fairly extensive collection of books mostly on Hawaiiana. Waipio Valley Artworks is also the meeting place for **Waipio Valley Shuttle,** tel. 775-7121, which will take you down to Waipio Valley.

Accommodations

A vintage home of a one-time plantation manager, **Waipio Wayside,** P.O. Box 840, Honokaa, HI 96727, tel. 775-0275 or (800) 833-8849, is now owned and operated by Jackie Horne as a congenial B&B. Look for the "Waipio Wayside" sign hung on a white picket fence exactly two miles toward Waipio from the Honokaa post office. You enter through double French doors, onto a rich wooden floor shining with a well-waxed patina. The walls are hand-laid vertical paneling, the prototype that modern paneling tries to emulate. The home contains five double bedrooms ranging in price $55-85 s, $65-95 d for multiple-night stays; $15 extra for single-night stays; $15 extra person. One large master bedroom is in its own little space out back, but attached to the house. The room, rich with knotty pine, is spacious and airy with plenty of windows. Every bedroom has beautiful Battenburg lace curtains. The back deck, where you will find hammocks in which to rock away your cares, overlooks manicured grounds that gently slope to a panoramic view of the coast. Jackie, whose

Jackie Horne at the Waipio Wayside

meticulous and tastefully appointed home is straight from the pages of *Ladies' Home Journal,* is also a gourmet cook. Breakfast is sometimes waffles with strawberries and whipped cream, sometimes omelettes and biscuits, with fresh fruit from the property. Beverages are pure Hamakua coffee—grown no more than 12 miles away—or Kona and Jamaican Blue Mountain coffee, juices, and an assortment of 24 gourmet teas from around the world. A stay at Waipio Wayside is guaranteed to be civilized, relaxing, and affordable. E-mail: wayside@ilhawaii.net; Web site: www.stayhawaii.com/wayside.html.

WAIPIO VALLEY

Waipio is the way the Lord would have liked to fashion the Garden of Eden, if he hadn't been on such a tight schedule. You can read about this incredible valley, but you really can't believe it until you see it for yourself. Route 240 ends a minute outside of Kukuihaele at an overlook, and 1,000 feet below is Waipio ("Arching Water"),

the island's largest and most southerly of the many that slice the harsh Kohala Mountains. The valley is a mile across where it fronts the sea at a series of high sand dunes. It's vibrantly green, always watered by Waipio Stream and lesser streams that spout as waterfalls from the *pali* at the rear of the valley. The green is offset by a

Waipio Valley

J.D. BISIGNANI

wide band of black-sand beach. The far side of the valley ends abruptly at a steep *pali* that is higher than the one on which you're standing. A six-mile trail leads over it to Waimanu Valley, smaller, more remote, and more luxuriant.

Travelers have long extolled the amazing abundance of Waipio. From the overlook you can make out the overgrown outlines of garden terraces, taro patches, and fish ponds in what was Hawaii's largest cultivated valley. Every foodstuff known to the Hawaiians once flourished here; even Waipio pigs were said to be bigger than anywhere else. In times of famine, the produce from Waipio could sustain the populace of the entire island (estimated at 100,000 people). On the valley floor and alongside the streams you'll still find avocados, bananas, coconuts, passion fruit, mountain apples, guavas, breadfruit, tapioca, lemons, limes, coffee, grapefruit, and pumpkins. The old fish ponds and streams are alive with prawns, wild pigs roam the interior, and there are abundant fish in the sea.

But the lovingly tended order, most homes, and the lifestyle were washed away in the tsunami of 1946. Now Waipio is unkempt, a wild jungle of mutated abundance. The valley is a neglected maiden with a dirty face and disheveled, wind-blown hair. Only love and nurturing can refresh her lingering beauty.

Getting There

The road leading down to Waipio is outrageously steep and narrow. If you attempt it in a regular car, it'll eat you up and spit out your bones. Over 20 fatalities have occurred since people started driving it, and it has only been paved since the early 1970s. You'll definitely need 4WD, low range, to make it; downhill vehicles yield to those coming up. There is very little traffic on the road except when surfing conditions are good. Sometimes Waipio Beach has the first good waves of the season and this brings out the surfers en masse. **Waipio Valley Shuttle,** tel. 775-7121, has their office at Waipio Valley Artworks in Kukuihaele. They use comfortable air-conditioned 4WD vans for their 90-minute descent and tour. The tour costs $30. Buy your ticket at the Artworks, and then proceed to the Waipio Overlook from where the vans leave every hour on the hour. This is the tamest, but safest, way to enjoy the valley. If you decide to hike down or stay overnight, you can make arrangements for the van to pick you up or drop you off for an added cost. The same company also offers a trip to the top of Mauna Kea.

If you have the energy, the hike down the paved section of the road is just over one mile, but it's a tough mile coming back up! Expect to take three to four hours down and back, adding more time to swim or look around.

ACTIVITIES

For a fun-filled experience guaranteed to please, try horseback riding with **Waipio Na'alapa Trail Rides,** tel. 775-0419. Sherri Hannum, a young mother of three who moved to Waipio from Missouri almost 30 years ago, and her husband Mark, own and operate the trail rides. Both are enamored with the valley, and as fate would have it, have become the old-timers of Waipio. They gladly accept the charge of keeping the ancient accounts and oral traditions alive. The adventure begins when Mark picks you up at 9:30 a.m. at Waipio Valley Artworks in Kukuihaele. You begin a 40-minute 4WD ride down to the ranch, which gives you an excellent tour of the valley in and of itself, since their spread is even deeper into the valley than the end of the line for the commercial valley tour! En route you cross three or four streams, as Mark tells you some of the history and lore of Waipio. When you arrive, Sherri has the horses ready to go. Sherri knows the trails of Waipio intimately. She puts you in the saddle of a sure-footed Waipio pony and spends all day telling you legends and stories while leading you to waterfalls, swimming holes, grave sites, and finally a *heiau*. The lineage of the horses of Waipio dates from the late 1700s. They were gifts to the *ali'i* from Capt. George Vancouver. Waipio was especially chosen because the horses were easy to corral and could not escape. Today, over 150 semi-wild progeny of the original stock roam the valley floor. Technically, you should bring your own lunch for the ride, since you can't always count on the fruits of Waipio to be happening. But if they are, Sherri will point them out and you can munch to your heart's delight. Tours lasting 2.5 hours cost $75 and start at 9:30 a.m. and 1 p.m. Full-day tours can be arranged, but a minimum of two and a maximum of four riders is required. Sorry, no children under 12 or riders weighing more than 230 pounds. Go prepared with long pants, shoes, and swimsuit. A ride with Sherri isn't just an adventure; it's an experience with memories that will last a lifetime.

Waipio Valley Wagon Tour, P.O. Box 1340, Honokaa, HI 96727, tel. 775-9518, owned and operated by Peter Tolin, is the newest and one of the most fun-filled ways of exploring Waipio. This surrey-type wagon, which can hold about a dozen people, is drawn by two Tennessee mules. The fascinating 1.5-hour tours depart five times daily at 9 a.m., 10:30 a.m., 12:30 p.m., 2 p.m., and 4 p.m. Cost is $35, children under 12 half price, children two and under free. To par-

ticipate, make reservations 24 hours in advance. Then check in 30 minutes before departure at the Waipio Overlook, where a 4WD vehicle will come to fetch you. The overlook also has a pay phone from which you can call the Wagon Tour to see if there is last-minute room for you, but a space is definitely not guaranteed. Lunch is not included, but if you bring your own, you can walk down to the beach and have a great picnic. The original wagon was built by Peter himself from parts that he ordered from the Mainland. Unfortunately, every part that he ordered broke down over a nine-month trial period. Peter had all new parts made at a local machine shop, only three times thicker than the originals! Now that the wagon has been *Waipionized,* the problems have ceased. The only high-tech aspect of the wagon ride is a set of small loudspeakers through which Peter narrates the history, biology, and myths of Waipio as you roll along.

Waipio Beach, stretching over a mile, is the longest black-sand beach on the island. The

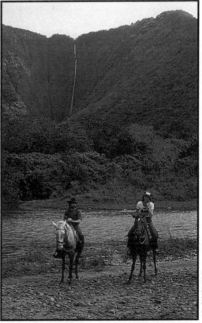

Sherri Hannum of Waipio Na'alapa Trail Rides

surf here can be very dangerous and there are many riptides. During the summer the sands drift to the western side of the valley; in winter they drift back east. If there is strong wave action, swimming is not advised. It is, however, a good place for surfing and fishing.

The **Waipio Valley Aqueduct Trail,** which follows the clearly marked water system of the recently defunct Hamakua Sugar Plantation, has just opened up to the public. Not overly vigorous, the rather flat trail (except for one spot that requires scrambling down a ladder) skirts the rear of the valley where the natural flora is still thriving. In some places, the sugar company followed an irrigation system laid by native Hawaiians over 1,000 years ago that watered ancient terraces growing wetland taro.

Aloha Distress
In the summer of 1992, the Bishop Museum requested an environmental impact survey on Waipio Valley because the frequency of visitors to the valley had increased tremendously. Old-time residents were complaining not only about the overuse of the valley, but about the loss of their quiet and secluded lifestyle. Sherri Hannum of Waipio Na'alapa Trail Rides and Peter Tolin of Waipio Valley Wagon Tour cooperated fully, and did their best to help in the preservation and reasonable use of one of Hawaii's grandest valleys. They have complied with the regulations imposed by the Bishop Museum even when it meant a significant financial loss to themselves. Because of the impact study, the commercial tours are not allowed to go to the beach area, which is now open to foot traffic only, and the valley is **closed on Sunday** to commercial tours. Other tour operators, resentful of the Bishop Museum, were not as cooperative as Sherri and Peter, and apparently have put personal gain above the preservation of Waipio.

There also seems to be some kind of socioethnic battle evolving in the valley. Long-term residents, mostly but not exclusively of Hawaiian decent, are staking out the valley as their own and have largely withdrawn the spirit of *aloha* from the melanin-challenged visitors to their wonderful valley. Their dissatisfaction is not wholly without basis, as some who have come to the valley have been quite disrespectful, trespassing on private property, threatening to sue landowners for injuries caused by themselves, or finding themselves stuck in a river that no one in their right mind would try to cross in a vehicle. Many wonderful, open, and loving people still live in the valley, but don't be too surprised to get the *stink face* treatment from others. Be respectful; and stay on public property. If the sign says *Kapu* or Keep Out, believe it. It is everyone's right to walk along the beach, the switchback that goes to Waimanu, and generally waterways. These are traditional free lands in Hawaii open to all people, and they remain so. It's really up to you. With proper treatment by visitors Waipio's mood will change again, and *aloha* will return.

HISTORY

Legend and Oral History
Waipio is a mystical place. Inhabited for over 1,000 years, it figures prominently in old Hawaiian lore. In the primordial past, Wakea, progenitor of all the islands, favored the valley, and oral tradition holds that the great gods Kane and Kanaloa dallied in Waipio intoxicating themselves on *awa*. One oral chant relates that the demigod Maui, that wild prankster, met his untimely end here by trying to steal baked bananas from these two drunken heavyweights. Lono, god of the Makahiki, came to Waipio in search of a bride. He found Kaikilani, a beautiful maiden who lived in a breadfruit tree near **Hiilawe Waterfall,** which tumbles 1,300 feet to the valley below and is Hawaii's highest single falls.

Nenewe, a shark-man, lived near a pool at the bottom of another waterfall on the west side of Waipio that has been recently fenced so that access is no longer available. The pool was connected to the sea by an underwater tunnel. All went well for Nenewe until his grandfather disobeyed a warning never to feed his grandson meat. Once Nenewe tasted meat, he began eating Waipio residents after first warning them about sharks as they passed his sea-connected pool on their way to fish. His constant warnings roused suspicions. Finally, a cape he always wore was ripped from his shoulders, and there on his back was a shark's mouth! He dove into his pool and left Waipio to hunt the waters of the other islands.

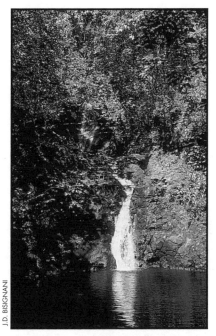

J.D. BISIGNANI

Nenewe's pool

ing flood in 1979 filled the valley with wild torrents of water. In both cases, the devastation to homes and the land was tremendous, but not one life was lost. Everyone who still lives in Waipio will tell you that somehow, they feel protected.

The remains of **Paka'alana Heiau** is in a grove of trees on the right-hand side of the beach as you face the sea. It dates from the 12th century and was a "temple of refuge" where *kapu* breakers, vanquished warriors, and the weak and infirm could find sanctuary. The other restored and more famous temple of this type is Pu'uhonua O Honaunau in Kona. Paka'alana was a huge *heiau* with tremendous walls that were mostly intact until the tsunami of 1946. The tidal wave sounded like an explosion when the waters hit the walls of Paka'alana, according to first-hand accounts. The rocks were scattered, and all was turned to ruins. Nearby, **Hanua'aloa** is another *heiau* that is in ruins. Archaeologists know even less about this *heiau,* but all agree that both were healing temples of body and spirit, and the local people feel that their positive mana is part of the protection in Waipio.

Recorded History

Great chiefs have dwelt in Waipio. King Umi-aliloa planted taro just like a commoner, and fished with his own hands. He went on to unite the island into one kingdom in the 15th century. Waipio was the traditional land of Kamehameha the Great and in many ways was the basis of his earthly and spiritual power. He came here to rest after heavy battles, and offshore was the scene of the first modern naval battle in Hawaii. Here, Kamehameha's war canoes faced those of his nemesis, Keoua. Both had recently acquired cannons bartered from passing sea captains. Kamehameha's artillery was manned by two white sailors, Davis and Young, who became trusted advisors. Kamehameha's forces won the engagement in what became known as the "Battle of the Red-Mouthed Gun."

When Captain Cook came to Hawaii, 4,000 natives lived in Waipio; a century later only 600 remained. At the turn of this century many Chinese and Japanese moved to Waipio and began raising rice and taro. People moved in and out of the valley by horse and mule and there were schools and a strong community spirit. Waipio

Pupualenalena, a *kupua* (nature spirit), takes the form of a yellow dog who can change his size from tiny to huge. He was sent by the chiefs of Waipio to steal a conch shell that mischievous water sprites were constantly blowing, just to irritate the people. The shell was inherited by Kamehameha and is now in the Bishop Museum. Another dog-spirit lives in a rock embedded in the hillside halfway down the road to Waipio. In times of danger, he comes out of his rock to stand in the middle of the road as a warning that bad things are about to happen.

Finally, a secret section of Waipio Beach is called **Lua o milu,** the legendary doorway to the land of the dead. At certain times, it is believed, ghosts of great *ali'i* come back to earth as "Marchers of the Night," and their strong chants and torch-lit processions fill the darkness in Waipio. Many great kings were buried in Waipio, and it's felt that because of their mana, no harm will come to the people that live here. Oddly enough, the horrible tsunami of 1946 and a ragwas painstakingly tended. The undergrowth was kept trimmed and you could see clearly from the back of the valley all the way to the sea.

WW II arrived and many people were lured away from the remoteness of the valley by a changing lifestyle and a desire for modernity. The tidal wave in 1946 swept away most of the homes, and the majority of the people pulled up stakes and moved away. For 25 years the valley lay virtually abandoned. The Peace Corps considered it a perfect place to build a compound in which to train volunteers headed for Southeast Asia. This too was abandoned. Then in the late '60s and early '70s a few "back to nature" hippies started trickling in. Most only played "Tarzan and Jane" and moved on, especially after Waipio served them a "reality sandwich" in the form of the flood of 1979.

Waipio is still very unpredictable. In a three-week period from late March to early April of 1989, 47 inches of rain drenched the valley. Roads were turned to quagmires, houses washed away, and more people left. Part of the problem is the imported trees in Waipio. Until the 1940s, the valley was a manicured garden, but now it's very heavily forested. All of the trees that you will see are new; the oldest are mangroves and coconuts. The trees are both a boon and a blight. They give shade and fruit, but when there are floods, they fall into the river, creating log jams that increase the flooding dramatically. Waipio takes care of itself best when humans do not interfere. Now the taro farmers are having problems because the irrigation system for their crops was washed away in the last flood. But, with hope and a prayer to Waipio's spirits, they'll rebuild, knowing full well that there will be a next time. And so it goes.

Waipio Now

Waipio is at a crossroads. Many of the old people are dying off or moving topside (above the valley) with relatives. Those who live here learned to accept life in Waipio and genuinely come to love

the valley, while others come only to exploit its beauty. Fortunately, the latter underestimate the raw power of Waipio. Developers have eyed the area for years as a magnificent spot in which to build a luxury resort. But even they are wise enough to realize that nature rules Waipio, not humankind. For now the valley is secure. A few gutsy families with a real commitment have stayed on and continue to revitalize Waipio. The valley now supports perhaps 50 residents. A handful of elderly Filipino bachelors who worked for the sugar plantation continue to live here. About 50 more people live topside but come down to Waipio to tend their gardens. On entering the valley, you'll see a lotus-flower pond, and if you're lucky enough to be there in December, it will be in bloom. It's tended by an 80-year-old Chinese gentleman, Mr. Nelson Chun, who wades into the chest-deep water to harvest the sausage-linked lotus roots by clipping them with his toes! Margaret Loo comes to harvest wild ferns served at the exclusive banquets at the Mauna Kea Beach Resort. Seiko Kaneshiro is perhaps the most famous taro farmer because of his poi factory that produces "Ono Ono Waipio Brand Taro." Another old-timer is Charlie Kawashima, who still grows taro the old-fashioned way, as an art form passed from father to son. He harvests the taro with an *o'o* (digging stick) and after it's harvested cuts off the corm and sticks the *huli* (stalk) back into the ground, where it begins to sprout again in a week or so.

taro

BOB RACE

Harrison Kanakoa, now deceased, mostly lived topside because of failing health in his later years. He was born in a house built in 1881 near Kauiki Heiau, one of the biggest and most powerful *heiau* in the valley. Harrison loved to "talk story," relating tales of when his family was the keeper of the *heiau*. When he was a small boy his grandfather took him to the *heiau*, where he rolled away an entrance stone to reveal a small tunnel that went deep inside. He followed his grandfather in a ways, but his child's courage failed, and he turned away and ran out. He said his grandfather yelled after him something in Hawaiian like "You coward," and refused to show him that place again. In 1952, C.H. Brewer, a very powerful sugarcane company in this area, bulldozed the *heiau* and planted macadamia nuts on top. The trees still bear nuts, but the *heiau* was obliterated.

STAYING IN THE VALLEY

Camping In Waipio

For camping in Waipio Valley you must get a permit from the Kamehameha Schools Bernice Pauahi Bishop Estate, Paauilo Office, tel. 776-1104. The office is located about 15 minutes from the overlook in Paauilo. To get the permit, you must call well in advance, giving the dates requested (4 day maximum) and number of people in your party. You will be faxed an application, and *all adult members* in your party must sign a "liability waiver" (parents or legal guardians must sign for any children) before the permit will be granted. Also, you must provide your own "Port-A-Potty" (yes it's true), that you must remove when you leave. A small "camper style" potty, available in Hawaii, is sufficient. Camping is allowed in designated areas only on the east side of Waipio Stream. Many hikers and campers have stayed in Waipio overnight without a permit and have had no problem, but it is illegal! Remember, however, that most of the land, except for the beach, *is* privately owned.

Accommodations

Waipio has a hotel! Owned and operated by Tom Araki, it was built by his dad to serve as a residence for teachers who came to teach at the local school, and was later used for instructors of a nearby, now defunct Peace Corps training camp. You'll find eight basic but clean rooms. Light is provided by kerosene lamps, and you must bring your own food to prepare in a communal kitchen. Tom, well into his 80s, is a treasure house of information about Waipio, and a "character" who's more interested in tending his taro patch, telling stories, and drinking wine than he is in running a hotel. His philosophy, which has enabled him to get along with everyone from

millionaires to hippies, is a simple "live and let live." The Waipio Hotel has become known and it's even fashionable to stay there. For reservations, write Tom Araki, 25 Malama Pl., Hilo, HI 96720, or call Tom down in Waipio Valley at tel. 775-0368. Expect to pay about $20 per person.

WAIMANU VALLEY, CAMPING AND HIKING

The hike down to Waipio and over the *pali* to Waimanu Valley 12 miles away is one of the top three treks in Hawaii. You must be fully prepared for camping and in excellent condition to attempt this hike. Also, water from the streams and falls is not always good for drinking due to irrigation and cattle grazing topside; bring purification tablets or boil or filter it to be safe. To get to Waimanu Valley, a switchback trail leads over the *pali* about 100 yards inland from Waipio Beach. The beginning of the switchback trail has a post with a painting that reads Warning Menehune. Waimanu

Waipio Beach

J.D. BISIGNANI

was bought by the State of Hawaii about 12 years ago, and they are responsible for trail maintenance. The trail ahead is rough, as you go up and down about 14 gulches before reaching Waimanu. At the ninth gulch is a trail shelter. Finally, below is Waimanu Valley, half the size of Waipio but more verdant, and even wilder because it has been uninhabited for a longer time. Cross Waimanu Stream in the shallows where it meets the sea. For drinking water (remember to treat it), walk along the west side of the *pali* until you find a likely waterfall. To stay overnight in Waimanu Valley you must have a (free) camping permit available through the Division of Forestry and Wildlife, P.O. Box 4849, Hilo, HI 96721, tel. 974-4221, open Tues.-Fri. 8 a.m.-4 p.m., Monday 10 a.m.-4 p.m. Your length of stay is limited to seven days and six nights. Each of the nine designated campsites has a fireplace and a composting outhouse. Carry out what you carry in!

Early this century, because of economic necessity brought on by the valley's remoteness, Waimanu was known for its *okolehau* (moonshine). Solomon, one of the elders of the community at the time, decided that Waimanu had to diversify for the good of its people. He decided to raise domesticated pigs introduced by the Chinese, who roasted them with spices in rock ovens as a great delicacy. Solomon began to raise and sell the pigs commercially, but when he died, out of respect, no one wanted to handle his pigs, so they let them run loose. The pigs began to interbreed with feral pigs, and after a while there were so many pigs in Waimanu that they ate all the taro, bananas, and breadfruit. The porkers' voracious appetites caused a famine which forced the last remaining families of Waimanu to leave in the late 1940s. Most of the trails that you will encounter are made by wild-pig hunters who still regularly go after Solomon's legacy.

According to oral tradition the first *kahuna lapa'au* (healing doctor) of Hawaii was from Waimanu Valley. His disciples crossed and recrossed Waipio Valley, greatly influencing the development of the area. Some of the *heiau* in Waipio are specifically dedicated to the healing of the human torso; their origins are traced to the healing *kahuna* of Waimanu.

DIANA LASICH HARPER

LOUISE FOOTE

PUNA

The Puna District was formed from rivers of lava spilling from Mauna Loa and Kilauea again and again over the last million years or so. The molten rivers stopped only when they hit the sea, where they fizzled and cooled, forming a chunk of semi-raw land that bulges into the Pacific—marking the state's easternmost point at **Cape Kumukahi.** These titanic lava flows have left phenomenal reminders of their power. **Lava Tree State Monument** was once a rainforest whose giant trees were covered with lava, like hot dogs dipped in batter. The encased wood burned, leaving a hollow stone skeleton. You can stroll through this lichen-green rock forest before you head farther east into the brilliant sunshine of the coast. Little-traveled side roads take you past a multitude of orchid, anthurium, and papaya farms, oases of color in a desert of solid black lava. A lighthouse sits atop Cape Kumukahi, and to the north an ancient paved trail passes beaches where no one ever goes.

Southward is a string of popular beaches—some white, some black. You can camp, swim, surf, or just play in the water to your heart's delight. Villages have gas and food, and all along the coast you can visit natural areas where the sea tortured the hot lava into caves, tubes, arches, and even a natural bathtub whose waters are flushed and replenished by the sea. There are historical sites where petroglyphs tell vague stories from the past, and where generations of families placed the umbilical cords of their newborn into manmade holes in the rock. On Puna's south coast are remains of ancient villages, including Kamoamoa where you can camp. The park **Visitors Center** that used to stand just before the beginning of Chain of Craters Road burned down in the summer of 1989 when lava surged across the road, severing its eastern gateway into Volcanoes National Park. (The road is still closed, with no opening scheduled for the near future.) The **Hawaii Belt Road** (Route 11) is a corridor cutting through the center of Puna. It goes through the highlands to Volcanoes National Park, passing well-established villages and scattered housing developments as new as

PUNA

SOME ROADS IN THIS AREA
MAY BE CLOSED DUE TO
VOLCANIC ACTIVITY.
CHECK STATUS LOCALLY.

© J.D. BISIGNANI AND MOON PUBLICATIONS, INC.

the lava on which they precariously sit. Back in these hills, new-wave gardeners grow "Puna Butter" *pakalolo,* as wild and raunchy as its name. On the border of Puna and the Kau District to the south is **Hawaii Volcanoes National Park.** Here the goddess Pele resides at Kilauea Caldera, center of one of the world's most active volcanoes.

ROUTE 130 AND THE SOUTHEAST COAST

The most enjoyable area in the Puna District is the southeast coast, with its beaches and points of natural and historical interest. If you take Route 130 south from Keaau, in about 12 miles you pass **Pahoa.** As in Keaau, Pahoa is primarily a crossroads. You can continue due south on Route 130 to the seaside villages of **Kaimu** and **Kalapana,** where Route 130 joins coastal Route 137, feeding into Chain of Craters Road which has been buried by recent lava flows and is impassable. Along Route 130, about halfway between Pahoa and Kaimu, look for a small, unobtrusive sign that reads "Scenic Overlook." Pull off and walk toward the sea until you find four hot steam vents. Many local people use them as natural saunas.

You might go directly east from Pahoa along Route 132. This lovely, tree-lined country road takes you past **Lava Tree State Monument,** which shouldn't be missed, and then branches northeast, intersecting Route 137 and terminating at **Cape Kumukahi.** If this seems *too* far out of the way, head down **Pohoiki Road,** just past Lava Tree. You bypass a controversial geothermal power station, then reach the coast at **Isaac Hale Beach Park.** From there, Route 137 heads southwest down the coast to Kalapana, passing the best Puna beaches en route. Fortunately for you, this area of Puna is one of those places where no matter which way you decide to go, you really can't go wrong.

KEAAU

Keaau, though technically not in Puna, is the first town south of Hilo (10 miles) on Route 11, and although pleasant enough, it's little more than a Y in the road. At the junction of Route 11 (Hawaii Belt Road) and Route 130 is **Keaau Town Center,** a small shopping mall with a handful of variety stores, a laundromat, a post office, restaurants, and a **Bank of America.**

Here, the **Sure Save Supermarket** not only has groceries but plenty of sundries and a decent camera department, along with a public fax service.

Note
Route 11 (Hawaii Belt Road) splits in Keaau and passes through the high mountain villages of Kurtistown, Mountain View, Glenwood, and Volcano, then enters Hawaii Volcanoes National Park. For a description of these villages see below.

Food
The local **Dairy Queen,** in the Keaau Town Center, not only makes malts and sundaes but serves breakfast, lunch, and dinner. Plate specials, burgers, and sandwiches like a Reuben with french fries go for $4.95. For those who want to try an island treat like crackseed or shave ice, the center's **Kaeo Krack Seed** is open daily except Sunday 9 a.m.-5 p.m. Also in the shopping center is **Keaau Natural Foods,** tel. 966-8877, with a large stock of organic food items, herbs, and grains but no juice or snack bar. However, pre-made sandwiches from the deli case are always available. Have a look at their bulletin board for information on alternative happenings in the community. Open Mon.-Fri. 9 a.m.-8 p.m., Saturday 9 a.m.-9 p.m., and Sunday 10 a.m.-5 p.m. Have a beer while you wait for your laundry to wash at the **Suds and Duds** laundromat. *Pu pu,* snacks, and simple meals are also available. The bar is open Mon.-Sat. 11 a.m.-9 p.m. with happy hour 3-6 p.m. weekdays and all day Saturday.

Keaau Cafe, tel. 966-6758, is basically a walk-up window that offers a variety of meat and vegetable *bento,* with hardly anything over $7.50. With only two little tables inside, the **Keaau Chop Suey House,** tel. 966-7573, is next door with everything on their menu under $6, including several vegetarian dishes.

A few hundred yards down Route 130 heading toward Pahoa, you'll see **Verna's Drive-In,** which serves plate lunches. Behind that is **Chief's Pizza.**

PAHOA AND VICINITY

You can breeze through this "one-street" town, but you won't regret stopping if even for a few minutes. A raised wooden sidewalk passing false-front shops is fun to walk along to get a feeling of the last century. Most of the shops lining it are family-run fruit and vegetable stands supplied by local gardeners. Selections depend upon whether the old pickup truck started and made it to town that day. At one time Pahoa boasted *the* largest sawmill in America. Its buzz saw ripped ohia railway ties for the Santa Fe and other railroads. It was into one of these ties that the *golden spike* uniting the East and West coasts of the Mainland was driven. Many local people earned their livelihood from ohia charcoal that they made and sold all over the island until it was made obsolete by the widespread use of kerosene and gas introduced in the early 1950s. Pahoa's commercial heart went up in flames in 1955. Along the main street was a tofu factory that had a wood-fired furnace. The old fellow who owned the factory banked his fires as usual before he went home for the night. Somehow, they got out of control and burned all the way down to the main alley dividing the commercial district. The only reason the fire didn't jump the alley was because a papaya farmer happened to be around and had a load of water on the back of his truck, which he used to douse the buildings and save the town.

Pahoa is attempting to become part of the *Main Street U.S.A. Project* which will protect and revitalize its commercial center and bring new life to vintage buildings like the Akebono Theater, where classic movies are once again being shown. Pahoa has one of the highest concentrations of old buildings still standing in Hawaii that are easily accessible. Although it has been bypassed by a new road, make sure to enter the town and stroll along the tiny back roads. The town is attempting to become the anthurium capital of the world, and they have a good start on it. In virtually every garden, surrounded by distinctive lava-rock walls, you'll see black shade mesh under which are magnificent specimens of the normal red flowers, plenty of white ones, a few green, and even black anthuriums.

Lava Tree State Monument
In 1790, slick, fast-flowing pahoehoe lava surged through this ohia forest, covering the tree trunks from the ground to about a 12-foot level. The moisture inside the trees cooled the lava, forming a hardened shell. At the same time, tremors and huge fissures cracked the earth in the area.

anthuriums under
protective shade

DAVID STANLEY

Tree mold formed when lava flowed around a banana tree.

When the eruption ended, the still-hot lava drained away through the fissures, leaving the encased tree trunks standing like sentinels. The floor of the forest is so smooth in some areas that the lava seems like asphalt. Each lava tree has its own personality; some resemble totem poles, and it doesn't take much imagination to see old, craggy faces staring back at you. The most spectacular part of the park is near the entrance. Immense trees loom over cavernous cracks *(puka)* in the earth and send their roots, like stilled waterfalls, tumbling down into them. To get to Lava Tree, take Route 132 east from Pahoa for three miles and look for the well-marked entrance on the left. Brochures are available as you enter. Drinking water is not available.

Cape Kumukahi

It's fitting that Kumukahi means "First Beginning" since it is the easternmost point of Hawaii and was recognized as such by the original Polynesian settlers. Follow Route 132 past Lava Tree for about 10 miles until it hits the coast, where a lighthouse sits like an exclamation point. Along the way, get an instant course in volcanology: you can easily chart the destructive and regenerative forces at work on Hawaii. At the five-mile marker an HVB Warrior points out the lava flow of 1955. Tiny plants give the lava a greenish cast, and shrubs are already eating into it, turning it to soil. Papaya orchards grow in the raw lava of an extensive flat basin. The contrast between the black, lifeless earth and the vibrant green trees is

startling. In the center of the flatland rises a cinder cone, a caldera of a much older mini-volcano unscathed by the modern flows; it is gorgeous with lush vegetation. An HVB Warrior points out the lava flow of 1960, and you can see at a glance how different it was from the flow of five years earlier. When Route 132 intersects Route 137, go straight ahead east down a paved road for two miles to the Cape Kumukahi Lighthouse. People in these parts swear that on the fateful night in 1960 when the nearby village of Kapoho was consumed by the lava flow, an old woman (a favorite guise of Madame Pele) came to town begging for food and was turned away by everyone. She next went to the lighthouse asking for help, and was cordially treated by the lighthouse keeper. When the flow was at its strongest, it came within yards of the lighthouse and then miraculously split, completely encircling the structure but leaving it unharmed as the flow continued out to sea for a considerable distance.

Accommodations

Out behind the Paradise Cafe is the **Pahoa Inn,** tel. 965-0066, a one-time house of ill repute. Japanese entertainment troupes used to lodge here while performing at one of three major theaters in town. The hotel has 14 rooms, a quiet courtyard filled with flowers and cacti, and a Japanese *ofuro* which is now an outside bath painted by a local artist to look like the inside of an aquarium. The classically designed redwood structure is in remarkably good shape. Monthly rates only are $250-300 including utilities. Shared bathrooms are clean and newly painted but basic. No reservations are accepted because of the limited number of rooms.

Right downtown, occupying the second floor of a building erected in 1910, is the **Village Inn,** tel. 965-6444. A stairway with brass hand rail leads to the second floor; as you ascend imagine how many others have grasped that very rail. You're greeted at the top by Koko—the resident parrot and king of his big cage—your musical entertainment during your stay here. This small hotel has five rooms, all with cable TV, lace curtains, and white wicker furniture like grandma used to have on her porch. Other furniture is reminiscent of the '30s and '40s and ceiling fans help cool the rooms. While simple, everything is neat and clean. Rooms start at $30 and go up from there; some share a bathroom. Owner Bill Male runs the **Whimseys** gift shop on the first floor. It's more like an antique shop; his stock is always changing but you can find such items as vintage jewelry, Hawaiian artifacts and stoneware, glassware, and aloha shirts.

Pahoa Natural Groceries rents out **The Bamboo House,** $45 d first night, $35 three nights or more, with rates for four people, just a minute's walk from the store. Small, basic, and clean, it features a bedroom with a queen-size bed, foldout couch, private bath, and cable color TV. Write the Bamboo House, P.O. Box 1429, Pahoa, HI 96778; or phone the health food store at tel. 965-8322. A 25% deposit is required.

Whittaker's B&B, P.O. Box 1324, Pahoa, HI 96778, tel. 965-7015, offers two bedrooms with private baths in a new home located in the Puna rainforest. Each room, large enough for a small family, rents for $50 double, children under 12 free.

Food

At the Pahoa Village Center is a **Dairy Queen,** open daily 7 a.m.-8:30 p.m. for breakfast, lunch, and dinner. They serve everything from banana splits to chicken, pizza, and plate lunches. Just down the street is **Pahoa Chop Suey,** a downhome restaurant where you can eat cheaply; and farther down is **Luquin's Place,** open daily 11 a.m.-9 p.m., tel. 965-9990, a reasonably priced Mexican restaurant that offers enchiladas, burritos, tacos, and combination platters

for $5-7. It now serves drinks; margaritas are a house specialty.

A block away is **Mady's Cafe Makana,** tel. 965-0608, open every day except Sunday 7:30 a.m.-3 p.m. Mady's is a full cafe and boutique. **Pareau** are one of the mainstays in the boutique and they run $7-35. Women's toiletries, candles, greeting cards, and carved wooden items are also sold. After shopping, stop in at the cafe for a bite to eat. Nearly everything is under $5. Fruit smoothies for $2.25, a bowl of hearty lentil soup for $3,95, a tamale for $1.75, a samosa for $3.35, or a veggie croissant for $2.75 are samplings from the menu. All choices are organic, healthy, and nutritious. Mady's also supplies baked goods and deli sandwiches to some of the health food stores in the area.

Try **Naung Mai Thai Food,** tel. 965-8186, open daily for lunch and dinner, where you can dine on Thai spring rolls $4.95; red, green, or yellow curried shrimp, chicken, or beef $8.95; or a hearty bowl of Thai chicken-coconut soup $6.95. A full vegetarian selection, including tofu and eggplant curry $5.95 and rice and noodles $7.95, completes the menu.

One of the best places to eat in Pahoa is **Paradise Cafe,** tel. 965-0066, open daily 7 a.m.-2 p.m., breakfast until noon, owned and operated by Dave and Carrie Marry. Dave has a remarkable knowledge of Pahoa's history that he is willing to share if time permits. Breakfast is served with hash browns, rice, and buttermilk biscuits, and includes eggs with bacon $5.50, two eggs with fresh catch priced daily, and their very famous hollandaise sauce that tops eggs Benedict. One of the best deals is *huevos rancheros* with tortillas, beans, and salsa for $5.95. The lunch menu is basic cheeseburgers, turkey sandwiches, and the like, all priced under $6.50. The menu changes daily, but you can count on fresh fish, tender steaks, and pasta for $8.95 that can be covered with sun-dried tomatoes, olive oil, parmesan, and fresh basil. They also take care of the vegetarians with tofu scramble and a daily veggie special.

Pahoa Sports Lounge, tel. 964-7488, features theme nights like jam night on Wednesday, Hawaiian on Thursday, rock and roll on Friday, and country western on Saturday. There are TVs everywhere, as they try to cover all the big sporting events. A barbecue grill serves up complimentary *pu pu* on Friday and Saturday evenings.

The main koa wood-topped bar is the heart of the lounge; the small back bar, looking out over the garden, opens when they are really busy. Out back is a tiny bamboo garden and a game room with regular and electronic darts, foosball, and a pool table. This place has been cleaned up and rejuvenated, creating a place where you can have a good time.

Next door is **Koho Okazuya,** open from 7 a.m., a window restaurant serving continental breakfast $2.60 and a variety of lunches like pineapple chicken, beef stew, and hamburger patties. A minute farther down the elevated sidewalk is **Da Store,** with groceries, a deli case, beer, and liquor.

Let your mind and stomach be soothed with cosmic vibrations and libations at **Huna Ohana,** open daily 8 a.m.-5 p.m., Sunday 9 a.m.-1 p.m., tel. 965-9661. The metaphysical bookstore (open until 6 p.m.) and cafe is owned and operated by Dawn Hurwitz. Vegetarian breakfast dishes include egg soufflé or tofu scramble served with cottage potatoes and multigrain toast at $3.95; bagels and cream cheese $1.75; and an assortment of croissants and blueberry muffins. Lunch brings veggie sandwiches $3.50, filling garden burgers (a blend of mushrooms, onions, rolled oats, lowfat mozzarella, brown rice, cottage cheese, eggs, cheddar, bulgur wheat, walnuts, and spices) $4.95, or filling tempeh burger made with ginger teriyaki sauce for $4.95. To get those cosmic vibes kicked into high gear, order a cup of espresso, mocha latte, or cappuccino, choose a likely tome from the bookstore section, and kick back on an overstuffed couch or outside in the garden area.

Yo Pizza, tel. 965-7033, open daily except Monday 11 a.m.-10 p.m., uses homemade sauces and dough to make small, medium, and large traditional pizzas costing $4.90-14.90. They also have Italian Caesar salads $4.50, garden salad $2.75, garlic bread $1.50, and hot, rich cappuccino and espresso, perfect with slices of homemade pie. Lunch can be sub sandwiches $4.50, or you can dine on dinner specials like lasagna or spaghetti and meatballs for $6.50. The decor is "basic pizza parlor," redolent of olive oil and garlic.

A newer place in town is **Paolo's** Italian restaurant, open Tues.-Sun. 5:30-9 p.m. Dine inside at tables topped with blue and white checkered tablecloths, or have a seat in the patio outside.

Start with an appetizer, like a bowl of minestrone soup for $2.95 or fresh mozzarella antipasto for $6.95, and follow that with pasta ravioli with spinach and ricotta for $7.95 or pasta with prawns for $12.95. Their special entrees, like chicken Marcella at $12.95, cioppino for$14.95, or pizza a la palios (gourmet pizza Italian style with capers, anchovies, tomato, oregano, and mozzarella) for $14.95, might be more to your taste. To round out the meal, have a cup of espresso or a caffe latte.

Shopping and Services

When you pull into Pahoa you are greeted by the **Pahoa Village Center,** a small shopping center where you'll find a **laundromat,** a video store, and the Dairy Queen. A minute down the road is the full-service **Pahoa Cash and Carry** grocery store, **7-Eleven,** and the **Pahoa Casherette,** which are enough for any supplies or incidentals that you may need. Right next to the Pahoa Village Center is the **Pahoa flea market** for reasonably priced secondhand goods.

Pahoa Natural Groceries, tel. 965-8322, open weekdays 9 a.m.-9 p.m., Sunday 9 a.m.-6 p.m., specializing in organic food items, is one of the finest health food stores on the Big Island. They have an excellent selection of fresh veggies, organic grains, herbs and minerals, deli items, and a very good bakery selection. There's a kitchen on premises, so what you get is not only heathful but very fresh.

Adjacent is **The Emporium,** tel. 965-6634, open daily 10 a.m.-6 p.m., with a small but excellent selection of jewelry, Guatemalan clothing, Balinese batik, Yucatán hammocks, gifts, magazines, and cards. The Emporium also displays artwork, some by local artists, and a colorful selection of rugs. Their shirts and dresses, all cotton and rayon, cost $25-50. Some of the clothing is either designed or handmade here in Puna. The back room displays a profusion of these vibrant rainbow-colored clothes.

Hale Mana, tel. 965-7783, open Mon.-Fri. 9 a.m.-5 p.m. or by appointment, adjacent to the health food store, is an acupuncture and massage clinic. The acupuncturists are Françoise Hesselink, Jocelyn Mayeux, and Rhonda Ashby. Relax as you lie on the table and breezes blow through the vintage rooms. Let one of these fine practitioners energize and revitalize your spirit and put spring back into your aching muscles.

For anyone interested in body art, **Kaleidoscope** tattoo parlor is a place to check out. Actually a club, the $10 entry fee allows you to hang out with others who have similarly adorned themselves and to attend their periodic parties. Joseph Gonsalves (a.k.a. TJ, a.k.a. Tattoo Joe) does only a few tattoos here but mostly makes house calls. Also in this shop you can pick up bullwhips, daggers, canes, handcarved chairs, and other such eccentric items.

If a permanent memento from the tattoo artist isn't what you had in mind, try next door at **Happily** antique shop for something more ordinary, like jewelry, wooden bowls, baskets, and hats. Open daily 10 a.m.-5 p.m. except Sunday, this shop has been around a long time and is almost an institution in town.

Along the elevated boardwalk, are numerous shops for gifts and other diversions. At **Pacific Mystics,** a new-age shop, you can consult the tarot while browsing among books, crystals, local crafts, surfboards, and a cosmic smattering of clothes and sunglasses. They now have a health food section as well.

KAIMU AND KALAPANA

Special Note
Kaimu and Kalapana have been annihilated by the advancing lava flow. For a full description of **Chain Of Craters Road** and recent volcanic activity, see the following chapter on Hawaii Volcanoes National Park. Parts of the road are still open, but only *from* the park.

The Painted Church
Star of the Sea Catholic Church is a small but famous structure better known as "The Painted Church." An effort to save the historic church from the lava was mounted, and it has been moved. A brief history of the area asserts that the now-inundated Kalapana was a spiritual magnet for Roman Catholic priests. Old Spanish documents support evidence that a Spanish priest, crossing the Pacific from Mexico, actually landed very near here in 1555. Father Damien, famous priest of the Molokai Leper Colony, established a grass church about two miles north and conducted a school when he first arrived in the islands in 1864. The present church dates from

inside The Painted Church

1928, when Father Everest Gielen began its construction. Like an inspired but much less talented Michelangelo, this priest painted the ceiling of the church, working mostly at night by oil lamp. Father Everest was transferred to Lanai in 1941, and the work wasn't completed until 1964, when Mr. George Heidler, an artist from Atlanta, Georgia, came to Kalapana and decided to paint the unfinished lower panels in the altar section. The artwork itself can only be described as gaudy but sincere. The colors are wild blues, purples, and oranges. The ceiling is adorned with symbols, portraits of Christ, the angel Gabriel, and scenes from the Nativity. Behind the altar, a painted perspective gives the impression that you're looking down a long hallway at an altar that hangs suspended in air. The church is definitely worth a few minutes at least.

End of the Road
Just near the lava-inundated village of Kalapana, Routes 130 and 137 come to an abrupt

halt where Madame Pele has repaved the road with lava. At the end of the line you come to a barricaded area. Volcanic activity has continued virtually unabated here since January 1983, when lava fountains soared 1,500 feet into the sky and produced a cone over 800 feet tall. The initial lava flow was localized at Pu'u O'o vent, but after dozens of eruptive episodes it shifted to Kupaianaha, which has continuously produced about half a million cubic yards of lava per day. Today it is mostly erupting once again from flank vents on Pu'u O'o. The lava flows eight miles to the sea, mostly through lava tubes. It has inundated almost 36.5 square miles, caused $61 million worth of property damage, and added more than 500 acres of new land to the Puna Coast—and it's still growing.

A sign strongly warns you against walking out onto the lava. Some hazards that you may encounter are brushfires, smoke, ash, and methane gas, which is extremely explosive. You can also fall through the thin-crusted lava into a tube which will immediately reduce you to a burnt offering to Pele and unceremoniously deposit your ashes into the sea! New lava can cut like broken glass, and molten lava can be flung through the air by steam explosions, especially near the coastline. Seacliffs collapse frequently, and huge boulders can be tossed several hundred feet into the air. The steam clouds contain minerals that can cause burning eyes, throat and skin irritations, and difficulty breathing.

If you are still intrigued, realize that you are on the most unstable piece of real estate on the face of the earth. For those maniacs, fools, adventurers, and thrill-seekers who just can't stay away, the walk to the sea takes about 25 minutes. Give yourself up for dead, and proceed. Follow the old roadbed, up and down, over the lava. When you can no longer discern the road, look off to your left and you'll see a large steam cloud rising. Pick your way to it, but don't get too close. Observers say that every day, huge chunks fall off into the sea in this area. As you look back at the mountain you can see heat waves rising from the land upon which you are standing. A camera with a zoom lens or a pair of binoculars accentuates this phenomenon. The whole mountain waves in front of you. As you walk closer to the sea, the lava cools and you can see every type there is: rope lava, lava toes, lava fingers. The tortured flow, which crinkles as you walk over it, has created many imaginative shapes: gargoyles, medieval faces, dolphins, and mythical creatures. At the coast, the lava pours into the sea, creating a white spume of steam lifting 200-300 feet into the air. No other place in the world gives you the opportunity to be the first person to tread upon the earth's newest land.

Accommodations
Kalani Honua Oceanside Eco-Resort, RR 2 Box 4500, Kehena Beach, HI 96778, tel. 965-7828 or (800) 800-6886, fax 965-9613, is a nonprofit, international conference and retreat center, a haven where people come when they truly want to get away from it all. The entrance is located a few miles northeast of Kalapana on Route 137 between mile markers 17 and 18. Look for a large Visitors Welcome sign and proceed until you see the office area and a gift and sundries shop. Depending upon the yearly schedule, they offer a variety of activities that include holistic massage, hula, meditation, yoga, and lei-making, for men, women, couples, and families. Contact them to find out what's happening when you'll be on the Big Island. The grounds have a botanical atmosphere, with a rain-fed swimming pool, hot tub, Jacuzzi, assembly studios, classrooms, cottages with views of the ocean and cedar lodges with kitchen facilities. It's the only place along the Puna Coast that offers lodging and vegetarian fare. Rates are $45 s for a dorm room with shared bath, $60 s and $70 d for a private room with shared bath, $75 s and $85 d for a private room with private bath, $85 s and $95 d for a guest cottage. You can also camp for $15 a night. A conch shell calls you to breakfast at 8 a.m., lunch at noon, and dinner at 6 p.m. (nonguests welcome). The meals cost $7, $8, and $12 respectively, with a meal ticket pre-purchased at the office; or guests can purchase a "meal plan" for $25 which entitles you to all three. Lights go out at 10:30 p.m., but candles are provided for night owls. Kalani Eco-Resort is not for everyone, but if you are looking for unpretentious peace and quiet and healthful food, there's no better place on the island. E-mail: kh@IL-Hawaii.net; Web site: www.randm.com/kh.html.

BEACHES, PARKS, AND CAMPGROUNDS

All of Puna's beaches, parks, and campgrounds lie along coastal Route 137 stretching for 20 miles from Pohoiki to Kamoamoa (recently wiped out by lava flow). Surfers, families, transients, even nude-sunbathing "buffs" have their favorite beaches along this southeast coast. For the most part, swimming is possible, but be cautious during high tide. There is plenty of sun, snorkeling sites, and good fishing, and the campgrounds are almost always available.

Pohoiki a.k.a. Isaac Hale County Beach Park

You can't miss this beach park located on Pohoiki Bay, at the junction of Route 137 and Pohoiki Road. Just look for a jumble of boats and trailers parked under the palms. At one time Pohoiki Bay served the Hawaiians as a canoe landing, then later became the site of a commercial wharf for the Puna Sugar Company. It remains the only boat launching area for the entire Puna Coast, used by pleasure boaters and commercial fishermen. Due to this dual role, it's often very crowded. Amenities include pavilions, restrooms, and a picnic area; potable water is not available. Camping is permitted with a county permit. Experienced surfers dodge the rip-current in the center of the bay, and swimming is generally good when the sea is

calm. Pohoiki Bay is also one of the best scuba and snorkel sites on the island. Within walking distance of the salt-and-pepper beach are hot springs that bubble into lava sinks surrounded by lush vegetation. They're popular with tourists and residents, and provide a unique and relaxing way to wash away sand and salt. To find them, face away from the sea and turn left, then look for a small but well-worn path that leads through the jungle. The pools are warm, small, and tranquil. Harmless, tiny brine shrimp nibble at your toes while you soak.

MacKenzie State Recreation Area

This popular state park was named for forest ranger A.J. MacKenzie, highly regarded throughout the Puna District and killed in the area in 1938. The park's 13 acres sit among a cool grove of ironwoods originally planted by MacKenzie. A portion of the old King's Highway, scratched out by prisoners last century as a form of community service, bisects the area. Many people who first arrive on the Big Island hang out at MacKenzie until they can get their start. Consequently, the park receives its share of hard-core types, which has earned it a reputation for rip-offs. Mostly it's safe, but if you're camping, take precautions with your valuables. The entire coastline along MacKenzie is bordered by rugged black-lava seacliffs. Swimming is dangerous, but the fishing is excellent. Be extremely careful when beach-walking, especially out on the fingers of lava; over the years,

the Puna Coast

J.D. BISIGNANI

Fire and steam mark the spot where lava meets the sea.

J.D. BISIGNANI

people have been swept away by freak waves. MacKenzie Park is located along Route 137, two miles south of Isaac Hale. Picnic facilities are available, but there is no drinking water. A state permit is required for overnight camping.

Puala'a Beach Park

Quietly opened by the County of Hawaii on July 4, 1993, this lovely, 1.3-acre beach park (short on parking) was an ancient fishing village on the boundary of the *ahupua'a* of Leapao'o and Puala'a. Located along the *red road* between Kapoho and Opihikao, the park features a pool thermally heated to a perfect temperature. Some people use the pond to do watsu, a type of in-water massage. The swimming is safe except during periods of very high surf, when ocean water washes in. The park is perfect for families with young children. The pond is now watched over by a life guard, and bathrooms have been set up for your convenience.

Kehena

Kehena is actually two pockets of black-sand beach below a low seacliff. Entrance to the beach is marked only by a scenic pulloff on Route 137, about five miles south of MacKenzie; usually a half-dozen cars are parked there. At one time Kehena was very popular, and a stone staircase led down to the beach. In 1975 a strong earthquake jolted the area, breaking up the stairway and lowering the beach by three feet. Now access is via a well-worn path, but make sure to wear sneakers because the lava is rough. The ocean here is dangerous, and often pebbles and rocks whisked along by the surf can injure legs. Once down on the beach, head north for the smaller patch of sand, because the larger patch is open to the sea and can often be awash in waves. The black sand is hot, but a row of coconut palms provides shade. The inaccessibility of Kehena makes it a favorite "no-hassle" nude beach with many "full" sunbathers congregating here.

Note: Unfortunately, recent lava flows have completely covered the very popular **Kaimu Beach Park,** also known as Black Sand Beach, and **Harry K. Brown Beach Park.** Now, raw and rugged lava meets the sea to be slowly turned into beach parks for future generations.

THE HAWAII BELT ROAD FROM HILO

Route 11 (Hawaii Belt Road) splits in Keaau and passes through several high mountain villages before entering Hawaii Volcanoes National Park. The Belt Road, although only two lanes, is straight, well-surfaced, and scrupulously maintained. At approximately 10-mile intervals are Kurtistown, Mountain View, Glenwood, and Volcano.

Fuku Bonsai Center, tel. 982-9880, open weekdays 8 a.m.-4 p.m. and by appointment, at 17-631 Volcano Highway (Belt Road), in Kurtistown behind the Post Office and B.J.'s Service Station, will sell you diminutive bonsai plants that are agriculturally inspected and mailable to the Mainland.

Mountain View is a village of nurseries specializing in anthuriums. Many of them sport signs inviting you to a free tour. Along Route 11 is a mini-mart and **Verna's Too Snack Shop** serving plate lunches, burgers, and shakes. As you pass through, take a minute to explore the short side-road into the village itself. Every house has a garden of ferns, flowers, and native trees. In the village is **Mt. View Bakery,** home of the famous stone cookies; and the **Mt. View Village Store,** which is fairly well supplied.

Look for a vintage plantation house painted blue between mile markers 12 and 13. This is **Tinny Fisher's Antique Shop,** owned and operated by Charles and Dorothy Wittig. What started as "yard sale treasures" about 10 years ago has turned into a unique curio, antique, and collectibles shop. Open daily except Monday, noon-6 p.m., the shop has all kinds of antiques and collectibles from Asia and Hawaii, including glass balls, Asian furniture, jewelry, and glassware galore. Tinny's also features a good Hawaiiana collection, with artifacts from the ancient days like *kukui* nut lamps, poi pounders, and stone knives.

Glenwood, between mile markers 19 and 20, offers a gas station and **Hirano's General Store** for basic provisions. A few minutes down the road you pass **Akatsuka Tropical Orchids and Flower Gardens,** tel. 967-8234, open daily 8:30 a.m.-5 p.m., except major holidays. They offer a complimentary orchid to all visitors. If tour buses don't overflow the parking lot, stop in for a look at how orchids are grown or to use the clean restrooms.

Just before you enter Volcanoes National Park, a sign points to the right down a short side road to **Volcano Village** where you will find accommodations, restaurants, and shopping (see below). The Hawaii Belt Road continues southwest through **Kau,** the southernmost district of the Big Island, eventually arriving in Kona. For a full description of Kau, its villages and sights, please refer to the Kau chapter.

LOUISE FOOTE

BOB RACE

HAWAII VOLCANOES NATIONAL PARK

INTRODUCTION

Hawaii Volcanoes National Park (HVNP) is an unparalleled experience in geological grandeur. The western end of the park is the summit of stupendous **Mauna Loa,** the most massive mountain on earth. The park's heart is **Kilauea Caldera,** encircled by 11 miles of **Crater Rim Drive.** At the park visitor center you can give yourself a crash course in geology while picking up park maps and information. Nearby is **Volcano House,** Hawaii's oldest hotel, which has hosted a steady stream of adventurers, luminaries, royalty, and heads of state ever since it opened its doors in the 1860s. Amidst all the natural wonders is a golf course—for those who want to boast they've done it all after hitting a sand wedge from a volcanic fissure. Just down the road is one of Hawaii's last remaining indigenous forests, providing the perfect setting for a bird sanctuary. Mauna Loa Road branches off Crater Rim Drive and ends at a foot trail for the hale and hearty who trek to the 13,679-foot summit.

The rim drive continues past steam vents, sulfur springs, and tortured fault lines that always seem on the verge of gaping wide and swallowing. You can peer into the maw of **Halemaumau Crater,** home of the fire goddess, Pele, and you'll pass **Hawaiian Volcano Observatory** (not open to public), which has been monitoring geologic activity since the turn of the century. Nearby is the **Thomas A. Jaggar Museum,** an excellent facility where you can educate yourself on the past and present volcanology of the park. A fantastic walk is **Devastation Trail,** a paved path across a desolate black lava field where gray, lifeless trunks of a suffocated forest lean like old gravestones. Within minutes is **Thurston Lava Tube,** a magnificent natural tunnel *"leid"* by amazingly vibrant fern grottoes at the entrance and exit.

VOLCANOES NATIONAL PARK

To Hilo

HAWAIIAN TROPICAL ORCHIDS

Volcano

AREA OF MAP

Pacific Ocean

VOLCANOES NATIONAL PARK

KALAPANA TRAIL

NAPAU CRATER TRAIL

Mauna Ulu (3,480 ft)

Aloi Crater (Site)

EAST RIFT ZONE

MAU LOA O MAUNA ULU

MULUWAI A PELE

To Coast

Hiiaka Crater

Devils Throat

Napau Crater

CHAIN OF CRATERS ROAD

KEAUHOU TRAIL

Kilauea

PARK HEADQUARTERS, MUSEUM, AND VISITOR AND ART CENTERS

KILAUEA STATE RECREATION AREA

KILAUEA IKI OVERLOOK

Thurston Lava Tube

TREE FERN AND OHIA FOREST

Puhimau Crater

Kokoolau Crater

Kalihanaokui Pali

AINAHOU RANCH

Pali Leie O Kali Hipoa

Kipuka Puhalinamoku Pali

VOLCANO COUNTRY CLUB/GOLF COURSE

MILITARY CAMP

PUU OO VOLCANO TRAIL (PRVT.)

VOLCANO WINERY

TREE MOLDS

Steaming Bluff

Volcano House

Waldron Ledge

HALEMAUMAU TR.

Kilauea Caldera

OVERLOOK

DEVASTATION TR.

Lua Manu Crater

DEVASTATION LOOKOUT

CRATER RIM DRIVE

Liia Manu Crater

Kau Desert

ROAD

PALI

HINA

TRAIL

MAUNA IKI TRAIL

KIPUKA NENE CAMPGROUND

BIRD PARK PICNIC AREA

NAMAKANI PAIO CAMPGROUND

VOLCANO OBSERVATORY

THOMAS A. JAGGAR MUSEUM

Halemaumau (3,412 ft)

CRATER RIM TRAIL

Cone Peak (3,652 ft)

KAU DESERT TRAIL

Cone Crater (3,652 ft)

1974 LAVA FLOW

Pit Craters

MAUNA IKI

VOLCANOES

NATIONAL PARK

SOUTHWEST RIFT ZONE

Puu Koae (3,250 ft)

Mauna Iki (3,032 ft)

To Hilina Pali Lookout

KIPUKA KULALIO

MAUNA LOA ROAD

Keamoku Lava Flow

HAWAII BELT ROAD

POWERLINE ROAD

To Lookout and Mauna Loa Trail

FOOTPRINTS IN ASH

To Naalehu and Kona

2 mi

2 km

© J.D. BISIGNANI AND MOON PUBLICATIONS, INC.

The indomitable power of Volcanoes National Park is apparent to all who come here. Mark Twain, enchanted by his sojourn through Volcanoes in the 1860s, quipped, "The smell of sulfur is strong, but not unpleasant to a sinner." Amen brother! Wherever you stop to gaze, realize that you are standing on a thin skin of cooled lava in an unstable earthquake zone atop one of the world's most active volcanoes.

Established in 1916 as the 13th U.S. national park, HVNP now covers 377 square miles. Based on its scientific and scenic value, the park was named an International Biosphere Reserve by UNESCO in 1980, giving it greater national and international prestige.

Admission to the park is $10 per vehicle (good for multiple entries over a seven-day period), $15 for an annual permit, $5 for bicycle traffic and hikers, and free to those 62 and over with a *Golden Age Passport* or *Golden Eagle Passport*. These "passports" are available at the park headquarters for a one-time fee of $10 and are good at any national park in the United States.

For information about the park, write or call HVNP, P.O. Box 52, HNP, HI 96718, tel. 985-6000; or check out their Web site at www.nps.gov/havo.

Geologic History:
Science Versus Madame Pele

The goddess Pele is an irascible old dame. Perhaps it's because she had such a bad childhood. All she wanted was a home of her own where she could house her family and entertain her lover, a handsome chief from Kauai. But her sea goddess sister, Namakaokaha'i, flooded her out

wherever she went after Pele seduced her husband, and the pig god, Kama Pu'a, ravished Pele for good measure. So Pele finally built her love nest at Halemaumau Crater at the south end of Kilauea Caldera. Being a goddess obviously isn't as heavenly as one would think, and whenever the pressures of life get too much for Pele, she blows her stack. These tempestuous outbursts made Pele one of the most revered gods in the Hawaiian pantheon because her presence and might were so easily felt.

For a thousand years Pele was appeased by offerings of pigs, dogs, sacred *ohelo* berries (her favorite) and now and again an outcast man or two (never women) who would hopefully turn her energy from destruction to more comfortable pursuits. Also, if Pele was your family's personal goddess, your remains were sometimes allowed to be thrown into the fire pit as a sign of great respect. In the early 1820s, the chieftess Kapiolani, an ardent convert to Christianity, officially challenged Pele in an attempt to topple her like the other gods of old. Kapiolani climbed down into Pele's crater and ate the sacred *ohelo* berries, flagrantly violating the ageless *kapu*. She then took large stones and defiantly hurled them into the fire pit below while bellowing, "Jehovah is my God. It is He, not Pele, that kindled these flames."

Yet today, most residents, regardless of background, have an inexplicable reverence for Pele. The goddess has modernized her tastes, switching from *ohelo* to juniper berries that she prefers in liquid form as bottles of gin! The Volcano Post Office receives an average of three packages a week containing lava rocks taken by tourists as souvenirs (sometimes 30 per day). Some hold that Pele looks upon these rocks as her children and taking them from her is kidnapping. The accompanying letters implore the officials to return the rocks because ever since the offender brought them home, luck has been bad. The officials take the requests very seriously, returning the rocks with the customary peace offering: a bottle of gin. Many follow-up "thank you" letters have been written to express relief that the bad luck has been lifted. There is no reference in Hawaiian folklore to this phenomenon, although Hawaiians did hold certain rocks sacred. Park rangers will tell you that the idea of "the bad-luck rocks" was initiated a few decades

---

VOLCANO ACTIVITY

For current information on volcano activity in the area, access the "Volcano Watch" Web site at www.soest.Hawaii.edu/hvo. Related volcano and earthquake information is also available at www.soest.Hawaii.edu/GG/HCV/eruption.html and hvo.wr.usgs.gov/geology/update2.hmtl; or call (808) 985-6000 for the Park Service's recorded message. Should there be any major increase in activity local radio stations give up-to-the-minute news.

river of lava from a recent flow

J.D. BISIGNANI

back by a tour bus driver who became sick and tired of tourists getting his bus dirty by piling aboard their souvenirs. *Voilà!* Another ancient Hawaiian myth! Know, however, that the rocks in Hawaii Volcanoes National Park are protected by federal law, much meaner and more vindictive than Pele ever imagined being.

Pele is believed to take human form. She customarily appears before an eruption as a ravishing beauty or a withered old hag, often accompanied by a little white dog. She expects to be treated cordially, and it's said that she will stand by the roadside at night hitching a ride. After a brief encounter, she departs and seems to mysteriously evaporate into the ether. Kindness on your part is the key; if you come across a strange woman at night, treat her well—it might not help, but it definitely won't hurt.

Eruptions

The first white man atop Kilauea was Rev. William Ellis, who scaled it in 1823. Until the 1920s, the floor of the caldera was exactly what people thought a volcano would be: a burning lake of fire. Then the forces of nature changed, and the fiery lava subsided and hardened over. Today, Kilauea is called the only "drive-in" volcano in the world, and in recent years has been one of the most active, erupting almost continuously since 1983. When it begins gushing, the result is not a nightmare scene of people scrambling away for their lives, but just the opposite; people flock *to* the volcano. Most thrill-seekers are in much greater

danger of being run over by a tour bus hustling to see the fireworks than of being entombed in lava. The volcanic action, while soul-shakingly powerful, is predictable and almost totally safe. The Hawaiian Volcano Observatory has been keeping watch since 1912, making Kilauea one of the best-understood volcanoes in the world. The vast volcanic field is creased by rift zones, or natural pressure valves. When the underground magma builds up, instead of *kaboom!* as in Mt. St. Helens, it bubbles to the surface like a spring and gushes out as a river of lava. Naturally, anyone or anything in its path would be burned to a cinder, but scientists routinely walk within a few feet of the still-flowing lava to take readings. In much the way canaries detect mine gas, longtime lava observers pay attention to their ears. When the skin on top begins to blister, they know that they are too close. The lava establishes a course that it follows much like an impromptu mountain stream caused by heavy rains.

This does not mean that the lava flows are entirely benign, or that anyone should visit the area during an eruption without prior approval by the park service. When anything is happening, the local radio stations give up-to-the-minute news, and the park service provides a recorded message at tel. 985-6000. In 1790 a puff of noxious gases was emitted from Kilauea and descended on the Kau Desert, asphyxiating a rival army of Kamehameha's that just happened to be in the area. Eighty people died in their tracks. In 1881 a flow of lava spilled toward undeveloped

Hilo and engulfed an area within today's city limits. In 1942, a heavy flow came within 12 miles of the city. Still, this was child's play in comparison with the unbelievable flow of 1950. Luckily, this went down the western rift zone where only scattered homes were in its path. It took no lives as it disgorged well over 600 million cubic yards of magma that covered 35 square miles! The flow continued for 23 days and produced seven huge torrents of lava that sliced across the Belt Road in three different areas. At its height, the lava front traveled six miles per hour and put out enough material to pave an eight-lane freeway twice around the world. In 1960, a flow swallowed the town of Kapoho on the east coast. In 1975, Hawaii's strongest earthquake since 1868 caused a tsunami to hit the southeast coast, killing two campers and sinking almost the entire Puna Coast by three feet.

The most recent, and very dramatic, series of eruptions that spectacularly began on January 3, 1983, have continued virtually unabated ever since, producing over one cubic kilometer of lava. Magma bubbled to the surface about two miles away from Pu'u O'o. The gigantic fissure fountained lava and formed Pu'u O'o Cinder Cone that is now 830 feet high and almost 1,000 feet across. Over a three-and-a-half-year period, there were 47 eruptions from this vent. On July 20, 1986, a new fissure, composed of approximately two miles of fountaining lava, broke upon the surface at Kupaianaha, and has since formed a lava lake about one acre in size and 180 feet deep. At the end of April 1987 all activity suddenly stopped and the lava drained from the lake and tube system, allowing scientists to accurately gauge the depth. About a week later, it all started up again when lava poured back into the lake, went through the tube system, and flowed back down to the ocean. The output was estimated at 650,000 cubic yards per day, which is equal to 55,000 truckloads of cement, enough to cover a football field 38 miles high.

From that point, the flow turned destructive and started taking homes. It moved to the coast in tubes, wiping out Kapaahu, parts of Kalapana, and most of the Royal Gardens Subdivision, with over 70 homes incinerated. In May 1989 it moved into the national park proper, and on June 22, it swallowed the park visitor center at Waha'ula. Since 1992, lava has been flowing into the ocean within the park. Unexpectedly, in January of 1997 the dramatic activity shifted two miles westward to the Napau Crater where lava erupted in spouts of fire and flows, and Pu'u O'o ceased spewing. From February of 1997, the majority of activity moved back to Pu'u O'o Cinder Cone where there has been a continual shift of vent locations on the west and southwestern flanks and constant renewed activity inside the crater. Until 1997, remote Waha'ula Heiau was spared, but in August of that year lava inundated and buried the sacred spot. The destruction has caused over $61 million worth of damage. Many of the homesteaders in the worst areas of the flow were rugged individualists and back-to-nature alternative types who lived in homes that generally had no electricity, running water, or telephones. The homes were wiped out. Some disreputable insurance companies with legitimate policy holders tried to wiggle out of paying premiums for lost homes, although the policies specifically stipulated loss by lava flow. The insurance compa-

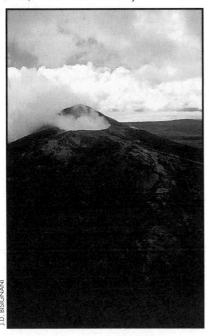

J.D. BISIGNANI

Pu'u O'o cinder cone

nies whined that the 2,000° lava never really touched some of the homes, and therefore they were exonerated from paying the coverage. Their claims were resoundingly repudiated in the courts, and people were paid for their losses. One gentleman, however, has been forced to continue living in the middle of the lava flow. He's been there from the beginning because his insurance company will not pay if he leaves, claiming that the house was abandoned and therefore not covered. He sits in the middle of the lava plain with the flows all around him. For the last seven years, he's ridden a bicycle out from his house to the road. From there he goes to work and goes about his business, then goes back in on his bicycle. Sometimes in the middle of the night, or while he's gone, a lava flow occurs and he has to wait a couple of days for it to crust over before he can get in and out. Makes you want to rush right out and pay your premium to your caring friends in the insurance business. A prayer to Pele would easily be more effective. There is only one way to treat the power of Hawaii's magnificent volcanoes: not with fear, but with the utmost respect.

Mauna Loa

At 13,679 feet, this magnificent mountain is a mere 117 feet shorter than its neighbor Mauna Kea, which is the tallest peak in the Pacific, and by some accounts, tallest in the world. Measured from its base, 18,000 feet beneath the sea, it would top even Mt. Everest. Mauna Loa is the most massive mountain on earth, containing 10,000 cubic miles of solid, iron-hard lava. This titan weighs more than California's entire Sierra Nevada range! In fact, Mauna Loa ("Long Mountain"), at 60 miles long and 30 wide, occupies the entire southern half of the Big Island, with Volcanoes National Park merely a section of its great expanse.

Special Note

Everything in the park—flora and fauna, rocks, buildings, trails, etc.—is protected by federal law. Be respectful! The **nene,** Hawaii's state bird, is endangered. By feeding these birds, visitors have taught them to stand in parking lots and by the roadside. What appears to be a humane and harmless practice actually helps kill these rare birds. Automobiles running them over has become the leading cause of death of adult birds in the park. Please look, but do not try to approach, feed, or harass the *nene* in any way.

KILAUEA CALDERA

The sights of Hawaii Volcanoes National Park are arranged one after another along **Crater Rim Drive.** Off the beaten track but worth a look are **Mauna Loa Road** (which takes you to places of special interest such as **Tree Molds** and **Bird Park**—10-minute detours) and **Kau Desert Trail,** about eight miles south of the visitor center on the Hawaii Belt Road, Hwy. 11. Most of the sights are the "drive-up" variety, but plenty of major and minor trails lead off here and there.

Tips

Expect to spend a long full day atop Kilauea to take in all the sights, and never forget that you're on a rumbling volcano where a misstep or loss of concentration at the wrong moment can lead to severe injury, or even loss of life. Try to arrive by 9 a.m. with a picnic lunch to save time and hassles. Kilauea Caldera, at 4,000 feet, is about 10° cooler than the coast. It's often overcast and

there can be showers. Wear your walking shoes and bring a sweater and/or windbreaker. Binoculars, sunglasses, and a hat will also come in handy.

Warning! Small children, pregnant women, and people with respiratory ailments should note that the fumes from the volcano can cause problems. Just stay away from areas of sulfur vents and don't overdo it, and you should be fine.

A very dramatic way to experience the awesome power of the volcano is to take a **helicopter tour.** The choppers are perfectly suited for the up-close maneuverability necessary to get an intimate bird's-eye view. The pilots will fly you over the areas offering the most activity, often dipping low over lava pools, skimming still-glowing flows, and circling the towering steam clouds rising from where lava meets the sea. When activity is really happening, tours are jammed, and prices, like lava fountains, go sky-high. Remember, however, that there is growing resentment by hikers or anyone else trying to have a quiet experience, and that new regulations might limit flights over the lava area. Also, choppers do go down, and it is the park rangers and their rescue units who must go to their aid.

VISITORS CENTER AREA

The best place to start is at the Visitors Center/Park Headquarters. The turnoff is clearly marked off Belt Road (Hwy. 11). By midmorning it's jammed, so try to be an early bird. The center is well run by the National Park Service. They offer a free lecture and film about geology and volcanism, with tremendous highlights of past eruptions, and with plenty of detail on Hawaiian culture and natural history. It runs every hour on the hour starting at 9 a.m. Also, a self-guided natural history museum gives more information about the geology of the area, with plenty of exhibits of the flora and fauna. You will greatly enrich your visit if you take a half-hour tour of the museum. Actually, the visitor center has been eclipsed by the state-of-the-art information available at the **Thomas A. Jaggar Museum** a few minutes up the road.

For safety's sake, anyone trekking to the backcountry *must* register with the rangers at the visitor center, especially during times of eruption. Do not be foolhardy! There is no charge for camping, and the rangers can give you up-to-the-minute information on trails, backcountry shelters, and cabins. Trails routinely close due to lava flows, tremors, and rock slides. The rangers cannot help you if they don't know where you are. Many day trails leading into the caldera from the rim road are easy walks that need no special preparation. The backcountry trails can be very challenging, and detailed maps (highly recommended) are sold at the center along with special-interest geology and natural history publications prepared by the Hawaii Natural History Association. The visitor center is open daily 7:45 a.m.-5 p.m.; call 985-6000 for trail, camping, or volcanic activity information.

Volcano House

Have you ever dreamed of sleeping with a goddess? Well, you can cuddle up with Pele by staying at Volcano House. If your plans don't include an overnight stop, go in for a look. Sometimes this is impossible, because not only do tour buses from the Big Island disgorge here, but tour groups are flown in from Honolulu as well. A stop at the bar provides refreshments and a tremendous view of the crater. Volcano House still has the feel of a country inn, although in reality it's a Sheraton Inn. This particular building dates from the 1940s, but the site has remained the same since a grass hut was perched on the rim of the crater by a sugar planter in 1846. He charged $1 a night. A steady stream of notable visitors has come ever since: almost all of Hawaii's kings and queens dating from the middle of last century, as well as royalty from Europe. Mark Twain was a guest, followed by Franklin Roosevelt. Most recently, a contingent of astronauts lodged here and used the crater floor to prepare for walking on the moon. In 1866 a large grass hut replaced the first, and in 1877 a wooden Victorian-style hotel was built. It is now the Volcano Art Center and has been moved just across the road. The longest owner/operator of Volcano House was George Lycurgus, who took over management of the hotel in the 1890s. His son, Nick, followed him and managed the hotel until the 1960s.

Volcano Art Center

Art and history buffs should walk across the street to the Volcano Art Center, tel. 967-8222, which is the original 1877 Volcano House, Hawaii's oldest hotel. You not only get to see some fine arts and crafts, you can take a self-guided tour of this mini-museum, open daily 9 a.m.-5 p.m. A new show featuring one of the many superlative island artists on display is presented monthly. Some prominent artists represented: Chiu Leong, who has a studio nearby where he turns out inspired *raku* pottery; Rick Mills, a master glass artist; Dietrich Varez, who makes affordable and distinctive wood block prints; Wilford Yamazawa, another amazing glassworker; Marion Burger, a young artist who lives in Volcano, known as one of the best naturalist painters around; George Allen, an oil painter whose themes are Hawaiian landscapes, flowers, and fish; Kathy Long, creator of insightful pencil drawings of local people; Pam Barton, who does whimsical fiber arts; woodworker Jack Straka, famous for his rich turned bowls; Kelly Dunn, who turns large bowls of Norfolk pine; Michael

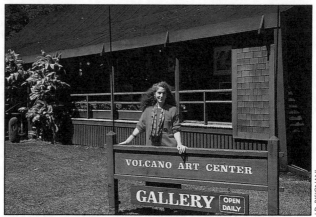

friendly and knowledgeable salesperson at the Volcano Art Center

Riley, a Volcano resident who does rocking chairs in koa and other exotic woods in a style that follows the master woodworker Sam Maloof; and Boone Morrison, the center's founder, a photographer and architect who apprenticed under Ansel Adams. There is also a profusion of less expensive but distinctive items like posters, cards, and earthy basketry made from natural fibers collected locally. One of the functions of the art center is to provide interpretation for the national park. All of the 250-plus artists who exhibit here do works that in some way relate to Hawaii's environment and culture. Volcano Art Center is one of the finest art galleries in the entire state, boasting works from the best that the islands have to offer. A new facility on recently acquired land will soon allow the Volcano Art Center to expand and provide greater space for future projects.

CRATER RIM DRIVE

There are so many intriguing nooks and crannies to stop at along Crater Rim Drive that you'll have to force yourself to be picky if you intend to cover the park in one day. Crater Rim Drive is a circular route; it matters little which way you proceed. Take your choice, but the following sights are listed counterclockwise beginning from Kilauea Visitors Center. Your biggest problem will be timing your arrival at the "drive-in" sights to avoid the steady stream of tour buses.

Sulphur Banks
You can easily walk to Sulfur Banks from Volcano Art Center along a 10-minute trail. If you're driving, signs along Rim Drive direct you, and your nose will tell you when you're close. As you approach these fumaroles, the earth surrounding them turns a deep reddish-brown, covered over in yellowish-green sulfur. The rising steam is caused by surface water leaking into the cracks where it becomes heated and rises as vapor. Kilauea releases hundreds of tons of sulfur gases every day, with Sulfur Banks being an example. This gaseous activity stunts the growth of vegetation. And when atmospheric conditions create a low ceiling, the gases sometimes cause the eyes and nose to water. The area is best avoided by those with heart and lung conditions.

Steam Vents
Next you'll come to Steam Vents, which are also fumaroles, but without sulfur. The entire field behind the partitioned area steams. The feeling is like being in a sauna. There are no strong fumes to contend with here, just the tour buses. **Kilauea Military Camp** beyond the vent is not open to the public. The camp serves as an R&R facility for military personnel.

Hawaii Volcano Observatory
This observatory has been keeping tabs on the volcanic activity in the area since the turn of the century. The actual observatory is filled with

delicate seismic equipment and is closed to the public, but a lookout nearby gives you a dentist's view into the mouth of Halemaumau Crater ("House of Ferns"), Pele's home. Steam rises and you can feel the power, but until 1924 the view was even more phenomenally spectacular: a lake of molten lava. The lava has since sunk below the surface, which is now crusted over. Scientists do not predict a recurrence in the near future, but no one knows Pele's mind. This is a major stop for the tour buses, but a two-minute saunter along the hiking trail gives you the view to yourself. Information plaques in the immediate area tell of the history and volcanology of the park. One points out a spot from which to observe the perfect shield volcano form of Mauna Loa—most times too cloudy to see. Another reminds you that you're in the middle of the Pacific, an incredible detail you tend to forget when atop these mountains. Here too is Uwekahuna ("Wailing Priest") Bluff, where the *kahuna* made offerings of appeasement to Pele. A Hawaiian prayer commemorates their religious rites.

Thomas A. Jaggar Museum

This newest addition to the national park is located next door to the Hawaiian Volcano Observatory, and offers a fantastic multimedia display of the amazing geology and volcanology of the area. The state-of-the-art museum, complete with a miniseries of spectacular photos on movable walls, topographical maps, inspired paintings, and TV videos, is open daily 8:30 a.m.-5 p.m., admission free. The expert staff constantly upgrades the displays to keep the public informed on the newest eruptions. The 30-45 minutes that it takes to explore the teaching museum will enhance your understanding of the volcanic area immeasurably. Do yourself a favor and visit this museum before setting out on any explorations.

Moon Walks

A string of interesting stops follows the observatory. One points out the **Kau Desert,** an inhospitable site of red-earth plains studded with a few scraggly plants. Next comes the **Southwest Rift,** a series of cracks running from Kilauea's summit to the sea. You can observe at a glance that you are standing directly over a major earthquake fault. Dated lava flows follow

in rapid succession until you arrive at **Halemaumau Trail.** The well-maintained trail is only one-quarter mile long and gives you an up-close view of the crater. The area is rife with fumaroles and should be avoided by those with respiratory problems. At the end you're treated to a full explanation of Halemaumau. Farther along the road, a roped-off area was once an observation point that caved in. You won't take the ground under your feet for granted! Close by is **Keanakakoi,** a prehistoric quarry from which superior stone was gathered to make tools. It was destroyed by a flow in 1877. If that seems in the remote past, realize that you are now on a section of road that was naturally paved over with lava from a "quickie" eruption in 1982!

Most visitors hike along **Devastation Trail,** which could aptly be renamed "Regeneration Trail." The half mile it covers is fascinating, one of the most-photographed areas in the park. It leads across a field devastated by a tremendous eruption from **Kilauea Iki** ("Little Kilauea") in 1959, when fountains of lava shot 1,900 feet into the air. The area was once an ohia forest that was denuded of limbs and leaves, then choked by black pumice and ash. The vegetation has regenerated since then, and the recuperative power of the flora is part of an ongoing study. Blackberries, not indigenous to Hawaii, are slowly taking over. The good news is that you'll be able to pick and eat blackberries as you hike along the paved trail, but note that the rangers are waging a mighty war against them. Notice that many of the trees have sprouted aerial roots trailing down from the branches: this is total adaptation to the situation, as these roots don't normally appear. As you move farther along the trail, tufts of grass and bushes peek out of the pumice. Then the surroundings become totally barren and look like the nightmare of a nuclear holocaust.

Thurston Lava Tube

If the Devastation Trail produced a sense of melancholy, the Thurston Lava Tube makes you feel like Alice walking through the looking glass. Inside is a fairy kingdom. As you approach, the expected billboard gives you the lowdown on the geology and flora and fauna of the area. Take the five minutes to educate yourself. The paved trail starts as a steep incline which quickly enters a fern forest. All about you are fern trees, vibrantly green, with native birds flitting here and there. As you approach the lava tube, it seems almost manmade, like a perfectly formed tunnel leading into a mine. Ferns and moss hang from the entrance, and if you stand just inside the entrance looking out, it's as if the very air is tinged with green. If there were such things as elves and gnomes, they would surely live here. The walk through takes about 10 minutes, and the tube rolls and undulates through narrow passages and into large "rooms." At the other end, the fantasy world of ferns and moss reappears.

SMALL DETOURS

Volcano Village

You shouldn't miss taking a ride through the village of Volcano, a beautiful settlement with truly charming houses and cottages outlined in ferns. Tiny gravel roads lace the development, which sits virtually atop one of the world's undeniable "power spots." The area is so green and so vibrant that it appears surrealistic. With flowers, ferns, and trees everywhere, it is hard to imagine a more picturesque village in all of America. But even in this little parcel of paradise, things are changing, if slowly. The town now boasts two general stores, a TrueValue Hardware store, a small art gallery, a post office, a farmers' market, a winery, and several accommodations and restaurants along with the old standbys.

Volcano Golf and Country Club

What's most amazing about this course is where it is. Imagine! You're teeing off atop an active volcano surrounded by one of the last pristine forests in the state. At the right time of year, the surrounding ohia turn scarlet when they are in bloom. The fairways are carved from lava, while in the distance Mauna Loa looms. A poor shot, and you can watch your ball disappear down a steam vent. The course began about 70 years ago when a group of local golfers hand-cleared three "greens," placing stakes that served as holes. Later this was improved to sand greens with tin cans for holes, and after an eruption in 1924 blanketed the area with volcanic ash that served as excellent fertilizer, the grass grew and the course became a lush green. After WW II

the course was extended to 18 holes, and a clubhouse was added. Finally, Jack Snyder, a well-known course architect, redesigned the course to its present par-72, 6,180-yard layout. Rates are $50 with shared cart. To beat the heavy lunch crowd at Volcano House, try the restaurant at the course. The course is located just north of the Belt Road, about two miles west of the park entrance. Phone 967-7331 for more information.

Volcano Winery

About one mile beyond the golf course (after the road turns to dirt) and off to your left are the brown buildings of the Volcano Winery, tel. 967-7479, owned by Dr. Lynn McKinney, a retired veterinarian from Honolulu. It's a hands-on winery where everything is done manually, even the bottling and corking. About 3.4 acres of this rough countryside are currently under cultivation, producing about three tons of grape per acre, yielding about 10,000 gallons a year. Because the land is at an elevation of about 4,000 feet, the patented Symphony grape is grown to take best advantage of the climatic conditions, which are similar to those in Oregon and Washington. Bottled are dry and semi-dry wines, guava/Chablis and Jaboticaba/Chablis blends, a lehua honey wine, and a macadamia nut honey wine. A local favorite, the Jaboticaba blend is made with a Brazilian fruit of that name. Although no tours of the winery are available, a tasting room is open daily 10 a.m.-5 p.m. Have a sip at the glass-covered koa bar and maybe you'll want to purchase a bottle for later in the evening or a 12-bottle case to share with friends when you get home. There also is a small boutique on the premises selling T-shirts, jewelry, *kukui* nut leis, postcards, and other gift items.

Mauna Loa Road

About 2.5 miles west of the park entrance on the Belt Rd., Mauna Loa Rd. turns off to the north. This road will lead you to the Tree Molds and a bird sanctuary, as well as to the trailhead for the Mauna Loa summit trail. As an added incentive, a minute down this road leaves 90% of the tourists behind.

Tree Molds is an ordinary name for an extraordinary place. Turn off Mauna Loa Rd. soon after leaving the Belt Rd. and follow the signs for five minutes to a cul-de-sac. At the entrance, a billboard tries hard to dramatically explain what occurred here. In a moment, you realize that you're standing atop a lava flow, and that the scattered potholes are entombed tree trunks, most likely the remains of a once-giant koa forest. Unlike at Lava Tree State Monument, where the magma encased the tree and flowed away, the opposite action happened here. The lava stayed put while the tree trunk burned away, leaving 15-to 18-foot-deep holes.

Kipuka Puaulu is a sanctuary for birds and nature lovers who want to leave the crowds behind, just under two miles from Route 11 down Mauna Loa Road. The sanctuary is an island atop an island. A *kipuka* is a piece of land that is surrounded by lava but has not been inundated by it, leaving the original vegetation and land contour intact. A few hundred yards away, small scrub vegetation struggles, but in the sanctuary the trees form a towering canopy a hundred feet tall. The first sign for Bird Park takes you to an ideal picnic area; the second, 100 yards beyond, takes you to Kipuka Puaulu Loop Trail. As you enter the trail, a bulletin board describes the birds and plants, some of the last remaining indigenous fauna and flora in Hawaii. Please follow all rules. The trail is self guided, and pamphlets describing the stations along the way are dispensed from a box 50 feet down the path. The loop is only one mile long, but to really assimilate the area, especially if you plan to do any birdwatching, expect to spend an hour minimum. It doesn't take long to realize that you are privileged to see some of the world's rarest plants, such as a small, nondescript bush called *aalii.* In the branches of the towering ohia trees you might see an *elepaio* or an *apapane,* two birds native to Hawaii. Common finches and Japanese white eyes are imported birds that are here to stay. There's a fine example of a lava tube, and an explanation of how ash from eruptions provided soil and nutrients for the forest. Blue morning glories have taken over entire hillsides. Once considered a pest and aggressively eradicated, they have recently been given a reprieve and are now considered good ground cover—perhaps even indigenous. When you do come across a native Hawaiian plant, it seems somehow older, almost prehistoric. If a pre-contact Hawaiian could come back today, he or she would recognize only a few plants and trees

even here in this preserve. More than four times as many plants and animals have become extinct in Hawaii in the last 200 years as on the entire North American continent. As you leave, listen for the melodies coming from the treetops, and hope the day never comes when no birds sing.

Mauna Loa Rd. continues westward and gains elevation for approximately 10 miles. At the end of the pavement, at 6,662 feet, you find a parking area and lookout. A trail leads from here to the summit of Mauna Loa. It takes three to four days to hike. Under no circumstances should it be attempted by novice hikers or those unprepared for cold alpine conditions.

Olaa Track

Off Route 11 close to Volcano village, turn on Wright Rd. (or County Rd. 148) heading toward Mauna Loa (on a clear morning you can see Mauna Kea). Continue for approximately three miles until you see a barbed-wire fence. The fence is distinctive because along it you'll see a profusion of *hapu'u* ferns which are in sharp contrast to the adjacent property. Here is an *ola'a* rainforest, part of the national park and open to the public, although park scientists like to keep it quiet. Be aware that the area is laced with lava tubes. Most are small ankle twisters, but others can open up under you like a glacial crevasse. Here is a true example of a quickly disappearing native forest. What's beautiful about an endemic forest is that virtually all species coexist wonderfully. The ground cover is a rich mulch of decomposing ferns and leaves, fragrant and amazingly soft. This walk is for the intrepid hiker or naturalist who is fascinated by Hawaii's unique foliage.

Remember, trails in this section of the park are poorly marked and quite confusing. You can get lost, and if no one knows that you're in there, it could be life threatening. Also, be aware that you may be trampling native species and could be inadvertently introducing alien species. The park service is trying to bring the area back to its native Hawaiian rainforest condition through eradication of alien plants and elimination of feral pigs.

Kau Desert Trail

Kau Desert Trail starts about eight miles south of the visitor center along Route 11, between mile markers 37 and 38. It's a short hike from the trailhead to the **Kau Desert Footprints.** People going to or from Kailua-Kona can see them en route, but those staying in Hilo should take the time to visit the footprints. The trek across the small section of desert is fascinating, and the history of the footprints makes the experience more evocative. The trail is only 1.6 miles roundtrip and can be hustled along in less than 30 minutes, but allow at least an hour, mostly for observation. The predominant foliage is a red bottlebrush that contrasts with the bleak surroundings—the feeling throughout the area is one of foreboding. You pass a wasteland of a'a and pahoehoe lava flows to arrive at the footprints. A metal fence in a sturdy pavilion surrounds the prints, that look as though they're cast in cement. Actually they're formed from pisolites: particles of ash stuck together with moisture, which formed mud that hardened like plaster.

In 1790 Kamehameha was waging war with Keoua over control of the Big Island. One of Keoua's warrior parties of approximately 80 people attempted to cross the desert while Kilauea was erupting. Toxic gases descended upon them and the warriors and their families were enveloped and suffocated. They literally died in their tracks, but the preserved footprints, although romanticism would wish otherwise, were probably made by a party of people who came well after the eruption. This unfortunate occurrence was regarded by the Hawaiians as a direct message from the gods proclaiming their support for Kamehameha. Keoua, who could not deny the sacred signs, felt abandoned and shortly thereafter became a human sacrifice at Puukohola Heiau, built by Kamehameha to honor his war god, Kukailimoku.

CHAIN OF CRATERS ROAD

The Chain of Craters Road that once linked Volcanoes National Park with Kalapana village on the east coast has been severed by an enormous lava flow, and can only be driven from Volcanoes down to where the flow crosses the road near the now-inundated and inaccessible Kamoamoa Campground. Remember that the volcanic activity in this area is unpredictable, and that the road can be closed at a moment's notice. Flying volcanic ash, mixed with the frequent drizzle, can be as slippery as ice. As you head down the road, every bend—and they are uncountable—offers a panoramic vista. There are dozens of pulloffs, many of which have names, like Naulu ("Sea Orchards"); plaques provide geological information about past eruptions and lava flows. The grandeur, power, and immensity of the forces that have been creating the earth from the beginning of time are right before your eyes. The lower part of the road is spectacular. Here, blacker-than-black seacliffs, covered by a thin layer of green, abruptly stop at the sea. The surf rolls in, sending up spumes of seawater. In the distance, steam billows into the air where the lava flows into the sea. At road's end you will find a barricade staffed by park rangers. Heed their warnings. The drive from atop the volcano to the barricade takes about 30 minutes. If you are going in the evening, when the spectacle is more apparent, bring a flashlight. When rangers

are there, they will escort you onto the flow, giving an interpretive talk as you walk along. To experience the lava flow from the Kalapana side, see "Kaimu and Kalapana" under "Route 130 and the Southeast Coast" in the Puna chapter.

When the road almost reaches the coast, look for a roadside marker that indicates the **Kau Puna Trail.** Just across the road is the **Pu'u Loa Petroglyph Field.** The Kau Puna Trail leads you along the coast, where you can find shelters at Keauhou and Halape. Rain catchment tanks provide drinking water. All campers must register at the Kilauea Visitors Center. In 1975 an earthquake rocked the area, generating a tidal wave that killed two campers; more than 30 others had to be helicoptered to safety. Only registering will alert authorities to your whereabouts in case of a disaster. A number of trails cross in this area and you can take them back up to Chain of Craters Road or continue on a real expedition through the Kau Desert. The Kau Puna Trail requires full trekking and camping gear.

Pu'u Loa Petroglyphs
The walk out to Pu'u Loa Petroglyphs is delightful and highly educational, and only takes one hour. The trail, although it traverses solid lava, is discernible. The tread of feet over the centuries has discolored the rock. As you walk

J.D. BISIGNANI

petroglyphs

along, note the *ahu,* traditional trail markers that are piles of stone shaped like little Christmas trees. Most of the lava field leading to the petroglyphs is undulating pa'hoehoe and looks like a frozen sea. You can climb bumps of lava, from eight to 10 feet high, to scout the immediate territory. Mountainside, the *pali* is quite visible and you can pick out the most recent lava flows—the blackest and least vegetated. As you approach the site, the lava changes dramatically and looks like long strands of braided rope.

The petroglyphs are in an area about the size of a soccer field. A wooden walkway encircles them and ensures their protection. A common motif of the petroglyphs is a circle with a hole in the middle, like a donut; you'll also see designs of men with triangular-shaped heads. Some rocks are entirely covered with designs while others have only a symbolic scratch or two. If you stand on the walkway and trek off at the two o'clock position, you'll see a small hill. Go over and down it, and you will discover even better petroglyphs that include a sailing canoe about two feet high. At the back end of the walkway a sign proclaims that Pu'u Loa meant "Long Hill," which the Hawaiians turned into the euphemism "Long Life." For countless generations, fathers would come here to place pieces of their infants' umbilical cords into small holes as offerings to the gods to grant long life to their children. Concentric circles were surrounded by the holes that held the umbilical cords. The entire area, an obvious power spot, screams in utter silence, and the still-strong mana is easi-ly felt. The Big Island has the largest concentration of this ancient art form in the state.

Waha'ula Heiau

Waha'ula Heiau, "Temple of the Red Mouth," radically changed the rituals and practices of the relatively benign Hawaiian religion by introducing the idea of human sacrifice. The 13th century marked the end of the frequent comings and goings between Hawaii and the "Lands to the South" (Tahiti), and began the isolation which would last 500 years until Captain Cook arrived. Unfortunately, this last influx of Polynesians brought a rash of conquering warriors carrying ferocious gods who lusted for human blood before they would be appeased. Paao, a powerful Tahitian priest, supervised the building of Waha'ula and brought in a new chief, Pili, to strengthen the diminished mana of the Hawaiian chiefs due to their practice of intermarriage with commoners. Waha'ula became the foremost *luakini* (human sacrifice) temple in the island kingdom and held this position until the demise of the old ways in 1819. Not at all grandiose, the *heiau* was merely an elevated rock platform smoothed over with pebbles.

Note: This entire area is now completely inundated by recent lava flows. Until 1997, the *heiau* itself was a small island in a sea of black lava that miraculously escaped destruction, but in August of that year lava oozed over these 700-year-old walls and filled the compound. Madame Pele has taken back her own.

PRACTICALITIES

CAMPING AND HIKING

Campgrounds and Cabins

The main campground in Volcanoes, **Namakani Paio,** clearly marked off Route 11, is situated in a stately eucalyptus grove. There is no charge for tent camping and no reservations are required. A cooking pavilion has fireplaces, but no wood or drinking water are provided. Also, there are no shower facilities for those camping and hiking within the park, so make sure that you're with people that like you a whole bunch. **Cabins** are available through Volcano House. Each accommodates four people and costs $35 s/d, $8 additional person. A $10 refundable key deposit gives access to the shower and toilet; and a $5 refundable deposit gets you linens, soap, towels, and a blanket (extra sleeping bag recommended). Each cabin contains one double bed and two single bunk beds and an electric light, but no electrical outlets. Outside are a picnic table and barbecue grill but you must provide your own charcoal and cooking utensils. Check in at Volcano House at 3 p.m. and check out by noon.

For backcountry overnight camping, apply at the Kilauea Visitors Center (7:45 a.m.-4:45 p.m.) for a free permit no earlier than the day before you plan to hike

Hiking

The slopes of Mauna Loa and HVNP are a trekker's paradise. You'll find trails that last for days or for an hour or two. Many have shelters, and those trails that require overnight stays provide cabins. Because of the possibility of an eruption or earthquake, it is *imperative* to check in at park headquarters, where you can also pick up current trail info. and maps.

The 18-mile hike to the summit of **Mauna Loa** (13,679 feet) is the most grueling. The trailhead is at the lookout at the end of the pavement of Mauna Loa Road. Hikers in excellent condition can make the summit (RT) in three days, but four would be more comfortable. There is a considerable elevation gain so expect freezing weather even in summer, and snow in winter. Altitude

sickness can also be a problem. En route you pass through *nene* country, with a good chance to spot these lava-adapted geese. Fences keep out feral goats, so remember to close gates after you. The first cabin is at Red Hill (10,035 feet) and the second is on the rim of Moku'aweoweo Crater (13,250 feet). Water is from roof catchment and should be boiled. The summit treats you to a sweeping panorama that includes Haleakala. Mauna Loa's Moku'aweoweo Caldera is over three miles long and has vertical walls towering 600 feet. From November to May, if there is snow, steam rises from the caldera.

The **Crater Rim Loop Trail** begins at park headquarters and follows Crater Rim Dr., crossing back and forth a number of times. Hiking the entire 11 miles takes a full day, but you can take it in sections as time and energy permit. It's a well-marked and maintained trail; all you need are warm clothing, water, and determination. For your efforts, you'll get an up-close view of all of the sights outlined along Crater Rim Drive.

Kilauea Iki Trail begins at the Thurston Lava Tube, or at park headquarters via the Waldron Ledge Trail. This four-mile trail generally takes 3-4 hours as it passes through the center of Kilauea Iki Caldera. It's easy to link up with the Byron Ledge Trail or with the Halemaumau Trail. You can return north to park headquarters or continue on either of these two trails to the Halemaumau parking area directly south of park headquarters.

Halemaumau Trail provides the best scenery for the effort. It begins at park headquarters and descends into Kilauea Caldera, covering seven miles there and back (five hours). If possible, arrange to be picked up at the Halemaumau parking area due south of park headquarters.

ACCOMMODATIONS, FOOD, AND SHOPPING

If you intend to spend the night atop Kilauea, your choices of accommodations are few and simple. Volcano House provides the only hotel, but cabins are available at the campgrounds, there are plenty of tenting sites, and there is a wonderful assortment of bed and breakfasts.

Volcano House

If you decide to lodge at Volcano House, P.O. Box 53, Hawaii Volcanoes National Park, HI 96718, tel. 967-7321 or (800) 325-3535, don't be frightened away by the daytime crowds. They disappear with the sun. Then Volcano House metamorphoses into what it has always been: a quiet country inn. The 42 rooms are comfy but old-fashioned. Who needs a pool or TV when you can look out your window into a volcano caldera? To the left of the reception area indoors, a crackling fireplace warms you from the chill in the mountain air. In front of the fireplace are stuffed leather chairs and a wonderful wooden rocker. One wall in the inn displays paintings and vintage photographs of the Hawaiian kings and queens of the Kamehameha line, while another wall holds magnificent photos of eruptions of the mountain. The management problems that afflicted the hotel over the past several years seem to have abated with the new owner and operator, Ken Fujiama. Although privately owned, it is the park service that sets the standards and pricing for the rooms. Room rates are: main building with crater view $131, noncrater view $105, Ohia Wing noncrater view $79, $10 additional person. No charge for children under 12 occupying the same room as their parents. Rooms include koa wood furniture, Hawaiian comforters, telephone, heater, and private bath and shower. Efficiently run, the hotel has a restaurant, lounge, shops, 24-hour front desk service, maid service, safety deposit boxes, city bus service, and fax machines. Besides that, you could hardly get closer to the crater if you tried.

Kilauea Military Camp

One mile west of the park entrance, within the park boundary, is the Kilauea Military Camp. Offering rooms and meals, this facility is only open to active duty and retired military personnel, civilian employees of the Department of Defense, and their families. Call 967-7315 for information and availability.

Kilauea Lodge

This superb addition to the Volcano area, P.O. Box 116, Volcano Village, HI 96785, tel. 967-7366, fax 967-7367, owned and operated by Lorna Larsen-Jeyte and Albert Jeyte, is the premier restaurant and lodge atop Volcano, as well as one of the very best on the island. The solid stone and timber structure was built in 1938 as a YMCA camp and functioned as such until 1962, when it became a "mom and pop operation," often failing and changing ownership. It faded into the ferns until Lorna and Albert revitalized it in 1987, opening in 1988. The lodge is a classic, with a vaulted, open-beamed ceiling. A warm and cozy "international fireplace" dating from the days of the YMCA camp is embedded with stones and plaques from all over the world, along with coins from countries such as Malaysia, Japan, Singapore, Australia, New Zealand, Finland, Germany, and Italy, to name a few.

Kilauea Lodge is an exquisite inn with an assortment of rooms ranging $105-195, including a complete breakfast for all guests. The architect, Virginia McDonald, a Volcano resident, worked magic in transforming the brooding rooms of the original section into bright, comfortable, and romantic suites. Each bathroom, with vaulted 18-foot ceilings, has a skylight. The sink and grooming area is one piece of Corian with a light built into it, so that the entire sink area glows. The rooms, all differently appointed, range in decor from Hawaiian-European to Asian with a motif of Japanese fans. Almost every room has original artwork by Gwendolyn O'Connor. Each has a working fireplace, queen-size bed, and swivel rocking chair. A separate one-bedroom cottage, set in the ferns at the back of the lodge, features a wood-burning stove (central heat too), wet bar, a queen-size bed, private bath with Jacuzzi, and small living room with queen-size pull-out sofa. In 1991, Kilauea Lodge opened seven new units centered around a commodious common room where you can read and snooze by a crackling fire. All rooms in the new section are tastefully furnished with wicker furniture, white curtains, vaulted ceilings, oak trim, Japanese and Hawaiian art prints, and fluffy quilts to keep off the evening chill. The Kilauea Lodge provides one of the most *civilized* atmospheres in Hawaii in one of its most powerful natural areas. The combination is hard to beat. E-mail: k-lodge@aloha.net.

Tutu's Place

Just up the road from the Kilauea Lodge is the

cute little two-bedroom cottage, Tutu's Place. Built in 1929 by the Uncle Billy of hotel chain fame for "tutu" (grandma), it was bought several decades later by the Warner family. Mr. Warner was a minister and was involved in Hawaiian politics. His wife, Ruth Warner, lived in the cottage for 30 years until in was bought in 1995 by Lorna Larson-Jeyte, the owner of the Kilauea Lodge. Although it's been completely refurbished, people in the know say that the cottage is still imbued with the spirit of Ruth Warner. It's done in a theme of rattan and koa, with a fireplace in the living room, a full kitchen, and a wonderful little bathroom. The rate is $135 for two people, including breakfast at the Kilauea Lodge; $15 for each additional person. To make reservations, call the Kilauea Lodge, tel. 967-7366, and ask for Tutu's Place.

Bonnie Goodell's Guest House

This very friendly hideaway, P.O. Box 6, Volcano, HI 96785, tel. 967-7775, is on the back roads of Volcano Village. The fully furnished house is designed as a self-sufficient unit where the guests are guaranteed peace and quiet on a lovely six-acre homesite. Bonnie grew up in Hawaii and was for many years the education director for the Honolulu Botanic Gardens. She *knows* her plants and is willing to chat with her guests. The place is particularly good for families. Children have plenty of room to play, while their parents can roam the orchards on the property. Bonnie and her husband have cut a two-mile long path from here to the Thurston lava tube, and if she has time, Bonnie may give you an interpretive tour describing the flora and fauna of the area. The two-story guest home is bright and airy. Enter into a combo living room, kitchen, and dining area with a large bathroom off to the right. Upstairs is a sleeping area with two twin beds and a queen-size fold-out bed; downstairs is another fold-out bed. Futons can sleep even more. Another cottage, smaller but more luxurious and wheelchair-accessible, is designed for honeymoon couples who want to be alone. The rate is $60 d, $10 for each additional person (off-season rates available). Sometimes Bonnie will allow an emergency one-night stay if the house is not booked, but she charges $10 extra because the entire house has to be cleaned.

Hale Ohia Cottages

Follow a private mountain lane for a few minutes into an enchanted clearing where the artwork of a meticulous Japanese garden surrounds a New England gabled-and-turreted home and its attendant cottages of red-on-brown rough-cut shingles. Once the hideaway of the Dillinghams, an old and influential *kama'aina* family, Hale Ohia, P.O. Box 758, Volcano Village, HI 96785, tel. 967-7986 or (800) 455-3803, fax 967-8610, is now owned and operated by Michael D. Tuttle, who recently purchased the property after falling hopelessly in love at first sight. The main house holds the Dillingham Suite ($85), with its own sitting room, bath, and glass-covered lanai. Simple and clean, with hardwood floors and wainscoted walls, the home is the epitome of country elegance, Hawaiian style. E-mail: haleohia@bigisland.com.

Hale Ohia, once the gardener's cottage, has two stories, with the bottom floor occupied by the Iiwi ($60) and Camellia ($75) suites, which are wheelchair-accessible and can be combined for larger groups ($85). Stained-glass windows with a calla lily-and-poppy motif add a special touch, while the low ceilings are reminiscent of the captain's quarters on a sailing ship. The first floor has a full kitchen and a covered lanai complete with barbecue grill that makes it perfect for evening relaxation. Narrow stairs lead to a full bath located on the first landing, from where you get a sweeping view of the grounds while performing your morning meditation. Upstairs opens into a bright and airy parlor and adjacent bedrooms that can sleep five comfortably.

Hale Lehua, once a private study, is secluded down its own lava footpath. Enter to find a wall of windows framing the green-on-green grounds. The interior is cozy with its own fireplace, bamboo and wicker furniture, self-contained bathroom, covered lanai, and partial kitchen with microwave, toaster, and refrigerator. Hale features a skylight, fireplace, and leaded glass windows through which the surrounding fern forest will emit its emerald radiance.

To make your stay even more delightful, room rates include an "extended" continental breakfast, and guests are welcome to immerse themselves in the bubbling Jacuzzi that awaits you under a canopy of Japanese cedars and glimmering stars.

Hale Ohia

J.D. BISIGNANI

Chalet Kilauea

Peeking from the *hapuu* fern forest in a manicured glen is Chalet Kilauea, P.O. Box 998, Volcano Village, HI 96785, tel. 967-7786, (800) 937-7786, where you will be cordially accommodated by owners Lisha and Brian Crawford. Enter the second level of the main house to find a guest living room where you can while away the hours playing chess, listening to a large collection of CDs, or gazing from the wraparound windows at a treetop view of the surrounding forest, ferns, and impeccable grounds. Just out the door, a make-over of a one-time Japanese *ofuro* resulted in an ornamental plant holder. Downstairs is an outdoor lounge area, and a black-and-white checkerboard dining room where wrought-iron tables sit before a huge picture window. On the lawn, a free-standing gazebo houses an eight-person Jacuzzi hot tub available 24-hours a day. Breakfasts (changeable daily), friendly and relaxed but with formal table settings, are remarkable: lox and bagels, fresh Volcano onions and tomatoes, macadamia nut or banana pancakes with strawberry topping, fresh papaya and squeezed juices, and Brian's own house blend Kona coffee with a hint of cinnamon. (E-mail: bchawaii@aol.com.)

The main house holds three suites and two additional rooms, $135-295. The Oriental Jade Room is richly appointed with Chinese folding screens, samurai murals, Oriental carpet, and jade-green bedspread. The green marble bathroom embellishes the green theme of the surrounding vegetation. Plush terry cloth robes are available for all guests. The lanai outside is shared with the Out of Africa Room, which has a strong color theme of burgundy and brass. The Continental Lei Suite is fluff and lace, the bridal suite. Here the colors are white, gold, and pink; a wedding dress hangs in the corner to accentuate the theme. Located on the first floor, the Owners Suite is designed for up to three people. Pink carpet covers the floor and a green floral spread covers the bed. With two shower heads in the shower stall, you can be happy showering together. Connected by a deck to the main house is the Treehouse Suite, a two-story unit with bath, sitting room, wet bar, and kitchenette downstairs, and a large bedroom on the upper floor. The surrounding glass makes the living forest part of the decor. A private lanai overlooks the garden, and a handcrafted wooden circular staircase connects the two floors.

Brian and Lisha have six other properties in and around Volcano ranging $95-225, including the Hide-a-way Cottage, Ginger House, and the Lodge at Volcano (big enough for a small business group). Give them a call and they will provide all the details. They also own and operate **Volcano Reservations,** a B&B reservation service with guest homes available statewide.

Hale Kilauea

Green pines and native ohia shade Hale Kilauea, P.O. Box 28, Volcano, HI 96785, tel. 967-7591, owned and operated by Maurice Thomas. In the main lodge, a central common room is very comfortable with reading materials, fireplace, parlor games, and TV. The spacious and airy rooms in the main lodge, $65-85 d, $20 extra person, all with private baths, are comfortable but not luxurious. Upstairs rooms are more deluxe with plush carpeting, knotty pine trim, refrigerator, small divan, and private lanai. Ask for a room in the rear so that you can overlook the quiet green forest instead of the parking area. Two rooms across from the main building are warm and cozy, although quite small. They are private and the least expensive at $55. The best deal, however, is a refurbished plantation cottage that sits across the road. The rate is $85 d, with special weekly and monthly rates. The wainscoted cottage provides a small but serviceable kitchen, separate bedroom, and living room that can sleep a few more. Don't expect luxury, but a night in the cottage is a window into Hawaii's past of humble workers in humble homes. With all the rooms, including the cottage, a hearty breakfast of hot and cold cereals, various breads, cheeses, plump sausages, and occasionally quiche, waffles, or pancakes is provided.

Lokahi Lodge
Built in 1992 specifically as a B&B by Patrick Dixon and Danny DiCastro, Lokahi Lodge, P.O. Box 7, Volcano, HI 96785, tel. 985-8647 (on Oahu, Maui and Kauai tel. 922-6597 or 800-457-6924), offers quiet country comfort. A rocking-chair veranda, perfect for keeping off sun and showers, completely surrounds the spacious ranch house. In the common sitting room (with 16-foot vaulted ceilings), you can relax on overstuffed couches and chairs while warming yourself in front of a red enameled free-standing stove. An old-fashioned, crank-handled telephone hangs on the wall, and an ensemble of organ, piano, and harp awaits anyone inclined to make their own music. A continental breakfast of homemade banana bread, fresh papaya and pineapple, fruit juices, jams, jellies, coffee, and tea assortment is offered at a huge banquet table surrounded by high-backed chairs. The stardust-speckled hallway is lined with vintage lei that have been collected by owner Danny DiCastro, a famous hula dancer. Rooms, $65 d, $15 extra person, are triple-insulated for guaranteed quiet, are fully carpeted, offer large clos-

ets, and have differing decor—for example, billowy paisley curtains and bedspreads with matching wallpaper. Comfortable furniture for private relaxation, tasteful oil prints, and bathrooms with tub, shower, and pedestal sink complete the rooms. For the most privacy request the "yellow or blue rooms" at the far end of the hallway. Each room has a private entrance leading onto the veranda, so that you may come and go without disturbing anyone. Lokahi Lodge definitely lives up to its name, which translates as "peace and harmony."

Carson's Volcano Cottages
Deep in the fern forest, Carson's Volcano Cottages, P.O. Box 503, Volcano, HI 96785, tel. 967-7683 or (800) 845-LAVA, fax. 967-8094, owned and operated by Tom and Brenda Carson, offers four B&B rooms, one in its own studio cottage, and the others in a three-room cottage. The accommodations all have private baths, entrances, and decks, and there's a hot tub for use by everyone on the deck of the main house. Two of the rooms have kitchens. The one-acre property is naturally landscaped with ohia and fern, while moss-covered sculptures of Balinese gods peek through the foliage. The studio cottage, $95 d, a miniature plantation house with corrugated roof, has a kitchen and a bath with a skylight. Appointed with fluffy pillows and downy quilts, this would be a perfect rendezvous for a "Victorian lady" and her paramour. The three-room cottage, $75-85 d per room, has vaulted ceilings, beds with wooden headboards, wicker furniture, and vintage photos on the walls. In one room, the crocheted bedspreads are helped by electric blankets, while a free-standing credenza from the '30s adds a touch of charm. Leaded glass windows open to a private porch. Another room, all in pink, also with its own vaulted ceiling and free-standing wardrobe, is appointed with vintage kitsch bric-a-brac like hula dancer glasses and lamps. A retired "lady of the evening" could easily relive memories in this room. Finally, the Oriental Room, striking in black and white, features Balinese masks and a Japanese doll mural. Located at the side of the cottage, this room has a more private entrance and a tiny kitchenette. Tom and Brenda provide an extended continental breakfast that might include banana bread, French toast, passion fruit juice, bagels and lox, or strawberry crepes. The Carsons also

rent out another home in the Volcano Village area called Koa Halei; it starts at $125. The house has two queen-size beds and is appointed in '30s and '40s vintage Hawaiian style. You'll be comfortable in front of the living room fireplace; or enjoy the evening sky from the hot tub on the back porch. E-mail: carsons@aloha.net; Web site: www.carsonscottage.com.

Other Lodging

A B&B with an excellent reputation is **My Island**, P.O. Box 100, Volcano, HI 96785, tel. 967-7216, fax. 967-7719. Rates range from a very reasonable $30 s with shared bath to $60 for a double with private bath, and there's even a private studio. E-mail: myisland@ilhawaii.net; Web site: ilhawaii.net/bnb/myisland.

Victoria Rose, a one-room B&B, tel. 967-8026, owned and operated by Lisa Farmer, is a fancy jewelry box done in maroon, pink, and lace, lots of lace. A four-poster "pineapple" bed and a private bath ensure privacy and comfort.

Volcano Country Cottages, P.O. Box 545, Volcano, HI 96785, tel. 967-7960 or (800) 967-7960, is another convenient place to try. Available are the Ohelo Berry studio cottage for $75 a night and the two-bedroom Artist's House for $120. Contact Kathleen Ing for information, reservations, and directions. E-mail: vccbnb@aloha.net.

Bed & Breakfast Mountain View, in the village of Mountain View, P.O. Box 963, Kurtistown, HI 96720, tel. 968-6868, fax 968-7017, is owned by Jane and Linus Chao, both accomplished artists. They offer rooms priced $55-75, all with private bath, TV and VCR, along with a hearty breakfast prepared and served in the family art gallery. The couple's inspired artwork graces the home. E-mail: info@bbmtview.com; Web site: www.bbmtview.com.

Located on 22 acres of macadamia nut and tropical fruit orchards, with views over Hilo and the ocean and the 120-foot Kulaniapia Waterfall on the property, is **The Inn at Kulaniapia.** This recently built B&B features large suites with private tiled baths and covered balconies. Private and serene, it's conveniently located near both Hilo and the lowlands and the upcountry volcano area. An introductory rate of $99 for double occupancy (with $25 for each additional adult up to four) is good until June 1998, after which the rates jump to $135-165 per couple. Call for reservations at 966-6373; or write The Inn at Kulaniapia at P.O. Box 204, Kurtistown, HI 96762. E-mail: waterfalls@prodigy.net.

Food

The **Kilauea Lodge Restaurant,** open for dinner 5:30-9 p.m. nightly, reservations a must, is an extraordinary restaurant serving gourmet continental cuisine at reasonable prices. Choose a seat below the neo-Victorian windows or at a table from which you can view the vibrant green ferns and manicured trees of the grounds. A very friendly and professional staff serves the excellent food prepared by Albert, and starts you off with a fresh "loafette" studded like their fireplace, but with sunflowers and sesame seeds. Appetizers such as mushroom caps stuffed with crab and cheese will titillate your palate. Entrees, ranging $13-26, include soup, salad, and vegetables. Vegetarians will be delighted with a stew of Mediterranean vegetables served atop fettuccine at $13.50, while shrimp tempura at $18.50 adds an Asian touch. Dinner features seafood Mauna Kea (succulent pieces of seafood served atop a bed of fettuccine) and paupiettes of beef (prime rib slices rolled around herbs and mushrooms in a special sauce), both for under $20. Always a great choice, the catch-of-the-day is baked, broiled, or sautéed with a savory sauce. Desserts are wonderful, and the meal is topped off with a cup of Irish or Italian coffee.

Volcano House Restaurant offers a breakfast buffet, $9.50 pp, $5.50 for children ages 2-11, daily 7-10:30 a.m., with hot and cold cereals, assorted juices, pancakes topped with fruit and macadamia nuts, sweet bread French toast, scrambled eggs, bacon, chili links, and Portuguese sausage. A lighter continental breakfast is $5.50. The lunch buffet ($12.50 adult, $7.50 child, served daily 11 a.m.-2 p.m.), often terribly crowded because of the tour buses, offers tossed greens and assorted vegetables, fresh fruit platters, stuffed mahimahi, teriyaki beef, pot roast, honey-dipped chicken, rolls and butter, soft drinks, coffee, and tea. Dinner nightly, 5:30-9 p.m., starts with appetizers like sautéed mushrooms $6.50 and fruit platter $8.50. It moves on to entrees like seafood linguine $18.50, roast prime rib $19.95, and Volcano House scampi $17.50. For the vegetarian, a steamed vegetable platter goes for $9.50. A child's menu is also available with dishes under $7.50.

The quality is fair and the prices reasonable; however, the lunchtime buffet is overwhelmingly crowded and should be avoided if possible.

You can get away from the crowds and have a satisfying meal at **Volcano Country Club Restaurant** at Volcano Golf Course. The green and white interior complements the fairways, which can be seen through the surrounding plate glass windows. The cuisine is quite good. Complete breakfast is served daily 7-10 a.m., a full lunch menu daily 10:30 a.m.-2:30 p.m., and light snacks and *pu pu* until 5 p.m. For breakfast choose from mahimahi and eggs for $6, Hawaiian stew with chunks of beef and vegetables for $7.25, or a short stack of pancakes for $4.75. Lunch selections include hearty ham, tuna, turkey, or chicken sandwiches for $6.25 and under ($7.75 when combined with a bowl of soup); clubhouse sandwich for $8.50; or burgers with trimmings for around $7.50. There is also a good selection of local favorites like loco moco or chili with rice for $7.25 and under. The bar is well stocked, serving name-brand liquor, exotic drinks, and beer and wine. Next to the Kilauea Lodge, this is the best place for lunch in the area.

Other Food and Shopping

If you are after an exquisite piece of art, a unique memento, or an inexpensive but distinctive souvenir, be sure to visit the **Volcano Art Center.**

A **farmers' market** open 8:30 a.m.-11 p.m. every Sunday of the month sells local produce, baked goods, used books, and other used items. It's located at the Cooper Center.

Volcano Store, tel. 967-7210, open 5 a.m.-7 p.m. daily, is in the middle of Volcano village and sells gasoline, film, a few camping supplies, and a good selection of basic foods. In front are a few **telephone booths,** and just next door is a full-service **post office.**

On the porch of Volcano Store is a window-service restaurant called **Ali Bakery,** open Mon.-Thurs. 8 a.m.-4:30 p.m., Fri.-Sat. until 5 p.m., Sunday until 4 p.m., with seating available. Breakfasts are everything from coffee and a sweet roll to ham and eggs for $3.95 to pancake and link sausage for $5.50. Lunches are burgers and fries for around $3, an assortment of plate lunches for under $6, or beef stew and rice for $4.95.

Just down the road, **Kilauea General Store,** open 6 a.m.-7:30 p.m., Sunday 6:30 a.m.-6:30 p.m., also sells gas, and although it is not as well stocked as a grocery, it does have a deli case, a good stock of beer and liquor, and an excellent community bulletin board.

BOB RACE

KAU

The Kau District is as simple and straightforward as the broad, open face of a country gentleman. It's not boring, and it does hold pleasant surprises for those willing to look. Formed entirely from the massive slopes of Mauna Loa, the district presents some of the most ecologically diverse land in the islands. The bulk of it stretches 50 miles from north to south and almost 40 miles from east to west, tumbling from the snowcapped mountain through the cool green canopy of highland forests. At lower elevations it becomes pastureland of belly-deep grass ending in blistering-hot black sands along the coast that are encircled by a necklace of foamy white sea. At the bottom of Kau is **Ka Lae** ("South Point"), the southernmost tip of Hawaii and the southernmost point in the U.S. It lies at a latitude 500 miles farther south than Miami and twice that below Los Angeles. Ka Lae was probably the first landfall made by the Polynesian explorers on the islands. A variety of archaeological remains supports this belief.

Most people dash through Kau on the Hawaii Belt Road, heading to or from Volcanoes National Park. Its main towns, **Pahala** and **Naalehu,** are little more than pit stops. The Belt Road

follows the old Mamalahoa Trail where, for centuries, nothing moved faster than a contented man's stroll. Kau's beauties, mostly tucked away down secondary roads, are hardly given a look by most unknowing visitors. If you take the time and get off the beaten track, you'll discover black- and green-sand beaches, the world's largest macadamia nut farm, Wild West rodeos, and an electricity farm sprouting windmill generators. The upper slopes and broad pasturelands are the domain of hunters, hikers, and *paniolo,* who still ride the range on sure-footed horses. In Kau are sleepy plantation towns that don't even know how quaint they are, and beach parks where you can count on finding a secluded spot to pitch a tent. Time in Kau moves slowly, and *aloha* still forms the basis of day-to-day life.

The majority of Kau's pleasures are accessible by standard rental car, but many secluded coastal spots can be reached only by 4WD. For example, **Kailiki,** just west of Ka Lae, was an important fishing village in times past. A few archaeological remains are found here, and the beach has a green cast due to the lava's high olivine content. Few tourists ever visit; only hardy fishermen come here to angle the coastal waters. Spots of this type abound, especially in Kau's remote sections. But civilization has found Kau as well: when you pass mile marker 63, look down to the coast and notice a stand of royal palms and a large brackish pond. This is Luahinivai Beach, one of the finest on the island, where country and western star Loretta Lynn has built a fabulous home. Those willing to abandon their cars and to hike the sparsely populated coast or interior of Kau are rewarded with areas unchanged and untouched for generations.

SIGHTS AND BEACHES

PAHALA

Some 22 miles west of Volcano is Pahala, clearly marked off Route 11. The Hawaii Belt Road flashes past this town, but if you drive into it, heading for the tall stack of the Kau Sugar Co., you'll find one of the best-preserved examples of a classic sugar town in the islands. It was once gospel that sugar would be "king" in these parts forever, but the huge stone stack of the sugar mill puffs no longer, while in the background the whir of a modern macadamia nut-processing plant breaks the stillness.

In Pahala you'll find the basics like a gas station, small shopping center, post office, Bank of Hawaii, Mizuno's Superette, and takeout plate lunch restaurant.

Wood Valley Temple
Also known as **Nechung Dorje Drayang Ling,** "Island of Melodious Sound," the Wood Valley Temple, P.O. Box 250, Pahala, HI 96777, tel. 928-8539, is true to its name. This Tibetan Buddhist temple sits like a sparkling jewel surrounded by the emerald-green velvet of its manicured grounds that are scented by an aromatic stand of majestic eucalyptus trees. Here Marya and Miguel, the caretakers and administrators, will greet you if they are not off on one of their frequent trips to Asia.

Note: Recently, sightseers have been coming to the temple, and although most respect the fact that it functions as a spiritual retreat center, a few have not. Marya and Miguel are very warm and open-hearted people who welcome all guests, but they have requested that directions not be given to the general public. If you wish to spend time at Wood Valley Temple, please contact them at the above address or by phone, and they will direct you.

Buddha gave the world essentially 84,000 different teachings to pacify, purify, and develop the mind. In Tibetan Buddhism there are four major lineages, and this temple, founded by Tibetan master Nechung Rinpoche, is a classic synthesis of all four. Monks, lama, and scholars from different schools of Buddhism are periodically invited to come and lecture as resident teachers. The Dalai Lama came in 1980 to dedicate the temple, and graced the temple once again in 1994 when he addressed an audience here of over 3,500 people. Two affiliate temples are located in Dharamsala, India, and in Lhasa, Tibet. Programs vary, but people genuinely interested in Buddhism come here for meditation and soul-searching as well as for peace, quiet, relaxation, and direction. Morning and evening services at 7 a.m. and 7 p.m. are led by Debala, the Tibetan monk in residence. Formal classes depend upon which invited teacher is in residence (write ahead for a schedule of programs).

The majority of the flowering and fruit trees on the premises are imports. Plenty of parishioners are into agriculture, and there is a strong movement by the temple members to slowly replant the grounds with native vegetation that they collect from various sites in and around Pahala. The grounds, like a botanical garden, vibrate with life and energy. Buddhism strives for its followers to become wise and compassionate people. The focus of the temple is to bring together all meditation and church groups in the community. Plenty of local Christian and Buddhist groups use the nonsectarian facilities. Any group that is spiritually, socially, and community oriented and that has a positive outlook is welcome. Wood Valley Temple can't promise *nirvana,* but they can point you to the path.

The retreat facility is called the **Tara Temple** and at one time housed a Japanese Shingon Temple in Pahala. When the Shingon sect moved

HAWAII VOLCANOES

NATIONAL PARK

To Hilo
Volcano

Kilauea
Caldera

HAWAII

VOLCANOES

NATIONAL PARK

Kau
Desert

MAMALANOA HIGHWAY

PAU RD.

HILINA

KAU DESERT TRAIL

FOOTPRINTS IN ASH

Ainapo

11

KAAHA
SHELTER

KIPUKA
PEPEIAO CABIN

Southwest Rift

PONONOHOA
CHASMS

KAU

Kapapala
Ranch

KAPAPALA CAVE

KEAIWA
CAMP

MACADAMIA NUT
ORCHARDS

HIGASHI
CAMP

Pahala

WAIOALA
SPRING

KAMEHAME
HILL

Punaluu

HENRY OPUKAHAIA SHRINE
KAU HISTORY AND CULTURE CENTER
PUNALUU BEACH COUNTY PARK
GOLF COURSE

Ninole

KAIEIE HEIAU

KEEKU HEIAU

Honuapo

LOOKOUT

WHITTINGTON BEACH COUTNY PARK

HAAO
SPRINGS

PARK

Honuapo Bay

Waipouli Bay

PUHIULA
CAVE

Kimo Point

Waiohinu

Naalehu

KAUAHAAO
CHURCH

MARK TWAIN
TREE

Manakaa Point

Waikapuna Bay

To Kailua-Kona

11

MANUKA
STATE
WAYSIDE

HAWAIIAN
OCEAN VIEW
ESTATES

HAWAII BELT RD.

Kahuku
Ranch

SOUTH POINT RD.

Kaalela

0   4 mi

0   4 km

MANUKA

NATURAL

AREA

RESERVE

RUINS

Kauna
Point

KAHAKAHAKEA TRAIL

PETROGLYPHS

Keawaiki

Kaimuuwala

Kaupuaa Bay

Pohakuloa

Pulehua

Kaalualu

Kalaleohoaiku Point

Onikinalu Cove

Papakolea Green
Sand Beach

Ka Lae
(South Point)

Kaulana Bay

PACIFIC OCEAN

© J.D. BISIGNANI AND MOON PUBLICATIONS, INC.

to a new facility in Kona, this building was abandoned and given to Wood Valley Temple. A local contractor moved it to its present location, cranked it up one story, and built the dormitories underneath. The grounds, hallowed and consecrated for decades, already held a Nichiren temple, the main temple here today, that was dismantled in 1919 and rebuilt on its present site to protect it from lowland flooding. Rates at the retreat facility are: private room $30-35 s, $40-45 d; bunk in the dorm $20 with use of a large communal kitchen and shared bath. All require a two-night minimum stay, $10 extra for only one night. Weekly discounts and group rates are available. Definitely call or write to make reservations, since you could be disappointed if you just turn up.

PUNALUU AND NINOLE

Just south of Pahala is Punaluu Beach Park (mile marker 56), famous for its black-sand beach. Punaluu was an important port during the sugar boom of the 1880s and even had a railroad. Notice the tall coconut palms in the vicinity, unusual for Kau. Punaluu means "Diving Spring," so-named because freshwater springs can be found on the floor of the bay. Native divers once paddled out to sea, then dove with calabashes that they filled with fresh water from the underwater springs. This was the main source of drinking water for the region.

Ninole is home to the **Seamountain Resort and Golf Course,** built in the early 1970s by a branch of the C. Brewer Company. The string of flat-topped hills in the background is the remains of volcanoes that became dormant about 100,000 years ago. In sharp contrast with them is **Loihi Seamount,** 20 miles offshore and about 3,000 feet below the surface of the sea. This very active submarine volcano is steadily building, and should reach the surface eventually. Near Ninole is **Hokuloa Church,** which houses a memorial to Henry Opukahaia, the Hawaiian most responsible for encouraging the first missionaries to go to Hawaii to save his people from damnation.

Punaluu Beach Park
Punaluu Beach Park is a county park with full amenities. Here you'll find a pavilion, bathrooms, showers, drinking water, telephone, and open camping area (permit required). During the day there are plenty of tourists around, but at night the beach park empties, and you virtually have it to yourself. Punaluu boasts some of the only safe swimming on the south coast, but that doesn't mean that it can't have its treacherous moments. Head for the northeast section of the black sand beach near the boat ramp. Stay close to shore because a prevailing rip current lurks just outside the bay.

Just near the beach is **Joe and Pauline's Curio Shop.** If you have time, stop in; these

black sands of Punaluu

J.D. BISIGNANI

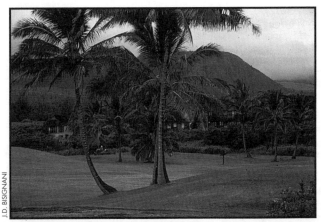

Seamountain
Golf Club Resort

J.D. BISIGNANI

people have a reputation for being more interested in offering *aloha* than in selling you a trinket. **Ninole Cove Park,** part of the Seamountain Resort, is within walking distance and open to the public. For day use, you might consider parking near the pro shop. As you walk to the beach from here you pass a freshwater pond, quite cold but good for swimming.

Practicalities
Seamountain Resort at Punaluu is now administered by Vacation Internationale, Ltd., P.O. Box 297, Kailua-Kona, HI 96745, tel. 928-6200 (direct resort local phone), (800) 344-7675 for reservations. Options at the condominium/hotel complex include a studio at $85-95 garden or ocean view, one bedroom $110-120, two bedrooms $140-150, (two-day minimum stay, off-season rates). Because of its rural location, Seamountain can offer secluded, deluxe accommodations for moderate prices. Your condo unit will be a low-rise, Polynesian-inspired bungalow with a shake roof. The above standard units, all tastefully furnished, offer remote color TVs, full kitchens, and full baths, while on the grounds are a swimming pool and a Jacuzzi. Although the units vary, all are furnished in island theme, typically with rattan couches and easy chairs, and all full kitchens have a full complement of dishes, silverware, and cookware. The feeling throughout the resort is a friendly, home away from home atmosphere where you are welcomed as part of a living community. Outside your door are the resort's fairways and greens, back-

dropped by the spectacular coast. If you're after peace and quiet, Seamountain is hard to beat. Besides golf, amenities include a nearby restaurant, tennis courts, pool, and weekly maid service.

Seamountain Golf Course Club House, open daily 10 a.m.-2 p.m., serves a limited menu of sandwiches and *pu pu* and also offers a full bar and morning coffee available at 7 a.m. A *kau kau* wagon parks daily except Monday at Punaluu Beach, offering island sandwiches, cold drinks, and snacks.

The only organized sporting facility in Kau is at the Seamountain Resort. Here you'll find four unlit tennis courts and a 6,500-yard, 18-hole, par-72 course. Greens fees are $30 ($40 for a visitor), cart $20, and clubs $15. Range balls are $5 a bucket and golf lessons $25 an hour.

NAALEHU AND VICINITY

Whittington Beach Park
Three miles north of Naalehu, is a county park with full amenities and camping. This park is tough to spot from the road because it's not clearly marked. As you're coming down a steep hill from Naalehu you'll see a bridge at the bottom. Turn right and you're there. The park is a bit run down, but never crowded. If you follow the dirt roads to its undeveloped sections you encounter many old ruins from the turn of the century when Honuapo Bay was an important sugar port.

Naalehu

Naalehu, the largest town in the area and the most southern town in the U.S., is lush. Check out the overhanging monkeypod trees. They form a magnificent living tunnel as you go down Route 11 through the center of town. Between Naalehu and Punaluu, the coastal area is majestic; stretching into the aqua-blue sea is a tableland of black lava with waves crashing against it in a surrealistic seascape that seems to go on forever. Every Fourth of July, a down-home rodeo is held in town for all the amateur riders of the district. Come and enjoy.

Waiohinu

A tall church steeple welcomes you to the small town of Waiohinu. There's nothing remarkable about this village, except that as you pass through you'll be seeing an example of the real Hawaiian lifestyle as it exists today. Just before the well-marked Shirakawa Motel on the *mauka* side of the road is the **Mark Twain Monkeypod Tree.** Unfortunately, Waiohinu's only claim to fame except for its undisturbed peace and quiet blew down in a heavy windstorm in 1957. Part of the original trunk, carved into a bust of Twain, is on display at the Lyman House Museum in Hilo. Now, a few shoots have begun sprouting from the original trunk and in years to come the Monkeypod Tree will be an attraction again.

Accommodations

The **Shirakawa Motel,** P.O. Box 467, Naalehu, HI 96772, tel. 929-7462, is a small, clean, comfortable, "hang loose bruddah" motel where your peace and quiet are guaranteed. It's been open since 1928; prices are a reasonable $30 s, $35 d, $42 with kitchen, $55 apartment complete with cardboard fireplace built by a man from Michigan who just couldn't forget the cold. There's a 10% discount for a one-week stay, 15% for longer, plus fees of $8 "roll away child," $10 "roll away adult" (if only it were that easy!). You'll be greeted by Kai, a golden Lab, who has given up aggression for the "hang loose, no worries" island lifestyle.

Becky's Bed & Breakfast, P.O. Box 673, Naalehu, HI 96772, tel./fax 929-9690 or (800) 235-1233, about 100 yards past the theater on the left, is owned and operated by Becky and Chuck McLinn. Available in this modest but cheery 60-year-old home are a spacious room with a queen bed and private bath for $50 s, $60 d; and a room with private entrance, two double beds, and private bath at $55 s, $65 d. There is no official policy, but if you stay four nights or longer, a discount can be arranged. To help you relax, the B&B features a backyard deck with a barbecue grill, inviting hammock, and hot tub to unjangle nerves. Becky serves a full breakfast of juice, fruit, and either Hawaiian French toast or hotcakes with bacon or sausage. Chuck serves as general handy man; he also takes a Polaroid photo of every guest and pastes it next to their comments in a guest book. Make sure to have a look at this ongoing account from visitors around the world. E-mail: beckys@interpac.net; Web site: hawaii-bnb.com/beckt.html.

Margo Hobbs and Philip Shaw of **Margo's Corner,** tel. 929-9614, P.O. Box 447, Naalehu, HI 96772, can accommodate you in a brightly painted pentagonal guesthouse for $50 s or $60 d, which includes two vegetarian meals with the family. The guesthouse, with a private bath and shower, has a queen-size bed. Two nights minimum preferred. Call for reservations and directions. Touring bicyclists and backpackers can camp ("on a donation basis") in the yard among Norfolk pines and an organic vegetable garden. No smoking and no excessive drinking, please.

Food

The Kau Drive-in Restaurant is open 7 a.m.-7 p.m. for breakfast, lunch, and dinner. You pass it between mile markers 78 and 77, near a Texaco gas station. The food is simple but good and makes a perfect lunch.

A mile farther south is **South Point Bar and Restaurant,** which is one of the best, albeit the "only" (which helps) restaurant and bar in the area. Actually, the bar and restaurant are separate establishments sharing the same roof. The restaurant is open daily noon-5 p.m. for lunch and 5-8 p.m. for dinner, with the bar open until 10 p.m. and live music on Friday night. Lunch can be sandwiches like ham and turkey for $5.95, clubhouse $6.75, garden burger $6, soup and small dinner salad $4.25, shrimp salad $8.95, mountainous chef salad $7.95, and a whopping one-third-pound burger with tomato, sprouts, choice of fresh cut fries or potato salad $6. For dinner try a 16-oz. rib eye steak at $15.95, seafood platter for $14.95, or vegetable lasagna

a local favorite

at $7.95. Sunday noon-2 p.m., the bar offers a barbecue out back that brings in the local people—always a good sign. The full bar serves wine, liquor, and draft and bottled beers, and there are pool tables and sports TVs to pass the time. Most patrons are friendly local people.

In Waiohinu, about a mile west of Naalehu, look for **Mark Twain's Square Café and Gift Shop,** open Mon.-Fri. 8 a.m.-5 p.m., Saturday 8 a.m.-4 p.m., owned and operated by the Fujikawa family. The luscious smells will lead you to fresh-baked bread, *manapua,* and an assortment of sandwiches all under $4, as well as plate lunches and daily specials like barbecue pork with rice and salad for $5.50.

As you are entering the west side of town, a large, easily spotted sign on the left marks the **Punaluu Bake Shop and Visitor's Center,** tel. 929-7343, open daily 9 a.m.-5 p.m. The bake shop, tempting with all kinds of pastries, is especially known for its *pao dolce,* sweet bread. Park and follow daily busloads of tourists down

a cement pathway to the retail shop for baked goods, sandwiches, coffee, cold drinks and a smattering of souvenirs.

Tabbada's Cafe, open daily for breakfast, lunch, and dinner 7 a.m.-9 p.m., dining room closed at 8 p.m., is a basic window restaurant with inside counter seating and a few booths. The reasonable menu offers a breakfast of two eggs, rice, bacon, ham, or Spam for $3.50; three-egg ham or Spam omelette for $3.95; and Punaluu French toast for $2.95. The lunch and dinner menu with everything priced $5.50-6.50 offers fried chicken, teriyaki steak, *kalua* pork, Korean chicken, and fresh fish.

For a quick sandwich or full meal try the **Naalehu Coffee Shop,** open daily, tel. 929-7238. Many of the local people call this restaurant "Roy's," after the owner's first name. The menu is typical island cuisine with a Japanese flavor; the best item is the fresh fish from local waters. The restaurant is basic and clean, with most meals on the menu around $7. They also have a wide assortment of souvenirs and tourist junk, and a large koi pond outside. Look for the big yellow building just near the shopping center as you enter town.

Naalehu Fruit Stand, tel. 929-9009, open Mon.-Thurs. 9 a.m.-6:30 p.m., Friday and Saturday till 7 p.m., Sunday till 5 p.m., is a favorite with local people, always a tip-off that the food is great. Along with fresh fruit, they sell submarines, hot dogs, pizza, salads, sodas, teas, coffee, fresh-baked goods, and a good selection of grains, minerals, vitamins, and health foods. The owners, John and Dorene Santangelo, are very friendly and willing to give advice about touring the Kau area (good bulletin board for local events). This is the best place on the south coast for a light meal or picnic lunch.

About 100 yards from the Naalehu Fruit Stand, notice the baseball park. Here **Kalaiki Plate Lunch,** open daily 5:30 a.m.-4 p.m., run by the Hanoa family, serves hearty sandwiches and island favorites ready to go. They are especially known for their full breakfasts, only $3-4.

Shopping and Supplies

In Naalehu you can gas yourself or your car at the **Luzon Liquor Store,** open daily 7 a.m.-9 p.m. You can also find basic groceries and supplies in this jam-packed, friendly local establishment (public telephone on porch).

Naalehu Shopping Center is along the road at the west end of town. In the small complex you'll find **Food Mart** and **Ed's Laundromat.**

The **Southern Star Theater** is a large building also at the west end of town. It's a classic old-time theater usually open on weekends, adults $3.25, children $1.75.

Kau Fishing Supply in Waiohinu offers fresh local fish that would make a perfect self-prepared meal for anyone heading out of town. Just down the road, you can pick up supplies at **Wong Yuen General Store and Gas Station,** open Mon.-Sat. 8:30 a.m.-5 p.m., Sunday to 3 p.m., tel. 929-7223.

Turtle Cove Woods, open daily 10 a.m.-6 p.m., is a souvenir and neat tourist junk shop across from Whittington Beach. Inside, along with hula skirts, wooden boxes, *kukui* nut lei, wooden platters, straw hats, and tiki carvings (done by owner J.D.), you'll find Nalani Kona Coffee at only $10 per pound.

SOUTH POINT

South Point

The Hawaiians simply called this Ka Lae, "The Point." Some scholars believe Polynesian sailors made landfall here as early as A.D. 150, and that their amazing exploits became navigating legend long before colonization began. A paved, narrow, but passable road branches off from Route 11 approximately six miles west of Naalehu, and drops directly south for 12 miles to land's end. Luckily the shoulders are firm, so you can pull over to let another car go by. The car-rental agencies warn against using this road, but their fears are unfounded. You proceed through a flat, treeless area trimmed by free-ranging herds of cattle and horses: more road obstacles to be aware of. Suddenly, incongruously, huge mechanical windmills appear, beating their arms against the sky. This is the **Kamoa Wind Farm.** Notice that this futuristic experiment at America's most southern point uses windmills made in Japan by Mitsubishi! The trees here are bent over by the prevailing wind, demonstrating the obviously excellent wind-power potential of the area. Farther along, a road sign informs you that the surrounding countryside is controlled by the **Hawaiian Homeland Agency,** and that you are forbidden to enter. That means that you are not welcome on the land, but you do have right-of-way on the road.

Here the road splits left and right. Go right until road's end, where you'll find a parking area usually filled with the pickup trucks of local fishermen. Walk to the cliff and notice attached ladders that plummet straight down to where the fishing boats are anchored. Local skippers moor their boats here and bring supplies and their catch up and down the ladders. Proceed south along the coast for only five minutes and you'll see a tall white structure with a big square sign

wind farm at South Point

J.D. BISIGNANI

on it turned sideways like a diamond. It marks the true *South Point,* the southernmost tip of the United States. Proceed to the sea and notice the tidepools, a warning that the swells can come high onto the rocks and that you can be swept away if you turn your back on *moana.* Usually, a few people are line-fishing for crevalle or pompano. The rocks are covered with Hawaiian dental floss—monofilament fishing line that has been snapped. Survey the mighty Pacific and realize that the closest continental landfall is Antarctica, 7,500 miles to the south.

Back at the Hawaiian Homes sign, follow the road left and pass a series of WW II barracks being reclaimed by nature. This road, too, leads to a parking area and a boat ramp where a few seaworthy craft are bobbing away at their moorings. Walk toward the navigational marker and you may notice small holes drilled into the stone. These were used by Hawaiian fishermen to secure their canoes to shore by long ropes while the current carried them a short way offshore. In this manner, they could fish without being swept away. Today fishermen still use these holes, but instead of canoes they use floats or tiny boats to carry only their lines out to sea. The *ulua,* tuna, and *ahi* fishing is renowned throughout this area. The fishing grounds here have always been extremely fertile, and thousands of shell and bone fishhooks have been found throughout the area. Scuba divers say that the rocks off South Point are covered with broken fishing line that the currents have woven into wild macramé.

When the Kona winds blow out of the South Pacific, South Point takes it on the chin. The weather should always be a consideration when you visit. In times past, any canoe caught in the wicked currents was considered lost. Even today, only experienced boaters brave South Point, and only during fine weather.

There is no official camping or facilities of any kind at South Point, but plenty of boat owners bivouac for a night to get an early start in the morning. The lava flow in this area is quite old and grass-covered, and the constant winds act like a natural lawn mower.

The best **windsurfing** in the area is at Kaulana Bay. Head down South Point Rd., and about a half mile before you get to the windmills is a passable dirt road to the left. You can only see about a half mile down it when you

first start out, but keep going. Pass through cattle gates and make absolutely sure to close them behind you. When you get to the bay, go to the left-hand side for the best entry. Remember that down here, no help is available, and you are totally on your own!

Green Sand Beach

From the boat ramp, a footpath leads east toward Kaulana Bay. All along here are remnants of pre-contact habitation, including the remains of a *heiau* foundation. If you walk for three miles, you'll come to Papakolea, better known as Green Sand Beach. The lava in this area contains olivine, a green semiprecious stone that weathered into sandlike particles distributed along the beach. The road heading down to Green Sand Beach is incredible. It begins as a very rugged jeep trail, and disintegrates from there. Do not attempt this walk unless you have close-toed shoes. Thongs will not make it. You're walking into the wind going down, but it's not a rough go—there's no elevation gain to speak of. The lava in the area is a'a, weathered and overlaid by a rather thick ground cover. Follow the road, and after 10 minutes, the lava ends and rich, green pastureland begins. An ancient eruption deposited 15-18 feet of ash right here, and the grasses grew.

Continue for approximately 35 minutes, until you see what is obviously an eroded cinder cone at the edge of the sea. (About 15 minutes back, you'll have noticed an area where many 4WDs have pulled off at an overlook. That isn't it!) Peer over the edge to see the beach with its definite green tinge. This is the only *beach* along the way, so it's hard to mistake. Getting down to it is absolutely treacherous. You'll be scrambling over tough lava rock, and you'll have to make drops of four to five feet in certain spots. The best approach is to go over the edge as soon as you come to the cinder cone area; don't walk around to what would be the south point of the caldera where the sand is. Once you get over the lip of heavy-duty rock, the trail down is not so bad. When you begin your descent, notice overhangs, almost like caves, where rocks have been piled up to extend them. These rocked-in areas make great shelters, and you can see remnants of recent campfires in spots perfect for a night's bivouac.

Green Sand Beach definitely lives up to its name, but don't expect emerald green. It's more like an army green, a dullish khaki green. Down at the beach, be very aware of the wave action. Watch for at least 15 minutes to be sure breakers are not inundating the entire beach. Then you can walk across it, but stay close to the lava rock wall. The currents can be wicked here and you should only enter the water on very calm days. No one is around to save you, and you don't want to wind up as flotsam in Antarctica.

Manuka State Wayside
The Manuka State Wayside is 12 miles west of South Point Rd. and just inside the Kau District. This civilized scene has restrooms, pavilions, and trails through manicured gardens surrounded by an arboretum. Shelter camping (no tents) is allowed on the grounds. All plants are identified. This is an excellent rest or picnic stop. The forested slopes above Manuka provide ample habitat for introduced, and now totally successful, colonies of wild pigs, pheasants, and turkeys.

DIANA LASICH HARPER

BOB RACE

KONA

Kona is long and lean, and takes its suntanned body for granted. This district *is* the west coast of the Big Island and lies in the rain shadows of both Mauna Loa and Mauna Kea. You can come here expecting brilliant sunny days and glorious sunsets, and you won't be disappointed; this reliable sunshine has earned Kona the nickname "The Gold Coast." Offshore, the fishing grounds are legendary, especially for marlin that lure game-fishing enthusiasts from around the world. There are actually two Konas, north and south, and both enjoy an upland interior of forests, ranches, and homesteads while most of the coastline is low, broad, and flat. If you've been fantasizing about swaying palms and tropical jungles dripping with wild orchids, you might be in for "Kona shock," especially if you fly directly into the Kona Airport. Around the airport the land is raw black lava that can appear as forbidding as the tailings from an old mining operation. Don't despair. Just north is one of the premier resorts in Hawaii, with a gorgeous white-sand beach lined with dancing coconut palms, and throughout Kona the lava has been transformed into beautiful gardens with just a little love and care.

Kailua-Kona is the heart of North Kona, by far the most developed area in the district. Its **Ali'i Drive** is lined with shops, hotels, and condos, but for the most part the shoreline vista remains intact because most of the buildings are low-rise. To show just how fertile lava can be when tended, miles of multihued bougainvillea and poinsettias line Ali'i Drive like a lei that leads to the flowerpot of the **Kona Gardens.** East of town is **Mount Hualalai** (8,271 feet), where local people still earn a living growing vegetables and taro on small truck farms high in the mountain coolness.

South Kona begins in the town of **Captain Cook.** Southward is a region of diminutive coffee plantations, the only ones in the U.S. The bushes grow to the shoulder of the road and the air is heady with the rich aroma of roasting coffee. Farther south, rough but passable roads branch from the main highway and tumble toward hidden beaches and tiny fishing villages where time just slips away. From north to south, Kona is awash in brilliant sunshine, and the rumble of surf and the plaintive cry of seabirds create the music of peace.

NORTH KONA

To Kawaihae

Kiholo Bay

Kiholo

Nawaikulua Point

Mahewalu Point
Kahuwai Bay
KONA VILLAGE RESORT
Waiakauhi Pond
FOUR SEASONS RESORT
Kukio

Puuanahulu

Kua Bay
Awakee Bay

Kawili Point
Mahaiula Bay
Makolea Point
Puu Kala Point

Makalawena

KONA BEACH STATE RECREATION AREA

Puu Nahaha ▲

LAVA TUBES

Huehue Ranch

Puu Waawaa ▲
(3,967 ft.)

Puu Iki ▲
(3,417 ft.)

Puu Paha ▲
(3,775 ft.)

Hainoa ▲
(4,083 ft.)

KEAHOLE AIRPORT

Keahole Point

OTEC FACILITY

KONA PALISADES ESTATES

KONA HILLS ESTATES

Potato Hill ▲

Hinaka Crater ▲

Hualalai ▲
(8,271 ft.)

KALOKO DR.

Puhili Point
Wawahiwaa Point
Kaloko Fishpond

KAMEHAMEHA PRESUMED BURIAL SITE

Honokohau
(Palani Junction)

Puu Laalaau ▲
(8,271 ft.)

HONOKOHAU MARINA
KALOKO-HONOKOHAU NATIONAL HISTORIC PARK
HALE O LONO HEIAU

OLD KONA AIRPORT STATE RECREATION AREA

Oneo Bay

Kailua (Kona)

KEALAKOWAA HEIAU

HOLUALOA MAUKA CAMP

COFFEE ORCHARDS

Holuaoa

Kahului Bay
KAUAKAIAKOLA HEIAU

Holualoa Bay

WHITE SANDS BEACH COUNTY PARK
Kahaluu Bay
ST. PETER'S CHURCH
KAPUANONI, HAPAI ALI'I AND KEEKU HEIAU
KEAUHOU-KONA GOLF COURSE
BIRTHPLACE OF KAMEHAMEHA III
Keauhou Bay
KONA SURF AND RESORT

Kahaluu

KONA GARDENS

HOLUA (SLIDE)

LOOKOUT

DAI FUKUJI BUDDHIST TEMPLE

Honalo

ANAKILA CHAPEL

Kainaliu

Kealakekua

Keikiwaha Point

0   3 mi
0   3 km

Captain Cook

To Naalehu and Volcanoes

To Waimea

© J.D. BISIGNANI AND MOON PUBLICATIONS, INC.

KAILUA-KONA AND VICINITY

SIGHTS

The entire Kona District is both old and historic. This was the land of Lono, god of fertility and patron of the Makahiki Festival. It was also the spot where the first missionary packet landed and changed Hawaii forever, and it's been a resort since the 19th century. In and around **Kailua** are restored *heiau,* a landmark lava church, and a royal palace where the monarchs of Hawaii came to relax. The coastline is rife with historical sites: lesser *heiau,* petroglyph fields, and curious amusement rides dating from the days of the Makahiki. Below the town of Captain Cook is **Kealakekua Bay,** the first and main *haole* anchorage in the islands until the development of Honolulu Harbor. This bay's historical significance is overwhelming, alternately being a place of life, death, and hope from where the spirit of Hawaii was changed for all time. Here on the southern coast is a Hawaiian "temple of refuge," restored and made into a National Historical Park. The majority of Kona's sights are strung along Route 11. Except for Kailua-Kona, where a walking tour is perfect, you need a rental car to visit the sights; the Big Island's Hele-On Bus is too infrequent to be feasible. If you're walking, pick up a copy of the pamphlet *Walking Tour of Historic Kailua Village,* put out by the Kona Historical Society.

Ali'i Shuttle

If you want to concentrate on the scenery and not the driving, take the Ali'i Shuttle, tel. 775-7121. Painted red, white, and blue, the bus runs daily every 30-45 minutes (more or less) along Ali'i Dr. 8:30 a.m.-10 p.m., and charges $2 each direction ($5 day pass, $20 weekly). The terminal points are Lanihau Shopping Center on the north end and Kona Surf Resort on the south end, with pickups at major hotels along the way. You can hail the bus and it will stop if possible.

Mokuaikaua Church

Kailua is one of those towns that would love to contemplate its own navel if it could only find it. It

Liholiho, Kamehameha II

JOHN HAYTER (HAWAII STATE ARCHIVES)

doesn't really have a center, but if you had to pick one, it would be the 112-foot steeple of Mokuaikaua ("The trees are felled, now let us eat") Church. This highest structure in town has been a landmark for travelers and seafarers ever since the church was completed in January 1838. The church claims to be the oldest house of Christian worship in Hawaii. The site was given by King Liholiho to the first Congregationalist missionaries who arrived on the brig *Thaddeus* in 1820. The actual construction was undertaken in 1836 by the Hawaiian congregation under the direction of Rev. Asa Thurston. Much thought was given to the orientation of the structure, designed so the prevailing winds blow through the entire length of the church to keep it cool and comfortable. The walls of the church are fashioned from massive, rough-hewn lava stone, mortared with plaster made from crushed and burned coral that was bound with *kukui* nut oil. The huge cornerstones are believed to have been salvaged from a *heiau* built in the 15th century by King Umi. The masonry is crude but effective—still sound after 150 years.

Inside, the church is extremely soothing, expressing a feeling of strength and simplicity. The resolute beams are native ohia, pegged together

KAILUA-KONA

To Honokohau and Waimea
To Holualoa and Captain Cook

To Airport and Kawaihae

To Captain Cook and Volcano

To Keauhou

NOT TO SCALE

Kailua Bay

© J.D. BISIGNANI AND MOON PUBLICATIONS, INC.

and closely resembling the fine beamwork used in barns throughout 19th-century New England. The pews, railings, pulpit, and trim are all fashioned from koa, a rich brown, lustrous wood that begs to be stroked. Although the church is still used as a house of worship, it also has the air of a museum, housing paintings of historical personages instrumental in Hawaii's Christian past. The crowning touch is an excellent model of the brig *Thaddeus,* painstakingly built by the men of the Pacific Fleet Command and presented to the church in 1934. The church is open daily from sunrise to sunset, and volunteer hostesses answer your questions 10 a.m.-noon and 1-3:30 p.m. Mokuaikaua Church is a few hundred yards south of Kailua Pier on the *mauka* side of Ali'i Drive.

Hulihee Palace

Go from the spiritual to the temporal by walking across the street from Mokuaikaua Church and entering Hulihee ("Turning Point") Palace. This two-story Victorian structure commissioned by Hawaii's second governor, John Kuakini, also dates from 1838. A favorite summer getaway for all the Hawaiian monarchs who followed, especially King Kalakaua, it was used as such until 1916. At first glance, the outside is unimpressive, but the more you look the more you realize how simple and grand it is. The architectural lines are those of an English country manor, and indeed Great Britain was held in high esteem by the

Hawaiian royalty. Inside, the palace is bright and airy. Most of the massive carved furniture is made from koa. The most magnificent pieces include a huge formal dining table, 70 inches in diameter, fashioned from one solid koa log. Upstairs is a tremendous four-poster bed that belonged to Queen Kapiolani, and two magnificent cabinets that were built by a Chinese convict who was serving a life sentence for smuggling opium. King Kalakaua heard of his talents and commissioned him to build the cabinets. They proved to be so wonderfully crafted that after they were completed the king pardoned the craftsman.

Prince Kuhio, who inherited the palace from his uncle, King Kalakaua, was the first Hawaiian delegate to Congress. He decided to auction off all the furniture and artifacts to raise money, supposedly for the benefit of the Hawaiian people. Providentially, the night before the auction each piece was painstakingly numbered by the royal ladies of the palace, and the name of the person bidding for the piece was dutifully recorded. In the years that followed, the **Daughters of Hawaii,** who now operate the palace as a museum, tracked down the owners and convinced many to return the items for display. Most of the pieces are privately owned, and because each is unique, the owners wish no duplicates to be made. It is for this reason, coupled with the fact that flashbulbs can fade the wood, that a strict *no photography* policy is enforced.

Delicate and priceless heirlooms on display include a tiger-claw necklace belonging to Kapiolani. You'll also see a portrait gallery of Hawaiian monarchs. Personal and mundane items are on exhibit as well—there's an old report card showing a 68 in philosophy for King Kalakaua—and lining the stairs is a collection of spears reputedly belonging to the great Kamehameha himself.

Hulihee Palace, tel. 329-1877, is on the *makai* side of Ali'i Dr., open Mon.-Fri. 9 a.m.-4 p.m., Saturday and Sunday 10 a.m.-4 p.m. You can look around on your own or ask the staff for a tour, which usually lasts 45 minutes. Admission is $5 adult, $4 seniors, $1 student. A hostess knowledgeable in Hawaiiana is usually on duty to answer most questions.

The **Palace Gift Shop,** small but with quality items, is on the grounds next door to the palace. It offers a fine selection of koa sculptures of fish, sharks, and even a turtle, along with Hawaiiana books and postcards. Just outside is a saltwater pond with tropical fish.

Ahuena Heiau

Directly behind the King Kamehameha's Kona Beach Hotel, at the north end of "downtown" Kailua, is the restored Ahuena Heiau. Built around Kamakahonu ("Eye of the Turtle") Beach, it's in a very important historical area. Kamehameha I, the great conqueror, came here to spend the last years of his life, settling down to a peaceful existence after many years of war and strife. The king, like all Hawaiians, reaffirmed his love of the *aina* and tended his own royal taro patch on the slopes of Mt. Hualalai. After he died, his bones were prepared according to ancient ritual on a stone platform within the temple, then taken to a secret burial place just north of town which is believed to be somewhere near Wawahiwaa Point. It was Kamehameha who initiated the first rebuilding of Ahuena Heiau, a temple of peace and prosperity dedicated to Lono, god of fertility. The rituals held here were a far cry from the bloody human sacrifices dedicated to the god of war, Kukailimoku, that were held at Puukohola Heiau, which Kamehameha had built a few leagues north and a few decades earlier. At Ahuena, Kamehameha gathered the sage *kahuna* of the land to discourse in the Hale Mana (main prayer house) on topics concerning wise government and statesmanship. It was here that Liholiho, Kamehameha's son and heir, was educated, and it was here that as a grown man he sat down with the great queens, Keopuolani and Kaahumanu, and broke the ancient *kapu* of eating with women, thereby destroying the old order.

The tallest structure on the temple grounds is the *anuu* (oracle tower), where the chief priest, in deep trance, received messages from the gods. Throughout the grounds are superbly carved *kia akua* (temple images) in the distinctive Kona style, considered some of the finest of all Polynesian art forms. The spiritual focus of the

J.D. BISIGNANI

Ahuena Heiau

heiau was humanity's higher nature, and the tallest figure, crowned with an image of the golden plover, was that of Koleamoku, a god of healing. Another interesting structure is a small thatched hut of sugarcane leaves, Hale Nana Mahina, which means "house from which to watch the farmland." Kamehameha would come here to meditate while a guard kept watch from a nearby shelter. The commanding view from the doorway affords a sweeping panorama from the sea to the king's plantations on the slopes of Mt. Hualalai. Though the temple grounds, reconstructed under the auspices of the Bishop Museum, are impressive, they are only one-third their original size. The *heiau* is open daily 9 a.m.-4 p.m., and admission is free. You can wander around following a self-guided tour, or take the free tour offered by the King Kamehameha's Kona Beach Hotel, tel. 329-2911, which includes a tour of their own hotel grounds as well. The hotel portion of the tour includes a walk through the lobby, where various artifacts are displayed, and features an extremely informative botanical tour that highlights the medicinal herbs of old Hawaii. The hotel tours begin at 1:30 p.m. weekdays. Don't miss this excellent educational opportunity, well worth the time and effort!

While in the area, make sure to visit the **Kailua Pier,** across the street from the *heiau.* Fishing boats are in and out all day, with most charters returning around 5 p.m. You'll have a chance to see some of the marlin for which Kona is noted, but if you have a sympathetic heart or weak stomach it might not be for you. This area is frantic with energy during the various "billfish tournaments" held throughout the year.

Honokohau Marina

Honokohau Harbor, three miles north of Kailua-Kona, is a small boat harbor and deep-sea fishing facility that has eclipsed the old Kailua Pier. The harbor area is full of fishing-oriented shops and is also home to the **Harbor House Restaurant,** where you can have a yarn with Kona's old salts. Primarily, this is where you come to see huge marlin caught that day, and to talk to the skippers of the deep-sea fishing boats that go after them. (For a description of **deep-sea fishing** see the "Sports and Recreation" section in the Out and About chapter) When you pull into the marina, you'll see a road that goes off to the left. Head that way toward the tan building with a Texaco sign, to where the pier and the weigh-station are located. The huge fish will be hoisted, measured, and photographed while the skippers and their crew clean and prepare the boat for the next day's outing. **Weigh in** is every day 11 a.m.-1 p.m., and 3-6 p.m., tel. 334-1881 for information. If you are fascinated by deep-sea fishing, this is your chance to pick a likely boat and to get acquainted with the crew.

Natural Energy Laboratory of Hawaii Authority (NELHA), a.k.a. OTEC

The future is now at these amazing Ocean Technology facilities located just south of the airport between mile markers 95 and 94, where you'll find a turnoff heading toward the sea. Incredible things are being done here. For example, cold water from several thousand feet below the surface of the ocean is placed in a turbine with warm surface water, a process that generates electricity and also provides desalinated water. In addition, the cold water is used for raising very un-Hawaiian things such as strawberries, lobsters, abalone, sea cucumbers, commercial black pearls, and Japanese flounder, as well as for raising *limu,* a local edible seaweed. Others use its alternative energy source to make fish jerky, to grow shiitake mushrooms, and even to raise tropical fish that will become living bouquets of color in fish tanks around the world. Cyanotech, a leading manufacturer of marine products for worldwide nutrition and pharmaceutical markets, uses the facilities to make spirulina, already available in health food stores. Tours are offered Thursdays at 10 a.m.; call 329-7341 for reservations. If you choose to take a tour, don't be overwhelmed by the size of the complex; the products are brought to a central area for your viewing. Afterward, you can request a tour of the facility. No tasting is offered, so bring your own snacks. For those who want to walk around on their own, maps are available.

Onizuka Space Center

Dedicated to Hawaii's own Col. Ellison S. Onizuka and to the men and women who tragically perished aboard the space craft *Challenger* on January 28, 1986, the center is located at Kona International Airport, P.O. Box 833, Kailua-Kona, HI 96745, tel. 329-3441. Hours are daily 8:30 a.m.-4:30 p.m. except Thanksgiving, Christmas, and New Year's Day; $2 admission. From this tragedy, a living memorial and space education facility was erected. Inside the modern, well-appointed building children and adults alike can marvel at human exploration of space by viewing exhibits like a "moon rock," scale model of a space shuttle and space station, an interactive staffed maneuvering unit, and a space theater with educational showings throughout the day. There is a gift shop with plenty of fascinating reading material concerning the international effort to explore the heavens. Stop in before flying out.

Along Ali'i Drive

Ali'i Dr. heads south from Kailua, passing the majority of Kona's resorts. On the mountain side of the road, a continuous flow of flowers drapes the shoulder like a femme fatale's seductive boa, while seaside the coastline slips along, rugged and bright, making Ali'i Dr. a soothing sight.

At your first stop, near White Sands Beach, look for the historic **Ohana Congregational Church** built in 1855 by Rev. John D. Paris. Services are still held every Sunday at 8 a.m. The base of the church is mostly original lava rock topped with a new roof. The cemetery area is peaceful and quiet and offers a perfect meditative perch from which to scan the coast below. Back on the road, look for signs to Kahaluu Beach Park; pull in and park here. On the rocky northern shore of this bay is **St. Peter's Catholic Church.** Its diminutive size, capped by a blue tin roof that winks at you from amidst the lava like a bright morning glory in an ebony vase, has earned it the nickname **Little Blue Church.** Built in 1889 on the site of an old, partially reclaimed *heiau,* the church is a favorite spot for snapshots. Inside, the epitome of simplicity reigns with bare wood walls and a simple crucifix. The only splash of color is a bouquet of fresh flowers on the altar. To the right of the church as you face it are the remains of **Kuemanu Heiau,** and within a 10-minute walk heading south from the church along the coast are strung the remains of **Kapuanoni, Hapai Ali'i,** and **Keeku** *heiau.* All are unrestored historical sites that still show signs of being used, and all offer fantastic vantage points from which to view the coast.

Do yourself a favor and visit the grounds of the **Kona Surf Hotel,** which have graciously been opened to the public. You're free to stroll

St. Peter's Church

J.D. BISIGNANI

around on your own, and nonguests can take a tour on Sunday, Tuesday, or Thursday at 3 p.m. Here are 14 acres of ponds and gardens glorious with the perfumes and blooms of over 30,000 plants, flowers, fruits, and shrubs gathered from throughout Polynesia. To complement the natural setting of the grounds, a profusion of Asian and Hawaiian artwork has been placed here and there. Inside, the main hallways of the hotel's four wings are resplendent with over a million dollars' worth of wall hangings and tapestries. For a special treat, visit in the evening, when the hotel shines spotlights on the water, bringing tiny crustaceans to the surface. Often, huge manta rays will also surface in the light to feed on this delectable buffet. Some local dive shops offer night dives especially for this thrilling experience.

A short stroll or a minute's drive south brings you to **Keauhou Bay.** Here you'll find a cluster of historical sites, and the pier for the Fair Winds Snorkel Dive and Charter. Look for a monument marking the birthplace of Kamehameha III in 1814. Local people come to fish from the pier around 5 p.m. for *halalu,* a tough little fish to catch. Ask at the Keauhou Bay Hotel for a free area map. Along the shoreline are a number of partially developed *heiau* sites. You'll also find a *holua,* grass-covered rocks that were slicked with water to form a slide. Hawaiians rode it on wooden sleds, especially during the Makahiki Festival. A small home stuck on a point of land on the edge of the bay is where John Wayne married his wife Pilar in 1954, and marks the site of the first modern house built on the bay.

BEACHES AND PARKS

If Kona is short on anything, it is beaches. The ones that it has are adequate and quite striking in their own way, but they tend to be small, few, and far between. Most people expecting a huge expanse of white sands will be disappointed. These beaches do exist on the Big Island's west coast, but they are north of Kailua-Kona in the Kohala District. Kona does, however, have beaches alive with marinelife, providing excellent and safe snorkeling and top-notch tidepooling.

Note: The following are the main beaches in Kailua-Kona and North Kona. For descriptions of South Kona beaches see below.

Kamakahonu Beach

You couldn't be more centrally located than at "Eye of the Turtle" Beach. Find it in downtown Kailua-Kona near Kailua Pier and the King Kamehameha's Kona Beach Hotel. Local people refer to it as "Kids' Beach" because it is so gentle and perfect for a refreshing dip. Big kids come here to play too, when every year world-class athletes churn the gentle waters into a fury at the start of the Ironman Triathlon. Rent snorkel gear, kayaks, and Hobie Cats for reasonable prices from the **Beach Shack,** located on the beach itself. Restrooms are on the pier.

Old Kona Airport State Recreation Area

In 1970 the old Kona Airport closed and the state of Hawaii turned it into a beach park. To get there, simply walk along the shoreline for a few hundred yards north of the King Kamehameha's Kona Beach Hotel. If driving, follow Ali'i Dr. to the junction just before the North Kona Shopping Center and turn left on the Kuakini Highway Extension.

Facilities include showers, restrooms, and picnic area. Parking is unlimited along the old runway, where you can also walk, bike, rollerblade, or jog. The park gate closes at 8 p.m. The white-sand beach is sandwiched between water's edge and the runway. You can enter the water at some shallow inlets, but the bottom is often rocky (be sure to wear water shoes) and the waters can be treacherous during high surf. The safest spot is a little sandy cove at the southern end of the beach. Snorkeling is good at the northern end of the beach, and offshore a break makes Old Airport popular with Kona surfers. There is no official camping at the park, but people often do camp at the north end. A heated controversy erupted when a developer purchased the land adjacent to the north end of the park, then closed it to camping. Local fishermen had camped here for years. Protesting in 1981, they raised a tent village named Kukai-limoku, which disbanded when the leaders were arrested for trespassing. It's also disputed whether the developer has claimed eight acres that actually belong to the state. The controversy goes on.

Honokohau Beach

All types of people come to Honokohau Beach, including fishermen, surfers, and snorkelers, but it's primarily known as a **clothes optional beach.** This status has been drastically changing ever since the area officially became part of **Kaloko-Honokohau National Historical Park.** Follow Route 19 north from Kailua-Kona for three miles and turn left on the marked road leading to the Honokohau Small Boat Harbor. Stay to the right and park almost at the end of the access road near the "boat graveyard" in a dirt parking lot. Don't walk straight ahead onto land being claimed by the Pai 'ohana, a local Hawaiian family trying to establish a homestead within the "sovereign jurisdiction of the Kingdom of Hawaii." Instead clamber over the berm, follow the well-worn path into the vegetation, and keep walking for a few minutes to the beach.

This area, more toward Kaloko, was heavily populated during old Hawaiian days, and plenty of archaeological sites—mostly fish ponds, ruins of houses, and a few petroglyphs—are found along the shoreline. Most of these sites are closed to protect them for posterity; if you come to an archaeological area, obey all posted signs and approach with great care and respect. Remember, it is imperative that you do not touch, disturb, or remove any historical artifacts. The coarse gray sand beach offers safe swimming in somewhat shallow water, and except for a composting toilet, has no facilities.

The status of nudity along the beach is changing, and as part of the General Management Plan, the "proposed action" is to make nudity illegal. Camping and open fires, now illegal, are citable offenses under federal regulations. Walk to the north end of the beach, where a trail leads inland through thick vegetation. Follow it to the "Queen's Bath" (officially called the "Anchialine Bath" by the park service), a brackish pond surrounded by rock cairns. Because it is under consideration as a historical site, swimming in the pond is not recommended. There's sometimes a ranger back in here, and although the park is officially open, visitation is neither encouraged nor discouraged. On the way out, pause at the active small-boat harbor. Although shark signs are posted, snorkelers frequent the bay.

Kaloko Beach, about a 10-minute hike north of Queen's Bath, has great snorkeling in only 10-20 feet of water. Here, you can explore a series of sea arches. The entire area is a favorite with green sea turtles, who make their presence known mainly in the evenings.

Dedicated in 1978, the 1,160-acre Kaloko-Honokohau National Historical Park can be entered either from Honokohau Small Boat Harbor or via Kaloko Gate, just off Hwy. 19 across from the Kaloko New Industrial Park. For information, call 329-6881.

North Kona Beaches

The first beach that you come to heading north from Kailua-Kona is the famous **Pine Trees** surfing beach, located near the OTEC facility just south of the airport between mile markers 95 and 94. Look for a well-worn dirt road leading to the left away from OTEC, and follow it to Pine Trees. Although famous with surfers and the site of many competitions, Pine Trees (none of which is in evidence) is not a good swimming beach. There are a few one-towel coves along the rocky shoreline where you can gain access to the water, but mostly it's a place from which to observe the action. You can also follow the road toward the OTEC facility until you find a large, sandy, public

beach, fronted by rock and coral. Here are a few volleyball nets, a restroom, and some picnic tables. Next come the numerous secluded beaches of the **Kona Coast State Park** (see below).

Finally, just before you get to the luxury resorts of South Kohala, you'll find **Kiholo Bay** and **Luahinewai Pond,** considered yet another Queen's Bath. Look for a stand of royal palms marking the spot, and follow the rough but passable road down to the beach, where you will find a large round wooden house that once belonged to Loretta Lynn. Close by, a path leads over the lava to a tiny cove made more dramatic by a black-sand beach.

Kona Coast State Park

Recently opened and well marked, the Kona Coast State Park stretches north encompassing several sandy secluded beaches. The first is about two miles north of the airport between mile markers 91 and 90. Follow the rugged but passable dirt road for about 1.5 miles to one of the closest beaches to Kailua-Kona. The semi-improved area has a lavatory and dilapidated picnic tables built around palm trees. The land rises before getting to the beach, and to the left are the remains of a concession stand. The swimming here is safe in season, but always be careful.

Before you get to the official parking area, notice a walking path off to the right. It is a five-minute walk to **Mahaiula Bay.** En route, you'll pass a portable toilet (clean), and about 200 yards further along is magnificent Mahaiula Beach. This crescent of white sand stretches for about 200 yards, with shade trees coming down almost to the water's edge. Completely unimproved and secluded, it's a great beach to "get away from it all" for the day.

Two miles further north, between mile markers 89 and 88, look for the Pu'u Ku'ili cinder cone whose vegetation has been given a crew cut by the trade winds. Turn here on a very rugged, 4WD-only dirt road that takes you down to **Makalawena Beach.** En route to this totally secluded area, you'll pass over rough lava and coral and eventually come to a gate, where you park. Proceed on foot, and you'll have your choice of three wonderful beaches ranging in size 30-100 yards long; all are frequented by green sea turtles. Walk to the left past the biggest beach, and look for a path behind it that leads to a brackish but mostly freshwater pond where you can rinse off. Don't be alarmed by the harmless brine shrimp that nibble at your toes. They're much too small to do any real damage. If you do not have 4WD, you can still enjoy this area, but it means a hike of about 30 minutes. Be sure to bring water, especially if you intend to spend the day. From Mahaiula Beach, walk north along a path and in about five minutes you'll come to the remains of an abandoned estate that once belonged to the Magoon Family, longtime island residents and major stockholders in Hawaiian Airlines. The state has purchased this land—which was at one time being eyed by a Japanese firm that wished to build a luxury resort—and it is now, thankfully, in the public domain. After enjoying your short coastal hike, you will come to Makalawena, where you will be totally secluded. Remember not to take any chances during high surf, since there is no safety supervision whatsoever.

Alternatively, a few minutes farther north by car, just past the cinder cone, you'll find another road that starts off paved but almost immediately turns to lava and coral. If you have 4WD you can go to the end of the road and then walk to the beach, but you can also walk for about 15 minutes from the turnout near the highway. The well-worn path leads you to **Kua Bay,** a famous swimming and boogie-boarding beach.

Ali'i Drive Beaches
The following beaches are strung one after the other along Kailua-Kona's Ali'i Drive. **White Sands Beach County Park** (a.k.a. **Magic Sands** or **Disappearing Sands**) is an excellent spot for a dip—if the sand is there. Every year, usually in March and April, the sands are stripped away by heavy seas and currents, exposing rough coral and making the area rugged for the average swimmer. People still come during those months because it's a good vantage point for observing migrating humpback whales. The sands always come back and when they do, the beach is terrific for all kinds of water sports, including bodysurfing and snorkeling. The annual **Magic Sands Bodysurfing Contest** is held during the winter months. The best board surfing is just north of the beach in a break the locals call "Banyans." White Sands' amenities include drinking water, showers, and restrooms, making the beach a favorite spot with local people and tourists.

Kahaluu Beach Park on Kahaluu Bay has always been a productive fishing area. Even today, fishermen come to "throw net." You'll occasionally see large family parties surrounding their favorite fish with a huge *hukilau* net, then sharing their bounty among all participants. Because of this age-old tradition, the area has not been designated a marine conservation district. Kahaluu became a beach park in 1966. This ensured that the people of Kona would always have access to this favorite spot, which quickly became surrounded by commercial development. Amenities include picnic tables, showers, restrooms, even a basketball court. The swimming is very good, but the real attraction is snorkeling. The waters are very gentle and Kahaluu is a perfect place for families or beginning snorkelers. However, stay *within* the bay because a powerful and dangerous rip current lurks outside, and more rescues are made on this beach than on any other in Kona. The shoreline waters are alive with tropical fish: angelfish, parrotfish, unicorn fish, the works. Bring bread or cheese with you, and in a minute you'll be surrounded by a living rainbow of colors. Some fish are even bold enough to nip your fingers. It's very curious that when these semi-tame fish spot a swimmer with a spear gun, they'll completely avoid him. They know the difference! Unfortunately, Kahaluu is often crowded, but it is still worth a visit.

ACCOMMODATIONS

Almost all of Kona's accommodations lie along the six miles of Ali'i Dr. from Kailua-Kona to Keauhou. Most hotels/condos fall in the moderate to expensive range, including one super-luxury hotel just north of Kailua-Kona. A few inexpensive hotels are scattered here and there along Ali'i Dr., and back up in the hills are a "sleeper" or two that are cheap but decent. The following list should provide you with a good cross section.

Camping Note
It's sad but true: except for the limited beach parks at Hookena and Miloli'i, south of Kailua-Kona, there is *no* official camping in all of the Kona District. Campers wishing to enjoy the Kona Coast must go north to the Kohala District to find

a campground, or south to Kau. Some unofficial camping does exist in Kona, but as always, this generates certain insecurities. Bivouacking for a night or two in any of the unofficial camp spots should be hassle free. Good luck!

Inexpensive

For a reasonable and homey hotel, try the **Kona Tiki,** 75-5968 Ali'i Dr., Kailua-Kona, HI 96745, tel. 329-1425, fax 327-9402, featuring refrigerators in all rooms (some kitchen units) and complimentary continental breakfast daily. Island fruits and a few old fishing poles are also furnished for the guests. The hotel is close to the road so it's a bit noisy in the day but quiets down at night except for the lullaby of the rolling surf. Rooms are clean, with ceiling fans but no phones or TVs, and have been recently refurnished with new curtains and bedspreads of pastel tropical design. All units face the ocean so everyone gets a view. There's a lovely lanai, a pool, and a trim little garden of raked sand. Prices are $56 s/d, kitchenette unit $62, extra person $8, three-day minimum.

The **Kona Bay Hotel,** at 75-5739 Ali'i Dr., Kailua-Kona, HI 96740, tel. 329-1393 or (800) 367-5102, is a locally owned downtown hotel run by Uncle Billy and his Kona family. Its best feature is the friendly and warm staff. The hotel is a remaining wing of the old Kona Inn, the rest of which was torn down to accommodate the shopping center across the road. The Kona Bay is built around a central courtyard and garden containing the Banana Cafe, pool, and bar. As at Uncle Billy's Hilo Bay Hotel, the motif is "cellophane Polynesian," highlighted by some artificial palms. The rooms are a combination of basic and superior with a/c, TV, green carpeting, one wall papered and the other bare cinder block. Each room has a mini-fridge, and some can be outfitted with kitchenettes. Rates begin at $77-92, and $87-97 for a kitchenette; car-rental package available. E-mail: unclebilly@aloha.net; Web site: www.aloha.net/~uncleb.

Kona Seaside Hotel is another basic but well-cared-for downtown hotel at 75-5646 Palani Rd., Kailua-Kona, HI 96740, tel. 329-2455 or (800) 367-7000. It's part of the island-owned Sands, Seaside, and Hukilau chain. Most rooms have a/c, cross ventilation, and lanai, but no TV. There's a sun deck and central area with enclosed courtyard and lobby. Prices range from $70 standard to $100 deluxe, double occupancy (car package available).

Patey's Place, 75-195 Ala Ona Ona St., Kailua-Kona, HI 96740, tel. 326-7018, , fax. 326-7640, is a reasonably priced, and traveler-friendly hostel. Upon arrival, it will appear as though a section of the living sea was taken from the coast, and moved whole into a residential area of Kona. You will be cohabiting with whales, mermaids, and dolphins, all rendered by airbrush *air*tist, Paul, Fullbrook, a resident Aussie artist, who was undoubtedly a green sea turtle in his past life. Robert Patey, manager/owner, is a long-time island resident, who has plenty of *aloha* and will point you in the right direction. He takes pride in his hostel, and it shows. Rates are: bunk room, $17.50; private room $31.50s, $41.50d; deluxe private with a/c and shared bath $70 at the Islander Inn (two private units owned by Patey's at this condo right on the beach). A $10 key and linen deposit is returned on departure. Patey's also provides: free transportation *from* the airport if you stay two or more nights; airport drop-off $5; various island tours from $40-55; body boards, fishing gear, and snorkel gear for a one time fee of $5; lockers; safe deposit box; and free and invaluable information. The bunk rooms (maximum four people) are clean, lockable, and cooled by cross ventilation and ceiling fans. The hostel is also outfitted with four full bathrooms, three kitchens, a tanning deck, laundry facilities, gas barbecues, and an activities desk. Patey's is an excellent choice for the adventurer, budget traveler, or anyone else who enjoys a dynamic international setting. Website: www.hostels.com/patey's; e-mail: patey@mail.gte.net.

Moderate

Kona by the Sea, 75-6106 Ali'i Dr., Kailua-Kona, HI 96740, tel. 327-2300 or (800) 922-7866 U.S. and Canada, (800) 321-2558 in Hawaii, is a rather new and beautifully situated condominium with extraordinary coastal views. Like many of Kona's properties, it has no beach, but there is a freshwater pool on the premises and a saltwater pool run by the state only a minute away. From the balcony of your suite overlooking a central courtyard, you can watch the aqua-blue surf crash onto the black lava rocks below. Each spacious one- or two-bedroom unit has two bathrooms, tiled lanai, modern kitchen complete with dishwasher and garbage disposal, living room with fold-out couch, dining room, color cable TV, and central air. Furniture differs slightly from unit to unit but is always tasteful and often includes rattan with plush cushions, and mauve and earthtoned rugs and walls. Prices are a reasonable $225-299 for one- and two-bedroom units. Kona by the Sea, like most properties managed by Aston Resorts, offers excellent value for a peaceful Kona vacation.

Kanaloa at Kona, 78-261 Manukai St., Kailua-Kona, HI 96740, tel. 322-9625 or (800) 688-7444, is situated in an upscale residential area at the southern end of Kailua-Kona and is one of those special places where you feel that you get more than what you pay for. The one- to three-bedroom units are enormous. Big isn't always better, but in this case it is. Each unit comes equipped with a complete and modern kitchen, two baths, a lanai with comfortable outdoor furniture, and a wet bar for entertaining. Rates for the tastefully furnished units range from $165 for one bedroom to $275 for two bedrooms; the rooms can accommodate four and six people respectively at no extra charge. A security officer is on duty, and on the grounds you'll find three pools, lighted tennis courts, Jacuzzis, gas barbecues, an activities desk with free morning coffee, and even a restaurant and cocktail lounge overlooking the black-sand beach. The complex itself is made up of lowrise units around a central courtyard. If you would like to escape the hustle and bustle but stay near the action, the Kanaloa at Kona is the place.

The **Keauhou Beach Hotel,** 78-6740 Ali'i Dr., Kailua-Kona, HI 96740, tel. 322-3441, (800) 367-6025, is built on a historic site that includes the remains of a *heiau* and a reconstruction of King Kamehameha III's summer cottage. The hotel is famous for its bougainvillea that plummets over the seven-story face of the hotel. Kahaluu Beach Park is adjacent, and the entire area is known for fantastic tidepools. This famous Kona hotel has recently undergone extensive changes. Rates range from $98 ocean view up to $170 for deluxe oceanfront. Each room has a/c, TV, phone, private lanai, and small refrigerator. The nightly buffets on the hotel's Kuakini Terrace are widely known and

well appreciated by guest and local alike. The hotel also offers a free shuttle service to local shopping, golfing, and dining. E-mail: keauhou @aloha.net; Web site: www.kbeach-hotel.com.

Casa De Emdeko is a condominium that receives the best possible praise: people who have lodged there once always return. It's a quiet, lowrise condo surrounding a central courtyard with freshwater and saltwater pools and an on-site convenience store. All units have a/c, full kitchen, and lanai. Prices start at $75 d, $10 extra person, for a garden-view apartment with every seventh night free. Contact Casa De Emdeko at 75-6082 Ali'i Dr., Kailua-Kona, HI 96740, tel. 329-2160 (resident manager); or the booking agent of SunQuest Vacations, tel. 329-6488, (800) 367-5168 Mainland, (800) 800-5662 Canada . Office hours are weekdays only 8 a.m.-5 p.m.; check in is at 1 p.m., checkout at 11 a.m. The office is closed on weekends and holidays but special arrangements can be made to accommodate you, and there is a buzzer at the front desk that summons the resident manager.

Kona Islander Inn condominium apartments are well appointed for a reasonable price. Conveniently located within walking distance of downtown Kailua-Kona, they're next door to the Spindrifter Restaurant. The style is "turn-of-the-century plantation" shaded by tall palms. All 22 rental units have phone, off-road parking, a/c, and TV. Rates run $99-129. For information write Kona Islander Inn, 75-5776 Kuakini Hwy., Kailua-Kona, HI 96740, tel. 329-3181, or Marc Resorts, tel. (800) 535-0085.

A few reasonably priced and attractive condominium apartments include the following. **Kona Mansion,** a quarter mile from downtown, offers one-bedroom suites for up to four persons $70. Each unit has a full kitchen. There's a swimming pool, parking, TV, and maid service on request, with a minimum stay of five nights. Contact Hawaiian Apartment Leasing, 1240 Cliff Dr., Laguna Beach, CA 92651, tel. (714) 497-4253, (800) 854-8843, (800) 472-8449 California. **Ali'i Villas,** oceanside just a half mile from Kailua-Kona, offers full kitchens, lanais, TVs, parking, a pool, and barbecues. Rates vary from one-bedroom units at $450-485 weekly (two to three guests) to two bedrooms (all units oceanfront) from $800-850 weekly (up to four guests). Additional guests cost extra. There is a 20% monthly discount during low season. For bookings, contact Norma C. Edens, Kona Sun Coast Properties, tel. (800) 326-4751. **Kona Billfisher,** tel. (808) 329-9277, near downtown, offers full kitchens, pool, barbecues, limited maid service, and gazebo. One-bedroom units cost $60 daily for up to four persons, two-bedroom units $80 for up to six guests. Weekly and monthly rates and discounts. **Kona Plaza,** tel. 329-1132, downtown, has a swimming pool and sun decks and is wheelchair accessible. Daily rates are $55 d, $65 up to four. Weekly, monthly, and off-season rates available.

High above Kailua-Kona on the road to Holualoa, surrounded by lush tropical foliage that permeates the air with a sweet perfume, perches **Hale Maluhia Country Inn Bed and Breakfast,** 76-770 Hualalai Rd., Kailua-Kona, HI 96740, tel. 329-5773, (800) 559-6627, fax 326-5487, a hideaway lovingly tended by hosts Ken and Ann Smith. Built and furnished in rustic Hawaiian style with a Victorian twist, the B&B offers accommodations in the main house or the separate Banyan Cottage. The interiors of the central house and cottage feature open-beamed ceilings, plenty of natural wood trim, koa cabinets, and full kitchens. There's even a functional working office with a computer, laser printer, and fax machine for those forced to mix business with pleasure. On the property are an outdoor stone-and-tile Japanese *ofuro* (spa) with massage jets, and a massage table where your cares and aches will float away on the evening breeze. Two relaxing common areas are outfitted with board games, a pool table, a large library, and surround sound color TV/VCR (large video library), while five lanais present the natural drama of a Michaelangelo sunset nightly; all are wheelchair friendly. Ken spoils you every morning with a sumptuous home-cooked breakfast buffet laden with tropical fruits and juices, fresh bread and pastries, savory breakfast meats, herbal teas, and robust Kona coffee. In the evenings, Ken, a man of earth and spirit, will gladly converse with you on the wonders of the Big Island, offering suggestions on how to enrich your journey. All rooms, painted a soothing mauve and teal, are decorated with Hawaiian and provincial antique furniture, and feature private baths. Rates are $75-110 d for a guest room in the main house, and $145 for the Banyan Cottage. Discounts for longer stays. Hale Maluhia (House of Peace) is all that its name implies. E-mail: hawaii-inns@aloha.net; Web site: www.hawaii-bnb.com/halemal.html.

Expensive

The **Aston Royal Sea Cliff Resort,** winner of an American Automobile Association Three Diamond Award, offers classy condo apartments. The white alabaster building features rooms fronting a central courtyard where you'll find the pool and spa. The unobstructed views of the coast from most rooms are glorious, with sunsets enjoyed on your private lanai a perfect day-ending activity. Amenities, such as free tennis, daily maid service, two swimming pools, cable color TV, activities desk, jet spa and sauna, and sundries shop are offered but there are no restaurants or activities. Rates start with a studio at $150 and move to one bedroom $165-215, two bedrooms $195-505; there's a special 15% rate reduction during the off-season as well as a "family plan." Contact Royal Sea Cliff Resort, 75-6040 Ali'i Dr., Kailua-Kona, HI 96740, tel. 329-8021 or (800) 922-7866.

The **Royal Kona Resort,** 75-5852 Ali'i Dr., Kailua-Kona, HI 96740, tel. 329-3111, (800) 919-8333, has figuratively and literally become a Kona landmark. The rooms are spacious and each includes a lanai (so protected from public view that it easily serves as an outdoor room). The tennis facilities are superb, and an ocean-fed pool is sheltered from the force of the waves by huge black lava boulders. Standard rates run from $130 for a garden view to $160 for a partial ocean view, $180 for an ocean view, and $210 for an ocean front, with the ocean front corner king rooms at $250. The hotel, built like rising steps with the floor below larger than the one above, commands a magnificent view from its perch atop a beautiful promontory of black lava. On the property, you can dine in the **Tropics Cafe Restaurant,** which has a lovely sun-soaked veranda with a sweeping view of the surrounding coastline. Executive chief Daniel Thiebaut has created a whole new menu for this establishment. The hotel also boasts a mini-shopping mall complete with a sundries store. The **Windjammer,** an open-air lounge, features entertainment several evenings each week. The hotel pool, completely refurbished, has an upper kiddies' pool and a lower re-tiled main pool adjacent to the rolling surf. Between the main building and the beach tower is the coconut grove. The *imu* is fired up every Monday, Friday, and Saturday evening, creating delectable morsels for the famous Kona sunset luau that comes complete with island entertainment that fills the grounds with music and laughter. Reservations are recommended (tel. 329-3111). The tennis courts, attended by a professional staff, are lit for nighttime play. Costs are a reasonable $6 hourly per court or $7 for all day; nonguests pay $7 and $9 respectively. Other full-service amenities include a laundry, free parking, beauty salon, baby-sitters, and no charge for children under 17 years of age sharing a room with their parents. The Royal Kona Resort keeps alive the tradition of quality service at a quality hotel. Website: www.royalkona.com.

King Kamehameha's Kona Beach Hotel is located in downtown Kailua-Kona at 75-5660 Palani Rd., Kailua-Kona, HI 96740, tel. 329-2911 or (800) 367-6060, on a spot favored by Hawaiian royalty; Kamehameha the Great spent the last days of his life here. It's one of the only Kona hotels that has its own beach, adjacent to the restored Ahuena Heiau. The walls of the lobby are lined with artifacts of ancient battles. Portraits of the Kamehameha royal family beginning with the great chief Kamehameha are displayed in the reception area, and two *kahili* stand nearby as signs of royalty. Hotel staff members give historical tours of the grounds. Rooms (each with a/c, TV, refrigerator, safe, and phone), are appointed in shades of blue with rattan furniture, each featuring a lanai with a sweeping panorama of the bay and Mt. Hualalai. Prices range from $110 for a standard room up to $500 for a three-bedroom suite, additional person $20, and children under 18 free when sharing their parents' room. The hotel features restaurants, a famous luau, cocktail lounges, tennis courts, shops, and a pool.

The **Kona Surf Resort**, 78-128 Ehukai St., Kailua-Kona, HI 96740, tel. 322-3411, (800) 367-8011, fax 322-3245, is located at Keauhou Bay, six miles south of Kailua-Kona. The building, comprised of four wings and lined with over $1 million worth of art, is architecturally superb. The impeccable hotel grounds are a magnificent match for the building and are open to the public. All 535 rooms have a/c, phones, and TVs. Prices

begin at $99 and go to $365 for a suite. There are two swimming pools, lighted tennis courts, and the Keauhou-Kona Golf Course next door, with special rates and starting times for hotel guests. E-mail: konasurf@ilhawaii.net; Web site: www.ilhawaii.net/konasurf.

FOOD

Inexpensive
"So, budget traveler," you've been asking yourself, "which is the best restaurant in town, with the most food at the lowest prices, with that down-home atmosphere?" **The Ocean View Inn**, tel. 329-9998, is it! The gigantic menu of Chinese, American, Japanese, and Hawaiian food is like a mini-directory. Lunch and dinner range $6-12, and a huge breakfast goes for about $3.50. The most expensive dinner is T-bone steak at $12.95. They're open daily except Monday, 6:30 a.m.-2:45 p.m. and 5:15-9 p.m., with the bar open daily 6:30 a.m.-9 p.m. Located across from the seawall near the King Kamehameha's Kona Beach Hotel, they're always crowded with local people, a sure sign that the food is good.

Stan's Restaurant, tel. 329-4500, is an open-air establishment one notch up in both price and atmosphere from the Ocean View Inn next door. Here you have a cocktail lounge and a stab at atmosphere with some cozy lighting and rattan furniture. Breakfast is pleasing, with an assortment of island-inspired hotcakes and a special for $3.95; no lunch is served. Dinner specials, starting at 5 p.m., are hibachi chicken or fillet of mahimahi $7.85, fresh island fish $9.95, the "daily special" at $7.95, and the captain's seafood dinner $11.50. All include salad, rice or whipped potatoes, fresh fruit, and dinner bread. However, the best items are their many Hawaiian foods like *kalua* pig and *lala poi* for under $6. The food is good, but not great, and you generally get a square meal for a very reasonable price.

The **Royal Jade Garden**, tel. 326-7288, open Sun.-Thurs.10:30 a.m.-9:30 p.m., Fri.-Sat. until 10 p.m., in the Lanihau Center, is a Chinese restaurant where you can get an amazing amount of well-prepared food for a moderate price. They have the normal run-of-the-mill chow meins for $5.50-7.50, noodle soups under $6, and meat dishes of chicken, duck, pork, or beef for $5.95-7.50. More expensive items include lobster with black bean sauce for $18.95 and a variety of fresh fish and seafoods for $8 and up. But they have an unbeatable special every night: you choose three entrees plus fried rice or fried noodles for only $6.50 (fewer choices less expensive). It's pre-prepared and placed on a hot table, but it's not cooked to death. You wind up with so much food that the most difficult part is keeping it on your plate. In the Royal Jade there's no decor, but if you are hungry and on a tight budget, this is one of the best values in town.

The **Big Island Bagel Company,** in the Kopiko Plaza along Palani Rd., open Mon.-Fri. 6 a.m.-7 p.m., Saturday 7 a.m.-4 p.m., is an upbeat bagelry with a Mediterranean touch achieved by overhanging porticos. The display case is filled with all kinds of bagels: chocolate chip, cinnamon, cinnamon raisin, banana nut, cinnamon apple. There are even bagel pastries, cheese bagels, pizza bagels, bagel sandwiches, and breakfast on a bagel. Pick one that looks yummy and enjoy it with a cup of Royal Kona coffee, iced latte, cafe mocha, or Italian soda. The food is inexpensive, freshly made, and delicious.

Kona's **old industrial area,** although it doesn't sound inviting, is a great place to find inexpensive food, along with stores where the *people* shop. To get to the industrial area, head for the airport, and about one minute north of the junction of Route 19 (the airport road) and Palani Rd., make a left on Kaiwi Street. Or follow Kuakini Rd., a major intersection off Palani Rd. just a minute from the seawall, to Kaiwi Street. The triangle formed by Kaiwi and Kuakini is primarily the old industrial area. The **French Bakery,** Kaahumanu Plaza, 74-5467 Kaiwi St., tel. 326-2688, open weekdays 5:30 a.m.-3 p.m., Saturday 5:30 a.m.-2 p.m., is a budget gourmet deli/restaurant where the food is great and the prices are low. Not only does it have the full range of pastries you would expect, it has wonderful sandwiches like pizza roll with cheese for only $1.75 and with ham or bacon for $2. All of the sandwiches are under $5, and the European-style coffee is full-bodied and rich.

Su's Thai Kitchen, in the industrial area at 74-5588A Pawai Pl. (just off Kaiwi St.), tel. 326-7808, open for lunch weekdays 11 a.m.-2:30 p.m. and for dinner nightly 5-9 p.m., is a semi-open-air restaurant with a distinctive touch of southeast Asia (also in Waimea at the Parker Ranch Shopping Plaza, tel. 885-8688). You can sit inside, but choose a spot on the veranda, where there is absolutely no view but where the breezes blow and bamboo curtains are dropped for a feeling of privacy. The extensive menu offers a *pu pu* platter (a combination of all the appetizers including spring roll, shrimp, and chicken sauté served with homemade plum sauce and peanut sauce) for $10.95. Other choices are lightly breaded and pan-fried shrimp combined with fresh mint, lime juice, garlic, and kafir for $8.95; savory Thai soups mostly with a coconut base, with morsels of fish, scallops, or pork $6.95-9.95; salads $4.95-9.95; and a full selection of curries $7.95-9.95. Vegetarians will be happy with vegetable curry, vegetable stir-fry, or sweet-and-sour vegetables. The daily lunch special for $5.95 might be a mini *pu pu* platter; green curry with chicken and eggplant accompanied by a bowl of white rice; or yellow curry with chicken, potatoes, carrots, and onions with a bowl of white rice. The service is friendly, the portions large for the money. Su's is a favorite with local people—the highest recommendation.

Magic Sands Café, tel. 334-1811, open Mon.-Fri. 11 a.m.-4 p.m., Saturday 11 a.m.-2 p.m., is out of the way—in the old industrial area at 74-5596 Pawai Place, Bay Q, not far from Su's Thai Kitchen—but is worth seeking out because it is inexpensive and gets the "thumbs-up" from local people, always a good sign. Both the decor and the food served are very basic, but portions are plentiful, inexpensive, and very good. The money-saving menu offers fresh catch for only $6.50, Big Island Garden Salad for $3.25, and a variety of plate lunches, vegetarian meals, and sandwiches, all reasonably priced.

A friendly gorilla greets you at the **Pot Belli Deli** (in the industrial area, see above) at 74-5543 Kaiwi St., tel. 329-9454, open weekdays 6 a.m.-4 p.m. The refrigerated deli case holds chicken, ham, or tuna salad sandwiches for $2.65 (jumbo $4.25); spinach pie $4.25; and bagels with cream cheese. The shelves hold all the condiments and extras you need for a terrific picnic lunch. You can get your order to go or eat at one of the few booths inside.

Tom Bombadill's menu takes its inspiration from Tolkien's Middle Earth, but its location is a lot noisier, perched over Ali'i Dr. and overlooking the Royal Kona Resort's tennis courts, open daily 11 a.m.-10 p.m., tel. 329-1292. They talk about the ocean view, but your neck will have to stretch like the mozzarella on their pizza to see it. The bar pours domestic beers at $2.50, imports at $3.50, and pitchers for $8.50. The menu includes all sorts of hamburgers for under $6; soups $3; soup and sandwich combination $5.75; island salad $4.25 small, $7.25 large; steak sandwich $10.25; chicken teriyaki dinner $11.95; shrimp plate $10.25. All of these meals are good but the real specialty is pizza, priced from only $3.25. They also deliver 11:30 a.m.-2:30 p.m., and then again 5-9 p.m., all the way from Keauhou to Palisades. Bombadill's has been around long enough to become a Kona institution.

Harbor House, formerly Attilla's Bar and Grill, at the Honokohau Small Boat Harbor, tel. 326-4166, open daily 10:30 a.m.-8:30 p.m., features Kona's longest bar. Harbor House is more or less an open-air pavilion, but it is actually quite picturesque as it overlooks the harbor. If you are interested in a charter fishing boat, this is the best place to come to spin a yarn with the local skippers who congregate here nightly at about 4:30 p.m. Over the bar hangs a gigantic 1,556-pound marlin, almost as big as the Budweiser sign. Strategically placed TVs make it a good sports bar, and the jukebox has a great selection of oldies and contemporary tunes. A variety of draft beers from Steinlager to Coors Light come in 16-ounce chilled schooners for only $2.50, with Heineken and Carlsburg $2.75. Sunday and Monday, the frothy schooners are only $2, with the same price daily during happy hour 3-6 p.m. The bill of fare offers grilled bacon cheeseburgers with fries for $6.50, shrimp and chips $6.75, crab-salad sandwich $5, clam chowder $3.25, and chili and rice $4.25. Try their delicious macadamia nut pie for $2.50. Harbor House is one of the truly *colorful* places in Kailua-Kona, and one of the best places to relax and have a hassle-free brew.

Giuseppe's, in the Kailua Bay Inn Shopping Plaza at 75-5699F Ali'i Dr. across from the Kona seawall, tel. 329-7888, open daily 11:30 a.m.-9 p.m. and until 4:30 p.m. on Sunday, serves dishes of savory pasta in a tiny but tasteful restaurant where you can dine in or take out. Lunch specials served until 4 p.m. range from spaghetti marinara for $5.50 to fettuccine with artichoke hearts for $6.50. Dinner is *delisioso,* with choices like chicken Marsala $12.75 and scampi Mediterranean $14.25, which includes pasta, dinner salad, and a choice of cheese bread. The minestrone soup served all day for $3.50 per bowl is excellent. The menu is rounded out with a small selection of sandwiches and various dishes from the children's menu for only $4.50 for lunch and $5.50 for dinner. Bring your own beer or wine (the new owners are in the process of getting a liquor license). During the triathlon, Giuseppe's offers all the pasta you can eat for $10.

Aki's Cafe, tel. 329-0090, also in the Kailua Bay Inn Shopping Plaza, is a moderately priced Japanese/American restaurant offering breakfast, lunch, and dinner. Breakfast can be three-egg omelettes $4.95-5.95, egg Benedict scramble $6.95, or pancakes around $3.95. A Japanese breakfast with eggs, miso soup, rice, and choice of meat is $6.95. Lunch can be California sushi $5.50, fried noodles to which you can add chicken or shrimp $5.95, or curry with rice $5.95. Or try the mahimahi burger $6.95, buffalo steak burger $6.95, or BLT or vegetarian sandwiches for under $5. The dinner menu offers marinated New York steak $15.50, chicken teriyaki $10.50, garlic pasta only $6.50, and fish 'n' chips $6.99. There are also cold drinks, ice cream, and coffee, including espresso, cappuccino, and caffe latte. Aki's is a centrally located, simple restaurant that adds a decent touch to ordinary food.

If you look up into the Kona night sky and the moon hits your eye like a big pizza pie, you've probably consumed one too many mai tais and are actually looking into the window of **Basil's Pizzeria and Restaurant** in downtown Kailua-Kona at 75-5707 Ali'i Dr., tel. 326-7836, open daily 11 a.m.-10 p.m., where they make their own pizza dough. Individual gourmet pizzas range $5.95-8.95, depending upon your choice of toppings; New York-style pizza, 14-inch and 16-inch, is $8.95-14.95. Besides pizza, Basil's offers soup of the day for $2.95,Italian antipasto $6.95, angel hair primavera $8.95, fettuccine Alfredo $8.95, and spaghetti with marinara sauce $6.95 (with meatballs $7.95). There is also seafood: shrimp marinara $12.95 and scallops scampi $13.95. Or try eggplant parmigiana at $8.95. A nightly "fresh catch special" is priced around $13.95, or you can order any number of sandwiches and burgers for under $6. Basil's offers free delivery of any item on the menu all along Ali'i Drive . So go ahead, recline on your condo lanai and call Basil's, and they'll be over *molto rapido.*

King Yee Lau, open Mon.-Sat. 11 a.m.-2 p.m., nightly 5-9 p.m., in the Ali'i Sunset Plaza at 75-5799 Ali'i Dr. across from the seawall at the south end of town, tel. 329-7100, offers an all-you-can-eat lunch buffet and the usual Chinese dishes like pressed crisp duck, beef with ginger sauce, and shrimp with seasoned vegetables, all priced under $7.95. Vegetarians can dine on tofu with oyster sauce or a variety of chow mein for under $6.50.

Thai Rin, tel. 329-2929, also in the Ali'i Sunset Plaza, open weekdays for lunch 11 a.m.-2:30 p.m., dinner 5-9:30 p.m., fills the air in the small plaza with the aromas of its savory Thai spices. The menu offers spring rolls $4.95; fried noodles Chinese-style $6.95; vegetarian dishes like Thai fried rice $7.95; stir-fried chicken, beef, or pork $7.95; and Thai garlic shrimp or squid $8.95. Thai Rin features a variety of lunch specials for about $5.95.

Mona's Barbecue, tel. 326-2532, also in the Ali'i Plaza, open Mon.-Fri. 11 a.m.-9 p.m., Saturday 12-9 p.m., is an eat in or takeout plate lunch restaurant where $6-7 will get you teriyaki chicken, chicken *katsu,* spicy pork ribs, or a barbecued burger with a variety of trimmings. Mona's is basic, clean, local, and cheap.

Fast Foods, Coffee, Delis, and Snacks

You can't get "hotter" than **Lava Java** in the **Ali'i Sunset Plaza** at 75-5799 Ali'i Dr., across from the seawall at the south end of town, open daily 7 a.m.-10 p.m., Kona's popular coffeehouse/restaurant. Here, local people and tourists alike come to kick back, read the papers, and actually engage in the lost art of conversation. Sandwiches are served 9 a.m.-7 p.m. on white or whole wheat bread or a freshly baked baguette. Try the turkey and cranberry sandwich for $5.95, a garden burger for $4.50, Polish hot dog for $3.25, or croissants topped with hot ham and cheese. Or try the pastrami and cheese melt for under $5. Lava Java has a counter offering muffins, cookies, root beer floats, Kona coolers made with tropical fruit sorbet, Italian sodas, and ice cream. Bulk coffee by the pound (about $18) is also available.

A Piece of the Apple, also in the Ali'i Sunset Plaza, open Mon.-Sat. 8 a.m.-4 p.m., is a New York-style deli with a healthful twist. Offered are fresh carrot juice, fresh-squeezed orange juice, smoothies, and fresh baked bagels. The deli section has two-fisted sandwiches like the Reuben $7.25, New Yorker (pastrami with Swiss cheese) $7.25, vegetarian $7.25, and "Seinfeld" (smoked turkey, roasted red peppers, mozzarella, and red onions) $7.25. Light appetites will enjoy a California salad with smoked turkey, avocado, and Swiss cheese $5.75, chef salad $5.75, garden salad $5.75, or house salad $2.50. You can sit inside, but the best spot is outside at a picnic table shaded by dwarf palms.

At the Kona Inn Shopping Village, try one of the following. **Mrs. Barry's Cookies** are homemade yummies that include macadamia nut, chocolate chip, and peanut butter, gift boxed to send home. Follow your nose to the **Coffee Cantata** and drink a cup in the little courtyard. **Kona Kai Farms Coffee House** features a sampler cup of Kona coffee.

To get your motor revved up on an early Kona morning, order a mug of locally grown coffee from **Hawaiian Angel Brand Coffee,** located next door to the Ocean View Inn, along Ali'i Dr. just near the pier. They serve coffee by the cup $1.25 and homemade lemonade $1.75, along with cappuccino, double espressos for Dr. Kevorkian failures, and farmer-direct coffee at $6.50 per pound. They're under a yellow umbrella in the little nook with a few tables on the front porch.

Around town, the **Bartender's Ocean Breeze** serves up 12-ounce mugs of ice-cold beer for $1 and grill-your-own burgers for $2.75. Other snacks are available on Ali'i Dr. near the Royal Kona Resort tennis courts, tel. 329-7622.

In the Kona Marketplace, **Chili by Max,** open Mon.-Sat. 10 a.m.-8 p.m., Sunday 11 a.m.-8 p.m., is famous for its award-winning oven-baked chili, made with beef or turkey. Also on the bill of fare are kosher hot dogs, chili dogs, chili nachos, baked potatoes, and ice cream.

Across Sarona Rd. from Kona Marketplace and down toward Kuakini Hwy. there's **Subway Sandwiches,** a chain selling double-fisted sandwiches to go. On Kuakini Hwy. next to **McDon-**

ald's golden arches is a **7-Eleven,** open 24 hours; and along Palani Rd. is **Taco Bell,** next door to **Pizza Hut,** which is across the road from **Burger King.**

In the Lanihau Center along Palani Rd., you can snack at **Buns In The Sun,** open Mon.-Fri. 5 a.m.-5 p.m., Saturday until 4 p.m., Sunday until 3 p.m., a bakery-deli serving everything from croissants to apple turnovers, along with espresso, cappuccino, and latte. Breakfast specials include a fried egg on a Kaiser roll for $2; or deviled egg and ham and cheese on a Kaiser for $3.70. Also enjoy sandwiches priced around $5.50, or homemade soups like garden vegetable or cream of mushroom, served with a roll for only $1.99. Sit, eat, and enjoy at a wrought-iron table under their outdoor canopy. The center's **Kona Grill,** open Mon.-Thurs. 6 a.m.-8 p.m., Friday to 10 p.m., Saturday 8 a.m.-10 p.m., and Sunday 8 a.m.-4 p.m., is a counter restaurant serving standard breakfasts and plates like teriyaki beef, *kalbi* ribs, and shrimp platter for about $6.50. The Kona Grill is not special, but the food is acceptable and inexpensive. The center also houses **Kentucky Fried Chicken,** where you can pick up a bucket Mon.-Thurs. 10 a.m.-9:30 p.m., Fri.-Sat. 10 a.m.-10 p.m., Sunday 10 a.m.-9:30 p.m.; and **Baskin-Robbins,** open daily 11 a.m.-10 p.m., selling cones of their famous 31 flavors. For an island treat try **Island Snow,** a kiosk outside of Long's selling shave ice with plenty of flavors to choose from.

Rocky's Pizza, tel. 322-3223, open daily 11 a.m.-9 p.m. at the Keauhou Shopping Village, offers whole pizzas for $9.95-14.95 or slices for $1.75 each. Rocky's also features delicious sub sandwiches like hot pastrami on crusty bread; they are favorites with the locals, who like good food at a good price.

In the Kopiko Plaza, along Palani Rd. and just down from the Lanihau Center, you'll find several places to eat: **Yuni's,** tel. 329-1018, is open daily 10:30 a.m.-8 p.m. This basic saimin stand offer *charsiu* saimin $4.39, seafood *udon* $5.75, and a variety of other noodle dishes under $6. **Domino's Pizza** offers eat in, takeout, or delivery; **Mask** is a bar and grill so new that it hasn't developed a personality yet; and **Kona Mix Plate** serves inexpensive plate lunches. The best, however, is **Big Island Bagel Co.**

The Kona Coast Shopping Center, also along Palani Rd., has a number of small local and ethnic restaurants in their "food court" where you can get inexpensive but savory meals. For the health-conscious, **Kona Health Ways** (see "Food Stores and Supermarkets" under "Shopping" in the Out and About chapter), open Mon.-Sat. 9 a.m.-8 p.m., Sunday to 7 p.m., is a full-service health food store that makes ready-to-eat sandwiches, salads, and soups geared toward the vegetarian. Other places are: **Poquito Mas,** a Mexican "window restaurant" with burritos, quesadillas, nachos, enchiladas, and tacos all priced well under $5; and **Betty's Kitchen,** open Mon.-Sat. 10 a.m.-9 p.m., Sunday 10 a.m.-7 p.m., offering Chinese food with plenty of vegetarian selections—many priced under $6.50. Inside, the interior is black-and-white tile and there's a walk-up counter. Next door is the **Kamuela Deli,** open Mon.-Sun.,10 a.m.-9 p.m., with plate lunches like teriyaki beef or breaded veal with "two scoop rice" and macaroni salad around $6. They also offer sandwiches ranging from a BLT to a mahi burger $2.45. Finally, for a quick snack, try **TCBY Yogurt,** open 11 a.m.-10 p.m.

You can perk up 24 hours a day at **Crusin Coffee Kona** at the King Kamehameha Mall, tucked away at the bottom of Pilani Road. The tasteful coffee shop is done in red, white, and black. Choose espresso, cappuccino, mocha, or just a good old cup of "joe" made from local Kahauloa coffee or SBC, a blend imported from Seattle. Also on the menu are Kona Natural Juices, ice cream, milk shakes, Italian cream sodas, cookies, cinnamon rolls, bagels, and sandwiches.

On your way to Pu'uhonua O Honaunau you might consider stopping at **Barry's Nut Farm** along Route 160. They'll give you a free tour of the gardens and nursery, or you can browse for pottery or buy sandwiches and drinks. Open daily 9 a.m.-5 p.m., tel. 329-6055.

Moderate

Cafe Sibu, in the Kona Banyan Court, open daily 11:30 a.m.-3 p.m. for lunch and 5-9 p.m. for dinner, tel. 329-1112, is an Indonesian restaurant serving savory marinated meats and vegetables spiced with zesty sauces and flame grilled. The restaurant, across from the seawall under the big banyan tree, has only a few outside tables and makes a light attempt at decor with a few antique Indonesian masks. They do, however, win the prize for the most ventilated restaurant in all of Hawaii, with nine ceiling fans whirring in a 10- by 10-foot room! To make the menu even more varied, the Italian owner offers a daily pasta dish, using recipes over 100 years old that have been handed down by her grandmother. *Delisioso!* If you're hungry, go for the *gado gado* for $9.50, an Indonesian salad layered with spices and peanut sauce that can be dinner for one or a salad entree for two or three. Stir-fried vegetables with chicken or tofu are $9.95; chicken and vegetable curries are $10.50 and $8 respectively; and Balinese chicken marinated in tarragon, garlic, and spices is $10.95. The combination plates are the best deals: you get a stir-fry, chicken curry, and choice of sauté for $11.95. Lunch prices on all of the above are about $2 cheaper. Cafe Sibu serves *the* best and *the* most interesting moderately priced food in Kailua-Kona.

Look for a bright *akachochin,* a red paper lantern, marking the entrance to **Restaurant Yokohama** in the Ali'i Sunset Plaza at 75-5799 Ali'i Dr., across from the seawall at the south end of town, tel. 329-9661, open Tuesday, Friday, and Sunday for lunch 11 a.m.-2 p.m., and Tues.-Sun. 5:30-9 p.m. Inside is simplicity: Japanese kites, light wood furniture, and a few glowing lanterns. Their classic lunches include *soba sukiyaki* for $7; *teishoku* or fixed-plate lunch such as *tonkatsu* pork cutlets that includes an appetizer, salad, rice, and miso soup for $7; a sushi combination for $8.50; and *donburi,* "something" on rice, like grilled beef for around $7. Start dinner with appetizers like sashimi $6.50, fried chicken $5.50, or *tsukemono* $4. Move on to traditional entrees cooked right at your table, like sukiyaki $21.25, or *shabu shabu,* thin slices of beef and assorted vegetables boiled in stock $23.50. Restaurant Yokohama also features sushi combination dinners $9.25-15.25. Although in a shopping plaza, both the atmosphere and cuisine are genuine.

The **Kona Ranch House** is a delightful restaurant with something for everyone. It has two rooms: the family-oriented *Paniolo* Room, where hearty appetites are filled family style; and the elegant Plantation Lanai, where both palate and sense of beauty are satiated. This restaurant, highlighted by copper drainpipes, brass ceiling fans, wicker furniture, and latticework, all against a natural wood-and-brick background, epitomizes plantation dining. The Kona Ranch House is a classy establishment where you get more than what you pay for. Prices range from reasonable to expensive, and the menus in the two separate rooms reflect this. Open daily 6:30 a.m.-10 p.m., and Sunday for brunch. Reservations are needed for the Plantation Lanai. The restaurant is located two minutes from downtown, at the corner of Kuakini Hwy. and Palani Rd., tel. 329-7061.

The **Jolly Roger,** walking distance from downtown at 75-5776 Ali'i Dr., tel. 329-1344, is another Kona restaurant with a remarkable seaside setting. The gently rolling surf lapping at the shore is like free dessert. Full breakfasts are served 6:30 a.m.-noon and start at $4, with waffles and pancakes cheaper. Lunch is served 11 a.m.-4 p.m., dinner 5:30-10 p.m. Sandwiches start at $3; assorted salads are $5; full salad bar is $5.95; and entrees of fresh fish, seafood, and beef are from $10. Happy hour daily, 11 a.m.-6 p.m., features an assortment of *pu pu.* A daily special of steak and eggs Benedict, available 6:30 a.m.-noon, costs $4.75. The decor is bent bamboo with puffy cushions, and the tile-floored veranda has marble-topped tables and white wrought-iron chairs.

Banana Bay Buffet, tel. 329-1393, is located in the courtyard of Uncle Billy's downtown Kona Bay Hotel. Following in the semi-plastic Polynesian tradition of Uncle Billy, they serve a fair to passable buffet for $8.95. A stuffed marlin, seemingly too huge and colorful to be real, gazes down at everyone from the wall. Sometimes free hula shows are part of the bargain. Open daily at 6:30 a.m. (breakfast special $4.95), this restaurant could be an "old reliable" with a touch more care in the food preparation.

Cassandra's Greek Taverna, tel. 334-1066, open Mon.-Sat. 11 a.m.-10 p.m., Sunday 4:30-9 p.m., tucked away along Ali'i Dr. in the Kona Plaza Shopping Center, uses a predominant blue and white motif reminiscent of the Greek Isles. A full bar features liquors, wines, and beer, while the lunch menu offered 11 a.m.-4 p.m. serves up omelettes with pita bread and feta cheese $5.95, a Greek pita pizza with spinach and feta cheese $6.95, and *souvlaki* made with chicken, beef, or pork $7.95-8.95. Traditional appetizers include *dolmades* (grape leaves stuffed with meat and rice) $5.95, *keftedes* (pan-fried Greek meatballs) with *satziki* $4.95, or stuffed kalamari $7.95 (no "c" in Greek). Entrees are savory: a *gyro* plate $12.95, Greek-style baby pork ribs $17.95, *souvlaki* kabobs of beef, chicken, pork or shrimp $12.95-21.95, garlic prawns $21.95, or steak and lobster $22. Cassandra's also features stir-fry "a la George" with chicken, beef, prawns, or vegetables $10.95-15.95, along with a sample platter for two $38.95. The interior is quite comfortable with white captain's chairs or bent back bamboo chairs with armrests and fluffy pillows. The bar is tucked in the corner. Earthy, vibrant Greek music to stir the soul wafts through the air.

Don Drysdale's Club 53, open daily 10 a.m.-2 a.m., tel. 329-6651, is owned by the famous Dodger pitcher and in the good sense of the word can best be described as a saloon. The amiable bar and grill serves reasonably priced beer, drinks, and sandwiches until 1 a.m. Sports fans away from home can always catch their favorite events on the bar's TV. Fare includes soup and salads from $2.50, a wide variety of *pu pu* from $4, sandwiches $3-5, plus the special peanut-butter cream pie at $2.35. Drysdale's is one of the most relaxing and casual bars in town, overlooking the bay at the Kona Inn Shopping Village.

Located on the second floor across from the pier, **Kona Galley,** tel. 329-5550, open for lunch 11:30 a.m.-4 p.m. and for dinner 4-9 p.m., features bright paintings of sunsets, flowers, and ferns reflecting the island mood of the beach and bay below. Lunchtime begins with gourmet burgers, from the simple and unadorned at $5.95 to the Cajun Burger for $6.95, or try a Chicken Sandwich $6.95, a New York Steak Sandwich $9.95, or the Galley Natural, a vegetarian sandwich $6.50. Dinner is more full-bodied, with dishes like chicken Jerusalem made with mushrooms, garlic, artichoke hearts, capers, and a Dijon dill sauce $12.95; scallops or shrimp Bombay $16.95; Pacific seafood medley, a mix of shrimp, scallops, and fresh fish, all sautéed with garlic and served with lemon butter $18.95; or a New York steak and lobster tail $32.95.

Quinn's is Kona's socially eclectic bar and grill where everyone from local bikers to pink-roasted tourists are welcomed. It's also a roost for nighthawks who come here to munch and have a beer when everything else in town is closed. Quinn's, across from the King Kamehameha's Kona Beach Hotel, is open daily for lunch 11 a.m.-5:30 p.m. and dinner 5:30 p.m.-1 a.m. (Sunday until 10 p.m.), tel. 329-3822. The local in-crowd comes to the patio for sandwiches, vegetarian specialties, and seafood. The inside bar is cozy, friendly, and sports oriented. For lunch, a gigantic mound of shrimp and crab salad for $8.95 is wonderful. The fresh catch-of-the-day sandwiches with salad for $8.25 are a deal, but they're not always available. Reasonably priced specialties include tenderloin tips sautéed in brandy with onions for $8.95, shrimp and chips for $8.95, and fish and chips for $6.95. Dinner entrees are savory: sautéed scallops $15.95, chicken stir-fry $12.95, and fresh catch sautéed or baked for $18.50 up. All include soup or dinner salad, vegetable, rice, and Quinn's homefried potatoes.

Cool down with a frosty margarita and watch life go by as you perch on a stool at the upstairs location of **Pancho and Lefty's,** 75-5719 Ali'i Dr., tel. 326-2171, open daily 11 a.m.-10 p.m., happy hour 3-6 p.m. with 12-ounce drafts for $1 and big, potent 16-ounce margaritas for $2.75. Menu selections begin with Buffalo wings $6.95, skinny dippers (potatoes covered with bacon and cheese or guacamole) $5.95, and nachos $7.95. Full dinners include taco salad $7.95; seafood salad with crisp greens $9.95; or fajitas—steak, chicken or seafood (fresh catch)—$15.95 (an order for two is $22.95). Specials are enchilada rancheros $10.95, carne asada $12.95, tostada $8.95, or Mexican burger $6.95. "Tight-Wad Tuesday" saves money with two entrees from the "Just Mexican Menu" for the price of one. Finish off your meal with ice cream, cheesecake, or cinnamon crisps. Pancho and Lefty's is a good-time place with satisfying food that's easy on the budget.

When you enter the Kaloko Industrial Park (not Kona's old industrial area near downtown), just past mile marker 97 and about three miles north from Kailua-Kona, the setting makes you think you're after plumbing supplies. What you'll find is terrific food prepared by one of Hawaii's greatest chefs at **Sam Choy's Restaurant,** tel. 326-1545, open weekdays 6 a.m.-2 p.m. and Wed.-Sat. 5-9 p.m. for dinner, reservations suggested. To get there, make a right along the main road as soon as you enter the industrial park, and pass a gas station (a good place to fuel if you're returning your rental car to the airport). About 50 yards past the gas station, make a left and look for Sam's in a nondescript gray building halfway up the hill on the right. The atmosphere is pleasant enough, but those in the know who have dined on Sam's sumptuous creations, either here or at the old Kona Hilton (where he used to be executive chef), come for the food! Breakfasts like the ultimate stew omelette (a three-egg omelette filled with Sam's beef stew) $6.95, steak and eggs $8.95, or the local favorite of fried rice and egg for $4, will keep you going most of the day. The regular menu also includes fresh island fish prepared poke style and then flash-fried for $6.95; Kaloko steak marinated in teriyaki sauce with grilled onions $8.95; and Kaloko noodle mania (chow mein noodles cooked with fresh vegetable and meat and served in a crispy wonton ball) for $6.75 Or try one of the specials, such as fresh *ahi* sauté $9.95, or homemade beef stew $6.50. For a gourmet dinner, choose oriental lamb chops with shiitake mushrooms $19.95, vegetable pasta $16.95, Sam Choy's Award Winning seafood *lau lau* made with fresh fish, assorted veggies, and Waipio Valley taro leaves for $23.95, or Chinese honey duck with Kau orange sauce for $17.95, all with soup and salad. Sam prepares wonderful food, and being a dad himself, he doesn't forget the kids—they have their own menu.

Under The Palms, tel. 329-7366, is an open-air bar and restaurant owned and operated by Brian Anderson, who also owns the Palm Café, tel. 329-7765, which is not only upscale, but literally upstairs. Their motto, "Please come in. If you don't we'll both starve," sets the tone for this much more casual and much less expensive yet good restaurant. Breakfast is traditional, with poached eggs on an English muffin $6.95, or da kine waffle with maple syrup $3.95, along with sticky bun pastries $1.50 and Kona coffee, both regular and flavored. Lunch brings specialties like Hawaiian wild boar green chili with tortilla rojas and hapa tomato stuffs $5.25; or shellfish antipasto marinated in white wine vinaigrette with sausage, olives, artichokes, assorted cheeses, and wild mushrooms $12.95. Or try the full plate salads, like Kona mixed greens $4.75 or **yaki soba** (fried noodle) salad with chicken, cucumbers, and Asian vegetables $8.25. Sandwiches include roast beef $7.95 and smoked turkey club $9.25. They also have a full bar where you can get beers like Budweiser, Coors, or Pacific Golden Ale for $3, Fire Rock Pale Ale made here in Kona for $3.75, or old favorites like Anchor Steam and Guinness for $4.50. Under the Palms has a small wine selection, exotic drinks, and a cappuccino bar to finish off your meal. Sit back and enjoy the nat-

Chef Sam Choy (left) and assistant

J.D. BISIGNANI

ural rhythm from the sea just across the road while local musicians blend their voices in lovely Hawaiian harmonies every night.

Calling **Bianelli's** "just a pizza shop" is like calling a Ferrari "just a car." Although they make pizza, and it is superb, they also have a full deli counter and plenty of delicious lunch and dinner entrees, all of which they deliver. Bianelli's has two locations, the main shop at the Pine Plaza at 75-240 Nani-Kailua between Hualalai Rd. and the Kona Belt Rd., tel. 326-4800, open Mon.-Fri. 11 a.m.-10 p.m., and Sat.-Sun. 5-11 p.m., dinner only; and a more limited shop at The Club in Kona, a fitness center located at the Kona Center where you can get protein drinks, juices, pizza by the slice, and salads (made with organic local greens when possible). The full menu includes specialty sandwiches like a scrumptious Philly cheese steak served on fresh-baked French bread, and meals such as manicotti, a variety of spaghetti dishes, and lasagna, all well under $10. A great deal is "all you can eat" homemade pasta for only $7.45, or $9.20 with salad. Bianelli's makes their own pizza dough, and they offer pizza pies ranging from $7.95 for a hand-tossed, New York-style mini-pizza to $15.95 for an exotic pie smothered in garlic and herb sauce, layered with Parmesan and buffalo-milk-mozzarella cheeses, and topped with whole peeled tomatoes and fresh herbs. Vegetarian pizza topped with artichoke hearts, eggplant, sun-dried tomatoes, and Maui onions costs about $14. The wine cellar is outstanding, with over 64 different selections ranging from California merlot to French pinot noir; prices range from about $14 to over $200 per bottle. Bianelli's also has a tremendous selection of domestic and imported beers. The interior is tastefully decorated in Italian-American style with the mandatory red-checkered tablecloths, while the walls are covered with posters ranging from blues legend Lead Belly to bicycle great Greg Le Monde. The food and service at both are excellent. *Delisioso!*

Kona Amigos, across the seawall in downtown Kailua-Kona at 75-5669 Ali'i Dr., tel. 326-2840, is open daily 11 a.m.-10 p.m. for food, with the bar open a little later. The cantina features special dishes like beef, chicken, fresh fish, or vegetarian fajitas priced $14-18 and enough for two; or enchilada rancheras for

$10.50. Less expensive but savory items include a fiesta tostada $9.95, chiles rellenos $11.95, and the Mauna Loa (roasted pork rolled in a flour tortilla) $11.95. The Southwestern Caesar salad for $9.95 comes with either grilled chicken breast or grilled fresh fish. Happy hour is 3-6 p.m. daily with bargains on well drinks and margaritas, while Bud Light Drafts are $1.50. Free tostada bar Mon.-Wed.-Fri., when you can have a snack whipped up before your eyes. Sit on the veranda to people-watch or to survey the entire harbor area. In season, the Kona Triathlon starts and finishes in front of this restaurant.

Kaminari's, open Mon.-Sat. 5:30-9 p.m., tel. 326-7799, is an authentic and moderately priced Japanese restaurant located in the Kopiko Plaza along Palani Rd. just near the Lanihau Center. The decor is functional cafeteria style, and the menu includes tempura or *tonkatsu donburi* (deep-fried shrimp, vegetables, and pork cutlet atop rice) $7; an assortment of *teishoku*, including soup, salad, pickles, and rice for $11.80; sashimi priced daily; Japanese-style steak $13.80; and yakitori (grilled chicken) $5.50.

Expensive

Oui oui monsieur, but of course we have zee restaurant *Français*. It is **La Bourgogne,** tel. 329-6711, open Mon.-Sat. 6-10 p.m., located in Kuakini Plaza South, five minutes from downtown Kailua-Kona along Route 11. Guy Chatelard, the original owner of La Bourgogne, has recently sold the restaurant to master chef Ron Gallagher and his manager wife Colleen Moore. Guy stayed on for a transition period, sharing his recipes and food philosophy with Ron and Colleen, who are dedicated to keeping up the fine service and cuisine. For those who just can't live without escargots, shrimp Provençal, or pheasant, you've been saved. How much? Plenty, *mon petit!* Cold and hot appetizers include *pâté du chef* for $6, jumbo shrimp cocktail for $12.50, and escargot d'Bourgogne $7.50. Soups of the day are scrumptious: French onion $4.50 and homemade lobster soup (when available) $6.00. For salads, order greens with choice of homemade dressing $4, or Caesar or wilted spinach salad both priced at $4.25. Titillating seafood and poultry entrees feature fresh catch-of-the-day $21; jumbo shrimp in butter, parsley, and garlic sauce $24.95; and breast of chicken filled with mousse of veal, ham, and morel mushrooms $15.95. Meat courses are delectable roast saddle of lamb with creamy mustard sauce $28.50, or tenderloin of venison with dried cherries and pomegranate sauce $28.50. Top off your gourmet meal with fresh, made-in-house desserts. This restaurant, small and slightly out of the way, is definitely worth a visit for those who enjoy exceptional food.

Jameson's-by-the Sea, open for lunch weekdays 11 a.m.-2:30 p.m. and dinner every evening 5:30-10 p.m., is located at 77-6452 Ali'i Dr. next to Kona Magic Sands Condo, tel. 329-3195. Jameson's makes a good attempt at elegance with high-backed wicker chairs, crystal everywhere, white linen table settings, and a back-lit fish tank in the entry. The sea foams white and crashes on the shore just outside the restaurant's open windows. The quality of the food is very good, just shy of gourmet. The bar serves domestic beer for $3, imported beer $3.75, well drinks $4, and exotics $5.50, which you can take to the veranda with some *pu pu* to enjoy the sunset. The lunch menu lists appetizers like sashimi, salmon pâté, fried calamari, and shrimp cocktail, all from $7.95. Lunch sandwiches are hearty fish of the day, grilled ham and cheese, or teriyaki steak for around $8. A number of seafood Louie salads made with crab, shrimp, or other seafood cost around $10. The dinner menu offers the same appetizers but adds a seafood platter with sashimi shrimp and fresh oysters $10.50. The dinner entrees range from fresh catches like *opakapaka, ono,* and mahimahi at market price, to fried shrimp and scallops with oyster sauce and Chinese pea pods $18.95. Other full meals include filet mignon with béarnaise sauce for $22.95, baked stuffed shrimp $18.95, and sesame chicken $17.95. There's also shrimp curry with mango chutney $18.95. For dessert save room for their assortment of homemade chiffon pies from $4.50.

At **Huggo's Restaurant,** tel. 329-1493, on Ali'i Dr. next door to the Royal Kona Resort, it's difficult to concentrate on the food because the setting is so spectacular. If you were any closer to the sea, you'd be in it, and of course the sunset is great. Because it is built on a pier, you can actually feel the floor rock. When you are having dinner, ask the waitperson for some bread between courses so that you can feed the fish. Huggo's is open Mon.-Fri. 11:30 a.m.-2:30 p.m. for full lunch service, 2:30-5 p.m. for late-lunch sandwiches only served at the bar, and 5:30-10 p.m. for dinner, with entertainment most nights. Waiters and waitresses are outfitted in alohawear, and the heavy wooden tables are inlaid with maps of the Pacific. Huggo's executive chef, Mark Painter, and the head chef, Peter Bartsch from Switzerland, have created a combination of continental, Hawaiian, and Pacific Rim cuisine that is extraordinarily good and affordable. Lunch is reasonable, with tasties like Huggo's club; or try a gourmet Boboli pizza with

Many of Kailua-Kona's restaurants are found in shopping plazas like Waterfront Row.

J.D. BISIGNANI

your choice of toppings for around $8. Huggo's burgers are around $8 and include the classic Huggo (with onions and mushrooms and your choice of Swiss or American cheese), the garden burger (a nonmeat patty with all the trimmings), the fresh-catch burger (priced daily), and the teriyaki chicken burger. Lunch salads include the Kona Caesar for $7.25 and the Chinese chicken salad $8.95. Meat-lovers must try Huggo's "almost world famous" barbecued ribs with beans $7.95—more on your plate than you can eat—served only on Tuesday and Thursday at lunchtime. The dinner menu is superb and starts with fresh *sashimi* (which can be seared on request) at market price; and seafood chowder made from clams and fresh fish and seasoned with sherry, cream sauce, and butter, a reasonable $3.50 per cup or $5.25 per bowl. The best entrees come from the sea just outside the door and are priced daily at around $22. A fantastic selection is the stuffed fish, delicious with an exotic blend of tender bay shrimp and Dijonaise sauce. Also worth trying is shrimp scampi $21.95; or Kona paella made with fresh fish, Maine lobster claw, shrimp, and chicken all tossed with lemon and saffron and served with rice pilaf $22.95. Huggo's has been in business for over 27 years, and is consistently outstanding. Enjoy free *pu pu* Mon.-Fri. 4-6 p.m. while sipping a cocktail as the red Kona sun dips into the azure sea.

The Kona Inn Restaurant at the Kona Inn Shopping Village, tel. 329-4455, open daily for lunch and dinner, is a lovely but lonely carry-over from the venerable old Kona Inn. Part of the deal for tearing down the Kona Inn and putting up the Kona Inn Shopping Village was giving the restaurant a prime location. On entering, notice the marlin over the doorway and a huge piece of hung glass through which the sunset sometimes forms prismatic rainbows. The bar and dining area are richly appointed in native koa and made more elegant with a mixture of turn-of-the-century wooden chairs, high-backed peacock thrones, polished hardwood floors, and sturdy open-beam ceilings. If you want to enjoy the view, try a cocktail and some of the *pu pu* served all day, or try one of the light choices like guacamole and chips $5.95, pasta and chicken salad $8.95, or shrimp salad $9.95. Lunch is reasonable: steak sandwich $11.95,

or Hawaiian chicken sandwich on whole-wheat bun with pineapple and cheese $6.95. The dinner menu starts with Boston chowder $3.45 and mixed green salad of crisp romaine tossed with Caesar dressing and topped with bay shrimp for a very reasonable $4.95. The specialties are local fish like *ono, ahi, opakapaka,* or mahimahi for around $20; and seafood pasta topped with shrimp, scallops, and mussels for $18.95. Less expensive selections include stir-fried chicken for $13.95 and chicken chardonnay (chicken lightly sautéed with chardonnay, simmered in a Dijon cream sauce, and served over fettuccine with leeks and mushrooms) for $15.95. The Kona Inn Restaurant epitomizes Kona beachside dining and the view is simply superb.

Michelangelo's, in Waterfront Row at 75-5770 Ali'i Dr., tel. 329-4436, is run by Mike Medeiros—a true Meditarraneo if there ever was one. It is open for lunch daily 11 a.m.-4 p.m., and for dinner until 10 p.m., with a limited late night supper menu until 1 a.m. Savory selections include antipasto for two at $6.95-11.95, clam chowder $4.95, and specialty salads that could make a meal, like scallops, crab, and shrimp marinated in olive oil, garlic, and fresh herbs for $10.95. For lunch, try seafood frutte d'mare $10.95, Kona crust pizza $7.95-8.95, Italian hamburger with feta cheese $6.95, risotto ala formagio $7.95, or fresh fish of the day sandwich sautéed or Cajun style $8.95. For pasta dishes choose penne or rigatoni $9.95, spaghetti and meatballs $8.95, or chicken parmesan $9.95. A great lunch special is chardonnay shrimp scampi $11.95. A children's menu with items all priced around $4.95 offers a bambino burger and spaghetti marinara, among other dishes. The dinner menu brings angel leaf Caesar salad $8.95, spaghetti boulinnaise $12.95, chicken parmesan $16.95, Lava Fire Calamari $17.95, or Norwegian smoked salmon $18.95. The extensive wine list offers varietals from Italy, France, Australia, and California. The large room is appointed with open-beam ceilings joined by distinctive copper couplings, and with Casablanca fans. Weekends bring live music, with Hawaiian headliners like Willie K.

Also in Waterfront Row, the **Chart House,** tel. 329-2451, open daily for dinner 5-10 p.m., is part of a small chain of restaurants that have built a good reputation for service, value, and well-prepared food. Primarily, they are a steak and seafood house with most meals costing $16-25. The location is very pleasant, away from the street noise and with a good view of the sea.

The Continent meets Asia on a Pacific island by way of the magnificent creations of master chef Daniel Thiebaut at the **Palm Cafe,** Coconut Grove Marketplace, 75-5819 Ali'i Dr., tel. 329-7765, open daily 5:30-10 p.m., reservations suggested. Perched above Ali'i Dr., with the sea in the distance, the restaurant has an elegant interior comfortably done in a soothing green-on-green motif with high-backed chairs, linen tablecloths, large louvered windows, and subdued lighting. Start with seared *ahi* served on a bed of crisp leeks and jicama stir-fry $7.50, or Chinese ravioli stuffed with ground pork, shiitake mushrooms, balsamic vinegar, and ginger butter sauce. Salads range from Big Island field greens with Portuguese sweet bread and croutons for $5.50 to the Palm Cafe Caesar for a very reasonable $4.50. Vegetarians will be pleased with vegetable and tofu tempura $16.50, or timbale of vegetables with a Hawaiian chili curry sauce and brown rice $15. The fresh fish dishes are the best, whether prepared with lemon and cilantro butter; Kona style, with ginger, green onions, shoyu, and hot peanut oil; or with an elegant vinaigrette of Kau orange and benishoga. The fish itself is grilled or steamed; daily quote about $22. Another specialty is baked *ono* with almond sesame crust, papaya, and Kona tomato relish, made piquant with ginger lime sauce. The wine selection is superb and can be counted on to complement the meal perfectly. To top off your meal, choose one of the devilish pastry selections, and end with the Earl Gray Tea liqueur.

The **Kona Beach Restaurant,** tel. 329-2911, at the King Kamehameha's Kona Beach Hotel, is open daily for breakfast, lunch, and dinner and is especially known for its Sunday brunch served 9 a.m.-1 p.m. Appetizers include crab cakes for $6.95 and sashimi medley $7.95, while entrées range from kiawe-smoked prime rib of beef at $17.95 to barbecued baby-back ribs for $13.95. More moderately priced pastas are made scrumptious with Cajun prawns or sautéed with herbs and spices. Fresh catch or broiled salmon combined with prime rib is $19.95. Hearty luncheon sandwiches are reasonably priced—served with french fries for

under $8. The restaurant itself is tasteful, but the best feature is an unobstructed view of the hotel's beach, especially fine at sunset.

Luaus, Buffets, Etc.

The **Keauhou Beach Hotel Buffet,** tel. 322-3441, at the hotel's Kuakini Terrace, is legendary. People in the know flock here especially for the Seafood Prime Rib Buffet for $21.95, children $9.95, served Fri.-Sunday. Fill your plate again and again with Alaskan snow crab legs, prime rib (excellent), seafood Newburg, sautéed mahimahi, fresh teriyaki marlin, deep-fried oysters, New England clam chowder, sashimi, *poki,* and boiled shrimp. They also have a great dessert bar with Boston cream pies, strawberry shortcake, rich double-chocolate carrot cake, and banana cream pie. A Chinese buffet is offered Monday and Tuesday for $13.95, children $7.95, and features roast duck, dim sum, Mandarin salad, and a medley of Cantonese and Sichuan selections. The restaurant has a beautiful view of the coast, and dinner is rounded off with live nightly entertainment. On Wednesday and Thursday, the Hawaiian Buffet is served with all the dishes that would have pleased King Kamehameha; $13.95 adults, $7.95 children. Each of the nightly buffets is served 5-9 p.m.

Tihati's Drums of Polynesia Luau at the Royal Kona Resort, tel. 329-3111, held every Monday, Friday, and Saturday, offers an authentic evening of entertainment and feasting, Hawaiian style. The luau begins at 5:30 p.m. and is followed by an open bar, lavish buffet, and thrilling entertainment for three fun-filled hours. Many supposedly authentic luaus play-act with the *imu*-baked pig, but here it is carved and served to the guests. Prices are $49 adults, $18 children ages 6-12, free for children under age five. Reservations are strongly recommended.

A sumptuous feast is held at the **Kona Village Resort,** just north of Kailua-Kona. It's worth attending this luau just to visit and be pampered at this private hotel beach. Adults pay around $63, children 6-12 $35, children 2-5 $21. Held every Friday, by reservation only, tel. 325-5555. The *imu* ceremony is at 6 p.m., followed by no-host cocktails; the luau and Hawaiian entertainment begin at 8 p.m. Also, limited reservations are accepted during the week for lunch, dinner, and special dinners and buffets.

The **Royal Waikoloan Hotel Luau,** tel. 885-6789, is offered on Sunday and Wednesday with the *imu* ceremony beginning at 6 p.m. followed by an open bar. Hawaiian entertainment and dinner begin at 6:30 p.m. Prices are: adults $52, children 6-2 $25, free for children 5 and under.

The King Kamehameha's Kona Beach Hotel, tel. 326-4969, sways with Hawaiian chants during its famous **Island Breeze Luau** held every Sunday, Tuesday, Wednesday, and Thursday on the beach and grounds of King Kamehameha's last residence, Ahu'Ena. The pig is placed into the *imu* every morning at 10 a.m. and the festivities begin in the evening with a lei greeting at 5:30 p.m. and a torch-lighting *imu* pageant at 6 p.m. Cocktails flow 6-8 p.m.; the 22-course luau dinner is served 6:30-8:30 p.m. Prices are $52 adults, $19.50 children 6-12, free for children five and under. Reservations are required. Call 326-4969 or stop by the luau desk in the lobby of the hotel. **Kona Beach Restaurant,** tel. 329-2911, also at the King Kamehameha's Kona Beach Hotel, features a breakfast buffet at $9.50, Mon.-Sat. 6:30-10 a.m., Sunday to 9:30 a.m. As good as the breakfast buffet may be, the restaurant is very famous for its **King's Brunch,** served Sunday 10 a.m.-1 p.m., $19.95 adults, $9.95 children 6-12. The long tables are laden with fruit, vegetables, pasta salad, peel-and-eat shrimp, omelettes, waffles, hot entrees from fresh catch to sashimi, and desserts so sinful

you'll be glad that someone's on their knees praying at Sunday services. Friday and Saturday nights are very special because of the **Prime Rib & Seafood Buffet** at $18.95, which brings hungry people from around the island.

Captain Beans' Dinner Cruise departs Kailua Pier daily at 5 p.m. and returns at 8 p.m. You are entertained while the bar dispenses liberal drinks and the deck groans with all-you-can-eat food. And you get a terrific panorama of the Kona Coast from the sea. You can't help having a good time on this cruise, and if the boat sinks with all that food and booze in your belly, you're a goner—but what a way to go! Minimum age is 18 years, $30 includes tax and tip. Reservations suggested; call 329-2955.

ENTERTAINMENT AND ACTIVITIES

Kona nights come alive mainly in the restaurants and dining rooms of the big hotels. The most memorable experience for most is free: watching the sunset from Kailua Pier, and taking a leisurely stroll along Ali'i Drive. All of the luaus previously mentioned have "Polynesian Revues" of one sort or another, which are generally good, clean, sexy fun, but of course these shows are limited only to the luau guests. For those who have "dancin' feet" or wish to spend the evening listening to live music, there's a small but varied selection from which to choose.

Enjoy the free spectacle as some of the island's best canoeists come to Kailua Bay to work out every evening.

J.D. BISIGNANI

Around Town

Huggo's Restaurant, with its romantic waterfront setting along Ali'i Dr., features music 8:30 p.m.-12:30 a.m. The entertainment changes nightly; *karaoke* on Tuesday features Juni Maderas. Excellent local bands like Mango, Nightlife, and Kona Blend offer smooth Jahwaiian and other mellow contemporary sounds with a touch of rock now and again.

The **Keauhou Beach Hotel** soothes you with easy listening, Hawaiian style, nightly at their famous buffet. Weekends bring live bands like Holua and Nightlife, who will rock you with everything from original tunes to classic Hawaiian numbers. Also, Uncle George Naope, a renowned *kumu hula,* delights audiences with members of his local dance troupe on the Kuakini Terrace, Friday 11 a.m.-1:30 p.m. and then again 5:30-9:30 p.m., Saturday 5:30-9 p.m., Sunday 10 a.m.-1 p.m. (usually!).

At the **Royal Kona Resort's Windjammer Lounge,** an open-air bar, sip a flavorful tropical concoction while watching the sun melt into the Pacific. Entertainment is offered several evenings a week, featuring jazz on Sunday afternoon. Call the resort at 329-3111 for a schedule of entertainment.

In downtown Kailua-Kona you can pick your fun at the **King Kamehameha's Kona Beach Hotel.** Here, the **Billfish Bar** has live entertainment on weekends 6-10:30 p.m., featuring mellow Hawaiian music by Pomaikai. The bar is open 10:30 a.m.-10:30 p.m. with happy hour 5-7 p.m.

Around town, the **Eclipse Restaurant** has dance music 10 p.m.-1:30 a.m. every night. **Jolly Roger Restaurant** offers a variety of live music throughout the week beginning at 8:30 p.m. At the **Keauhou-Kona Golf Course Restaurant** you can enjoy live contemporary Hawaiian music performed by local artists every evening from 7 p.m. For a quiet beer, sports talk, or just hanging out with the local people try **Quinn's, Drysdale's, Ocean View Inn,** or **Sam's Hideaway,** all in downtown Kailua-Kona.

At **Fisherman's Landing Restaurant,** *karaoke* is presented every Wednesday 9 p.m.-midnight. They also have live music and dancing nightly to the tunes of Sugar Sugar, a local dance band; Fri.-Sat. 6-9 p.m. a solo musician plays a mixed bag of country, classic rock-and-roll, and Hawaiian music.

For movies try the **World Square Theater** in the Kona Marketplace or the **Hualalai Theater** in Kailua-Kona.

The **Aloha Theater** in Kainaliu has a semi-professional local repertory company, the Aloha Community Theater, that puts on plays about six times per year that run for about three weeks each. Showtime in the completely refurbished and well-appointed theater is usually 8 p.m., and admission is a very reasonable $8 (senior discount). Check the local newspaper or the HVB office, or look for posters here and there around town.

SHOPPING

Below is an overview of Kona-area malls, including a general idea of what they contain.

Kailua-Kona Malls

The Kailua-Kona area has an abundance of two commodities near and dear to a tourist's heart: sunshine and shopping malls.

One of the largest malls in Kailua is the **Kona Inn Shopping Village** at 75-5744 Ali'i Drive. This shopping village boasts more than 40 shops selling fabrics, fashions, art, fruits, gems and jewelry, photo and music needs, food, and even exotic skins.

Kona Banyan Court, in central Kailua-Kona, has a dozen shops with a medley of goods and services. Distinctive shops include: **Kona Fine Woods** for souvenir-quality woodcarvings; **Unison,** a surfing shop with T-shirts, sandals, hats, and boogie boards; and **Paradise Antiques,** filled with Hawaiian-style treasures and bric-a-brac. To gain control of your hair in the wild Kona breeze, put it in the hands of Darlene, who owns **Hair We Are,** open daily 9 a.m.-7 p.m., Sunday 10 a.m.-4 p.m. Men, women, and children are welcome. The most impressive shop in the complex is **Big Island Jewelers,** tel. 329-8571, open Mon.-Sat. 9 a.m.-9 p.m., Sunday 10 a.m.-6 p.m., owned and operated by brothers Flint and Gale Carpenter, master goldsmiths. The shop motto, "Have your jewelry made by a Carpenter," applies to custom-made jewelry fashioned to their or your personal design. Big Island Jewelers, in business for over 15 years, does repairs and also carries a full line of pearls and loose stones that they will mount into any setting you wish.

You'll also find **Kailua Bay Inn Shopping Plaza** along Ali'i Dr., with shops like **Mil-Rose** filled with sun and fun wear, swimwear, and accessories mostly for women; **Kona Jog and Gift,** with official Ironman Triathlon products along with running shorts, biking shorts, sweat shirts, T-shirts, waterproof watches, hats, incidental bags, and even some aloha shirts; **Waiting for the Sun Petroglyph Jewelry** specializing in glassware and gifts; and **Kona Arts and Crafts,** offering genuine Hawaiian gifts. The **Akona Kai Mall** lies across from Kailua Pier, and the **Kona Marketplace** in central Kailua-Kona offers a variety of shops selling everything from burgers to bathing suits.

The **King Kamehameha's Kona Beach Hotel Mall,** fully air-conditioned, features a cluster of specialty shops and a **Liberty House.** Shops include: **Resort Sundries,** selling wine, liquor, and beer along with suntan lotions, gift items, magazines, novels, and T-shirts; **Jewel Palace,** sparkling with watches and fine jewelry fashioned from gold and silver; **Liberty House Kids,** featuring aloha and resort wear especially designed for children; **Silver Reef,** featuring Hawaiian-motif jewelry, glassware, Japanese dolls, and porcelain wear; **Ali'i Artwear,** specializing in distinctive resort and beach wear for women; and **Kailua Village Artists,** hung with paintings and prints.

Catercorner to King Kamehameha's Hotel is the **Seaside Mall,** with most shops open daily 9 a.m.-6 p.m. Here you'll find **Neptune's Garden** creating rainbows with its display of stained glass art fashioned into lamps, creative hangings, vases, and a few paintings. Here, too, is **Tropical Tees,** where you can outfit yourself with distinctive T-shirts and sunglasses; and the **Sandal Stop,** where your tootsies will purr in a new pair of sandals, dress shoes, or Birkenstocks for men, women, or children. Across the way is **Eel Skin Liquidators;** no, they don't juice eels, but they do sell eelskin accessories like purses and belts, along with an assortment of souvenir-quality artifacts, jewelry, and knickknacks. Other shops are the **Kona Coast Sunglass Company,** who will help your eyes filter out those harmful rays; **Gold Fish,** selling painted fish, necklaces, back scratchers, toe rings,

bracelets, and hanging mobiles; **Starshine,** with its distinctive T-shirts; and **Bubi's Sportswear** for T-shirts, sweatshirts, towels, hats, and tourist niceties for beach, sun, and surf.

The **Kona Square Shopping Center,** next to the Seaside Mall with most shops open daily 9 a.m.-6 p.m., features **Mermaid's By The Sea,** a distinctive ladies' and children's clothing boutique bright with alohawear, pareau, sun and evening dresses, and a ceiling hung with cherubic angels if you're not sharing your Hawaii vacation with one of your own. Directly across from Mermaids is **Island Silversmiths,** Kona's oldest modern-day shop, in business since 1973, so you know they're doing something right. To complete your ensemble from Mermaids, peruse the display cases filled with bracelets, rings, and necklaces fashioned from silver and gold. Motifs are pure Hawaiian, with geckos, fish hooks, dolphins, whales, and the odd unicorn or scorpion thrown in just to be worldly. Here too is **Gems of the Sea,** displaying shoreline treasures . . . shells of all types from all over the world. Inside you can also choose from coral jewelry, fish hooks, necklaces of all kinds, troll dolls, sea urchin night lights, and wind chimes.

The **Lanihau Center,** tel. 329-9333, at 75-5595 Palani Rd., is one of Kailua-Kona's newest shopping meccas. It offers **Longs Drugs** for sundries and photo supplies; an assortment of restaurants; apparel and shoe stores including **Feet First; Waldenbooks,** an excellent all-purpose bookstore; **Radio Shack** for electronic gizmos of all sorts; and **H2O Action Surf Shop** for jeans, surf boards, boogie boards, sporting goods, in-line skates, shirts, T-shirts, hats, and sunglasses.

Kopiko Plaza, along Palani Rd. just down from the Lanihau Center, is a small mall containing **Scott's Knife Center** for fine cutlery from carving knives to Swiss Army knives; **Action Sports** for the largest selection of sporting equipment in town; and, **Tempo Music,** where you can get all of your music needs, including plenty of island sounds. The mall also has a smattering of inexpensive restaurants, both for takeout and eat in.

Waterfront Row is a relatively new shopping and food complex at the south end of downtown Kailua-Kona. Built of rough-cut lumber, it's done in period architecture reminiscent of an outdoor promenade in a Boston shipyard at the turn of the century. **Pacific Vibrations,** a surf shop, sells everything from postcards to hats, backpacks, and aloha shirts. **Pleasant Hawaiian Holidays** maintains a booth here from where you can book a wide range of activities. **Crazy Shirts** sells unique island creations, and **Kona Jack's** offers distinctive unisex apparel featuring its logo. Restaurants include the **Chart House** for steaks and seafood, **Michelangelo's** for Italian cuisine, and **Jolly Roger** for American and Hawaiian cuisine.

Rawson Plaza, at 74-5563 Kaiwi St., is just past the King Kamehameha's Kona Beach Hotel in the industrial area. This practical, no-frills area abounds in "no-name" shops selling everything you'll find in town but at substantial savings.

Kona Coast Shopping Center along Palani Rd. features **Pay 'n' Save** for sundries and everything from scuba gear to Styrofoam coolers; **KTA Market;** the **Undercover Shop,** with fine lingerie; **Hallmark Cards; Marshals,** open Mon.-Sat. 10 a.m.-9 p.m., Sunday 10 a.m.-6 p.m., a family oriented clothing store with decent prices; **Blockbuster Video,** where you can rent a movie for the evening, open daily 10 a.m.-midnight; **Men's Shop,** open Mon.-Sat. 9 a.m.-6 p.m., Sunday 10 a.m.-5 p.m., with alohawear, shirts, shorts, slacks, jackets, and big men's sizes; and **Fantastic Sams,** a hair salon open Mon.-Thurs. 9 a.m.-6 p.m., Fri.-Sat. 9 a.m.-7 p.m., Sunday 9 a.m.-5 p.m., no appointment necessary.

South of Kailua Malls

If, god forbid, you haven't found what you need in Kailua, or if you suddenly need a "shopping fix," even more malls are south on Route 11. **Keauhou Shopping Village** is at the corner of Ali'i Dr. and Kamehameha III Road. Look for flags waving in the breeze high on the hill marking the entrance. This mall houses apparel shops, restaurants, a post office, and photo-processing booths. You can find all your food and prescription needs at **KTA Supermarket,** the largest in the area. **Keauhou Village Bookshop** is a full-service bookstore. **Kona-kai Cafe,** an espresso and coffee shop open daily 8:30 a.m.-6 p.m., will take care of your sweet tooth and drooping energy; you can also buy a pound or two of fresh Kona coffee there. **Drysdale's** is

an indoor/outdoor bar and grill where you can relax over a cold beer or choose from their extensive sandwich menu. Other shops include: the **Showcase Gallery,** for glassware, paintings, ceramics, and local crafts; **Long's Drugstore,** for everything from foot care products to photography; **Ace Hardware** for nuts and bolts; **Radio Shack** to tune in; **Liberty House** for family fashions; and **Alapaki's,** for island goods from black coral jewelry to colorful muumuus.

Continuing south on Route 11, you'll spot the **Kainaliu Village Mall** along the main drag.

Food Markets

KTA Supermarket, open daily 6 a.m.-midnight, is generally the cheapest market in town and is located at the Kona Coast Shopping Center along Palani Road; there's another one at the Keauhou Village Mall, at the extreme south end of Ali'i Dr. at its junction with Kamehameha III Road. They're well stocked with sundries; an excellent selection of Asian foods, fresh veggies, fish, and fruit; and a smattering of health food. The market also contains a full-service pharmacy.

The **Kailua Village Farmers Market** along Ali'i Dr. just across from Waterfront Row, open Wednesday, Friday, Saturday, and Sunday 6 a.m.-3 p.m., tel. 329-1393, sells locally grown (some organic) fruits and vegetables, nuts, flowers, and coffee. Every Wednesday, Friday, Saturday, and Sunday 6 a.m.-2 p.m. **Uncle Billy's Farmers Market** is held in the parking lot across the street from Uncle Billy's Kona Bay Hotel. Lots of local produce, flowers, and coffee.

Across the road, **Sack 'n' Save,** in the Lanihau Center, open 5 a.m.-midnight, is one of the main supermarkets in town.

Kona Wine Market, in the small King Kamehameha Mall, 75-5626 Kuakini Hwy., tel. 329-9400, open daily 10 a.m.-8 p.m., Sunday noon-6 p.m., is the best wine shop on the Kona coast. They feature an impressive international selection of wine and varietals from California, Italy, Spain, France, Chile, and Australia. Prices range from $4.95 for a table wine to $200 for a bottle of select boutique wine. A large cooler holds a fine selection of beer, both domestic and imported, and the store shelves hold wonderful gourmet munchies like Indian chutney, Sicilian olives, mustards, dressings, marinades, smoked salmon, hearty cheeses, and even pasta imported from

Italy. Cigar smokers will also appreciate the humidor filled with fine cigars from around the world.

Casa De Emdeko Liquor and Deli is south of town center at 75-6082 Ali'i Drive. It's well stocked with liquor and groceries, but at convenience-store prices. Other markets include **King Kamehameha Pantry**, tel. 329-9191, selling liquors, groceries, and sundries; and **Keauhou Pantry**, tel. 322-3066, in Keauhou along Ali'i Dr., selling more of the same.

Health Food Stores

Kona keeps you healthy with **Kona Healthways** in the Kona Coast Shopping Center, tel. 329-2296, open Mon.-Sat. 9 a.m.-8 p.m., Sunday to 7 p.m. Besides a good assortment of health foods, they have cosmetics, books, and dietary supplements. Vegetarians will like their ready-to-eat sandwiches, salads, and soups. Shelves are lined with teas and organic vitamins. They also have a cooler with organic juices, cheeses, and soy milk. A refrigerator holds organic produce, while bins are filled with bulk grains.

A **General Nutrition Center**, located in the Lanihau Center along Palani Rd., open Mon.-Fri. 10 a.m.-8 p.m., Sat.-Sun. 10 a.m.-6 p.m., is stocked with vitamins, food supplements, and minerals.

Bookstores

Waldenbooks, in the Lanihau Center on Palani Rd., tel. 329-0015, open Mon.-Thurs. 9:30 a.m.-7 p.m., Friday 9:30 a.m.-9 p.m., Sunday 10 a.m.-5 p.m., not only has the well-stocked and far-ranging selection for which this national chain has become famous, but also features an in-depth Hawaiiana collection and even some Hawaiian music tapes.

In Kailua-Kona be sure to venture into **Middle Earth Bookshop** at 75-5719 Ali'i Dr., in the Kona Plaza Shopping Arcade, tel. 329-2123, open Mon.-Sat. 9 a.m.-9 p.m., Sunday to 6 p.m. This jam-packed bookstore has shelves laden with fiction, nonfiction, paperbacks, hardbacks, travel books, maps, and Hawaiiana. A great place to browse.

Keauhou Village Bookshop at Keauhou Shopping Village, tel. 322-8111, open Mon.-Sat. 9 a.m.-6 p.m., Sunday 9 a.m.-5 p.m., is a full-service bookstore with plenty of Hawaiiana selections, general reading material, a children's

section, and a superb travel section, along with an excellent selection of maps, especially on Hawaii. They also sell CDs and cassettes.

Photo Needs

Zac's Photo, in the North Kona Shopping Center, tel. 329-0006, open daily 7 a.m.-9 p.m., develops prints in one hour and slides in two days. Zac, a native of Belgium, will even make minor camera repairs free of charge. Prices are very competitive and you can save more by clipping two-for-one and 20% discount coupons from the free tourist brochure, *This Week, Big Island.*

Longs Drugs, in the Lanihau Center along Palani Rd., also has excellent prices on film and camera supplies.

Kona Photo Arts in the North Kona Shopping Plaza, at the corner of Palani Rd. and Kuakini Hwy., tel. 329-2566, is open Mon.-Sat. 8 a.m.-6 p.m. It is a *real* photography store where you can get lenses, cameras, filters, and even telescopes and binoculars. Their processing is competitive, and they also offer custom developing.

More Malls: Art and Specialty Shops

In the King Kamehameha's Kona Beach Hotel, **The Shellery** lives up to its name with baubles, bangles, and beads made from shells, along with a selection of fine jewelry and pearls; and **Kailua Village Artists** displays paintings and prints for sale.

Island Togs, tel. 329-2144, is across from the Kona Beach Restaurant at the King Kamehameha's Kona Beach Hotel. This long-established shop hidden from the main tourist gauntlet is known by the locals as one of the best places to purchase women's bathing suits and bikinis. They also feature very reasonable prices on resortwear, shorts, and an assortment of tops.

In the World Square Shopping Center visit **Coral Isle Art Shop** for modern versions of traditional Hawaiian carvings. You'll find everything from tikis to scrimshaw, with exceptionally good carvings of sharks and whales for a pricey $75 or so.

Enjoy the beauty of Hawaii with flowers from **Editha's Lei Stand,** a.k.a. **Oriental Flower Decor,** tel. 334-1194, located in front of Huggo's Restaurant, open daily 10:30 a.m.-6 p.m., except Sunday with a slightly earlier closing. Editha creates lovely lei that run from $3.75 for a basic

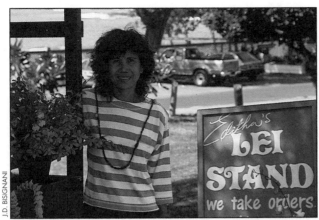

J.D. BISIGNANI

Editha's Lei Stand

strand to $20 for a magnificent triple lei, along with a variety of fresh-cut flower arrangements. All of Editha's flowers are "certified" so if you want to take them home, you'll have no hassle with agricultural inspection. If you prefer direct shipping to the Mainland, there'll be no problem with a minimum cost of $37 including shipping.

Also in the parking lot in front of Huggo's Restaurant, along Ali'i Dr., look for a little truck business called **Nikki's** that sells Kona coffee at $8.49 per pound and macadamia nuts at $6.95 per pound, both decent prices.

At the **Kona Inn Shopping Village** you can buy custom jewelry at **Jim Bill's Gemfire.** Featured at the **T-shirt Company,** a.k.a. **Island Salsa,** are designer tee's that are some of the best in Kona. Prices are normally around $18, but they run specials all the time. You can pick up one-of-a-kind creations by Roberta, the owner/artist, for around $10. **Collectors Fine Art** is a perfect labyrinth of rooms and hallways showcasing the acclaimed works of international artists. Not a shop at which to buy trinkets; prices range from $300 to $250,000 for some of the finer paintings and sculptures by internationally acclaimed artists. **Hula Heaven,** open daily 9 a.m.-9 p.m., is situated in a stone tower dating from 1927 and specializes in vintage Hawaiian shirts and modern reproductions. Prices range from $50 for the "look alikes" to $1,000 for the rarest of the classics. Because many of the items on display date from the '40s and '50s, the shop is like a trip back in time. Other shops include: **Noa Noa,** featuring hand-painted, one-of-a-kind origi-

nal clothing, mostly from Indonesia; **Kona Jewelry Factory,** featuring island-inspired jewelry; **Hawaiian Fruit and Flower Company** for sweets and sweet-smelling flowers; **Fare Tahiti Fabrics** for incidental travel bags, pareau, and fabrics; **Golden Orchid,** a women's resort wear and casual wear shop; **Kona Inn Children's Wear,** featuring Hawaiian fashions for the little ones; **Limited Editions Hawaii,** with original designs on T-shirts; and **Kona Inn General Store,** with sundries, beer, and liquor.

At **Kona Inn Flower and Lei** you can pick up flowers to add that perfect touch to a romantic evening. Nearby **Christel's Collectibles** has stuffed toys, stuffed pillows, and some clothing. **Kona Inn Jewelry,** for worldwide treasures, is one of the oldest and best-known shops for a square deal in Kona. Owned and operated by Joe Goldscharek and his family, they take time to help you choose just the right gift. Inside you'll find stained-glass hangings, jewelry, fine gemstones, and a collection of hand-painted fish. The family tries to pick unique items from around the world that can be found in no other Kona shop. Be aware that the shop is protected by Mama Cat, a sleeping ball of fur honored with her own postcard, who if you're not careful will purr you to death.

Other shops in the center include: **Flamingo's** for contemporary island clothing and evening wear mainly for women; **Big Island Hat Co.** for headgear ranging from pith helmets to sombreros; **The Treasury,** specializing in jewelry, T-shirts, beachwear, hats, sunglasses, backpacks, shoulder bags, and postcards; **Tahiti Fabrics,** offering bolts of cloth and a nice collection of Hawaiian shirts; **Alley Gecko's,** showcasing colorful gifts from around the world; and the **Old Hawaiian Gold Co.,** which can bedeck you in gold chains or pearl and coral jewelry.

At the **Kona Marketplace** in the downtown area, look for **Kona Jewelers,** specializing in fine jewelry and ceramics. The jam-packed **Aloha From Kona** specializes in baubles, bangles, postcards, handbags, and purses. In contrast is **Ali'i Nexus,** for fine jewelry, one of the nicest and most low-key shops in town. The **Kona Flea Market** stuck to the rear of the mall sells inexpensive travel bags, shells, beach mats, suntan lotion, and all the junk that you could want. **Island Salsa** features original silk-screened T-shirts, alohawear for the entire family, ladies' evening wear, swimwear, and dinner clothes.

Kona Gold, tel. 327-9373, in the Kailua Bay Inn Shopping Plaza, open daily except Sunday 9 a.m.-9 p.m., has excellent prices on custom-made jewelry by Harold Booton, the goldsmith and proprietor. Harold also imports jewelry from around the world, especially silver, and if it's not on sale, bargaining is definitely okay! The store stocks coral jewelry, a smattering of T-shirts, and lifelike wooden sculptures of whales and marine animals, many of which come from Indonesia. Kona Gold is a perfect shop in which to purchase a lifelong memento at a very reasonable price.

Alapaki's, at Keauhou Shopping Village, sells distinctive island arts and crafts. Inside you'll find pink, gold, and black coral jewelry; lei of shells and seeds; and *tutu* dolls bedecked in colorful muumuus. Distinctive items include koa bowls, each signed by the artist; and a replica of a Hawaiian double-hulled canoe made of coconut and cloth with traditional crab-claw sails. Original paintings by R.K. McGuire feature Hawaiian animals; basketry, fans, and jewelry made from ironwood needles are by local artist Barb Walls. Some of the finest artworks displayed are feather lei by Eloise Deshea and woodcarvings by Thomas Baboza.

For some practical purchases at wholesale prices, check **Liberty House Penthouse** at Keauhou Shopping Village; it will appeal to bargain hunters. This outlet store sells items that have been cleared and reduced from the famous Liberty House stores. You can save on everything from alohawear to formal dresses.

Kailua Candy Company, in the industrial section on the corner of Kurakini and Kiawi Streets, tel. 329-2522 or (800) 622-2462, is open daily 8 a.m.-6 p.m. It was recognized as one of the "top 10 chocolate shops in the United States" in the February 1993 issue of *Bon Appetit* magazine. All the chocolates are made of the finest ingredients available, and all would try the willpower of Gandhi, but the specialty is the macadamia nut *honu,* Hawaiian for turtle. The best sampler is the one-pound Kailua Candy Company Assortment, hand-packed with a quarter pound each of *honu,* the award-winning Kona coffee swirl, dark macadamia nut clusters, and white coconut Mauna Kea snowballs. It costs $17.10, or $21 shipped anywhere on the Mainland. Shipping of all the candy is available at the cost of postage plus $1 handling fee; shipments are guaranteed to be in perfect condition or they will be replaced free. Every day 8 a.m.-6 p.m., have a free look into the kitchen and nibble samples of their products.

Poor soul! If your lover's run off with an escaped felon, your life savings can fit into a change purse, a birthday party you threw for all your friends fit at a table for one, and you've already suffered the ultimate humiliation of hurling yourself off Kona Pier only to splat onto damp sand at low tide, perhaps you should head for **Ancient Wisdoms,** in the Ali'i Sunset Plaza at 75-5799 Ali'i Dr., across from the seawall at the south end of town, tel. 329-9412, open Sun.-Mon. 10 a.m.-6 p.m., Tues.-Sat. 10 a.m.-9 p.m. On its shelves you will find metaphysical and "old-age" books, new-age music, basketry, aromatherapy, crystals, crystal balls, jewelry, incense, paintings from local artists, a Native American section, posters, postcards, and souvenirs. Saturday nights (call for details), Ancient Wisdoms shows foreign and classic films, free, at 7 p.m. You can also arrange a massage ranging from *lomi lomi* to Swedish in the shop's massage room. If this doesn't lift your spirits, try the last resort . . . whining and wishful thinking.

Along Ali'i Dr., diagonally across from Hulihee Palace, is **Hawaiian Wear Unlimited,** where you can pick up alohawear for a very reasonable price. Just up the road, across from the seawall along Likana Ln., is **Ululani Fresh Cut Flowers,** a reasonably priced lei stand. **Goodies** just up the alley has gift boxes of jams and jellies, Maui onion mustard, macadamia nuts, an assortment of coffees, and various perfumes and scents.

Real treasure hunters will love the **Kona Gardens Flea Market** held every Wednesday and Saturday 8 a.m.-2 p.m. in the parking lot next to St. Michael's Church along Ali'i Drive. Unfortunately, this formerly huge flea market is now only a shadow of its former self and is always tottering on the brink of closure.

The **Banyan Tree Bazaar** (not really the name, but no one has bothered to give it one yet) is along Ali'i Dr. next to Stan's Restaurant across from the seawall. Look for blue and white umbrellas under which local merchants sell handcrafted and locally made necklaces, earrings, and bracelets. Others sell various artworks like stuffed animals, along with an array of inexpensive but neat tourist junk.

SERVICES AND INFORMATION

Emergencies
For **ambulance, fire,** and **police** emergencies call 911. The **Kona Hospital** is in Kealakekua, tel. 322-9311. The most convenient **pharmacy** is Longs Drugs, tel. 329-1380. For **alternative health care services and massage,** both well established in Kailua-Kona, see the "Health and Conduct" section in the Out and About chapter.

Information and Services
An **information gazebo** is open daily 7 a.m.-9 p.m. along the boardwalk in the Kona Inn Shopping Village. They can handle your questions about everything from dining to diving. The **Hawaii Visitors Bureau** maintains an office in the Kona Plaza Shopping Arcade, at 75-5719 Ali'i Dr., tel. 329-7787, open Mon.-Fri. 8 a.m.-noon, then again 1-4:30 p.m. The staff is friendly, helpful, and extremely knowledgeable about touring the Big Island.

The **library** is at 75-140 Hualalai Rd., tel. 327-3077. The **Hele Mai Laundromat** is near King Kamehameha's Kona Beach Hotel.

An excellent **tourist map** that highlights restaurants, accommodations, and businesses is available free at the HVB office and at many shops in Kona and throughout the Big Island. The map is published by the Island Map Company, 159 Kiawe St., Suite 1, Hilo, HI 96720, tel. 934-9007.

Banks, Post Office, Etc.
First Hawaiian Bank, in the Lanihau Center on Palani Rd., can be reached at tel. 329-2461. Also in the center at Sack 'n' Save, **Bank of America** maintains a 24-hour Versatel machine. **Bank of Hawaii** maintains two area offices, one in Kailua at tel. 326-3927, the other in Kealakekua at tel. 322-9377. The main **post office** is on Palani Rd., tel. 329-1927, just past the Lanihau Center. **Mail Boxes ETC** at the Crossroads Shopping center provides postal, shipping, and wrapping services.

CENTRAL AND SOUTH KONA

Kailua-Kona's Ali'i Drive eventually turns up the mountainside and joins Route 11, which in its central section is called the **Kuakini Highway.** This road, heading south, quickly passes the towns of **Honalo, Kainaliu** ("Bail the Bilge"), **Kealakekua,** and **Captain Cook.** You'll have ample opportunity to stop along the way for gas, picnic supplies, or browsing. These towns have some terrific restaurants, specialty shops, and boutiques. At Captain Cook, you can dip down to the coast and visit a working coffee mill, or continue south to **Pu'uhonua O Honaunau,** a reconstructed temple of refuge, the best in the state. Farther south still, little-traveled side roads take you to the sleepy seaside villages of **Hookena** and **Milolii,** where traditional lifestyles are still the norm.

Or for an alternative, instead of heading directly south out of Kailua-Kona on Route 11, take Hualalai Rd. (Route 182) to Route 180, a high mountain road that parallels Route 11 and takes you to the artists' community of **Holualoa,** from where you get an expansive view of the coastline below. When leaving Holualoa for points south, stay on Route 180, the Mamalahoa Highway, a gorgeous road with great views from the heights.

HOLUALOA

Holualoa ("The Sledding Course") is an undisturbed mountain community perched high above the Kailua-Kona Coast with many of the island's most famous artists creating art in galleries which

To Kailua-Kona

180
11 Holualoa
Holualoa Bay

WHITE SANDS BEACH
COUNTY PARK
Kahaluu
KONA GARDENS
Keauhou
Keauhou Bay
LOOKOUT
DAI FUKUJU
BUDDHIST TEMPLE
Honalo
Kainaliu

**CENTRAL AND
SOUTH KONA**

*Keikiwaha
Point*

Kealakekua

Captain Cook

KAAWALOA
PALI KAPU O KEAUA
Napoopoo
COFFEE MILL
KEALAKEKUA BAY STATE UNDERWATER PARK
HIKIAU HEIAU STATE MONUMENT
NAPOOPOO BEACH COUNTY PARK
Keei

Honaunau
ST. BENEDICT'S
PAINTED CHURCH
160

PU UHONUA O HONAUNAU
NATIONAL HISTORIC PARK
(CITY OF REFUGE)
Keokea
Loa Point
Kealia
Kealia Beach
Hookena
HOOKENA BEACH
COUNTY PARK

Kapilo Bay

*Lepeamoa
Rock*

*Kau Loa
Point*

Auau Point
Puoa Point

Keananuionaha Point

KIPAHOEHOE
NATIONAL AREA
RESERVE

0   4 mi
0   4 km

Kipahoehoe Bay
Arched Rock

Milolii Beach

MILOLII BEACH
COUNTY PARK
Hoopuloa

Milolii

Milolii Bay
*Moku o Kahailani
Rock*
Puu Hinahina Bay

HOLUA (SLIDE)
PETROGLYPHS/CAVES
RUINS
Lava Tubes

MANUKA STATE
WAYSIDE

HAWAIIAN
OCEAN VIEW
ESTATES

11
To Volcano

PACIFIC

OCEAN

© J.D. BISIGNANI AND MOON PUBLICATIONS, INC.

line paintbrush to easel along its vintage main street. Prior to its transformation to an art community Holualoa had another history. In days past, general stores, hotels, restaurants, bars, and pool halls lined its streets. Before Hawaii found its potential for tourism and started to develop its coastal areas, rural Hawaii was primarily agricultural, and the farms, and consequently most of the population, was located on the mountainsides. Large agricultural areas sustained working communities and Holualoa was one such population center. While agriculture is still a part of the local economy, it has been eclipsed by tourism and the arts. Get there by taking the spur Route 182, known as **Hualalai Road,** off Route 11 (Queen Kaahumanu Hwy.) from Kailua-Kona, or by taking Route 180 (Mamalahoa Hwy.) from Honalo in the south or from Honokohau in the north (junction with Route 190, Palani Road from Kailua-Kona). Climbing Hualalai Road (Route 182), the best route, affords glorious views of the coast below. Notice the immediate contrast of the lush foliage against the scant vegetation of the lowland area. On the mountainside, bathed in tropical mists, are tall forest trees interspersed with banana, papaya, and mango trees. Flowering trees pulsating in the green canopy explode in vibrant reds, yellows, oranges, and purples. If you want to get away from the Kona heat and dryness, head up to the well-watered coolness of Holualoa.

Note: Keep in mind that it is customary for most of the galleries to be *closed on Monday.*

Shops and Other Sights

After you wind your way up Route 182 through this verdant jungle area, you suddenly enter the village and are greeted by **Kimura's Lauhala Shop,** tel. 324-0053, open daily 9 a.m.-5 p.m., closed Sunday. The shop, still tended by Mrs. Kimura and her daughters, Alfreida and Ella, has been in existence since 1915. In the beginning, Kimura's was a general store, but they always sold *lau hala* and became famous for their hats, which local people would make to barter for groceries. Famous, on and later off island, only *Kona-side* hats have a distinctive pull-string that makes the hat larger or smaller. Mrs. Kimura, and most of her friends who helped manufacture the hats, are getting on in age and can no longer keep up with the demand. Many hatmakers have passed away, and there are few young people interested in keeping the dying art alive. They still have hats, but the stock is dwindling. All *lau hala* weavings are done on the premises, while some of the other gift items are brought in. Choose from authentic baskets, floor mats, handbags, slippers, and of course an assortment of the classic sun hats that start at $35. A terrific purchase is a *lau hala* tote bag, lined with 100% cotton tapa style cloth. This new specialty item, priced around $45, with two big pouches and a zippered pouch, works equally well as a day bag, beach bag, or picnic basket. Also for an authentic souvenir, look for a round basket with a strap, the original Kona coffee basket,

After Kimura's follow the road for a minute or so to enter the actual village, where the **post office** and a cross atop a white steeple welcome you to town. The tiny village, complete with its own elementary school, is well kept, with an obvious double helping of pride put into this artists' community by its citizens. Just here is **Paul's Place,** a well-stocked country store, open weekdays 7:30 a.m.-8 p.m., weekends 8 a.m.-8 p.m.

Along the main road is a converted coffee mill, gaily painted and decorated, and currently the home of the nonprofit **Kona Art Center,** open Tues.-Sat. 10 a.m.-4 p.m., which began as a labor of love by husband and wife artist team Robert and Carol Rogers. Uncle Bob, as he was affectionately known, passed away recently, but Aunt Carol is still creating art at the center. Both had an extensive background in art teaching. They moved from San Francisco to Holualoa in 1965 and began offering community workshop classes. Carol says, "I love Kona because we share, care, and love with our people here." Across the road is a restored building, a one-time country church rescued from the ravages of weather and termites, that now proudly displays the works of the center's members. In here you will find everything from hobby crafts to serious renderings that might include paintings, basketry, sculptures, and even tie-dyed shirts. The center is very friendly and welcomes guests with a cup of Kona coffee. The building is rickety and old, but it's obviously filled with good vibrations and love. However, time moves on and things change. The building has been recently sold, and the new owners—who tried to cooperate with the center by keeping it housed here—were advised by a number of outside architects that the building is beyond saving and must be torn down. The idea is to replace it with a new center that will house a restaurant and various shops and provide space for the art center in the rear. This is in the planning stage.

Across the road from the Kona Art Center is **Dahlia's Flower Shop,** tel. 322-3189, open daily except Sunday 9:30 a.m.-3 p.m., specializing in tropical flower arrangements, mums, and fresh *maile* lei. The prices are excellent and Dahlia offers shipping to the Mainland and Canada. All of her flowers are "certified" so there is no hassle with agricultural inspection.

Opposite the Holualoa Library is the **Country Frame Shop,** tel. 324-1590, open Mon.-Fri. 9:30 a.m.-4:30 p.m., Saturday 9:30 a.m.-1:30 p.m. It specializes in framing artwork in koa but also displays works by famous local artists including: Carla Sachi-Nifash, a watercolor artist who renders Hawaii in everything from still life to underwater scenes; furniture artist Mike Felig, who turns koa into contemporary and traditional pieces of furniture; Sue Swerdlow, who is a master at capturing color as it bursts from the jungle; Jennifer Pontz, who etches glass with Hawaiian motifs; and, Tom Breeze and Mary Jo Lake, who create affordable, functional pieces, such as cutting boards, that you can use every day and will remind you of your trip to the Big Island. The owner, Chuck Hart, accepts credit cards and will ship anywhere. The Country Frame Shop is well worth a visit, if only just to browse.

"He's a potter, I'm a painter," is the understatement, uttered by Mary Lovein, the female half of the artistic husband and wife team of Mary and Matthew Lovein. They produce and display their lovely and inspired artwork at **Holualoa Gallery,** tel. 322-8484, open Tues.-Sat., 10 a.m.-5 p.m., which is easily spotted along Holualoa's main thoroughfare. Mary uses her acrylics and airbrush to create large, bold, and bright seascapes and landscapes of Hawaii. Matthew specializes in *raku:* magnificent works of waist-high vases, classic Japanese-style ceramics glazed in deep rose, iridescent greens, crinkled gray, and deep periwinkle blue. Mary and Matthew collaborate on some of the larger pieces. Matt creates the vessel and, while it is still greenware, its underglaze is painted by

Mary. Other artists featured in the shop are: Herb Kane, world renowned for his dream-reality paintings of Hawaii and its people; Cecilia Faith Black, who does delicate jewelry; Patricia Van Asperen-Hume, who creates fused glassworks; and Frances Dennis, who hand-paints romantic Hawaiian imagery on porcelain.

The flora and fauna of Hawaii, both aboveground and beneath the waves, come alive in the **White Garden Gallery,** open Tues.-Sat., 10 a.m.-4 p.m., tel. 322-7733. The bright and airy studio, once the home of "grease monkeys," showcases the fantastic works of accomplished watercolorist Shelley Maudsley-White. Her original and state-of-the art *giclé* prints of hibiscus, exotic birds, plumeria-scented forests, and hilarious yet pointed marine works with titles like *Confrontation Between a Manta Ray and Puffer Fish* confirm her philosophy that "there is more happening on this earth than what meets the eye." Working in the gallery, both as salesperson and artist, is Alexis Wilson, whose creations complement those of White. Alexis's fertile imagination has created, among others, a work entitled *Who Ever Heard of a Blue Papaya?* Both artists sucessfully strive to capture the spiritual and physical aspects of reality.

A premier shop in town, **Studio 7,** open Tues.-Sat. 10 a.m.-5 p.m., tel. 324-1335, is owned and operated by Hiroki and Setsuko Morinoue, who both studied at the Kona Art Center. The shop showcases Setsuko and Hiroki's work along with that of about 20 Big Island artists. Hiroki works in many media but primarily does large watercolors or woodblock prints. Setsuko, Hiroki's wife, is a ceramicist and displays her work with about six other potters, including the famous Chiu Leong. Check out the "neoclassical" silk-screen by contemporary Japanese artists Hideo Takeda and Taika Kinoshita. Affordable items include freeform bowls, signed by the artist, and wooden bracelets. To the rear of the shop is a wooden walkway over gray lava gravel that looks out onto a Japanese-style garden. Strolling from room to room in Studio 7 is like following a magic walkway where the art is displayed simply but elegantly, a legacy of the owners' very Japanese sense of style. Viewing the mastery of the fine artists of Kailua-Kona displayed at Studio 7 is an uplifting experience that you will long remember, and is in itself worth the trip to Holualoa.

A separate shop in the same building is **Koa T Gallery,** woodworking by Thomas A. Stoudt, tel. 322-7755. Tom works small. His pieces are extremely functional, including salt and pepper shakers, stamp dispensers, ladies' vanity mirrors, bowls, koa walking sticks, koa-based lamps, lazy Susans, and little night-stand clocks.

Hale O Kula, along Holualoa's main road in Holualoa's original post office, houses both **Goldsmithing by Sam Rosen,** tel. 324-1688, and **Chesnut and Co. Gallery,** tel. 324-1446, both open Mon.-Sat. (an exception for Holualoa artists) 10 a.m.-4 p.m. Sam, who doesn't need much room, is kind of stuck in the back. When you put your head through the open Dutch door and yell out "Sam," he appears. Sam works mostly in gold, silver, and precious stones; he also creates bronze sculptures and ceramics . . . very, very small sculptures. One of his sculptures, entitled *Things About Trees,* is a poignant reminder of the ravages done by overcutting our forests. This miniature, with a sad but clear "voice," is a leafless dead tree and around it, in a dance of sympathy and bereavement, are three Hawaiian "night marchers." All hold their bowed heads in their hands while one points outward, seemingly to ask, "Who is responsible? You?" If the message makes a difference, then indeed, "Good things do come in small packages." Sam can also supply stones from his collection, which includes amazing specimens like malachite and polyhedroid, a quartz from Brazil. **Chesnut & Company** is small but jam-packed with treasures like *tansu,* Japanese furniture known for its joinery; bamboo and *lau hala* lamps by Gerald Ben; free-form prints in splendid colors of cobalt blue and rose by Nora Yamanoha; spirit masks and "garden goddesses" by Volcano artist Ira Ono; basketry from Bali and Holualoa; placemats fashioned from supple twigs and coconut fiber; and distinctive weavings, wall hangings, and original design tables by Peggy Chesnut (her loom is on the premises).

The **Holualoa Foundation for Art and Culture** is a nonprofit organization begun by local artists Sam Rosen, Setsuko Morinoue, and her husband Hiroki Morinoue, the current president. The foundation plans to offer public classes including painting, drawing, photography, and ceramics, taught by working artists. These workshops will be offered at a nominal charge. Members, and

tourists alike will be welcomed. For information call 324-1688 or 324-1335.

A side road, easily spotted along Holualoa's main street, leads you to **Koyasan Daishiji Shingon,** a Japanese Buddhist mission with distinctive red-orange buildings and a stone-lantern lined entrance. The mission is basic, simple, and unpretentious, combining Japanese Buddhism with a Hawaiian air. The roof has the distinctive shape of a temple, but unlike those found in Japan, which are fashioned from wood, this is corrugated iron. Getting to the temple takes only a few minutes, and coming back down the road rewards you with an inspiring vista of Kona and the sea.

Practicalities

The enticing aroma of rich coffee has been wafting on the breeze in this mountain community ever since the **Holuakoa Cafe,** owned and operated by Meggi Worbach, opened its doors in mid-1992. Just up the hill from the Kona Hotel, the cafe, open Mon.-Sat. 6:30 a.m.-5 p.m., tel. 322-2233, serves wonderful apple coffee cake, bagels, muffins, and coffee and espresso from mocha frappés to double cappuccinos. Other offerings include smoothies, juices, and herbal teas. The cafe also serves as a revolving art gallery for local artists who may include Bob Smith, known for carving koa canoe paddles in the ancient tradition. The cafe displays a few boutique and souvenir items, including jewelry from Indonesia, and a smattering of wooden art pieces. You can sit inside at a table, perch at the counter, or enjoy your coffee and pastry alfresco on the veranda, from where the two-block metropolis of Holualoa sprawls at your feet.

A wooden jewel box nestled in velvet greenery waits to be opened as it rests on the edge of Holualoa high above the wide, rippling, cerulean Pacific. **The Holualoa Inn Bed and Breakfast** at 76-5932 Mamalahoa Hwy., P.O. Box 222, Holualoa, HI 96725, tel. 324-1121 or (800) 392-1812, fax 322-2472, is the retirement home of Thurston Twigg-Smith, CEO of the *Honolulu Advertiser* and member of an old *kama'aina* family. Mr. Twigg-Smith built the original home in 1978, but tragically, it burned to the ground. Undaunted, he rebuilt, exactly duplicating the original. After living here a few years Mr. Twigg-Smith decided it was too quiet and peaceful and went back to live in Honolulu. Following its conversion to a B&B in 1987, it is now operated by grandson, Michael Twigg-Smith, and his wife, Leia. The home is a marvel of taste and charm—light, airy, and open. Follow the serpentine drive from Holualoa's main road into the midst of vibrant foliage daubed with red hibiscus, manicured thickets of ripening green coffee, sun-yellow papaya, and wind-swirled palms. The home at the end of the drive pleasantly shocks the senses. Top to bottom, it is the natural burnished red of cedar and eucalyptus. Here the Hawaiian tradition of removing your shoes upon entering is made a pleasure. The floors, softly polished, cool, and smooth, massage your feet; the roof rides above the walls so that the air circulates easily. The front lanai is pure relaxation, with koa rocking chairs and a queen-size leather *punee;* stained glass puncturing the walls here and there creates swirls of rainbow light. Throughout the home are original artworks done by the Twigg-Smith family. A pool table holds king's court in the commodious games room, as doors open to a casual yet elegant sitting room where breakfast is served. A back staircase leads to a gazebo, floored with tile and brazenly open to the elements, while the back lanai is encircled by a roof made of copper. From here, Kailua-Kona glows with the imaginative mistiness of an impressionist painting, and, closer by, 40 acres are dotted with cattle raised by the family. Just below is the inn's pool, tiled in blue with a torch ginger motif. A plan is afoot to install a Jacuzzi in the coffee grove. All six rooms $130-170, differ in size and decor. The Polynesian Room, on ground level, is a mini-suite with sitting room, bedroom, and large bath. Another, the Bali Room, floored with reed mats, opens its windows to the splendid view. A few years back, Mr. Twigg-Smith was offered $7 million for the home. Much to our benefit, he said no. E-mail: holualoa@il-hawaii.net.

The **Kona Hotel,** along Holualoa's main street, tel. 324-1155, primarily rents its 11 units to local people who spend the work-week in Kailua-Kona's seaside resorts and then go home on weekends. They are more than happy, however, to rent to any visitor passing through, and are a particular favorite with Europeans. The Inaba family opened the hotel in 1926, and it is still owned and operated by Goro Inaba and his wife Yayoko, who will greet you at the front desk upon arrival. A clean room with bare wooden floors, a bed and dresser, and a shared bath down the hall goes for $20 s, $26 d, and $30 twin. Call ahead for reservations. No meals are served, but Mrs. Inaba will make coffee in the morning if you wish. The hotel is simple, clean, and safe.

SIGHTS FROM HONALO TO CAPTAIN COOK AND VICINITY

The mountainside communities of Honalo, Kainaliu, Kealakekua, and Captain Cook lie along a five-mile strip of Route 11, and if it weren't for the road signs, it would be difficult for the itinerant traveler to know where one village ends and the next begins. If you are after budget accommodations, unique boutique shopping, inexpensive island cuisine, and some off-the-beaten-track sightseeing, you won't be disappointed. About five miles south of Captain Cook is the small community of Honaunau and the road leading down to Pu'uhonua O Honaunau Historical Park.

Honalo
This dot on the map is at the junction of Routes 11 and 180. Not much changes here, and the town is primarily known for **Dai Fukuji Buddhist Temple** along the road. It's open daily 9 a.m.-4:30 p.m., free. Inside are two ornate altars; feel free to take photos but please remember to remove your shoes.

Kona Historical Society Museum
The main building of the Kona Historical Society Museum was originally a general store built around 1875 by local landowner and businessman H.N. Greenwell using native stone and lime mortar made from burnt coral. Now on both the Hawaiian and national registers of historic places, the building served many uses, including the warehousing and packaging of sweet oranges raised by Greenwell, purported to be the largest, sweetest, and juiciest in the world. The Kona Museum, P.O. Box 398, Captain Cook, HI 96704, tel. 323-3222 (for tour reservations tel. 323-2005), is open weekdays 8 a.m.-4 p.m. and Saturday 10 a.m.-2 p.m. if a guide is available; admission is $2. To get there, as you ap-

proach Kealakekua along Route 11, look on the right for a sign that reads "Kona Specialty Meat Co." Pull into this road and follow it around to the back of the meat market, where you will find the parking lot for the museum.

The main artifact is the building itself, but inside, you will find a few antiques like a surrey and glassware, and the usual photographic exhibit with themes like coffee-growing—part of the legacy of Kona. The basement of the building houses archives filled with birth and death records of local people, photographs both personal and official, home movies, books, and maps, most of which were donated by the families of Kona. The archives are open to the public by appointment only. According to the director, Jill Olson, the main purpose of the Historical Society is the preservation of Kona's history and the dissemination of historical information. Sometimes the society sponsors lectures and films (nominal charge), which are listed in the local newspapers. They also offer 4WD tours of the Kona area ($55) three times per year, usually in March, July, and November, and a historical boat tour in late January ($20) that takes you from Kailua-Kona south along the coast. There is no fixed schedule, but if you are in the area during those times of year, it would be well worth the trouble to contact the museum to find out if these excellent tours are being offered. However, historic walking tours of Kailua-Kona ($10), are regularly scheduled Tues.-Sat. at 9:30 a.m. The tours usually last about one hour at a leisurely pace, but they do have a tendency to take on a personality of their own, and may go longer.

Another excellent tour that gets to the heart of the area is the walking tour conducted at the historic **D. Uchida Coffee Farm** (listed on the National Register of Historic Places), begun by Japanese immigrants in 1925. Located in Mahukona, not far from Kealakekua, the 90-minute tour ($15) is offered Tuesday and Thursday at 9 a.m., with special tours by appointment; for reservations call 323-2005.

Amy B.H. Greenwell Ethnobotanical Garden
You can not only smell the flowers but feel the history of the region at the Amy B. H. Greenwell Ethnobotanical Garden, tel. 323-3318, along Route 11 just past mile marker 110 and marked by an HVB Warrior between the communities of Kealakekua and Captain Cook. The garden is open Mon.-Fri., 7 a.m.-3:30 p.m., with guided tours on the second Saturday of every month at 10 a.m., but visitors are welcome anytime during daylight hours—free. Amy B.H. Greenwell died in 1974 and left her lands to the Bishop Museum, which then opened a 10-acre interpretive ethnobotanical garden, planting it with indigenous Hawaiian plants, Polynesian introduced plants, and Hawaiian medicinal plants. When you step up to the office, take a fact sheet that describes the garden, complete with self-guiding map. The garden has remnants of the Kona field system, dating from pre-contact times when a fantastic network of stone ridges linked 50 square miles of intensive agriculture.

Royal Kona Coffee Mill and Museum
In the town of Captain Cook, Napoopoo Road branches off Route 11 and begins a roller-coaster ride down to the sea, where it ends at Kealakekua Bay. En route it passes the well-marked **Royal Kona Coffee Mill.** Along the way you can't help noticing the trim coffee bushes planted along the hillside. Many counterculture types have taken up residence in semi-abandoned "coffee shacks" throughout this hard-pressed economic area, but the cheap, idyllic, and convenience-free life isn't as easy to arrange as it once was. The area is being "rediscovered" and getting more popular. For those just visiting, the tantalizing smell of roasting coffee and the lure of a "free cup" are more than enough stimulus to make you stop. Mark Twain did! The museum is small, of the nontouchable variety with most exhibits behind glass. Mostly they're old black-and-white prints of the way Kona coffee country used to be. Some heavy machinery is displayed out on the back porch. The most interesting is a homemade husker built from an old automobile. While walking around be careful not to step on a couple of lazy old cats so lethargic they might as well be stuffed. Perhaps a cup of the local "java" in their milk bowl would put spring in their feline steps! Inside, more or less integrated into the museum, is a small gift shop. You can pick up the usual souvenirs, but the real treats are gourmet honeys, jellies, jams, candies, and of course coffee. Buy a pound of Royal Kona Blend for about $15, or 100% Royal Kona for around $27.89. Actually, it's cheaper at

Royal Kona Coffee Mill and Museum

DAVID STANLEY

other retail outlets and supermarkets around the island, but you can't beat the freshness of getting it right from the source. Refill anyone? The museum is open for self-guided tours daily 8 a.m.-5 p.m., tel. 328-2511.

Kealakekua Bay

Continue down Napoopoo Rd. through the once-thriving fishing village of Napoopoo ("Holes"), now just a circle on the map with a few houses fronted by neat gardens. At road's end, you arrive at Kealakekua ("Road of the God") Bay. Relax a minute and tune in all your sensors because you're in for a treat. The bay is not only a **Marine Life Conservation District** with a fine beach and top-notch snorkeling, but it drips with history. *Mauka,* at the parking lot, is the well-preserved **Hikiau Heiau,** dedicated to the god Lono, who had long been prophesied to return from the heavens to usher in a "new order." Perhaps the soothsaying *kahuna* were a bit vague on the points of the new order, but it is undeniable that at this spot of initial contact between Europeans and Hawaiians, great changes occurred that radically altered the course of Hawaiian history.

The *heiau* is carved into the steep *pali* that form a well-engineered wall. From these heights the temple priests had a panoramic view of the ocean to mark the approach of Lono's "floating island," heralded by tall white tapa banners. The *heiau* platform was meticulously backfilled with smooth, small stones; a series of stone footings, once the bases of grass and thatch houses used in the religious rites, is still very much intact. The *pali* above the bay is pocked with numerous burial caves that still hold the bones of the ancients.

Captain James Cook, leading his ships *Resolution* and *Discovery* under billowing white sails, entered the bay on the morning of January 17, 1778, during the height of the Makahiki Festival, and the awestruck natives were sure that Lono had returned. Immediately, traditional ways were challenged. An old crew member, William Watman, had just died, and Cook went ashore to perform a Christian burial atop the *heiau.* This was, of course, the first Christian ceremony in the islands, and a plaque at the *heiau* entrance commemorates the event. On February 4, 1778, a few weeks after open-armed welcome, the goodwill camaraderie that had developed between the English voyagers and their island hosts turned sour, due to terrible cultural misunderstandings. The sad result was the death of Captain Cook. During a final conflict, this magnificent man, who had resolutely sailed and explored the greatest sea on earth, stood helplessly in knee-deep water, unable to swim to rescue-boats sent from his waiting ships. Hawaiians, provoked to a furious frenzy because of an unintentional insult, beat, stabbed, and clubbed the great captain and four of his marines to death. (For a full accounting of these events, see the "History" section in the Introduction.) A 27-foot obelisk of white marble erected to Cook's memory in 1874 "by some of his fellow countrymen" is at the far northern end of the bay. Another plaque is dedicated to Henry Opukahaia, a young native boy taken to New England, where he was educated and converted to Christianity. Through impassioned speeches begging for salvation for his pagan countrymen, he convinced the first Congregationalist missionaries to come to the islands in 1820.

The land around the monument is actually under British rule, somewhat like the grounds of a foreign consulate. Once a year, an Australian ship comes to tend it, and sometimes local people are hired to clear the weeds. The monument fence is fashioned from old cannons topped with cannon balls. Here too is a bronze plaque often awash by the waves that marks the exact spot where Cook fell. You can see the marble obelisk from the *heiau*, but actually getting to it is tough. Expert snorkelers have braved the mile swim to the point, but be advised it's through open ocean, and Kealakekua Bay is known for sharks that come in during the evening to feed. A rugged jeep/foot trail leads down the *pali* to the monument, but it's poorly marked and starts way back near the town of Captain Cook, almost immediately after Napoopoo Road branches off from Route 11. If you opt for this route, you'll have to backtrack to visit the coffee museum and the *heiau* side of the bay.

Napoopoo Beach County Park

Kealakekua Bay has been known as a safe anchorage since long before the arrival of Captain Cook and still draws boats of all descriptions. The area, designated a **Marine Life Conservation District,** lives up to its title by being an excellent scuba and snorkeling site. Organized tours from Kailua-Kona often flood the area with boats and divers, but the ocean expanse is vast and you can generally find your own secluded spot to enjoy the underwater show. If you've just come for a quick dip or to enjoy the sunset, look for beautiful, yellow-tailed tropic birds that frequent the bay. Napoopoo Beach County Park has full amenities, including showers, picnic tables, and restrooms. Lifeguards are on duty during the weekends.

Heading for Pu'uhonua O Honaunau

This historical park, the main attraction in the area, shouldn't be missed. Though it was once known as City of Refuge Park, the official name is coming into more use in keeping with the emergence of Hawaiian heritage. The best way to get there is to bounce along the four miles of coastal road from Kealakekua Bay. En route, you pass a smaller, more rugged road to **Keei;** this side trip ends at a black-sand canoe launch area and a cozy white-sand beach good for swimming. A channel to an underwater grotto has been sliced through the coral. On the shore

Captain Cook's Monument

J.D. BISIGNANI

are the remains of Kamaiko Heiau, where humans were once sacrificed.

The other, more direct way to Pu'uhonua O Honaunau is Route 160 at Keokea, where it branches off Route 11 at mile marker 104, a short distance past Honaunau. Whether you are going or coming this way, make sure to take a five-minute side trip off Route 160 to **St. Benedict's Painted Church.** This small house of worship is fronted by latticework, and with its gothic-style belfry looks like a little castle. Inside, a Belgian priest, John Berchman Velghe, took house paint and, with a fair measure of talent and religious fervor, painted biblical scenes on the walls. His masterpiece is a painted illusion behind the altar that gives you the impression of being in the famous Spanish cathedral in Burgos. Father John was pastor here from 1899 until 1904, during which time he did these paintings, similar to others that he did in small churches throughout Polynesia. Before leaving, visit the cemetery to see its petroglyphs and homemade pipe crosses.

Pu'uhonua O Honaunau
National Historical Park

The setting of Pu'uhonua O Honaunau couldn't be more idyllic. It's a picture-perfect cove with many paths leading out onto the sea-washed lava flow. The tall royal palms surrounding this compound shimmer like neon against the black lava so prevalent in this part of Kona. Planted for this purpose, these beacons promised safety and salvation to the vanquished, weak, and war-tossed, as well as to the *kapu*-breakers of old Hawaii. If you made it to this "temple of refuge," scurrying frantically ahead of avenging warriors or leaping into the sea to swim the last desperate miles, the attendant *kahuna,* under pain of their own death, had to offer you sanctuary. *Kapu*-breakers were particularly pursued because their misdeeds could anger the always moody gods, who might send a lava flow or tidal wave to punish all. Only the *kahuna* could perform the rituals that would bathe you in the sacred mana and thus absolve you from all wrongdoing. This *pu'uhonua* ("temple of refuge") was the largest in all Hawaii, and be it fact or fancy, you can feel its power to this day.

The temple complex sits on a 20-acre finger of lava bordered by the sea on all sides. A massive, 1,000-foot-long mortarless wall, measuring 10

feet high and 17 feet thick, borders the site on the landward side and marks it as a temple of refuge. Archaeological evidence dates use of the temple from the mid-16th century, and some scholars argue that it was a well-known sacred spot as much as 200 years earlier. Actually, three separate *heiau* are within the enclosure. In the mid-16th century, Keawe, a great chief of Kona and the great-grandfather of Kamehameha, ruled here. After his death, he was entombed in *Hale O Keawe Heiau* at the end of the great wall, and his mana reinfused the temple with cleansing powers. For 250 years the *ali'i* of Kona continued to be buried here, making the spot more and more powerful. Even the great Queen Kaahumanu came here seeking sanctuary. As a 17-year-old bride, she refused to submit to the will of her husband, Kamehameha, and defied him openly, often wantonly giving herself to lesser chiefs. To escape Kamehameha's rampage, she made for the temple. Kaahumanu chose a large rock to hide under, and she couldn't be found until her pet dog barked and gave her away. Kaahumanu was coaxed out only after a lengthy intercession by Capt. George Vancouver, who had become a friend of the king. The last royal personage buried here was a son of Kamehameha who died in 1818. Soon afterwards, the "old religion" of Hawaii died and the temple grounds were abandoned but not entirely destroyed. The foundations of this largest city of refuge in the Hawaiian Islands were left intact.

In 1961, the National Park Service opened Pu'uhonua O Honaunau after a complete and faithful restoration was carried out. Careful consultation of old records and vintage sketches from early ships' artists gave the restoration a true sense of authenticity. Local artists used traditional tools and techniques to carve giant ohia logs into faithful renditions of the temple gods. They now stand again, protecting the *heiau* from evil. One of the most curious is a god-figure, with his maleness erect, glaring out to sea as if looking for some voluptuous mermaid. (Perhaps a sign of mermaid luck, good or bad, the erect member disappears from time to time, but more likely it just becomes the ill-gotten booty of weenie vandals . . . a sign reading "Hands Off" is a bit improprietous!) All the buildings are painstakingly lashed together in the Hawaiian fashion, but with nylon rope instead of traditional cordage, which would have added the perfect touch.

Stop at the visitor center to pick up a map and brochure for a self-guided tour. Exhibits line a wall, complete with murals done in heroic style. Push a button and the recorded messages give you a brief history of Hawaiian beliefs and the system governing daily life. Educate yourself; the visitor center, tel. 328-2288, is open daily 7:30 a.m.-5:30 p.m. Entrance to the 180-acre park is $2 per person. The beach park section is open 6 a.m.-midnight. Follow the refuge wall toward the northwest to a large, flat rock perfect for lying back and watching the sun set.

Every year on the weekend closest to the 1st of July, a free three-day cultural festival is held here, featuring traditional Hawaiian arts, crafts, music, and dance. Be sure to stop by for a peek into the past if you are in the area during this time.

ACCOMMODATIONS

So you came to Kona for the sun, surf, and scenery and couldn't care less about your room so long as it's clean and the people running the hotel are friendly? Well, you can't go wrong with any of the following out-of-the-mainstream hotels. They're all basic, but not fleabags. At all of these inexpensive hotels, it is very important to get your rooms first thing in the morning, if you don't have reservations. They are very, very, tough to get into. People know about them, so the rooms are at a premium.

Teshima's Inn, tel. 322-9140, is a small, clean, family-run affair in Honalo. Operated by Mr. and Mrs. Harry Teshima and family, it's somewhat like a Japanese *minshuku* with all rooms fronting a Japanese garden. To be sure of getting a room, call three days to a week in advance, and to reserve you must send at least one night's deposit (no credit cards accepted). If you just turn up, you have a slim chance of getting one of the 11 rooms. Check in is at the restaurant section. The rooms, at $20 s, $30 d, $250-300 monthly, are Spartan but very clean.

Merryman's Bed and Breakfast, owned by Don and Penny Merryman, P.O. Box 474, Kealakekua HI 96750, tel. 323-2276 or (800) 545-4390, is considered, even by others with B&Bs, to be one of the best on the island. The Merrymans, snow-birds from Alaska, came to the Big Island and built their cedar dream house, which they are willing to share with other people. The extra large knotty pine and glass rooms, always perfumed by fresh cut flowers and furnished with antiques, are made private with bamboo curtains. The bedspreads are thick, white quilts in a floral design, while the floors are covered with textured carpet. Your relaxation is ensured by rattan chairs with "Miss Muffet-like" puffed pillows into which you can sink with the setting sun. There are an outdoor Jacuzzi and a deck with comfortable lounging furniture, the premier spot on the property. Rates range $75-95. E-mail: merryman@ilhawaii.net; Web site: www.hawaii-bnb.com/merymn.html.

Manago Hotel, P.O. Box 145, Captain Cook, Kona, HI 96704, tel. 323-2642, fax. 323-3451, has been in the Manago family for 75 years, and anyone who puts his name on a place and keeps it there that long is doing something right. The old section of the hotel along the road is clean but a little worse for wear and doesn't impress much because it looks like a storefront. The rooms in the old section are small with wooden floors, double beds, and utilitarian dressers. Walk in to find a bridgeway into a garden area that's open, bright, and secluded away from the road. The new section features rooms with wall-to-wall carpeting, new furniture, private bath, louvered windows, and private lanai. The rates are $35 shared bath, $41 new section, plus $3 for an extra person. There is also one Japanese room that goes for $52 s, $55 d; weekly and monthly discount on all rooms. The views of the Kona Coast from the hotel grounds are terrific. You can dine in a restaurant in the old section, open for breakfast Tues.-Thurs. 7-9 a.m., lunch 11 a.m.-2 p.m., dinner 5-7:30 p.m., Fri.-Sun. 5-7 p.m., closed Monday. People come from all over the island for the legendary pork chop dinners.

RBR Farms Bed and Breakfast, P.O. Box 930, Captain Cook, HI 96704, tel./fax 328-9212 or (800) 328-9212, can accommodate you on a working coffee and macadamia nut farm. The cottage with fully equipped kitchen rents for $150 per couple ($175 holiday rate). Rooms are also available in the main house for $75-90. The upstairs rooms have the best view over the coast. All rooms have private entrance, TV, and ceiling fan. Everyone shares the pool and

Jacuzzi. E-mail: rbrfarms@gte.net; Web site: www.konaweb.com/rbr.

Similarly, **Lion's Gate,** owned by Diane and Bill Shriner, P.O. Box 761, Honaunau, HI 96726, tel./fax 328-2335, offers rooms on a working macadamia nut and Kona coffee farm. Only minutes from the Pu'uhonua O Honaunau National Historical Park, Lion's Gate features a Jacuzzi, refrigerator, and TV in all rooms, great views of the coast, a gazebo for relaxing, and, of course, complimentary Kona coffee and macadamia nuts. Rooms run $60-75. E-mail: liongate@aloha.net; Web site: www.stayhawaii.com/liongte.html.

A Dragonfly Ranch, P.O. Box 675, Honaunau, HI 96762, tel. 328-2159, (800) 487-2159, fax. 328-9570, owned and operated by David and Barbara Link, offers "tropical fantasy lodging" at a country estate. Rooms are remarkable and range from the "Hale in the Trees" to the "Honeymoon Suite" featuring an outdoor water bed. All rooms include a wet bar and refrigerator, private outdoor shower, cable TV, stereo, and small Hawaiiana library. Rates run $70 for a suite in the main house, $120 for the Redwood Cottage and Writer's Studio, and $160 for the Honeymoon Suite (substantial discounts for longer stays). However, be aware that A Dragonfly Ranch is the epitome of the adage "beauty is in the eye of the beholder." To some, the touted tropical fantasy may be a "tropical nightmare." The hosts are very friendly and inviting, indeed, but definitely have an alternative philosophy. The "Honeymoon Suite," for example is almost "open air." Dragonfly Ranch is one of those places that people totally adore or else dash away from. E-mail: dfly@aloha.net.

FOOD

All of the restaurants in this section happen to fall in the inexpensive range. All are worth a stop if you're hungry when you go by. Some are great, especially for breakfast and brunch. For markets and health food stores, see the following "Shopping" section.

Teshima's Restaurant in Honalo, open daily 6:30 a.m.-1:45 p.m. and 5-9:30 p.m., is just like the homey Inn that adjoins it. Here, in unpretentious surroundings, you can enjoy a full American, Hawaiian, or Japanese lunch for about $7, a filling daily special for $7.50, and dinner at $7.50-11. Another specialty is a *bento,* a box lunch for $5.50 that includes riceballs, luncheon meat, fried fish, teriyaki beef, *kamaboku* (fish cake), and Japanese roll. If you're interested in a good square meal, you can't go wrong.

Aloha Theater Cafe, open daily 8 a.m.-9 p.m., Sunday for brunch only 9 a.m.-2 p.m., tel. 322-3383, is part of the lobby of the Aloha Theater in Kainaliu. The enormous breakfasts ($5-8) feature locally grown eggs, homemade muffins, and potatoes. Lunchtime sandwiches, $6-8.50, are super-stuffed with varied morsels, from tofu and avocado to vegetarian tempeh burgers. There's also a variety of soups and salads and Mexican dishes like a quesadilla *especial* for $7.50. Full dinners like fresh *ahi* and *ono* are $15.95, filet mignon goes for $15.95, and pasta and shells are $12.95. For a snack choose from an assortment of homemade baked goods that you'll enjoy with an espresso or cappuccino. Order at the counter first (table service for dinner), and then sit

Lance of Tropical Temptations

on the lanai that overlooks a bucolic scene of cows at a watering trough, with the coast below. This is an excellent place to have breakfast or to pick up a picnic lunch on your way south. Also, check out the bulletin board for local happenings, sales, services, and the like.

The **Korner Pocket Bar and Grill,** tel. 322-2994, serving lunch and dinner weekdays 11 a.m.-10 p.m., until midnight Friday and Saturday, is a family-oriented/friendly biker bar where you can get excellent food at very reasonable prices. To get there, turn left off Route 11 in Kealakekua onto Halekii St., a half block before McDonald's, and look for the Korner Pocket in the small shopping center on the left. Start with *pu pu* like twice-baked potato for $2.50, calamari strips $4.25, chicken hot wings $4.95, and chilled shrimp cocktail $6.95. Grill selections are a poolroom burger $4.95, fresh catch about $7.50, or scrumptious bistro burger of grilled beef on crusty sourdough topped with fresh mushrooms sautéed in wine garlic sauce $6.50. Dinners are tempting: garlic scampi $12.95; chicken aiko accented with zesty Japanese sauce of lemon, apple, laurel, and spices; and prime rib eight ball, their encore entree at $11.95. The complete bar is well stocked with wines and spirits, or you can wash down your sandwich with an assortment of draft beers. The Pocket rocks with live music Friday night featuring various local rock bands, while Saturday usually brings jazz for quieter dining and dancing. The Korner Pocket looks as ordinary as a Ford station wagon, both inside and out, but the food is surprisingly good, and the owners, Paul and Judy, are very friendly.

Just beyond **McDonald's** golden arches as you enter Kealakekua, look for the **Canaan Deli,** tel. 323-2577, open Mon.-Fri. 7 a.m.-7 p.m. and Sat.-Sun. 7 a.m.-1 p.m., a luncheonette with an Italian flair. The owners, Geegee and Dawn Gambone, hail from Philadelphia and bring the "back East" deli tradition of a lot of food for little money along with them. You can't go wrong with a Philly cheese-steak sub for $5.50; or try a pizza smothered in cheese and delectables, ranging from a 10-inch cheese to a 17-inch Master for $28. All sauces, breads, and the pizza dough are homemade. Breakfast specials include a three-egg omelette for $5.50, toasted bagels for as little as $1.25, or steak and eggs $6. Lunch is deli sandwiches (it is a *full* deli), from pastrami to a good old

BLT costing $4-5.50, big fatso hoagies priced around $6-7, a meatball sandwich for $6, a loco moco for those a quart low on cholesterol, and various burgers. Free deliveries (minimum purchase $15) are provided from Keauhou to Honaunau in South Kona. Don't forget, you are dealing with an Italian guy from Philadelphia, so you have to treat him with respect, or you'll be swimming with the fishes all right . . . permanently!

There are very few places in Captain Cook where you can get a meal. On the right as you enter town is a takeout restaurant with barbecued ribs, chicken, hot biscuits, coleslaw, and salad. You can also try **Hong Kong Chop Suey** in the Ranch Center, which is as basic as can be, with most items at $5, including sides. Also, try the legendary pork chop dinner served at the **Manago Hotel** restaurant in downtown Captain Cook. Limited hours for breakfast, lunch, and dinner, Tues.-Sunday. Another place to try in Captain Cook is the **Kahauloa Coffee Company Coffee Shack,** offering bulk coffee, deli sandwiches, pastries, fresh baked bread, pizza, salad, and soup d'jour.

You'll be dancing like Zorba, singing like Caruso, and leisurely digesting like a *lomi lomi*ed Kamehameha after entering **The Kona Theater Cafe,** open daily 6 a.m.-6 p.m., tel. 328-2244, in Captain Cook just across from the post office. Reopened and revitalized by Ted Georgakis, a half-Italian, half- Greek man with an island flair, the ethnic atmosphere allows you to casually yet passionately philosophize over a menu that offers breakfast all day, fresh baked sweets, hot lunches, deli sandwiches, full entrées, and espresso. The cafe is still in transition, figuratively; a brick is laid daily, as in Roma, to create an atmosphere of restaurant, deli, theater, and espresso bar. Ted offers steamed fritatta and toast $4.25; a breakfast sandwich consisting of a bagel with egg, melted cheese, and Italian ham—a farmer's breakfast at $4.99; fresh waffles $3.25; specialty Greek or Italian salads $5.65; Hawaiian, Greek, or Italian chicken sandwiches on home-baked bread $5.95; healthful tempeh burgers $4.99; deli-style hot pastrami on rye $4.99; Italian sausage and peppers $4.95; or turkey and Swiss $5.49 (takeout available). Ted also handmakes fresh carrot juice, smoothies, and ginger lemonade, along with coffee selections from the espresso bar. He gets organic greens from a transplanted Florentine, Barbara Cappelli, a lady not only of innate beauty and artistry, but a woman with working hands that coax 18 different types of leafy edibles from the rich but tough local soil. Ted plans to revitalize the theater but will work on keeping it as close to original as possible. When it's complete (call to find out when), you will be able to enjoy art films, foreign films, community theater, and small concerts. Ted, being the Italian-Greek that he is, will feed not only your body, but your artistic soul as well. *Bravissimo!*

SHOPPING

Kainaliu

Next door to the Aloha Cafe, the **Aloha Store,** tel. 322-1717, open daily Mon.-Sat. 9 a.m.-8 p.m., Sunday 10 a.m.-2 p.m., sells gifts and sundries. The store has a wonderful selection ranging from stuffed teddy bears to teapots, along with local clothing and jewelry. You can also find items like koa barrettes and bracelets, children's games and books, music tapes, necklaces, earrings, and sterling silver jewelry. There's a rack of aloha shirts, candle holders, pottery, a smattering of honey and fruit gift items, and lotions and potions locally made. The bulletin board is great for letting you know what's happening, especially alternatively, in the area.

The Blue Ginger Gallery, tel. 322-3898, open Mon.-Sat. 9 a.m.-5 p.m., showcases the art of owners Jill and David Bever, as well as artists' works from all over the island. David creates art pieces in stained glass, fused glass, and wood. Jill paints on silk, creating fantasy works in strong primary colors. Using her creations as base art, she then designs one-of-a-kind clothing items that can be worn as living art pieces. The small but well-appointed shop brims over with paintings, ceramics, sculptures, woodworking, and jewelry. A section holds Asian artworks, including Polynesian masks, carved elephants, Buddha heads, and batiks from Indonesia. The Blue Ginger Gallery is a perfect place to find a memorable souvenir of Hawaii.

The Rainbow Path is in downtown Kainaliu in the Basque Bldg. at 79-7407 Hawaii Belt Rd., P.O. Box 2208, Kealakekua, HI 96750, tel. 322-0651, open Mon.-Fri. 9 a.m.-6 p.m., Saturday 10 a.m.-6 p.m. Monday, Wednesday, and Saturday, metaphysical readings are given by appointment. The Rainbow Path specializes in books on Hawaii, metaphysics, self-help, and personal discovery, and in books for children. You can also find tapes and CDs that include Hawaiian chants, Native American Indian music, Celtic music, and music especially composed to induce relaxation and relieve stress. Your body is taken care of with Ayurvedic medicine, incense, beeswax candles, bath and body products made by the Island Massage Company, and natural perfumes of island scents. The soul will stir with crystal pendants, pyramids, beaded necklaces, and dream catchers. All who are on the path will find this bookstore an oasis.

Badass Coffee Company, tel. 322-9196, open daily 7 a.m.-9 p.m., is a coffee and espresso bar where they roast their own beans on the premises in a *Royal No. 4 Roaster* manufactured in 1910, probably the last operational roaster of its type left in the state. Pure Kona coffee of the best grade sells for $29.95 per pound. After watching the roasting, take your cup of coffee and a homemade pastry to the rear of the shop, where you'll find an indoor stone grotto area away from the noise of the street.

Don't let the tourist junk piled outside **Hawaiian Crafts & Gifts,** in downtown Kainaliu across from the Bad Ass Coffee Co., tel. 322-0642, stop you from going in. Owned by Jeffrey Matias and open Mon.-Sat. 9 a.m.-5 p.m., the shop has a very surprising interior, filled as it is with authentic jewelry, shells, and Jeff's own beadwork. Many of the items are purchased from local people and include hula instruments, *lau hala* weavings, Niihau shellwork, Hawaiian fishhook pendants, *kukui* nut lei, and even an assortment of Hawaiian food products like mustard and salad dressings. Hanging on the walls are carvings of tikis, dolphins, turtles, and owls, the *amakua* of ancient Hawaii. For the children, there are Hawaiian dolls, and children of all ages will love a replica of a sea-going canoe with the distinctive crab claw sail. Jeff also imports unique jewelry from the Balkans! For those who can't live without another T-shirt, you'll find them as well as artificial flower lei.

At the south end of town, in the new Mango Court, is **Ohana O Ka Aina Food Co-op,** open 9 a.m.-6 p.m. weekdays, 10 a.m.-5 p.m. Saturday. This full-range health food store serves freshly made sandwiches from their deli. You can buy fresh orange and ginger lemonade made on the premises. The co-op, the last of its kind in Hawaii, has a large supply of herbs, plenty of vitamins and minerals, a smattering of fresh produce, and an excellent assortment of bulk grains. If you are a bona fide member of an organic foods co-op, and you have your card along with you, they will give you a reciprocal member discount.

This is one time that you'll enjoy an outbreak of **Pandamonium,** in downtown Kainaliu, open Mon.-Sat. 10 a.m.-6 p.m., tel. 324-7799, a shop filled with locally handcrafted artwear and crafts. Racks also hold high quality hand-painted Indonesian clothing, a designer line of T-shirts by Dr. Bill, and, if you just happen to be feeling a bit peaked after a long day of shopping, Chinese herbs, vitamins, and minerals in a side concession room. Not only can you come here and dress your body, you can address what ails you as well.

As you are leaving the built-up area of Kainaliu, look to see a sign for **Island Books,** "Used Books Bought and Sold," owned by Jev and Jonathan Thompson, open Mon.-Sat. 10 a.m.-6 p.m., P.O. Box 645, Kealakekua, Hawaii 96750,tel. 322-2006. They stock a general mix of titles, but history, geography, Hawaiiana, and a good selection of used travel books are the specialty. Here's a great place to purchase some casual reading material and save money at the same time.

Oshima's General Store is well stocked with cameras and film, drugs, fishing supplies, magazines, and some wines and spirits. Also in town is **Kimura's Market,** a general grocery store with some sundries.

Kealakekua

Right next door to the Kona Central Union Church is **Changing Hands,** a resale shop owned by Norma Hand that specializes in vintage clothing, glassware, and mostly Hawaiian antiques and bric-a-brac. It's open weekdays 10:30 a.m.-4:30 p.m., occasionally Saturday. You can pick up a treasure ranging in cost from a dollar or two to a few hundred.

The **Kahanahou Hawaiian Foundation,** tel. 322-3901, deals in ancient Hawaiian handicrafts, including masks, hula drums, and hula accoutrements. This nonprofit organization serves as an apprenticeship school for native Hawaiians who are trying to revitalize traditional arts. Unfortunately, no one seems to be in attendance in the shop, and you are instructed to ring the buzzer. A sign says, "If you're just here to browse and to kill

time don't kill ours; we can't afford the luxury." That sets the tone of your greeting when someone finally appears to scowl at you. Obviously the foundation is not into preserving *aloha.*

The Grass Shack, a.k.a. Little Grass Shack, open Mon.-Sat. 9 a.m.-5 p.m., sometimes Sunday noon-5 p.m., tel. 323-2877, is an institution in Kealakekua, owned and operated by *kama'aina* Lish Jens. It looks like a tourist trap, but don't let that stop you from going in and finding some authentic souvenirs, most of which come from the area or from Ms. Jens's many years of traveling and collecting. The items *not* from Hawaii are clearly marked with a big orange sign that says, "Sorry These Items Were Not Made In Hawaii." But the price is right. There are plenty of trinkets and souvenir items, as well as a fine assortment of artistic pieces, especially wooden bowls, hula items, exquisite Niihau shellwork, and Hawaiian masks. A shop specialty is items made from curly koa. Each piece is signed with the craftsperson-'s name and the type of wood used. One of the artisans displayed here is master woodworker Jack Straka. Items are also made from Norfolk pine and milo. A showcase holds jewelry and tapa cloth imported from Fiji, and a rack holds tapes of classic Hawaiian musicians from the '40s and '50s. The shop is famous for its distinctive *lau hala* hats, the best hat for the tropics.

Tropical Temptations, tel. 323-3131, open Mon.-Sat. 10 a.m.-5 p.m., is housed in a gaily painted yellow and green building. Climb the steps to the porch, where you'll find a service buzzer that will summon owner and chief tempter Lance Dassance, who will smile a welcome into his candy kitchen. Remember, however, that most of the business is wholesale and not really set up for drop-in visitors. Lance turns the best available grade of local fruits, nuts, and coffee beans·into delicious candies. The fresh-fruit process uses no preservatives, additives, waxes, or extenders and no sugars except in the chocolate, which is the best grade possible. A slow-drying process is used, so as few nutrients as possible are lost. A shop specialty is candy made from rare white pineapple, which grows for only eight weeks per year. Lance, if not too busy, will be happy to take you on a tour of the facility. He takes a personal pride in making the best candy possible and stresses that he uses only fruit ripened in the last 24 hours. Tropical Temptations, the healthiest candy store in Hawaii, has an

the Blue Ginger Gallery in Kainaliu

J.D. BISIGNANI

outlet booth in Kailua-Kona at the Kona Inn Shopping Village.

Konakai Coffee Farms has a tasting room and restaurant at the south end of Kealakekua. They produce and serve cups of Kona coffee plain or as espresso, cappuccino, and caffe latte. Check the racks of fresh-roasted pure Kona coffee.

The **Kamigaki Market** is also in Kealakekua.

Captain Cook

The **Kealakekua Ranch Center,** in Captain Cook, is a two-story mall with fashions, food, general supplies, and a Sure Save Supermarket.

Honaunau

Bong Brothers, 84-5227 Mamalahoa Hwy., on the *makai* side of the road near mile marker 106, tel. 328-9289, is open Mon.-Fri. 8:30 a.m.-6 p.m., Sunday 10 a.m.-6 p.m. It's housed in a coffee mill complex circa 1920, one of the oldest in Honaunau, and sells not only coffee but organic produce and health food deli items. Jay Koerner, the manager, is knowledgeable about both the area and about coffee and will show you around, time permitting. Ricardo, a local chef, makes pesto, "Ricardo's Revenge Salsa" with red hot habaneros, mango chutney, black bean and brown rice burritos and, on Thursdays, fresh pizza with a crust of five-grain flour, flax meal, or whole wheat; it's spiced with pesto made out of four kinds of basil and with a six-nut mix, and topped with a seven-cheese blend and all kinds of diced organic goodies. The shelves hold dried mango, candied ginger, bulk coffee, chocolate-covered coffee beans, Puna honey, Sam's Organic Gourmet salad dressings, dried pineapple, apples, and bananas, special sauces, and the "no shop is complete without them" T-shirts. Also look for a stack of burlap coffee bags, some bearing the Bong Brothers logo, that cost only $3 and make a nifty souvenir. Adjacent is **Gold Mountain Mill,** a functional roasting mill tended by Tom Bong and his dog Bear; if time permits they'll will show you around the operation. Coffee from the surrounding area comes in about three times per week to be roasted. The process that you will see includes pulping the bean, where the inside portion is squeezed out after soaking and then placed on the sun decks to dry. When nearly dry, the beans are placed in a large, turning drum, which blows hot air throughout to achieve the perfect moisture level. Next, a parchmentlike inner skin is removed from the beans; then they're ready for roasting in the still functional, vintage 1930s roaster.

Also in Honaunau is the **Shimizu Market.**

HOOKENA AND MILOLII

Hookena

If you want to see how the people of Kona still live, visit Hookena. A mile or two south of the Pu'uhonua O Honaunau turnoff, or 20 miles south of Kailua-Kona, take a well-marked spur road *makai* off Route 11 and follow it to the sea. The village is in a state of disrepair, but a number of homey cottages and some semi-permanent tents are used mostly on weekends by local fishermen. Hookena also boasts the **Hookena Beach County Park** with pavilions, restrooms, and picnic tables, but no potable water. Camping is allowed with county permit. For drinking water, a tap is attached to the telephone pole near the beginning of your descent down the spur road. The black-sand (actually gray) beach is broad, long, and probably *the* best in South Kona for both swimming and bodysurfing. If the sun gets too hot, plenty of palms lining the beach provide not only shade but a picture-perfect setting. Until the road connecting Kona to Hilo was finally finished in the 1930s, Hookena shipped the produce of the surrounding area from its bustling wharf. At one time, Hookena was the main port in South Kona and even hosted Robert Louis Stevenson when he passed through the islands in 1889. Part of the wharf still remains, and nearby a fleet of outrigger fishing canoes is pulled up on shore. The surrounding cliffs are honeycombed with burial caves. If you walk a half mile north, you'll find the crumpled walls and steeple of Maria

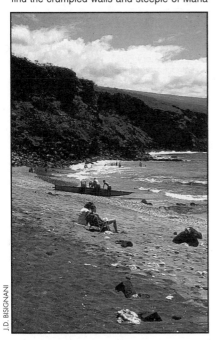

secluded Hookena Beach

Lanakila Church, leveled in an earthquake in 1950. The church was another "painted church" done by Father John Velghe in the same style as St. Benedict's.

Milolii
This active fishing village is approximately 15 miles south of Pu'uhonua O Honaunau. Again, look for signs to a spur road off Route 11 heading *makai.* The road, leading through bleak lava flows, is extremely narrow but worth the detour. Miloli ("Fine Twist") earned its name from times past when it was famous for producing *'aha,* a sennit made from coconut-husk fibers; and *olona,* a twine made from the *olona* plant and best for fishnets. This is one of the last villages in Hawaii where traditional fishing is the major source of income and where old-timers are heard speaking Hawaiian. Fishermen still use small outrigger canoes, now powered by outboards, to catch *opelu,* a type of mackerel that schools in these waters. The method of catching the *opelu* has remained unchanged for centuries. Boats gather and drop packets of chum made primarily from poi, sweet potatoes, or rice. No meat is used so sharks won't be attracted. In the village, a small, understocked store is operated by Willie Kaupiko, though the whole family pitches in. The **Miloli Beach County Park** is a favorite with local people on the weekends; camping by permit. Tents are pitched in and around the parking lot, just under the ironwoods at road's end. Notice that a number of the tents appear to be semi-permanent. There are flushing toilets, a basketball court, and a brackish pond in which to rinse off, but no drinking water, so bring some. Swimming is safe inside the reef and the tidepooling in the area is some of the best on the south coast. A 15-minute trail leads south to Honomalino Bay, where a white-sand beach is secluded and great for swimming. But always check with the local people first about conditions!

Accommodations to the South
Bougainvillea Bed and Breakfast, P.O. Box 6045, Ocean View, HI 96737, tel./fax 929-7089 or (800) 688-1763, has views of the ocean and South Point. The inn is quiet and romantic; each room has a private entrance and bath. Guests share the pool, hot tub, TV, and video library. Great stargazing. E-mail: peaceful@interpac.net; Web site: www.hawaii-bnb.com/bougvl.hmtl.

J.D. BISIGNANI

BOB RACE

SOUTH KOHALA

The Kohala District is the peninsular thumb in the northwestern portion of the Big Island. At its tip is **Upolu Point,** only 40 miles from Maui across the **Alenuihaha Channel.** Kohala was the first section of the Big Island to rise from beneath the sea. The long-extinct volcanoes of the Kohala Mountains running down its spine have been reduced by time and the elements from lofty, ragged peaks to rounded domes of 5,000 feet or so. Kohala is divided into North and South Kohala. South Kohala boasts *the* most beautiful swimming beaches on the Big Island, along with good camping and world-class hotels. Inland is **Waimea** (Kamuela), the *paniolo* town and center of the massive Parker Ranch. Founded last century by John Parker, its 200,000 plus acres on the western slopes of Mauna Kea made it the largest privately owned ranch in America. However, since the death of Richard Smart, the heir to the ranch, in 1992, it is now in transition and being held partially as a public trust.

Getting There from Hilo
If you're approaching Kohala from Hilo or the

east side of the island, you can take two routes. **The Saddle Road** (Route 200) comes directly west from Hilo and bypasses Mauna Kea and the Observatory Road. This very scenic road has the alluring distinction of being the least favorite route of the car-rental agencies. The Saddle Road intersects Route 190, where you can turn north for six miles to Waimea or south for 32 miles to Kailua-Kona. **Route 19,** the main artery connecting Hilo with the west coast, changes its "locally known" name quite often, but it's always posted as Route 19. Directly north from Hilo as it hugs the Hamakua Coast, it's called the "Hawaii Belt Road." When it turns west in Honokaa, heading for Waimea, it's called the "Mamalahoa Highway." From Waimea directly west to Waikui on the coast Route 19 becomes "Kawaihae Road," and when it turns due south along the coast heading for Kailua-Kona its moniker changes again to "Queen Kaahumanu Highway." The routes heading to Kohala from Kailua-Kona are discussed in the following sections. Many are "sights" in and of themselves, with lovely panoramas and leisurely back-lane rides.

© J.D. BISIGNANI AND MOON PUBLICATIONS, INC.

SOUTH KOHALA

PACIFIC OCEAN

To Hawi

KAWAIHAE ROAD

Waimea

To Hilo

SADDLE ROAD 200

SADDLE ROAD JUNCTION

Puu Opelu

Waiaka

ROAD

250 To Hawi

19

Kawaihae

Kawaihae Bay

270 To Hawi

PUUKOHOLA HEIAU NATIONAL HISTORIC SITE

MAILEKINI HEIAU

SAMUEL M. SPENCER BEACH COUNTY PARK

MAUNA KEA BEACH HOTEL AND GOLF COURSE

HAPUNA BEACH STATE RECREATION AREA

HAPUNA BEACH PRINCE HOTEL AND GOLF COURSE

Hapuna Bay

Waialea Bay

Puako Bay

Puako

PUAKO RD.

19

Lahuipuaa

Kamahoa

Gulch

Kamahoa

WAIKOLOA ROAD

Waikoloa Village

WAIKOLOA VILLAGE GOLF COURSE

Puu Hinai (1,439 ft.)

HAWAII BELT HIGHWAY

190

To Kailua-Kona

MAMALAHOA

Lava Flow

Puuanahulu

THE ORCHID AT MAUNA LANI
MAUNA LANI BAY HOTEL
GOLF COURSE

Honokaope Bay

WAIKOLOA BEACH RESORT
HILTON WAIKOLOA VILLAGE
SHERATON ROYAL WAIKOLOAN
THE SHORES AT WAIKOLOA
GOLF COURSE
THE KINGS SHOPS

HELIPORT

Anaehoomalu

Kapalaoa

Weliweli

Puco Bay

Keawaiki Bay

Ohiki Bay

Kiholo Bay

Kiholo

Nawaikulua Point

KAAHUMANU HIGHWAY

Keawaiki

19

QUEEN

Kaupulehu

KONA VILLAGE RESORT

Kahuwai Bay

FOUR SEASONS RESORT/HUALALAI GOLF COURSE

To Kailua-Kona

2.5 mi

2.5 km

0

THE COAST

The shoreline of South Kohala, from Anae-hoomalu Bay north to Kawaihae Bay, is rich in perhaps the finest super-deluxe resorts in the state. This coast's fabulous beaches are known not only for swimming and surfing, but for tide-pooling and awe-inspiring sunsets as well. Also, the two main beaches offer camping and even rental cabins. There are little-disturbed and rarely visited archaeological sites, expressive petroglyph fields well off the beaten track, the educational **Puukohola Heiau,** and even a rodeo. No "towns" lie along the coast, in the sense of a laid-out community with a main street and attendant businesses and services. The closest facsimile is Kawaihae, with a small cluster of restaurants, shops, and gas station. Waikoloa Village also provides some services, with exclusive boutique shopping.

Route 19, Queen Kaahumanu Highway

As you begin heading north from Kailua-Kona on coastal Route 19 (Queen Kaahumanu Highway), you leave civilization behind. There won't be a house or any structures at all, and you'll understand why they call it the "Big Island." Perhaps to soften the shock of what's ahead, magnificent bushes loaded with pink and purple flowers line the roadway for a while. Notice too that friends and lovers have gathered and placed white coral rocks on the black lava, forming pleasant graffiti messages such as "Aloha Mary" and "Love Kevin."

Suddenly you're in the midst of enormous flows of old a'a and pahoehoe as you pass through a huge and desolate lava desert. At first it appears ugly and uninviting, but the subtle beauty begins to grow. On clear days you can see Maui floating on the horizon, and *mauka* looms the formidable presence of Mauna Kea streaked by sunlight filtering through its crown of clouds. Along the roadside, wisps of grass have broken through the lava. Their color, a shade of pinkish gold, is quite extraordinary, and made more striking juxtaposed against the inky-black lava. Caught by your headlights at night, or especially in the magical light of dusk, the grass wisps come alive, giving the illusion of wild-haired gnomes rising from the earth. In actuality, it's fountain grass imported from Africa.

Around mile marker 70, the land softens and changes. The lava is older, carpeted in rich green grass appearing as rolling hills of pastureland. No cows are in evidence, but be aware of "Kona nightingales," wild jackasses that roam throughout this area and can be road hazards. Also, these long, flat stretches of road can give you "lead foot." Be careful! The police patrol this strip heavily, using unmarked cars (high-performance Trans Ams and the like are favorites) and looking for unsuspecting tourists who have been "road hypnotized." From Kailua-Kona to the Royal Waikoloan Hotel at Anaehoomalu is about 30 miles, with another 10 miles to the Mauna Kea Beach Hotel near Kawaihae. If you're day-tripping to the beaches, expect to spend an hour each way.

SIGHTS AND NEARBY COMMUNITIES

The following sights and beaches are listed from south to north. All, except for Waikoloa Village, lie along coastal Route 19, which is posted with mile markers, so finding the spots where you want to stop is easy.

Waikoloa Village

If you're interested in visiting Waimea (Kamuela) as well as seeing the South Kohala coast, you might consider turning right off Route 19 between mile markers 74 and 75 onto Waikoloa Road. This is a great deal of territory to cover in one day! This route cuts inland for 13 miles, connecting coastal Route 19 with inland Route 190, which leads to Waimea. About halfway, you pass the planned and quickly growing community of Waikoloa Village (about six miles inland from Waikoloa Resorts) that is unfortunately heralded by a condo complex of stark gray in neo-Alcatraz design which would aptly be called "Prisoners of Paradise" but is misnamed "The Greens." Try to overlook them, and head for the village itself, which is low-rise and quite tasteful.

J.D. BISIGNANI

the wide expanses of Kohala

The village is serviced by the **Waikoloa Highlands Center,** a small but adequate shopping mall with a gas station, full-service supermarket, First Hawaiian Bank, postal service store, small medical center, and a few restaurants and shops. This is also the home of **Waikoloa Stables,** tel. 883-9335, which hosts a number of rodeos and Wild West shows. They offer saddle horses and a variety of trail rides for the visitor. Here too is the **Waikoloa Village Golf Club,** tel. 883-9621, a private course open to the public; and **Roussels** restaurant at the clubhouse.

Puako

This alluring area is located *makai* on a side road off Route 19 about four miles south of Kawaihae. Hawaiians lived here in times past, but a modern community has been building along the three miles of Puako Bay since the 1950s. A thin ribbon of white sand runs the length of the beach that provides fair swimming, good fishing and snorkeling, and terrific tidepooling. Sunsets here are magnificent and you'll usually have a large stretch of beach to yourself, but remember your flashlight for the walk back because there's no lighting. Near-shore scuba diving is excellent, with huge caverns and caves to explore, and a colorful concentration of coral and marinelife.

Along Puako Road is **Hokuloa Church,** built by Rev. Lorenzo Lyons in 1859. This musically talented reverend mastered the Hawaiian language and composed lovely ballads such as

"Hawaii Aloha," which has become the unofficial anthem of the islands.

Puako Petroglyphs

These rock carvings, approximately 3,000 individual designs, are considered some of the finest and oldest in Hawaii, but carvings of horses and cattle signify ongoing art that happened long after Westerners appeared. Circles outlined by a series of small holes belonged to families who placed the umbilical cords of their infants into these indentations to tie them to the *aina* and give them strength for a long and good life. State archaeologists and anthropologists have reported a deterioration of the site due to vandalism, so please look but don't deface, and stay on all established paths. Access is by a well-marked, self-guiding trail starting from Holoholo Kai Beach Park. Other nearby groupings are located near the Royal Waikoloan Hotel. Any of the large Kohala hotels here offer brochures and information concerning the petroglyph field.

Organized tours of the nearby petroglyphs start daily at 8:30 a.m. from the food pavilion at the King's Shops. The Royal Waikoloan Hotel also offers a free guided tour of petroglyphs near its property on Tuesday and Thursday at 8:15 a.m. Be sure to bring plenty of water and wear good walking shoes and a hat.

Puukohola Heiau

Don't miss this completely restored Hawaiian temple, a National Historical Site located one

HAWAII STATE ARCHIVES

John Young, by ship's artist A. Pellion

mile south of Kawaihae where coastal Route 19 turns into Route 270 heading into North Kohala. This site, covering 77 acres, includes **Mailekini Heiau** and the nearby **John Young House** site. Administered by the National Park Service, it is open daily 7:30 a.m.-4 p.m.; admission is free. As you enter, pick up a map highlighting the main points of interest. It's worthwhile checking out the visitor center (tel. 882-7218), where Ranger Benjamin Saldua and others provide excellent information. Puukohola ("Whale Hill") received its name either because the hill itself resembles a whale, or because migrating whales pass very close offshore every year. It was fated to become a hill of destiny.

Kamehameha I built this *heiau* in 1790 on the advice of Kapoukahi, a prophet from Kauai who said that Kamehameha would unify all the islands only after he built a temple to his war-god Kukailimoku. Kamehameha complied, building this last of the great Hawaiian *heiau* from mortarless stone that when finished measured 100 by 224 feet. The dedication ceremony of the *heiau* is fascinating history. Kamehameha's last rival was his cousin, Keoua Kuahuula. This warlike chief, through prophecy and advice from his own *kahuna,* realized that it was Kame-

hameha who would rise to be sovereign of all the islands. Kamehameha invited him to the dedication ceremony, but en route Keoua, in preparation for the inevitable outcome, performed a death purification ceremony by circumcising his own penis. When his canoes came into view, they were met by a hail of spears and musket balls. Keoua's body was carried to Kukailimoku's altar. Kamehameha became the unopposed sovereign of the Big Island and, within a few years, of all of Hawaii.

Every August on the weekend closest to Establishment Day, a free two-day cultural festival is held on the *heiau* grounds, including arts and crafts exhibitions, games, hula demonstrations, music, and dance.

Near the *heiau* is the house site of John Young, an English seaman who became a close adviser to Kamehameha, who dubbed him Olohana, "All Hands." Young taught the Hawaiians how to use cannons and muskets and fought alongside Kamehameha in many battles. He turned Mailekini Heiau into a fort, and over a century later it was used during WW II by the U.S. Army as an observation area. Young became a respected Hawaiian chief and grandfather of Queen Emma. He's one of only two white men buried at the Royal Mausoleum in Nuuanu Valley on Oahu.

Kawaihae Town
The port marks the northern end of the South Kohala coast. Here Route 19 turns eastward toward Waimea, or turns into Route 270 heading up the coast into North Kohala. Kawaihae town is basically utilitarian, with wharves and fuel tanks. A service cluster has numerous shops and restaurants.

BEACHES, PARKS, AND CAMPGROUNDS

Anaehoomalu Bay
After almost 30 miles of the transfixing monochrome blackness of Kohala's lava flows, a green standout of palm trees beckons in the distance. Between mile markers 76 and 77, on the Waikoloa Resorts road, another well-marked access road heads *makai* to the Royal Waikoloan Hotel and historic Anaehoomalu Bay. The bay area, with its

freshwater springs, coconut trees, blue lagoon, and white-sand beach, is a picture-perfect seaside oasis. Between the large coconut grove and the beach are two well-preserved fish ponds where mullet was raised *only* for consumption by the royalty who lived nearby or were happening by in seagoing canoes. Throughout the area along well-marked trails are **petroglyphs,** a segment of the cobblestoned **King's Highway,** and numerous archaeological sites including house sites and some hard-to-find burial caves. The white-sand beach is open to the public, with access, parking, and beautiful lava stone showers/bathhouses. Although the sand is a bit grainy, the swimming, snorkeling, scuba, and windsurfing are fine. A walk north along the bay brings you to an area of excellent tidepools and waters heavily populated by marinelife. The next beach north is at Puako Bay.

Holoholokai Beach Park

Located near the Orchid at Mauna Lani Hotel on a well-marked access road, the picturesque beach park, open to the public daily 6:30 a.m.-7 p.m., is improved with a bathroom, running water, picnic tables, and resort-quality landscaping. Unfortunately, the beach itself is mostly coral boulders with only tiny pockets offering very limited water access. However, the park is used very little and is perfect for relaxing under a palm tree or for a leisurely stroll to explore the many tidepools.

Hapuna Beach State Recreation Area

Approximately 12 miles north of Anaehoomalu is the *second*-best, but most accessible, white-sand beach on the island. (The best, Kauna'oa, is listed next.) **Camping** is available in six A-frame screened shelters that rent for $20 per night and accommodate up to four. Provided are sleeping platforms (no bedding), electric outlets, cold-water showers, and toilets in separate comfort stations, plus a shared range and refrigerator in a central pavilion. Check in at 2 p.m., checkout at 10 a.m. The A-frames are very popular, so reservations and deposit are required. You can receive full information by contacting the Division of State Parks, P.O. Box 936 (75 Aupuni St.), Hilo, HI 96721, tel. 974-6200. There is unofficial camping south along **Waialea Bay** that you can get to by walking or taking the turnoff at mile marker 69.

Hapuna Beach is wide and spacious, almost 700 yards long by 70 wide in summer, with a reduction by heavy surf in winter. A lava finger divides the beach into almost equal halves. During good weather the swimming is excellent and lifeguards are on duty. During heavy weather, usually in winter, the rips are fierce, and Hapuna has claimed more lives than any other beach park on all of Hawaii! At the north end is a small cove almost forming a pool that is always safe, a favorite with families and children. Many classes in beginning scuba and snorkeling are held in this area, and shore fishing is good throughout. At the south end, good breaks make for tremendous bodysurfing (no boards allowed), and those familiar with the area make spectacular leaps from the seacliffs.

Kauna'oa Beach

Better known as **Mauna Kea Beach** because of the nearby luxury hotel of the same name, Kauna'oa is less than a mile north of Hapuna Beach and is considered to be the best beach on the Big Island by not only the local population, but also by those who judge such things from a broader perspective. In 1997, the National Geographic Traveler magazine ranked it one of the five best beaches in the United States. In times past, it was a nesting and mating ground for green sea turtles, and although these activities no longer occur because of human pressure on the habitat, turtles still visit the south end of the beach. Mauna Kea Beach is long and wide, and the sandy bottom makes for excellent swimming. It is more sheltered than Hapuna, but can still be dangerous. Hotel beach boys, always in attendance, are unofficial lifeguards who have saved many unsuspecting tourists. During high surf, the shoreline is a favorite with surfers. All beaches in Hawaii are public, but *access* to this beach was won only by a lawsuit against the Mauna Kea Beach Hotel in 1973. The ruling forced the hotel to open the beach to the public, which they did in the form of 10 parking spaces, a right of way, public shower, and toilet facilities. To keep the number of nonguests down, only 10 parking passes are handed out each day on a first-come, first-served basis. Pick them up at the guardhouse as you enter the hotel grounds. These entitle you to spend the day on the beach, but on weekends they're gone by

9:30 a.m. You can wait for someone to leave and then get the pass, but that's unreliable. The hotel also issues a pass for a one-hour visit to the hotel grounds (overstaying results in a $10 fine). You can use this pass to drop off family, friends, beach paraphernalia, and picnic supplies, then park at Hapuna and return via an easy mile-long **nature trail** connecting Hapuna and Mauna Kea Beaches, the route used by the majority of people unable to get a pass. Also, the hotel issues a "food and drink" pass that entitles you to stay as long as you wish, if you get it validated at one of the restaurants or snack bars. So as long as you're in there, you might as well use the beach for the price of a soft drink. In time the hotel will catch on, so test the waters before winding up with a fine.

Spencer Beach County Park
Look for the entrance a minute or two past Puukohola Heiau on Route 19 just before entering Kawaihae. Trails lead from the beach park up to the *heiau,* so you can combine a day at the beach with a cultural education. The park is named after Samuel Mahuka Spencer, a long-time island resident who was born in Waimea, served as county mayor for 20 years, and died in 1960 at Honokaa. The park provides pavilions, restrooms, cold-water showers, electricity, picnic facilities, and even tennis courts. Day use is free, but tent and trailer **camping** is by county permit only. Spencer Beach is protected from wind and heavy wave action by an offshore reef and by breakwaters built around Kawaihae Bay. These make it the safest and best swimming beach along South Kohala's shore and a favorite with local families with small children. The wide, shallow reef is home to a wide spectrum of marinelife, making the snorkeling easy. The shoreline fishing is also excellent.

PRACTICALITIES

RESORTS

Kona Village Resort
So you want to go "native," and you're dreaming of a "little grass shack" along a secluded beach? No problem! The Kona Village Resort is a once-in-a-lifetime dream experience. Located on Kahuwai Bay, a perfect-perfect cove of white sand dotted with coconut palms, the village lies seven miles north of the Kona Airport, surrounded by 82 open acres promising seclusion. The accommodations are distinctive "hales," individual renditions of thatch-roofed huts found throughout Polynesia and Hawaii. They are simple but luxurious, and in keeping with the idea of getting away from it all have no TVs, radios, or telephones. All, however, do have ceiling fans and louvered windows to let the tropical breezes blow through. Beds are covered with distinctive quilts and pillows. Each hut features a wet bar, fridge, coffee-making machine, and extra-large bathroom. Your "Do Not Disturb" sign is a coconut that you place upon your private lanai, and messages are hand-delivered and placed in a basket, also on the lanai. At one time you had to fly into the hotel's private airstrip, but today you can arrive by car. Almost ex-

actly at mile marker 87 look for a sign reading "Hualalai" where you turn in, and then make a right within 100 yards; actually, Hualalai is the name of the mountain to your back, and the area down by the sea was called *Kaupulehu* ("Roasted Breadfruit") by the native Hawaiians who lived in this once thriving village area.

Return guests will find the entrance changed from when the Kona Village was the only hotel in the area. You enter by an access road that leads through the coal black lava fields of South Kohala. Don't despair! Down by the sea you can see the shimmering green palm trees as they beckon you to the resort. Kona Village gives you your money's worth, with tennis, Ping-Pong, lei greetings, water sports, and a variety of cocktail parties and luau. Guided tours are also offered to the many historic sites in the area, along with classes in lei making, shoreline tidepool exploring, *lau hala* weaving, Hawaiian quilting, and even a botanical tour of the grounds complete with legends and explanations of the ancient medicinal uses of the plants. Rates start at $395 d, full American plan (three meals), and go up to $680 for oceanfront. Deduct $90 for single occupancy and add $25 for children under age two, $55 for children 2-5, $110 for children 6-12, and $160

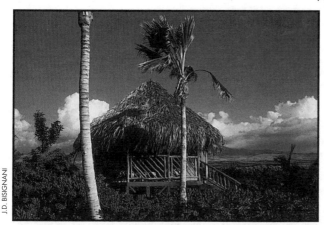

J.D. BISIGNANI

hale *at Kona Village Resort*

for an extra adult. The hotel's "Keikis in Paradise" is a children's program included in the price of a room that will entertain and educate children ages six and up throughout the day. There is a strict reservations and refund policy, so check. For information, contact Kona Village Resort, P.O. Box 1299, Kailua-Kona, HI 96745, tel. 325-5555, (800) 432-5450 from anywhere in the state, or (800) 367-5290 from the Mainland. E-mail: kvr@aloha.net; Web site: www.konavillage.com.

Meals are served in the Hale Moana, the main dining room; and at the Hale Moana Terrace, where a famous luncheon buffet is served daily 12:30-2 p.m. Hale Samoa is the fine dining restaurant, open daily except Wednesday and Friday, for dinner. Upon entering Hale Samoa, your spirits rise immediately with the sweep of cathedral ceiling. On the walls is an original painting by Herb Kane, Hawaii's foremost artist, that depicts *The Fair American,* a tiny ship commandeered by King Kamehameha that was instrumental in changing the history of old Hawaii. The walls also hold portraits of the hotel's original owner, Johnno Jackson, an oil driller from California, who in 1960 sailed in with his wife Helen, their Labrador dog, a monkey, and a parrot-all in a 42-foot schooner-landing on these shores and declaring, "This is the spot!" Also on the grounds are Hale H'ookipa "House of Hospitality," where a luau is held on Friday nights, and a steak-fry every Wednesday. Drinks and tropical libations are offered at the Hale Samoa Terrace, Shipwreck Bar, and Bora Bora Bar at the poolside.

A public tour is offered weekdays from 11 a.m. that includes a 15-acre petroglyph field on the property that you can inspect if you make prior arrangements. You will be instructed to meet a tour guide at the main gate at about 10:50 a.m. The hotel manager is Fred Duerr, who's been at the facility since 1966, along with most of his highly professional and seasoned personnel. They take pride in the hotel and do everything to help you have a rewarding, enjoyable, and relaxing stay at this premier resort. The Kona Village is a Hawaiian classic that deserves its well-earned reputation for excellence.

Four Seasons Resort

The Four Seasons Resort, Hualalai at Historic Ka'upulehu, opened in late 1996 as the newcomer to this coast. Located at 8 Queen Kaahumanu Hwy., this 243-room resort is split into 36 low-rise bungalows in four crescent groups that front a half-mile beach just up from Kona Village Resort. Located in amongst old lava flows from the Hualalai volcano, thirty-two of these units have ocean access and four are located along the 18th green of the accompanying golf course. Polynesian in style, they are a mixture of dark mahogany wood, light wall colors and carpeting, pleasing medium brown rattan furniture, and gray slate flooring. Authentic Hawaiian art pieces from the late 1700s to the present are displayed throughout the hotel. With all the greenery around, the lobby exudes a feeling of the outdoors. Plate glass windows behind the front desk allow the slope of Hualalai to sit unobstructed before you. Be sure to check out the interpretive center just downstairs from the lobby, where Mr. Kaleo will enlighten you about the surrounding waters, this area of Hawaii, and the life and lifestyle of ancient Hawaiians. A 1,200-gallon reef aquarium approximates the offshore ocean environment with live coral and fish from the local area. Before you snorkel, have a look in here to see what you'll encounter.

Rooms are over 600 square feet and filled with furniture and decorations. King-size beds predominate and are accompanied by freestanding credenzas, desks, couches, walk-in closets, an entertainment center, a fax line, and a refrigerated wet bar. Large as well are the bathrooms, each of which looks out onto a private garden, lanai, or patio. The slate floors of the main rooms are covered with seagrass mats and the beds with material reminiscent of tapa cloth. An exceptional place, it's not cheap. Rooms run $450-550 a night, suites $550-750 a night; $90 for an extra adult. From December 20 through January 3, there is a seven-night minimum for all stays. For information and reservations, contact the resort at P.O. Box 1269, Kailua-Kona, HI 96745, tel. 325-8000, (888) 340-5662, or (800) 332-3442, fax 325-8100.

The resort's two restaurants will certainly fill your every culinary need for all three meals of the day. Both the elegant **Puhu I'a Restaurant** and the casual **Beach Tree Bar and Grill** are set at oceanside. The more formal Puhu I'a features Hawaiian, Western, and Asian cuisine and includes many fish dishes, vegetarian entrees, and plenty of desserts and wine.

Located near the tennis courts is the Sports Club and Spa, a full-service facility open 7 a.m.-7 p.m., seven days a week. Pick from tai chi or aerobics instruction, a 25-meter lap pool, or Nautilus machines for a workout, then soothe those muscles on the massage table. A half basketball court is available for all the aspiring Magic Johnsons, and mountain bikes are conveniently for rent. After your exercise, stop in at the Trading Company store a few steps away for munchable supplies to bring back to the room, or for a noontime picnic. Hualalai Tennis Club is open 7 a.m.-9 p.m. only for hotel guests; reservations are required. Court fees are $10 per person per day. Private lessons are available

and ball machines can be rented. The Hualalai Golf Club offers an 18-hole, par-72 golf course designed by Jack Nicklaus that lies along the ocean. Green fees run $105 per person. The clubhouse holds the pro shop, locker rooms, cart and bag storage area and, for refreshment, the **Hualalai Club Grille and Bar.**

On the ocean side of the meeting room building is **Kids for all Seasons,** the hotel's service to take care of your children while you have fun yourself. Open 9 a.m.-5 p.m. for those 5-12 years old, the service provides a wide variety of fun-filled and supervised indoor and outdoor activities.

Royal Waikoloan Hotel

The Sheraton chain wanted to enter the luxury hotel market with a splash, so in 1981 they opened the $70-million, 545-room Sheraton Royal Waikoloan Hotel. They found the perfect spot at Anaehoomalu Bay (between mile markers 77 and 78), and produced a class act. The hotel lobby is a spacious open-air affair, beautifully appointed in koa and objets d'art. All rooms are tastefully decorated and provide a/c, color TV, king-size beds, and private lanais. Rates range $135-190 d for a standard, $250 for a cabana, and $350-450 for a suite; $20 additional person. For reservations, write: Royal Waikoloan, 69-275 Waikoloa Beach Drive, Kamuela, HI 96743-9763, tel. 885-6789, or phone Mainland Central Reservations at (800) 462-6262. On the superbly kept grounds are six tennis courts, numerous ponds, and a swimming pool. Special features include a small shopping arcade, (King's Shops a minute across the road) horseback riding (off property), and free shuttle service throughout Waikoloa. The focal points, however, are two marvelous golf courses. The Beach Course was designed by Robert Trent Jones Jr.; he learned his trade from his dad, whose masterpiece is just up the road at the Mauna Kea Resort. The King's Course is also known as the Weiskopf-Morrish Course after its designers, Tom Weiskopf and Jim Morrish.

You have a choice of dining facilities. The **Royal Terrace** opens its doors to the sea and features American cuisine daily for breakfast, lunch, and dinner. The atmosphere is relaxed and the prices are affordable for such a hotel. **The Tiare,** elegant dining in elegant surroundings for elegant prices, offers signature dishes such as Waikoloa seafood trio, a fisherman's stew made with fresh catch and fish from these wonderful Hawaiian waters just off Kona, fresh fish prepared in a variety of ways, and rack of lamb. Open daily except Wednesday and Sunday 6:30-9:30 p.m., tel. 885-6789, reservations recommended.

For those interested in the wonderful petroglyphs that are found throughout the area, you are invited to come to the Royal Waikoloa on Tuesdays and Thursdays at 8:15 a.m., when a knowledgeable staff member will take you on a petroglyph tour that includes petroglyph rubbing. A Ku'uali'i Fish Pond Tour is also offered on a variable schedule throughout the week. A special fish called the Ku'uali'i still thrives in the ponds that were *kapu* except to the *ali'i,* and were raised for their consumption alone.

The Shores at Waikoloa

The Shores at Waikoloa are secluded luxury condominiums nestled away in the planned community of Waikoloa at 69-1035 Keana Place, P.O. Box 5460, Waikoloa, HI 96743, tel. 885-5001; for reservations phone Aston Hotel and Resorts, tel. (800) 922-7866 Mainland, (800) 445-6633 Canada, (800) 321-2558 Hawaii. To get there, turn off Route 19 into well-marked Waikoloa at mile marker 76, and proceed straight ahead past the King's Shops, a small shopping area. Keep going for a few minutes and you will come to a sign that says Condominiums and another marker that points you to The Shores at Waikoloa. Enter through a security gate to see the peaceful and beautifully manicured grounds of the low-rise condominium. A few minutes away are the best beaches on Hawaii and all of the activities offered by the large luxury hotels, if you wish to participate. The condominium offers an "activities desk" where you can arrange a snorkeling or sailing excursion or hire a baby-sitter. A swimming pool and Jacuzzi are open until 10 p.m., and two complimentary tennis courts (and a few rackets too) are available. The condos are decorated by the individual owners so each room is unique, but there are guidelines and standards so that every unit is tastefully and comfortably decorated, mostly in an island motif. All units are extremely spacious, with many boasting

marble and terra-cotta floors; huge bathrooms with double tubs, showers, and sinks; full modern kitchens; and light and airy sitting rooms complete with state-of-the-art entertainment centers. Rates range $215 for a one-bedroom to $505 for a three-bedroom golf villa. Low season brings a 25% reduction, and The Shores offers an unbeatable low-season "golf package." If you are after a luxury vacation within a vacation where you can get away from it all after you've gotten away from it all, The Shores at Waikoloa is a superb choice.

Hilton Waikoloa Village

At the Hilton Waikoloa Village (formerly Hyatt Regency Waikoloa), 69-425 Waikoloa Beach Dr., Kamuela, HI 96743, tel. 885-1234 or (800) 445-8667, the idea was to create a reality so beautiful and naturally harmonious that anyone who came here, sinner and saint alike, would be guaranteed a glimpse of paradise.

From Kona airport, travel north on Route 19 for about 15 minutes. Look for mile marker 76, and turn beachside toward Waikoloa. Follow the roadway through the lava fields until you arrive at the hotel. Valets will park your car.

The architecture, "fantasy grand," is subdued and understated, not gaudy. The three main towers, each enclosing a miniature fern-filled botanical garden, are spread over the grounds almost a mile apart and are linked by pink flagstone walkways, canals navigated by hotel launches, and a quiet, space-age tram. Everywhere sculptures, art treasures, and brilliant flowers soothe the eyes. Songs of rare tropical birds and the wind whispering through a bamboo forest create the natural melody that surrounds you. You can swim in a private lagoon accompanied by dolphins, dine in magnificent restaurants, explore surrounding ranchlands, or just let your cares slip away as you lounge in perfect tranquillity.

Inside, attention to the smallest detail is immediately apparent. Elevators are done in rich woods and burnished brass. An alcove may hold a dozen superbly hand-carved puppets from Indonesia. Halls are bedecked with chandeliers, marble-topped tables, and immense floral displays. Even cigarette receptacles are artworks: large Asian pots or ceramic dolphins with mouths agape, filled with black sand.

the dolphin pool
at the Hilton

J.D. BISIGNANI

A museum promenade displays a Hawaiiana collection of carved koa bowls and feather lei, along with carvings from Thailand, paintings from Japan, and porcelains from China. Fantastic pots, taller than a person, are topped with two handles of gold elephant faces and tusks. Look through archways at perfectly framed grottoes harboring koi ponds and waterfalls. Sit on royal thrones and benches next to intricately carved credenzas and tables and simply delight at the beauty.

The hotel's restaurants are culinary extravaganzas, and every taste is provided for. **Donatoni's** features classic Italian; **Cascades** presents a different theme nightly which includes Polynesian, Chinese, Italian, and Mexican; **Imari** serves traditional Japanese fare; **Kamuela Provision Co.** specializes in steak and seafood; and the hotel's bars, lounges, and casual poolside dining options are surprisingly moderately priced. In addition, try the evening **Kamehameha Court Luau** for food, dinner show, and dancing.

The beach fronting the property offers excellent snorkeling, while three gigantic pools and a series of lagoons are perfect for water activities and sunbathing.

Take the amazing "Behind the House" tour of the facility (free). You are led below ground, deep into the heart of the hotel, where you get to see how everything works. An underground service roadway, complete with stop signs and traffic cops, runs for over a mile and is traveled by employees on bicycles and motorized utility carts. As you pass offices with signs that read *Wildlife Director, Curator of Art, Astronomer,* you come to realize how distinctive an undertaking the hotel is. Next come the florist shop, the butcher, the baker, the laundry (with more output than any other laundry in the state of Hawaii-22 pounds of linen go in each room) and wardrobe, responsible for outfitting the hotel's 2,000 employees. You're given staggering figures: 750,000 gallons of fresh water is needed for the pools; over 18 million gallons of seawater is pumped through the canals daily; each motor launch costs $300,000; the 41 chandeliers weigh over 24 tons; the hotel's 300 computers are linked by over 28 miles of cable. On and on, the statistics match the magnificence of what you see.

With all this splendor, the most talked-about feature at the hotel is still **Dolphin Quest.** A specially constructed saltwater pond, 65 times larger than federal regulations require, is home to Atlantic bottlenose dolphins from Florida's Gulf Coast, where they're found in bays and lagoons living most of their lives in water 16-20 feet deep. Here, their pond is 22 feet deep in the center, measures 350 feet long, and contains 2.5 million gallons of naturally filtered seawater.

Daily, on a lottery basis for adults, but with "two months in advance reservations available to children up to 19 years of age" (arranged through your travel agent or by phoning the hotel), guests are allowed to "interact with the dolphins." Dolphin Quest is trying to steer the program away from the concept of "swimming with dolphins," and more toward an educational experience. The program was founded by two highly respected marine veterinarians, Drs. Jay Sweeney and Rae Stone, both prominent in their field for their efforts to protect and preserve marine mammal populations. It was their idea to bring a new experience to the public in which the interaction was from the dolphin's point of view. Instead of a typical stadium-type setting where the dolphins are performers and the people are spectators, they created something more natural.

Here you don't ride the dolphins and they don't do tricks for you. In the half-hour session, the guests wade in chest-deep water with the dolphins gliding by while a staff member imparts information concerning not only dolphins, but all marinelife and human interdependence with it. If the dolphins want to be petted they stop, if not they move past like a torpedo. The experience is voluntary on the dolphins' part—*they* choose to swim with *you* as a guest in their domain.

Artwork surrounds you at the Hilton Waikoloa Village.

Much of the proceeds from the program goes toward marine research. At one time, a team from the University of California at Santa Cruz was housed, funded, and provided with boats to investigate a way to save the more than 100,000 spinner dolphins that are caught in tuna nets every year. Pointing to success, four baby dolphins have been born on the property since the inception of "Dolphin Quest." There are two male dolphins: one an immature "teenager" and the other a full-grown adult, Hobie, who keeps company with four female dolphins, dubbed "Hobie's Harem."

This futuristic and fantastic hotel complex has set a new standard against which all future resorts will be measured. Of course, as you would expect, all this luxury comes at a price; rates are $210-360 standard and $550-3,950 suites. Experience and time has matured the Hilton Waikoloa Village into one of the finest resorts in Kohala.

The Orchid at Mauna Lani

In a tortured field of coal-black lava made more dramatic by free-form pockets of jade-green lawn rises ivory-white The Orchid at Mauna Lani, a proud new addition to Sheraton's Luxury Collection, at One N. Kaniku Dr., Kohala Coast, HI 96743, tel. 885-2000, hotel direct at (800) 845-9905, or Sheraton Inns at (800) 325-3589. A rolling drive lined with *haku lei* of flowering shrubs entwined with stately palms leads to the open-air porte cochere. Enter to find koa and marble reflecting the diffused and soothing light of the interior. Straight ahead, off the thrust-proscenium Sunset Terrace, a living blue-on-blue still-life of sea and sky is perfectly framed. Nature, powerful yet soothing, surrounds the hotel. Stroll the grounds, where gentle breezes always blow and where the ever-present surf is the back beat of a melody created by trickling rivulets and falling waters as they meander past a magnificent free-form pool and trimmed tropical gardens of ferns and flowers. The Orchid At Mauna Lani was formerly a Ritz-Carlton Hotel, and although "the body" has not changed, "the soul" has. The Orchid is now much more casually elegant, a place to relax in luxury "island style." Gone is the sense of formality, and in its place is warm *aloha*.

The hallways and lobbies open from the central area like the delicate ribs of a geisha's fan.

Overhead hang magnificent cut-crystal chandeliers of differing designs. The walls are graced with Hawaiian quilts and exquisite art rendered by some of Hawaii's most famous artists, including Susan Hansen, Betty Freeland, Russell Lowrey, Fabienne Blanc, Nancy Poes, and Ken Bushnell. There are excellent artworks on view everywhere, from the walls of the superb Grill Restaurant to the Fitness Center. Elevators are koa-paneled, and every set of stairs boasts a velvety smooth koa banister carved with the pineapple motif, the Hawaiian symbol of hospitality.

Located in two six-story wings off the main reception hall, the 539 hotel rooms, each with private lanai and sensational view, are a mixture of kings, doubles, and suites. Done in neutral tones, the stylish and refined rooms feature handcrafted quilts, twice-daily room attendance, turndown service complete with a complimentary orchid and locally made chocolates, remote-control color TV, 24-hour room service, fully stocked honor bar, and in-room safe. Wardrobes, featuring automatic lighting, are hung with plush terry robes and plump satin hangers. The spacious marble bathrooms, with wide, deep tubs, separate commodes, and shower stalls are appointed with dressing and vanity mirrors, double sinks, hair dryers, and name-brand grooming products. Rates begin at $310 for a garden view to $440 for a deluxe oceanfront room . The Club Level, an exclusive floor with its own concierge, offers extra amenities—$510 will get you a room as well as continental breakfast, light lunch, cocktails, cordials, and a full spread of evening hors d'oeuvres. Suites range from an executive one-bedroom to the magnificent Presidential Suite and cost $495-2,800.

The hotel offers first-rate guest services, amenities, and activities that include a small shopping mall with everything from sundries to designer boutiques, complimentary shuttle to and from Mauna Lani's famous championship golf courses (to Waikoloa if time permits), bag storage, 11 tennis courts (with seven lit for evening play), complimentary use of fitness center and snorkel equipment, an enormous swimming pool and sun deck, bicycles for short tours, safe-deposit boxes, on-property car rental, and baby-sitting. **Keiki Aloha** is a special instructional day-camp program for children ages 5-12. Reasonably priced and offered half or full days, Keiki Aloha, in its secure and separate "children's room," includes lunch and lets kids engage in a variety of fascinating activities such as making shell jewelry, stringing lei, exploring petroglyphs, painting, and playing Hawaiian games and water sports.

Dining at the The Orchid can be everything from poolside casual (burgers and fries) to haute cuisine (fine delectables from around the world.) Executive Chef David Reardon and his staff prepare island cuisine in various styles, using locally grown produce, herbs, meats, and seafood. The culinary results are not only mouth-watering, but healthy and wonderfully nutritious.

At **The Grill,** open for dinner 6:30-9:30 p.m., cocktails and dancing until closing, most dishes are either Hawaiian style or northern Mediterranean influenced. Whet your appetite with crab cakes, vegetable raviolis, or guava grilled pork tenderloin $10-13, and move on to Maui onion soup gratiné, grilled corn and seafood chowder, or any of several salads $7-10. Entrées include a selection of grilled fresh island fish, beef, poultry, and vegetarian dishes. Specialties include rack of lamb, pan-seared sea scallops, and roasted onaga with saffron linguine. Entrées range $26-36.

The **Orchid Court** is open daily for breakfast and dinner and also serves an extraordinary Sunday brunch. The Orchid Court is a casual restaurant featuring Pacific Rim and local fare, and including both a children's and a you-can-run-but-you-can't-hide fitness menu. Prices for standard complete breakfasts are $15-16, the fitness breakfast $13, and a complete breakfast buffet $19. A la carte dishes are also available. Dinner entrees include sesame crusted mahimahi and red miso and pineapple glazed chicken breast.

The poolside **Brown's Beach House,** open daily for lunch and dinner, is the hotel's most casual restaurant, where you dine alfresco in a garden setting. Lunch offerings range from American standards and healthful salads to pizza and pasta. The dinner menu includes entrées like pumpkin seed and coriander crusted onaga and Asian spiced roast rack of lamb. At your feet, a perfect crescent white-sand beach opens to the great Pacific.

Mauna Lani Bay Hotel

As soon as you turn off Route 19, the entrance road, trimmed in purple bougainvillea, sets the mood for this $70-million, 350-room hotel that opened in 1983. The per-unit cost of $200,000 was the most ever spent in Hawaii up to that time, and it shows in the oversized rooms emphasizing relaxation and luxury, the majority with an ocean view. The hotel has a tennis garden with 10 courts, a lovely beach and lagoon area, a health spa, exclusive shops, and swimming pools. Enter through a grand portico, whose blue tile floor, a mimic of the ever-present sea and sky, immediately creates a sense of sedate but beautiful grandeur. Below is a central courtyard, where full-sized palms sway amidst a lava-rock water garden; cascading sheets of clear water splash through a series of koi ponds, making naturally soothing music. A short stroll leads you through a virtual botanical garden to a white-sand beach perfect for island relaxation.

Surrounding the hotel is the marvelous **Francis I'i Brown Golf Course** (North and South Courses), whose artistically laid-out fairways, greens, and sand traps make it a modern landscape sculpture. The courses are carved from lava, with striking ocean views in every direction; the 15th hole of the South Course requires a drive over a finger of ocean. Both are challenging, but not *too* much so, though they measure over 6,300 yards each, par 72. Greens fees are expensive, with preferred starting times given to hotel guests. Terrific savings with special "Room and Golf Packages" are offered by the hotel. (Call the Pro Shop at 885-6655 for more information.)

The prestigious *Tennis Magazine* has also rated the Mauna Lani's 10 *plexi-pav* courts among the "top 50 greatest tennis courts in the U.S." Special "Tennis Packages" offer reduced room rates along with a can of balls per room per day, a round robin tournament daily, a one-hour usage of the ball machine, and complimentary unlimited court time daily.

For parents with young children who have come to the realization that "families who want to stay together, don't always play together," the hotel offers a break from those little bundles of joy with **Camp Mauna Lani Bay,** for children ages 5-12. Day camp, 9 a.m.-3 p.m., is $25 including lunch and snacks, with a reduction in fee for additional children from the same family. Evening camp, 5-10 p.m., which is more responsible for romance then even a bottle of fine wine, is $20 per child with dinner and snacks. Full day camp, 9 a.m.-10 p.m., is $40 with lunch, dinner, and snacks for the first child, discounted thereafter. In-room baby-sitters are available on a per-hour basis. Throughout the day, the children at camp learn about Hawaiiana with coconut frond weaving, nature walks, and Hawaiian games, and develop their artistic skills with sand paintings, cookie decorating, and beadwork. Also, to work off some excess energy, there are lawn games, scavenger hunts, sand castle building and, for "couch potatoes in training," video games.

Don't forget about the teens. The hotel has initiated the **Eco-Teen Island Bound Adventures** program for kids 13-17 who want to explore ways to spend their time. Day-long activities include a hike along the Kohala coast, sea kayak trip, petroglyph tour, introduction to deep-sea fishing, volleyball tournaments, hula dancing, and more. This program is offered only from late March to late April, from mid-June to early September, and during Thanksgiving and Christmas vacation times.

The Mauna Lani's rooms begin at $415 ocean view to $520 oceanfront, with suites from $835 and royal bungalows for $3,200-4,100 (includes a personal chef, valet, live-in maid, and swimming pool). The hotel also offers one- to three-bedroom ocean villas, weekly and monthly rates available and three-night minimum required. Each room includes a private lanai, remote color TV and VCR, honor bar, in-room safe, make-up mirrors, and fluffy his/her robes. Guest privileges include complimentary use of the health spa (massage extra), snorkeling equipment, classes on Hawaiiana such as lei making and hula lessons, fish feeding, complimentary morning coffee and newspapers in the Bay Terrace Restaurant, and resort and historic tours. For full information, contact: Mauna Lani Bay Hotel, 68-1400 Mauna Lani Dr., Kohala Coast, HI 96743, tel. 885-6622 or (800) 367-2323, (800) 992-7987 Hawaii. E-mail: maunalani@maunalani.com.

The **Bay Terrace**, open daily for breakfast and dinner, offers the most casual but still superb dining. Daily offerings include everything from full-course breakfasts to dinner entrées like rack of lamb. Weekend nights feature a fabulous seafood buffet that shouldn't be missed, and the Sunday brunch served 9 a.m.-2 p.m. is legendary.

The oceanfront **Canoe House,** open daily for dinner, delights you with Pacific Rim cuisine. The koa menus (always changing with new items) feature special *pu pu* like nori-wrapped tempura *ahi* with soy-mustard sauce and toma-to-ginger relish $18.50, fresh corn risotto $10. A variety of soups and salads include creamy lobster leek and potato soup $7.50, miso-style avocado salad $12, or fresh asparagus and buffalo mozzarella with Kalamata-olive vinaigrette dressing $9.50. Main dishes tantalize you, with items like fresh seared mahimahi $29, pesto-seared scallops with roasted eggplant and calamatta olives $29, or grilled Korean-style chicken $29. Of course, there are also herb-crusted rack of lamb $30, and a wonderful Thai style seafood curry with lobster, shrimp, and Chinese vegetable stir-fry $36.50.

The **Ocean Grill,** where you'll be comfortable in bathing suit and cover-up, serves lunches and cocktails, while **The Gallery Restaurant and Knickers Bar,** at the Golf Pro Shop, serves lunch 11 a.m.-3 p.m. and dinner 5:30-9 p.m. (complimentary coffee and pastries for early tee times), closed Sun.-Monday. The award-winning restaurant is probably the least expensive fine-dining restaurant at the resort. Lunch can be Caesar salad $7 (with seared peppered *ahi* $9.50), smoked chicken salad $9.50, club house sandwich $8, roasted turkey sandwich $7.50, or specialties like curry *Indienne,* beef slowly cooked in spicy Madras curry and served with rice and condiments for $10.50. Dinner starts with tomato and Maui onions with balsamic dressing $7, peppered *ahi* $13.50, and onion bisque with *fontina* croutons $5. "Wannabe Italians," and who wouldn't, will enjoy ravioli with pesto sauce $18, or the always popular spaghetti with clams, garlic, white wine, and Italian parsley $19. Other gourmet fare includes New York steak $26, rib eye $23, roasted rack of lamb with sweet potato purée on thyme juice $24, the fresh catch (which can be broiled with shrimp, grilled in a citrus five-spice butter sauce, or baked with a macadamia nut crust) $22-24, and a one-pound, Kona-raised lobster served with shrimp and clams in a basil shellfish broth $29.

The **Honu Bar** is a perfect place to relax after a day of golf or tennis; there you will find a pool table and an excellent selection of liqueurs, wine, and fine cigars.

The Mauna Kea Beach Hotel

This hotel has set the standard of excellence along Kohala's coast ever since former Hawaii Governor William Quinn interested Laurence Rockefeller in the lucrative possibilities of building a luxury hideaway for the rich and famous. Beautiful coastal land was leased from the Parker Ranch, and the resort opened in 1965. The Mauna Kea was the only one of its kind for a few years until other luxury hotels were built along this coast. It's getting a bit older, and getting stiff competition from newer nearby luxury resorts, but class is always class and the Mauna Kea receives very high accolades as a fine resort. After an extensive restoration, the Mauna Kea reopened with youthful enthusiasm in December 1995.

The hotel's classic, trend-setting **golf course** designed by the master, Robert Trent Jones, has been voted among America's 100 greatest courses and Hawaii's finest. Also, *Tennis Magazine* includes the hotel among the "50 greatest U.S. tennis resorts." The hotel itself is an eight-story terraced complex of simple, clean-cut design. The grounds and lobbies showcase over 1,000 museum-quality art pieces from throughout the Pacific, and over a half-million plants add greenery and beauty to the surroundings. The landings and lobbies, open and large enough to hold full-grown palm trees, also display beautiful tapestries, bird cages with their singing captives, and huge copper pots on polished brick floors. The Mauna Kea offers a modified American plan (breakfast and dinner), the best beach on the island, and its own dive boat for seagoing adventure. Million-dollar condos also grace the grounds. Guests tend to come back year after year. The beautifully appointed rooms, starting at $280, $45 extra person, feature an extra-large lanai and specially made wicker furniture. From there, rates go up to $1,050 for a suite. A television-free resort at its inception, the hotel now has TVs in most of the rooms as part of the recent restoration. For full information contact Mauna Kea Beach Hotel, One Mauna Kea Beach Dr., Kohala Coast, HI 96743, tel. 882-7222 or (800) 882-6060.

Sumptuous dining is presented in the **Batik Room,** dinner nightly 7-10 p.m., where the Sri Lankan-inspired decor adds a touch of Eastern

the Mauna Kea Beach
Resort, an enclave of
class and elegance
along the Kohala coast

mystery and romance. Intricate *batik* tapestries, brass liner plates, and regal *houdah* (elephant thrones) set the mood for the exotic menu. Begin your feast with whole roasted garlic and escargot with wild mushrooms $14.50, or with island *ahi* tartar cake $17.00. Soups ranging from a salmon broth with fresh vegetables to lobster bisque armagnac cost $7-8.50. Entrees, magnificent creations from around the world starting at $28, include roasted duck with sweet corn polenta; a variety of island fish grilled, steamed and sautéed; and zesty curries made from lamb, veal, chicken, or shrimp. A titillating dessert is chocolate soufflé topped with macadamia nuts, champagne sauce, Grand Marnier, or fresh blueberries.

The Garden, another of the hotel's fine dining restaurants, open nightly for dinner 6:30-9:30 p.m., set the standards in the mid-1980s when it was one of the first restaurants to offer Hawaiian regional cuisine. Now it serves authentic Italian cuisine in its garden setting. **The Terrace,** informal and alfresco, is well-known along this coast for its Sunday buffet, $32. The choices seem endless at the serving table and you come away feeling like you won't need to eat for a week. The Terrace also serves a daily lunch buffet for $24 and has an à la carte menu of appetizers, soups, and salads.

For breakfast, lunch, or dinner in an open-air setting, try the **Pavilion** restaurant. Breakfast can be à la carte, from a simple continental breakfast to a traditional American meal with eggs, potatoes, juice, and bacon; or choose a lavish buffet offering fresh fruits, cereals, French toast, Belgian waffles, the finest and most delectable breakfast meats, steaming pots of Kona coffee, pineapple crepes, and even *huevos rancheros*. Lunch can similarly be à la carte—club sandwich or Cobb salad, for example—or a magnificent buffet of chilled seafood, sashimi, salmon, steaks, chops, lox, a cornucopia of island fruits and vegetables, and a dessert bar. Dinner offers starters like sesame seed prawns with green papaya salad and Waimea spring vegetables and mushroom risotto, all under $12.50. Baked onion soup or egg noodle soup with braised duck and shiitake mushrooms are sure to please. Entrées are a variety of pasta, fish, and meat dishes, most for under $30.

For light fare and quick snacks try the hotel's beachside **Hau Tree Cafe,** serving lunch and cocktails 11:30 a.m.-3:30 p.m.; or try **The 19th Hole,** adjoining the pro shop, where you can snack on everything from burgers to sushi daily 11 a.m.-4:30 p.m. The Mauna Kea is also famous for its 6 p.m. Saturday-evening **clambake** at the Hau Tree Cafe, where you can feast on Maine lobster, garlic shrimp, and sumptuous steamed clams while the sun sets to the melodious strains of musician extraordinaire George Kahumoku and Friends. Tuesday is extra special, featuring the Mauna Kea's world-famous **Old Hawaiian Aha'aina Luau.** As the sun sends blazing shafts of red and gold over the Luau Gardens at North Pointe, you dine on island favorites like *laulau, hulihuli* pork, Korean short ribs, island-grown steaks, and snow crab claws. The evening entertainment includes a torch lighting ceremony, traditional hula presented by *kumu hula* Nani Lim, and the dramatic Samoan fire dance.

Hapuna Beach Prince Hotel

Opened in 1994, the low-slung Hapuna Beach Prince Hotel fronts Hapuna Beach about one mile down the coast from the Mauna Kea Hotel. These two hotels, owned and operated by the Westin Hotel chain, are separate entities but function as one resort, joined as if in marriage. The princess, Mauna Kea, has finally found her prince. Long and lean, this hotel steps down the hillside toward the beach in eight levels. A formal portico fronts the main entryway through which you have a splendid view of palm trees and the ocean. This entryway is simple in design yet welcoming in spirit. Chinese flagstone, stained reddish by iron oxide, paves the main entry floor. Walls are the color of sand, and the wood throughout is light brown or dark teak. Lines are simple and decoration subtle. An attempt has been made to simplify and let surrounding nature become part of the whole. As at the Mauna Kea, visitors are not overwhelmed by sensory overload. A shuttle connects the Hapuna Beach Hotel to the Mauna Kea and all services available at one are open to guests of the other.

Carpeted bedrooms are spacious, allowing for king-size beds, and the bathrooms have marble floors. Each well-appointed room has an entertainment center, comfy chairs, live plants, prints on the walls, and a lanai with table, chaise lounge, and rack to dry clothes. Although each room is air conditioned, they all have louvered doors, allowing you to keep out the sun while letting breezes flow through. Rates for the 350 guest rooms start at $325 and go up to $460 a night; suites run $900-6,000. For information and reservations, contact the hotel at 62-100 Kaunaoa Dr., Kohala Coast, HI 96743, tel. 880-1111 or (800) 882-6060.

Of the hotel's four restaurants, the **Coast Grill** is its signature establishment. It specializes in fresh seafood and meat dishes and is only open for dinner; reservations are recommended. Starters, like Manila clam and Waimea

corn chowder or smoked duck *lumpia,* generally run $6-12. Move on to snapper wrapped in ti leaves, tenderloin of beef and marinated jumbo shrimp, smoked baby back ribs, or any other entree for $23-35. **Ocean Terrace** serves breakfast and dinner in a casual, open-air setting. Breakfast is either the buffet or from the menu; most dinner entrees, either from the sea or from the range, are grilled. The **Hakone** serves not only a Japanese buffet—an unusual treat and perfect opportunity to sample a variety of Japanese foods at one sitting—but offers individual entrées and items from its sushi bar. Resort evening attire is required. Located in the clubhouse, **Arnie's** serves standard American and health-conscious food and caters mainly to the golfers. In addition, you can get drinks, lunch items, and afternoon snacks at the **Beach Bar** down by the pool. The resort's executive chef, Corey Waite, and his staff do a superb job in the preparation and presentation of each meal and pride themselves on the Hawaiian regional cuisine that they serve. All restaurants except Hakone have children's menus.

The **Westin Kids Club** ($20 half day, $40 full day) offers a reprieve to parents who desire some time away from their energetic kids. The kids' time is filled not only with fun activities but with educational projects. Staffed by accredited nannies, the kids' club accepts children 5-12 years old. A baby-sitting service is also available for infants.

The **Hapuna Golf Course** clubhouse on the premises has Arnie's restaurant and the hotel's physical fitness center. While the fitness center has weights, its main focus is on dance, yoga, stretching, and alignment techniques. Various massage therapies are available. The staff is certified and fully licensed. Massages are $80 an hour and $40 a half hour. Open to the public, the fitness center costs $15 a day, $20 a week, or $50 a month.

Kenai Helicopters has a heliport on the hotel grounds, so if Madame Pele decides to blow her stack again you can be the first in line to go up and see the spectacle. **Mauna Kea Stable,** the resort's private stables located up the hill in Waimea, offers various rides and is the only stable allowed to ride on the huge Parker Ranch. Guests are given priority for rides but nonguests can also make use of the services.

OTHER ACCOMMODATIONS

Puako Beach Condos

Puako village has the only reasonably priced accommodations in this diamond-studded neck of the woods. The units go for $100 a night; three-night minimum. All units have a kitchen, laundry facilities, lanai, and charged maid service. There are ample parking, TV, and a swimming pool. Write Puako Beach Condos, 3 Puako Beach Dr., Kamuela, HI 96743, tel. 882-7711 or tel./fax 965-9446.

Waikoloa Villas

Up the hill in Waikoloa Village you'll find Waikoloa Villas, P.O. Box 385134, Waikoloa, HI 96738, tel. 883-9144, or call Marc Resorts (800) 535-0085 for reservations. Rates for these condo units are one bedroom $159-169, two bedrooms $179-189, three bedrooms $229-239; two-night minimum stay. Amenities include swimming pool, nearby golf, and weekly maid service. All units are fully furnished with complete kitchens. The condo offers a money-saving condo/car package.

FOOD

Except for a few community-oriented restaurants in Waikoloa Village, and a few reasonably priced roadside restaurants in Kawaihae, all of the food in South Kohala is served in the elegant but expensive restaurants of the luxury hotels. These hotels also provide the **entertainment** along the coast, mostly in the form of quiet musical combos and dinner shows. The following is a list of the very limited food options in South Kohala, independent of that offered at the luxury resorts, hotels, and condominiums.

Restaurants at the King's Shops

Hama Yu Japanese Restaurant is open daily 11:30 a.m.-3 p.m. and 5:30-9 p.m. Choose appetizers ($4.50-7) like soft-shell crab, yakitori, and a variety of sashimi and sushi. Dinners include tempura $24, Japanese steak $26, and *tonkatsu* $19.

For a smaller and more moderately priced meal try **Hawaiian Chili by Max,** a window restaurant where you can have a variety of chilis and hot dogs, all well prepared and health-conscious. A separate area called **The Food Pavilion** will satisfy anyone on the run with everything from a Subway Sandwich to pizza and espresso coffee.

The Grand Palace Chinese Restaurant, open daily 11 a.m.-9:30 p.m., serves appetizers ranging from $6.95 for deep fried chicken wings to $12.95 for a cold platter. Soups are from $7.50 for pork with mustard cabbage all the way up to $43 for shark's fin soup. Chicken and duck dishes range from $7.95 for sweet and sour chicken to $38 for a whole Peking duck. Seafood includes sautéed shrimp with asparagus $12.95, steamed fresh oysters in the shell with black bean sauce $14.95, and Kung Pao squid $8.95. There are also your standard beef, pork, and vegetable dishes like egg fu yung $5.95 or spinach with garlic sauce $6.95. Specialties are clay pot dishes such as stewed beef brisket $9.95 and the "house special" fried rice $8.95.

The **Big Island Steakhouse,** featuring the Merry Wahine Bar, is open daily from 5 p.m., serving items like a *pu pu* platter with baby back ribs $8.95, sashimi at market price, and a variety of salads from simple onion and tomato $4.95, to aloha salads with fish, chicken, or beef $10.95-13.95. Entrees are prime rib (10 oz) $16.95, 12 oz $18.95, Thai pasta with stir-fry vegetables $14.95, and coconut prawns $16.95.

Golf Cart Vendor

You can actually buy a well-made sandwich, hot dog with all the trimmings, and a variety of soft drinks and beer from the strategically placed and gaily canopied Golf Cart Vendor at the Mauna Lani Resort Golf Course. Follow Kaniku Dr. toward the hotel and look for the access road pointing to Holoholokai Beach Park. Follow it, and in about 100 yards just where the golf cart track crosses the road, look to the right for the cart. This makes a perfect stop if you're heading to the Puako Petroglyphs or to the beach park. The sandwiches, fairly hearty, are under $4, the hot dogs $2.50, and the beer, soda and snacks are priced amazingly right for this exclusive neck of the woods!

Blue Dolphin

In Kawaihae Village along Route 270 is the Blue Dolphin, run by husband-and-wife team Randy and Leona Roberts, tel. 882-7771, open for lunch Mon.-Fri. 10:30 a.m.-2 p.m., for dinner Mon.-Sat 5-9 p.m. Their menu features the house shrimp salad $7.50, a variety of burgers ranging $5-8.50, and sandwiches like turkey with Swiss cheese $4.95. They also serve plate lunches such as teriyaki beef $7.50, teriyaki chicken $6.75, and chicken luau $7.95. For dinner, the soup of the day is $1.95 for a cup, $3.25 for a bowl, with appetizers like sautéed mushrooms $5.95 and fresh ceviche $3.95. Hawaiian entrées include *kalua* pork $9.95 and mixed Hawaiian plate $10.95, with specialties like sautéed prawns and scallops $14.95, barbecued ribs $10.95, and a vegetarian mixed plate $8.95. If you're heading north and want to picnic along the way, the Blue Dolphin will be happy to pack things to go.

The Blue Dolphin Restaurant keeps the beat cool with jazz Friday nights from 7 p.m. and the first Tuesday of the month, when a local group, *Almost A Capella,* comes to perform their ensemble of oldies.

Cafe Pesto

Who'd expect a yuppie upscale restaurant in the sleepy village of Kawaihae? Cafe Pesto, tel. 882-1071, open Sun.-Thurs. 11 a.m.-9 p.m., Fri.-Sat. 11 a.m.-10 p.m., has a chic interior design with black-and-white checkerboard flooring and black tables trimmed with wood, similar to its sister cafe in Hilo. The bold gourmet menu tantalizes you with starters like *crostini* (French bread with a fresh, creamy herb garlic butter) $2.95 and freshly made soups from $3.25. Daily specials might be wild green salad $3.50, blue Caesar salad $3.95, or Greek pasta salad $6.95. Pasta dishes are scrumptious: smoked-salmon pasta with spinach, capers, and sun-dried tomatoes; and fettuccine in saffron cream sauce $12.95. Lunch, served 11 a.m.-4 p.m., brings an assortment of hot sandwiches that includes everything from smoked ham to a chicken pita for under $8. Cafe Pesto also serves gourmet pizza with crust and sauces made fresh daily. Among their best pizzas are shiitake mushrooms and artichokes with rosemary and Gorgonzola sauce, seafood pesto pizza, and pizza luau, all ranging in price from $5.95 for a small to $16.95 for a large. Dinner entrees are wild, with North Kohala fresh catch which can be grilled, seared, or sautéed $19-21.95, and seafood risotto sumptuous with morsels of Keahole lobster, tiger prawns, jumbo scallops, and Pahoa corn all seared with sweet chili $18.95. Cafe Pesto is *the* perfect place to stop for a civilized meal as you explore the Kohala coast.

Kawaihae Harbor Grill

This new addition to Kawaihae serves lunch daily 11:30 a.m.-2:30 p.m., and dinner 5:30-9:30 p.m. Climb the steps to the large veranda from where you have a bird's-eye view of Kawaihae and unfortunately an unobstructed view of the petrochemical tanks across the road. The lunch menu offers calamari $6.95, seared island poke $8.95, a steak sandwich $10.95, and chicken and chips $9.95. Light dining consisting of a veggie *pu pu* platter is $6.95, the house salad $3.95, and a chicken sandwich $7.25. In the evening, dinners include harbor grill *lau lau,* which is fresh catch, scallops, and crab steamed in ti leaves $18.95, steak and seafood combo $20.95, grilled chicken, half $9.95, whole $16.95, and charbroiled rib eye steak $18.95. Inside, the one-time village store is quite tasteful, with *lau hala mats,* mood lamps, and a glass partition that has been etched with an octopus and tropical fish. Although not quite elegant, the Kawaihae Harbor Grill is tasteful and presented with pride.

Tres Hombres Beach Grill

Pancho Villa in aloha shirt and sombrero and riding a surfboard (!) would be instantly at home in Tres Hombres, tel. 882-1031, located in the Kawaihae Center, open 11:30 a.m.-midnight, dinners to 9 p.m. on weekdays and to 10 p.m. weekends. Besides being a south-of-the-border restaurant run by *hombre* Rafael Cifuentes, Tres Hombres is an unofficial surfing museum filled with a fine collection of surfboards and surfing memorabilia donated by such legendary greats as Dewey Weber, Greg Knoll, and Jack Wise. Some of the tables are fashioned from wooden surfboards made of balsa wood with mahogany striping, others from green-and-white Mexican tiles. Bar stools are of provincial Mexican design topped with leather. The bamboo-appointed interior has a relaxed tropical effect. The extensive menu offers savories like nachos $8.95, nachitos $5.95, calamari $8.95, chimichangas $5.95 and $8.95. Substantial meals include Island Salad with boneless breast of chicken over greens with avocado and fresh papaya $11.95; tostada grande with beef or chicken $10.95, with shrimp $15.95 or, for the vegetarian, black bean $9.95. Burritos go from $7.25 for a bean and cheese to $9.95 for a beef or chicken. The beach grill also offers fish $13.95, filet mignon $17.95, crab enchiladas $16.95, and combination dinners made up from a choice of enchiladas, tacos, tostadas, and chiles rellenos $10.95-13.95. For dessert, try their deep-fried ice cream $5.95. The full bar serves not only all the island favorites, but adds special concoctions like K-38s, Swamis, mango margaritas, Kawaihae Sunsets that will help you go down for the evening, and Mauna Kea Sunrises that, with a great deal of wishful thinking, will pop you back up. *Pu pu* are served 3-6 p.m. daily. Relax with an ice-cold margarita on the lanai of this tastefully casual restaurant, and experience an excellent change of pace from the luxury hotels just down the road.

Roussels Waikoloa Village
A few years ago, the well-respected Roussels Restaurant in Hilo closed its doors and some time later opened again in Waikoloa, to everyone's delight. Roussels, tel. 883-9644, is open seven days a week; lunch 11 a.m.-2 p.m., appetizers 2-9:30 p.m., and dinner Tues.-Sat. only 5-9:30 p.m. Reservations recommended. For those wanting to stay along the coast, Roussels is a bit out of the way, but for those willing to venture inland, the restaurant lies like a pot of gold at the end of the rainbow. In Waikoloa Village, turn onto Malia St. and follow it to the golf course clubhouse where the old Roussels sign will direct you to the new restaurant.

Still in partnership with head chef Spencer Oliver, Roussels' niche is spicy Cajun food. It's the only restaurant on the island whose main emphasis is food from New Orleans and the Creole South. The shrimp and oyster gumbo at $4.95 a cup is outstanding, as is the shrimp Creole for $16.25. Whet your appetite with escargot in a garlic and tomato sauce $6.75, blackened sashimi at market price, or crab and shrimp cocktail $8.25. Delightful salads are Waimea greens *beaucoup* (local greens with crumbled blue cheese and a shallot vinaigrette), tempting avocado and seafood salad with a remoulade mayonnaise dressing $12.85 as an entree, or a Cre-

ole Caesar salad $3.95. Move on to the Cajun entrees of chicken Pontalba (sautéed boneless chicken breast with Bearnaise sauce) $14.95, duck in orange sauce $18.75, or prime rib seasoned and flash-cooked $19.75. Seafood entrees include fresh local catch done by your choice of preparation at market price, soft shell crab meunière also at market price, or prawns scampi $21.95. All entrees are served with salad, vegetables, and fresh-baked bread. Complement the meal with a choice wine, choose from an assortment of cakes, pies, and mousses baked daily, and end with a wonderful liqueur. While the dinner menu hasn't changed much, lunches are now a bit faster and geared toward the local golf clientele. Salads, hamburgers, po'boy and other sandwiches, soups, gumbo, fish, chicken, and pasta are on the menu. This is upscale Cajun cooking in an upcountry island setting.

SHOPPING AND ACTIVITIES

The King's Shops
The Waikoloa Beach Resort community has its own small but adequate shopping center, The King's Shops, open daily 9:30 a.m.-9:30 p.m., that features over 35 different shops and restaurants, along with entertainment, special events, and a **tourist information center.** A number of the shops feature Hawaiian artifacts, with museum-quality exhibits displayed here and there, and even some petroglyphs that offer a link to the mythology of ancient Hawaii. The shops include: **Benetton** and **Crazy Shirts** for distinctive tops, shirts, and tees; **Zac's** for your photo and copy needs; **Liberty House** for department-store merchandise; **Whaler's General Store** for light groceries and sundries; and **Noa Noa** for an excellent selection of imported fashions from throughout Southeast Asia, especially Indonesia. Fabrics range from rayon to silk; the batik prints were individually designed. Excellent prices. **Endangered Species** welcomes you with a python overhead. Most items, from T-shirts to sculptures, have an animal or floral motif. A portion of the proceeds from all sales goes to the World Wildlife Foundation. **Kunahs** mainly offers casual tropical wear for men, such as shorts, T-shirts, hats, aloha shirts, and classic aloha shirts for $40-78. **Dolphin Galleries Artwork**

sails the high seas with marine art, lures the ladies with fine jewelry, and even offers a few distinctive 3D sculptures. **Island Shells** is hung with dolphins, fish, shellwork, and jewelry; **Pacific Rim Collections** is where you will find Hawaiian quilts, masks from throughout the South Pacific, and carved whales and dolphins; **Malia** offers fine women's wear; and **Under the Koa Tree** showcases Hawaiian artists who have turned their hands to koa woodwork and fine jewelry.

Free **entertainment** is offered at the King's Shops every Tuesday 6-8 p.m. when a local *hula halau* comes to perform, and Thursday 6-8 p.m. when local musicians come to perform contemporary Hawaiian music. The Royal Waikoloan Hotel offers *pu pu* and refreshments at the event for a nominal charge. The evening is popular with both tourists and local people, and is an excellent chance to have fun Hawaiian style.

Organized tours of nearby **petroglyphs** start at 8:30 a.m. daily from in front of the food pavilion. Wear comfortable clothing and bring water for this hour to hour-and-a-half walk.

Kawaihae Center

The Kawaihae Shopping Center can take care of your rudimentary shopping needs. It sits at the Y-junction of Routes 19 and 270 and is situated so that the upper floors face Route 19 and the lower floors are along Route 270. There's a **7-Eleven** convenience store, the **Cactus Tree** for alohawear, and **Tropical Dreams** for homemade ice creams and sorbets. You'll also find the **Upstairs Gallery** featuring porcelain, paintings, and prints by Pegge Hopper. For a mid-day pick-me-up caffeine blast try the **Kawaihae Bad Ass Coffee Shack.** Restaurants are on both levels.

Across the road are a **76 gas station** and **Laau's Fish Market,** open Mon.-Sat. 6 a.m.-6 p.m., offering fresh fish from local waters.

An excellent art shop is **Kohala Collections,** tel. 882-1510, open daily 11:30 a.m.-8:30 p.m. and on Tuesday in the evenings only 6-8:30 p.m. It displays mostly Big Island artists. The gallery's features include works by Jurgen Wilms, who does Big Island landscapes in oils; distinctive bamboo lamps by Cal Hashimoto; fine carvings of sea turtles done in milo wood by Greg Pontius; Hawaiian theme paintings in pastel by Jeremiah Cordero; folding screens by Kalalani; koa frames by Tai Lake; distinctive furniture by master craftsman Don Wilkinson; oil paintings by Avi Kiriaty; fused glass by Patricia Van Aspern-Hume; bronze sculpture by Deborah Fellows; and the fine pottery of Matt Lovein. Less expensive items include petroglyph coasters, koa bookmarks, wooden turtles, and island jewelry. Kohala Collections is an excellent gallery featuring some of the very best artists on the Big Island today.

Kohala Divers

Located along Route 270 in Kawaihae, open daily 8 a.m.-5 p.m., tel. 882-7774, Kohala Divers offers scuba certification for $350, snorkel rentals for $10 (24 hours), and scuba rentals for $22. They lead two-tank dives for $75, and will take snorkelers along if they have room on the boat ($25). Kohala Divers is also a retail shop where you can buy boogie boards, fins, masks, snorkels, and scuba equipment. If you are a scuba enthusiast, you can come here to get your tanks refilled for $4, or overhaul your diving gear for $35 plus parts. It's a bit far to go from Kailua-Kona, but they offer big savings, and they're the only dive company along the Kohala coast.

DIANA LASICH HARPER

BOB RACE

WAIMEA (KAMUELA)

Waimea is in the South Kohala District, but because of its inland topography of high mountain pasture, mostly covering Mauna Kea's western slopes, Waimea can be considered a district in its own right. It also has a unique culture inspired by the range-riding *paniolo* of the expansive **Parker Ranch.** This spread, founded early last century by John Palmer Parker, dominates the heart and soul of the region. Waimea revolves around ranch life and livestock. A herd of rodeos and "Wild West shows" is scheduled throughout the year. But a visit here isn't one-dimensional. In town are homey accommodations and inspired country dining. For fun and relaxation there's a visitor and ranch center; Puuopelu, the Parker mansion and art collection; a wonderful museum operated by John Parker's great-great granddaughter and her husband; a litany of historic shrines and churches; and an abundance of fresh-air and wide-open spaces, the latter not so easily found in the islands.

The town, elev. 2,670 feet, is split almost directly down the center—the east side is the wet side, and the west is the dry side. Houses on the east side are easy to find and reasonable to rent; houses on the dry side are expensive and usual-ly unavailable. You can literally walk from verdant green fields and tall trees to dry desert in a matter of minutes. This imaginary line also demarcates the local social order: upper-class ranch managers (dry), and working-class *paniolo* (wet). However, the air of Waimea, refreshed and cooled by fine mists *(kipuupuu),* combines with only 20 inches of rainfall a year into the best mountain weather in Hawaii. Waimea is equally known as Kamuela, the Hawaiianized version of Samuel, after one of John Parker's grandsons. Kamuela is used as the post office address, so as not to confuse Waimea with a town of the same name on the island of Kauai. The village is experiencing a growth spurt. In 1980 it had no traffic lights and was home to about 2,000 people. Now the population has grown fivefold and there are traffic jams. Waimea is modernizing, and its cowboy backwoods character is rapidly changing.

Getting There
The main artery connecting Waimea and Kailua-Kona is Route 190, also known as the Hawaii Belt Road. This stretch is locally called the Mamalahoa Highway. From Kailua-Kona, head out on Palani Road until it turns into Route 190. As

WAIMEA

To Hilo

KUHIO HALE
HAWAIIAN HOMES
HALL

KUHIO VILLAGE

MANA RD.

HAWAII BELT RD.

POLICE

FIRE STATION

IMIOLA CHURCH

CATTLEMANS STEAKHOUSE

MEDICAL CENTER

STATE OFFICES

PARKER SCHOOL

WAIMEA CENTER

NEW POST OFFICE

KAHILU THEATER

PARKER RANCH STABLES

TOWN HALL

PARKER RANCH CENTER MALL

VISITOR CENTER

KAPIOLANI RD.

HOKUULA RD.

Waimea Park

WAIMEA COUNTRY LODGE

PARKER SQUARE MALL

KAMUELA INN

LINDSEY RD.

KAMUELA OFFICE CENTER

LIBRARY

PARKER RANCH GYM

WAIMEA SCHOOL

KOHALA HWY

PANIOLO PARK

RACE TRACK

WAIMEA KOHALA AIRPORT

EDEWEISS

OPELO RD.

OPELO PLAZA

WAIMEA VISITOR CENTER

LAE LAE RD.

KAWAIHAE RD.

Kohakohau Str.

Waikoloa Str.

Haleaha Gulch

PARKER RANCH HISTORIC HOMES

MAMALAHOA

To Kona

POWER PLANT

WALAKA BRIDGE

DUMP

HAWAII PREP ACADEMY

KAMUELA MUSEUM

Keanuiomano Str.

To Kawaihae and Hale Kea

To Hawi

© J.D. BISIGNANI AND MOON PUBLICATIONS, INC.

0.5 mi

0.5 km

you gain elevation heading into the interior, look left to see the broad and flat coastal lava flows. Seven miles before reaching Waimea, Saddle Road (Route 200) intersects the road from the right, and now the highlands, with grazing cattle amidst fields of cactus, look much more like Marlboro Country than the land of aloha. The **Waimea-Kohala Airport,** tel. 885-4520, is along Route 190 just a mile or so before you enter town. Facilities amount to a basic restroom and waiting area with a few car-rental windows. Unless a flight is scheduled, even these are closed.

SIGHTS

HISTORIC HOMES AND ART COLLECTION AT PUUOPELU

Richard Smart, last heir to the fantastic Parker Ranch, opened **Puuopelu,** a century-old family mansion, to the public just a few years before he passed away on November 12, 1992. Inside this living museum, the works of prominent artists are displayed, but since his death, the artworks are being sold off and the collection is rapidly diminishing. On the grounds, original and reconstructed Parker Ranch homes are also open to visitors. Puuopelu is located along Route 190 a few minutes south of town and is open daily 10 a.m.-5 p.m., admission $7.50 adults, $5 children.

A formal drive lined with stately eucalyptus leads to the mansion. Enter an elegant sitting room illuminated by a crystal chandelier to begin your tour. The home was begun in 1852 by John Palmer Parker II. In 1910 Richard Smart's grandmother, Aunt Tootsie, added the living room, kitchen, and fireplace. In 1969 Richard Smart, who inherited the ranch lands and home from Aunt Tootsie, gutted the home and raised the ceiling to 19 feet to accommodate his art collection. He added elegant French doors and skylights. Part of the kitchen was converted into a dining room, the Gold Room was created, and the koa doorways were raised to match. Richard Smart became a well-known actor. He studied at the Pasadena Playhouse in the late '20s, and appeared on Broadway with famous names such as Carol Channing and Nannette Fabray. Mr. Smart performed in plays all over the U.S., and recordings of him singing songs in Italian, French, and Spanish provide the background music as you tour the art collection. You've heard of actors becoming ranchers; well, he was a rancher who became an actor. Recently opened is Richard Smart's bedroom, which is loaded with memorabilia from his stage performances, and with mementos given by the people that he knew on Broadway. The tour is self guided with all art pieces named. Besides works of famous artists, there are magnificent pieces like a tall wooden cabinet with carved yellow Chinese Peiping glass from the 19th century, silver tea sets, decanters for pouring wine at elegant functions, large cut-crystal punch bowls, and magnificent chandeliers hung from the skylights overhead. Make sure to see the little side bedroom, called the Venetian Room, aptly decorated with paintings of gondolas and appointed with treasures from Venice. Lighting the room are two chandeliers, one pink and the other turquoise. Here, the filigreed art-deco mirrors are also fabulous. The feeling is of genteel elegance, but notice that the walls are rather rough board-and-batten covered with beautiful artwork. You get a feeling of class, but it's obvious that you are on a ranch. In the emerald-green kingdom that is the Parker Ranch, Puuopelu is the crowning jewel.

Just outside Puuopelu is the reconstructed **Mana Home** (admission included), the original Parker Ranch homestead. A knowledgeable tour guide, Judy Apo, leads you through and provides historical anecdotes about the Parker family. The home was built in 1847 by family patriarch John Palmer Parker from the durable native koa found at high elevations on the ranch lands. The exterior of the original home, covered by a heavy slate roof, was too brittle to move from its original site 12 miles away, but the interior was removed, numbered, and put back together again like a giant jigsaw puzzle in the reconstructed home. A model in the living room shows you what the original site looked like back in the 1800s. To preserve the rich wood interior of the home, all that's required is to wipe it down once a year with lemon oil. At first the home seems like a small cabin, just what you'd expect from the

1850s, but in actuality it's a two-story home with one bedroom downstairs and three upstairs.

The Parker dynasty began when John Palmer Parker jumped ship and married Kipikani, the granddaughter of King Kamehameha. They bought two acres of land for $10, and Parker with his two sons built the Mana Home. In later years Kipikani, being the granddaughter of the king, received 640 acres. The two sons, John Palmer Parker II and Ebenezer, who were by then married, built two homes on it, and as children came, added more rooms in the sprawling New England tradition. They also built one large community kitchen, at which the entire family cooked and dined. A replica shows how the home grew over the years, and it is a good indicator of how the Parker fortunes grew along with it. As the children's children got older, they needed a schoolhouse, so they built one at the corner of the original site. It still stands and is maintained by a *paniolo* and his family who live there. Unfortunately, many members of the Parker family died young. The first-born, John Palmer Parker II, married Hanai. His brother, Ebenezer, married Kilea, a woman from Maui, who bore him four children. One of their boys was Samuel Parker, known in Hawaiian as Kamuela, the co-name of Waimea. Samuel married Napela, and together they had nine children. Samuel's father Ebenezer died at age 26 after swallowing the bone of a flubber (a little bird the size of a pigeon) that punctured his intestine. Kilea could never get over his death and visited his grave daily. Finally, she decided that she wanted to return to her family on Maui. She was advised by the people of the island not to go because of rough seas. Kilea did not heed the advice, and along with her entourage was lost at sea. Meanwhile, John Palmer Parker II and Hanai gave birth to only one boy who died within 12 months. Childless, they adopted one of their nephew Samuel's nine children as a *hanai* child, in a practice that continues to this day. He was the fifth child, John, who became John Palmer Parker III and who later married Elizabeth Dowsick, known as Aunt Tootsie. They had one girl, Thelma Parker, before John III died of pneumonia at age 19. Aunt Tootsie raised Thelma as a single parent, and somehow managed to purchase Samuel Parker's and his eight children's half of the ranch. Thelma Parker married Gillian Smart. They had one boy, Mr. Richard Smart, before

a modern paniolo *of Waimea*

J.D. BISIGNANI

his mother Thelma died at age 20 of tuberculosis. Aunt Tootsie literally took the bull by the horns to keep the ranch going, and when she passed away in 1943, she left everything to her grandson Richard. The ranch prospered under his ownership and spread to its present 225,000 acres with 50,000 head of cattle that supply fully one-third of the beef in the Hawaiian Islands. After his death, the ranch, although still producing cattle, has become a charitable trust called **The Parker Ranch Charitable Foundations** that benefits the people of Waimea and local communities long associated with its operation. The Parker Ranch is the second largest private landowner in the state, following the Bishop Estate.

SIGHTS IN TOWN

Parker Ranch Visitor Center And Museum

This is the first place to stop while in town. The visitor center, at the Parker Ranch Shopping

Center, is open daily 9 a.m.-5 p.m., tel. 885-7655, adults $5, children $3.75 (joint admission to Puuopelu available). After spending an hour at the center's two museums and taking in the slide presentation, you'll have a good overview of the history of the Parker Ranch and, by extension, Waimea. Exhibits at the **John Palmer Parker Museum** depict the history and genealogy of the six generations of Parkers who have owned the ranch. At the entrance is a photo of the founder, John Parker, a seaman who left Newton, Massachusetts, on a trading vessel in 1809 and landed in Kealakekua, becoming a fast friend of Kamehameha the Great. Parker, then only 19, continued his voyages, returning in 1814 and marrying Kipikane, a chieftess and granddaughter of Kamehameha. In the interim, domesticated cattle, a present from Captain Vancouver to Kamehameha, had gone wild due to neglect and were becoming a dangerous nuisance all over the Big Island. Parker was hired to round up the best of them and to exterminate the rest. While doing so, he chose the finest head for his own herd. In 1847 King Kamehameha III divided the land by what was known as the Great *Mahele,* and John Parker was granted Royal Deed No. 7, for a two-acre parcel on the northeast slopes of Mauna Kea. His wife, being royal born, was entitled to 640 acres, and with these lands and tough determination, the mighty 225,000-acre Parker Ranch began. It was, until the death of Richard Smart, the largest privately owned ranch in the

U.S., and on its fertile pastures over 50,000 cattle and 1,000 horses were raised. The ranch is now a charitable trust whose proceeds benefit the community of Waimea.

In the museum, old family photos include one of Rev. Elias Bond, who presided over the Christian marriage of Parker and his Hawaiian wife in 1820. Preserved also are old Bibles, clothing from the era, and an entire koa hut once occupied by woodcutters and range riders. There are fine examples of quilting, stuffed animals, an arsenal of old weapons, and even a vintage printing press. The 15-minute video in the comfortable **Thelma Parker Theater** begins whenever enough people have assembled after going through the museum. The video presents a thorough and professional rendition of the Parker Ranch history, along with sensitive glimpses of ranch life of the still very active *paniolo.*

There isn't much happening around the old town entertainment-wise, but **free hula lessons** are given at the Parker Ranch Visitor Center on Monday afternoons.

Imiola Church

Head east on Route 19 to "church row," a cluster of New England-style structures on the left, a few minutes past the Parker Ranch Shopping Center. Most famous among them is Imiola ("Seeking Life") Church. It was built in 1855 by the Rev. Lorenzo Lyons, who mastered the Hawaiian language and translated some of the

Ranch life still dominates Waimea.

J.D. BISIGNANI

great old Christian hymns into Hawaiian, as well as melodic Hawaiian chants into English. The current minister is a friendly and urbane man, Rev. Bill Hawk, a new arrival who is assisted by his wife Sandra. Restored in 1976, the yellow clapboard church with white trim would be at home along any New England village green. When you enter, you'll notice an oddity: the pulpit is at the near side and you walk around it to face the rear of the church. The walls and ceilings are of rich brown koa, but the pews, supposedly of the same lustrous wood, have been painted pink! The hymnals contain many of the songs translated by Father Lyons. Outside is a simple monument to Rev. Lyons, along with a number of his children's gravesites. A tour of the church is free, and definitely worth the time.

Kamuela Museum

The Kamuela Museum, largest privately owned museum in Hawaii, is a fantastic labor of love. For the octogenarian owners, founders, and curators, Albert and Harriet Solomon, it's a vocation that began in 1968 and fulfilled a prophecy of Albert's grandmother, who was pure Hawaiian and a renowned *kahuna* from Pololu Valley. When Albert was only eight years old, his grandmother foretold that he would build "a great longhouse near three mountains and that he would become famous, visited by people from all over the world." This prediction struck him so much that he wrote it down and kept it throughout his life. When grown, he married Harriet, the great-great granddaughter of John Palmer Parker, and the two lived in Honolulu for most of their adult lives, where Albert was a policeman. For 50 years the Solomons collected, collected, and collected! Harriet, being a Parker, was given heirlooms by family members which are also on exhibit. The museum is west of town center on Route 19, 50 yards after the junction with Route 250 heading toward Hawi. The museum, dedicated to Mary Ann Parker, John Parker's only daughter, is open every day of the year 8 a.m.-5 p.m., tel. 885-4724; admission $5, children under 12, $2. Plan on at least an hour.

As you enter, the screen door bangs like a shot to signal Albert and Harriet that another visitor has arrived. Although the tour is self guided, Mrs. Solomon directs you through the museum, almost like a stern "schoolmarm" who knows what's best for you, but actually she's a sweetheart who has plenty of time for her guests and is willing to "talk story." Inside it's easy to become overwhelmed as you're confronted with everything from sombreros to a stuffed albatross, moose head, and South American lizard. An extensive weapons collection includes Khyber rifles, Japanese machine guns, swords, and knives. If you enjoy Hawaiiana, there's *kahili* and *konane* boards, poi pounders, stone sinkers and hooks, wooden surfboards, and a very unique "canoe buster." The museum has a few extremely rare stone idols and a good collection of furniture from the Hawaiian nobility, including Prince Kuhio's council table. Antiques of every description include Japanese and Hawaiian feathered fans, carved Chinese furniture, a brass diving helmet, some of the first Hawaiian Bibles, and even buffalo robes used by the pioneers. Everywhere are old photos commemorating the lives of the Parkers down through the years. Before you leave, go into the front room, where the view through a huge picture window perfectly frames a pond and three round-topped mountains in *paniolo* country.

PRACTICALITIES

ACCOMMODATIONS

As far as staying in Waimea is concerned, you won't be plagued with indecision. Of the two hotels in town, both are basic and clean, one inexpensive and the other upscale.

The **Kamuela Inn,** tel. 885-4243, fax 885-8857, P.O. Box 1994, Kamuela, HI 96743, a one-time basic cinder-block motel with 19 units, has been transformed into a bright and airy 31-unit boutique hotel. It is located down a small cul-de-sac off Route 19 just before Opelu Road. Office hours are 7 a.m.-8 p.m., but a key and instructions will be left for late arrivals. The new owner, Carolyn Cascavilla, takes personal pride in the hotel and offers each guest a complimentary continental breakfast. The small but pleasant grounds are appointed with flowers and manicured trees and you'll find a swing to lull you into relaxation. A new wing features the deluxe "Executive Suite" and a "Penthouse" where Governor John Waihee, among other dignitaries, has found peace and quiet. The new wing is comfortable and tasteful with hardwood floors, queen-size beds, a full kitchen, and a small anteroom that opens onto a private lanai, perfect for a quiet morning breakfast. The Penthouse is upstairs, and breaks into two joinable units that can accommodate up to five guests. The basic motel rooms are small, neat, and tidy with twin beds with wicker headboards, private bathrooms, and color TV, but no a/c (not needed) or phones. About one third of the units have kitchens. Prices range from $59 for a basic room to $185 for the deluxe suites.

The Waimea Country Lodge, tel. 885-4100, P.O. Box 2559, Kamuela, HI 96743, is located along Lindsey Rd. in "downtown" Waimea, but don't let "downtown" fool you because it's very quiet. The rooms, most with kitchenettes and vaulted ceilings, have full baths, and are well appointed with rich brown carpeting, a pine credenza and writing desk, king-size bed (twins in some rooms) with turned pine lamps at each end, wicker easy chairs, phones, and TVs. The barn-red board-and-batten inn sits off by itself and lives up to being in *paniolo* country by giving the impression of a gentleman's bunkhouse. Rates are $80 standard, $84 superior (refrigerators), $93 with a kitchenette, $100 deluxe, $10 additional person.

FOOD

Inexpensive/Moderate

Mean Cuisine, tel. 885-6325, open Mon.-Sat. 6 a.m.-8 p.m. and Sunday 8 a.m.-2 p.m., in the Opelo Plaza along Route 19 west of town center, would be just as well served if it called itself "Queen's Cuisine," because it not only serves food fit for such a noble personage, but its owner, Ann Sutherland, former executive chef at the exclusive Mauna Lani, has built a well-earned reputation as one of Hawaii's culinary royalty. Chef Sutherland prepares different specials daily, such as a breakfast spinach, mushroom, and onion croissant covered with ricotta, mozzarella, and parmesan cheeses $3.50. At

lunch try the smoked turkey chef salad $6.75, roast boneless pork loin $6.95, the Kawaihae catch, sautéed ono, with walnut pesto and local tomatoes on pasta with marinara $9.50. A bowl of homemade split pea soup with Canadian bacon or of Southwestern corn chowder is only $2.50, with bread $2.75. For those on the run, a hot table holds *kalua* pork and cabbage, Tex-Mex ravioli, and spinach crepes, all priced $6-7. Fresh-made pastries include almond bear claws $1.35, apple strudel $2.60, lilikoi cheesecake, banana cake, and Dutch apple pie. The bread-basket is filled with loaves of Parisian, honey wheat, squaw, *paniolo,* and seven grain. Lilikoi house iced tea $1 is a terrific beverage. The menu in this tiny, amazing one-woman-show is as varied as the one that wows guests at the Mauna Lani. Make sure to dine at Mean Cuisine. For the money, it serves the best food on the island.

Maha's, sharing space with Cook's Discovery in the vintage Spencer House, tel. 885-0693, open daily except Tuesday 6 a.m.-4:30 p.m., offers island style food made fresh daily. Maha—a name given her by her three sons when they were children—learned to cook for her large Hawaiian family. Maha worked professionally for many years as a pastry chef and then cooked at Knickers at the Mauna Lani Resort. From her diminutive kitchen comes breakfast of poi pancakes with coconut syrup $3.50, and an assortment of too tempting pastries including homestyle banana bread, papaya coffeecake, croissants, or pan biscuits $2.50, and always-fresh Kona coffee. Lunch can be "Waipio Ways," a plate of broiled fresh fish with sliced and steamed Waipio taro and sweet potato on a bed of Kahua greens with ginger vinaigrette dressing $9, smoked ahi with lilikoi salsa, or ahi marinated in a honey smoked sauce and baked in a flour tortilla with shredded cheese, both at $10.50, "Kahala Harvest" is a vegetarian delight mounded with vine-ripened tomatoes, Waimea broccoli, mushrooms, cucumbers, bell peppers, sweet onions, spinach, and clover sprouts $7.50; or try one of the sandwiches, like roasted lamb with chutney on squaw bread. *Aloha Ahiahi,* a version of afternoon tea served 3-4:30 p.m., brings a sampler of Maha's pastries, including croissants, Cook's Discoveries jams, open faced finger sandwiches, shortbreads, or cobblers (assortment changes) $12. This is an instance in which you can mix pleasure with pleasure, shopping at Cook's Discoveries and dining at Maha's.

Seek out **Kelei's Kama'aina Kitchen,** tel. 885-0344, in the Holomua Center near the first stoplight, open Wed.-Sat. 10 a.m.-6 p.m., and sometimes on Sunday if they haven't decided to go fishing. This is where the people of Waimea go to get home-cooked food at down-home prices (primarily takeout, but you can eat there). Plate lunches include *kalua* plate with *kalua* pig, *lomi* salmon, and Waipio salad $6.25; or the Waimea Special, which is *kalua* pig, *lau lau,* *lomi* salmon, fried fish, and poi $7. Sandwiches are fresh *ahi* burger for an unbelievable $3.50, shrimp burger $2.75, or a *kalua* pig sandwich $3.50. Salads are Chinese chicken salad $5, or Kelei's original crab sweet potato salad $1.25! *Lomi* salmon also sells for $6 per pound, and they make *poke* fresh daily, the variety depending upon the availability of local fish. But, what everyone really comes for is the *kiawe* barbecue chicken, available all day Saturday, and sold the moment it comes off the grill!

Su's Thai Kitchen, long known in Kailua-Kona for its delicious and moderately priced Thai cuisine, has opened a branch restaurant in the Parker Ranch Center, open daily 9 a.m.-9 p.m. American and island style breakfast, served until 11 a.m., can be two eggs over easy $4.95, hot oatmeal $2.95, cinnamon rolls $2, three-egg omelettes with a choice of three ingredients $5.95, and French toast with cinnamon and powdered sugar $4.95. For lunch, served 10 a.m.-3 p.m., Su's offers Japanese specials like a mini-tempura platter $6.95 and sukiyaki $6.95, along with Hunan beef $5.95 and an assortment of Thai lunch specials priced around $5.95. Dinner starts with an extra-large *pu pu* platter $10.95, chicken wings $4.95, shrimp toast $4.95, and steaming bowls of different Thai soups $6.95-9.95. Salads are Su's House Salad $4.95, or *yumyai* shrimp and chicken with bean thread noodle $9.95. Savory curries, red, yellow, or green, can be made with a with a combination of scallops, crab, fish, and shrimp $16.95, with most priced around $9.95. A specialty is Volcano fish, flash-fried and then topped with Su's homemade sweet and sour sauce $16.95. Su's, although very basic in its decor at the Parker Ranch Center location, continues to enjoy a well-deserved reputation for excellent food.

Also in the Parker Ranch Center is **Morelli's Pizza,** tel. 885-6100, open Mon.-Sat. 11 a.m.-8 p.m., and Sunday 11 a.m.-7 p.m. Besides trays of pizza, their oven yields pizza by the slice for only $1.85, garlic bread $1, garlic bread with cheese $1.50, and oven baked sandwiches like turkey, pastrami, ham, or veggie $6. The pizzas range from a small cheese pizza $5.75 to a three-topping monster tray $17.50. To round out your meal, you can also order garden and chef salads, and homemade soup. A small dining room with picnic tables is provided if you choose to eat at the pizza parlor.

For mid-range fare try **Great Wall Chopsui** at the Waimea Center along the Mamalahoa Hwy. (Route 19), tel. 885-7252, open daily except Wednesday 11 a.m.-8:30 p.m., lunch 11 a.m.-3 p.m. Its appealing selection of standard Chinese dishes includes a lunch special of one, two, or three choices for $4.95, $5.95, and $6.95, respectively. Dinner specials are an all-you-can-eat buffet at $6.95, and fresh *manapua* made daily. For entrees try a variety of beef, chicken, and pork dishes all around $5.50, or lobster with black bean sauce at $12.50, the most expensive item on the menu. Karaoke nightly.

Also in the Waimea Center is **Young's Kalbi,** a Korean restaurant open daily except Monday, 10:30 a.m.-9 p.m., that serves dishes like *kalbi* chicken, shrimp tempura, oyster-sauce chicken, and spicy pork, all priced under $7. The most expensive item is three *kalbi* beef short ribs for $7.50. Young's is very basic but clean, and the food is good.

And for those who insist on taking their nourishment from portion-controlled frozen patties served in Styrofoam boxes, you'll find **McDonald's** clearly marked by its arches along the highway at the entrance to the Waimea Center. Here, too, are **Subway** and **TCBY Yogurt.** Also look for the cafeteria-style **Kamuela Deli,** offering sirloin steak, grilled ham steak, and boneless spicy chicken, all priced around $6.50. They also do breakfast like corned beef hash or hamburger patties with eggs and hash browns, both priced at $4.50. Deli sandwiches, priced $2-3, include teri beef, shrimp burgers, and ham sandwiches. Plate lunches are also available. **Leilani Bakery,** open weekdays 5:30 a.m.-6:30 p.m., Sunday 6 a.m.-6 p.m., tantalizes with fresh-baked rolls and breads, cookies, cakes, pies, and pastries.

Paniolo Country Inn, tel. 885-4377, in the town center, open daily for breakfast 7-11 a.m., lunch 11 a.m.-5 p.m., dinner 5-8:45 p.m., specializes in full breakfasts, flame-broiled steaks, burgers, and plate lunches. Breakfast selections include omelettes with one item $3.75, and the *wikiwiki* breakfast of English muffin, banana bread or wheat toast, coffee, and small fruit juice $3.25. Lunches can be the Rodeo Special (a bun heaped with pepperoni, salami, bell peppers, mushrooms, and onions and smothered with pizza sauce and melted cheese) $5.95, or the *Paniolo* Country (a sandwich made with layers of spiced ham, turkey breast, bacon, tomato, onion, melted cheese, mayonnaise, and sprouts) $6.50. Hamburgers range from $5.75 for a regular burger to $6.95 for the deluxe with the works. Soups and salads are $4.25, the *paniolo* taco salad $6.25, and the tostada grande salad $6.95. Plate lunches are standards like teriyaki short ribs $7.25, while a dinner plate could be top sirloin $12.50. The Paniolo Country Inn even has pizza and a children's menu to keep prices down. The food is wholesome, the atmosphere American standard, and the service prompt and friendly.

Don's Pake Kitchen, about two miles east of town on Route 19, open daily 10 a.m.-9 p.m., has a good reputation for food at reasonable prices even though most of their selections are of the steam-table variety. Chef's specials are ginger beef, oyster chicken, and shrimp-sauce pork all priced under $6. Steamed rice sold by the pint is $1.20. Don's also specializes in large pans of food that can feed entire families. Next door is **The Vegetable Stop,** open Monday, Wednesday, Saturday 9 a.m.-5 p.m. Most of the best veggies and fruits, homegrown but not necessarily organic, are gone by noon.

Waimea Coffee Company, in the Parker Square Shopping Mall, is open Mon.-Fri. 7 a.m.-5 p.m., Saturday 8 a.m.-4 p.m. Order coffee both in bulk and by the cup. Lunch is served 11 a.m.-3 p.m.: sandwiches of turkey, ham, or tuna; Caesar salad; quiche; and homemade soups. The pastries come from Kona's French Bakery, one of the very best on the island.

The **Hawaiian Style Café,** in a modest pink and blue building across from Parker Square, open Mon.-Fri. 6 a.m.-1 p.m., Sunday 7 a.m.-11 p.m., closed the last Sunday and Monday of each month, offers local and American standard food at very reasonable prices. Inside the blue painted interior, short diner stools line a counter where the menu offers breakfasts of two eggs with Spam or bacon $2.95, a three-egg omelette with a side of pancakes $5, Hawaiian-style loco moco $5.25, and Belgian waffles with whipped butter, strawberries, and maple syrup $4.50. Plate lunches served with rice and potato or macaroni salad include broiled *mahimahi* $6.95, beef and tripe stew, or a steak plate $6.75. Daily specials include Friday's *luau plate* $8.95. A little short on Martha Stewart panache but long on pride, the Hawaiian Style Cafe will fill you up while being easy on your wallet.

Perhaps slightly ignominiously located across from the Opelo Plaza along Route 19 at Waimea "Express Gas," **Aloha Luigi Restaurant,** open Mon.-Sat. 11 a.m.-8 p.m. and Sunday 1-7 p.m., serves inexpensive pasta, pizza, and salads.

Fine Dining

One of the best benefits of Waimea's coming of age is the number of excellent restaurants that have recently opened. The competition among gourmet-food establishments is stiff, so each one tries to find its culinary niche.

The Edelweiss on Route 19 across from the Kamuela Inn is Waimea's established gourmet restaurant, where chef Hans-Peter Hager, formerly of the super-exclusive Mauna Kea Beach Hotel, serves gourmet food in rustic but elegant surroundings. The Edelweiss is open Tues.-Sat. for lunch 11:30 a.m.-1:30 p.m. and for dinner 5-9 p.m., tel. 885-6800. Inside, heavy posts and beams exude that "country feeling," but fine crystal and pure white tablecloths let you know you're in for some superb dining. The wine cellar is quite extensive, with selections of domestic, French, Italian, and German wines. Affordable lunches include offerings like soup, turkey sandwiches, and chicken salad in papaya for under $8.50. Dinner starts with melon with prosciutto $4.95, escargot $6.25, onion soup $4.25, and Caesar salad $4.25. Some Edelweiss specialties are sautéed veal, lamb, beef, and bacon with pfefferling $20.75; roast duck braised with a light orange sauce $18.50; half spring chicken diablo $16.50; and of course German favorites like Wiener schnitzel $16.50, and roast pork and sauerkraut $16.50. The cooking is rich and delicious; the proof a loyal clientele who return again and again.

Merriman's, tel. 885-6822, open for lunch weekdays 11:30 a.m.-1:30 p.m., dinner 5:30-9 p.m., in the Opelo Plaza along Route 19, has received a great deal of well-deserved praise from travelers and residents alike for its excellent food. The restaurant, resembling a small house from the outside, is stylish with pink and gray tablecloths, multicolored Fiestaware settings, and blue-green cushioned chairs of bent bamboo. Chef Sandra Rivera creates classical European and American haute cuisine from local ingredients like Kohala lamb, Ulupalakua Ranch beef, Waimea lettuce, Puna goat cheese, and vine-ripened tomatoes. The menu changes every few months, but perennial appetizer favorites are corn and Kahuku shrimp fritters 7.95, vine-ripened Lokelani tomatoes with Maui onions $5.95, and spinach salad with balsamic vinaigrette dressing $5.95. Lunch fare is coconut grilled chicken with peanut dipping sauce and rice $7.95; grilled eggplant with Puna goat cheese, basil, and hot sauce $5.95; and grilled shrimp on Asian linguine for $9.95. Entrees are superb: Oahu chicken ginger-grilled with Indonesian peanut sauce $17.50; seafood sausage, chicken, fish, and shellfish in a saffron sauce at $23.95; and Thai-style shrimp curry for $22.95. Vegetarians can graze on linguine with tomato capers and snow peas $15.50, or on stir-fried vegetables with spicy curry for $14.50. Some of the most delicious offerings, however, are the fresh catch at market price, prepared in various gourmet styles including wrapped in *nori* and sautéed with wasabi, or herb-marinated and grilled with mango-lime sauce, banana, mango, and coconut relish. Merriman's is a Big Island classic. Enjoy!

The **Island Bistro,** along Route 19, tel. 885-1222, open daily for lunch, dinner. and cocktails, is owned and operated by Stanley Monsef, an original founder of the highly acclaimed Merriman's, who presents through his talented chef, Michael Neff, wonderful dishes of Hawaiian regional cuisine. Pass through the covered lanai where you can choose to dine alfresco, and enter the intimate off-white and pastel appointed bistro shining with glass-topped tables and alive with the green of plants and the tinkling of a background piano. In the bar area, a rack holds bottles of vintage wines offered on the menu. Here you can order a pre-dinner cocktail or a frothy mug of draft beer from selected microbreweries. Lunch can be bistro sandwiches like herb roasted lamb $6.95, big bistro burger $5.50, a special half sandwich with small green salad $5.95, grilled fish of the day with lemon basil at market price, or grilled chicken breast $6.50. Dinner, always served with a special touch such as edible flowers or volcano-shaped rice cones, is excellent with choices like *pu pu* vegetable summer rolls $5.75, *kalua* pork ribs $6.95, grilled vegetable sauté $5.50, five onion garlic soup $3.95, Waimea field greens $6.95, and Szechwan sesame Caesar salad $7.50. Entrees are mouth-watering pork tenderloin, small plate $12.95, entrée $19.95; Thai marinated grilled chicken, small plate $10.95, entrée $17.95; fresh catch of the day at market price; nori-sautéed salmon $14.95 and $22.95; and scampi $13.95 and $21.95. The Island Bistro, with its combination of fine cuisine, tasteful decor, and the tutelage of a proven restaurateur, can't help becoming a Big Island classic.

SHOPPING

Waimea's accelerated growth can be measured by the shopping centers springing up around town. One new center across from the Parker Ranch Shopping Center has some people concerned as it will surround the Spencer House, a classical home from the ranch period. People were not thrilled when this area was denuded of its stately trees to accommodate the shopping center.

The Parker Ranch Shopping Center

This long-established mall has over 30 specialty stores selling shoes, apparel, sporting goods, toys, and food. The **Parker Ranch Store** sells boots, cowboy hats, shirts, skirts, and buckles and bows. Many handcrafted items are made on the premises. Open daily. The **Big Island Coffee Company,** open daily 8 a.m.-5 p.m., offers samples of pure Kona coffee that you can then choose to purchase off the rack. Bulk coffee comes in tiny burlap bags holding 8 oz. of whole beans, or in a gift pack for $10. Other savories include pineapple cookies, macadamia nuts, and chocolate-covered whole coffee beans that'll keep you zipping right along. Displays hold souvenirs like carved tikis, hula dancers, straw hats for men and women, T-shirts, and sweatshirts, with 90% from the Big Island, or at least from Hawaii. **Keep In Touch** offers distinctive T-shirts and resortwear; **Blue Sky** sells art and distinctive apparel; **Malia Kamuela** has racks of resortwear for women; **Ali'i Creations** shines with glassware and small gift items; and **Collectibles** has women's clothing along with art items like carved ivory and koa, and a display case holding locally made jewelry. **Setay,** a unique fine-jewelry shop, sells china, crystal, silver, and gold; and **Waimea Design Center and Art Gallery** tel. 885-6171, has Asian handicrafts and Hawaiian koa bowls and furniture.

Waimea Center

Well marked along the Mamalahoa Hwy. near McDonald's, Waimea's newest mall opens most of its stores weekdays 9 a.m.-5 p.m. and Saturday 10 a.m.-5 p.m. Among its shops you will find a **KTA Superstore** with everything from groceries to pharmaceuticals; **Zac's Photo** for developing and all photo needs, open Mon.-Fri. 9 a.m.- 6 p.m., Saturday 9 a.m.-5 p.m., Sunday 10 a.m.- 4 p.m.; **Natural Foods,** open Mon.-Sat. 9:30 a.m.- 6 p.m., Sunday 10 a.m.-4 p.m. (well stocked with natural canned and boxed items, bulk foods including grain, flour, and pasta, a good selection of organic vegetables and produce, a cold case holding drinks and cheeses, and an excellent supply of vitamins and minerals); the **Men's Shop,** whose name says it all; **Kamuela Kids** for children's clothing; **Mailboxes Etc.,** open Mon.- Fri. 9 a.m.-6 p.m., Saturday 9 a.m.-3 p.m., for all mailing and packaging needs including fax service; **Rhythm and Reading,** open Mon.-Thurs. 9 a.m.-7 p.m., Friday 9 a.m.-8 p.m., Saturday 9 a.m.-7 p.m., Sunday 9 a.m.-6 p.m., selling tapes, CDs, records, videos, and gifts; **Pueo Book Shop,** open Mon.-Sat. 10 a.m.-5 p.m., and sometimes on Sunday 10 a.m.-3 p.m., small, but well stocked with "new-age" books, bestsellers, and a good selection of Hawaiiana; the **Kamuela Hat Company,** who will cover your dome with Stetson hats, straw hats, and planter's hats for both men and women (*paniolo* oriented, this store is excellent if you're after Western wear); and **Quality Discount Shoes** for men,

women, and children.The Waimea Center also has some fast-food eateries and inexpensive restaurants.

The word *kama'aina* was invented with Patti Cook in mind. The proprietor of **Cook's Discoveries,** tel. 885-3633, open daily 10 a.m.-6 p.m., Patti has filled her shop with personally chosen items displaying her impeccable taste and knowledge about all things relating to Hawaii. Cook's Discoveries fills the classic and restored **Spencer House,** the first frame house ever built in Waimea, in 1852. The house was once surrounded by the lush green grasses of *paniolo* country but is now in the middle of the black asphalt of The Waimea Center's parking lot! Everything inside, fashioned by craftspeople from throughout the state, says Hawaii. Shelves hold lustrous koa boxes, bracelets, cribbage boards, and pen sets, all easily transportable. Look for traditional pieces, including a carved ivory pendant (fossilized walrus tusk) representing a human tongue, the "voice of authority," traditionally worn only by the highest *ali'i*, and hung from a necklace of woven black silk (subsituting for human hair); this ancient weaving process is known only to a handful of people in the entire state. Other traditional pieces are *lei o mano* (lei of sharks' teeth), a clublike war weapon yielded in battle or when absolute and immediate persuasion was necessary, *kukui* nut lei, distinctive warrior helmets with mushroomlike protuberances atop, poi bowls, and decorated gourds once used for food storage. Contemporary "made in Hawaii" articles include: handmade coconut lotion soap; plenty of jewelry; carved tiki walking sticks; and brush and mirror sets. A room in the rear can best be described as the "fashion room." Here, you'll find muumuu; *pareau* in tropical designs and colors; T-shirts emblazoned with Nenewe, the shark god; exquisite Hawaiian quilts; and also decorator jars of jams, jellies, and sauces made from lilikoi, *ohelo* berries (Pele's favorite), and Waimea's famous strawberries. A nook on the front porch houses **Alice's Lei and Garden Shop,** where you'll find Alice using her nimble fingers to make fresh flower bouquets and lei. Along with her flower arrangements, Alice uses all natural ingredients to blend lotions and potions that include, among others, a gardener's hand cream made with macadamia nut oil, aloe, and Hawaiian beeswax; mosquito bite cream made with chickweed, citronella and lemon balm; mango lip balm; and pure lavender oil, which is good for sunburn. Two front rooms in the Spencer House are filled with delicious aromas coming from the kitchen (about as big as your car's dashboard) of **Maha's,** where you can enjoy everything from smoked *ahi* to afternoon "high tea."

The Parker Square Shopping Mall

Located along Route 19, heading west from town center, this small mall has a collection of fine boutiques and shops. Here, the **Gallery of Great Things,** tel. 885-7706, open Mon.-Sat. 9:30 a.m.-5:30 p.m., Sunday 10 a.m.-4 p.m., really is loaded with great things. Inside you'll find novelty items like a carousel horse, silk dresses—pricey at $200—straw hats, koa paddles for $700, Niihau shellwork priced $100-25,000, vintage kimonos, an antique water jar from the Chiang Mai area of northern Thailand for $925, Japanese woodblock prints, and less expensive items like shell earrings for $8 and koa hair sticks for $4. The Gallery of Great Things represents about 200 local artists on a revolving basis, and the owner, Maria Brick, also travels throughout the Pacific collecting art. A recent trip yielded a rare and authentic "Palauan story board" priced at $3,500. With its museum-quality items, the Gallery of Great Things is definitely worth a browse. But remember, all items are one of a kind and "now you see them, now you don't."

Sweet Wind, tel. 885-0562, open Mon.-Fri. 9:30 a.m.-5:30 p.m., Saturday 9 a.m.-4 p.m., Sunday 11 a.m.-4 p.m., owned and operated by Wendy Gilliam, is packed with books, beads, and unique gifts. This "alternative thought and resource center" also sells incense, aromatherapy tinctures, and crystals. The beads come from the world over and a display case holds Native American rattles, drums, and silver and amber jewelry. Visiting Wendy at Sweet Wind is soothing for body and soul.

The **Silk Road Gallery,** tel. 885-7474, open Mon.-Sat. 9:30 a.m.-5:30 p.m., owned and operated by Geoffrey and Helena Orme, is resplendent with Asian antiques, specializing in ancient creations from Japan, China, and Korea. In this tasteful shop you will discover such treasures as

carved ivory netsuke, a favorite of the well-dressed samurai; ornate silk kimonos; Sung Dynasty vases; and *Satsumayaki* painted pottery from Japan. As you look around you may spot lacquer tables and bowls, ornate *tansu* (chests), straw sandals, an actual water wheel, sacred scrolls that hang in a place of honor in Japanese homes, a Chinese jade bowl with elaborate dragon handles, and an 18th-century Chinese moghul lotus bowl. Geoffrey and Helena, experts in Asian antiques, make frequent trips to Asia, where they personally hand-pick all the items in their shop—at which the artistic wonders of the ancient Silk Road are still on display.

Other stores in the center include **Bentley's,** with crockery, glassware, books, *lau hala* bags, and ceramics; and **Imagination Toys,** hung with kites, Hawaiian dolls, stuffed gorillas, parrots, and puzzles.

Don't be fooled by the name: the **Waimea General Store** sells mostly sundries with plenty of stationery, children's games, stuffed toys, and books on Hawaiiana. Gadgets include porcelain coffeepots, corn-on-the-cob holders, crochet needles and yarn, garlic crushers, hand-held food grinders, mugs, and incidental kitchenware.

The Opelo Plaza

Also along Route 19 heading west from town center is one of Waimea's newest shopping malls. **Waimea Booksellers,** tel. 885-8616, open Tues.-Fri. 11 a.m.-7 p.m., Saturday 10 a.m.-5 p.m., Sunday 10 a.m.-2 p.m., primarily a "used" bookstore owned by Fred Fortin and Anita Gerhard, also stocks new books. The shelves hold mysteries, adventure novels, women's books, gay and lesbian books, travel guides, music, westerns (the largest selection on the Big Island), many books on oceanography and sailing ships, fiction, and fantasy. Choose a tome and enjoy your read while sitting on a comfy wooden bench facing a minigarden bright with flowers. Waimea Booksellers hosts special events like author readings, publishes a newsletter with reviews of new books, will do special orders, and will also search for out-of-print books free of charge.

Here too are **Mean Cuisine** and **Merriman's,** two of Waimea's best restaurants in their categories (see "Food," above).

Food Markets and Sundries

For food shopping at the Parker Ranch Shopping Center there's **Sure Save Supermarket** and **Kamuela Meat Market,** featuring fine cuts of Parker Ranch beef. At the Waimea Center, look for the **KTA Superstore,** with everything from groceries to pharmaceuticals.

A **farmers' market** is held in Waimea every Saturday 7:30 a.m.-noon, when local farmers come to sell their produce, much of which is organic. Look for a dozen or so stalls in the parking lot of the Hawaiian Homelands Building located along Route 19 about two miles east of town center heading toward Honokaa. In one of the first stalls is Marie McDonald, a Hawaiian woman (don't let the name fool you) who is an expert at fashioning *haku lei,* a beautiful and intricate form of lei-making with multiple strands of intertwined flowers and ferns. Ms. McDonald and her daughter, who often helps at the stand, will take time to "talk story" and to inform you about medicinal herbs and some of the unique produce found at the market.

SERVICES AND INFORMATION

Health

Physicians are available at Lucy Henriques Medical Center, tel. 885-7921.

Angela Longo, Ph.D., tel. 885-7886, located in the Kamuela Office Center, is a practitioner of **acupuncture** and a Chinese herbalist. Angela, who graduated from U.C. Berkeley with a Ph.D. in biochemistry, combines principles from both East and West into a holistic approach to health and well-being. Besides attending to her demanding practice, Angela is a devoted single parent and a classical Indian dancer who performs at special functions around the island. She is one of the most amazing health practitioners in the entire state.

Chiropractic care is available from Dr. Ken Williams at the **Waimea Chiropractic Clinic,** tel. 885-7719.

Stillpoint Therapies, tel. 885-7383, in Waimea's Ironwood Bldg., in association with chiropractor J. Michael Beard, is a team made up of Wendy Rundell and John Worcester, who practice the healing arts of hypnotherapy, massage, trigger massage, and craniosacral massage.

Transpersonal psychologist Dr. Dominie Cappadona, Ph.D., tel. 885-8446, specializes in solutions for mid-life crisis and menopause, employing various techniques including dream work, conceptual therapy, shamanistic practices, and psychological analysis.

Information/Services

The **post office** is located in the Parker Ranch Shopping Center. Mailing address for Waimea is Kamuela, so as not to confuse it with the Waimeas on Oahu and Kauai.

The **Waimea visitor center** is west of town along Route 19, almost directly across from the Opelo Shopping Center. They hand out free maps and brochures of the area and provide public restrooms.

BOB RACE

NORTH KOHALA

Jungle trees with crocheted shawls of hanging vines stand in shadowed silence as tiny stores and humble homes abandoned by time melt slowly back into the muted North Kohala earth. This secluded region changes very little, and very slowly. It also has an eastward list toward the wetter side of the island, so if you're suffering from "Kona shock" and want to see flowers, palms, banana trees, and Hawaiian jungle, head for the north coast. Here the island of Hawaii lives up to its reputation of being not only big, but bold and beautiful as well.

North Kohala was the home of Kamehameha the Great. From this fiefdom he launched his conquest of all the islands. The shores and lands of North Kohala are rife with historical significance, and with beach parks where no one but a few local people ever go. Here cattle were introduced to the islands in the 1790s by Captain Vancouver, an early explorer and friend of Kamehameha. Among North Kohala's cultural treasures are **Lapakahi State Historical Park,** a must-stop offering "touchable" exhibits that allow you to become actively involved in Hawaii's tra-

ditional past; and **Puukohola Heiau,** one of the last great traditional temples built in Hawaii. Northward is **Kamehameha's birthplace**—the very spot—and within walking distance is **Mookini Heiau,** one of the oldest in Hawaii and still actively ministered by the current generation of a long line of *kahuna.*

Hawi was a sugar town whose economy turned sour when the sugar company drastically cut back its local operations. Hawi is making a comeback, along with this entire northern shore, which has seen an influx of small, boutiquelike businesses and art shops. In **Kapaau,** a statue of Kamehameha I peering over the chief's ancestral dominions fulfills an old *kahuna* prophecy. On a nearby side road stands historic **Kalahikiola Church,** established in 1855 by Rev. Elias Bond. On the same side road is the old **Bond Homestead,** the most authentic yet virtually unvisited missionary home in all of Hawaii. Financially strapped, but lovingly tended by the remaining members of the Bond family, it's on the National Historical Record. The main coastal road ends at **Pololu Valley Lookout,** where you can overlook one of the premier taro-growing valleys of old Hawaii. A walk down the steep *pali* into this valley is a walk into timelessness, with civilization disappearing like an ebbing tide.

Getting There

In Kawaihae, at the base of the North Kohala peninsula, Route 19 turns east and coastal Route 270, known as the Akoni Pule Highway, heads north along the coast. It passes through both of North Kohala's two major towns, Hawi and Kapaau, and ends at the *pali* overlooking Pololu Valley. All the historical sites, beach parks, and towns in the following sections are along this route, listed from south to north.

Route 250, the back road to Hawi, is a delightful country lane that winds through gloriously green grazing lands for almost 20 miles along the leeward side of the Kohala Mountains. It begins in the western outskirts of Waimea and ends in Hawi on the far north coast. One of the most picturesque roads on the island, it's dotted with mood-setting cactus and small "line shacks." Suddenly vistas open to your left, and far below are expansive panoramas of rolling hills tumbling to the sea. At mile marker 8 is **Von Holt Memorial Park,** a scenic overlook perfect for a high mountain picnic. Around mile marker 19, keep your eyes peeled for a herd of llamas on the left. At the coast,

NORTH KOHALA

Route 250 splits. Right takes you to Kapaau, and left to Hawi. If you're coming along the coastal Route 270 from Kapaau toward Hawi, look for the H. Naito Store, and make a left there to go back over Route 250 to Waimea; you don't have to go all the way to Hawi to catch Route 250.

Upolu Airport, tel. 889-9958, is a lonely strip at Upolu Point, the closest spot to Maui. A sign points the way at mile marker 20 along coastal Route 270. Here, you'll find only a bench and a public telephone. The strip is serviced only on request by the small propeller planes of charter and commuter airlines.

SIGHTS, BEACHES, AND TOWNS

KAWAIHAE COAST

Lapakahi State Historical Park
This 600-year-old reconstructed Hawaiian fishing village, combined with adjacent **Koai'e Cove Marine Conservation District,** is a standout hunk of coastline 12 miles north of Kawaihae. Gates are open daily except holidays 8 a.m.-4 p.m. for a self-guided tour, but the ranger's knowledgeable anecdotes make a guided tour much more educational.

The small grass shack near some *lau hala* trees at the entrance stocks annotated brochures and yellow water jugs. As you walk counterclockwise around the numbered stations, you pass canoe sheds and a fish shrine dedicated to Ku'ula, to whom the fishermen always dedicated a portion of their catch. A salt-making area demonstrates how the Hawaiians evaporated seawater by moving it into progres-

sively smaller "pans" carved in the rock. There are numerous homesites along the wood-chip trail. Particularly interesting to children are exhibits of games like *konane* (Hawaiian checkers) and *ulimika* (a form of bowling using stones) that the children are encouraged to try. Throughout the area, all trees, flowers, and shrubs are identified, and as an extra treat, migrating whales come close to shore Dec.-April. Don't leave without finding a shady spot and taking the time to look out to sea. For information write Lapakahi State Historical Park, P.O. Box 100, Kapaau, HI 96755, tel. 889-5566.

Mahukona and Kapaa Beach County Parks
Mahukona Beach County Park is a few minutes north of Lapakahi down a well-marked side road. As you approach, notice a number of abandoned buildings and warehouses; Mahukona was once an important port from which the Kohala Sugar Co. shipped its goods. Still there is a pier with a

konane *board*

J.D. BISIGNANI

hoist used by local fishermen to launch their boats. The harbor is filled with industrial debris which makes for some good underwater exploring, and snorkeling the offshore reef is rewarded with an abundance of sealife. Only 150 yards off shore (follow the anchor chain from the landing) in only 20 feet of water lie the remains of a wrecked steamboat, the only wreck in Hawaii that's accessible from shore. The wooden boat has almost completely deteriorated, but you will find a huge boiler, engine, shaft, and propeller. Swimming off the pier is also good, but all water activities are dangerous during winter months and high surf. Picnic facilities include a large pavilion and tables. There are also cold-water showers and restrooms, and electricity is available in the pavilion. Although numerous signs close to the pavilion say No Camping, both tent and trailer camping are allowed with a county permit near the parking lot.

Kapaa Beach County Park is five minutes farther north. Turn *makai* on a side road and cross a cattle grate as you head toward the sea. This park is even less visited than Mahukona. The rocky beach makes water entry difficult. It's primarily for day use and fishing, but there are showers, a restroom, and a pavilion. Camping is allowed with a county permit. Neither of these two beaches is spectacular, but they are secluded and accessible. If you're interested in a very quiet spot to contemplate a lovely panorama of Maui in the distance, this is it.

Mookini Heiau
and Kamehameha's Birthplace

At mile marker 20, turn down a one-lane road to Upolu Airport. Follow it until it reaches the dead end at the runway. Turn left here on a *very* rough dirt road to Mookini Heiau. This entire area is one of the most rugged and isolated on the Big Island, with wide, windswept fields; steep seacliffs; and pounding surf. Pull off at any likely spot along the road and keep your eyes peeled for signs of cavorting humpback whales that frequent this coast yearly Nov.-May. After bumping down the road for about two miles, look for a tall transmission tower pointing its bony metal finger skyward that marks the road to the *heiau*. Sometimes the road is closed with a locked gate and you'll have to walk five minutes uphill to gain access, but if the gate is open, you can drive in.

Only *ali'i* came to the *heiau* to purify themselves and worship, sometimes offering human sacrifices. In 1963, Mookini Heiau was the first Hawaiian site to be listed in the National Historical Sites Registry. Legend says that the very first temple at Mookini was built as early as A.D. 480. This incredible date implies that Mookini must have been built immediately upon the arrival of the first Polynesian explorers, who many scholars maintain arrived in large numbers a full two centuries later. More believable oral history relates that the still-standing foundation of the temple was built by the Tahitian high priest Paao, who came with conquering warriors from the south in the 12th century, bringing the powerful mana of the fierce war-god Kukailimoku. The oral tale relates that the stones for the temple were fitted in a single night, passed hand to hand by a human chain of 18,000 warriors for a distance of 14 miles from Pololu Valley. They created an irregular rectangle measuring 125 by 250 feet, with 30-foot-high and 15-foot-thick walls all around.

When you visit the *heiau,* pick up a brochure from a box at the entrance (often empty); if none is available, a signboard nearby gives general information. Notice that the leeward stones are covered in lichens, giving them a greenish cast and testifying to the age of the *heiau.* Notice a huge, flat stone near another embedded in the ground with the menacing atmosphere of a sacrificial altar. Nearby is a clone of the famous "Phallic Rock" on Molokai. Please be respectful as you walk around, as this temple is still in use, and stay on the designated paths that are cordoned off by woven rope. To the rear is an altar area where recent offerings are often seen; the floor of the temple is carpeted with well-placed stones and tiny green plants that give a natural mosaic effect. For at least eight and perhaps 15 centuries, members of the Mookini family have been the priests and priestesses of the temple. Today, the inherited title of *kahuna nui* rests with Leimomi Mookini Lum, a nearby resident. The entire *heiau* is surrounded by a wavelike hump, perhaps the remnant of an earlier structure, that resembles a castle moat. Be sure to visit the nearby "little grass shack," one of the best examples of this traditional Hawaiian architecture in the islands. Check how sturdy the walls are, and what excellent protection is pro-

Mookini Heiau

J.D. BISIGNANI

vided by the grass-shingled roof. Also, be aware of the integration of its stone platform and how perfectly suited the shack is to provide comfort against the elements in Hawaii. Look through the door at a timeless panorama of the sea and surf.

A minute from the *heiau* along the dirt road, an HVB Warrior points to Kamehameha's birthplace, **Kamehameha Akahi Aina Hanau.** The entrance to the area is at the back side, away from the sea. Inside the low stone wall, which always seems to radiate heat, are some large boulders believed to be the actual "birthing stones" where the high chieftess Kekuiapoiwa, wife of the warrior *ali'i* Keoua, gave birth to Kamehameha sometime around 1752. This male child, born as his father prepared a battle fleet to invade Maui, would grow to be the greatest of the Hawaiian chiefs—a brave, powerful, but lonely man, like the flat plateau upon which he drew his first breath. The temple's ritual drums and haunting chants dedicated to Ku were the infant's first lullabies. He would grow to accept Ku as his god, and together they would subjugate all of Hawaii. In this expansive North Kohala area, Kamehameha was confronted with unencumbered vistas and sweeping views of neighboring islands, unlike most Hawaiians, whose outlooks were held in check by the narrow, confining, but secure walls of steep-sided valleys. Only this man with this background could rise to become "The Lonely One," high chief of a unified kingdom.

Together, Mookini Heiau and King Kamehameha's birthplace make up the seven-acre **Kohala Historical Sites State Monument.**

HAWI

As you come into Hawi along Route 270, you'll see a line of false-front buildings leaning shoulder-to-shoulder like patient old men knowing that something *will* happen, and it has! One of the buildings is an ancient movie theater that still shows films. Introducing you to the town are Sacred Heart Church and Hawi Jodo Buddhist Mission, two lovely temples of worship and symbols of Hawaii's diversified spirituality. In the middle of town, Route 250, crossing the Kohala Mountains from Waimea, intersects the main road.

Hawi was once a bustling sugar town that boasted four movie theaters in its heyday. In the early 1970s, the Kohala Sugar Co. pulled up stakes, leaving the one-industry town high and dry. Still standing is the monumental stack of the sugarworks, a dormant reminder of what once was. The people of Hawi have always had grit, and instead of moving away they toughed it out, and have revitalized their town. Spirit, elbow grease, and paint were their chief allies. Hawi has risen from its slumber and is now making a comeback with new restaurants, and shops opening their doors. Here, too, is a handful of local shops selling food and household goods, an information center, a hotel (the only functional one in North Kohala), and some remarkable crafts shops and boutiques.

Accommodation

The 18-room **Kohala Village Inn,** 55-514 Hawi Road, Hawi, HI 96755, tel. 889-0419, was long known as Luke's Hotel. The hotel has always catered to local working people or island families visiting the area, as well as passing tourists. Located in central Hawi, it has a quiet little courtyard, nearby restaurant, and in-room TVs (extra charge). Rooms are a reasonable $47-95. Clean and adequate, the hotel has a friendly, quiet atmosphere.

Food

A glowing example of Hawi's modern restoration and revitalization is the **Bamboo Restaurant,** tel. 889-5555, open Tues.-Sat. 11 a.m.-2 p.m. for lunch, 6-9 p.m. for dinner, and Sunday for breakfast from 11:30 until mid-afternoon. Recently opened by Jim and Joan Channon in the N. Takata Store, this venerable old building was built by the Harada Family between 1911-1915, serving as a hotel that housed contract workers brought to North Kohala by buckboard and later relocated to work camps. As the sugar trade took root, merchants came to town, and the hotel began catering to this more upscale clientele. These traveling salesmen were the epitome of the stereotype, and desired evening entertainment. "Ladies of the night" took up residence in a few back rooms, and, with the proximity to the cane fields, might aptly have been known as "sugar babies." The fortunes of the Harada family took a turn for the worse, and the building was bought in 1926 by the Takata family, who converted it to a grocery and dry goods store that served the community until 1991, when they moved, building a new store just down the road. The old building fell into disrepair until Jim and Joan purchased it, opening their restaurant after 16 months of restoration. Touches were added, like the old wicker chairs that once rocked wealthy vacationers into a light slumber at Waikiki's Moana Hotel, but they left the best alone, preserving the original feel of the building. Upon entering, notice the floor, heavily trodden over the decades, every nick marking a memory. The original wavy window glass is intact and still bears the original painted signs reading,

"Fruits, Groceries, Cigars, Candy, Meats, and Coca Cola." The restaurant section, to the left, seats you in high-backed chairs with armrests, where you will feel very comfortable for an evening of dining. The tables themselves, although not technically made from bamboo, have bamboo inlaid under Plexiglas, and are bright with flowers. A mural ascends the central stairway; vintage photos hang on the walls and greenery hangs from an indoor awning. In the rear a dory hangs over rough wood tables that rest on the trunks of stout bamboo stalks; other tables are black bent-back bamboo set with floral tablecloths. Lunch can be a homemade soup of the day; or try one of the salads, like the Bamboo Salad, a Kohala tradition, with locally grown organic greens and spicy macadamia nuts and Maui onions at $3.50 and $5.50, or a Caesar classic at $3.25 and $4.95. More substantial dishes are *kalua* pork and cabbage $5.95, stir-fried noodles $5.95, calamari strips $4.25, Hawaiian tostada with vegetarian chili $5.95, or Kohala coconut chicken with lemongrass, garlic, ginger, and lime $7.95. There is also an assortment of sandwiches and burgers all priced around $6. Dinner begins with *pu pu* such as margarita prawns $6.95 and *kalua* pork quesadilla $5.25. From the ocean comes fresh catch at market price, broiled, sautéed, or baked in a sesame and nori crust, with a choice of sauce like Thai coconut or margarita sauce. From the land comes flame-broiled New York steak at market price, or local favorites like teriyaki beef at a reasonable $9.95. Breakfast, offered on Sunday along with Sunday brunch, can be platters like eggs Bamboo—poached egg on toasted English muffin with a slice of smoked ham or vegetables and topped with lilikoi hollandaise sauce, $5.95 one egg, $7.95 two; or *Mo Mona Palaoa* toast, a sweet bread dipped in special egg batter $2.95; or two eggs with smoked ham or pork $5.50. A limited lunch menu always features fresh fish.

You can also get a good, inexpensive meal at **Kohala Village Restaurant,** tel. 889-0105, in the "food wing" of the Kohala Village Inn in downtown Hawi. It's open Monday 11 a.m.-2 p.m., Wed.-Sun. 8 a.m.-2 p.m., closed Tuesday; dinner is served Mon.-Sat. 5:30-9 p.m. Monday is "Family Night" with reduced prices on special menu items. Start the day with homemade buttermilk pancakes $4.25; two eggs with bacon, ham, Spam, or Portuguese sausage, rice or home fries, coffee, tea, milk, or juice for a reasonable $5.50; a three-egg omelette from the omelette station with choice of ingredients $5.25; or the breakfast sandwich $3.95. Lunch brings you appetizers like fried wonton $3.75, California BLT sandwiches $5.50, or grilled ham and Swiss $5.50. There are also salads, like an Oriental chicken salad $6.50, and more substantial entrées like red pesto pizza, veggie pasta, or chicken stir-fry, each $6.95. The dinner menu offers chips and salsa $3.50, quesadilla $4.75, or Cajun crab cakes with chili mayonnaise $6.50, along with entrees like shrimp pasta $13.50, grilled chicken and Italian sausage over pasta $10.95, herb roasted chicken $9.50, and a chicken and ribs combo $10.95. The Kohala Village Restaurant is priced right and family-oriented.

Ohana Pizza & Beer Garden, tel. 889-5888, also in downtown Hawi, features very good pizza for $5.50-10.75 depending upon size and toppings. This clean, friendly restaurant also offers hefty sandwiches for $2.95, and pasta dinners (like homemade lasagna) served with dinner salad and homemade garlic bread for $6. Salads are $1.50, and homemade garlic bread $1. You can order wine or a chilled domestic beer for $1.75, or an import for $2.50. The staff of local people is friendly and hospitable. A great place to pick up a picnic lunch.

Sun, surf, and the trek to Hawi made you a bit droopy? Salvation is at hand at the **Kohala Coffee Mill** in downtown Hawi, open Mon.-Fri. 6:30 a.m.-4 p.m., Saturday 8 a.m.-4 p.m., and Sun 8-?, according to the sign. Inside the remodeled vintage building, order Kona coffee, espresso, cappuccino, pastry, and soft drinks. Shelves hold T-shirts, herbal teas, fruit jelly and jam, and honey.

Matthew's Place, tel. 889-5500 or 889-0630, open daily (one of the few open all day on Sunday in Hawi), operated by the Cerezo family, offers local food, seafood, and pizza. You can't go wrong at this simple, clean, good, and inexpensive restaurant.

Shopping

K. Takata is a well-stocked grocery store in Hawi, tel. 889-5261. **Kohala Health Food,** in downtown Hawi, tel. 889-0277, is open daily except Sunday 10:30 a.m.-6:30 p.m.; its shelves are filled with herbs, vitamins, minerals, and local organic produce when available. **Pumehana Flowers,** tel. 889-5541, next to Kohala Health Food, is alive with flowers and plants. Inside are small gift items and a cooler holding lei, perfect for brightening the day for that "special person," and perhaps for brightening the evening prospects for you. **Kohala Trade Center,** a basic convenience store in downtown Hawi, is open Mon.-Fri. 10 a.m.-10 p.m., Saturday 11 a.m.-10 p.m., and Sunday 12 a.m.-8 p.m.

Proof that two establishments can occupy the same place at the same time, the **Kohala Koa Gallery,** tel. 889-0055, open Monday 10 a.m.-5 p.m., Tues.-Sat. 10 a.m.-9 p.m., Sunday 10 a.m.-4 p.m., owned and operated by Michael and Robin Felig, is housed in the vintage Hawi, N. Takata Building along with the Bamboo Restaurant. Living up to its name, the gallery is lustrous with all types of koa artwork: furniture, covered photo albums, jewelry boxes, and sculptures, representing the work of over 70 island artists. The furniture is mainly by Michael Felig, who creates rocking chairs that beg to be sat in, and fine koa dining room tables, both of which carry price tags of over $2,000. Works of other well-known artists on display: lazy Susans, cribbage boards, and lovely boxes by John Glasser; creamy white hand thrown crystalline glazed ceramics with flower or fish motifs by Jon and Pam Pacini; and smaller and less expensive items like tapa-covered notebooks, replicas of sailing canoes, a smattering of aloha shirts, hand-painted silkwares from Kalalani Studio, jewelry with an ocean motif, and bright prints.

Look for a brightly painted sign on the left, as you enter Hawi, marking the entrance to **Hawaii Moon** (no relation), tel. 889-0880, open Mon.-Sat. 10 a.m.-5 p.m., Sunday 10 a.m.-4 p.m., owned and operated by Robin Fetig, co-owner of Kohala Koa Gallery, just next door. Small, but packed with arts, crafts, and clothing, the shop displays the artistic woman's touch. Racks hold sundresses, pareau, shoulder bags, aloha shirts, and shorts. Look for a shelf of chubby women dolls, their hair done in silver and red foil, that are as cute as . . . chubby little women dolls! Artists include: **Omodt,** a husband and wife team that creates very distinctive low-fired pottery pieces, primarily in black and white or blue, that includes paperweights, earrings, and clocks, all with an "island" motif; **Himani,** who does hand-tinted, original black-and-white photos of Hawaiian dancers; **Pacini,** another husband and wife ceramic artist team making vases and sculptures with Hawaiian themes; and **Steven Hatland** (how did he pass the one-name requirement?), a ceramic artist who employs a distinctive blue and blue-green glaze on everything from fruit bowls to water pitchers. Smaller souvenir items include: shell keychains, stuffed fish, leather bracelets, jewelry, and paperweights.

Hale Wood, tel. 889-5075, (800) 664-5075, in Hawi across from the launderette, open Mon.-Fri. 9 a.m.-7 p.m., Saturday 10 a.m.-6 p.m., and Sunday 11 a.m.-5 p.m., is owned and operated by husband-and-wife team Buck and Juli, woodworker and finisher, respectively. They work mostly in koa, fashioning everything from hope chests to coat racks, along with curly koa chop sticks for only $5. Besides their work, you will also find pieces by Jane Haggardt, a Kau artist who fashions palm baskets, adorning them with protea, dried flowers, and shells; Nalani, a creator of fiber baskets who uses twigs and bits of bark and fallen leaves. A small rack in the back room holds pareau, and a nearby case is filled with jewelry. Although quite small, Hale Koa is a great place to browse, and Buck and Juli are very friendly and helpful.

The last laugh won't be on you if you turn up a small alley in downtown Hawi (just near the Kohala Coffee Mill Espresso Bar) and seek out **First Laugh,** a name derived from a Navajo Indian legend (ask), tel. 889-0183, open daily 9 a.m.-5 p.m. The shop is owned and operated by Victoria Woollard, a mom herself, who sells new and used children's clothing (infants to 12 years), along with items like homemade soaps, toys, works of local artists, and children's books. The prices can't be beat.

Services and Information

The **Kohala Visitor Center** dispenses maps, information, and *aloha*. It's open daily and located just near the junction of Routes 270 and 250 in Hawi. Next door is the local **laundromat,** a semi-open-aired affair that can be used just about all the time. **Police** can be reached at 889-6225, emergency **fire** and **ambulance** at 961-6022.

The area **post office** is a new and large facility on Route 270 between Hawi and Kapaau just near the H. Naito Store.

The full-service **Kamehameha Pharmacy** is along Route 270 in downtown Kapaau.

KAPAAU

Kapaau is a sleepy community, the last town for any amenities on Route 270 before you reach the end of the line at Pololu Overlook. There's a gas station, grocery store, library, bank, and police station. Most young people have moved away seeking economic opportunity, but the old folks remain, and macadamia nuts are bringing some vitality back into the area. Here too, but on a smaller scale than in Hawi, local artists and some new folks are starting shops and businesses catering to tourists. The main attraction in town is **Kamehameha's Statue,** in front of the Kapaau Courthouse. The statue was commissioned by King Kalakaua in 1878, at which time an old *kahuna* said that the statue would feel at home only in the lands of Kamehameha's birth. Thomas Gould, an American sculptor living in Italy, was hired to do the statue, and he used John Baker, a part Hawaiian and close friend of Kalakaua, as the model. Gould was paid $10,000 to produce the remarkable and heroic sculpture, which was sent to Paris to be bronzed. It was freighted to Hawaii, but the ship carrying the original statue sank just off Port Stanley in the Falkland Islands, and the nine-ton statue was thought lost forever. With the insurance money, Gould was recommissioned and he produced another statue that arrived in Honolulu in 1883, where it still stands in front of the Judiciary Building. Within a few weeks, however, a British ship arrived in Honolulu, carrying the original statue that had somehow been salvaged and unceremoniously dumped in a Port Stanley junkyard. The English captain bought it there and sold it to King Kalakaua for $850. There was only one place where the statue could be sent: to the then-thriving town of Kapaau in the heart of Kamehameha's ancestral homelands. Every year, on the night before Kamehameha Day, the statue is freshly painted with a new coat of house paint; the bronze underneath remains as strong as the great king's will.

J.D. BISIGNANI

original Kamehameha statue

Kamehameha County Park, down a marked side road, has a full recreation area, including an Olympic pool open to the public, basketball courts, and weight rooms in the main building along with outside tennis courts with night lighting and a driving range. There are a kiddie area, restrooms, and picnic tables, all free.

Kalahikiola Church

A few minutes east of town an HVB Warrior points to a county lane leading to Kalahikiola Congregational Church. The road is delightfully lined with palm trees, pines, and macadamias like the formal driveway that it once was. Pass the weathering buildings of the Bond Estate and follow the road to the church on the hill. This church was built by Rev. Elias Bond and his wife Ellen, who arrived at Kohala in 1841 and dedicated the church in 1855. Rev. Bond and his parishioners were determined to overcome many formidable obstacles in building Kalahikiola ("Life from the Sun") Church, so that they could "sit in a dry and

decent house in Jehovah's presence." They hauled timber for miles, quarried and carried stone from distant gulches, raised lime from the sea floor, and brought sand by the jarful all the way from Kawaihae to mix their mortar. After two years of backbreaking work and $8,000, the church finally stood in God's praise, 85 feet long by 45 wide. The attached bell tower, oddly out of place, looks like a shoe box standing on end topped by four mean-looking spikes. Note that the doors don't swing, but slide—some visitors leave because they think it's locked. Inside, the church is dark and cool and, inexplicably, the same type of spikes as on the bell tower flank both sides of the altar. There is also a remarkable koa table. Pamphlets (25 cents) describe the history of the church.

The Bond Estate

The *most* remarkable and undisturbed missionary estate still extant in Hawaii (and one of two undisturbed mission districts in the world—the other is in Nepal) is the old Bond Homestead and its attendant buildings, including the now defunct but partially renovated Kohala Girl's School and the Kalahikiola Church. All three of these wonderful structures are on the National Historical Register. The community-based, nonprofit organization Ho'omau O Iole is working toward the restoration and preservation of this mission district, with the goal of eventually opening the home to public tours. Currently, only outside walking tours of the homestead grounds, the girl's school, and the church are conducted. One to one and a half-hour guided tours are offered Mon.-Sat. (Sunday on request) at 10 a.m., 11:30 a.m., 1 p.m., and 2:30 p.m. (with an additional summer tour at 4 p.m.). Reservations are requested, but those who just show up are not turned away. The tour costs $20 adult, $10 kids ages 6-13; ask about the cost of a family pass. A shortened (30- to 45-minute) guided tour is also available for $12 and $6, respectively. Self-guided tours run $8 and $4. For information, contact the Bond Historic Tours, tel. 889-0883, 10 a.m.-5 p.m.; or (888) BOND888 from the Western U.S. or Canada.

When you enter the grounds, the clock turns back 100 years. The first buildings were completed in 1841 by Rev. Isaac Bliss, who preceded Elias and Ellen Bond. The main buildings, connected in New England farm fashion and made with barn-style peg and beam construction, have steep-pitched roofs designed to keep off the "back East" snows. They worked equally well here to keep rainwater out, as they were originally covered in thatch. The original furniture and family possessions are placed as if the residents are out for the afternoon, although the family has not lived in the house since 1925, when it was occupied by Dr. Benjamin Bond. In the majority of missionary homes and museums in Hawaii, suitable period furniture had to be purchased or replicas made to fill the houses, but here it is all original! The homey dining and writing room is dominated by a large table that can take six leaves because the Bonds never knew how many there would be for dinner—four, or 60 (who might have landed by schooner in the middle of the afternoon). A full set of dishes waits undisturbed in the sideboard. A cozy little parlor has comfortable wicker rocking chairs and a settee under a photo of Elias Bond himself. The reverend built the settee and most of the furniture in the house. His furniture from New England arrived on a ship after he did, but because it was the Sabbath, the reverend refused to have it unloaded. Unfortunately, the ship caught fire and all the Bond's personal possessions were lost. In the kitchen area a refrigerator dating from the '20s looks like a bank vault. It ran on electricity from a generator on the homestead that was frequently used by local plantation owners to recharge their batteries. Off in a side room, an old wooden bathtub is as sound as the day it was built. In Rev. Bond's bedroom is a crocheted "primer" dated 1817, made by his sister Eliza who died before he came to Hawaii; he brought it as a memento and it still hangs on the wall. Upstairs are two large rooms in disrepair, which contain a treasure trove of antiques.

The small wing attached to the main house, called "The Cottage," was built when Dr. Benjamin Bond was first married. The family ate together in the main house, using the cottage as a Victorian bedroom and sitting room that now abounds with photos and antiques. The attached bathroom was once a summerhouse that was dragged to the present location by a steam tractor, then plumbed. As you look around, you'll feel that everything is here except for the people.

Keokea Beach County Park

Two miles past Kapaau toward Pololu you pass a small fruit stand and an access road heading *makai* to secluded Keokea Beach County Park. The park, on the side of the hill going down to the sea, is very picturesque and luxuriant. It is a favorite spot of North Kohala residents, especially on weekends, but it receives little use during the week. The rocky shoreline faces the open ocean, so swimming is not advised except during summer calm. There are a pavilion, restrooms, showers, and picnic tables. A county permit is required for tent and trailer camping.

Accommodation and Food

There are no established hotels in Kapaau but you can find a room at **Don's Tropical Valley Vacation Rentals,** P.O. Box 1333, Kapaau, HI 96755, tel. 889-0369. Located in the quiet residential community of Makapala at mile marker no. 27, this hostel is walking distance from Keokea Beach and the Pololu Valley overlook. The house has two private bedrooms for one or two persons and a dorm room that sleeps up to four. Rates start at $15 a night. Reservations should be made three days in advance. Web site: www.comevisit.com/tropical or e-mail: tropical@pacific-ocean.com. Guest rentals and studio apartments are also available from the following individuals and families: D. Chapon, tel. 889-6440 or 882-1510; Nani, tel. 889-5606; or the Brown family, tel. 884-5122.

Don's Family Deli, tel. 889-5822, open daily for breakfast and lunch until 6 p.m., across the street from the Kamehameha Statue in Kapaau, is a taste of New York in North Kohala. How can a visit to tropical paradise be complete without bagels and lox, lasagna, or a thick slice of quiche? Don's features Dreyer's ice cream, coffee and cappuccino, and homemade biscotti filled with nuts and that zesty anisette flavor. Don Rich, a longtime Kohala resident, will also fix you up with a tofu or mahimahi burger, and offers a wide selection of meats and breads if you prefer to make your own picnic lunch.

Shopping

For food shopping in Kapaau try **Union Market,** tel. 889-6450, along Route 270 coming into Kapaau, which sells not only general merchandise and meats, but also a hefty assortment of

Pololu Valley

J.D. BISIGNANI

grains, nuts, fruits, and locally made pastries and breads. **H. Naito Store** is a general grocery, dry goods, and fishing supplies store in Kapaau, tel. 889-6851.

David Gomes, tel. 889-5100, is a local guitar and ukulele maker. He works in koa and other woods and does inlay in shell, abalone, and wood. His beautiful instruments take 4-6 months to complete. His small shop is located about a half mile on the Kapaau side of the junction of Routes 270 and 250.

In Kapaau, across from the Kamehameha statue, is **Ackerman Gallery,** open daily 9 a.m.-5:30 p.m., tel. 889-5971, owned and operated by artist Gary Ackerman. Besides showcasing his own sensitive, island-inspired paintings, he displays local pottery, carvings, and one-of-a-kind jewelry. He also carries a smattering of artwork from throughout the Pacific. The artwork selections are tasteful, but expensive. You can also choose a reasonably priced gift item, especially from the handmade jewelry section. Make sure to check out the beautiful hand-blown glass display by a local artist named Yamazawa. The distinctive, iridescent glaze is achieved by using volcanic cinders—you can bring home a true island memento that includes a bit of Madame Pele herself. Gary has expanded and has opened another Ackerman Gallery in Kapaau. This lovely gallery, housed in a turn-of-the-century building, showcases the fine art of local island artists like Greg Pontius, Kelly Dunn, and Gary Ackerman.

Wo On Gallery, tel. 889-5002, is owned and operated by Leslie Patten, P.O. Box 1065, Kapaau, HI 96755. This gallery, dedicated to local artists, occupies the historic Wo On ("Harmony and Peace") General Store that served the Chinese community during plantation days. Next door is lovely and historically significant Tong Wo Cemetery and Temple, well worth a visit.

POLOLU VALLEY AND BEYOND

Finally you come to Pololu Valley Overlook. Off to the right is a small home belonging to Bill Sproat, a man of mixed Hawaiian ancestry and a longtime resident of Pololu. Bill, whose vim and vigor belie his 80-plus years, was a mule skinner throughout the area for 50 years. He is a treasure house of knowledge and homespun wisdom, and still speaks fluent Hawaiian. His mother was a Hawaiian who became a schoolteacher down in Pololu, and his dad was an adventurer who came to Hawaii in the 1890s. Bill's grandmother was a *kahuna* who lived in the valley and never converted to Christianity. Most of the folks feared her dark powers, but not Bill who, although a strong Christian, learned much about Hawaii and its ways from his grandmother. If Bill is in his yard, perhaps tending a mule, make sure to stop and talk with him.

It's about 12 miles from Pololu to Waipio Valley, with five U-shaped valleys in between, including Honokea and Waimanu, two of the largest. From the lookout it takes about 15 minutes to walk down to the floor of Pololu. The trail is well maintained as you pass through a heavy growth of *lau hala,* but it can be slippery when wet. At the bottom is a gate that keeps grazing animals in; make sure to close it after you! **Kohala Ditch,** a monument to labor-intensive engineering, is to the rear of these valleys. It carried precious water to the sugar plantations, and today carries adventurous kayakers for a very unusual thrill ride. Pololu and the other valleys were once inhabited and were among the richest wet taro plantations of old Hawaii. Today, abandoned and neglected, they have been taken over by introduced vegetation. The

black-sand beach fronting Pololu is lined with sand dunes, with a small sandbar offshore. The rip current here can be very dangerous, so enter the water only in summer months. The rip fortunately weakens not too far from shore; if you're caught, go with it and ride the waves back in. Many people hike into Pololu for seclusion and back-to-nature camping. Make sure to boil the stream water before drinking. Plenty of wild fruits can augment your food supply, and the shoreline fishing is excellent. The trails leading eastward to the other valleys are in disrepair and should not be attempted unless you are *totally* prepared, and better yet, accompanied by someone who knows the terrain.

BOOKLIST

ASTRONOMY

Bryan, E.H. *Stars over Hawaii.* Hilo, HI: Petroglyph Press, 1977. Charts featuring the stars filling the night sky in Hawaii.

Rhoads, Samuel. *The Sky Tonight—A Guided Tour of the Stars over Hawaii.* Honolulu: Bishop Museum, 1993. Four pages per month of star charts—one each for the horizon in every cardinal direction. Exceptional!

COOKING

Alexander, Agnes. *How to Use Hawaiian Fruit.* Hilo, HI: Petroglyph Press, 1984. A full range of recipes using delicious and different Hawaiian fruits.

Beeman, Judy, and Martin Beeman. *Joys of Hawaiian Cooking.* Hilo, HI: Petroglyph Press, 1977. A collection of favorite recipes from Big Island chefs.

Choy, Sam. *Cooking From the Heart with Sam Choy.* Honolulu, HI: Mutual Publishing, 1995. This beautiful, handbound cookbook contains many color photos by Douglas Peebles.

Fukuda, Sachi. *Pupus, An Island Tradition.* Honolulu, HI: Bess Press, 1995.

Margah, Irish, and Elvira Monroe. *Hawaii, Cooking with Aloha.* San Carlos, CA: Wide World, 1984. Island recipes including *kalua* pig, *lomi* salmon, and hints on decor.

Rizzto, Shirley. *Fish Dishes of the Pacific from the Fishwife.* Honolulu, HI: Hawaii Fishing News, 1986. Features recipes using all the fish commonly caught in Hawaiian waters (husband Jim Rizzuto is the author of *Fishing, Hawaiian Style*).

CULTURE

Hartwell, Jay. *Na Mamo: Hawaiian People Today.* Ai Pohaku Press, 1996. Profiles 12 people practicing Hawaiian traditions in the modern world.

Heyerdahl, Thor. *American Indians in the Pacific.* London: Allen and Unwin Ltd., 1952. Theoretical and anthropological accounts of the influence on Polynesia of the Indians along the Pacific coast of North and South America. Though no longer in print, this book is fascinating reading, presenting unsubstantiated yet intriguing theories.

Kirch, Patrick V. *Feathered Gods and Fishhooks: An Introduction to Hawaiian Archaeology and Prehistory.* Honolulu: University of Hawaii Press, 1985. This scholarly, lavishly illustrated, yet readable book gives new insight into the development of pre-contact Hawaiian civilization. It focuses on the sites and major settlements of old Hawaii and chronicles the main cultural developments while weaving in the social climate that contributed to change. A very worthwhile read.

FAUNA

Boom, Robert. *Hawaiian Seashells.* Honolulu: Waikiki Aquarium, 1972. Photos by Jerry Kringle. A collection of 137 seashells found in Hawaiian waters, many found nowhere else on earth. Broken into categories with accompanying text including common and scientific names, physical descriptions, and likely habitats. A must for shell collectors.

Carpenter, Blyth, and Russell Carpenter. *Fish Watching in Hawaii.* San Mateo, CA: Natural World Press, 1981. A color guide to many of the reef fish found in Hawaii and often spotted by snorkelers. If you're interested in the fish that you'll be looking at, this guide will be very helpful.

Fielding, Ann, and Ed Robinson. *An Underwater Guide to Hawaii.* Honolulu: University of Hawaii Press, 1987. If you've ever had a desire to snorkel/scuba the living reef waters of Hawaii and to be familiar with what you're seeing, get this small but fact-packed book. The amazing array of marinelife found throughout the archipelago is captured in glossy photos with accompanying informative text. Both the scientific and common names of specimens are given. This book will enrich your underwater experience and serve as an easily understood reference guide for many years.

Goodson, Gar. *The Many-Splendored Fishes of Hawaii.* Stanford, CA: Stanford University Press, 1985. This small but thorough "fish-watchers" book includes entries on some deep-sea fish.

Hobson, Edmend, and E.H. Chave. *Hawaiian Reef Animals.* Honolulu: University of Hawaii Press, 1987. Colorful photos and descriptions of the fish, invertebrates, turtles, and seals that call Hawaiian reefs their home.

Hosaka, Edward. *Shore Fishing in Hawaii.* Hilo, HI: Petroglyph Press, 1984. Known as the best book on Hawaiian fishing since 1944. This book receives the highest praise because it has borne and bred many Hawaiian fishermen.

Kay, Alison, and Olive Schoenberg-Dole. *Shells of Hawaii.* Honolulu: University of Hawaii Press, 1991. Color photos and tips on where to look for certain shells.

Mahaney, Casey. *Hawaiian Reef Fish, The Identification Book.* 1993. A spiral-bound reference work featuring many color photos and descriptions of common reef fish found in Hawaiian waters.

Nickerson, Roy. *Brother Whale, A Pacific Whalewatcher's Log.* San Francisco: Chronicle Books, 1977. Introduces the average person to the life of earth's greatest mammals. Provides historical accounts, photos, and tips on whalewatching. Well written, descriptive, and the best "first time" book on whales.

H.D. Pratt, P.L. Bruner, and D.G. Berrett. *The Birds of Hawaii and the Tropical Pacific.* Princeton, N.J. Princeton University Press, 1987. Useful field guide for novice and expert birdwatchers, covering Hawaii as well as other Pacific Island groups.

van Riper, Charles, and Sandra van Riper. *A Field Guide to the Mammals of Hawaii.* Honolulu: Oriental Publishing. A guide to the surprising number of mammals introduced into Hawaii. Full-color pages document description, uses, tendencies, and habitat. Small and thin, this book makes a worthwhile addition to any serious trekker's backpack.

FLORA

Kepler, Angela. *Exotic Tropicals of Hawaii.* Honolulu, HI: Mutual Publishing, 1989. This small-format book features many color photos of exotic tropical flowers.

Kuck, Lorraine, and Richard Togg. *Hawaiian Flowers and Flowering Trees.* Rutland, VT: Tuttle, 1960. A classic, though no longer in print, field guide to tropical and subtropical flora illustrated in watercolor. A "to the point" description of Hawaiian plants and flowers with a brief history of their places of origin and their introduction to Hawaii.

Merrill, Elmer. *Plant Life of the Pacific World.* Rutland, VT: Tuttle, 1983. The definitive book for anyone planning a botanical tour to the entire Pacific Basin. Originally published in the 1930s, it remains a tremendous work, worth tracking down through the out-of-print book services.

Miyano, Leland. *Hawaii, A Floral Paradise.* Honolulu, HI: Mutual Publising, 1995. Photographed by Douglas Peebles, this large-format book is filled with informative text and beautiful color shots of tropical flowers commonly seen in Hawaii.

Sohmer, S.H., and R. Gustafson. *Plants and Flowers of Hawaii.* Honolulu: University of Hawaii Press, 1987. Sohmer and Gustafson cover the vegetation zones of Hawaii, from mountains to coast, introducing you to the wide and varied floral biology of the islands. They give a good introduction to the history and unique evolution of Hawaiian plantlife. Beautiful color plates are accompanied by clear and concise plant descriptions, with the scientific and common Hawaiian names listed.

Teho, Fortunato. *Plants of Hawaii—How to grow them.* Hilo, HI: Petroglyph Press, 1992. A small but useful book for those who want their backyards to bloom into tropical paradises.

HEALTH

McBride, L.R. *Practical Folk Medicine of Hawaii.* Hilo, HI: Petroglyph Press, 1975. An illustrated guide to Hawaii's medicinal plants as used by the *kahuna lapa'au* (medical healers). Includes a thorough section on ailments, diagnosis, and the proper folk remedy. Illustrated by the author, a renowned botanical researcher and former ranger at Volcanoes National Park.

Wilkerson, James A., M.D., ed. *Medicine for Mountaineering and Other Wilderness.* 4th ed. Seattle: The Mountaineers, 1992. Don't let the title fool you. Although the book focuses on specific health problems that may be encountered while mountaineering, it is the best first-aid and general health guide available today. Written by doctors for the layperson to use until help arrives, it is jam-packed with easily understandable techniques and procedures. For those intending extended treks, it is a must.

HISTORY

Apple, Russell A. *Trails: From Steppingstones to Kerbstones.* Honolulu: Bishop Museum Press, 1965. This "Special Publication #53" is a special-interest archaeological survey focusing on trails, roadways, footpaths, and highways and how they were designed and maintained throughout the years. Many "royal highways" from pre-contact Hawaii are cited.

Ashdown, Inez MacPhee. *Old Lahaina.* Honolulu: Hawaiian Service Inc., 1976. A small pamphlet-type book listing most of the historical at-

tractions of Lahaina Town, past and present. Ashdown is a life-long resident of Hawaii and gathered her information firsthand by listening to and recording stories told by ethnic Hawaiians and old *kama'aina* families.

—*Ke Alaloa o Maui.* Wailuku, HI: Kama'aina Historians Inc., 1971. A compilation of the history and legends connected to sites on the island of Maui. Ashdown was at one time a "lady in waiting" for Queen Liliuokalani and has since been proclaimed Maui's "Historian Emeritus."

Cameron, Roderick. *The Golden Haze.* New York: World Publishing, 1964. An account of Capt. James Cook's voyages of discovery throughout the South Seas. Uses original diaries and journals for an "on the spot" reconstruction of this great seafaring adventure.

Daws, Gavan. *Shoal of Time, A History of the Hawaiian Islands.* Honolulu: University of Hawaii Press, 1974. A highly readable history of Hawaii dating from its "discovery" by the Western world down to its acceptance as the 50th state. Good insight into the psychological makeup of influential characters who helped form Hawaii's past.

Finney, Ben, and James D. Houston. *Surfing, A History of the Ancient Hawaiian Sport.* Los Angeles: Pomegranate, 1996. Features many early etchings and old photos of Hawaiian surfers practicing their native sport.

Free, David. *Vignettes of Old Hawaii.* Honolulu: Crossroads Press,1994. A collection of short essays on a variety of subjects.

Fuchs, Lawrence. *Hawaii Pono.* New York: Harcourt, Brace and World, 1961. A detailed, scholarly work presenting an overview of Hawaii's history, based upon psychological and sociological interpretations. Encompasses most socio-ethnological groups from native Hawaiians to modern entrepreneurs. A must for social historical background.

Handy, E.S., and Elizabeth Handy. *Native Planters in Old Hawaii.* Honolulu: Bishop Museum Press, 1972. A superbly written, easily understood scholarly work on the intimate relationship of pre-contact Hawaiians and the *aina* (land). Much more than its title implies, this book should be read by anyone seriously interested in Polynesian Hawaii.

Ii, John Papa. *Fragments of Hawaiian History*. Honolulu: Bishop Museum, 1959. Hawaii's history under Kamehameha I as told by a Hawaiian who actually experienced it.

Joesting, Edward. *Hawaii: An Uncommon History*. New York: W.W. Norton Co., 1978. A truly uncommon history told in a series of vignettes relating to the lives and personalities of the first white men in Hawaii, Hawaiian nobility, sea captains, writers, and adventurers. Brings history to life. Absolutely excellent!

Kurisu, Yasushi. *Sugar Town, Hawaiian Plantation Days Remembered*. Honolulu: Watermark Publishing,1995. Reminiscences of life gowing up on sugar plantations on the Hamakua Coast of the Big Island. Features many old photos.

Liliuokalani. *Hawaii's Story By Hawaii's Queen*. 1964. Reprint, Rutland, VT: Tuttle, 1991. A moving personal account of Hawaii's inevitable move from monarchy to U.S. Territory by its last queen, Liliuokalani. The facts can be found in other histories, but none provides the emotion or point of view expressed by Hawaii's deposed monarch. A "must-read" to get the whole picture.

McBride, Likeke. *Petroglyphs of Hawaii*. Hilo, HI: Petroglyph Press, 1996. A revised and updated guide to petroglyphs found in the Hawaiian Islands.

Nickerson, Roy. *Lahaina, Royal Capital of Hawaii*. Honolulu: Hawaiian Service, 1978. The story of Lahaina from whaling days to present, spiced with ample photographs.

INTRODUCTORY

Cohen, David, and Rick Smolan. *A Day in the Life of Hawaii*. New York: Workman, 1984. On December 2, 1983, 50 of the world's top photojournalists were invited to Hawaii to photograph the variety of daily life on the islands. The photos are excellently reproduced, and accompanied by a minimum of text.

Day, A.G., and C. Stroven. *A Hawaiian Reader*. 1959. Reprint, New York: Appleton, Century, Crofts, 1985. A poignant compilation of essays, diary entries, and fictitious writings that takes you from the death of Captain Cook through the "statehood services."

Department of Geography, University of Hawaii. *Atlas of Hawaii*. 2nd ed. Honolulu: University of Hawaii Press, 1983. Much more than an atlas filled with reference maps, this also contains commentary on the natural environment, culture, and sociology: a gazetteer: and statistical tables. Actually a mini-encyclopedia.

Michener, James A. *Hawaii*. New York: Random House, 1959. Michener's fictionalized historical novel has done more to inform *and* misinform readers about Hawaii than any other book ever written. A great tale with plenty of local color and information, but read it for pleasure, not facts.

Piercy, LaRue. *Hawaii This and That*. Honolulu, HI: Mutual Publishing, 1994. Illustrated by Scot Ebanez. A 60-page book filled with one-sentence facts and oddities about all manner of things Hawaiian. Informative, amazing, and fun to read.

LANGUAGE

Elbert, Samuel, and Mary Pukui. *Hawaiian Dictionary*. Honolulu: University of Hawaii, 1986. The best dictionary available on the Hawaiian language. The *Pocket Hawaiian Dictionary* is a less expensive, condensed version of this dictionary, and adequate for most travelers with a general interest in the language.

Elbert, Samuel. *Spoken Hawaiian*. Honolulu: University of Hawaii Press, 1970. Progressive conversational lessons.

MYTHOLOGY AND LEGENDS

Beckwith, Martha. *Hawaiian Mythology.* 1970. Reprint, Honolulu: University of Hawaii Press, 1977. Forty-five years after its original printing, this work remains the definitive text on Hawaiian mythology. Beckwith compiled this book from many sources, giving exhaustive cross-references to genealogies and legends expressed in the oral tradition. If you are going to read one book on Hawaii's folklore, this should be it.

Colum, Padraic. *Legends of Hawaii.* New Haven: Yale University Press, 1937. Selected legends of old Hawaii, reinterpreted but closely based upon the originals.

Elbert, S., comp. *Hawaiian Antiquities and Folklore.* Honolulu: Univerity of Hawaii Press, 1959. Illustrated by Jean Charlot. A selection of the main legends from Abraham Fornander's great work, *An Account of the Polynesian Race.*

Kalakaua, His Hawaiian Majesty, King David. *The Legends and Myths of Hawaii.* Edited by R.M. Daggett, with a foreword by Glen Grant. Honolulu: Mutual Publishing, 1990. Originally published in 1888, Hawaii's own King Kalakaua draws upon his scholarly and formidable knowledge of the classic oral tradition to bring alive ancient tales from pre-contact Hawaii. A powerful yet somewhat Victorian voice from Hawaii's past speaks clearly and boldly, especially about the intimate role of pre-Christian religion in the lives of the Hawaiian·people.

Melville, Leinanai. *Children of the Rainbow.* Wheaton, IL: Theosophical Publishing, 1969. A book on higher spiritual consciousness attuned to nature, which was the basic belief of pre-Christian Hawaii. The appendix contains illustrations of mystical symbols used by the *kahuna.* An enlightening book in many ways.

Thrum, Thomas. *Hawaiian Folk Tales.* 1907. Reprint, Chicago: McClurg and Co., 1950. A collection of Hawaiian tales from the oral tradition as told to the author from various sources.

Westervelt, W.D. *Hawaiian Legends of Volcanoes.* 1916. Reprint, Boston: Ellis Press, 1991. A small book concerning the volcanic legends of Hawaii and how they related to the fledgling field of volcanism at the turn of the century. The vintage photos alone are worth a look.

NATURAL SCIENCES

Abbott, Agatin, Gordon MacDonald, and Frank Peterson. *Volcanoes in the Sea.* Honolulu: University of Hawaii Press, 1983. A simplified yet comprehensive text covering the geology and volcanism of the Hawaiian Islands. Focuses upon the forces of nature (wind, rain, and surf) that shape the islands.

Carlquist, Sherwin. *Hawaii: A Natural History,* 2nd ed. National Tropical Botany, 1980. Definitive account of Hawaii's natural history.

Hazlett, Richard, and Donald Hyndman. *Roadside Geology of Hawaii.* Missoula, MT: Mountain Press Publishing, 1996. Begins with a general discusion of the geology of the Hawaiian Islands, followed by a road guide to the individual islands offering descriptions of easily seen features.

Hubbard, Douglass, and Gordon MacDonald. *Volcanoes of the National Parks of Hawaii.* 1982. Reprint, Volcanoes, HI: Hawaii Natural History Association, 1989. The volcanology of Hawaii, documenting the major lava flows and their geological effect on the state.

Kay, E. Alison, comp. *A Natural History of the Hawaiian Islands.* Honolulu: University of Hawaii Press, 1994. A selection of concise articles by experts in the fields of volcanism, oceanography, meteorology, and biology. An excellent reference source.

PERIODICALS

Aloha, The Magazine of Hawaii and the Pacific. Davick Publications, P.O. Box 49035, Escondido, CA 92046. This excellent bimonthly magazine is much more than glossy photography. Special features may focus on sports, the arts, history, flora and fauna, or just pure island adventure. *Aloha* is equally useful as a "dream book" for those who wish that they could visit Hawaii, and as a current resource for those actually going. One of the best for an overall view of Hawaii, and well worth the subscription price.

Hawaii Magazine. 1400 Kapiolani Blvd., Suite B, Honolulu, HI 96814. This magazine covers the Hawaiian Islands like a tropical breeze. Feature articles on all aspects of life in the islands, with special departments on travel, events, exhibits, and restaurant reviews. Up-to-the-minute information, and a fine read.

Naturist Society Magazine. P.O. Box 132, Oshkosh, WI 54920. This excellent magazine not only *uncovers* bathing-suit-optional beaches throughout the islands, giving tips for naturalists visiting Hawaii, but also reports on local politics, environment, and conservation measures from the health-conscious nudist point of view. A fine publication.

PICTORIALS

La Brucherie, Roger. *Hawaiian World, Hawaiian Heart.*Pine Valley, CA: Imagenes Press, 1989.

Grant, Glenn. *Hawaii The Big Island.* Honolulu: Mutual Publishing, 1988. Includes the historic, social, and nature photos of many photographers.

POLITICAL SCIENCE

Albertini, Jim, et al. *The Dark Side of Paradise, Hawaii in a Nuclear War.* Honolulu: cAtholic Action of Hawaii. Well-documented research outlining Hawaii's role and vulnerability in a nuclear world. This book presents the antinuclear and antimilitary side of the political issue in Hawaii.

Bell, Roger. *Last Among Equals: Hawaiian Statehood and American Politics.* Honolulu: University of Hawaii, 1984. Documents Hawaii's

long and rocky road to statehood, tracing political partisanship, racism, and social change.

SPORTS

Ambrose, Greg. *Surfer's Guide to Hawaii.* Honolulu: Bess Press, 1991. Island-by-island guide to surfing spots.

Rosenberg, Steve. *Diving Hawaii.* Aqua Quest, 1990. Describes diving locations on the major islands as well as the marinelife divers are likely to see. Includes many color photos.

Wallin, Doug. *Diving & Snorkeling guide to the Hawaiian Islands,* 2nd ed. Pisces Books, 1991. A guide offering brief descriptions of diving locations on the four major islands.

TRAVEL

Clark, John. *Beaches of the Big Island.* Honolulu: University of Hawaii Press, 1985. Definitive guide to beaches, including many off the beaten path. Features maps and black & white photos.

Morey, Kathy. *Hawaii Trails.* Berkeley: Wilderness Press, 1993. Morey's books are specialized, detailed trekker's guides to Hawaii's outdoors. Complete with useful maps, historical references, official procedures, and plants and animals encountered along the way. If you're focused on hiking, these are the best to take along. *Maui Trails, Kauai Trails,* and *Oahu Trails* are also available.

Riegert, Ray. *Hidden Hawaii.* Berkeley, CA: And/Or Press, 1992. Ray offers a "user friendly" guide to the islands.

Stanley, David. *South Pacific Handbook.* 6th ed. Chico, CA: Moon Publications, 1995. The model upon which all travel guides should be based. Simply the best travel book in the world for travel throughout the South Pacific.

Thorne, Chuck, and Lou Zitnik. *A Divers' Guide to Hawaii.* Kihei, HI: Hawaii's Diver's Guide,

1984. An expanded diver's and snorkeler's guide to the waters of the six main Hawaiian Islands. Complete list of maps with full descriptions, tips, and ability levels. A must for all levels of snorkelers and divers.

Thorne, Chuck. *The Diver's Guide to Maui.* Kahului, HI: Maui Dive Guide, 1984. A no-nonsense snorkeler's and diver's guide to Maui waters. Extensive maps, descriptions, and "straight from the shoulder" advice by one of Maui's best and most experienced divers. A must for all levels of divers and snorkelers.

Warner, Evie, and Al Davies. *Bed and Breakfast Goes Hawaiian.* Kapa'a, HI: Island Bed and Breakfast, 1990. A combination bed and breakfast directory and guide to sights, activities, events, and restaurants on the six major islands.

CAPSULE HAWAIIAN GLOSSARY

The list on the following pages gives you a "taste" of Hawaiian and provides a basic vocabulary of words in common usage which you are likely to hear. Becoming familiar with them is not a strict necessity, but they will definitely enhance your experience and make talking with local people more congenial. You'll soon notice that many islanders spice their speech with certain words, especially when they're speaking "pidgin," and you too can use them just as soon as you feel comfortable. You might even discover some Hawaiian words that are so perfectly expressive they'll become regular parts of your vocabulary. Many Hawaiian words have been absorbed into the English dictionary.

Also see the "Language" and "Food and Drink" sections in the Introduction for other applicable Hawaiian words and phrases. The definitions given are not exhaustive, but are generally considered the most common.

Words marked with an asterisk (*) are used commonly throughout the islands.

a'a*—rough clinker lava. A'a has become the correct geological term to describe this type of lava found anywhere in the world.

ae—yes

ahupua'a—pie-shaped land divisions running from mountain to sea that were governed by *konohiki,* local *ali'i* who owed their allegiance to a reigning chief

aikane—friend; pal; buddy

aina—land; the binding spirit to all Hawaiians. Love of the land is paramount in traditional Hawaiian beliefs.

akamai—smart; clever; wise

akua—a god, or simply "divine." You'll hear people speak of their family or personal *amakua* (ancestral spirit). Favorites are the shark or the *pueo* (Hawaiian owl).

ali'i*—a Hawaiian chief or noble

aloha*—the most common greeting in the islands; can mean both hello or goodbye, welcome or farewell. It can also mean romantic love, affection, or best wishes.

amakua—a personal or family spirit, usually an ancestral spirit

aole—no

auwe—alas; ouch! When a great chief or loved one died, it was a traditional wail of mourning.

awa, also known as *kava,* a mildly intoxicating traditional drink made from the juice of chewed awa root, spat into a bowl, and used in religious ceremonies

halakahiki—pineapple

hale*—house or building; often combined with other words to name a specific place, such as Haleakala ("House of the Sun"), or Hale Pai at Lahainaluna, meaning "printing house"

hana*—work; combined with *pau* means end of work or quitting time

hanai—literally "to feed." Part of the true aloha spirit. A *hanai* is a permanent guest, or an adopted family member, usually an old person or a child. This is an enduring cultural phenomenon in Hawaii, in which a child from one family (perhaps that of a brother or sister, and quite often one's grandchild) is raised as one's own without formal adoption.

haole*—a word that at one time meant foreigner, but which now means a white person or Caucasian. Many etymological definitions have been put forth, but none satisfies everyone. Some feel that it signified a person without a background, because the first white men could not chant their genealogies as was common to Hawaiians.

hapa*—half, as in a mixed-blooded person being referred to as *hapa haole*

hapai*—pregnant; used by all ethnic groups when a *keiki* is on the way

haupia*—a coconut custard dessert often served at a luau

heiau*—A platform made of skillfully fitted rocks, upon which temporary structures were built as temples and offerings made to the gods.

holomuu*—an ankle-length dress that is much more fitted than a muumuu, and which is often worn on formal occasions

hono—bay, as in Honolulu ("Sheltered Bay")

honu—green sea turtle; endangered

ho'oilo—traditional Hawaiian winter that began in November

hoolaulea—any happy event, but especially a family outing or picnic

hoomalimali*—sweet talk; flattery

huhu*—angry; irritated

hui*—a group; meeting; society. Often used to refer to Chinese businesspeople or family members who pool their money to get businesses started.

hukilau—traditional shoreline fish-gathering in which everyone lends a hand to *huki* (pull) the huge net. Anyone taking part shares in the *lau* (food). It is much more like a party than hard work, and if you're lucky you'll be able to take part in one.

hula*—a native Hawaiian dance in which the rhythm of the islands is captured by swaying hips and stories told by lyrically moving hands. A *halau* is a group or school of hula.

huli huli—barbecue, as in *huli huli* chicken

i'a—fish in general. *I'a maka* is raw fish.

imu*—underground oven filled with hot rocks and used for baking. The main cooking method featured at a luau, used to steam-bake pork and other succulent dishes. The tending of the *imu* was traditionally for men only.

ipo—sweetheart; lover; girl- or boyfriend

kahili—a tall pole topped with feathers, resembling a huge feather duster. It was used by an *ali'i* to announce his or her presence.

kahuna*—priest; sorcerer; doctor; skillful person. In old Hawaii *kahuna* had tremendous power, which they used for both good and evil. The *kahuna ana'ana* was a feared individual because he practiced "black magic" and could pray a person to death, while the *kahuna lapa'au* was a medical practitioner bringing aid and comfort to the people.

kai—the sea. Many businesses and hotels employ *kai* as part of their name.

kalua—means roasted underground in an *imu*. A favorite island food is *kalua* pork.

kama'aina*—a child of the land; an old-timer; a longtime island resident of any ethnic background; a resident of Hawaii or native son or daughter. Hotels and airlines often offer discounts called *"kama'aina* rates" to anyone who can prove island residency.

kanaka—man or commoner; later used to distinguish a Hawaiian from other races. Tone of voice can make it a derisive expression.

kane*—means man, but actually used to signify a relationship such as husband or boyfriend. Written on a lavatory door it means "Men's Room."

kaola*—any food that has been broiled or barbecued

kapu*—forbidden; taboo; keep out; do not touch

kapuna—a grandparent or old-timer; usually means someone who has gained wisdom. The statewide school system now invites *kapuna* to talk to the children about the old ways and methods.

kaukau*—slang word meaning food or chow; grub. Some of the best food in Hawaii comes from the *"kaukau* wagons," trucks that sell plate lunches and other morsels.

kauwa—a landless, untouchable caste once confined to living on reservations. Members of this caste were often used as human sacrifices at *heiau*. Calling someone *kauwa* is still considered a grave insult.

kava—also known as *awa,* a mildly intoxicating traditional drink made from the juice of chewed awa root, spat into a bowl, and used in religious ceremonies

keiki*—child or children; used by all ethnic groups. "Have you hugged your *keiki* today?"

kiawe—an algaroba tree from South America commonly found in Hawaii along the shore. It grows a nasty long thorn that can easily puncture a tire. Legend has it that the trees were introduced to the islands by a misguided missionary who hoped the thorns would coerce natives into wearing shoes. Actually, they are good for fuel, as fodder for hogs and cattle, and for reforestation, none of which you'll appreciate if you step on one of their thorns or flatten a tire on your rental car!

kokua—help. As in "Your *kokua* is needed to keep Hawaii free from litter."

kona wind*—a muggy subtropical wind that blows from the south and hits the leeward side of the islands. It usually brings sticky hot weather and one of the few times when air-conditioning will be appreciated.

konane—a traditional Hawaiian game, similar to checkers, played with pebbles on a large flat stone used as a board

koolau—windward side of the island

kukui—a candlenut tree whose pods are polished and then strung together to make a beautiful *lei*. Traditionally the oil-rich nuts were strung on the rib of a coconut leaf and used as a candle.

kuleana—homesite; the old homestead; small farms. Especially used to describe the small spreads on Hawaiian Homes Lands on Molokai.

Kumulipo*—ancient Hawaiian genealogical chant that records the pantheon of gods, creation, and the beginning of humankind

la—the sun. Often combined with other words to be more descriptive, such as *La*haina ("Merciless Sun") or Haleaka*la* ("House of the Sun").

lanai*—veranda or porch. You'll pay more for a hotel room if it has a lanai with an ocean view.

lani—sky or the heavens

lau hala*—traditional Hawaiian weaving of mats, hats, etc., from the prepared fronds of the pandanus (screw pine)

lei*—a traditional garland of flowers or vines. One of Hawaii's most beautiful customs. Given at any auspicious occasion, but especially when arriving or leaving Hawaii.

lele—the stone altar at a *heiau*

limu—edible seaweed of various types. Gathered from the shoreline, it makes an excellent salad. It's used to garnish many island dishes and is a favorite at luau.

lomi lomi—traditional Hawaiian massage; also, raw salmon made into a vinegared salad with chopped onion and spices

lua*—the toilet; the head; the bathroom

luakini—a human-sacrifice temple. Introduced to Hawaii in the 13th century at Wahaula Heiau on the Big Island.

luau*—a Hawaiian feast featuring poi, *imu*-baked pork, and other traditional foods. Good ones provide some of the best gastronomical delights in the world.

luna—foreman or overseer in the plantation fields. They were often mounted on horseback and were renowned for either their fairness or their cruelty. Representing the middle class , they served as a buffer between plantation workers and white plantation owners.

mahalo*—thank you. *Mahalo nui* means "big thanks" or "thank you very much."

mahele—division. The "Great Mahele" of 1848 changed Hawaii forever when the traditional common lands were broken up into privately owned plots.

mahimahi*—a favorite eating fish. Often called a dolphin, but a mahimahi is a true fish, not a cetacean.

mahu—a homosexual; often used derisively like "fag" or "queer"

maile—a fragrant vine used in traditional *lei*. It looks ordinary but smells delightful.

makaainana—a commoner; a person "belonging" to the *aina* (land), who supported the *ali'i* by fishing and farming and as a warrior

makai*—toward the sea; used by most islanders when giving directions

make—dead; deceased

malihini*—what you are if you have just arrived: a newcomer; a tenderfoot; a recent arrival

malo—the native Hawaiian loincloth. Never worn anymore except at festivals or pageants.

mana*—power from the spirit world; innate energy of all things animate or inanimate; the grace of god. Mana could be passed on from one person to another, or even stolen. Great care was taken to protect the *ali'i* from having their mana defiled. Commoners were required to lie flat on the ground and cover their faces whenever a great *ali'i* approached. *Kahuna* were often employed in the regaining or transference of mana.

manauahi—free; gratis; extra

manini—stingy; tight; a Hawaiianized word taken from the name of Don Francisco *Marin,* who was instrumental in bringing many fruits and plants to Hawaii. He was known for never sharing any of the bounty from his substantial gardens on Vineyard Street in Honolulu, therefore his name came to mean "stingy."

mauka*—toward the mountains; used by most islanders when giving directions

mauna—mountain. Often combined with other words to be more descriptive, such as Mauna Kea ("White Mountain")

mele—a song or chant in the Hawaiian oral tradition that records the history and genealogies of the *ali'i*

menehune—the legendary "little people" of Hawaii. Like leprechauns, they are said to have shunned humans and possess magical powers. Stone walls said to have been completed in one night are often attributed to them. Some historians argue that they actually existed and were the aboriginals of Hawaii, inhabiting the islands before the coming of the Polynesians.

moa—chicken; fowl

moana*—the ocean; the sea. Many businesses and hotels as well as places have *moana* as part of their name.

moe—sleep

moolelo—ancient tales kept alive by the oral tradition and recited only by day

muumuu*—a "Mother Hubbard," an ankle-length dress with a high neckline introduced by the missionaries to cover the nakedness of the Hawaiians. It has become fashionable attire for almost any occasion in Hawaii.

nani—beautiful

nui—big; great; large; as in *mahalo nui* (thank you very much)

ohana—a family; the fundamental social division; extended family. Now used to denote a social organization with grass-roots overtones, as in the "Protect Kahoolawe Ohana."

okolehau—literally "iron bottom"; a traditional booze made from ti root. *Okole* means "rear end" and *hau* means "iron," which was descriptive of the huge blubber pots in which *okolehau* was made. Also, if you drink too much it'll surely knock you on your *okole.*

ono*—delicious; delightful; the best. *Ono ono* means "extra or absolutely delicious."

opihi—a shellfish or limpet that clings to rocks and is gathered as one of the islands' favorite *pu pu.* Custom dictates that you never remove all of the *opihi* from a rock; some are always left to grow for future generations.

opu—belly; stomach

pahoehoe*—smooth, ropey lava that looks like burnt pancake batter. It is now the correct geological term used to describe this type of lava found anywhere in the world.

pakalolo—"crazy smoke"; grass; smoke; dope; marijuana

pake—a Chinese person. Can be derisive, depending on tone in which it is used. It is a bastardization of the Chinese word meaning "uncle."

pali*—a cliff; precipice. Hawaii's geology makes them quite common. The most famous are the *pali* of Oahu where a major battle was fought.

paniolo*—a Hawaiian cowboy. Derived from the Spanish *espaniola.* The first cowboys brought to Hawaii during the early 19th century were Mexicans from California.

papale—hat. Except for the feathered helmets of the *ali'i* warriors of old Hawaii, hats were generally not worn. However, once the islanders saw their practical uses and how fashionable they were, they began weaving them from various materials and quickly became experts at manufacture and design.

pa'u—long split skirt often worn by women when horseback riding. Last century, an island treat was *pa'u* riders in their beautiful dresses at Kapiolani Park in Honolulu. The tradition is carried on today at many of Hawaii's rodeos.

pau*—finished; done; completed. Often combined into *pau hana,* which means end of work or quitting time.

pilau—stink; bad smell; stench

pilikia—trouble of any kind, big or small; bad times

poi*—a glutinous paste made from the pounded corm of taro which ferments slightly and has a light sour taste. Purplish in color, it's a staple at luaus, where it is called "one-, two-, or three-finger" poi, depending upon its thickness.

pono—righteous or excellent

pua—flower

puka*—a hole of any size. *Puka* is used by all island residents, whether talking about a pinhole in a rubber boat or a tunnel through a mountain.

punalua—a traditional practice, before the missionaries arrived, of sharing mates. Western seamen took advantage of it, leading to the spread of contagious diseases and eventually to the ultimate demise of the Hawaiian people.

punee*—bed; narrow couch. Used by all ethnic groups. To recline on a *punee* on a breezy lanai is a true island treat.

pu pu*—an appetizer; a snack; hors d'oeuvres; can be anything from cheese and crackers to sushi. Oftentimes, bars or nightclubs offer them free.

pupule—crazy; nuts; out of your mind

pu'u*—hill, as in Pu'u Ulaula ("Red Hill")

tapa*—a traditional paper cloth made from beaten bark. Intricate designs were stamped in using beaters, and natural dyes added color. The tradition was lost for many years but is now making a comeback, and provides some of the most beautiful folk art in the islands.

taro*—the staple of old Hawaii. A plant with a distinctive broad leaf that produces a starchy root. It was brought by the first Polynesians and was grown on magnificently irrigated plantations. According to the oral tradition, the life-giving properties of taro hold mystical significance for Hawaiians, since it was created by the gods at about the same time as humans.

ti—a broad-leafed plant that was used for many purposes, from plates to hula skirts (never grass). Especially used to wrap religious offerings presented at the *heiau*.

tutu*—grandmother; granny; older woman. Used by all as a term of respect and endearment.

ukulele*—*uku* means "flea" and *lele* means "jumping," so literally "jumping flea"—the way the Hawaiians perceived the quick finger movements used on the banjolike Portuguese folk instrument called a *cavaquinho*. The ukulele quickly became synonymous with the islands.

wahine*—young woman; female; girl; wife. Used by all ethnic groups. When written on a lavatory door it means "Women's Room."

wai—fresh water; drinking water

wela—hot. *Wela kahao* is a "hot time" or "making whoopee."

wiki*—quickly; fast; in a hurry. Often seen as *wiki wiki* (very fast), as in "Wiki Wiki Messenger Service."

USEFUL PHRASES

Aloha ahiahi—Good evening.
Aloha au ia oe—I love you!
Aloha kakahiaka—Good morning.
Aloha nui loa—much love; fondest regards
Hauoli la hanau—Happy birthday.

Hauoli makahiki hou—Happy New Year.
Komo mai—please come in; enter; welcome
Mele kalikimaka—Merry Christmas.
Okole maluna—bottoms up; salute; cheers; kampai

ACCOMMODATIONS INDEX

Akaka Falls Inn, Gift Gallery and Cafe: 184
Ali'i Villas: 252-253
Arnott's Lodge: 107, 163
Aston Royal Sea Cliff Resort: 253
Bamboo House: 204
Becky's Bed & Breakfast: 236
Bed & Breakfast Mountain View: 229
Bonnie Goodell's Guest House: 226
Bougainvillea Bed and Breakfast: 289
Carson's Volcano Cottages: 228-229
Cas De Emdeko: 252
Chalet Kilauea: 227
Country Club Condo Hotel: 160
Dolphin Bay Hotel: 160-161
Don's Tropical Valley Vacation Rentals: 333
Dragonfly Ranch, A: 284
Four Seasons Resort: 297-298
Hale Kilauea: 227-228
Hale Maluhia Country Inn Bed and Breakfast:
  253
Hale Ohia Cottages: 226
Hapuna Beach Prince Hotel: 306
Hawaii Naniloa Resort: 159
Hilo Hawaiian Hotel: 159
Hilo Seaside Hotel: 160
Hilton Waikoloa Village: 299-301
Holmes' Sweet Home B&B: 163
Holualoa Inn Bed and Breakfast: 277-278
Hotel Honokaa Club: 107, 187
Inn at Kulaniapia: 229
Kalani Honua Oceanside Eco-Resort: 207
Kamuela Inn: 316-317
Kanaloa at Kona: 252
Keauhou Beach Hotel: 252
Kilauea Lodge: 225
Kilauea Military Camp: 225
King Kamehameha's Kona Beach Hotel: 254
Kohala Village Inn: 329
Kona Bay Hotel: 251
Kona Billfisher: 253
Kona by the Sead: 251-252

Kona Hotel: 278
Kona Islander: 252
Kona Mansion: 252
Kona Plaza: 253
Kona Seaside Hotel: 251
Kona Surf Resort: 254
Kona Tiki: 251
Kona Village Resort: 296-297
Lion's Gate: 284
Lokahi Lodge: 228
Luana Ola B&B and Cottages: 187-188
Manago Hotel: 283
Margo's Corner: 236
Mauna Kea Beach Hotel: 304-306
Mauna Lani Bay Hotel: 303-304
Merryman's Bed and Breakfast: 283
My Island: 229
Orchid at Mauna Lani, The: 301-302
Our Place Papaikou's B&B: 163
Pahoa Inn: 203
Patey's Place: 107, 251
Puako Beach Condos: 307
RBR Farms Bed and Breakfast: 283-284
Royal Kona Resort: 253-254
Royal Waikoloan Hotel: 298-299
Seamountain Resort: 235
Shipman House B&B: 161
Shirakawa Motel: 235
Shores at Waikoloa, The: 299
Teshima's Inn: 283
Tutu's Place: 225-226
Uncle Billy's Hilo Bay Hotel: 159-160
Victoria Rose: 229
Village Inn: 204
Volcano House: 42, 217, 225
Waikoloa Villas: 307
Waimea Country Lodge: 317
Waipio Hotel: 197
Waipio Wayside: 191
Whittaker's B&B: 204
Wild Ginger Inn: 161

RESTAURANT INDEX

Abundant Life Natural Foods: 172
Akaka Falls Inn, Gift Gallery and Cafe: 184
Aki's Cafe: 256
Ali Bakery: 230
Aloha Akaka Plate Lunch: 182-183
Aloha Luigi Restaurant: 319
Aloha Theater Cafe: 284-285
Arnie's: 306
Bamboo Restaurant: 329
Banana Bay Buffet: 259
Banyan Snack Shop: 167
Barry's Nut Farm: 258
Bartender's Ocean Breeze: 257
Basil's Pizzeria and Restaurant: 256-257
Batik Room: 304-305
Bay Terrace: 303
Beach Bar: 306
Beach Tree Bar and Grill: 298
Bear's Coffee Shop: 165
Betty's Kitchen: 258
Bianelli's: 262
Big Island Bagel Company: 255, 258
Big Island Steakhouse: 307
Blue Dolphin: 307-308
Broke the Mouth: 164
Brown's Beach House: 302
Buns In The Sun: 258
Burger King: Kailua-Kona 258
Cafe 100: 164
Cafe Pesto (Hilo): 168
Cafe Pesto (Kawaihae): 308
Cafe Sibu: 258-259
Canaan Deli: 285
Canoe House: 304
Captain Beans' Dinner Cruise: 266
Cascades: 300
Cassandra's Greek Taverna: 259-260
Cathy's Lunch Shop: 167
C.C. Jon's: 189
Chart House: 264-265
Chief's Pizza: 202
Chili by Max: 257
Coast Grill: 306
Crusin Coffee Kona: 258
Dairy Queen: Keaau 201; Pahoa 204
Domino's Pizza: Kailua-Kona 258

Donatoni's: 300
Don Drysdale's Club 53: 260
Don's Family Deli: 333
Don's Grill: 166-167
Don's Pake Kitchen: 319
Dotty's Coffee Shop and Restaurant: 165
Edelweiss, The: 319-320
Fiasco's: 168
Five Spice: 165
Freddie's: 164
French Bakery: 255
Gallery Restaurant and Knickers Bar: 304
Garden, The: 305
Grand Palace Chinese Restaurant: 307
Great Wall Chopsui: 318
Grill, The: 302
Guissepe's: 256
Hakone: 306
Hama Yu Japanese Restaurant: 307
Harbor House: 256
Harrington's: 171
Hau Tree Cafe: 305
Hawaiian Chili by Max: 307
Hawaiian Style Café: 319
Herb's Place: 188-189
Hilo Lunch Shop: 166
Hilo Seeds and Snacks: 167
Holuakoa Cafe: 277
Hong Kong Chop Suey: 285
Hotel Honokaa Club: 187
Hualalai Club Grille and Bar: 298
Huggo's Restaurant: 263-264
Hukilau Restaurant: 166
Huna Ohana: 205
Ichiban Deli: 166
Ishigo's General Store: 184
Island Bistro: 320
Island Grinds: 167
Jameson's-by-the-Sea: 263
Jolene's Kau Kau Corner: 188
Jolly Roger: 259
Kahauloa Coffe Company Coffee Shack: 285
Kalaiki Plate Lunch: 237
Kaminari's: 262
Kamuela Deli (Kona): 258

Kamuela Deli (Waimea): 318
Kamuela Provision Co.: 300
Kau Drive-in Restaurant: 236-237
Kawaihae Harbor Grill: 308
Kay's Lunch Center: 165-166
Keaau Cafe: 201
Keaau Chop Suey House: 201
Keauhou Beach Hotel Buffet: 265
Kelei's Kama'aina Kitchen: 318
Ken's House of Pancakes: 169
Kentucky Fried Chicken: 258
Keoki's Place: 186
Kilauea Lodge Restaurant: 229
King Yee Lau: 257
KK Tei Restaurant: 170
Kohala Village Restaurant: 329-330
Koho Okazuya: 205
Kona Amigos: 262
Kona Beach Restaurant: 265, 266
Kona Galley: 260
Kona Grill: 258
Kona Health Ways: 258
Kona Inn Restaurant: 264
Kona Mix Plate: 258
Kona Ranch House: 259
Kona Theater Cafe: 285-286
Korner Pocket Bar and Grill: 285
La Bourgogne: 262-263
Lanky's Pastries and Deli: 167
Lava Java: 257
Lehua's Bar and Restaurant: 170
Low's International Food: 164
Luquin's Place: 204

LUAU

Hale Ho'okipa—Friday Night Luau
  (Kona Village Resort): 109, 265
Island Breeze Luau: 109, 266
Kamehameha Court Luau: 109, 300
Old Hawaiian Aha'aina Luau: 109, 305-
  306
Royal Waikoloan Hotel Luau: 109, 266
Tihati's Drums of Polynesia Luau: 109,
  265

Mady's Cafe Makana: 204
Magic Sands Café: 255
Maha's: 317
Mamane Street Bakery & Café: 188

Manago Hotel Restaurant: 285
Mark Twain's Square Café: 237
Mask: 258
Matthew's Place: 330
McDonald's: Hilo 167; Kailua Kona 257-258;
  Kealakekua 285; Waimea 318
Mean Cuisine: 317
Merriman's: 320
Michelangelo's: 264
Mona's Barbecue: 257
Morelli's Pizza: 318
Mun Cheong Lau: 165
Naalehu Coffee Shop: 237
Naalehu Fruit Stand: 237
Naung Mai Thai Food: 204
New China Restaurant: 166
Nihon Culture Center: 169
19th Hole, The: 305
Nori's Saimin and Snacks: 164-165
Ocean Grill: 304
Ocean Terrace: 306
Ocean View Inn: 254
Ohana Pizza & Beer Garden: 330
Orchid Court: 302
Pahoa Chop Suey: 204
Palm Cafe: 265
Pancho and Lefty's: 260
Paniolo Country Inn: 319
Paolo's: 205
Paradise Cafe: 204
Pavilion: 305
Pescatore Ristorante: 169-170
Piece of the Apple, A: 257
Pizza Hut: Hilo 167; Kailua-Kona 258
Poquito Mas: 258
Pot Belli Deli: 255
Puhu I'a Restaurant: 298
Punaluu Bake Shop: 237
Queen's Court Restaurant: 169
Quinn's: 260
Restaurant Miwa: 167-168
Restaurant Yokohama: 259
Rocky's Pizza: 258
Roussels Waikoloa Village: 3009
Royal Jade Garden: 254-255
Royal Siam Thai Restaurant: 168
Royal Terrace: 298
Sachi's Gourmet: 166
Sam Choy's Restaurant: 260-261
Sandalwood Room: 170
Satsuki's: 166

Seamountain Golf Course Club House: 235
Shooter's: 167
Simply Natural Ice Cream Parlor, and More: 188
Stan's Restaurant: 254
Su's Thai Kitchen: Kona 255; Waimea 318
Subway Sandwiches: Hilo 167; Kailua-Kona 257; Waimea 318
Tabbada's Cafe: 237
Taco Bell: 258
Terrace, The: 305
Teshima's Restaurant: 284
Texas Drive-In and Restaurant: 188
Thai Rin: 257
Tiare, The: 298-299
Ting Hao Mandarin Kitchen: 165

Tom Bombadill's: 256
Tres Hombres Beach Grill: 308-309
Tropics Cafe Restaurant: 253
Uncle Billy's: 168-169
Under The Palms: 261
Vegetable Stop, The: 319
Verna's Drive-In: 202
Verna's Too Snack Shop: 210
Volcano Country Club Restaurant: 230
Volcano House Restaurant: 229-230
Wai'ole Lounge: 167
Waimea Coffee Company: 319
Yo Pizza: 205
Young's Kalbi: 318
Yuni's: 258

INDEX

Italicized page numbers indicate information in captions, charts, illustrations, maps, or special topics.

A

a'ama: 113
accommodations: 102-107; *see also specific place;* Accommodations Index
Ackerman Gallery: 334
acupuncture: 138
Admission Day: 101
agricultural inspection: 120
agriculture: 44-45
ahi: 111
Ahuena Heiau: 245-246
airfares 118-119
airlines: 120-124
airports: 120
air travel: 117-124
AJAs: 51-52
Akaka Falls State Park: 185
Akatsuka Tropical Orchids and Flower Gardens: 210
akepa: 19
akiapola'au: 18
Akona Kai Mall: 93
alae ke'oke'o: 18
alala: 17
alcohol: 113-114
ali'i: 48
Aloha Festivals: 101
alohawear: 97
amakihi: 18
Amaury St. Giles Modern Art Gallery: 189
Amy B.H. Greenwell Ethnobotanical Garden: 279
Anaehoomalu Bay: 294-295
animals: *see* fauna; *specific animal*
annexation: 38
anthuriums: 153
'a'o: 18
apapane: 18
area: 5-6
arts: 63-69, *66, 69;* buying 95-99
Arts Council of Hawaii: *69*
Astronaut Grove: 155
astronomy: 178-179
ATM machines: 146

ART CENTERS GALLERIES, AND MUSEUMS

Ackerman Gallery: 334
Amaury St. Giles Modern Art Gallery: 189
Blue Ginger Gallery: 286
Collectors Fine Art: 271
Hale O Kula: 277
Hawaii Artists O'Hana: 183
Holualoa Foundation for Art and Culture: 277
Holualoa Gallery: 276
Kona Art Center: 275-276
Studio 7: 276
Volcano Art Center: 217-218
White Garden Gallery: 276
Wo On Gallery: 334
Woodshop Gallery: 183

a'u: 111
automatic-teller machines: 146
avocados: 109-110

B

backpacking: *see* hiking
baggage: 119-120
bananas: 109
banks: 146
bats: 19
beaches: 8
beauty pageants: 99, 101
bed and breakfasts: 105-107; *see also specific place*
beer: 113-114
bicycling: 90-91
'Big Five': 45
Big Island Bonsai Show: 100
billfish: 20
birds: 16-18, 92
birdwatching: 73-74
black marlins: 20

Bligh, Lt. William: 26
Blue Ginger Gallery: 286
blue marlins: 20
boat travel: 124-125
Bodhi Day: 102
Boiling Pots: 151
Bond Estate: 332-333
Bon Odori: 100
bookstores: 95
breadfruit: 110
breweries: 113-114
Buddha Day: 100
Burney, James: 26
bus travel: 130-131

C
California Institute of Technology 10.4-meter
   Submillimeter Telescope: 179
camping: 70-75, 142; Hawaii Volcanoes
   National Park 224; Kona 250-251;
   Waimanu Valley 197-198; Waipio Valley
   197
candlenut trees: *137*
canoes: 63-64, 101
Cape Kumukahi: 203
Captain Cook: 283, 285-286, 288
Captain Cook Festival: 100
car rentals: 127-130
carving: 64, 97-98
caste system: 48-49
cattle: 20, 45
Caucasians: 52-54
Cayetano, Benjamin J.: 40
Chain of Craters Road: 222-223
charters, fishing: 76-77
charters, flight 119
children, traveling with: 119
Chinese: 50-51
chiropractors: 139
Christmas Fantasyland of Trees: 101-102
Christmas in the Country: 101
Christmas Tradition, A: 101-102
climate: 10-12
clothes: 141-143
cocaine: 139
cockroaches: 135
Coconut Island: 152
coconuts: 110
coffee: 44-45, 114, 279-280
Collectors Fine Art: 271
condominiums: 104-105; *see also specific*
   place

Cook, Capt. James: 23-27, 280-281
coots: 18
coral: 98, 136
coral reef: 8
costs: hotel rates 103-104; money-savers
   114-115
county parks: 71-72; *see also specific park*
crackseed: 114
crafts: *see* arts; *specific craft*
Crater Rim Drive: 218
Crater Rim Loop Trail: 224
Crater Rim Run and Marathon: 101
credit cards: 146
cruises: 124-125
Culture Center Nihon: 152
currency: 145
cyclones: 12, *12*

D
Dai Fukuji Buddhist Temple: 278
dance: 64-65
Daughters of Hawaii: 244
David Douglas Historical Monument: 185-186
Davis, Isaac: 29
death marches: 61-62
deep-sea fishing: *see* fishing
Department of Land and Natural Resources: 74
Devastation Trail: 219
disabled traveler services: 126, 134-135
diving: *see* scuba diving
dogs: 19
Dole, Sanford B.: 38
donkeys: 20
driving: 129
drugs: 139
drugstores: 138
D. Uchida Coffee Farm: 279
ducks: 18

E
Earth Heritage Gallery: 150
Earthjustice Legal Defense Fund: 10
earthquakes: 8
East Hawaii Cultural Center:
East Hawaii Cultural Council: *69*, 150
economy: 41-46
ecotours: 126, 133-134
education: 38
electricity: 145
elepaio: 18
emergencies: 144
endangered species: 16-19

environmental issues: 8-10, 44
environmental resource groups: 10
equipment: 141-143; camping 72-73, 142;
    water sports 83-84
Establishment Day: 101
ethnicity: 47
events: 99-102; see also specific event

F
farmers' markets: 94-95
fauna: 16-20; see also specific animal
featherwork: 64
feral animals: 19-20, 92
ferns: 15
festivals: 99-102; see also specific festival
fiddlehead ferns: 15
Filipino Fiesta: 100
Filipinos: 54
fishing: 75-78, 77, 101
flies: 20
flora: 13-16
folk medicine: 137-138
food: 107-115; see also specific place;
    Restaurant Index
food stores: 94-95
Fornander, Abraham: 48
freshwater fishing: see fishing
fruit stores: 94-95

G
game animals: 92
game birds: 92
game fish: 75-76, 112
Gemini Northern 8-meter Telescope: 179
geography: see land
geology: see land
geothermal energy: 8-10
gesneriad: 16
ghosts: 61
Glenwood: 210
glossary: 343-347
golf: 85, 86, 87-88, 100, 102
government: 40, 41
Great Mahele, The: 35-36
Great Waikoloa Horse Races and Rodeo:
    99
Greenpeace: 10
Green Sand Beach: 239-240
guavas: 111

H
Hakalau Forest National Wildlife Refuge: 20-21

Halemaumau Trail: 219, 224
Hale O Kula: 277
Hale Pohaku: 177
Hamakua Coast: 2, 181-198, 182
Hamakua Music Festival: 101
handicapped traveler services: 126, 134-
    135
handicrafts: see arts; specific craft
haole rot: 135
Hapai Heiau: 247
Hapuna Beach State Recreation Area: 295
Harry K. Brown Beach Park: 209
Hawaiian Audubon Society: 74
Hawaiian Bill of Rights: 35
Hawaiian crow: 17
Hawaiian dark-rumped petrel: 18
Hawaiian drosophila fly: 20
Hawaiian halk: 17-18
Hawaiian hoary bat: 19
Hawaiian Holiday Macadamia Nut Factory:
    187
Hawaiian Homeland Agency: 238
Hawaiian International Billfish Tournament:
    101
Hawaiian language: 57-58
Hawaiians: 47-50
Hawaiian thrush: 18-19
Hawaii Antenna of the Very Long Baseline
    Array: 179
Hawaii Artists O'Hana: 183
Hawaii Belt Road: 210
Hawaii County Fair: 101
Hawaii County: 40
Hawaii creeper: 19
Hawaii on Horseback: 100
Hawaii Tropical Botanical Gardens: 155-157
Hawaii Visitors Bureau: 143-144
Hawaii Volcano Observatory: 218-219
Hawaii Volcanoes National Park: 211-230,
    212, 213; camping 72; Chain of Craters
    Road 222-223; geology 213-216; hiking 73;
    Kilauea Caldera 216-222; practicalities
    224-230; Visitors Center 217-218
Hawi: 328-331
hawksbill turtles: 20
health: 135-139; see also safety
health food stores: 94-95
heiau: 61
helicopter tours: 132-133
Hiilawe Waterfall: 194
Hikiau Heiau: 280
hiking: 70-75, 197-198, 224

Hilo: 2, 147-175, *149, 156*; accommodations 159-163; beaches 157-159; entertainment 171; food 164-171; services and information 174-175; shopping 171-174; sights 148-157
Hilo Arboretum: 153
Hilo Bayfront Park: 157-158
Hilo International Airport: 120
Hilo Orchid Society Show: 100
Hilo Shopping Center: 93
Hilo Tropical Gardens and Gallery: 152-153
Hilo Tsunami Museum: *97*, 150
history: 21-40; annexation 38; exploration 24-27; migration 21-24; missionaries 31-36; revolution 37-38; statehood 39-40; sugar industry 36-37; unification 28-31; whaling 33-34; World War II
hitchhiking: 131
Hokuloa Church (Ninole): 234
Hokuloa Church (Puako): 293
holidays: 99-102; *see also specific holiday*
Holoholokai Beach Park: 295
Holualoa: 273-278
Holualoa Foundation for Art and Culture: 277
Holualoa Gallery: 276
home exchanges: 107
Honalo: 278, 283, 284
Honaunau: 284, 288
honeycreepers: 18
Honokaa 186-190
Honokohau Beach: 248-249
Honokohau Marina: 246
Honomu: 182-185
Hookena: 288-289
Hoolulu County Park: 152
horseback riding: 85-90, 192-193
hospitals: 138
hostels: 107
hotels: 102-104; *see also specific place*
hotel tax: 103
Hualalai, Mt.: 6
hula: 64-65
Hulihee Palace: *97*, 244-245
humpback whales: 20
hunting: 91-92
hurricanes: 12, *12*
hydrangea: 16

I
idols: 61
iiwi: 18
Imiola Church: 315-316

information: 143-146
insects: 135
insurance: 129
interisland travel: 122-124
International Festival of the Pacific: 101
'io: 17-18
Ironman World Triathlon Championship: 101
Isaac Hale County Beach Park: 208
Island Heritage Gallery: 150

J
James Clerk Maxwell Telescope: 178
James Kealoha Park: 158
Japanese: 51
Japanese Boys' Day: 100
jewelry: 98
John Palmer Parker Museum: 315
John Young House: 294
July 4 Parker Ranch Rodeo and Horseraces: 100

K
Kaahumanu: 30, 31, 32-33, 34
Kaeo: 28, 30-31
Kahaluu Beach Park: 250
Kahekili: 28, 29, 30
kahuna: 48
Kaiko'o Mall: 93
Kailua Bay Inn Shopping Plaza: 93
Kailua-Kona: 243-273, *244;* accommodations 250-254; beaches and parks 248-250; entertainment and activities 266-267; food 254-266; services and information 273; shopping 267-273; sights 243-248
Kailua Pier: 246
Kaimu: 206-207
Kaimu Beach Park: 209
Kainaliu: 284-285, 286-287
Kainaliu Village Mall: 93
Kalahikiola Church: 332
Kalakaua, David: 37
Kalanikupule: 30-31
Kalaniopuu: 28
Kalapana: 206-207
Kaloko Beach: 249
Kaloko-Honokohau National Historical Park: 248-249
Kalopa State Recreation Area: 187
Kamakahonu Beach: 248
Kamehameha Akahi Aina Hanau: 328
Kamehameha County Park: 332
Kamehameha, Lot: *see* Kamehameha V

KAMEHAMEHAS

Kamehameha I: 28-31, 245, 294, 328
Kamehameha II: 32-33, 246
Kamehameha III: 34-36
Kamehameha IV: 37
Kamehameha V: 37

Kamehameha Ski Meet: 100
Kamehameha's Statue: 331
Kameiamoku: 29
Kamoa Wind Farm: 238
Kamuela Museum: *97*, 316
Kapaa Beach County Park: 326-327
Kapaau: 331-334
Kapiolani: 213
kapu: 49
Kapuanoni Heiau: 247
Kau: 4, 231-240, *233*
Kau Desert: 219
Kau Desert Trail: 221-222
Kauikeaouli: *see* Kamehameha III
kaukau wagons: 115
Kaumana Caves: 155
Kauna'oa Beach: 295-296
Kau Puna Trail: 222
kauwa: 49
Kawaihae: 294
kayaking: 84-85
Keaau: 201-202
Kealakekua: 283, 285, 287-288
Keauhou-Kona Triathlon: 99
Kealakekua Bay: 243, 280-281
Kealakekua Ranch Center: 93
Keanakakoi: 219
Keauhou Bay: 247-248
Keauhou Shopping Center: 93
Keaukaha Beach: 158
Keeku Heiau: 247
Kehena: 209
Keokea Beach County Park: 333
Keopuolani: 32-33
Keoua: 29-30
Kilauea: 6-7
Kilauea Caldera: 216-222; Visitors Center 217-218; Crater Rim Drive 218-220
Kilauea Iki: 219
Kilauea Iki Trail: 224
King Kalakaua Keiki Hula Festival: 101
King Kamehameha Day: 100

King Kamehameha's Kona Beach Hotel Mall: 93
King's Highway: 295
Kipuka Puaulu: 221
Kiwalao: 29
Koai'e Cove Marine Conservation District: 326
koa trees: 14
Kohala: 4, 290-235, *291, 312, 325;* North 324-335; South 290-310; Waimea 311-323
Kohala Ditch: 335
Kohala Historical Sites State Monument: 327-328
Kohala Mountains: 6
Kolekole Beach Park: 185
koloa maoli: 18
Kona: 4, 241-289, *242, 244, 274*
Kona Art Center: 275-276
Kona Banyan Court: 93
Kona Brewing Company: 113
Kona Coast Shopping Plaza: 93
Kona Coast State Park: 249
Kona Coffee Cultural Festival: 101
Kona Historical Society Museum: *97*, 278-279
Kona Inn Shopping Village: 93
Kona International Airport: 120
Kona International Brewers' Festival: 113
Kona Sports Festival: 100
Kona Stampede: 99
kona winds: 11-12
Koreans: 54
Koyasan Daishiji Shingon: 277
Ku: 29, 30
Kua Bay: 250
Kualoa Farms: 154
Kuemanu Heiau: 247
Kuhio, Prince: 99-100
kukui: 137
Kukuihaele: 190-191
Kumulipo, The: 21-22
Kurtistown: 210

L
Lake Waiau: 6, 177
land: 5-10, *6*, 213-216
land ownership: 45-46, *46*
language: 55-58, *56*, 343-347
Lanihau Center: 93
Lapakahi State Historical Park: 326
laundromats: 144
Laupahoehoe: 185-186
Laupahoehoe Beach Park: 185

lava: 7, 206-207
Lava Tree State Monument: 202-203
Lehia Park: 159
lei: 65-66, *66*
Leleiwi Beach Park: 159
Liholiho: *see* Kamehameha II
Liholiho, Alexander: *see* Kamehameha IV
Liliuokalani Gardens: 152
Liliuokalani, Lydia: 37-38
limu: 113
litchis: 111
Little Blue Church: 247
lobelia: 15
Loihi Seamount: 234
lomi lomi: 114
Lua o milu: 195
luau: 109; *see also* Restaurant Index
luggage: 119-120
Lunalilo, William: 37
Lyman, David and Sarah: 148
Lyman Mission House and Museum: *97*, 148-150

M
Macadamia Nut Harvest Festival: 101
macadamia nuts: 44, 111, 154, 187
MacKenzie State Recreation Area: 208-209
Magic Sands Bodysurfing Contest: 250
Mahaiula Bay: 249
Mahele Book: 35-36
mahimahi: 111
Mahukona Beach County Park: 326-327
Mailekini Heiau: 294
mail services: 144
makaainana: 48-49
Makalawena Beach: 249-250
malasadas: 114
Mana Home: 313-314
mangos: 110
manini: 111
Manuka State Wayside: 240
marathons: 99, 101
marijuana: 44, 139
marine birds: 18-19
marinelife: 20
Marine Life Conservation District: 280, 281
Mark Twain Monkeypod Tree: 236
marlins: 20
Marquesans: 23
massage: 139
Massie Rape Case: 53
Masters and Servants Act of 1850: 36

Maui: 60-61
Mauna Kea: 6, 176-180
Mauna Kea Beach: 295-296
Mauna Kea Beach Hotel's Annual Invitational Golf Tournament: 102
Mauna Kea Beach Hotel's Annual Pro-Am Golf Tournament: 100
Mauna Kea Observatory Complex: 178-179
Mauna Kea Ski Meet: 99
Mauna Kea State Recreation Area: 179-180
Mauna Kea Support Services: 179
Mauna Loa: 6, 216, 224
Mauna Loa Macadamia Nut Factory: 154
Mauna Loa Road: 220-221
measurements: 145
mele: 21
Menzies, Archibald: 30
Merrie Monarch Festival: 100
Metcalfe, Simon: 29
Metcalfe, Thomas: 29
methamphetamine: 139
migration: 22-23
military presence: 43-44
Million Dollar Golden Marlin Fishing Tournament: 101
Milolii: 289
Miss Aloha Hawaii Pageant: 99
Miss Hawaii Filipina Pageant: 101
missionaries: 33, 35, 62
Mochi Pounding Festival: 99
moi: 111

MUSEUMS

museums: *97*
John Palmer Parker Museum: 315
Hilo Tsunami Museum: 150
Hulihee Palace: 244-245
Kamuela Museum: 316
Kona Historical Society Museum: 278-279
Lyman Mission House and Museum: 148-150
Onizuka Space Center: 246-247
Parker Ranch Visitor Center and Museum: 314-315
Puuopelu: 313-314
Royal Kona Coffee Mill and Museum: 279-280
Thomas A. Jaggar Museum: 219

Moikeha Hawaiian Sailing Canoe Race: 101
Mokuaikaua Church: 243-244
money: 145-146
Mookini Heiau: 327-328
mopeds: 130
moray eels: 137
mosquitoes: 35, 135
motorcycles: 130
mouflon sheep: 19-20
mountain biking: *see* bicycling
mountains: *5,* 6-7
Mountain View: 210
Mt. Hualalai: 6
music: 64-69, 101
mythology: 21-22, 60-61, 194-195

N
Naalehu: 235-238
Naalehu Rodeo: 100
Naha Stone: 151
Nahienaena: 34-35
Na Hoku Hanohano awards: 58-69
Nani Mau Gardens: 153-154
Napoopoo Beach County Park: 281
NASA Infrared Telescope Facility: 178
Natural Energy Laboratory of Hawaii
    Authority: 246
Nature Conservancy, The: 10
nature tours: 125-126
nautical charts: 74-75
Nechung Dorje Drayan Ling: 232-234
nene: 16, 17, 216
Newell's shearwater: 18
Ninole: 234-235
Ninole Cove Park: 235
North Kona Shopping Center: 93
nuclear controversy: 44

O
observatories: 178-179, 218-219
ocean tours: 78-79
Odaishasan: 182
Ohana Congregational Church: 247
ohia trees: 14-15
Olaa Track: 221
Old Kona Airport State Recreation Area: 248
Olowalu Massacre: 29
oma'o: 18-19
Onekahakaha Beach Park: 158
Onizuka, Ellison: 155, 179, 246-247
Onizuka Space Center: *97* 246-247

Onizuka Visitor Center: 179
ono: 111
oral tradition: 21
OTEC: 246

P
package tours: 118
packing: 141-143
Pahala: 232-234
Pahoa: 202-206
Painted Church: 206
Paka'alana Heiau: 195
pakalolo: see marijuana
palila: 19
Panaewa Rainforest Zoo: 154-155
panini: 15
Paniolo Ski Meet: 100
pao dolce: 114
papayas: 110
parasailing: 84
Parker, John Palmer: 314, 315
Parker Ranch: 313-314
Parker Ranch Historic Homes: *97*
Parker Ranch Round-Up Rodeo: 101
Parker Ranch Shopping Center: 93
Parker Ranch Visitor Center and Museum:
    314-315
Parker Square Shopping Mall: 93
passion fruit: 110
Pearl Harbor: 39
Pe'epe'e Falls: 151
Pele: 7, 213-214
Pele Defense Fund: 9-10

PEOPLE

people: 47-55
Caucasians 52-54
Chinese 50-51
Filipinos 54
Hawaiians 47-50
Japanese 51-52
Koreans 54-55
Samoans 55

---

petroglyphs: 222-223, 293, 295
pets: 143
pharmacies: 138
pidgin: 55-57, *56*
Pine Trees: 249

plants: *see* flora
plate lunches: 115
Pohoiki Beach: 208
Pololu Valley: 334-335
Polynesians: 48
ponds: 8
po'ouli: 19
population: 47
Portuguese: 53-54
Portuguese man-o-wars: 136
postal services: 144
precipitation: 10, *11*
prickly pear cactus: 15
Prince Kuhio Day: 100
Prince Kuhio Plaza: 93
Pro-Am Billfish Tournament: 101
pronunciation: 58
puahanui: 16
Puainako Town Center: 93
Puako: 293
Puala'a Beach Park: 209
Puerto Ricans: 54
Puna: 3-4, 199-210, *200*
Punaluu: 234-235
Punaluu Beach Park: 234-235
pu pu: 114
Pu'uhonua O Honaunau: 281-282
Pu'uhonua O Honaunau National Historical
    Park: 282-283
Puukohola Heiau: 293-294
Pu'u Loa Petroglyphs: 222-223
Puuopelu: 313-314

Q
Queen Liliuokalani Long Distance Canoe
    Race: 101

R
radio: 145
Rainbow Falls: 151
rainfall: 10, *11*
Rainforest Action Network: 10
rainforests: 16
Rawson Plaza: 93
Reciprocity Act: 36
recreation: *see* sports and recreation; *specific
    activity*
Reeds Bay Beach Park: 158
religion: 59-62
restaurants: *see the* Restaurant Index
revolution: 37-38

Richardson's Beach: 159
rodeos: 99, 100, 101
room tax: 103
Royal Kona Coffee Mill and Museum: 279-280

S
Saddle Road: 2, 176-180, *177*
safety: 73, 136-137
sailboarding: 84, 239
saimin: 115
salmon: 114
Samoans: 55
scuba diving: 79-84
seafood: 111-113
sea urchins: 136-137
Shakespeare in the Park: 171
sharks: 136
shave ice: 114
sheep: 19-20, 92
shells: 98-99
shoes: 142
shopping: 93-99; arts to buy 96-99;
    bookstores 95; food stores and
    supermarkets 94-95; shopping centers 93-
    94; specialty shops 95-96
shopping centers: 93-94
Sierra Club Hawaii Chapter: 10, 74
size: 5-6
skiing: 85, 99, 100
slack-key guitar: 67-68
snorkeling: 79-84, *82*
snuba: 82-84
South Point: 238-240
Southwest Rift: 219

SPORTS AND RECREATION

sports and recreation: 70-97
bicycling: 90-91
camping and hiking: 70-75
deep-sea and freshwater fishing: 75-78
golf: 85, *86, 87-88*
horseback riding: 85-90
hunting: 91-92
ocean tours: 78-79
skiing: 85
tennis: 85, *89*
water sports: 79-85; *see also specific
    activity*

Spencer Beach County Park: 296
Star of the Sea Catholic Church: 206
statehood: 39-40
state parks: 72; Akaka Falls 185; Kona Coast 249; Lapakahi Historical 326
state recreation areas: Hapuna Beach 295; Kalopa 187; MacKenzie 208-209; Mauna Kea 179-180; Old Kona Airport 248; Wailoa River 158
St. Benedict's Painted Church: 282
Steam Vents: 218
St. Peter's Catholic Church: 247
striped marlins: 20
Studio 7: 276
Subaru (Japan National Large Telescope): 179
Submillimeter Array: 179
sugar industry: 36-37, 45
Suisan Fish Market: 152
Sulphur Banks: 218
sunburn: 135
supermarkets: 94-95
surfing: 84, 249

T
taboos: 49
Tahitians: 23
tanning: 135
tapa cloth: 64
taxis: 131
telephone services: 145
tennis: 85, *89*
theft: 140
Thelma Parker Theater: 315
Thomas A. Jaggar Museum: 219
Thurston Lava Lube: 219-220
Thurston, Lorrin: 37
tidal waves: 7-8
time zone: 145
topographical charts: 74-75
tourism: 41-43
tours: 125-126; bicycling 91; ocean 78-79; package 118; sightseeing 131-134
trade winds: 11
transportation: 115-135; air 117-124; bus 130-131; car 127-131; getting around 127-135; getting there 115-126; taxi 131; tours 125-126, 131-134; water 124-125
travel agents: 117-118
traveler's checks: 146
Tree Molds: 220-221
trees: 14-15

triathlons: 99, 101
tropical depression: *12*
tropical storm: *12*
Tsunami Museum: *97,* 150
tsunamis: 7-8
turtles: 20

U
'ua'u: 18
uku: 111
ulua: 111
United Kingdom Infrared Telescope: 178
University of Hawaii 2.2-meter Telescope: 179
Upolu Airport: 120, 326

V
Vancouver, George: 26, 30
visas: 120
Volcano Art Center: 217-218
volcanoes: 6-7, 206-207, 211-230
Volcano House: 217
Volcano Village: 210, 220
Volcano Wilderness Marathon and Rim Runs: 99
Volcano Winery: 220
Von Holt Memorial Park: 326

W
wagon rides: 90, 193
Waha'ula Heiau: 223-224
Waiakea Kai Shopping Plaza: 93
Waiakea Pond: 152
Waialea Bay: 295
Waiau, Lake: 6, 177
Waikoloa Village: 292-293
Wailoa Center: 152
Wailoa River State Recreation Area: 158
Waimea (Kamuela): 4, 311-323, *312;* accommodations 316-317; food 317-320; services and information 323; shopping 320-323; sights 313-316
Waimea-Kohala Airport: 120, 313
Waimea Shopping Center: 93
Wainee Church: 37
Waiohinu: 236
Waipio Beach: 193-194
Waipio Valley: 191-198; activities 192-194; camping 197-198; hiking 197-198; history 194-197; practicalities 197-198
Waipio Valley Aqueduct Trail: 194
Wao Kele O Puna Rainforest: 8-9

weather: *see* climate
weaving: 64, 98
Webber, John: 26
Wesak: 100
Western Week: 100
whales: 20
whalewatching: 79
whaling: 33-34, 35
what to take: 141-143
White Garden Gallery: 276
White Sands Beach County Park: 250
Whittington Beach Park: 235
winds: 11-12
windsurfing: 84, 239

wineries: 220
W.M. Keck Observatory: 178
woodcarving: *see* carving
Woodshop Gallery: 183
Wood Valley Temple: 232-234
Wo On Gallery: 334
World Square: 93
World War II: 39-40

Y
Young, John: 29, 30, 294

Z
zoos: 154-155

ABOUT THE AUTHORS

J.D. BISIGNANI 1947-1997

Joe Bisignani was a fortunate man because he made his living doing the two things that he liked best: traveling and writing. He will be greatly missed.

A mainstay of Moon Publications since 1979, he was best known in the travel world for his wildly successful, five-volume Hawaii Handbook series, of which *Maui Handbook* won the Hawaii Visitors Bureau's Best Guidebook Award in 1991, while *Hawaii Handbook* earned Best Guidebook as well as the Grand Award for Excellence in 1988. His *Japan Handbook* won the Lowell Thomas Travel Journalism Gold Award in 1993. Together with founder Bill Dalton and other writers, "Joe Biz" profoundly influenced the company's success in the travel publishing world.

ROBERT NILSEN

Robert Nilsen was born and raised in Minnesota. His first major excursion from the Midwest was a two-year stint in South Korea with the Peace Corps. Following that eye-opening service, he stayed on in Korea independently, teaching and traveling for another two years. Setting his sights on other lands and other cultures, he made his way through Asia during 1978-80, first heading south from Seoul to Bali and then west as far as the Kyber Pass before returning home to the United States. Over the intervening years, he has had the good fortune to return five times to various countries in Asia and the Pacific. Robert has written *South Korea Handbook* for Moon Publications, revised both the *Kauai Handbook* and *Maui Handbook,* and contributed to the *Indonesia Handbook.* Since the passing of his good friend J.D. Bisignani, he has shouldered full responsibility for the revision of the Hawaii series of Moon Travel Handbooks, which also includes *Hawaii Handbook, The Big Island of Hawaii Handbook,* and the *Honolulu-Waikiki Handbook.*

ABOUT THE COVER ARTIST

Artist Roy Gonzalez Tabora, whose art is featured on the cover of this handbook, was born into a family of painters. At the age of 20, already an accomplished realist painter, he continued his education and received his degree in fine arts from the University of Hawaii. He never simply copies from a photograph or relies solely upon his imagination, choosing instead to render an artful blend using his heart and mind to produce what are considered some of the finest and most unforgettable seascapes in the world. He is currently represented by Kahn Galleries, 4569 Kukui St., Kapa'a, HI 96746, tel. (808) 822-5281, fax (808) 822-2756.

LOSE YOURSELF IN THE EXPERIENCE, NOT THE CROWD

For 25 years, Moon Travel Handbooks have been the guidebooks of choice for adventurous travelers. Our award-winning Handbook series provides focused, comprehensive coverage of distinct destinations all over the world. Each Handbook is like an entire bookcase of cultural insight and introductory information in one portable volume. Our goal at Moon is to give travelers all the background and practical information they'll need for an extraordinary travel experience.

The following pages include a complete list of Handbooks, covering North America and Hawaii, Mexico, Latin America and the Caribbean, and Asia and the Pacific.To purchase Moon Travel Handbooks, check your local bookstore or order by phone: (800) 345-5473 M-F 8 am.-5 p.m. PST or outside the U.S. phone: (530) 345-5473.

"An in-depth dunk into the land, the people and their history, arts, and politics."
—*Student Travels*

"I consider these books to be superior to Lonely Planet. When Moon produces a book it is more humorous, incisive, and off-beat."
—*Toronto Sun*

"Outdoor enthusiasts gravitate to the well-written Moon Travel Handbooks. In addition to politically correct historic and cultural features, the series focuses on flora, fauna and outdoor recreation. Maps and meticulous directions also are a trademark of Moon guides."
—*Houston Chronicle*

"Moon [Travel Handbooks] . . . bring a healthy respect to the places they investigate. Best of all, they provide a host of odd nuggets that give a place texture and prod the wary traveler from the beaten path. The finest are written with such care and insight they deserve listing as literature."
—*American Geographical Society*

"Moon Travel Handbooks offer in-depth historical essays and useful maps, enhanced by a sense of humor and a neat, compact format."
—*Swing*

"Perfect for the more adventurous, these are long on history, sightseeing and nitty-gritty information and very price-specific."
—*Columbus Dispatch*

"Moon guides manage to be comprehensive and countercultural at the same time . . . Handbooks are packed with maps, photographs, drawings, and sidebars that constitute a college-level introduction to each country's history, culture, people, and crafts."
—*National Geographic Traveler*

"Few travel guides do a better job helping travelers create their own itineraries than the Moon Travel Handbook series. The authors have a knack for homing in on the essentials."
—**Colorado Springs** *Gazette Telegraph*

MEXICO

"These books will delight the armchair traveler, aid the undecided person in selecting a destination, and guide the seasoned road warrior looking for lesser-known hideaways."

—*Mexican Meanderings* Newsletter

"From tourist traps to off-the-beaten track hideaways, these guides offer consistent, accurate details without pretension."

—*Foreign Service Journal*

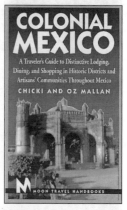

Archaeological Mexico	$19.95
Andrew Coe	450 pages, 25 maps
Baja Handbook	$15.95
Joe Cummings	380 pages, 44 maps
Cabo Handbook	$14.95
Joe Cummings	265 pages, 18 maps
Cancun Handbook	$13.95
Chicki Mallan	270 pages, 25 maps
Colonial Mexico	$16.95
Chicki Mallan	300 pages, 38 maps
Mexico Handbook	$21.95
Joe Cummings and Chicki Mallan	1,200 pages, 232 maps
Northern Mexico Handbook	$16.95
Joe Cummings	590 pages, 68 maps
Pacific Mexico Handbook	$17.95
Bruce Whipperman	580 pages, 69 maps
Puerto Vallarta Handbook	$14.95
Bruce Whipperman	330 pages, 36 maps
Yucatan Handbook	$15.95
Chicki Mallan	470 pages, 62 maps

LATIN AMERICA AND THE CARIBBEAN

"Solidly packed with practical information and full of significant cultural asides that will enlighten you on the whys and wherefores of things you might easily see but not easily grasp."

—*Boston Globe*

Belize Handbook	$15.95
Chicki Mallan	390 pages, 45 maps
Caribbean Handbook	$16.95
Karl Luntta	400 pages, 56 maps
Costa Rica Handbook	$19.95
Christopher P. Baker	780 pages, 74 maps
Cuba Handbook	$19.95
Christopher P. Baker	740 pages, 70 maps
Dominican Republic Handbook	$15.95
Gaylord Dold	420 pages, 24 maps
Ecuador Handbook	$16.95
Julian Smith	450 pages, 43 maps
Honduras Handbook	$15.95
Chris Humphrey	330 pages, 40 maps
Jamaica Handbook	$15.95
Karl Luntta	330 pages, 17 maps
Virgin Islands Handbook	$13.95
Karl Luntta	220 pages, 19 maps

NORTH AMERICA AND HAWAII

"These domestic guides convey the same sense of exoticism that their foreign counterparts do, making home-country travel seem like far-flung adventure."

—*Sierra Magazine*

Alaska-Yukon Handbook	$17.95
Deke Castleman and Don Pitcher	530 pages, 92 maps
Alberta and the Northwest Territories Handbook	$17.95
Andrew Hempstead and Nadina Purdon	530 pages, 72 maps,
Arizona Traveler's Handbook	$17.95
Bill Weir and Robert Blake	512 pages,54 maps
Atlantic Canada Handbook	$17.95
Nan Drosdick and Mark Morris	460 pages, 61 maps
Big Island of Hawaii Handbook	$15.95
J.D. Bisignani	370 pages, 23 maps
British Columbia Handbook	$16.95
Jane King and Andrew Hempstead	430 pages, 69 maps

Colorado Handbook	**$18.95**
Stephen Metzger	480 pages, 59 maps
Georgia Handbook	**$17.95**
Kap Stann	370 pages, 50 maps
Hawaii Handbook	**$19.95**
J.D. Bisignani	1,030 pages, 90 maps
Honolulu-Waikiki Handbook	**$14.95**
J.D. Bisignani	380 pages, 20 maps
Idaho Handbook	**$18.95**
Don Root	610 pages, 42 maps
Kauai Handbook	**$15.95**
J.D. Bisignani	320 pages, 23 maps
Maine Handbook	**$18.95**
Kathleen M. Brandes	660 pages, 27 maps
Massachusetts Handbook	**$18.95**
Jeff Perk	600 pages, 23 maps
Maui Handbook	**$14.95**
J.D. Bisignani	410 pages, 35 maps
Montana Handbook	**$17.95**
Judy Jewell and W.C. McRae	480 pages, 52 maps
Nevada Handbook	**$18.95**
Deke Castleman	530 pages, 40 maps
New Hampshire Handbook	**$18.95**
Steve Lantos	500 pages, 18 maps
New Mexico Handbook	**$15.95**
Stephen Metzger	360 pages, 47 maps
New York City Handbook	**$13.95**
Christiane Bird	300 pages, 20 maps
New York Handbook	**$19.95**
Christiane Bird	780 pages, 95 maps
Northern California Handbook	**$19.95**
Kim Weir	800 pages, 50 maps
Oregon Handbook	**$17.95**
Stuart Warren and Ted Long Ishikawa	588 pages, 34 maps
Pennsylvania Handbook	**$18.95**
Joanne Miller	448 pages, 40 maps
Road Trip USA	**$22.50**
Jamie Jensen	800 pages, 165 maps
Southern California Handbook	**$19.95**
Kim Weir	750 pages, 30 maps
Tennessee Handbook	**$17.95**
Jeff Bradley	530 pages, 44 maps
Texas Handbook	**$18.95**
Joe Cummings	692 pages, 70 maps
Utah Handbook	**$17.95**
Bill Weir and W.C. McRae	490 pages, 40 maps

Washington Handbook	$19.95
Don Pitcher	870 pages, 113 maps
Wisconsin Handbook	$18.95
Thomas Huhti	590 pages, 69 maps
Wyoming Handbook	$17.95
Don Pitcher	610 pages, 80 maps

ASIA AND THE PACIFIC

"Scores of maps, detailed practical info down to business hours of small-town libraries. You can't beat the Asian titles for sheer heft. (The) series is sort of an American Lonely Planet, with better writing but fewer titles. (The) individual voice of researchers comes through."

—Travel & Leisure

Australia Handbook	$21.95
Marael Johnson, Andrew Hempstead, and Nadina Purdon	940 pages, 141 maps
Bali Handbook	$19.95
Bill Dalton	750 pages, 54 maps
Bangkok Handbook	$13.95
Michael Buckley	244 pages, 30 maps
Fiji Islands Handbook	$13.95
David Stanley	280 pages, 38 maps
Hong Kong Handbook	$16.95
Kerry Moran	378 pages, 49 maps
Indonesia Handbook	$25.00
Bill Dalton	1,380 pages, 249 maps
Japan Handbook	$22.50
J.D. Bisignani	970 pages, 213 maps
Micronesia Handbook	$14.95
Neil M. Levy	340 pages, 70 maps
Nepal Handbook	$18.95
Kerry Moran	490 pages, 51 maps
New Zealand Handbook	$19.95
Jane King	620 pages, 81 maps
Outback Australia Handbook	$18.95
Marael Johnson	450 pages, 57 maps
Philippines Handbook	$17.95
Peter Harper and Laurie Fullerton	670 pages, 116 maps
Singapore Handbook	$15.95
Carl Parkes	350 pages, 29 maps
Southeast Asia Handbook	$21.95
Carl Parkes	1,000 pages, 196 maps

South Korea Handbook	**$19.95**
Robert Nilsen	820 pages, 141 maps
South Pacific Handbook	**$22.95**
David Stanley	920 pages, 147 maps
Tahiti-Polynesia Handbook	**$13.95**
David Stanley	270 pages, 35 maps
Thailand Handbook	**$19.95**
Carl Parkes	860 pages, 142 maps
Vietnam, Cambodia & Laos Handbook	**$18.95**
Michael Buckley	720 pages, 112 maps

OTHER GREAT TITLES FROM MOON

"For hardy wanderers, few guides come more highly
recommended than the Handbooks. They include
good maps, steer clear of fluff and flackery, and offer
plenty of money-saving tips. They also give you the
kind of information that visitors to strange lands—on
any budget—need to survive."

—*US News & World Report*

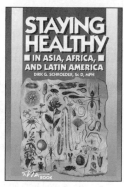

Moon Handbook	**$10.00**
Carl Koppeschaar	141 pages, 8 maps
Moscow-St. Petersburg Handbook	**$13.95**
Masha Nordbye	259 pages, 16 maps
The Practical Nomad: How to Travel Around the World	**$17.95**
Edward Hasbrouck	575 pages
Staying Healthy in Asia, Africa, and Latin America	**$11.95**
Dirk Schroeder	197 pages, 4 maps

MOONBELT

A new concept in moneybelts.
Made of heavy-duty Cordura
nylon, the Moonbelt offers
maximum protection for your money
and important papers. This pouch,

designed for all-weather comfort, slips under your shirt or waistband, rendering it virtually
undetectable and inaccessible to pickpockets. It features a one-inch high-test quick-release
buckle so there's no more fumbling around for the strap or repeated adjustments. This
handy plastic buckle opens and closes with a touch but won't come undone until you want
it to. Moonbelts accommodate traveler's checks, passports, cash, photos, etc.
Size 5 x 9 inches. Available in black only. **$8.95**

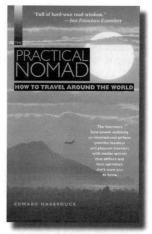

WHERE TO BUY MOON TRAVEL HANDBOOKS

BOOKSTORES AND LIBRARIES: Moon Travel Handbooks are distributed worldwide. Please contact our sales manager for a list of wholesalers and distributors in your area.

TRAVELERS: We would like to have Moon Travel Handbooks available throughout the world. Please ask your bookstore to write or call us for ordering information. If your bookstore will not order our guides for you, please contact us for a free catalog.

> **Moon Travel Handbooks**
> **P.O. Box 3040**
> **Chico, CA 95927-3040 U.S.A.**
> **tel.: (800) 345-5473, outside the U.S. (530) 345-5473**
> **fax: (530) 345-6751**
> **e-mail: travel@moon.com**

IMPORTANT ORDERING INFORMATION

PRICES: All prices are subject to change. We always ship the most current edition. We will let you know if there is a price increase on the book you order.

SHIPPING AND HANDLING OPTIONS: Domestic UPS or USPS first class (allow 10 working days for delivery): $4.50 for the first item, $1.00 for each additional item.

Moonbelt shipping is $1.50 for one, 50 cents for each additional belt.

UPS 2nd Day Air or Printed Airmail requires a special quote.

International Surface Bookrate 8-12 weeks delivery: $3.00 for the first item, $1.00 for each additional item. Note: We cannot guarantee international surface bookrate shipping. We recommends sending international orders via air mail, which requires a special quote.

FOREIGN ORDERS: Orders that originate outside the U.S.A. must be paid for with an international money order, a check in U.S. currency drawn on a major U.S. bank based in the U.S.A., or Visa, MasterCard, or Discover.

TELEPHONE ORDERS: We accept Visa, MasterCard, or Discover payments. Call in your order: (800) 345-5473, 8 a.m.-5 p.m. Pacific standard time. Outside the U.S. the number is (530) 345-5473.

INTERNET ORDERS: Visit our site at: www.moon.com